W9-ADR-998

Praise for Norman L. Macht's
Connie Mack and the Early Years of Baseball
WINNER OF THE 2008 LARRY RITTER AWARD

"A compelling look at a legend and an era."
    —*Kirkus Reviews*

"From the early beginnings of baseball into the modern era, no figure dominated the game like Connie Mack. In Norman Macht's book the legendary patriarch finally gets his deserved recognition from a serious historian. Macht has turned out a book that provides a true insight into baseball and its beginning as the national pastime."
    —**Ernie Harwell,** Hall of Fame broadcaster for fifty-four years

"A biography of Mack cannot help but be a history of baseball in the first half of the twentieth century, and this biography is a feast of interesting facts and judgments."
    —**George F. Will,** syndicated columnist and author of
    Men at Work: The Craft of Baseball

"The tale Macht offers is often riveting."
    —*Library Journal*

"A mother lode of data, stories, perceptions about one of the legendary figures in the history of the national pastime. . . . If you are into baseball, get into this tome."
    —*Dr. Harvey Frommer on Sports*

"[Includes] many fascinating details of baseball from the 1880s to 1914."
    —*Boston Globe*

"Richly enjoyable."
    —*Roanoke Times*

"Masterful. . . . A must-read for all historians of the national pastime, particularly those with an interest in Philadelphia sports."
    —*Pennsylvania Magazine of History and Biography*

"[Macht] tells Mack's story with incredible detail, with liberal helpings of personal anecdotes and descriptions and on-the-field summaries. . . . To know Mack's life story is to know much of the personalities and politics behind the birth of the American League. . . . An excellent story of an amazing American."
—*Dubuque (IA) Telegraph-Herald*

"As a catcher and manager, Connie Mack deserves much of the credit for writing 'The Book' on baseball strategy and the managing of men. How he did it all is told here for the first time."
—**Roland Hemond,** three-time winner of Major League Baseball's Executive of the Year award

Praise for Norman L. Macht's *Connie Mack: The Turbulent and Triumphant Years, 1915–1931*

"A major addition to the study of the game and its longest-serving icon."
—*NINE: A Journal of Baseball History and Culture*

"Macht has done such meticulous research that readers will discover the precise layout of Mack's office at Shibe Park as well as his home. . . . [Mack] was a respected husband, father, leader, role model, and humanitarian—maybe even a hero."
—*Kirkus,* starred review

"This book will please anyone who likes the hits, runs, and errors of baseball."
—**R. W. Roberts,** *Choice*

"If you are a fan of the early days of baseball or just want to learn more about them, I'd highly recommend picking up this book. It was extremely enjoyable to sit and read and will increase your knowledge of that time period immensely."
—**Daniel Shoptaw,** *Cardinal70.com*

"Like the man he continues to so capably chronicle, Norman Macht is astute, authoritative, and meticulous. If you want to learn about twentieth-century baseball, you'll have to read this book."
—**Bob Edmonds,** *McCormick Messenger*

CONNIE MACK

THE GRAND OLD MAN

OF BASEBALL

NORMAN L. MACHT

THE GRAND OLD MAN
OF BASEBALL

CONNIE
MACK

IN HIS FINAL YEARS

1932–1956

UNIVERSITY OF NEBRASKA PRESS | LINCOLN AND LONDON

Library of Congress
Cataloging-in-Publication Data
Macht, Norman L. (Norman Lee), 1929–
The grand old man of baseball: Connie Mack
in his final years, 1932–1956 / Norman L. Macht.
pages   cm
Includes index.
ISBN 978-0-8032-3765-0 (cloth: alk. paper)
ISBN 978-0-8032-7896-7 (epub)
ISBN 978-0-8032-7897-4 (mobi)
ISBN 978-0-8032-7898-1 (pdf)
1. Mack, Connie, 1862–1956. 2. Baseball
managers—United States—Biography.
3. Philadelphia Athletics (Baseball team)—
History. 4. Baseball—United States—History.
I. Title.
GV865.M27M33 2015
796.357092—dc23
[B]
2015019427

Set in Minion by L. Auten.
Designed by A. Shahan.

To
Andrew M. "Butters" Budenz
Major, USMC
1979–2013

—————————————

JOOST TO SUDER TO FAIN

Voluminous prose has been written by those
Who have this one thought to advance:
That the greatest combine in the double play line
Was Tinker to Evers to Chance.

Those three famous Cubs were surely not dubs.
Their fielding was something sublime.
They were far and away the class of their day,
The double play kings of their time.

But they've since been dethroned and partly disowned.
No longer as kings do they reign.
For a new DP team is ruling supreme,
Known as Joost to Suder to Fain.

These sensational A's have perfected their ways
To the point where they lead all the rest.
As twin killings go, three years in a row
They've ranked as the Major Leagues' best.

There's never a worry; they'll comply in a hurry,
When a quick double play is desired.
A roller or liner just couldn't be finer,
You can bet that two men are retired.

You may already know what the record books show,
Three years they've continued to shine,
All others surpassing this record amassing:
A total of six twenty-nine!

Eddie Joost rings the bell as a shortstop as well
As a mighty good man with the stick.
To select someone who has an arm that's as true,
It would be an impossible pick.

On second there stands "the man with the hands."
If a ball's hit to Pete there's no doubt.
You never need look, jot it down in the book,
It's a cinch that the batter is out.

A hitter's accursed with Ferris on first.
There's no one as clever as he,
At spearing a bounder or sizzling grounder
And completing that tough three-six-three.

A long time from now, when they're telling of how
So and so could get two with no strain,
We'll think of the days of Connie Mack's A's,
And of Joost and Suder and Fain.

—**Dick Armstrong**, 1950

CONTENTS

ILLUSTRATIONS

PREFACE This project began as a 350-page biography of a legendary baseball manager. Thirty years later it had grown into a 2,000-page trilogy of the life and times of a fascinating, complicated man who experienced extraordinary successes and devastating failures during the first half of America's most chaotic century. Why did it take me thirty years to write the story of one man's life?

- The rereading of sentences whose warts stuck out where previously they had lain hidden, leading to the moving about of words like a home decorator rearranging furniture or studying patches of paint for the right color combination.
- The discovery, while working on chapter 18, of a fact or a revealing anecdote that required my revisiting chapter 5.
- The determination to rely on primary sources, seeking sometimes elusive evidence to support a memory or, as was often the case, disprove a tall tale.

Hindsight can be an obstacle to objectivity. I have tried to look at a situation as it was faced at the time while blocking out the knowledge of how it turned out.

So can preconceived opinions. What you read is what I learned, everything I learned, and nothing but what I learned about Mr. Mack.

So who was Connie Mack? If you want to knock him, he was a money-grasping skinflint who lost more games than he won. If you admire him, he was generous, a prudent businessman, and a successful leader of men. It's not unusual for someone to be both generous in big matters and difficult in small ones. He could be petty; he could be quickly angered; he was rarely ungracious or unkind.

What does that make him? Human.

It has been said that my affection and admiration for Connie Mack is evident in my writing. This is not accurate. I didn't know the man. I met him once, briefly, when he was eighty-five and I was eighteen. What I have tried to convey is the love and respect I found among the people who knew him best: men and women who worked for him on and off the field, beat writers and columnists throughout the country, baseball fans of all ages, family, friends of many years, and strangers who never met him.

The entire truth of a man's character—his motivations and secret thoughts banked in the recesses of his mind like embers in a coal furnace—is a mystery that cannot be captured in a few words—or even a few thousand; indeed it cannot be completely known by anyone. A historian often must rely on an educated guess, based on years of research and hundreds of interviews, to explain a person's actions.

A man's life is a tapestry, not a chart. Some readers are interested only in the baseball part of the story. But this is about a man's life, not just his work. The ways in which an extraordinary life may hold some lessons for our ordinary lives lie in the details of that life.

Francis Bacon wrote, "The human understanding when it has once adopted an opinion . . . draws all things else to support and agree with it. And though there be a greater number and weight of instances to be found on the other side, yet these it either neglects or else by some distinction sets aside or rejects."

Try to set aside the impressions you may have absorbed about Connie Mack and come to this play seeking to understand for yourself the man behind the myths.

A Note on Sources

If I had endnoted in detail every printed or oral quote, this book would be too heavy to lift. In addition to my own interviews, I combed through newspapers from Philadelphia, Washington DC, New York, Chicago, Los Angeles, St. Louis, Kansas City, and a lot more cities, large and small. I have tried to identify sources within the text without impeding the narrative.

Many former players were interviewed for this work. Some of their memories were translations from stories they had read or heard that metamorphosed in their minds into something they had experienced firsthand. These the historian is wise to ignore. As to their recollections of events they witnessed or were involved in, nobody expects them to remember conversations word for word, or to tell them the same way every time. As Theodore H. White aptly put it, "It is a trap of history to believe that eyewitnesses remember accurately what they have lived through." Or done themselves.

Connie Mack fielded the same questions over and over as time passed. With his telling and retelling of the same anecdotes, it was natural that each telling might be a little different. Gradually, embellishment might lead to exaggeration and occasionally to invention. With age, the filters of the mind comb out the unpleasant, block out the gray, leaving a more roseate hue in the sunset of life.

When I report someone's thoughts, it is based on what they told me or told someone else or wrote.

No conversations have been manufactured. All convey the thoughts and meanings of the speakers. They come from personal interviews and newspaper accounts of the time, records that in the days of pencils and notepads are not expected to be verbatim. Writers admitted paraphrasing interviewees, an accepted practice that does not impair validity. Some accounts are pieced together from various interviews. This is not an exact science. It's an art, resulting in what feels right and appropriate given the circumstances and the people involved. The dialogue used reflects the gist of what happened, consistent with the participants.

Among Philadelphia writers, Gordon Mackay, Bill Dooly, Ed Pollock, Art Morrow, and Bill Brandt were considered accurate, reliable, objective reporters by their peers. Some baseball writers are adept at creative writing. James Isaminger, ghosting for Connie Mack, was an accomplished embroiderer.

Among national writers, Frank Graham of New York was known as an accurate, understated reporter. Westbrook Pegler's quotes of Connie Mack ring true.

The need to confirm every story you're told rides shotgun on every interview. If no evidence could be found to support a story, it usually wasn't used (An apocryphal story, identified as such, can sometimes be more effective in illuminating a personality than a string of adjectives.)

Roger Angell once wrote about asking Willie Mays in 1991 to recall his favorite home run. Mays rattled off, "Against Claude Raymond. Astrodome. Somebody was on first and it tied the game. Jim Davenport won it for us in the eleventh or twelfth inning. Raymond threw me thirteen fastballs and I fouled them off. The ball went over the fence in left-center field. What year? You'd have to look that up. Ask Claude Raymond—he probably knows it better than I do."

Roger Angell did as Mays suggested. He asked Claude Raymond, who said without hesitation, "I threw Mays thirteen straight fastballs and he fouled off thirteen."

Now more interested in the thirteen fouled-off fastballs than the home run, Angell checked with a San Francisco Giants media person, who found the game—September 14, 1965—and confirmed that Davenport had won it in the tenth. But the game account said Mays had fouled off only four pitches, not thirteen.

After his story ran, Angell received a letter from Charles Einstein, noted chronicler of Mays's career, who happened to have a tape recording of the game broadcast.

"It was four fouls," Einstein wrote. "Nothing impeaches the memory of an old ballplayer more than another old ballplayer who remembers the moment the same way."

And that's why stories like the one often told by Paul Richards about the mental lapse he suffered while catching for the Athletics in 1935 that caused Connie Mack to put him on a train to Atlanta the next day—an incident "witnessed" by pitcher Randy Gumpert and described by him fifty years later—didn't make it into this book. No evidence could be found that it happened the way they told it.

But a lot of stories did pass inspection. I hope you enjoy them.

ACKNOWLEDGMENTS One day in 1985 I called Connie Mack Jr. in Fort Myers, Florida. "I intend to write a biography of your father," I said. "Will you help me?" He said, "If you had told me, 'I want to write a biography *if* you'll help me,' I would have said no. But since you said you *intend* to write it and asked if I would help you, the answer is yes."

Thus began my thirty-year friendship with the children, grandchildren, nephews, and nieces of Connie Mack—the Macks, McGillicuddys, Nolens, McCambridges, and Cunninghams—to whom I owe more than the United States owes China for their memories and support in this marathon project.

I am especially indebted to Philadelphia baseball historian Robert Warrington for his insightful critiquing of the manuscript which clarified muddy waters and corrected inaccuracies.

For the years 1932–1950 there were many more players available to provide firsthand impressions and experiences than for the earlier years. Those I interviewed included Wayne Ambler, Joe Astroth, John Babich, Al Brancato, Lou Brissie, Joe Cascarella, Sam Chapman, Allie Clark, Joe Coleman, Eddie Collins Jr., Bobby Coombs, Doc Cramer, Crash Davis, Joe DeMaestri, Roberto Estalella, Nick Etten, Ferris Fain, Tom Ferrick, Tony Freitas, Randy Gumpert, Irv Hall, Bill Hockenbury, Eddie Joost, George Kell, Skeeter Kell, Alex Kellner, Dario Lodigiani, Ed Madjeski, Barney McCosky, Benny McCoy, Les McCrabb, Charlie Metro, Wally Moses, Bill Nicholson, Ace Parker, Nelson Potter, Bob Savage, Carl Scheib, Bobby Shantz, Roy Sievers, Pete Suder, Billy Sullivan Jr., Bud Thomas, Tommy Thomas, Elmer Valo, John Welaj, Bill Werber, Dib Williams, Ted Williams, and Gene Woodling.

A special thanks to Dick Armstrong, the Athletics' public relations director 1949–1952, who worked closely with Connie Mack and witnessed the infighting among the younger Macks; to longtime Athletics attorney Frank Schillp for providing me with illuminating legal documents; and to him and Arthur Gallagher for their firsthand accounts of the events surrounding the 1954 sale of the A's.

The reappearance after fifty years of the Athletics' business ledgers and the willingness of their owner, Rob Rodriguez (with an assist from Senator Connie Mack III), to lend them to me provided a wealth of information enabling me to replace financial guesses and rumors with facts. A tip of the hat to Ed Norton for his countless hours in Philadelphia's libraries, archives, and city offices tracking down the stuff of story verifications and legal documents, and to Liz Ackert (Texas State University), Freddy Berowski, Craig Budner, Bob Buege, Warren Corbett, Sr. Helen Forge (Sisters of Charity), Cynthia Franco of the DeGolyer Library at Southern Methodist University, Joe Gross, Dan Lambert, Lincoln Landis, Todd Lebowitz, Dan Levitt, Gilbert Martinez, John McCormack, William McMahon, Kathy Muller, Mark Pankin, Tom Ruane and Retrosheet, Ira Siegel, Steve Steinberg, Richard Trumbull, Pat Williams, and John Zajc for their contributions.

If there were a copy editor hall of fame, eagle-eyed, astute but gracious grammarian Bojana Ristich would be in it, having perused and improved more than three thousand of this trilogy's manuscript pages in the quest for perfection.

I am indebted to the University of Chicago for teaching me the importance of primary sources and the art of asking questions and evaluating answers.

And to Tom Hall at IT Data Recovery of Austin, Texas, who really made this book possible by recovering it from a crashed computer.

CONNIE MACK

THE GRAND OLD MAN

OF BASEBALL

1 | CONNIE MACK, FINANCIAL FAILURE

The wheels fell off the world in 1932. Early signs of global economic recovery in the spring of '31 had been erased by social and financial chaos in Europe. Disarmament talks were going nowhere. Europe was in turmoil, its governments collapsing. Germans who had money were shipping it out of their country as Hitler's brownshirts destroyed people's lives and the nation's stability.

A devastating drought in the American southwest was in its second year. Farmers who could grow a crop couldn't sell what they grew and couldn't find any place to store it. There was so much old surplus wheat, corn, and cotton that it was priced by the penny a bushel or bale. By the end of the year one of every four farmers would lose his land. Panic drove people who heard that banks were closing to rush to their local banks and withdraw all their money—the average account had $140 in it—causing more banks to close, cutting off loans to farmers, shops, and businesses. People were putting their money into mattresses—not investing in mattress makers but stuffing it into the bedding they slept on.

Gold flowed out of the United States, much of it shipped out by wealthy Americans who had no faith in the dollar. Nineteen countries, including England, went off the gold standard, and America was on the brink of doing the same. Currencies fluctuated wildly. Old war loans made by America to its allies went unpaid. Nobody knew how to foreclose on a foreign country.

Federal revenues nosedived to less than half the budgeted expenses. Income in Pennsylvania had topped $2 billion in 1929; by 1932 it was less than half. Net income reported by Pennsylvania residents who earned enough to file 1932 tax returns averaged $3,006, the lowest since 1917. Taxes went up. The Commerce Department reported that anyone lucky enough to have a job was working sixty-one days a year to pay federal, state, and local taxes. President Herbert Hoover tried to cut government spending, proclaiming, "You can't spend the country into prosperity," while Congress continued to fill the pork barrels. In June 1932 all government employees, including Congressmen, earning at least $10,000 a year would take a 10 percent pay cut. President Hoover led the way, turning back 20 percent of his salary.

After rallying in the spring of 1930, the stock market had been sliding, the Dow falling below 300, then 200, then 100. It finally hit bottom at 41.22 in July 1932. Connie Mack didn't fare well in the stock market after that. His investments more often went bankrupt than prospered.

Mack continued to help his extended family with money and jobs as best he could. His brother Dennis's widow, Annie, always needed help. He hired her brother, Tom Monahan, to work the gates at Shibe Park. Until they were older, two of Annie's six children and Annie were regulars at the Macks' Sunday dinner table.

Any of Mack's nephews and nieces could walk through the press gate with their friends unimpeded or visit Uncle Connie in his office. Mack's favorite nephew may have been Dennis's son Cornelius, who used the name Neil. In 1932, after working as an actuary and a claims adjuster, he was unemployed. He asked his uncle to help him find a job: "He sent me to a sports editor and then an advertising agency, but I had no experience. Then he sent me to his friend Judge McDevitt, a Republican big shot, and he hired me and I worked in the courthouse."

During World War II Neil was in the merchant marine for two years, then became a transit workers' union organizer, a position that earned him a personal FBI file. That didn't faze Uncle Con; Neil remained a favorite nephew.

Baseball was going in for farming. The Cardinals expanded their farm system faster than anyone else. The Yankees hired George Weiss from Baltimore to begin theirs.

Connie Mack had built his 1929–1931 championship teams by buying high-priced minor league stars. But as farm systems began to corner most of the top prospects for their own use, the quality of excess players for sale went down. The more the chains expanded, the slimmer the pickings became. Twenty-five years ago Mack had been able to take inexperienced youths and successfully develop them at the major league level. But the business had changed. He was still trying to run his baseball school at Shibe Park while other clubs were doing their teaching and weeding in the minor leagues.

The Athletics fell behind, operating a sort of ad hoc farm system in which Mack would option players to minor league teams in exchange for the right to choose one or more players at the end of the season.

An AP survey concluded that major league payrolls would drop by a million dollars (the average salary in 1931 had been $7,350, totaling about $2.8 million). Some of the biggest stars faced a 40 percent axe. Even though Babe Ruth had had a better year than Hoover, he took a $5,000 cut, partly made up by a slice of revenues from exhibition games in which he played at least 5 innings. To limit expenses the player limit was kept at twenty-three. Ticket prices remained unchanged, based on the reasoning that they had not been raised during the boom years. Even so, some clubs were scrambling to find a bank that would lend them the money to go to spring training and start the season.

The Commissioner's Office budget was also hurting. Financed entirely by 15 percent of World Series and some city series' receipts, it had been pinched by short series: of the 6 most recent World Series, only the 1931 set had gone 7 games. The rest had taken only 19 of a possible 35 games to produce a winner, and the 1932 Series would play to plenty of empty seats. Commissioner Kenesaw M. Landis retroactively cut his 1932 salary to $50,000 and would drop it to $40,000 for 1933.

As a cost-cutting step, the leagues cut out their $50,000 annual subsidy for American Legion ball, despite Landis's pleas to continue supporting the program. (The leagues also ignored Landis's vehement opposition to farm systems by unanimously approving unlimited transfers of players between major league clubs and their affiliates.)

Connie Mack had no salary leeway with his top stars. Mickey Cochrane, Jimmy Foxx, and Al Simmons had three-year contracts. The salaries of those three, plus those of Robert Moses "Lefty" Grove and George "Moose" Earnshaw, totaled more than $100,000. None of the Athletics' regulars took a cut. The A's player payroll remained above $250,000. In the circumstances, the 1931 pennant winners did well, whether or not they agreed.

Second baseman Max "Camera Eye" Bishop went to Mack's office from nearby Waynesboro in January 1932 to talk contract. He had been earning $10,000 a year for the last three years. Mack said, "You made ten thousand last year and another three thousand from the World Series. That's a pretty good contract."

Bishop said, "Mr. Mack, Esther and I are contemplating buying a home. If I could make $11,000, I'd be on easy street."

Flustered, Mack said, "Max, you epitomize to me the team player. If you get $11,000, that will foul up my entire salary structure. I can't do it."

Bishop signed for $10,000 again.

Jimmie Dykes remained at $12,000, making him the highest-paid third baseman in the league. (Willie Kamm, at $11,500, was next, followed by Ossie Bluege's $9,000 at Washington. Joe Sewell of the Yankees earned $8,000.)

Mack had two holdouts. Grove wanted a $10,000 raise to $30,000. (Mack had given him a $3,000 bonus after the 1930 season, then a raise to $20,000 in 1931.) Rube Walberg wanted a $5,000 boost to $15,000. They were both in Fort Myers on February 22, when pitchers and catchers held their first workout. Barred from practice until they signed, they stayed at the hotel and watched the others file onto the bus to Terry Park. A United Press reporter asked Mack about their status. Usually reluctant to talk about salaries and holdouts, Mack was surprisingly outspoken. Acknowledging that Grove and Walberg were refusing to sign, he was quoted as saying, "They are smart fellows but big fools for not signing. They will sign on my terms or sit out. They are not for sale or trade. We didn't cut them any but neither are they going to get an increase. They've been offered all we can pay. I don't expect to hold any conferences with them. I'll talk to them when they sign."

Bob Paul of the *Daily News* maintained friendly ties with the players. He once sent this wire to Hollywood producer Sol Lesser: "If you're looking for a new Tarzan, I offer for your consideration Jimmy Foxx who has ideal physique, splendid radio-tested voice, screen-tested features and is the idol of America's youth. Wire me instructions if interested."

By now Foxx was too beefy for swinging through the treetops on vines.

Paul often took the side of players holding out. A few days after spring training began, Paul approached Connie Mack. He described what followed in his column:

Out at the ballpark, I came across Connie sitting with the Rev. Frank A. Shore, an Episcopal minister who seldom missed a practice session. They were sitting on one of the wooden benches that served as an open-air dugout. As I approached to tell Connie that Grove offered to play him 18 holes of golf for the difference in salary—reported to be $10,000—the veteran manager opened fire. He might have hit an all-time high in the explosive language familiar to a dugout had he not remembered the presence of the Fort Myers clergyman.

"You and the rest of the blankety-blank baseball writers are the real cause for all these holdouts!" fairly shouted Connie. "You write only the side of the x#%* players in your blankety-blank papers and those x#%* players are just dumb enough to believe what they read. Why, your x#%* writings stand to cost me thousands of hard-earned money. If I had my way, you blankety—oh, Rev. Shores, why, I must have forgotten you were here. You know how upset these baseball writers get me some days. What was that you said, Paul?"

(This could have happened; columnist Red Smith would later attest that such outbursts were not foreign to Mr. Mack, despite his reputation for uttering nothing stronger than "gosh" or "pshaw." Players hearing the story agreed. "He could use the language when he wanted to," recalled Roger "Flit" Cramer, "but he didn't do it often. He could cuss good as anybody, no question about it." But the story appears here with a caveat: several years later Bob Paul wrote an identical account concerning the 1934 holdout of Jimmy Foxx.)

Neither Grove nor Walberg received a raise. On March 1 Grove signed for two years at $20,000 and Walberg for $10,000, saying he was satisfied to avoid a cut.

Mack sent pitcher Waite Hoyt a contract for $7,500. Hoyt demanded $10,000. Neither man budged. On February 8 Hoyt cleared waivers, and Mack released him. Hoyt signed with Brooklyn and pitched another seven years.

Coach William "Kid" Gleason, sixty-six, was absent from spring training, too ill to make the trip. He had been injured in an auto accident a month ago. Mack sent him a telegram: "Regret to hear of your being ill. Would advise you to take things easy for a couple weeks. By taking good care of yourself for ten days you will be better than ever. Don't worry. Get ready for opening of championship season and we will go after that bunch like the A's can go."

Gleason never fully recovered. He died on January 2, 1933. More than five thousand people gathered outside the funeral home on Lehigh Avenue in Philadelphia and watched as hundreds of players, including a dozen former and present Athletics, officials, umpires, Mack and the Shibes, John McGraw, and Commissioner Landis arrived. The Reverend Thomas Davis, the unofficial A's chaplain, extolled Gleason's "honesty, cheerfulness, gratitude, and generosity."

The list of people influential in Connie Mack's career who would pre-decease him now included Charles F. Daniels, the Hartford manager who had sold Mack and three other players to Washington in 1888. Daniels died on March 23.

Ford Frick once said that in the 1930s club owners could still get away with things that were later impossible to put across. Some things. In February Connie Mack and Cleveland general manager Billy Evans tried to slip an illegal deal past Commissioner Landis and failed. Counting on Dib Williams and Eric McNair to rejuvenate the middle infield, Mack sold veteran short-stop Joe Boley to Cleveland for $10,000, half down and the rest if Cleveland kept him after May 15. Landis nixed the deal, likening it to optioning a player to a club in the same league, a no-no under the league constitution. Mack wound up giving Boley his release in June. The Indians signed him, but he appeared in only one game before they let him go.

Connie Mack was worried about his youngest star, Jimmy Foxx.

The Maryland farm boy had gone uptown in a big way. He was making more money than anybody in his hometown of Sudlersville had ever seen, and he enjoyed spending it. He drove a block-long Studebaker President Brougham, wore silk shirts and fancy shoes, and rented a house in the posh Philadelphia suburb of Jenkintown. The Foxxes employed a butler, and the genial Jimmy took plenty of clubhouse riding about that.

Jimmy took to the night life. He went to the best places. According to Mike "Pinky" Higgins, Foxx's roommate in 1933, "Jimmy relaxed a little too late one night. The next morning Connie Mack stopped him in the lobby. Mack said, 'By golly, Jim, you were out after curfew last night, and don't you deny it. Some of the best people in the city saw you there.' And Foxx said, 'Mr. Mack, if the best people go there, why can't I?' It was the only time I saw Mr. Mack at a loss for words."

Generous by nature, Jimmy always had a roll of cash in his pocket. He grabbed the tab at nightclubs and restaurants no matter who he was with. "The hangers-on at the local taprooms seemed to know when he was coming in," recalled scout Ira Thomas's nephew Jim Morrow. He tipped so lavishly that waiters, hatcheck girls, Pullman porters, and bellhops found it hard to believe he was a member of the tight-fisted baseball tribe. He supported his younger brother Sammy and bought an in-town house for his parents in Sudlersville.

One day in Chicago in 1931 Foxx was watching a rookie catcher for the White Sox working out at first base during infield practice. Billy Sullivan Jr. had just graduated from Notre Dame. When he was done, Sullivan threw his glove on the ground. Foxx picked it up.

"We don't use gloves like this up here," he said. "It's too small."

"It's the only one I could find in South Bend," Sullivan said.

The next day Foxx handed the rookie a big league glove, well broken in, and said, "Take it, it's yours."

Jimmy Foxx was a guess hitter, and that bothered Connie Mack. All hitters guess to some extent. They all look for the fastball, but the good ones can adjust for the curve or change-up in time to hit it. With all his power, Foxx could make pitchers suffer for their mistakes. But it seemed to Mack that they had begun to outfox the young slugger more last year, and the numbers showed it. He had struck out more and walked less.

Mack talked to him and Foxx listened. He spent hours in batting practice, trying to clear his head and concentrate on picking up the pitch out of the pitcher's hand.

A dozen rookie pitchers kept Mack busy. Lew Krausse's batting practice pitching in '31 had earned him a chance to start a game late that year. He had beaten the Red Sox, 7–1, and was the center of plenty of attention this spring. Mickey Cochrane and Jimmie Dykes were pulling for him to make good because the nineteen-year-old was the best golfer in camp, and they rushed through practice to get to the golf course with him. But none of the rookies really impressed Mack. "Maybe," Washington outfielder Sam Rice observed, "Connie's been looking at Grove, Earnshaw, and Walberg for so long that any others look just ordinary to him."

Cochrane was the only spring casualty; a blister on his foot became infected, and he was sidelined until the season opened.

On March 18 the A's were in St. Pete to play the Braves. Connie Mack sat in the stands before the game and was carried back eighteen years as he watched three of the men who had swept his great 1914 team in the World Series—the batting star Hank Gowdy (now a coach), hitting fungos to Rabbit Maranville (still a full-time infielder), and pitching coach Dick Rudolph, who had beaten the A's twice in 1914—showing a youngster how to hold a runner on first.

At noon that day Mack had told the Rotary Club, "I am afraid of those Yankees. They are a very powerful club and will have better pitching than the experts say." New York had closed strong in 1931, going 14-2 down the stretch to finish second with 94 wins. On opening day the Yankees proved Mack's point, hitting 5 home runs, 4 off George Earnshaw. For the A's, Foxx and Simmons connected and Max Bishop walked four times, but the Yankees won, 12–6.

New York was loaded with a veteran lineup of stars still a few years from showing their age, a slick-fielding new shortstop, Frank Crosetti, and a solid pitching staff augmented by a fiery, head-hunting twenty-six-year-old rookie, Johnny Allen. (Fifty years later Roger Cramer recalled, "Johnny Allen told me once he was going to throw at me and he burned the hair right off my head. You can still see the mark.")

The Athletics also had a veteran lineup, virtually unchanged from its World Series roster. In September Mack had recalled outfielder Lou Finney from York, Bob Johnson from Portland, Mike Higgins from San Antonio, pitcher Jimmy DeShong from Jersey City, and pitcher Merritt "Sugar" Cain and shortstop Ed Cihocki from Harrisburg. He sent Jim Moore, Joe Palmisano, and Jim Peterson to Portland for outfielder Ed Coleman and pitcher Joe Bowman. As part payment for Bowman, the A's cancelled an October 20, 1930, demand note for $10,000, indicating that they had been advancing money to Portland club owner Tom Turner.

Now Mack decided that Johnson, Higgins, and Finney would benefit from more playing time than they would see in Philadelphia. He sent them to Portland. He kept Ed Coleman, who would start out strong until he broke an ankle in June, and Flit Cramer for outfield depth. (Roger Cramer had picked up the name "Doc" as a youngster when he made house calls with the local doctor. But in Philadelphia he was more commonly known as Flit, a nickname put on him because he was death on flies, like "Flit," a common insect spray of the time. The earliest use of the nickname "Doc" among ballplayers seems to have appeared in 1934.) Unlike the Yankees, Mack's pitching was a question mark after Grove, Walberg, Earnshaw, and Roy Mahaffey—and it would be asking a lot for Grove to duplicate his phenomenal 31-4 season of 1931.

The other thing Mack's boys lacked and the Yankees had was hunger. Nobody knew better than Connie Mack how tough it was to keep a team keyed up enough to win three pennants in a row. As for a fourth, that had been done only once, by John McGraw's 1921–1924 Giants. (Hughie Jennings led them for one-third of the 1924 season.) The Yankees had been in front in 1926, '27, and '28; they hadn't liked riding in the back seat for the past three years. They got off to a fast start and were never threatened.

After losing 6 in a row the Athletics were 4-10 on April 30.

Dib Williams and Eric McNair were often in the lineup at second or short. Cramer was seen in right field more often than the thirty-seven-year-old Bing Miller.

None of the young pitchers came through. They were soon back in the minors for further seasoning.

Eddie Rommel appeared to be at the end of the line. Although he was only thirty-four, the fire seemed to have gone out of him. Used occasionally in relief, Rommel worked only 65 ineffective innings. Six of the 84 hits off him were home runs, the highest ratio of his career.

Jimmie Dykes, who had been Rommel's teammate for thirteen years, believed the knuckleballer had lost his confidence, a career killer for any pitcher. "He got it into his head that he could not win," Dykes said after the season. "If he can chase the depression out of his system and pitch as he once did, he can help a team."

Once again the burden fell on Lefty Grove and the two broadbacks, as Cochrane called Walberg and Earnshaw. Grove kept them afloat. After a 2–1 loss to Washington on April 30, he won 11 in a row through June 13. Walberg and Mahaffey got off to slow starts; by the time they were in midseason form, it was too late. Mahaffey became one of Earnshaw's drinking buddies. Connie Mack knew it; he knew everything his boys were up to. At one point Mack fined Mahaffey $500, but it was later forgiven.

Ed Pollock covered the A's for the *Philadelphia Bulletin* in 1932. A story he later related probably starred Earnshaw. The place was the Alamac Hotel in New York:

Ron Nolan of the *Bulletin* staff and I were sitting in the lobby with Mack. At about 10:45 one of his star pitchers strolled in, went to the desk, and in a voice loud enough for us to hear, asked for his room key. Then he came over and joined the group. He yawned a few times, said he was tired, bid his goodnights, and got into the elevator. Connie straightened up, put a hand on my knee, gestured for silence and waited for about a minute. Then he jumped to his feet and cautioned for Nolan and me to follow him. He went to a side window and pointed to a waiting taxicab. In a moment out came the pitcher and hurriedly entered the cab. He got out of the elevator on the second floor—Connie had noticed where the indicator stopped—and came down the fire escape stairs. "You see," said Mack, "the hotel clerks don't have to tell me everything."

Mack even knew the nighttime activities of the writers. Pollock wrote:

One night in Detroit in the company of other writers and one of the club's officials [probably traveling secretary Rudy Ohl], I ferried across to Canada and visited some of the spots across the border where there was no prohibition. It was very late when we returned. Next night at dinner Mack went out of his way to pass the table. He stopped and inquired with a smile, "Did you have a good time last night across the river?" I told him I didn't think he was checking on us. "I wasn't," he replied. "Sometimes I see things and other times people tell me things." Then as though mind-reading he added, "The hotel clerk didn't say a word."

To bolster his pitching with a string of doubleheaders coming up, Mack bought left-hander Tony Freitas, who had just pitched a no-hitter against Oakland, paying Sacramento $25,000 and Jimmy DeShong for him on May 20. Ira Thomas had scouted Freitas. Mack didn't know anything about him other than "He's the best pitcher in the [Pacific] Coast League from what I hear." Freitas, twenty-four, turned out to be the opposite of Grove—a junk-ball pitcher. If he hit a batter, it wouldn't leave a mark.

Freitas arrived in Boston and went to Fenway Park, where he met "some of the greatest ballplayers who ever lived. . . . I was greeted very cordially, no hazing. I was scared stiff, didn't know how to act."

He made his first start on May 31 against Washington. Before the game Cochrane went over the hitters with him. Freitas took a 3–2 lead into the ninth. With 1 out, Joe Cronin was the batter. Cochrane went out to the mound and reminded Freitas, "Whatever you do, don't give this fellow anything above the belt."

"I threw Cronin just what he liked," Freitas recalled, "and he hit a home run to tie the game. The worst I ever heard Connie Mack say if you made a mistake was, 'Is that the best you can do?' But he said nothing to me on that occasion when I got back to the dugout."

Mack decided to pair Freitas with Grove in doubleheaders, Lefty blazing his fastball in the opener and Freitas following with his soft stuff. The first few times they tried it, it didn't work; they split the games. Eventually they both won on August 13 at Boston.

On June 1 the A's were fourth, 6 games behind New York, who came in for a six-game series at Shibe Park. That morning Connie Mack summed up the season—and what can drive club owners and managers up the wall—in a letter to one of his ardent supporters and correspondents, Sister Florence Cloonan of the Sisters of Charity:

> It seems to be one of those years where our club just can't get started in the right direction, but I have always considered baseball a rather hard game, due to the fact that a club one year will play exceptionally great ball and then the next year the same players will play just the opposite kind.
>
> I am sure that our boys would like to play good ball all the time, but things just don't seem to break right, and, of course, the boys become a little discouraged and then are not in a position to give their best.
>
> Jimmy Foxx has been playing wonderful ball of late, but in the last few days he has not done quite so well. While Simmons, the man upon whom we depend so much, has not done anything for us this year. In fact, none of the players have been playing as good as in years past, and there is no account of it as they are all taking exceptionally good care of themselves.

Mack hoped the six games coming up against the Yankees would give them a boost, but the best they could do was split the series.

On June 3 John McGraw, in poor health for several years, resigned as manager of the Giants. He had last won a pennant in 1924 and had lost the big headlines in New York to Babe Ruth and the Yankees. Among the many tributes, Mack, who had always rated McGraw number one among managers, said, "All baseball will feel keenly the passing of such a man from active participation in it. To lose his brilliant mind is a blow to the game."

On that same day the Yankees defeated the A's at Shibe Park, 20–13, dropping them into fifth place. The story of the game was not the Yankees' 7 home runs or record 50 total bases or Tony Lazzeri's hitting for the cycle or Foxx's major-league-leading nineteenth home run or the teams' combined 77 total bases, tying the league record. It was Lou Gehrig's becoming the first American Leaguer to hit 4 home runs in a game. The first three, in the first, fourth, and fifth innings, were hit off Earnshaw; the last, in the seventh, off Mahaffey. (Earnshaw's favorite story of his tiffs with Connie Mack concerned this game. After being pinch-hit for in the fifth, he started for the clubhouse. "Sit right down here, young fellow," Mack said. "I want you to watch how you should pitch to Gehrig." When Gehrig homered off Mahaffey, Earnshaw said, "I see what you mean, Mr. Mack," and departed.)

In the bottom of the eighth Mack sent Oscar Roettger up to pinch-hit for center fielder Roger Cramer. When Gehrig came up in the ninth, Al Simmons moved from left to center field, and Bing Miller went to left. Ed Rommel was now on the mound.

Recalled rookie catcher Ed Madjeski, "All the A's on the bench wanted to see Gehrig hit number five. They wanted [Rommel] to groove one for him." Whether Rommel did or not, Gehrig got hold of it, and the five thousand in attendance saw what Al Simmons would call the greatest catch he ever made. He raced to the farthest corner in center field, leaped, and caught it. A few feet to either side and it might have been out of the park.

Despite that memorable catch, being out of the pennant race for the first time in four years was taking a toll on Al Simmons. A self-admitted "gruff and ornery" sort of guy (an attitude he had adopted to emulate his idol, Ty Cobb), his mood soured, said some writers, out of jealousy over the headlines going to Jimmy Foxx. In a 4-game series at Detroit June 11–14, Simmons had 4 singles and no RBIS while Foxx was leading the A's to 3 wins. Simmons was popping up, striking out, and hitting into double plays instead of rattling the fences with line drives. Two weeks later, when he struck out 3 times in a game in New York, he "certainly didn't look like the champion batsman of the American League," wrote Joe Vila of the *New York Evening Sun*. Wags in the press box sniped that running out ground balls was a job for his valet. His play in the outfield was sometimes indifferent. Having compiled a .363 average over the past eight years, something more than his current .304 was expected of him.

Simmons later admitted that once he had it made financially, he had lost some of his fire: "I was never again the ballplayer I was when I was hungry." Connie Mack saw it too. But at the time Simmons burned over the writers' comments. He didn't think he deserved them. Before a game at Shibe Park he and Dykes were sitting in the dugout. Bob Paul entered and sat down beside them. Simmons unloaded his opinion of the press. Dykes, who never complained about the writers, stood up. "If you're going to bore Bob with that stuff," he said, "I'm leaving. Why don't you make those fellows in the press box eat their words by your actions on the field instead of crying the blues?"

Connie Mack was with the team in Cleveland on June 10 when Connie Jr. graduated from Germantown Academy, winning the school's Robert E. Lamberton medal as "best in athletics and scholarship." He was headed for Duke to play first base for coach John "Colby Jack" Coombs and center for the Blue Devils' basketball team. Mack had rarely talked about his son's athletic exploits and never saw him play. It was as if he didn't want to put any pressure on young Connie.

Lefty Grove twisted his ankle shagging flies in St. Louis on June 15 and was lost for three weeks. Earnshaw picked up the slack and won 5 in a row. Cochrane had a bad ankle and could hardly walk on it. Dib Williams, after starring in the World Series, was suffering hitting and fielding lapses. He was hitting vertical line drives and throwing erratically with a limp-wristed motion.

The A's went into New York on June 25 and lost a pair. They fell 9½ games back, farther out of first place than the National League's last place Reds. They were finished. Playing in front of caverns of silent, empty seats didn't help. "We saw the beginning of the end," Dykes said, "and some of us did nothing to put it off."

By mid-July the predictions of a close three-way race were forgotten. Washington was struggling to hold fourth place. Only the Yankees had consistent hitting and pitching. Joe McCarthy was using his pitchers in the same way that his idol, Connie Mack, had sometimes been criticized for. The Yankees' frontline starters—Lefty Gomez, Red Ruffing, Johnny Allen, and George Pipgras—were used regularly in relief.

With no Sunday games at Shibe Park, the A's often interrupted home stands to travel to more liberal cities for the day. It was customary for clubs making those one-day trips to leave some players at home. On July 10 Mack gave Cochrane, Bing Miller, and all but two pitchers the day off. Eddie Rommel had pitched 2 innings on Friday and 3 on Saturday, so he was surprised when he and Lew Krausse were the only pitchers on the train to Cleveland.

After the A's scored 2 in the top of the first, Krausse walked 1 and gave up 4 hits, including a 3-run home run by Earl Averill. That was enough for Mack. Rommel started the second. Both teams had their batting eyes. The A's appeared to put the game away with a 7-run seventh and led, 13–8, before Indians ace Wes Ferrell was rushed in to end the uprising. But the Indians scored 6 in their half to take the lead, 14–13. At one point during the inning Mack called time. In the press box the guess was that Mack would send Dykes to the mound to finish it (he had done so twice in 1927), but Mack replaced the catcher instead.

In the ninth an error opened the way for Foxx's double to drive in 2 and give the A's the lead, 15–14. Then the Indians tied it and almost won it. George "Mule" Haas's diving catch in right field took Rommel and Ferrell into the tenth and eleventh and twelfth—to the sixteenth, when Foxx hit a 2-run home run. But it still wasn't over. The Indians tied it with 4 hits, and again Haas came up with a leaping catch against the right-field wall to send them to the seventeenth. In the eighteenth Foxx singled and McNair doubled to make it 18–17.

The Indians ran out of gas before Rommel did, going out in order in the last of the eighteenth.

Records fell like tenpins: Rommel's 17-inning relief chore (Ferrell pitched 11⅓) and 29 hits allowed; 33 hits by the Indians—9 of them by shortstop Johnny Burnett; 58 hits by both teams.

Foxx led the A's with 3 home runs and 8 RBIs. John Heving and Ed Madjeski split the catching chores. Everybody else in the A's lineup played the entire 4:05 game.

To Eddie Rommel the oddest thing about the game was a play he had thought about for years but never used—until he messed it up in this game. Had it worked, the game would have been just another 9-inning win. With men on first and second and no outs, if the batter popped a bunt toward the pitcher, he planned to trap it, not catch it, then throw to second for a force, and a throw to first would make it two outs. "Nine times out of ten the man on second will head for third, and the first baseman could easily get the ball over there for a triple play." After years of Rommel's talking about it, the situation occurred in the sixth inning. The bunt hung low in front of the mound. Rommel trapped it and threw it into center field. A run scored.

This was Eddie Rommel's last win. One-third of his innings pitched for the year had come in that three-day span. After the season Rommel cleared waivers and was released. Nobody signed him, and Mack brought him back as a coach. In 1935 the A's had a working agreement with Richmond in the Piedmont League. Mack arranged for Rommel to manage the team. At thirty-seven, Eddie also played 18 games at second base. The next year Rommel was asked to take a pay cut. "I was so astounded I went right to Connie," Rommel told the *Philadelphia Inquirer.* "He smiled and said, 'Eddie, that sometimes happens in the big leagues. Forget the idea of managing. I have a job for you if you want to take it. How would you like to try umpiring?' I told him it suited me if there was a chance to get into the big leagues. 'That is entirely up to you,' he replied."

After two years in the minor leagues, Rommel began a twenty-two-year umpiring career in the American League.

Three weeks later the A's were back in Cleveland to inaugurate the city's new $2.6 million Municipal Stadium before a paid attendance of 76,979, a welcome payday for both clubs. An eighth-inning walk to Bishop and an RBI single by Cochrane led to the only run in a duel between Lefty Grove and Mel Harder. (The Indians would use both League Park and Municipal Stadium until 1946.)

Hard times were devastating the minor leagues. They were folding like nomads' tents. Nineteen started the season; thirteen would finish. In July the Eastern League disbanded. Johnny Jones, a thirty-one-year-old outfielder hitting .370 at Albany, came home to Philadelphia without a job. On the morning of July 25 he went to Shibe Park to see Connie Mack. Jones had had a cup of coffee with the A's back in 1923 and had been in the minors ever since. "I have no openings right now," Mack told him, "but if I happen to need an outfielder I'll give you a tryout."

The Yankees were in town, and Jones stayed to watch the game. In the sixth inning Roger Cramer dove for a line drive and broke his collarbone. Mule Haas replaced him. Ed Coleman and now Cramer were out of action. At the end of the inning Babe O'Rourke's sonorous voice was heard on the loudspeaker: "Will Johnny Jones please report to Mr. Mack's office?"

After the game Mack signed Jones for $500 a month. The A's left for Detroit right after the game. Jones had no time to go home. He called his wife to pack a bag and bring it to him. Jones appeared in 4 games, 3 as a pinch hitter, and was released on September 1.

The Athletics weren't a bad team. Enough of them continued to hustle to enable them to play at a pennant-winning pace in the second half of the season, going 51-29 after July 4. They won 4 more games than the National League champion Cubs. But the Yankees kept on winning. The final standings reversed those of 1931: New York won 107, the second-place A's 94. The Yankees' home record of 62-15 surpassed the A's 60-15 of a year ago.

Twenty-four-year-old Jimmy Foxx had replaced Ruth and Simmons as the most feared batter in the league All around the circuit fans gasped at the longest drives ever hit out of their ballparks. Unlike Babe Ruth's breathtakingly high fly balls, Foxx's line drives disappeared in a hurry. On June 25 he hit one off Lefty Gomez in New York. It landed in the last section of the third tier in left field, splintering the back of a seat. Gomez, who fed off Foxx tales in his long career as an after-dinner speaker, said of this one, "I thought it was a fastball when I threw it, but it was going a lot faster after Foxx hit it. After the game it took me twenty minutes to walk to where it took him a split second to hit it."

Foxx was on his way to topping Ruth's 60 home runs in a season when he fell off a ladder at home in late July and hurt his wrist. After a slow start, hitting only 4 in April, he had been averaging 12 a month. After the injury he hit only 3 from July 27 to August 20 and had 47 through August 26. Giving up all notions of catching Ruth, he hit 10 more by the last day of the season. That day, swinging for the fences every time up, he connected on his last try to finish with 58. Foxx had two handicaps in chasing Ruth's record. He batted right-handed; the left-field fence was farther than the right in five of the eight ballparks. After 1927 wire screens had been put up in front of the right-field pavilion in St. Louis and the right-field seats in League Park in Cleveland. SABR researcher Bob Schaefer documented one time that Foxx hit the St. Louis screen and wound up with a double. In 1932 a few strands of barbed wire were strung above the right-field wall in Shibe Park to prevent boys from climbing over the wall. On at least one occasion (July 1) a Foxx drive hit the wire and bounced back onto the field for a triple. Two more home runs were nullified by games called on account of rain.

Foxx scored 151 runs, drove in 169, and had a .749 slugging average. He missed the batting title (and triple crown) by three points at .364. It all earned him the first of his three Most Valuable Player (MVP) honors. He would end his career with the highest on-base percentage plus slugging average of all right-handed batters.

Once Al Simmons got over his piques and valleys, his play picked up. (Years later, as a coach with the Athletics, he would tell Stan Musial, "Go after the 3,000 hits, kid. When I looked back on games I missed that I might have played, times at bat I wasted carelessly, it was too late. I didn't have enough left to make it and just missed by 73. So stay in there and bear down all the way.")

Simmons's final numbers for the year defined what an "off-year" can look like for a star: a .322 batting average with 216 hits, 35 home runs, 144 runs scored, and 151 RBIs.

Cochrane caught 137 games, many of them with aching eyes and ankles. His batting average fell 56 points, but he had career highs of 23 home runs and 112 RBIs.

Eric McNair led the league with 47 doubles. At the start of the season he had tightened up whenever he made an error, a situation that often led to another boot. Coached by Jimmie Dykes to forget the errors—"Once made, they're done"—McNair now stood out as an infield fixture of the future.

Lefty Grove started and finished his own games and others' starts, relieving more often than Walberg and Earnshaw together, and never complained. Well, hardly ever. Ed Madjeski said, "Sometimes if a game was getting close and Grove was on the bench cutting up, Connie Mack would not say a word, just look down at him. Grove would grab his glove and say, 'Dammit, you'd think I was the only pitcher on this club' as he went to the bullpen."

When the A's lost 4 in a row in early September and their hold on second place slipped to 2 games over Washington, Grove declared, "We're not going to be beat out of second place if I have to pitch every day."

He didn't have to. It was like old times: Grove, Earnshaw, and Walberg went the route seven times in the next 13 games. Grove worked in only 5 of the 13—three complete game wins and two relief jobs, including the last 2 innings in the clincher against Washington on September 23.

Their second-place finish earned the A's $998 each from the World Series receipts. Tony Freitas used his for a down payment on a $2,600 house in Sacramento.

For the second year in a row Grove completed 27 of 30 starts and led the league in ERA for the fourth consecutive year while winning 25 and pitching 1 out shy of 292 innings. Although Grove's strikeout total went up, Red Ruffing fanned two more to lead the league.

Earnshaw, Mahaffey, and Walberg had control problems and higher ERAs than the league average. Earnshaw's heart wasn't in it once the Yankees pulled away. Roy Mahaffey worked over 200 innings, most of the time pitching with men on base. He was 13-13; did that make him consistent or inconsistent? Tony Freitas pitched well—11-3 as a starter—and was an excellent fielder. On July 18 the Browns had men on second and third with 1 out in the sixth inning. "[Fred] Schulte hit the ball back to me," Freitas recalled. "I headed off [Jim] Levey from third and tagged him just before he got back to the bag. [George] Blaeholder on second was almost to third and he started back. I bluffed a throw and tagged him before he could get to second for an unassisted double play. Blaeholder cut my right ankle with his spikes on the play." Freitas was out for three weeks.

On September 2 Lew Krausse shut out the Red Sox, 15–0. He developed a sore arm, never pitched in the big leagues again, and spent most of the next ten years in the Class A bushes.

According to Bill Dooly of the *Philadelphia Record*, considered by other writers to be an accurate reporter, Connie Mack had begun his cost-cutting efforts in June, putting everybody but Grove, Cochrane, and Foxx up for bids, with no takers. One deal—Simmons and any pitcher except Grove to the Browns for Leon "Goose" Goslin and George Blaeholder—apparently snagged on Simmons's $100,000 three-year contract. The Browns had lost over $110,000 in 1931 and were reluctant to take on more payroll baggage.

Connie Mack's attitude toward trades narrowed his options: "None of the five ranking clubs in the league will ever be able to buy or trade with me for a player as long as I am a manager. They are always well-supplied with players and that's as strong as I want to see them."

Fortunately for Mack, some of the wealthiest club owners had the worst teams. The White Sox had been in the second division since the mass expulsion of its stars in 1920. Lou Comiskey, president of the Sox since the death of his father in 1931, and business manager Harry Grabiner had given up trying to revive the once-dominant club by developing young players. They were ready to spend. In August they expressed interest in Simmons and Haas. Mack put a $75,000 tag on the pair. In the course of the discussions, Comiskey added Jimmie Dykes to his wish list. When Mack said no, the negotiations ended. Rumors persisted, Dykes's name appearing in some of the speculations.

The A's closed the season in Washington on September 25. On the train to Philadelphia, Dykes asked Connie Mack about the stories of impending player sales. His home was in Philadelphia. He had bought a bowling alley with his World Series shares. Now thirty-five, he had been with Mr. Mack for fifteen years. He didn't want to go anywhere. "Don't worry about what the papers say," Mack told him. "You'll be with me next year."

Joe McCarthy was back in the World Series, opposing his old team, the Cubs. Connie Mack went to New York the day before the Series opened on September 28. At some time during the next twenty-four hours he met with Comiskey and Grabiner, who told him they would raise the price considerably for Simmons and Haas if he tossed in Dykes.

The Athletics' final financial numbers weren't in yet, but Connie Mack knew they would be big and bright red. Home attendance had dropped 33 percent to 405,500, the lowest in eleven years. Home and road receipts were down almost $300,000. The A's still drew big paydays at Yankee Stadium, but they were lucky to be paid on attendance of 1,000 in St. Louis, Boston, or Chicago, where the White Sox had been the "other team" in town since the Cubs started winning in 1926. Simmons, Foxx, and Cochrane were on multiyear contracts, but other salaries would have to be cut.

The country was still in the dumps. A presidential election was going on.

There was uncertainty, even panic, over what kind of experiments an unknown Roosevelt administration might try in order to revive the nation if Hoover was defeated.

Still, Mack was reluctant to part with Dykes until Comiskey assured Mack that he intended to make Dykes the manager when Lew Fonseca's contract expired after the '33 season. But of course Mack had to keep that a secret, which he did. And of course when the deal was announced, the papers were full of speculation that Dykes was included only because he would be the next Sox manager.

After the Yankees won the Series opener, 12–6 (before a sparse crowd that left twenty thousand seats empty), American League magnates met for dinner at the Commodore Hotel. Mack stopped in at the busy press room on his way to the dinner and informed the writers that he had sold the three players to Chicago for cash.

No price was announced. Comiskey said only that it was the biggest cash outlay for players in White Sox history, topping the $100,000 they had paid for Willie Kamm. Some headlines blared $250,000; others guessed it was probably less. The price was $150,000.

Connie Mack then escaped the barrage of questions temporarily. When the dinner was over, the Philadelphia writers were waiting for him.

"You can write whatever you want," he told them. "All I'll say now is that we were in a mood to sell those three men. The chance came, the offer was acceptable, and we took it." He would have nothing more to say until after the Series, when he would hold a press conference and answer questions at Shibe Park.

Reporters raced to the phones to get comments from the three former A's. They caught up with Simmons, who was barnstorming with Foxx and Cochrane in Sheboygan, Wisconsin. Cochrane and Foxx were sorry to hear the news. Simmons was delighted to be going to Chicago, just ninety miles from his Mitchell Street home in Milwaukee. "Mr. Mack was a good boss," he said. "I have some regrets at leaving him. But as long as he decided to sell me I'm glad he sent me to the White Sox."

Simmons told the *Chicago Tribune,* "Mack and I are on the best of terms, and we've had no falling out. The White Sox probably offered a lot of money and Mack gave in, I think, because he and the other owners need cash."

Mule Haas expressed similar sentiments but doubted that the deal would make the White Sox contenders. He was right.

Jimmie Dykes was in his room at the Alamac Hotel, preparing to go out with his wife for dinner and the hit musical *Of Thee I Sing*. He was shaving when somebody called him with the news. The next day he said the shock almost caused him to cut his throat. He knew nothing about any rumors that he would become a manager.

Later Dykes wrote that when he returned to the Alamac after the show, he was still "boiling mad." He confronted Connie Mack in the lobby:

"Am I going to the White Sox?"

"Yes, Jimmie," said Mack. "I've sold you to Chicago."

Furious, Dykes turned and left.

Some weeks later Dykes went to Shibe Park to say goodbye to the club-house attendants. Connie Mack heard he was there and asked him to come up to the office. There Mack explained. "By the time last season was over the Athletics were deep in debt. I had no choice. To save the club I had to let you go. I want to repeat what I told you on the train from Washington. At that time I had every intention of keeping you next year."

Dykes wrote that he considered Grabiner a cheapskate (a term he never applied to Connie Mack), but A's coach Eddie Collins, who had been with the White Sox for twelve years, assured him that Grabiner was one of the squarest shooters in baseball. In Chicago Dykes would take a 33 percent pay cut, to $8,000, and would get a $1,000 bonus for 1933.

At noon on October 4 every Philadelphia paper and wire service was represented in Connie Mack's tower office for the promised briefing.

"I had to let them go for financial reasons," Mack said. "Attendance this season was much lower than in prior seasons. We had one of the highest salaried clubs in the league. We went into the red heavily."

The A's were the only team in the league with four men earning over $20,000 and five over $10,000. Before the sale the club faced a loss of more than $140,000.

The sale enabled the A's to report a profit of $6,777.01, but it didn't help the cash flow immediately. Although the full amount was entered in the ledgers at the time, only one-third was payable January 1, 1933, and the rest in installments on January 1 of '34 and '35.

No columnists or letters to the editor lit into Connie Mack. When times are tough for everybody, understanding thrives. Al Simmons was the best outfielder the A's would ever have, but nobody lamented his departure. His surly, swaggering attitude had turned off the denizens of the press box and bleachers alike. Jimmie Dykes, however, was everybody's favorite. He would be missed.

But the lack of criticism didn't assuage Mack's sorrow. He never liked to sell players he wanted to keep.

It didn't make Connie Mack feel any better that every other team in the league reported a loss. "I feel that I've been a failure, not in playing results but financially, and that failure forced me to sell those players. Any man who can't make both ends meet must be a failure. And I didn't make ends meet for the A's."

2 | CONNIE MACK'S INCOME

Accurate information about the early days of the business of baseball is hard to pin down. Newspaper accounts were often estimates—or just guesses. Recently discovered A's ledgers—found since the publication of the first two volumes in this trilogy—give us what seems to be an accurate, authentic source. But the profit and loss figures, for example, differ—sometimes drastically—from other sources such as the official report of the congressional Organized Baseball Hearings of 1951, the so-called Celler Committee. Maybe different bookkeeping methods account for the differences. So a researcher seeking accuracy has to make choices.

I have chosen to go with the unaudited entries made by longtime A's secretary Bob Schroeder in the ledgers that begin in 1910. Where other sources are used, I identify them.

Was Connie Mack a financial failure?

Not when you consider that every American League team operated at a loss in 1932. Only the sale of Simmons, Haas, and Dykes enabled the A's to show a profit.

Measured by the preceding thirty-one years, Mr. Mack was a very successful businessman.

When Connie Mack rode into Philadelphia in 1901, he was staking a claim on a gold mine richer than anything the forty-niners had found in California. Big league baseball was a very profitable business, a fact that led tycoons in other businesses to invest in the Federal League. Baseball was the only form of professional sports entertainment for the masses. Horse racing ran a distant second, and prize fighting was far behind in the competition for the dimes of the sporting crowd.

As much as he scoffed at writers' estimates of how much money he had

taken out of the business, by the standards of the time—especially the pre–World War I time—Mack was a wealthy man.

He did not become wealthy on his salary, which was never more than $20,000 a year. He started in Philadelphia at $3,500. In 1902 his partners raised him to $5,000. Club ledgers show his salary at $10,000 in 1910, remaining there until 1922, when it was doubled. (He later took a cut in pay from 1934 through 1936 and again in 1943.)

The bulk of his early income probably came from dividends declared by the club's board of directors. A 1907 *Sporting News* article signed "Veteran" estimated that in the first six years of their existence, 1901–1906, the Athletics earned over $100,000 in each of their pennant-winning years, 1902 and 1905, and "big profits" in the other years. At that time Mack owned 25 percent of the stock; therefore his share of the dividends "must total over $100,000." This is guesswork and assumes that all the profits were paid out in dividends, an assumption for which we have no confirmation. The A's were probably just as profitable in 1907 and 1909, when they finished second, but they may have lost money in 1908, when they finished sixth and attendance fell almost 30 percent.

In 1913 Ben Shibe loaned Mack $113,000 to buy out the newspapermen who had been given a 25 percent interest in the team in 1901. After giving five shares each to his sons, Roy and Earle, Mack now owned just under 50 percent of the stock.

The ledgers show profits totaling about $250,000 for 1910 through 1914 but do not show any dividends paid until November 1914, when $12,000 was distributed. Another dividend of $50,000 was paid on January 2, 1915.

From 1914 through January 12, 1931, Connie Mack received $255,011 in dividends, most of them in the 1920s. None were paid thereafter.

Mack also profited from outside investments. He opened a bowling alley in 1903 and sold it at a profit a few years later. He and John Shibe bought five acres in the exclusive Bala neighborhood of Philadelphia in 1906 and built twelve homes.

Owning a piece of the Athletics provided another source of income. The sale of food and drinks and scorecards, advertising in scorecards and on outfield fences, and the renting of cushions was an important part of the baseball business from the beginning. In the nineteenth century the ballgame was sometimes an incidental attraction to lure patrons to an adjacent beer garden. As early as the 1880s a club could earn a thousand dollars for

scorecard rights alone. Even minor league teams received offers every spring for scorecard and refreshment privileges.

Some clubs ran their own concessions operations; some leased the scorecard and concessions privileges to pioneers in the catering business, such as Harry M. Stevens, Ed Barrow, and the Jacobs brothers (Marvin, Charles, and Louis), who went on to create Sportservice, for a percentage of the gross or a fee based on attendance.

The Athletics may have been unique: they did both. Connie Mack and the Shibes formed a separate partnership to manage the concessions and paid the club a pittance to lease the privileges. There is no record of when the Athletics' owners decided to take this direction. They may have started the business that way in 1901. It might have coincided with the opening of Shibe Park in 1909.

The 1910 club entries show $3,000 in income from the sale of privileges, two-thirds for refreshments and one-third for scorecard advertising. The same annual payments were made by John Shibe, who ran the catering business until his death in 1937, when a new Shibe Park Concessions Company was formed. While the Pirates might earn $35,000 a year from concessions privileges at seven cents a head in the 1930s and the Yankees $159,000 at eighteen cents a head in the 1940s, the new partnership of the Macks and Shibes paid the same $3,000 a year to the Athletics until 1939, when they raised it to $5,000. In 1941 it was raised to $5,500 and remained there through 1945, when it went up to $20,000.

A 1929 survey estimated that 5.5 percent of major league revenue came from concessions; for some clubs they were the most profitable part of the business. Those profits never appeared on the Athletics' profit and loss statements. They were distributed to the Athletics' stockholders on a per-share basis. Prior to 1914 Connie Mack owned 25 percent; after that, 50 percent, until his distribution of stock to his sons in 1946, when he was left with 20 percent.

What did Connie Mack's share of those concessions profits amount to from 1910 through 1950? We can only estimate based on various bits of information from occasional *Sporting News* articles on this side of the business, a 1937 *Fortune* article, and citations from the work of Steven A. Reiss in *Baseball in America and America in Baseball*.

To begin, it's necessary to understand that the Athletics never sold outfield fence signs, which were worth as much as $25,000 in some cities. They gave away scorecards for many years, and they never sold beer. A 1959 *Inquirer*

story (when there was talk of the Phillies' building a new park in New Jersey because of Pennsylvania's Sunday curfew law and ban on the selling of beer in ballparks) cited "recent figures" that the average fan spent seventy-five cents during a game. "In Philadelphia it's only twenty-five cents. The difference is beer."

So the anecdotal figures—the reported 1929 Cubs' sales of sixteen cents a head and profits per head of more than twenty cents in 1946; the 1937 *Fortune* estimate that on a hot day sales might be eighteen cents a head; the fifty or fifty-five cents a head reported sales at big doubleheaders in the 1940s; the 1949 Cardinals reporting sales of sixty-three cents a head—must be discounted for the A's.

From the day the Phillies moved into Shibe Park in August 1938, the concessions company split the profits from sales at the Phillies' games with their tenants. It kept all the receipts from the Eagles and Villanova football games played at Shibe Park and catered events at other venues.

So what figures should we use? We're talking about a long-ago world of nickels and dimes. Hot dogs, sodas, and peanuts sold for ten cents until the 1940s, when Durk's hot dogs went up to fifteen cents. A 1940 Shibe Park menu lists sandwiches at fifteen and twenty cents, a hot plate of ham or steak with two vegetables for forty cents.

Let's go with an average gross of eight cents a head from 1910 to 1920, twelve cents in the 1920s, ten cents in the 1930s, and twenty cents in the 1940s, with a 50 percent profit margin.

For 1910–1919 Connie Mack would have received an average of $4,700 a year. For the 1920s the average would have been $17,400 a year. For the 1930s the average would have been $10,000 a year. For 1940 through 1945 Connie Mack would receive $34,000 a year; in 1946, $49,000. After he gave shares to his sons in 1946, Mack held 302 shares. In the postwar boom years, 1947–1949, he received 20 percent of $135,000 or $27,000 a year. Each of his sons got $90 a share on 163 shares or $14,670.

So over forty years Connie Mack received a total of about $655,000 as his share of the concessions profits. Had the total profits gone to the club, they would have added more than $1.5 million to the working capital.

In 1951 Penn Sportservice began paying $200,000 to the club for the concessions privileges.

By the 1920s Connie Mack was proud to be worth a million dollars. In a revocable trust dated April 23, 1928, Mack provided for his wife and three adult children, all from his first marriage. His wife, Katherine, had a ⅝ interest, and Roy, Earle, and daughter Marguerite, ⅛ each. Mack put into the trust his 747 shares of the Athletics. Dividends totaling almost $50,000, paid in 1928 and 1929, and Mack's income from the concessions went into the trust.

The farsighted trust, effective for the life of the beneficiaries, described all sorts of contingencies on the death of any of them, with the A's stock or (if sold) the proceeds passing to grandchildren and their heirs.

Then the stock market crashed and cleaned him out. He never made back the million. Mack revoked the trust in 1930. The securities were returned to him, and all accumulated income was distributed to the four beneficiaries.

From the day he arrived in Philadelphia, Mack had supported his mother and three children, along with various relatives and in-laws. In 1910 he started a second family, which produced five children. By the end of his life he was still subsidizing some of his children and was generous with relatives, grandchildren, old-time players, and countless others. When Connie Mack died in 1956, his estate, except for the proceeds from the 1954 sale of the team, would total less than $60,000.

3 | DISMANTLING THE A'S

Despite the woes of the world at large and the world of baseball, Connie Mack enjoyed his seventieth birthday on December 23, 1932, as much as any he had ever celebrated. He arrived at his office at the usual 10 a.m. and found it filled with letters, telegrams, and floral arrangements. The first notes he showed to visitors came from friends in Hartford, where he had played in 1886 before going to the major leagues.

Then he put aside the reminiscing and looked ahead. The way he saw it, he had one more year of experience than he'd had a year ago, making his judgment that much better. "We'll have a great ball club next year," he said. "I don't think anyone will run away with the next pennant."

In his inaugural address on March 4, 1933, President Franklin D. Roosevelt said, "The only thing we have to fear is fear itself."

A lot of people had a lot more to fear than just fear itself. The next day the Nazis gained control of the German government and handed Hitler unlimited power.

Japan had overrun northern China and Manchuria and was seen as America's biggest threat of war.

Fifteen million Americans were looking for work. Nobody knew what steps the new administration would take to boost employment or what would work, including the new administration itself. Money and gold were being withdrawn from banks, which in turn were foreclosing on farmers and small shop owners. In the month before Roosevelt took office, governors of one state after another ordered their banks to close.

When Roosevelt closed all the banks on March 6, 1933, Connie Mack had no access to cash for players' meal money and other expenses for spring training in Fort Myers. Dick Richards, who had brought the A's to Fort Myers in 1925, supplied the team with office space in his Royal Pharmacy and invited Mack to dip into the pharmacy's till and use the daily receipts for expenses. This went on for nearly two weeks when, according to Dick Richards's son Joe, "Finally Dad had to pay some of his bills too. Connie Mack called someone he knew in Philadelphia and put Dad on a train going up there. The man met Dad at the train and handed him an envelope with $5,000 in it. When he got back, Connie Mack paid Dad back and used the rest to get his team back to Philadelphia. I think Mr. Mack looked at my father almost as a son."

The story is plausible. Mack had plenty of wealthy friends around Philadelphia with ready access to that amount of money, banks or no banks. This might have been the kernel of the Glennon family story that their father, coal transporter Eddie Glennon, once loaned Mr. Mack some money to meet his payroll.

One of the first acts of Congress after the new administration took over was the repeal of Prohibition. Although it wouldn't take effect until the thirty-sixth state—Utah—ratified the amendment on December 5, Congress immediately legalized 3.2 percent beer.

April 7 was declared Beer Day in Pennsylvania. Suds lovers rushed to the saloons almost as fast as the legislature rushed to tax it.

An ad read: "Someday you'll tell your children and children's children that the beer I drank on Beer Day was good old Esslinger."

About half the major league clubs decided to sell beer; the Athletics and Phillies did not. John Shibe said, "Beer trade belongs to hotels, restaurants, and bars who have had to struggle along without it all these years. They've suffered a lot of losses and now have a chance to get some of their money back. We're not going to try to cut in on them. Our business is baseball. Let other people have theirs."

A year later that gesture of generosity was forgotten. The Athletics applied to city treasurer Willis Hadley for a license to sell beer at an upper-deck concession stand. They ran into opposition from the anti-Sunday-baseball forces, as well as an 1881 law banning the sale of beer or liquor at places of amusement. It didn't matter that the state Liquor Control Board had licensed some such places to sell beer and liquor; Hadley said he wasn't going to do it for Shibe Park.

A's Attorney Charles G. Gartling took this evidence of inconsistency to a higher court but got nowhere. The legislature still feared the wrath of the churches over the Sunday baseball issue. It had no belly for a beer fight.

From time to time the Athletics would lobby for the ban to be lifted, but it wouldn't happen until after they had left the state.

But there was beer in the Shibe Park clubhouse after games. Mack preferred to give his boys a chance to relax with a beer or two there rather than head for the neighborhood saloons to find it.

And of course the fans could bring their own beer in bottles and cans, which, when emptied, made handy messengers of disapproval over umpires' decisions on the field.

To add to the club's financial burden, the city council imposed a fee of $5.50 per day for each policeman assigned to game-day duty at Shibe Park and Baker Bowl—more than the regular full day's pay for cops. The clubs had no say as to how many might be assigned. Gartling went to court and had the act overturned. But the state supreme court reversed the decision. Connie Mack was now 0-3 vs. the Supremes in Philadelphia.

One day in 1927, after a game in New York, Ty Cobb introduced Eddie Collins to Tom Yawkey, whose uncle had owned the Detroit club during most of Cobb's tenure there. Collins and Yawkey found they had both attended the Irving prep school in Tarrytown about fifteen years apart. After that, whenever the A's were in New York, Collins visited Yawkey at his apartment.

One evening in 1932, after dinner at Mack's favorite New York restaurant (the Alexandria Room of Schrafft's at Fifth Avenue and Forty-Sixth Street), Collins invited Connie Mack to go with him to see Yawkey. The A's had lost that day; the three men sat replaying the game, Tom Yawkey bemoaning the loss more than the others.

As Collins later remembered it, Mrs. Yawkey said, "Well, Tom, get a club for yourself someday and you can make it do as you like."

On their way back to the Alamac Hotel, Mack asked Collins if he thought Mrs. Yawkey was serious about Tom's buying a ball club. "If he has got such a notion in his mind," said Mack, "there's one club in the American League I think he could buy. I know the owners want to sell."

"What club is that?"

"Boston."

Collins said he'd ask Tom.

Yawkey told Collins he was willing to meet with Red Sox president Bob Quinn to explore the idea.

That was the end of it as far as Collins was concerned. But when Connie

Mack took him to the winter meetings in December 1932, AL president Will Harridge asked Collins if Yawkey had said anything more about buying the Boston club. "No," said Collins. "He's down south right now. I'll write and ask him."

Back in New York in January 1933, Yawkey, Collins, Quinn, and Yawkey's partner, a Mr. DeFoe, met at Yawkey's office. After the meeting Yawkey asked Collins for information about the baseball industry.

With Connie Mack's help, Collins collected some data. "Connie Mack sent me from Philadelphia a half dozen times with facts about this curious kind of business," Collins wrote.

Later that month Yawkey and Collins met at the funeral of their former Irving headmaster. On the train back to New York, Yawkey asked Collins, "If the Athletics would release you, would you come to Boston if I bought the club and took you in for a piece of it?"

"Flabbergasted, I went to Connie Mack the next morning," Collins recalled, "and told him something funny had come up about the Boston deal.

"Connie began to laugh. 'I know,' he said. 'Yawkey wants you to go to Boston. I've seen it coming for a month. It's a grand opportunity.'"

Will Harridge, eager to see new money rescue the broke Red Sox, urged Collins to go. "If you go along with Yawkey, the deal will go through."

Collins agreed to go as general manager, and the deal went through.

"The day I said goodbye to Connie Mack to go to Boston," wrote Collins, "I had something in my throat that felt like a baseball."

At his first league meeting in the spring of 1933, Yawkey let it be known he had money to spend. He didn't know any more about the price of ballplayers than the price of a dozen eggs (twenty-five cents). According to *Sporting News* editor J. G. Taylor Spink, Yawkey told the league directors, "I don't know much about the technique of trading and buying and all that sort of thing. They tell me it is a special study in itself. I haven't time to go through the apprenticeship. Who has any real good ball players for sale? The money is on the table."

To the starving club owners who were humming the hit song, "Brother, Can You Spare a Dime," he was greeted like manna from heaven to Moses and the Israelites wandering in the desert.

Within a week Yawkey gave the Browns $55,000 for catcher Rick Ferrell and pitcher Lloyd Brown, and paid the Yankees, who weren't starving, $100,000 for third baseman Bill Werber and pitcher George Pipgras.

Every club's payroll was now below its 1929 level. The 1951 congressional Celler Committee report on the business of baseball would show the Athletics fourth highest in the league for 1933 at $166,533, down 35 percent from 1929.

Max Bishop took a 50 percent cut to $5,000. Bing Miller went from $10,000 to $6,000. Foxx, Cochrane, and Grove were still on long-term contracts. Rare raises went to Mike Higgins and Eric McNair.

After winning 12 games in 1932, Tony Freitas was shocked to open his mail and find a contract for $1,400 less than he'd made in '32.

"I fired it back," Freitas said. "He [Mack] told me he had too many high-priced players on the club. I thought, 'Don't take it out on me, the little potato.' I wound up signing for the same $4,000."

In California George Earnshaw was telling reporters the Yankees would clinch the pennant by the Fourth of July. That rankled Mack as much as Moose's resistance to taking a 50 percent pay cut. Earnshaw was unable to move Mack and signed for $7,500. Rube Walberg was the last to sign, taking a 40 percent cut to $6,000.

(The sportswriters who chronicled the players' salary woes were in the same boat. Stanley Woodward, sports editor of the *New York Herald-Tribune*, wrote, "Newspaper owners paid employees as little as possible and every five-dollar raise was attended by a battle between the employee and the managing editor." It would take Red Smith ten years, until 1945, to reach $90 a week at the *Philadelphia Record*.)

Unemployed baseball fans were unmoved by the players' complaints. Ballplayers could afford the $1.50 lobster dinner at the Palmer House in Chicago, while a family of five got by on a dollar a day—if they had the dollar.

Players could walk into a tobacco store and buy cigarettes by the pack. The working or nonworking stiff bought his "loosie" smokes one at a time, for a penny if he wanted to splurge on Camels, or Marvels at two for a penny. No need to buy matches; a gas lighter sat on the counter to light up. "If you wanted to act like a big shot," said one smoker, "you could light a Marvel at the end where the name was and tell people it was a Camel."

In such ways were dignity and self-respect preserved.

Connie Mack had been in Fort Myers a few weeks when he was hit with the news that his forty-year-old daughter, Peggy McCambridge, was gravely ill.

Peggy and her two sons, Cornelius (Connie) and Bob, had lived in Philadelphia for a year in 1930 after her husband died. Then she and Connie had moved to Chicago. Bob McCambridge stayed, and Connie Mack sent him to Germantown Academy with Connie Jr. for a year, where he played third base. In August 1932 the family moved to Asheville, North Carolina, for Peggy's health.

"We are about settled and I enjoy it here very much," Peggy wrote her brother-in-law in Chicago that fall. "No more pleurisy and no stomach trouble. My strength is returning and am putting on a little weight. Naturally with such results in such short time it is most gratifying. . . . Well, your Cubs won the flag. That's fine. You will have some excitement. I hope our radio works better than it has been. Reception is very poor. Who is going to win the election? Conditions are terrible here. Our Depression meat is chicken. Can get two spring chickens for less than a dollar. The roses are beautiful in the back yard. I pick some every day. . . . The air is so different from Chicago and the water is good. We are out in a subdivision and view the mountains all around."

Peggy did well until the winter. On Sunday, March 5, she began to weaken. A strep infection set in. Her doctor, George Alexander, called Connie Mack to come immediately. Mack was on the train from Fort Myers when she died at midnight on March 8. Minutes later Dr. Alexander, who was at the house awaiting Mack, was talking to a local reporter when he dropped dead from a heart attack.

"That was some night," recalled Connie McCambridge, who was fifteen at the time.

More than fifty years later he said, "I look back at her now and see how strong she was to keep us boys and look after us. She was only 4-foot-10 and she went through a lot. After my father died she wore black for so long until one of the dresses was ripped in the laundry and she took that as a sign that she didn't have to wear black anymore."

Connie Mack escorted Peggy's body to Worcester for burial in the family plot. The two boys went to live with their uncle in Manitowoc, Wisconsin. For the next several years, whenever the A's were in Chicago, Mack would invite his grandsons to come down to stay with him, or he would go to visit them.

Years later the boys' cousin, Ellen McCambridge Bargmann, recalled those visits fondly: "The boys called him Dad, but I called him Uncle Mack. We were in awe of him. We never saw those high collars in Manitowoc. Straight as a die. He was kind to us, soft-spoken, and had little conversations with us, which to me shows what a wonderful father he must have been.

"He stayed at the Hotel Manitowoc. My mother fixed dinner and he always asked for creamed onions—typical Irish.

"Once in 1933 when the A's were in Chicago we all went down and stayed at the Del Prado with them. Katherine was there but she didn't like the McCambridges. I was nine. After a game we were in the game room playing Ping-Pong. We played against Mickey Cochrane—he never had the stogie out of his mouth even when he talked, then Jimmy Foxx. They hit the ball easy to us."

Connie McCambridge remembered those visits: "One Sunday in Manitowoc we were coming home from Mass in the car and we saw a girl walking up the street and my cousin said, 'That's Connie's girlfriend.' Dad said, 'What? Drive around the block so I can get a look at her.' He was always teasing me."

He recalled the trip to Chicago that year too: "We were eating in the dining room with Connie Mack, and Katherine came in and sat somewhere else. He didn't bring it to our attention that she was sitting elsewhere. More power to him. He would just go on. She was a tough cat."

Connie Mack remained very close to them, as he did with his brother Tom's children, corresponding with them, usually with a check enclosed, for the rest of his life.

On March 13 Mack learned of the death of Mike Drennan, his chief scout. It was Drennan who had sent Jimmie Dykes for a tryout at Shibe Park, made the purchase of Jimmy Foxx, and scouted Mickey Cochrane in Dover.

The Athletics had a new coaching staff. Connie Mack hired Lena Blackburne to replace Kid Gleason. Blackburne was cut from the same rawhide as Gleason—all baseball. A scrappy, light-hitting infielder, Blackburne had been signed by Mack off the New Jersey sandlots thirty years earlier but had never played for the A's. He had managed the White Sox in 1928–1929. Pitcher Red Faber said of him, "Lena never wanted to leave the field, not even at practice."

Bing Miller replaced Collins as the captain and part-time player, primarily as a pinch hitter. Ed Rommel became the pitching and third base coach at $3,000, a big saving from Eddie Collins's $15,000. Earle Mack, a coach on the baselines or in the dugout since 1924, was relegated to the bullpen.

Dave Keefe had been a pitcher for the A's in 1921–1922. After bouncing around in the minors for ten years, he was still a baseball lifer at thirty-six. One day at Shibe Park he asked Connie Mack if he could work out by pitching batting practice. Mack sometimes used area high school prospects for that chore when the team was at home, but they often lacked the desired control for the job. Keefe, who threw a natural forkball as the result of having lost the middle finger of his right hand in a childhood accident, proved just the ticket. Mack signed him as probably the first full-time batting practice pitcher in the big leagues. Keefe filled that role for the AL team at nine All-Star Games starting in 1937. The job was hazardous in those days; there was no screen in front of the batting practice tossers. Keefe took plenty of hits to all parts of his body for his $1,500 salary but stayed with it, becoming a coach in 1941 and traveling secretary for ten years beginning in 1950.

Connie Mack had some qualms about his pitching staff. He knew how pay cuts could sap a player's motivation. He counted on Lefty Grove to be as effective as ever, but Walberg and Earnshaw had gone downhill last year. He didn't know if there was any fire left in them.

Beyond the veteran trio lay the great unknown. Maybe Roy Mahaffey would improve. Maybe Sugar Cain would come through. Maybe Hank McDonald, bought from Portland in 1931 and sent down again in '32, would do the job.

Even if he didn't have the money, Mack couldn't resist buying pitchers, especially big ones. In 1931 he had given Harrisburg $12,044 for 6-foot, 200-pound right-hander Bill Dietrich, a former Philadelphia high school athlete. Dietrich spent 1932 in Portland and Wilkes-Barre. Maybe, at twenty-three, he was ready. Dietrich wore glasses—not a first but a rarity in the big leagues. Danny MacFayden of the Yankees was the only other active pitcher using them.

Mack paid $26,667 and first baseman Oscar Roettger for 6-foot-3, 210-pound lefty Gowell Claset, 23-13 at Montreal last year.

The rest of his team looked solid: the infield of Foxx, Bishop, McNair, and Higgins was as good as any in the league. When McNair went down with a sore arm, Dib Williams was given another chance and made the most of it. In Fort Myers Bing Miller changed Dib's stance and his bat position. Lena Blackburne told him, "That limp wrist throw is okay for a second baseman. But to play short you have to stiffen that wrist." Williams worked harder than anybody and became not only a dependable fielder, but also a productive hitter.

Mike Higgins, after hitting .327 with 83 extra-base hits at Portland, was ready to take over third base. (Growing up in Dallas, he had picked up the nickname "Pinky" because of his ruddy-cheeked complexion. But to the A's he was Mike.) Higgins had always wanted to play for Mack and now had his chance. He was one ballyhooed rookie who would live up to his minor league records.

One reason so many minor league worldbeaters failed to maintain their stats as big league hitters was the use of cheap baseballs—known as nickel rockets—in some leagues that produced exaggerated numbers. Three leagues—the Pacific Coast, Mississippi Valley, and New England (with three)—would have .400 hitters in 1933. Will Harridge said in December that only two of the many minor leaguers bought by AL clubs in 1933 had lived up to expectations. He succeeded in getting a standardized baseball adopted by all leagues.

Higgins found it easier to field ground balls on the well-kept big league infields. It was harder adjusting to big league pitching. "In the Pacific Coast League [PCL], there were only one or two good pitchers on a team," he said. "The rest were mediocre. In the majors you only see good pitching so you get used to it. They are always working the corners on you. Ordinary pitchers in the Coast League with a 2-0 count would always throw you a kelly down the middle. I always laid back looking for it. That's how I hit a lot of my home runs. Here whether the pitcher is in the hole or not he keeps shooting for the corners. I haven't seen one down the middle yet."

Observers were impressed with the speed and range of the young outfielders Coleman, Cramer, Finney, and Johnson.

Bob Johnson, twenty-seven, was born in Pryor, Oklahoma. He would usually be tabbed Indian Bob Johnson; the story was that his mother was half Cherokee, but Shirley Povich of the *Washington Post* once quoted him as saying that his mother was only one-sixteenth Cherokee. Johnson moved to Tacoma, where he worked for a contractor and pitched for the company team, then made his way to southern California. His older brother, Roy, was making good money as a big league outfielder in 1929. Bob was a husky six-footer with strong arms and wrists, so he tried out with the Los Angeles Angels, who suggested he try the Wichita club, which was looking for players. Johnson broke in with Wichita, where Tom Turner saw him and bought him for Portland. On a visit to Portland in 1930, John Shibe saw him and recommended him to Mack, who bought him, then optioned him to Portland for the next two years because he couldn't hit a curve. After countless hours of extra batting practice against curve ball specialists, Johnson became a .330 hitter with power. He had a flat-footed stance and used a 38-ounce bat.

Johnson was the star of the spring games in Fort Myers. He won a place in the lineup and the confidence of the other players, who preferred him to Ed Coleman.

"It's a funny thing," Mack mused one day. "In the first game Johnson muffed two fly balls. If it had been Coleman they would have said he's a poor fielder. But of Johnson they say he never makes a muff. I think they are right. I don't think Johnson lets many get away from him. But it goes to show how the players figure things out. I am enthusiastic about Coleman. I like the way he hits and I think he is a good fielder. But I can't leave Johnson out."

Mack was easier on Coleman than his men were. It wasn't that they disliked Coleman, an affable, easygoing fellow. They didn't trust him in the outfield because he tried to make basket catches and dropped too many of them. They'd been taught to "catch the ball in front of your eyes, not down below the waist," said Flit Cramer. "With a man on third and one out, catch the ball moving in so you're in position to throw and get rid of it."

The one who spent the most time on the bench would be Lou Finney, who was optioned to Montreal to play every day.

"What we gave away in power, we gained in speed," said Mack. He ordered the sliding pit restored. They worked on base running and stretching hits.

In an April 9 exhibition game in Brooklyn, Johnson hit 2 home runs and was part of a triple steal. Bill Dooly enthused about the running game, promising his readers, "The A's will lift you out of your seat with the thrill of their adventures on the base paths."

But in the end they relied on power again and were last in stolen bases.

Connie Mack thought there would be little room between New York and Washington in the 1933 pennant race. The Senators had added two veteran pitchers in Earl Whitehill and Lefty Stewart. Owner Clark Griffith had another boy wonder manager, his twenty-six-year-old shortstop son-in-law, Joe Cronin.

Mack was not surprised by Griffith's choice. Whenever the A's had been in Washington for the past three or four years, Cronin had made a point of seeking out Mack in the hotel lobby and plying him with questions. "I don't know if I could tell him anything he didn't know," Mack told the AP. "But he used to ask all kinds of questions and I'd answer them. Finally I began to think he'd be using what I told him against my own club. He's a smart young fellow, nice mannered chap too."

Joe Cronin would prove to be a staunch ally when Connie Mack needed him twenty years later.

Mack left Fort Myers with confidence. "We had a fine training season. I can't remember a better one. If we can't win with this team, we couldn't win with the club I had last year."

If, he added, the pitchers come through.

Of course this was the usual kind of spring talk for publication, even from managers who knew they had a second division team. Privately and in letters Connie Mack was always realistic in his assessment of his team. This time he spoke as confidently in private as he did in public.

He wasn't alone. Six of those polled by the AP picked the Athletics to win. The majority picked the Yankees; they didn't see what Joe McCarthy saw—that most of his stars had aged significantly over the winter. The Pirates were the favorites in the NL.

The Athletics opened in Washington on April 12 with McNair out with a sore arm, Foxx with a spike wound in his leg, and the lightly regarded Ed Cihocki (who would underhit his weight by 20 points) at shortstop.

For the first time in fifty years Connie Mack was not there for his team's opener. He was in Harrisburg, urging Governor Gifford Pinchot to sign a bill introduced by Senator Louis A. Schwartz that had finally passed, allowing a referendum on Sunday baseball.

It wasn't a pleasant task for Mack. In 1930 he had campaigned for Democrat John M. Hemphill, a supporter of Sunday baseball, against Pinchot, a staunch Prohibitionist and defender of the Sunday Blue Laws. Pinchot won. Late that summer a Philadelphia court chipped away at the Blue Laws, declaring that amateur and semipro teams could play on Sundays, even take up a collection, as long as the games weren't too near a church.

The A's didn't give up. John Shibe was a power in state Democratic circles. Mack's longtime friend Judge Harry S. McDevitt was equally high among Republicans.

In 1931 a Sunday bill had passed the House but never came to a vote in the Senate. In March of 1932 the House approved a new version 127–75, and it reached the Senate floor, where it was fiercely debated, both sides quoting Scripture to support their opposing views. The league had two schedules prepared but released neither, awaiting the outcome of the vote. Mack expected the bill's approval and was shocked when two Republicans on whom he was counting from nearby Delaware and Tioga Counties switched their votes to defeat it, 26–24.

"It means a terrible battle for us to exist," said Mack.

Reintroduced in 1933, a bill requiring local referenda in November passed on April 11. The whole issue was something Governor Pinchot wished would go away. He didn't want to antagonize the Sabbatarians, who were against it, or the baseball enthusiasts, who were for it. Connie Mack decided he had better make a final pitch to the reluctant Pinchot. He sent the team to Washington with Bing Miller in charge and went to Harrisburg, where he, Schwartz, and Philadelphia councilman William Roper met with the governor to urge him to sign the bill. The meeting took longer than Mack expected. He didn't get any commitment, and he didn't get to Washington until after the game.

Two weeks went by before the governor signed the bill on April 25. He felt it necessary to make a radio address to the voters that night to explain his action. To placate the opposition, he promised that if a referendum was approved in November, 10 percent of Sunday admission receipts would go to unemployment relief. That made him appear to be doing something for the 13 percent of the state's population on relief and making the Sabbath-wreckers pay for it. (After the election the state passed a 4 percent relief tax, which, with the 10 percent federal tax, raised general admission tickets to $1.14, the highest in any big league city.)

After the A's lost 4 of the first 5, Connie Mack blamed himself for not working his pitchers enough in the exhibition games. "I thought I was doing the right thing by not letting them go more than 3 or 4 innings. I can see that the more years I stay in this game, the more I learn about it. Now we have to get our pitchers in shape to stay nine."

It was so cold when the A's opened at home, Mack sat bundled in a heavy dark overcoat against the fierce wind blowing in from the outfield. Lefty Grove wore kid gloves when he batted, not as batting gloves but to keep his hands warm. A mere five thousand hardy souls were rewarded by Grove's four-hitter and Foxx's 2 home runs.

George Earnshaw quickly began what would turn into a season-long soap opera, As the New Leaf Turns. He would turn over more of them than hungry thrips in a garden. Earnshaw arrived at Fort Myers full of apologies and promises of good behavior. He was through fooling around. He was determined to get into condition and stay that way. He had even left his golf clubs at home. His mouth said all the right things, but his heart was not in his mouth. His behavior pattern began when the A's went to Miami to play the Cardinals; he and Bob Paul visited the Two Bits Club, a gambling speakeasy in a big barn where it cost two bits to get in.

Earnshaw started the second game in Washington and was wild, driven out in the 6-run sixth inning of an 11–4 loss. Five days later he pitched his heart out giving up only 3 hits in New York. But Lefty Gomez matched him and the Yankees won it, 2–1. After that disheartening loss he went on a tear and committed the sin of taking younger players with him, notably Gowell Claset and Roy Mahaffey, who didn't need any arm-twisting to go boozing.

On April 24 Earnshaw gave up 6 runs in 8 innings, but the A's bats saved him, and the team eventually won, 16–10.

Then they went west, and it was cold and it was wet, and they played only two games in the first nine days of May. During two idle days in Chicago old teammates Dykes, Simmons, and Haas came to visit, Dykes as usual the nonstop life of the party. Some of them went to the racetracks; others played a marathon Ping-Pong tournament. Eric McNair got up a casino game. There were bridge or pinochle games in the rooms of Mike Higgins and Bob Johnson.

After lunch one day McNair, Finney, and Cain walked the two blocks to the rocky shore of Lake Michigan. As Bill Werber related the story (possibly having heard it from McNair), "McNair didn't like Cain for some reason. They were both southerners, McNair from Mississippi, Cain from Georgia. They stood at the lakeshore watching the icy water dashing against the rocks. Cain said, 'I'd bet a hundred dollars nobody would jump in there with their clothes on.'

"McNair saw a way to get a hundred dollars from Cain. He took off his overcoat and wristwatch and put up the money. Finney held the bet. McNair jumped into the water, climbed out onto the rocks, and ran back to the hotel. He paid a dollar to get his shoes shined and two to get his suit pressed. That night at dinner he crowed about how he had come out ninety-seven dollars to the good over Sugar Cain."

Connie Mack went to the Century of Progress Exposition one day. "I was standing at a railing," he wrote to a friend, "when an old fellow standing next to me began to push and said I was taking up too much room. I looked up and there stood Deacon White." He and White, eighty-five, had been teammates at Buffalo in 1890. "I recognized him at once though I hadn't seen him for forty years."

It was still raining on Monday morning, May 8, in Detroit. Earnshaw was sitting in the hotel lobby chatting with a friend when Connie Mack beckoned to him.

"I'm sending you home to get into shape," Mack said.

The surprised Earnshaw said, "I am in shape."

"Go home and work out at Shibe Park," Mack said. "You can't possibly get in enough work to stay sharp in this weather. It won't be any better in Cleveland. You'll be ready to pitch when we get home in a week."

Reporters heard about it. They found Earnshaw at the train station. "It was a complete surprise and shock to me," he said. "I expected to pitch this afternoon."

Mack knew his man. Earnshaw had written a letter to his wife two days earlier in St. Louis, admitting that he was in poor condition because of the bad weather. The many postponements didn't give him a chance to pitch and stay in shape. He told her that he didn't expect to pitch for the rest of the trip.

When the writers caught up with Mack he said, "George may feel he is in shape to pitch but a big fellow like him needs lots of work, at least 50 percent more than the ordinary pitcher and it's been impossible to get. I could have pitched George here, yes, but I think we'd have had to take him out in 3 or 4 innings and that sort of thing wouldn't bring him around to condition."

Mack also knew that Earnshaw hadn't just been playing billiards in the evenings. But he wasn't ready to say anything about that yet.

The A's came home and went 9-2 against the west, and suddenly only 3 games separated the top five teams. The workouts seemed to have helped Earnshaw. On May 18 he beat Chicago, 9–1. A week later he pitched a solid 7 innings against Detroit. After Jim Peterson pitched the eighth, Grove worked the last 4 innings in the 12-inning 4–3 win.

When Mack told Earnshaw he'd be pitching on May 30 in Boston, Moose stunned Mack by saying, "I don't know if I'll be ready."

He wasn't. He started the second game of a doubleheader and lasted 3 innings. Lefty Grove had worked 3 innings in the first game and was tired. His arm was stiff and achy. Still, with the score 6–6 he went in and pitched the ninth and tenth; the A's won in the twelfth. "I wasn't loose until the last man I faced," Grove said.

The Athletics went to New York and had two days off. On Thursday afternoon Mack confronted Earnshaw again about his condition. Another new leaf was turned. George promised he would stop drinking and running around. Mack told him to be ready to pitch on Sunday.

They started a 4-game series on Friday, June 2, trailing the Yankees by 3½ games. When Mahaffey got into trouble in the eighth, Grove got up, beckoned for a catcher to go with him, and headed for the bullpen. This time he gave up the hit that drove in the winning runs.

That night George Earnshaw went on a toot and took Gowell Claset with him.

The next day they were both in the bullpen. Rube Walberg started and walked 4 in the first, but a double play saved him temporarily. He got into more trouble in the second. Eddie Rommel stepped in front of the dugout and held his arms far apart to call in the rotund Claset. Earnshaw was taking a nap. He slept soundly, right through the A's scoring 11 runs in the third, right through Claset's being bombarded in the fifth and Rommel's signaling for George to come in, right through Jim Peterson's being rushed in instead and the Yankees scoring 10 runs and going on to win, 17–11.

Mack was furious. He was also bitterly disappointed, He suspended Earnshaw for ten days without pay and fined him $500 and sent him home.

"For the sake of George's family I held off as long as I could," Mack told reporters. "George promised me on Thursday afternoon that his drinking and running around were over. I thought he meant it. I thought our troubles were over. I even thought we had a good chance for the pennant. Friday night he was on a tear as bad as ever. He broke faith again. He came to the park on Saturday in such condition he was asleep during the whole 11-run rally we put out. I had no further choice."

On Sunday, before the biggest crowd of the year—sixty-five thousand— the Athletics lost twice to the Yankees. They made one first-inning hit off Johnny Allen in the second game and left town 7½ games out. They were 0-8 against New York so far.

"If it weren't for those Yankees," Mack lamented in a letter to Sr. Florence, "we could still be well up in the race, but we don't seem to be able to do anything with that crowd of players. It just seems as tho our youngsters get a little stage fright when playing New York."

Back at Shibe Park on Monday, June 5, Earnshaw called Mack and asked if he could work out on the field. Mack said okay. He was banned from the clubhouse, his gear moved to an unused dressing room under the left-field stands. He ran, pitched batting practice for the pitchers, and shagged flies but was generally ignored by the rest of the players. As far as they were concerned, Moose had thrown down the team and Mr. Mack. He had pitched only 41 innings so far. Two years ago that would have been a few weeks' work.

Al Simmons pinned the Athletics' woes squarely on his old teammate. "If George were pitching in his old form the A's would be right up there," he said. "But he isn't the old Earnshaw and it's too bad."

Connie Mack often thanked Sr. Florence for "the many prayers you are saying for our success." But his pitching didn't have a prayer.

It wasn't just the starters. The guys in the bullpen—Claset and Peterson and McDonald and Tim McKeithan and Dietrich—weren't getting the job done. Mack recovered $4,000 by selling McDonald to the Browns. He shipped Claset to Baltimore; for his $26,667 investment, Mack had gotten a return of 11⅓ innings pitched, 11 walks, and 23 hits allowed. Dietrich was farmed out to Montreal, in response to a plea for help from Royals' president Frank Shaughnessy.

"We only have pitchers who can go six or seven innings," Mack lamented. "We need somebody who can go in and hold the other fellows for the last few innings. It's the only way I know we can stay up in the race.

"Until the rest of the pitchers prove to me they can go the distance, I'm going to hold Grove back and shoot him in there to save games for us."

From May 20 through June 2 Grove worked in 9 games without starting. The A's won 8 of them. Pitching in 6 games in a week, he gave up 1 run in 18 innings. But they gained no ground on the leaders. On June 5 Lefty went back to pitching complete victories. He would lead the league with a 24-8 record and 21 complete games while relieving 17 times. He reached his peak on August 3, striking out Babe Ruth three times and Gehrig twice while handing the Yankees their first shutout in 309 games.

Grove never complained about the workload. But he still simmered and occasionally boiled over about shoddy fielding behind him. On August 15 in Cleveland his defense made him work for an 8–7 win; 4 errors—2 by Dib Williams and 1 each by Higgins and McNair—and a single that Bob Johnson played into a triple led to 3 unearned runs in the first five innings. After the fifth inning, Grove stormed into the dugout flinging his glove. "Some of these goddamn infielders ought to wear aprons."

McNair jumped up, ready to swing at him. "You mean that?"

"There, there, boys," Mack said. That ended it.

Desperate for pitchers, Mack signed a local semipro, Dick Oliver, whose real name was Tracy Barrett. He became better known as Kewpie Barrett, a wartime pitcher for the Phillies, than for anything he did for the A's.

Duke University coach Jack Coombs had Connie Jr., Mickey Cochrane's brother Archie, and the coach's nephew, Bobby Coombs, playing for the Blue Devils. When Bobby, a 5-foot-9 right-hander, shut out Fordham on 3 hits, a scout recommended him to Connie Mack. After graduation, Bobby reported on June 5. Connie Mack watched him throw and told Eddie Rommel, "Put him in the bullpen."

Three days later the A's led the Yankees, 14–9, after 8 innings. Mack decided to take a look at his new reliever. He told Rommel to bring in Coombs to pitch the ninth. Rommel stood up and held his hands about two feet off the ground, the signal for "the short guy."

"I ran to the mound like I was eager to face the Yankees," Coombs said. "First man up was Babe Ruth. Cochrane came out and said, 'Forget your curve with this guy. Just rear back and throw it.'

"As a kid I had watched Jack Russell in Boston getting Ruth out with slow curves. I got a 2-2 count on him and I threw a changeup that froze Ruth. It was right down the middle of the plate. I thought I had him struck out, but umpire Bill Summers called it a ball. Cochrane got into Summers's face and I learned some new language that day. I threw another change-up and Ruth hit it over the fence. I thought it was a pop-up but it never stopped going."

By now Ruth's legs were complaining about his weight. To give them a rest he would sometimes sit in the A's left-field bullpen between innings if he didn't expect to bat. The next day Coombs was there when Ruth paid them a visit. He remembered Ruth saying, "I'd be a much better hitter if I wasn't afraid of killing the pitcher."

Coombs also learned what it was like to be the target of one of Mr. Mack's zingers. One day Boston had a man on second. The batter singled to left field. "In college," Coombs said, "the pitcher was a cutoff man because the arms weren't so good. Nobody ever told me to back up home plate. So Bob Johnson threw the ball in and I cut it off and threw to Foxx at first and we caught that guy off the bag. But the run scored. When I came in, Mr. Mack said to me, 'I thought you were smart.' That's all he said."

Another chapter in *As the New Leaf Turns*, starring George Earnshaw, began. A contrite Earnshaw admitted that Connie Mack had been right to fine him, told Mr. Mack that he knew his future depended on his ability to deliver, and told Bill Dooly, "I'm intensely sorry about it all. Mr. Mack has been very kind to me. In fact, he's been wonderful. From here on I'm going to prove myself out there on the pitchers' mound."

He told Westbrook Pegler, "I can leave the sauce alone, like I did in '30 and '31."

On June 17, Bunker Hill Day in Boston, Earnshaw won, 15–3, one of his 4 complete games all year.

Mack kept using him with mixed results.

According to Dan Levitt's research, all of major league baseball lost $1,651,530 in 1933. Only two teams made money—the Phillies, who were $3,184 in the black, probably from player sales, and the Giants. (Depreciation of players' contracts, introduced in 1927, was sometimes the difference between showing a profit or loss. But depreciation didn't pay the salaries and bills.)

Baseball, predicted Carl Chaffee, vice-president of Philadelphia's First National Bank, would soon be a rich man's hobby.

You didn't have to see the books to know how the baseball business was doing. Where attendance was down, it was down a lot. On their first Sunday in New York the A's played before about fourteen thousand, their smallest Sunday crowd at Yankee Stadium in five years. A Saturday ladies' day attracted only fifteen hundred into Sportsman's Park in St. Louis in May. Convinced that St. Louis was no longer an American League city, Browns owner Phil Ball said he would welcome a bid for the team from Montreal interests, who had been seeking a big league franchise for years. He began to cancel weekday games to create Sunday doubleheaders. There was talk of combining the teams in St. Louis, Boston, and Philadelphia and condensing the major leagues into one twelve-team circuit. Another idea was to play two six-inning games every day.

Cubs president William Veeck suggested a midseason month of interleague play to boost attendance, an idea *The Sporting News* called "quackery."

Stoney McLinn of the *Public Ledger* advocated an early form of revenue sharing, a percentage of all receipts to go into a fund from which struggling clubs could draw so they wouldn't have to sell players to meet expenses. "But I fear the baseball owners have the sleeping sickness," he wrote.

Sixteen minor leagues were struggling to survive. The decline in the lower leagues forced Connie Mack to pass up youngsters he would formerly have taken a chance on because places to send them for experience had dried up. Frank Shaughnessy came up with a scheme to help attendance: a postseason playoff involving the top four teams in a league, thus giving towns whose clubs had no shot at first a reason to maintain their interest in the race.

Anybody who went to a game at Shibe Park could see it was easier to count the occupied seats than the empty ones. It wasn't a sign of lack of interest in the team. There was far more enthusiasm over the arrival of the rookies Mike Higgins and Bob Johnson than dismay over the departure of Dykes and Simmons. It wasn't because the team was so bad or so good that the outcome was seldom in doubt. It was just over .500 but in the thick of a five-team bunch within 3 games of the lead.

The *Record* summed it up in a May 27 editorial:

The Athletics have another amazing team this year. Seven straight victories up to Thursday. If they play only 70 percent as well the rest of the season they'll win the pennant. There's a thrill nearly every inning at Shibe Park. . . .

Yet only a scant 1,200 or 1,500 spectators a day have been watching this great team in a home stand of exciting games.

Why?

Has Philadelphia, one of the best baseball towns in America, lost its interest in one of the greatest teams ever developed? Are Philadelphia fans indifferent to the success of one of Connie Mack's 'miracle' teams?

The answer to both questions is no.

The *Record* is flooded with telephone calls every evening from excited men and women with anxious voices. They ask, 'Did the A's win today? What was the score?' And every night thousands of extra copies of the sport Bulldog edition are sold to fans who want the details about the Athletics' games. Thousands of people are intensely interested in the games of the A's and Phillies who never see the inside of Shibe Park or Baker Bowl. Why? Because they can't afford to pay present-day admission prices. It costs a dollar and a dime to sit in the grandstand. It costs $2.20 to sit in a box seat. Add to that 15 or 20 cents for transportation and the answer to poor attendance at Philadelphia's ballparks is easy. Baseball is too expensive in a depression year. A dollar bill was small change in 1929. Now it seems as big as the scoreboard in right field.

Connie Mack agreed; when economic conditions improved, the fans would come back. Until then he would work with what money he had to improve his team.

The *Record* advocated cutting ticket prices to fill the ballparks. "Baseball is a public institution that can't stand the strain much longer under the present setup."

Bill Dooly put the blame on everybody: "Owners are to blame for paying big salaries and fans are to blame for supporting their favorites getting big money, but now complain about high ticket prices." Some things never change.

But it wasn't that easy. No individual club owner could cut prices; the league had to approve it. Some club owners doubted that cutting prices would increase attendance enough to cover expenses. Besides, they hadn't raised prices during the good years. Why reduce them now?

So they didn't.

The seats weren't always empty. When the Yankees came to town in early June, a Thursday 14-10 win in which Foxx hit 3 home runs inspired thirty-five thousand to find the funds to see the A's sweep a Saturday doubleheader.

Connie Mack wasn't just whistling when he had said he thought he had a chance for the pennant. By midseason nobody had taken charge of the race. During June and July the Yankees led by 6, then trailed Washington by 4½, then regained a share of first. Cleveland, Chicago, and the A's were bunched together in third. At one point only 8 games separated first-place New York from sixth-place Detroit. St. Louis and Boston were deep in the cellar.

Al Simmons thought New York had the best team. "If they don't win they have only themselves to blame. They dislike the [Senators] so heartily that they've been pressing themselves out of a lot of games with them." They would lose 14 of 22 against Washington.

The Athletics' lineup was nothing shabby: Bishop, Cramer, Cochrane, Foxx, Coleman, Johnson, Higgins, and McNair or Williams. Either Johnson or Higgins would have been a deserving rookie of the year. Johnson hit 21 home runs, fourth in the league. Higgins hit .314 with 14 home runs. Foxx won the triple crown with a .356 batting average, 48 homers, and 163 RBIs and was awarded his second straight MVP trophy. He was held hitless in only 27 games. He also led first basemen in assists. Mack called it "a splendid team" and said he had never had a team that could hit so well through eight men in the batting order. Three times in August one of them hit for the cycle: Cochrane (for the second time), Foxx, and Higgins. The Athletics would score more runs than the pennant-winning Senators, lead in doubles and slugging average, and hit only 4 fewer home runs than the Yankees.

Cleveland general manager Billy Evans marveled at Connie Mack's coming up with youngsters like Higgins and Johnson to replace the stars he had sold. "You can't beat old Connie," he said. "I didn't see how anyone could let players like those fellows go, come back with a ball club like he's got this year. He's a wonder. I tell you if he gets pitching he'll just about walk in with the pennant."

So Connie Mack was still optimistic when the Athletics went on the road on June 11 in third place, 5½ games out. They came home on July 4 still third but 9 games out.

A disheartened Mack called a rare pregame meeting at home. "You're a much better ball club than you've shown," he said. "I expect you to do better."

He had reason for great expectations. The team had a home record of 18-5 so far. They would be home for three weeks. But they won only 11 of 23 and left home 12½ games and another year out of the race.

"No club can win today without pitching," Mack wrote to a fan on August 8, "so I feel that our club is not going places this year."

"Throw strikes," Mack implored his hurlers. "Get the ball over. Even a .330 hitter will be out two out of three times. Maybe you'll get him out the third time too."

It didn't help.

The three-man staff of stalwarts was down to one—Grove. Otherwise Sugar Cain was the closest to what you might call dependable, and he allowed about 16 base runners per 9 innings. Walberg was primarily a reliever; he would win only 6 starts. Two years ago Mahaffey was a budding star. This year he'd have the highest ERA in the league. Last year Tony Freitas fooled batters with his slop. And now? "The bats got too big," he said. "I couldn't get anybody out."

On July 30 in Boston Connie Mack gave Earnshaw another start. But he had no confidence in him. Before the game he said to Bobby Coombs, "Earnshaw is starting. But I want you to warm up and be ready from the first batter. Don't say a word to anybody. If you do you'll never pitch for me again. Earle is waiting for you under the stands."

Coombs was excited. His father had come down from Maine and would get to see him pitch.

Mack's hunch was right. Earnshaw never got out of the first inning. Coombs went in and pitched to one batter to end the inning. Then Rube Walberg finished the game.

"It was the only time my father saw me pitch in the major leagues," Coombs said. "One batter."

Three days later Moose went 7 innings and beat the Yankees, 16–3. On August 7 he lasted 2 innings. Five days later he lost to New York, 8–6. A game at Cleveland on August 17 captured the season in 8 innings: Earnshaw, Peterson, Walberg, and Coombs all contributed to a 15–3 shellacking. It was the last time George Earnshaw pitched for the Athletics. Two weeks later Mack sent him home for the year.

For three weeks after August 17 Bobby Coombs was warming up almost every day. He was arm-weary and hyperextended his elbow. When Connie

Mack said, "I want you to pitch in an exhibition game tomorrow," he didn't know what to say.

"Whatever I said would set my status as a big leaguer," he said later. "Now I know I should have said yes and hoped it rained. But I didn't. I said, 'Mr. Mack, I'm sorry. I've got to take a rest.' He didn't use me again."

He never started or won a game, but for Bobby Coombs those four months with the Athletics were full of good times. He shared a room with Eddie Rommel at a boarding house on Lehigh two blocks from Shibe Park. Biscuits and gravy for breakfast, three meals a day.

Lefty Grove had a room nearby. The press portrayed Grove as a loner, gruff—even insulting—to friendly overtures from players and fans, caring nothing for popularity. And he did come off that way to most writers and strangers. To the players and the beat writers who were familiar with him, that wasn't the Grove they knew.

Bobby Coombs remembered him fondly. "In the evenings he'd stroll over and smoke a cigar and talk. On the road he and I went to zoos in the morning and burlesque shows—he liked the comics—in the evening. Sometimes I'd see him on the hotel porch talking with Cochrane and Mr. Mack, smoking his cigar.

"Some mornings coming down in the elevator Lefty would call me 'Son.' Other mornings, if there were women in the elevator, he'd call me 'Pisspot.' You never knew with him."

On the train rides, there were card games: low-stakes poker, pinochle, hearts. Grove, Walberg, Higgins, and McNair, occasionally joined by one or two others, played a rogue mutation of an old game called pisha pasha. As Coombs recalled it, "The hands were dealt, then somebody would put down the two of a suit and if you didn't have the three on your turn you put a dime in the pot, and so on till the first one with no cards won the pot."

Mack sold Bobby Coombs to Syracuse; after ten years in the minors he made it back briefly with the Giants in 1943, then coached baseball and freshman football for twenty-eight years at Williams College (where one of his freshmen was George Steinbrenner).

The A's were a slugging, error-prone, pitching-poor team, finishing a distant third behind Washington and New York. The bats produced hits by the peck, while the pitchers gave them up by the bushel. They gave up more runs and more walks than anybody in either league.

When Washington clinched the pennant on September 21, Connie Mack was the first to wire Joe Cronin: "Congratulations. You are a great boy, Joe. Will be pulling for you on October 3." In the National League, the Giants, who had finished sixth the year before, surprised all the experts by finishing first.

Sr. Florence had been transferred from Denver to St. Francis Hospital in Topeka, Kansas, where she listened to the Series on the radio, praying for Mel Ott of the Giants to hit a home run (he hit two).

"The Giants played wonderful ball and deserved to win," Mack wrote. "The Washington team was not quite up to its standard."

On September 12 a dinner marked Connie Mack's fiftieth year in baseball. Two days later Mack received a package from Sr. Florence containing an engraved gold cigarette case for Mack. Though he didn't smoke, Mack kept it for the rest of his life.

When Arch Ward of the *Chicago Tribune* came up with the idea of an all-star game to be played in Chicago as part of the city's world's fair that summer, most major league magnates were cool, even hostile, to the idea. It would disrupt the season, put their top stars at risk of injury in an exhibition game, and cost them money. The net proceeds—more than $46,000—were to go to the Association of Professional Ball Players of America, founded in 1924 and funded primarily by players' ten-dollar annual dues to aid aged and needy former players and umpires. (In 1933 the Athletics and Yankees were the only clubs with 100 percent enrollment.) Commissioner Landis's support for Ward's idea helped to make it happen on July 6 at Comiskey Park.

Members of the public voted for the starters, and they voted on the basis of current performance, not popularity. Al Simmons led all players with 346,291 votes, 25,000 ahead of Babe Ruth. Some voters who wanted to see both Lou Gehrig and Jimmy Foxx in the lineup put Foxx down for third base, even though he had not played there all year. As a result, he led at neither position.

In a sentimental gesture the league presidents invited Connie Mack and John McGraw to manage the teams. It had been twenty years since McGraw and Mack had last met in a World Series. Nothing else could have lured McGraw from his retirement porch in Pelham, New York.

Mack picked Eddie Collins, Art Fletcher, and Joe McCarthy to serve as coaches. In the 10 a.m. meeting at the Del Prado Hotel on the morning of the game, McCarthy gave them what information he could on the NL stars from his five years of leading the Cubs. Forty-two years later Lefty Gomez, the starting pitcher, described his version of the meeting.

"They started through the roster of the National League club—Pepper Martin fastball hitter, Frank Frisch fastball hitter, Chuck Klein fastball hitter, Chick Hafey fastball hitter. I said, 'May I ask a question?'

"Mr. Mack looked at me. I said, 'I'm a fastball pitcher. Are you sure you really want me to start this game?'"

From the day Ban Johnson had launched the American League as a major league in 1901, he had stressed the importance of demonstrating its superiority over the National League at every opportunity. Connie Mack had never forgotten that. He wouldn't root for a National League team in the World Series even if his son Earle was managing it. He went into this All-Star Game with the same attitude. It wasn't "just an exhibition game" to him.

John McGraw felt the same way. The drive to win was in him as strong as ever, although the energy wasn't. He held no pregame meeting. Dressed in a brown suit, he put up the starting lineup and said there would be some changes during the game. He was quiet on the bench, sometimes talking with one of his coaches, Max Carey.

Players not in the starting lineup were introduced by the public address announcer as they took batting practice, which Eddie Rommel pitched for the AL. Eighteen-year-old Bill Conroy, just signed by Mack out of Illinois Wesleyan, had the thrill of his life by catching batting practice for the AL-ers until he cut his hand.

After Gomez pitched three scoreless innings and drove in the first run, Mack switched to the slow stuff of Alvin "General" Crowder, then finished with Lefty Grove. The people's choice of catcher, Bill Dickey, bruised his thumb in batting practice. Mickey Cochrane had been out for two weeks with broken ribs. That left only Rick Ferrell to do the catching.

McGraw started Bill Hallahan and closed with Dizzy Dean.

The highlight of the game was Babe Ruth's third-inning home run with a man on to give the Americans a 3–0 lead. When Ruth connected, Eddie Collins danced and hollered in the first base coach's box while the fans in the stands did the same.

Behind 4–2 with 2 out in the ninth, McGraw sent in Tony Cuccinello to pinch-hit. "Take a strike," said McGraw, for the millionth and last time. "Geez," Tony thought, "with 'Mose' Grove pitching he ought to *give* me a strike." Cuccinello went down swinging.

The fans were disappointed that they hadn't seen Jimmy Foxx, who was coming off a hot week. In a doubleheader in St. Louis on July 2 he had hit 4 home runs, a double, and a triple; the triple and double were inches from being home runs.

In answer to complaints that he had not given the fans a look at Foxx or Tony Lazzeri, Mack said, "I didn't shake the team up because it's against all my instincts to disturb a winning combination. Nothing made me feel more badly than the fact I didn't use them. After all, I was chosen manager of this team to win the game, and I resolutely followed my own methods once the game was under way. The players understood."

After the last out McGraw made his way through the crowd to the American clubhouse. He praised Ruth's overhead catch of Hafey's long fly ball near the fence in the eighth inning more than his home run. He and Mack chatted for a few minutes, surrounded by wide-eyed players thrusting baseballs at them for autographs.

John McGraw died seven months later.

As the season drew to a close, Connie Mack felt more like a financial failure than ever. Like all successful businessmen, he had tried to operate on the principle that income must exceed outgo. And it hadn't. He had been forced to borrow just to get through the year, taking a loan against his life insurance, according to Shirley Povich. With two more home dates remaining, the A's would be lucky to draw three hundred thousand for the year. (They didn't.) It was a baseball axiom that it took four hundred thousand to break even. Households were cutting expenses wherever they could. Businesses were cutting payrolls, if not closing their doors. Where was it written that a baseball team couldn't go out of business too?

On Thursday morning, September 28, Lefty Grove went up to Mack's office before the game against the Red Sox. He was interested in getting some World Series tickets for the Washington games.

"Sit down," Mack said. "As long as you're here, let's talk about next year. Our attendance has been so low we are no longer in a position to pay you what you're accustomed to." Grove's two-year contract at $20,000 was up, along with the multiyear contracts of Foxx and Cochrane.

Mack told him what he could afford to pay. Grove said nothing.

"Well, you think it over," Mack said, "and let me know what you think tomorrow morning."

That afternoon, after a 4–3 loss, Mack went around the clubhouse and asked each man to be in his office at eleven Saturday morning before the doubleheader that would close the home season—except Grove, whom he already expected to see, and Walberg and Earnshaw, whom he didn't plan to keep.

Mack may have remembered a similar meeting in 1892, when he was on the other side of the desk, a catcher with the Pirates seeking a raise. The club president had called the players into his office after the last game and told them the club was broke. If they didn't sign for what was being offered right then and there, they'd get contracts in the mail for less.

It didn't matter where Mack sat; such situations were painful to him either way.

On Saturday morning Mack gave his boys the financial facts of life. He explained that he had no alternative but to cut salaries. "If anyone is not willing to accept what the club can offer you and would be more content elsewhere, I'll do what I can to sell or trade you to a club that might pay you more."

He had seen the effects of such pay cuts on players' morale during his playing days.

"In baseball," he once said, "it is always better to let your players go elsewhere rather than reduce their salaries and keep them on."

But of course he couldn't let them all go. And raises were scarce everywhere these days.

None of the players said anything. Lefty Grove didn't show up.

Only one player expressed a wish to be traded. A few days after the season closed Mack received a letter from Max Bishop. Ten years was long enough with one club, Bishop wrote. Mack said he would do what he could for him.

Word spread quickly that Connie Mack would be selling players. It didn't matter that a month ago he had stated flatly that he wouldn't consider any offers for Cochrane and Foxx, no matter how attractive. All he had talked about was the need to rebuild his pitching staff around Grove.

One day his telephone rang. Detroit president Frank Navin was on the line.

"I understand you're willing to sell some players," Navin said.

"Some of my pitchers, maybe," Mack said.

"How about Mickey Cochrane?" Navin said.

"Not a chance," said Mack.

"I want Cochrane for the Tigers' manager," Navin said. The Tigers hadn't won a pennant since 1909. After five second-division finishes Stanley "Bucky" Harris had resigned with a nudge from Navin.

"He's not for sale," Mack said.

The conversation kept repeating itself until Navin said, "I'll see you at the World Series."

Many accounts have Navin approaching the Yankees at the World Series to acquire Babe Ruth as the Tigers' playing manager. The Yankees, looking for a graceful way to dump the aging Babe, were willing to release Ruth to become a manager, but they wanted something in return if he was going to play. Ruth was still a draw at the gate, but not without a bat in his hands. Nobody goes to the ballpark to watch a manager think, not even (or especially) Babe Ruth. The Yankees gave Navin permission to talk to Ruth about the deal. But, the story goes, Ruth put off seeing Navin to go barnstorming in Hawaii, a choice that soured Navin on him. Yet during that same World Series, Navin buttonholed Mack and reiterated his desire to make Cochrane the Tigers' manager, ostensibly at the same time he was getting the Yankees' permission to talk to Ruth. If Navin was really serious about pursuing Ruth, it could only mean that Navin had become convinced that Mack had no intention of letting Cochrane go.

Anticipating that something was going to happen, writers indulged in all kinds of permutations of A's players going to Cleveland or Detroit or Chicago or Boston. Connie Mack didn't bother with daily denials. But he tried to avoid "No comment," which he knew would be translated as a confirmation of whatever concoction a writer had put forth.

On October 27 Shirley Povich declared that Grove had been sold to Tom Yawkey for $200,000. Every Philadelphia paper interrupted Connie Mack's breakfast with a call for comment. Mack laughed. The gist of what he told them was as follows:

That's very nice of Washington to dispose of my players. Yes, and I like the price very much. But since they say Boston has gone that far—what was it, two hundred thousand?—well, I think I'll hold out a while longer. Maybe I can get the ante raised. You know, that's the kind of money I've heard about but I haven't seen lately. If I hold out long enough, maybe Washington will sell the whole club for me and get me right out of the financial hole. As it is, however, I guess I'll just have to sigh my regrets. No sales were made. And if I do make one I'll let the

Philadelphia fans know myself. They won't have to go to Washington for the news.

On October 31 the *Philadelphia Public Ledger* claimed that Cochrane had been sold to Detroit and agreed to terms to manage the Tigers. It hedged on Grove, saying he was going to either Boston or Chicago.

That morning Grove, Miller, Foxx, Cochrane, and Edward E. "Doc" Ebling were in town on their way to a hunting trip, taking golf champion Walter Hagen with them. (Hagen said he would rather have been a big league ballplayer than a pro golfer. The players wished they could play golf like Hagen.) Grove said he had had no contract conversation with Mack.

Meanwhile, the campaign to pass the Sunday baseball referendum was heating up. The ballot would read: "Do you favor the conduct, staging and playing of baseball and football games, regardless of whether an admission charge is made, or incidental thereto, or whether labor or business is necessary to conduct, stage or operate the game, between the hours of 2 and 6 post meridian on Sunday?"

The *Record,* which had been advocating the overthrow of the ancient Blue Laws since 1928, sent out a million survey cards to voters. Seventy-five percent were returned, of which 90 percent checked yes to Sunday baseball.

The repeal of Prohibition, which had already been passed in thirty-three other states, was also on the ballot. The two questions were expected to bring out a lot of voters. In addition, John B. "Jack" Kelly, local Democratic chairman, often pictured with his four-year-old daughter Grace by his side, was actively campaigning to throw out the corrupt Republican hold on local government controlled by the Vare brothers, who had been running things since before Connie Mack's arrival in 1901.

Gerry Nugent, president of the Phillies since the death of his father-in-law William F. Baker in 1932, had played no part in the lobbying for the Sunday sports law. But now he joined in the campaigning. On Friday, November 3, he and Mack spoke at a rally of local amateur and semipro clubs in the ballroom of the Boulevard Hotel along with Senator Schwartz, Jimmie Dykes, and Jimmy Wilson, soon to be named Phillies manager. The night before, Mack, Dykes, Schwartz, and local big leaguer Bucky Walters had appeared before an overflow crowd at the Philadelphia Baseball League banquet.

The churches were holding their own parades and mass meetings, scorching Connie Mack for consorting with the devil in the struggle for the souls of the youth of the country.

Mack was constantly on the defensive against the hints that he was holding back announcing the sale of his stars until after the election. "All of these persons who say I have made deals and am holding off the announcements until after election day; why don't they come to me for the facts? I want to say now that I have made no deal with any club. What the future will bring forth is something I cannot tell. . . . If I had already made a deal I would quickly announce it and not wait. Deals once made quickly leak out. Even if I wanted to withhold a deal the other club would be very quick to object."

(It was accepted among the writers that in many cases when they had good reason to believe Mack was being less than truthful in denying a deal, Mack had no choice. He was bound by his promise to the other party to say nothing until the other club owner wanted the news released.)

On October 31 Stoney McLinn quoted him: "I have not closed a deal of any kind. If I had made any deal I would tell you about it right now. What benefits would it be to me to withhold the information until after election day?"

McLinn then wrote, "Asked if he had already sold Grove and Cochrane, he wouldn't say."

It is likely that as of that date no such deals had been closed. There were reports that Mack was asking for $125,000 and catcher Ray Hayworth for Cochrane, and Navin countered with $100,000 and catcher John Pasek.

On speculation about his "wrecking" his team again, Mack was even more sensitive. "I cannot deny too strongly the preposterous statement that I am going to wreck my club as I did after the close of the season in 1914. We are not out to tear down, but build."

But he was most infuriated by the preachers who accused him of campaigning for the commercialism of the Sabbath solely for his own financial benefit.

"That's what hurts me," he told McLinn. "To think that at my age and after devoting a lifetime to the grand old game of baseball, our national pastime, there should be even the slightest intimation that I was playing politics or bringing commercialization into something I so sincerely believe will add to the health, contentment and enjoyment of our community. He continued:

I regard it as unfair to the thousands of Philadelphians who may never see the Phillies or Athletics play ball to becloud the issue by bringing in my name as the chief beneficiary all the time. It is a slap at me that I resent. Of course our club wants to stage games of baseball on Sunday.

We hope to draw big crowds, too. But only to provide entertainment and relaxation for our citizens such as they may enjoy in any other city in the country. . . . But we did not start this movement. It was started by the people who seek such freedom of action on Sunday as is enjoyed in all the large cities outside of Pennsylvania. The chief beneficiary is to be the thousands of boys and young men who play in the lot games and the countless additional thousands who will spend the afternoon in the open watching those ball games. Yes, I do resent this attempt to becloud the real issue by branding me with the stamp of commercialism. And to start these nasty rumors about trades which we are holding back until Sunday baseball is assured—that is an insult to my sportsmanship.

The Philadelphia city council announced its intention to charge a $15 fee for Sunday games, even for a kids' pick-up game, if the referendum passed.

"Outrageous," said Connie Mack. "So far as our club is concerned I'm not complaining about a fifteen dollar tax. I don't say that is too much for us to pay. But to tax lot games any such prohibitive sum is a mistake. I would not favor it even if it were a help to my club. Why, to put any tax on the boys who go out on a lot to enjoy themselves by playing a game of baseball and perhaps amuse some of their friends and neighbors who go out to watch them and perhaps drop a little change in the hat to pay for baseballs and equipment is entirely out of line as I see it."

Perhaps he was thinking back to his youth in East Brookfield when that was how the town team had operated.

"I hope they make these little neighborhood games free from taxes, or make the tax so low it can easily be paid."

The council dropped the fee for amateur games to one dollar.

Fans who opened their morning paper on election day November 7 were surprised to see a headline that the A's were buying a player, not selling:

A'S BUY RADCLIFF. ST. PAUL SLUGGER, 24, MISSED AMERICAN ASSOCIATION BATTING TITLE BY 6 POINTS, HIT .364

After voting in the twenty-second ward Connie Mack headed for Sudlersville, Maryland, where the locals were putting on the biggest event in the little town's history, a dinner for their hometown hero, Jimmy Foxx. That evening reporters telephoned Mack with the election results, an overwhelming six to one vote for Sunday games. Only the repeal of prohibition won by a larger margin. (The entire Vare machine was also tossed out, an event that shook the political gods more than the passage of Sunday baseball.)

"This is the most agreeable news but I am not at all surprised," Mack said, "because I knew what the voters would do. Personally it is a big boost to us but I want to say that it also means joy and recreation for thousands of players and followers of semipro and amateur teams. It is a big thing for the city and the state."

Five days later the Philadelphia Eagles held the defending NFL champion Chicago Bears to a 3–3 tie at Baker Bowl before a freezing crowd of eighteen thousand in the first legal professional Sunday sports event in the city.

Contrary to the doom prophesied by the preachers if Sunday baseball became legal, Philadelphia did not go to hell. The A's and Phillies maybe—but not the city's youth.

On November 29 Connie Mack tracked down Lefty Grove captaining a bowling team in Hagerstown and asked him to come to Shibe Park. It's possible that Mack made one last effort to reach a salary agreement. A more likely reason for the meeting is that he wanted to let Lefty know of his probable sale to Boston during the upcoming winter meetings.

Mack's eldest son, Roy, was also in town from Portland, Oregon, where he was the Beavers' business manager. The Beavers, despite a winning team, had lost money for two years. Some reports said Tom Turner was looking to sell, but others—more accurate—had him buying out John Shibe's interest.

Tom Shibe was in the hospital for surgery, so John Shibe accompanied Mack to Chicago for the winter meetings. Accounts of what took place were limned in the kind of lachrymose tones usually reserved for the passing of a benevolent monarch.

On Tuesday evening, December 12, Mack, Yawkey, and Collins were closeted in a meeting room at the Palmer House. Once Mack came out. Writers crowded around him. "I can't tell you yet. I'm not yet sure myself." He went back into the room. A half hour passed.

"Perhaps," wrote Cy Peterman of the *Evening Bulletin*, "in that final half-hour which must have been something of a Gethsemane, he remembered, with terrifying effect, the clamor of the bankers, those relentless bankers who, according to report, have become loudly insistent of late. At any rate, he gave in."

When Connie Mack called them into the now empty meeting room, Peterman described Mack as "white as paper ashes." "His bony hand shook" as he told the Philly writers of the sales of Bishop, Grove, and Walberg to Boston; Cochrane to Detroit; and Earnshaw to Chicago. He did not mention the amounts, just the players involved.

Mack was quoted by William Brandt as declaring that the deals "were not definitely closed until today."

Al Horwits of the *Public Ledger* had Mack "nervously pacing the floor and tearing away at a piece of paper, highly emotional" as he faced the writers. "Don't leave me, John," he quoted Mack as saying more than once to John Shibe, who assured Mack he would stay with him.

"And so a very nervous Mack sat down, braced himself, and started to reel off names. He completed his announcement and slowly but unsteadily stood up. He held onto the chair for a moment, then steadied himself."

Reporters threw questions at him. "I have nothing further to say. The deals are made," said Mack. As he started to walk away, Mack said, "I'll meet you at Shibe Park Monday at eleven o'clock and discuss everything with you."

Mack then went down the hall to the suite of Collins and Yawkey where, according to Horwits and Peterman, Yawkey handed the shaken Mack a drink, the seventy-one-year-old looking "a little startled, a little afraid."

About twenty minutes later, Mack was seen going to his own room. Nobody bothered him.

It all seems overwritten. Or was it just an act? There's something peculiar about these melodramatics if it was true that the deals had been agreed on in November, as these same reporters continued to assert. But if the scene took place as described, it appears that Connie Mack had resisted the need to make the sales for as long as he could before concluding them at the meeting.

Headlines had the total proceeds ranging up to $300,000 "from sources in the buying cities." Cochrane went to Detroit for $100,000. Grove went to Boston for $125,000, George Earnshaw and catcher John Pasek to the White Sox for $25,000 and catcher Charlie Berry. Some reports had Tom Yawkey paying $50,000 and two players (pitcher Bob Kline and infielder Rabbit Warstler) for Rube Walberg and Max Bishop. But the A's transaction records show no cash involved in that trade.

Mack made it clear that Jimmy Foxx was not for sale at any price, "even if it were a record breaker." "Fawksie" was still only twenty-five. He was one of the men Mack planned to build around.

So when were the deals actually made? After the sales were announced in

December the *Record* reported, "It is no secret among club owners that Mack and his associates were forced to sell to raise money, and the announcements were withheld until after Sunday baseball was voted in. It is reported that the club had financial obligations of $200,000 that had to be paid before January 1. It is no secret that the deals were made and the money paid in most instances more than two months ago."

Although the comments about when the money was paid and the withholding of the news pending the election were just conjecture, league records seem to support the belief that the deals were closed well ahead of Mack's "ashen-faced, highly emotional" announcement, and it was deny, deny, deny by all parties until the meetings in Chicago.

The agreement on Cochrane filed with the league office was recorded November 4. The Grove agreement was recorded November 8. The players' notices, however, were dated December 14. (Frank Navin's saying on December 8 that he hadn't talked to Mack since October but would see him at the Chicago meeting doesn't square with the records or with Mack's statement on December 11 that "after the World Series we were in constant contact over the long distance phone.")

It's doubtful that any trade involving Walberg or Earnshaw or Bishop would have affected the vote. Even the sale of Cochrane and Grove before election day would not have put much of a dent in the 6–1 margin.

Did the bankers force the sale? According to James Isaminger, "Notes held by banks had to be satisfied without further delay. Banks would grant no extension and declined to wait until next fall to see if the coming of Sunday baseball might improve the financial condition of the A's."

It's true that banks were calling in loans in order to meet their reserve requirements and stay open, and there is no reason to expect that they would have exempted the Athletics from that pressure. So while it was true, as Connie Mack said, that "they didn't tell us to sell our players," it was equally true that "there was no other way to raise the money."

Mack's children understood that their father's back was against the financial wall. In Richmond, Virginia, reporters cornered Connie Jr. before the Duke sophomore's first basketball game. "There was no other way," they quoted him. "It was the banks," he added laconically.

Years later Mack's daughter Ruth remembered it as "strictly financial. He owed the banks so much money and had to get money to hold onto the club."

Where did the bank debt come from? In 1925–1926 the A's had spent $593,936.09 on the upper-deck left-field and right-field pavilions and left-field bleachers. In June 1925 they owed the First National Bank $545,000. After a big profit in 1925, that debt was down to $114,735. It was back up to $364,000 by August 1928.

Connie Mack had paid out about $460,000 cash—equal to about $6 million today—(and sixteen players valued at $160,000) to create the 1929 world champions. The debt had reached $700,000 before being paid down to $400,000. (Estimates from "baseball men in a position to know" put the bankers' repayment demands at $250,000.)

For the year 1933 the A's paid interest on $325,000. The debt would be down to zero by October 22, 1934.

Awaiting a few late arrivals on the Monday morning after the sales had been announced, Mack sat in his high-backed black swivel chair, an array of tiny white alabaster elephants in front of him and the cutout photo of Al Simmons that still sat atop the green metal file cabinet behind him a year after Al's departure—and would remain there as long as Mr. Mack occupied the office.

He smiled as he recounted the sob stories picturing him in tears and agonizing over the selling of his stars, calling it "horsefeathers."

Then for an hour he described each of the transactions in so much detail there were no questions left to be asked when he finished. Inability to pay his stars what they wanted and the need to rebuild his pitching staff led to the sales, he said.

"I mulled [Navin's offer] over in my mind for quite a while. I thought of Cochrane knowing he would have to take a cut in salary. Mickey had been with the club nine years and had given great service and I started to wonder if I was doing the right thing in depriving him of the chance to become the manager of a major league club. I decided I wouldn't stand in his way.

"Then I decided if I let Cochrane go, I'd also let [Grove] go. Both had been with me a number of years and would have to take a cut in salary."

Mack had intended to rebuild his pitching staff around Grove with Mickey Cochrane's help. But Lefty had been clearly miffed at the idea of taking a pay cut. And you couldn't build a young pitching staff around an unhappy centerpiece.

(Cochrane received a raise to $20,000 at Detroit. Grove would take a cut from $20,000 to $15,000 in Boston.)

"After much thought I resolved to let him go. All along Eddie Collins had been after me for Grove. I said no but if I ever did he would have first refusal. I told Eddie I was ready. Negotiations began but were not completed."

Mack pleaded with the press to "do what you can to correct this impression" that he was forced by bankers to sell the players. "We assume full responsibility for our transactions. The banks have been very fair with us. . . . We acted on our own initiative and will take all the criticism. . . . I think the banks have been done a great injustice."

Nevertheless, paying down the debt was part of the reason for the sales. Reducing the payroll was equally urgent. In a birthday interview with Isaminger a week later Mack acknowledged, "I sold these players to reduce my overhead and pay off debts that have accumulated since 1930. I felt that we have to make a fresh start. If I told you how many paid admissions we received at home and abroad it would knock you off your seat. We had to pull in our oars because we did not have the attendance to support the salaries some of the departing stars wanted. Rather than have disgruntled players on my hands next season, I sold them. Best illustration is seen in Earnshaw's record. His salary was cut last year and he turned in 5 victories when he normally is good for 20 or more."

At another time Mack claimed that Earnshaw had never indicated any dissatisfaction over his 50 percent salary cut. "If he had said he didn't like to play for that kind of money, I would have tried to make a deal for him. But not once did he give me to understand that he wasn't satisfied." Mack also said he had considered keeping Moose until the last minute.

With all the sales, when the books were closed for the year, the club would still show a $25,754 loss. That was the second best bottom line in the league. To understand the cash flow consequences on the operation of the club, it's necessary to deduct the entry of a $107,225 loss on the sale of stock in the Portland club and depreciation charges of $66,000, and remove the $253,500 net gain on the purchase and sale of players. That leaves outgo exceeding income by almost $106,000.

As for the story that the club would retain only $25,000 from the sales to cover spring training costs, which normally ran to twice that amount, Mack said, "We spent a large portion of the money received in the big deals to pay for four young pitchers."

He named Al Benton, Harry Matuzak, and Vern Kennedy from Oklahoma City, and Joe Cascarella from Jersey City. In fact, Mack had been spending money as if he had had it all year. By August Johnny Marcum, a right-hander with Louisville, had a 20-13 record. Mack had been watching him by scanning the box scores each week in *The Sporting News*. He sent Earle down to size him up and agreed to pay $30,000 and Jim Peterson for the twenty-four-year-old while other scouts were still watching him. Marcum arrived in September and pitched shutouts in his first two starts. Mack had shelled out cash (and Tony Freitas and Gowell Claset) to St. Paul for outfielder Rip Radcliff.

"We have to rebuild our battery department," Mack said. "We have to get a first-class catcher. That's what we intend to do—to strengthen our ball club. As far as I am concerned, I don't expect it to be ever necessary for me to again dispose of a player Philadelphians would like to see on the team."

It was a rash statement, one that would have been better left unsaid.

Seeking reactions from the departing players, Philadelphia writers found Lefty Grove at his bowling alley. "A change is good for most of us after we've been a long time in one city," he said. "No reflection on Mack or the A's. Connie had not talked to me about it because he is very careful about that sort of thing."

(At the annual New York Baseball Writers' dinner that winter, columnist Henry McLemore sang a parody, "Lefty Doesn't Live Here Any More.")

George Earnshaw had nothing but good things to say about Connie Mack, calling him "one of the finest characters in baseball, a great man to work for."

There's no doubt that it was a very emotional time for Connie Mack. He was through with Walberg and Earnshaw, as he had been with Eddie Plank and Chief Bender nineteen years ago. After ten years Max Bishop wanted a change of scenery. Mack could announce those deals offhandedly. Walberg was thirty-seven, Bishop thirty-four. Earnshaw would soon be thirty-four. Their best days were clearly behind them.

Grove would be thirty-four in March, Cochrane thirty-one in April. But they had been the heart and soul of Mack's Athletics since 1925. Those partings were painful.

Looking back, some historians lazily label the sales as "Mack wrecked his team for the second time." Some continue the myth that he did it to line his pockets à la Cardinals general manager Branch Rickey, who would have pocketed 10 percent of the proceeds. But at the time—and given the economic times—Mack's actions drew more praise than condemnation.

William Brandt did some cruising for comments in the hotel lobby after the announcement of the sales and reported the following:

"Mack's canny," expressed the views of a large percentage of the lobby fraternity. "If money had to come from somewhere," one said, "Connie picked the right men to sell. All the stars he put on the block were men who had already reached the peaks of their careers. The time to sell a star is before he slips. Grove and Cochrane may have one, two, or five great years left in them. When you stay with a player who has been as outstanding as each of these has been in each department, there's a large margin of likelihood that next year or the year after might mark the turning of the tide for him. Mack is building a new team around Foxx and a nucleus of the old players. I do not see what this deal leaves him in the way of a battery, but if he were forced to make deals for cash I certainly admire his wisdom in choosing these men and his courage in going through with the propositions in the face of the enormous criticism from his home fans which is seemingly inevitable."

But the enormous criticism didn't happen. Philadelphia fans understood. Out-of-town writers did too. Bill Corum of the *New York Evening Journal* thought Mack might have sacrificed a chance at the 1934 pennant by doing some adding instead of subtracting.

"But would the fans have come to see them even if they were winning the flag? I take it that Mr. Mack thought not. And Mr. Mack has been sitting in that tower at Shibe Park thinking, or something, for a lot of years now. Who am I to second-guess him, if so minded? Which I am not. For $250,000 I'd sell all the ball players I ever saw in a paper sack. If I had the ball players— and if I had the paper sack."

A week later at his annual birthday interview, Connie Mack said, "Maybe I made the wrong move in selling those five players, but the more I think of the deal the more I am convinced I did the right thing."

As if he had a choice.

One writer, Perry Lewis, jumped on Mack, the start of a long-running Lewis anti-Mack campaign. Writing as "Old Sport's Musings" in the *Inquirer* (a column headed by the motto "If you can't boost don't knock), Lewis knocked: "It seems that Boston can afford to pay the greatest pitcher in baseball and Philadelphia cannot. It seems that Detroit can afford to employ baseball's greatest maskman and Philadelphia cannot. In short, these three great players [Grove, Cochrane, and Bishop] were traded because they wanted to be traded. Very nice for Mickey, Max and Lefty, but rather tough on the baseball fans of Philadelphia."

Eighty years later major league clubs would still be releasing or trading high-priced stars because they "couldn't afford" to keep them.

Dick Bircher was a pilot who pulled advertising banners in the air, among other occupations. He had recently purchased an airfield on Roosevelt Boulevard in northeast Philadelphia and renamed it Boulevard Field. Bircher was married to Katherine Mack's niece, Marian. One day in December 1933 Bircher arrived at the Mack home. "I'd like to take you up in my airplane for your birthday," Bircher said to Connie Mack.

"No, no, no," said Mack. "I've refused to make any such trip before."

Bircher said, "You're seventy-one years old, but you still have a lot of pep in you. Let's show everybody you're not an old man."

Mack gave in. "I never had any idea I would go into a plane," he said a few days later. "I always told them they'd never get me off the ground. But then I never thought I'd sell Lefty Grove either."

At ten o'clock on the morning of December 23 Bircher and his wife picked up Mack and his daughter Ruth and drove to Boulevard Field. Mack, clad in an overcoat against the forty-degree chill, and the others stood with a few reporters on the field while Bircher took his five-passenger Stinson up for a demonstration of aerial acrobatics: loop the loop, slide slip, falling leaves. Then he landed, and Mack and Ruth got into the plane. They climbed to two thousand feet and flew over Shibe Park and Baker Bowl and Mack's home at 604 W. Cliveden. Mack peered out the window and gestured excitedly to Ruth when he spotted the house.

Dick Bircher asked them how they were doing. "It's fun," said Ruth, "but I don't like the idea of landing."

To tease her Bircher headed across the Delaware River, touched down at Central Airport in Camden, and took off again. After a forty-five-minute ride, they landed back at Boulevard Field.

That afternoon Isaminger visited Mack in his office.

"It's the greatest experience I ever had," Mack was quoted as saying, and he went on:

I can well understand now why men and women are so strongly inclined toward aviation. . . . [Shibe Park] from the sky looked like somebody's backyard. We also flew over golf courses and they looked so small you think you could cover the course in one shot. . . . I can't describe the thrills my first ride in a plane gave me and I can now well understand why Judge Landis does virtually all of his traveling by air. . . . Dick, our pilot, was wonderful. He never seemed to exert himself and talked to me constantly, often with his hands off the steering apparatus. It looks to me that piloting a plane is far easier than driving a Ford. I hope this is not the last time I am in a plane. I can understand why everybody once up wants to be in the air all the time.

He even went so far as to predict that big league clubs would travel by air someday. (Six months later Larry MacPhail fulfilled that prediction, dividing the Cincinnati Reds into two groups that flew from Cincinnati to Chicago.) Mack then described his formula for good health and a long life and made it clear that retiring was far from his thoughts:

I never felt better in my life, and feel at seventy-one no different than I was twenty years ago. I eat two fairly good meals a day with a light luncheon. For breakfast I have fruit, a cereal, and one of three meats. It is either a chop or bacon and eggs or calf's liver and bacon. I never vary on these three meats except on Fridays I confine myself to eggs. Then I drink one cup of coffee, the only time during the day I do this.

My luncheon consists solely of a pint of milk and some graham crackers. For dinner I have soup, some kind of meat, plenty of vegetables, dessert, and a cup of tea. I eat more vegetables than meat. I have no desire for any alcoholic drinks.

Every day I relax on my [office] couch for fifteen minutes to a half hour and I attribute my good health to this fact. In the baseball season I always rest at 1:30 and at two I go down to the bench and feel as fresh as I do when I awake in the morning. I advise everybody more than fifty years old to do this. I have derived the greatest benefit from this rest.

I do a lot of walking in summertime and in some cities where the ballpark is not too remote I make the practice of walking there. I don't do so much walking in winter except when I go to Florida early.

Everybody my age should golf. I made a serious mistake a year ago when I did not go to make my early start in Florida as I did in previous years. I am going to Florida next January 15 and have six weeks of golfing before the players arrive.

Anyone over fifty should get at least eight hours sleep. A man should worry as little as possible. Nothing ages one more than worries. We all must worry a little as a result of the stern realities of life, but we should never let anything prey on our minds too much. Try to cultivate a serene mind at all times.

At the minor league meeting in Galveston in November, Commissioner Landis said, "Steel factories, railroads, newspapers, agricultural livestock, baseball—we all rode down together and we'll all ride back together. Fans can't go to a baseball game if they don't have any money and they don't have any money if they don't have a job."

Rear Admiral Richard L. Byrd turned his back on all this and departed from Norfolk on his flagship steamer the *Jacob Ruppert*, headed for the South Pole. (Jacob Ruppert was the main sponsor of the expedition, an early case of buying naming rights.)

President Roosevelt had the bulliest pulpit from which to preach optimism, but Connie Mack had long been its prominent symbol and salesman. Addressing fifteen thousand Red Cross volunteer fund raisers that winter, he told them, "Keep your chins up. Don't let a few turn-downs from people who don't understand the value of your organization discourage you. Keep at it with that will prevailing which knows no defeat. I think the example of the New York Giants this year is an example of a group of players who put their heart and soul into the game determined to come through winners. When the season started a majority of writers picked them for a cellar position this year. But nothing daunted them. They went in to win and they did. . . . It is this spirit that wins in life and in sport."

With this spirit Connie Mack looked forward to the fight for financial survival—and the search for a first-class catcher and pitchers who could throw strikes.

4 | FROM EAST BROOKFIELD TO JAPAN

Connie Mack had been so busy he had not played a round of golf in almost two years. After the hectic transactions of the past winter he was determined to relax. He and Mrs. Mack took off on January 15, 1934, for six weeks at Mount Plymouth, Florida, before going to Fort Myers. At seventy-one, he was still turning strangers into friends. A man named George F. Johnson, wintering in Daytona Beach, had sent him a Christmas card wishing him more future success. Connie Mack didn't know Johnson, but he invited the man "and your friends [to] come over some day for a game of golf and lunch with me any day after January 15th. If that will suit you, you can give me a ring a few hours before coming."

The Athletics who reported to Fort Myers in 1934 did not resemble a wrecked team. Mike Higgins and Bob Johnson had had spectacular rookie seasons. They and Lou Finney received raises, Higgins wringing a $2,000 jump to $6,000 out of Connie Mack. Dib Williams would miss the first two weeks of the season, with Rabbit Warstler, a lightly regarded throw-in in the Grove deal, filling in at second. The infield looked strong enough for Mack to predict they would fool the experts who expected them to finish seventh. (Williams wound up missing most of the season; Warstler became the regular second baseman.)

In his syndicated column, Babe Ruth picked the A's to finish third, based on their hitting and defense. The outfield of Cramer, Coleman, and Johnson was strong-armed and potent at the plate.

Flit Cramer was the best center fielder in the league. He had learned from the former best, Tris Speaker. "Two-thirds of being a good outfielder is getting a jump on the ball," Cramer said. "Speaker told me to start after every ball that was hit, whether or not it was coming into my territory. I practiced this until I was unconsciously in motion with the crack of the bat."

If the ball wasn't hit to him, he was right there warning another outfielder if he was getting close to the wall or telling him where to throw when he chased down a base hit.

He had no power, but Cramer was good for 200-plus hits a year.

When Mack grew tired of Ed Coleman's nocturnal habits, singles-hitting Lou Finney would finish the year in right field.

With the Red Sox in Sarasota, Lefty Grove was suffering from his first sore arm. He'd been unable to do any more than lob the ball all spring. He told Boston manager Bucky Harris, "I'll let you know when I'm ready."

The weeks went by. Grove didn't say, "I'm ready." Instead, according to *Sporting News* correspondent Paul Shannon, a disgusted Grove said, "I'm through."

Shannon speculated that Eddie Collins talked Grove out of quitting, reminding him that it would look like Connie Mack had foisted a lame-armed pitcher on Tom Yawkey, who would demand his money back. And Collins knew that Mack needed the money.

"Lefty still thinks the world of Connie Mack," Shannon wrote, "as does every player who ever wore an Athletics uniform."

Maybe that's the way it happened. The fact is that when the Tigers came to Fort Myers, Lefty Grove and Eddie Collins drove from Sarasota with Tom Yawkey to visit with Mickey Cochrane and their old Athletics teammates. Grove took advantage of the chance to be examined by Doc Ebling, who assured him that his arm was sound. It turned out that three infected wisdom teeth were the cause of Grove's miseries.

Jimmy Foxx was not there for the reunion. Foxx had spent the winter in Coral Gables, Florida, with his family, maid, and chauffeur. He was living high (and gaining weight) and wanted to be paid high. His three-year contract for $50,000 had ended. He wanted $20,000, the papers said. After winning the triple crown by wide margins in every department and his second MVP award in two years, he deserved it. But the times were against him.

When Prohibition had ended, thirty-five thousand applicants signed up to take the civil service exam in Pennsylvania for the twenty-five hundred jobs created for truck drivers for the state board of liquor control, which operated the liquor stores in the state. The average annual income for full-time workers was just over a thousand dollars. Unemployed architects stood in long lines to apply for jobs that paid $3,000 a year. Only 342,308 people had earned enough to file a tax return in Pennsylvania for 1933. The average net income for those filing returns was $3,125.42 after deductions, requiring $124.90 in taxes. Attendance at Shibe Park had been under three hundred thousand, and there was no reason to expect it to be any better this year. Although attendance would almost triple in Detroit and more than double in Boston, there would be days on the road in other cities when the visitors' share wouldn't cover the hotel bill.

Mack's initial offer to Foxx was said to be $11,000. That went nowhere. He went up to $15,000 with a bonus based on attendance. Foxx wasn't interested in any bonus deals, just a straight contract. When the A's went to Miami Beach on March 9 to play the world champion Giants, Foxx and Mack met at the McAllister Hotel in Miami and agreed on $17,500. That put the Sudlersville farm boy in exclusive company; a Treasury report to Congress would show that only eighteen thousand employees at over eight thousand corporations earned more than $15,000 that year.

For the first time in thirty-four years, the A's had no left-handed pitchers. "But I'd just as soon have none as a poor one," Mack told visiting New York writer Bill Corum. The staff was led by Roy Mahaffey, Johnny Marcum on the strength of his 2 fall shutouts, and Sugar Cain, and it didn't inspire Mack. Asked to name his big four pitchers, he told John Kieran of the *New York Times*, "Big four? We'll be modest and hope we get a medium-sized four."

Unless a pitcher goes into a game believing he can win, said Connie Mack, he won't. Pitchers' minds were fragile, quirky, inscrutable. Connie Mack had been instilling confidence in men for forty years. Trying to, anyhow. If a man was willing to learn, you could teach him a new pitch or refine his delivery so that every pitch came off the same motion. Those were the teachable mechanics.

Stoney McLinn observed that Sugar Cain had a case of "ingrown disposition. Until he finds a silver lining in life he will not be an important winner." McLinn found Johnny Marcum "easygoing, lacking in imagination. If a transfusion could be arranged between Marcum and Cain it might make a pitcher of them both." Cain was incurably wild and Marcum eminently hittable. Mahaffey would be "out of condition" on and off all season.

The rest of the staff was notable, though not necessarily for pitching. Joe Cascarella had a fine tenor voice that would be heard on national radio. Harry Matuzak had been an elementary school teacher for three years while trying to make the big leagues.

Bill Dietrich was somewhat like Lefty Grove at the same age: he would have a tantrum whenever an error or mistake cost him a run or a game. He had the best fastball but the worst control. And he was tipping his pitches. Mack worked with him on using the same motion for every pitch. It wasn't easy. Finally he taught Dietrich to be aware that he was tipping his pitches and make adjustments to throw the opposite of what the hitters were expecting. "When they stepped into a few curves that didn't curve," Mack said, "they stopped." Dietrich would be 11-12 with 4 shutouts, but he walked too many—5 per 9 innings.

George Caster was an early no-windup pitcher. He extended his arms in front of him, then brought them in and delivered. Bought from Seattle, he wasn't ready. Mack sent him to Portland, where he had a 13-15 record. Taking another look at Caster in 1935, Mack told the tall twenty-seven-year-old right-hander he didn't have the stuff to win in the big leagues.

But Mack didn't give up on him. He had found over the years that of all the players he had given thorough tryouts and sent back to the minors, most of those who came back and made good were pitchers. "The best any other player can do is polish his natural talents," he said, "A pitcher can always change his style or pick up a new pitch."

Mack sent Caster to Albany to work on a new pitch. It took Caster all season to master the knuckleball. The next year he went to Portland and learned to control it, winning 25 games. In late 1936 Eddie Collins tried to buy him from Portland, but Connie Mack had a string on him.

Duke graduate Tim McKeithan was back for a third and final look. Jack Coombs sent a side-arming southpaw, Mort Flohr, to Mack. Like his fellow Blue Devil Bobby Coombs, the first batter Flohr faced was Babe Ruth on June 8, one year to the day after Coombs had given up a Ruthian homer. This time Ruth didn't hit Flohr; Flohr's first pitch hit Ruth on the right wrist, the most memorable event in Flohr's 0-2 career. (Expected to be out at least a week, Ruth missed only one game.)

Vern Kennedy was a college graduate who had been the decathlon champion in the 1927 Penn Relays. Bought on a trial basis, he would be returned to Oklahoma City. Kennedy was the only one of the bunch who would have a 20-win season in the big leagues—but for another team.

Bob Kline, obtained from Boston in the Grove deal, was a 6-foot-3, 200-pound sinker ball pitcher used primarily as a reliever. Working out of the bullpen, as of May 15, he would be 5-1, winning more games than Grove, Earnshaw, and Walberg combined. But most of those wins came in slugfests in which Kline was hit as hard as anybody. In June Mack sent him to Washington for the $7,500 waiver price.

Al Benton, the most inexperienced, displayed the most confidence. Mack considered him the best prospect of the bunch "if he doesn't take a beating and lose his confidence."

Mack may have been tempted to sign Mildred "Babe" Didrikson, the world's greatest woman athlete. The 1932 Olympic gold medalist and golf pro had signed with the House of David, a barnstorming team of mostly bearded players, to pitch the first inning of their games as they traveled around the country. In the spring she made the rounds of the Florida camps, pitching an inning for various teams for publicity. Always the showman, Mack agreed to let her pitch an inning against the Dodgers on March 20. She walked one batter and hit another, and then the A's made a Williams-Warstler-Foxx triple play on a line drive by Joe Stripp.

Building a new pitching staff was daunting enough, but doing it with new catchers made it worse. Connie Mack was often quoted as saying that pitching was 70 or 80 percent of baseball, but he also said that catching was 40 percent of pitching. He no longer had Mickey Cochrane. He had Ed Madjeski, described by Bill Dooly as having "much to learn but [without] the time to listen," and Charlie Berry, a Lafayette football star who had signed with the A's in 1925 and been with Boston and Chicago since 1928.

Mack's third catcher was a nineteen-year-old rookie, Frank Hayes. Soon after graduating from Pennington Prep School in New Jersey in 1933, Hayes had shown up at Shibe Park for a tryout as an outfielder. Mack sized up the 6-foot-1, 195-pound youngster, envisioned him as a Gibraltar-like impediment to runners trying to reach home plate, and suggested he become a catcher. But there was a rule that barred major league clubs from signing sandlotters. Mack had helped his friend, Frank Shaughnessy, president of the Montreal club, by sending him Bill Dietrich on option. He asked Shaughnessy to return the favor by abetting him in a little rule-bending. Hayes signed a Montreal contract, removing him from the sandlot ranks, spent about a week with the Royals, and was released. (In 1936 it became legal for a major league club to recommend a sandlot player to a minor league club.) Hayes then joined the A's and caught in three games at the end of the season.

Brand new to catching, Hayes had no idea how to play a foul pop-up. Just as Ralph "Cy" Perkins had done for a green Mickey Cochrane nine years earlier, Lena Blackburne worked with the youngster, hitting pop-ups to him for hours at a time, until Hayes went from the worst to one of the best behind the plate. Hayes impressed Mack with his bat in exhibition games, winning one city series game with a ninth-inning home run and another with a two-run single.

Seeking a veteran catcher, Mack ran afoul of Judge Landis again, and it cost him his $35,000 outfielder Rip Radcliff. He sent Radcliff and George Detore to Louisville for a $15,000 option on catcher Hank Erickson. Mack apparently figured he would get the players back if he didn't exercise the option. Then Mack learned that Louisville wouldn't let Erickson go until after the season. In May Landis ruled that Radcliff and Detore belonged to Louisville outright even if Mack didn't pick up the option. Mack wrote them off and never exercised the option. Radcliff was bought by the White Sox and had a productive ten-year career. Erickson caught 25 games for Cincinnati in 1935. (Had Mahaffey and Erickson ever formed a battery for the A's, the writers would have made much of the fact that both bore the nickname "Popeye.")

In Fort Myers Henry Ford stopped by to say goodbye to Mr. Mack. Since his friend Thomas Edison had died a few years ago, Ford had found less of interest to keep him in Florida.

"He said that baseball was the greatest game of all," Mack told Bill Corum, "and that other American industries might well be proud to have such a fine reputation with the public for honesty and square dealing."

April 8 was a beautiful warm Sunday. Even though it was a city series game, Mack and the Shibes expected a full house for their first legal Sunday game. They were disappointed when little more than half the seats were occupied. Philadelphia police refused to allow the gates to open until an hour before the three o'clock game time.

Two weeks later they played their first official Sunday game, a 4–3 loss to Washington, before 20,306, many of them out-of-towners who had to park as far as eight blocks away.

The major leagues had their highest opening day attendance since 1931. The alphabet soup of New Deal programs had cut unemployment from over 25 percent to under 15 percent. (Twenty minor leagues started and finished the year.) The A's opened at home against the Yankees before the smallest crowd in the league, about ten thousand frozen fans who went home happy when Bing Miller pinch-hit in the ninth and drove in the winning run. But the game began with a bad omen for both teams: starting pitchers Sugar Cain and Lefty Gomez each walked the first batter they faced on four pitches. There were 18 bases on balls in the game. Gomez was relieved for the first of many times to come by rookie Johnny Murphy.

In the fifth inning Charlie Berry split a finger stopping a wild pitch. Ed Madjeski replaced him. Don Heffner was on third base. Earle Combs tapped back to Cain, who rushed at Heffner between third and home, then threw home to Madjeski. Heffner was a gone goose; Madjeski had only to bluff a throw and tag him. But instead the catcher threw the ball over everybody into left field and Heffner scored.

On the bench Connie Mack was seething. Errant throws are part of the game. But throwing at all in that situation was inexcusable to the old ex-catcher. Madjeski singled and scored in the bottom of the fifth, but Mack sent Frank Hayes in to finish the game. Afterward a few writers asked him about Madjeski's throw, which Mack said was the dumbest play he had ever seen. "Dammit," he said, "if you ever see [Madjeski] back there again, then the next time you see me and you have a gun in your hand, shoot me."

Ed Madjeski never caught another pitch for Connie Mack. He delivered some timely pinch hits but was released on May 14 and signed with the White Sox.

Frank Hayes was headed for a year's experience in the minors. But with Berry out for at least ten days, there was nobody else to catch. The next day the youngster had three hits, including his first home run. He caught the next eight games until Berry came back, and they shared the job the rest of the year.

Like the perennial flowers that bloom in the spring, sportswriters could be counted on to begin their annual complaints about the slow pace of the games, blaming "slow motion players." Most games were taking more than two hours, they carped, and some as long as two and a half.

Perhaps to change his luck in New York, Mack switched to the Governor Clinton Hotel across from Penn Station. It didn't help. At the April 24 opener at Yankee Stadium, after Mayor Fiorello LaGuardia went to the mound wearing a glove and a turned-around cap, imitated a pitcher soaking a spitter, and threw a strike to Bill Dickey, Red Ruffing and John Marcum pitched 4-hitters, but one of the hits off Marcum was a home run by Frank Crosetti.

Despite Mack's misgivings, his pitchers started off surprisingly effective—Cascarella picked up 2 wins against the Yankees—but light hitting led to a 3-6 record. That balance soon changed. Jimmy Foxx and Bob Johnson replaced Ruth and Gehrig as the most productive home run duo in the majors. Foxx hit the first home run ever into Comiskey Park's newly shortened center-field bleachers. As of mid-July Mack's number three and four hitters were one-two in the home run department. Johnson would finish fourth with 34, behind Gehrig, Foxx, and Hal Trosky. The Athletics led the league in home runs and slugging average, but it wasn't enough to overcome the pitchers giving up the most walks and second-most runs.

Connie Mack trolled the college campuses for pitchers—especially left-handers—and other prospects. He felt unarmed without a southpaw. On a day off he watched Indiana University left-hander Vernon Wilshere strike out 15 and beat Temple, 6–4, signed him, and started him against the Tigers. But Wilshere wasn't ready.

Mack's efforts weren't always appreciated. In August scout Phil Haggerty sent a Mercer College athlete named Gerald McQuaig to New York to work out with the A's. McQuaig, a sophomore, was the star fullback for Mercer. When the Mercer football coach, Lake Russell, heard that Mack had signed the youngster, he called Mack and pleaded for the boy's return to school. Mack refused. Russell appealed to Judge Landis, claiming McQuaig was a minor (he was twenty-two). McQuaig got into 7 games and had 1 hit, and that was the end of his big league days.

The A's quickly settled into seventh place and slumbered there. By the end of August Connie Mack had written off the season. "We have just about wound up our season tho we have quite a number of games to play," he wrote to Sr. Florence. "Felt on Wednesday last, when our pitcher Marcum defeated School Boy Row [sic] and prevented him from breaking the record made by Johnson and Groves with a crowd of something like over 30,000 and every seat being taken and standing room at a premium, that we might say our season was closed."

Detroit rookie pitcher Schoolboy Rowe had won 16 in a row, matching the record held by Walter Johnson and Lefty Grove, when the first-place Tigers arrived in Philadelphia on Sunday, August 26. Rowe's record was 20-4. The pressure had been building on him and the entire Detroit team every time he pitched. The 1930s version of the media hounds were after him en masse. The hotel telephone switchboard fielded a constant stream of calls for the twenty-four-year-old. Six-inch stacks of telegrams for him piled up at the front desk. After a rainout on Tuesday, Cochrane decided to start Rowe in the second game of a doubleheader on Wednesday, giving him a few extra hours to relax.

The last-place White Sox were in New York to play the second-place

Yankees. Some Chicago and New York writers passed up that game to take a train to Philly to cover the expected record-breaker. "It's a break for Connie Mack," said one. "With Detroit and a doubleheader, they might draw a good weekday crowd, maybe 15,000."

When the writers arrived at the Tigers' hotel, they thought a convention was in town. The place was mobbed. They headed for Shibe Park and had to push and shove their way through the milling crowd. Fans who couldn't get inside were moving toward the houses with rooftop bleachers. Inside the writers waited in line to climb the 129 steps to the press box, which was already filled.

Detroit won the first game, 12–7. Cain, Mahaffey, and Cascarella were battered for 20 hits. In El Dorado, Arkansas, where Rowe had excelled at every sport played by the local high school, all sixteen thousand residents were pulling for him. All 33,718 in Shibe Park and the uncounted fans on the rooftops across Twentieth Street were pulling, yelling, and hooting against him. (One of those rooftop fans was twelve-year-old Roy Campanella.) Detroit scored 2 in the first off John Marcum, but it was not to be nearly enough for Rowe. The A's came out swinging, tied it in the fourth, almost knocked Rowe out in a 5-run fifth (capped by a Higgins home run), and finally finished him in the seventh. Having gotten their wish, the crowd cheered the downcast Rowe all the way into the dugout.

The Athletics woke up in September. Cain, Dietrich, Benton, and Cascarella looked like world-beaters. Dietrich, who on September 3 had given up the last of Babe Ruth's career 108 home runs hit against the A's, shut out Chicago and Washington in his last two starts.

Their 18-12 September finish vaulted the A's into fifth place. But by then the fans had become indifferent and deserted them, even on Sundays. The results of the A's first experience with Sunday baseball after so many years of fighting for it had been disappointing. That winter Mack expressed his surprise at its lack of success to Frank Navin, who told him:

You won't find business good on Sundays for at least three years. That was our experience when we were allowed to play Sunday ball in Detroit. It took three years before we saw financial advantage. The reason is plain. It takes time to change the habits of the people. In Detroit nearly everybody was in the habit of doing certain things on Sundays. They did not willingly relinquish their programs. The Detroit team had to show them something before they started changing their habits. It took us three years before Sunday attendance came up to expectations. It's going to take you that long, too.

Navin was right.

Total attendance was up a mere 2 percent. But given the dire economic times, the bottom line could have been a lot worse without it. Mack sold no high-priced players, so the loss of almost $142,000 for the year put the club deeper in debt.

Despite cries that Connie Mack had sold the 1934 pennant to Tom Yawkey, the Red Sox finished fourth, just 7 games ahead of the A's. Devastated by injuries, Washington fell to seventh, 33 games off its pennant-winning pace of 1933. Attendance plummeted. Clark Griffith was in financial trouble. Winning in 1933 had produced no profits because the Senators had won too easily. After September 1 attendance had dropped off. The last four games against the Yankees would have netted each team about $150,000 if the race had been close. With the pennant clinched the Senators drew only about four thousand a game. The five-game World Series, while a testament to the game's honesty, denied the teams about $125,000 in revenue from additional games. So when Tom Yawkey offered $250,000 for Joe Cronin to be the player-manager for the Red Sox, Griffith took it. He also unloaded his other high-salaried stars who had performed like bored prima donnas in '34.

(When Connie Mack was unable to attend a welcoming dinner for Cronin in Boston on May 20, 1935, he sent a telegram: "Regret greatly my being unable to attend your friendship and welcome dinner given in honor of that great ballplayer and manager Joe Cronin who is out to give the Boston baseball fans what they have been looking for. A real champion is Joe.")

Simmons, Haas, Dykes, and Earnshaw couldn't raise the White Sox out of the cellar.

The Tigers had lacked a good catcher for five years under Bucky Harris. Most of the team had been developed by Harris before Mickey Cochrane arrived. But Cochrane made an immediate difference with at least one Detroit pitcher, Tommy Bridges. Ed Rommel had learned to read the curveball specialist's delivery when a curve was coming. The A's had been 7-1 against him since '31. (Dykes, Haas, and Simmons had taken the information to the White Sox, who blasted Bridges, 12–0, the first time they saw him in '33.) Cochrane corrected Bridges's flaw, and the A's were 0-2 against him in 1934. Black Mike sparked the Tigers to the pennant, 7 games ahead of the Yankees.

Two years after the Cardinals had finished seventh, Branch Rickey, called the "Piggly-Wiggly of baseball" for his chain store system, produced a new "Gashouse Gang" for St. Louis. Led by Dizzy and Paul Dean and managed by Frank Frisch, the Gang edged the defending champion Giants on the last day of the season. The World Series would be an all-western show for the first time in fifteen years, the Cardinals winning it in seven games.

For Connie Mack, there were a few personal highlights in the otherwise lackluster season.

The White Sox were in Washington, where they lost their fifth in a row on May 8, when manager Lew Fonseca was fired and Jimmie Dykes replaced him. Dykes inherited a pitching staff that was worse than any he had seen even in the cellar days in Philadelphia. One day in Washington the Sox were losing, 17–1, in the eighth inning when the public address announcer sounded a call for all Congressmen at the game to report to the Capitol for a roll call vote. One press box observer quipped, "They're going to investigate charges that four White Sox pitchers are impersonating big league pitchers."

The next stop for the Sox was New York. On the way Dykes stopped off to get some words of advice from Connie Mack. "Always play your hunches," said the premier riverboat gambler of baseball, "no matter how unorthodox they are. And whether or not they work, don't second-guess yourself."

(Mack gave the same advice to Leo Durocher when he became manager of the Dodgers in 1939. In 1987 Durocher told George Vecsey of the *New York Times*, "I was in a hotel in Chicago and there was Mr. Mack. He said, 'Leo, can you come up to my room?' and I did and he said, 'Don't be afraid to take a chance. One day it works. One day it doesn't.'")

Dykes asked Mack about handling pitchers, specifically when to take them out.

"You'll know, never fear. Something will tell you. And when you do make up your mind to take 'em out, take 'em out. Don't ever change your mind. If you've said to yourself: 'Now, if the next man gets a hit, out he goes,' and the next man gets a hit, take him out. Don't weaken. Ninety percent of the time you'll be right; the other 10 percent you'll be wrong, of course, but the percentage is way in your favor."

And finally Mack reminded him, "You're just one of the twenty-five players on the team. The only difference between you and the others is that you have authority. Let them question your judgment but never let them doubt your authority."

Dykes was the ninth man who had played for Mack and become a big league manager. Twenty-one others had managed in the minors so far, and another half-dozen were coaching at colleges.

On June 20 Connie Jr. married Susan Sheppard, whom he had met at Duke. The daughter of Senator Morris Sheppard of Texas, she had just graduated; Connie Jr. left Duke after two years and would join the family business in 1935. The ceremony took place at the Sheppards' Washington home. Connie Mack was best man. (Mack's cousin May Dempsey said, "I remember Connie Mack telling mother that he stood up for Connie Jr. It was a Protestant ceremony and the Catholics got mad at him and he heard about it from them.") Among the guests was Monte Cross, who had jumped from the National League when Mack started the A's, played on his 1902 and 1905 pennant winners, and remained a close friend of the family ever since. The next day Cross, sixty-three, had a fatal heart attack at his Philadelphia home.

The second All-Star Game was played on July 10 in New York. Connie Mack wasn't there. He was back where he had begun, in East Brookfield, Massachusetts, with the Athletics for a gala Connie Mack Day. It was the biggest event in the history of the four Brookfield villages. Showman George M. Cohan, who had spent the summers of his youth at his grandparents' home in North Brookfield and had watched Mack catch for the East Brookfield team, drove over from Boston with a song he had written for the occasion. Cohan was sixteen years younger than Mack; they had become friends around 1910. Whenever Mack was in New York and Cohan was appearing in a show, Cohan always had tickets for him and would invite him and his party backstage. Ruth Mack remembered on one occasion being there with her mother and dad, and Cohan had them come up on stage and introduced them to the audience.

Connie Mack's thoughts were very much on his youth leading up to the festivities. The A's were in Boston on July 6 when Mack wrote to Eddie Drake, the underage Civil War drummer boy who had returned from the war to his home near the Mack house and befriended young Connie. The A's train was scheduled to arrive in East Brookfield at eleven in the morning. Mack wrote, "Would like to shake your hand once more if you can see your way clear to come down to the East station."

There was no report of their meeting.

From the East Station the team's three Pullman cars traveled on the branch line to North Brookfield that ran behind Mack's boyhood home.

Nostalgia was as thick as the New England humidity when Mack stepped down from the Pullman car. Wearing a gray suit, panama hat, and sporty brown and white shoes, he was greeted by a thousand cheering admirers. The 181st Infantry band from Fort Devens led a motorcade to the town center. On the Brookfield common, bordered by houses decked with colorful banners, the band and a trio of veterans of the Great War performed Cohan's patriotic songs. The Congregational Church ladies provided a lunch for the players while Mack went to the home of Pat Carter for lunch with Carter, Gene Daniels, and Joe Doyle, who had played second and short and pitched respectively for North Brookfield against Mack's East Brookfield nine in 1883. Afterward Mack visited the grave of Marty Bergen, a catcher for Boston in the 1890s who had slain his family, then himself, in North Brookfield in 1900. Proceeds of the game that afternoon against the North Brookfield Armortreds went partly for a grave-site monument for Bergen and partly for the benefit of Frank Bird, another local catcher who had played briefly for the Browns in 1892 until he had been paralyzed by an on-field accident.

When the Athletics and Cohan appeared on the field at 3:10, thirty-seven state troopers tried but failed to keep order. More than ten thousand screaming autograph seekers battled for access to Mack and Cohan, along with a pack of photographers that outnumbered the swarm attending a presidential appearance. Standing on the home grounds of his ancient rivals, Mack told New York sportswriter John Kieran, "I kinda flinched . . . because of the battles and the fierce feeling in the old days, when it was worth a fellow's life almost to be caught there if he was from East Brookfield."

Mack smiled broadly when he greeted Jesse Burkett, whom he had played against in the 1890s. The longtime minor league manager had been at Worcester back in 1908, when Connie Mack had sent a New Jersey sandlot shortstop to him: Lena Blackburne, now a coach for the A's.

The game began, but the crowd control never took hold. Every foul ball was fought for and taken to Mack and Cohan to be signed. Connie Mack sat on a chair between home and first and was kept busy by signature hunters, obliging every one with a smile and handshake, talking about the old days with those who remembered them. Wherever Cohan went, to buy peanuts or umpire briefly at first base, youngsters pursued him—even onto the field. In the sixth inning a posse of boys with shirts reading Cohan's Disturbers marched by him, reminding the composer of the team he had organized when he had been the young terror of North Brookfield.

Players who were not in the lineup sat on the grass embankment and visited with the residents. Boston mayor James M. Curley, running for governor, worked the crowd.

The overloaded bleachers gradually sagged until they collapsed altogether, so gently that nobody was hurt. The surrounding rooftops held up under their human loads.

Meanwhile the local semipros beat the A's, 9–5. Mack watched the Armortreds' pitcher, Bill Graham, with interest: Graham didn't walk anybody.

"We can't always win in these country towns," Mack said to the members of the press seated nearby, "especially in North Brookfield."

The game was stopped in the middle of the eighth inning for an NBC radio broadcast. Connie Mack, trying to hold back tears, stepped to the microphone on the field. "I cannot begin to tell you the pleasure it has given me to come back to North Brookfield today. It was fifty-one years ago the Fourth of July that I played my last ball game on this common. We lost that game, too. I don't know that I've been on this ball field since. What an experience it has been to come here today to receive this greeting and to meet the old friends and old ballplayers of other days."

After Cohan said a few words, a local girl, Jean Rooney, presented them with bound copies of the day's program. Fifty years later she still treasured a photo of the presentation.

Tax assessor Fred Grabert summed up the day: "I think the people in town were in awe because it was an event that would never happen again in the life of the town."

After the game Mack and Cohan went to the home of the Reverend James F. McGillicuddy, a distant relative, for dinner while the teams were feted at the Knights of Columbus Hall. Connie Mack may have wished he could remain for the dance that followed at the town hall, where he had attended many such galas during his courting days more than fifty years ago. But at 8:30 a motorcycle escort led the team back to the train, back to the future, headed for Chicago.

In October 1930 a wildcatter had discovered an ocean of crude oil under Rusk County in east Texas. That touched off an invasion of independent oilmen buying up leases on the mineral rights to farmers' properties, paying cash to hard-up farmers for a share of any future income they might get from anybody who actually drilled wells and found oil. Even a little piece of a big gusher could make a man rich. If no oil was ever found, at least the farmer was ahead. These rights were sliced and diced into little pieces, which were actively bought and sold, going from $1.50 an acre to as high as $3,000 whenever a gusher came in nearby. Big operators wound up with rights to tens of thousands of acres all over the state. Then everything slowed when oil hit a low of four cents a barrel in May 1933. Connie Mack's friend Hyman Pearlstone joined in the speculation. When he sold land holdings, he retained the mineral rights. In March 1934 he signed over to Mack one-third of his ⁹⁄₄₀ share of the lease on 279 acres in Leon County. It was like scouting a dozen Lefty Groves and picking the one who would come up with a dead arm. While everybody around them seemed to be getting rich, nothing happened in their Leon County fields, a situation that left Pearlstone open to some good-natured kidding from his family. Occasionally a wildcatter leased some of the holdings, but nobody drilled anything there for more than sixty years. Connie Mack never saw more than an annual check for $18.59 for "deferred rental" under the lease.

Earle Mack was the Athletics' organizer of postseason barnstorming expeditions. He had begun planning a trip to Japan in October 1933. Earle wrote to the trip's sponsor, Matsutaro Shoriki, publisher of the *Yomiuri Shimbun* newspaper, alerting him that Lefty O'Doul, who had led previous tours to Japan, would arrive that winter to negotiate the terms. Shoriki guaranteed 150,000 yen, 80 percent of all receipts above that amount, and all expenses, including boat fares. (Eleven years later Babe Ruth said, "Shoriki didn't pay us what he promised to pay. Most of us spent more money in Japan than we made.")

Earle wrote to other clubs requesting the participation of their players. Not all were inclined to go along. William Benswanger, president of the Pirates, mentioned "the boat hazard; the danger of Oriental disease, etc., and the possibility of playing too much baseball, thereby unfitting the player for his summer's work." But, he wrote, "We are not opposed to the idea." In other words, go ahead but don't count on us for players.

In the end no National League clubs agreed to participate. The players, most of whom brought their wives, included Hayes, Foxx, Warstler, Cascarella, McNair, and Miller from the A's; Gehrig, Gomez, and Ruth from the Yankees; Moe Berg and Earl Whitehill from Washington; Clint Brown and Earl Averill from Cleveland; and Charlie Gehringer from Detroit The umpire was John Picus "Jack" Quinn. The trainer was Doc Ebling.

Connie Mack didn't expect to go. Babe Ruth would be the big draw and would manage the team. Mack never tired of rattling around the United States, where he knew he could get home in a day if he had to. Being more than two weeks' travel time away made him nervous. But Tom Shibe, Katherine Mack, and Earle talked him into the trip. Sr. Florence sent him prayer beads to take with him. Babe Ruth would still manage the team. Earle led the team on a westward barnstorming tour to Vancouver, then went home. The players brought him a gold watch from Japan.

There were two mishaps before they left North America. Jimmy Foxx was hit in the head by a pitch in Winnipeg and was left to recover for a few days before being pronounced fit to continue the trip. (Bill Jenkinson traced Foxx's later debilitating, career-shortening sinus problems to this concussion.) Charlie Berry was hit by appendicitis in North Dakota and never got any farther. He was replaced by Frank Hayes.

They sailed on the *Empress of Japan* from Vancouver on October 20 and stopped at Honolulu, where they found Al Simmons on his honeymoon. Connie Mack thoroughly enjoyed the voyage. He eagerly accepted an invitation to go below for a tour of the engine room, where the European members of the crew surprised him by producing a dozen baseballs to sign. He was undaunted by reports that a typhoon was headed their way; they experienced only a little rain.

Even in the middle of the Pacific Ocean, Mack couldn't avoid being assailed by rumors. Like nature, baseball writers abhorred a vacuum of off-season news. They filled it by writing fiction. With nine newspapers struggling to survive in New York, the competition was fierce. A story about Babe Ruth's being hired to manage the A's in 1935 sprouted from the imagination of George Kenney and appeared in the early edition of the *New York Daily News* on the night of October 25. It led with the unequivocal statement, "Babe Ruth will manage the Philadelphia Athletics next year," and was picked up the next morning by the *Los Angeles Times* and *Chicago Tribune*.

Kenney was not the first to indulge in such speculation. In the April 1934 *Baseball Magazine*, Stetson Palmer had written, "Mack is on the verge of stepping down." Nothing new there. Writers had been making the same assertion for at least ten years, secure in the belief that someday it would happen.

In Kenney's fantasy, Mack had "hinted toward the close of the recent season that he would retire soon." Ruth had spurned the Yankees' offer to remain as a pinch hitter and "indicated that a managing post had been offered him."

While not exactly science fiction, Kenney's story did show a clever imagination: "To conceal the real offer, however, [Ruth] indicated that the team which he had been offered was a National League team.

"In order to school the Babe in the Connie Mack system of diamond strategy," Kenney continued, "he made Babe field manager of the all-star team on the current tour of the Orient. By the time the jaunt is done, the Babe will have had a thorough course in the Connie Mack way of doing things and will be ready to blossom forth in his new role as manager."

Never mind that Ruth had been named to manage the all-stars before Mack had even decided to go with them.

Kenney added that Ruth would receive stock in the Athletics.

The next day Bill Corum in the *New York Evening Journal* said Ruth was going to the Boston Braves but not to replace Bill McKechnie as the manager. He got it right. But nobody noticed.

Newspapers across the country picked up the Kenney story. The wire services immediately sent cablegrams to the *Empress of Japan* seeking comments from Ruth and Mack. The AP said Mack replied that he would manage until he was eighty. The UP's embroidery said Mack had thought about Ruth but decided he couldn't afford the rumored $35,000 salary Ruth would demand.

Ruth denied knowing anything about anything.

John Shibe said, "New York writers have been trying to find a job for Ruth for years. There's apparently none open so they decided to make him manager of the Athletics."

Mack scoffed at the suggestion that Ruth might join the A's to learn about managing. "That's silly," he said. "Besides, you can't teach anybody to manage a team."

Ed Barrow doubted there was anything to it. "Under baseball law, no club has the right to dicker with Ruth without first obtaining our permission. As no such request has come to us, and knowing what a stickler Connie Mack is for observing the rules of baseball, I feel certain there is nothing to this." He said if anybody wanted Ruth as a manager—but not as a player—the Yankees would give him his release. But nobody had approached the Yankees.

On the ship and throughout the tour, Mack and Ruth got along fine. The Ruths and Gehrigs avoided each other, but so what? That didn't bother Mack, who never had any plans to hire Ruth, so there was no way anything could happen to cause him to change his mind.

According to Doc Ebling, Ruth so enjoyed the three-week tour, he didn't think his playing days were over. Looking out at the sea from the deck of a Dutch liner bound for Bali after the Japanese tour, Ruth said to him, "I think the old dogs will stand another season after all."

The all-stars landed at Yokohama on Friday morning, November 2. The crush for autographs began even before they left the ship. Boatloads of reporters, photographers, police, and passport officials met the ship before it docked. At the pier about twenty-five young girls in kimonos boarded and presented each player with a robe with his name embroidered on it in Japanese characters. A short train ride took them into Tokyo. From the moment they arrived, they were mobbed by millions of people wherever they went, all of them trying to get to "Babu Rusu." For two weeks they swarmed around him. Anybody who didn't have something to sign held a camera. Some had both. The Babe signed everything they thrust at him. Young ladies in kimonos even followed the players into the men's room in the hotel seeking autographs. The first day the visitors worked out at a field eighteen miles out of town, about twenty thousand people came out to watch them.

On the morning of the first game in Tokyo, Harold Amos, principal of the American school in Tokyo, was in the lobby of the Imperial Hotel with his son William, thirteen. Connie Mack walked in. A friend of Amos's called him over and introduced them.

Mack said to the boy, "Billy, are you going to the game this afternoon?"

"No, sir. We weren't able to get tickets, even a couple months ago."

"Mr. Amos," said Mack, "will you leave Billy with us for the rest of the day? I think we can do something for him."

Mack took the boy into the dining room and ordered lunch for him, then left to attend to some business. He returned and they went out and got into the back seat of a huge touring car. A big man in a tan polo coat squeezed in beside Billy. Babe Ruth grinned and stuck out his hand. "Hiya, kid. Let's show 'em how to do it."

Other limousines carrying the Americans followed them as police with lights flashing led them slowly through the dense cheering throngs. As Ruth passed, waving to the crowd, the roar of "Babu-Rusu" shook the Ginza like an earthquake.

Billy Amos recalled, "Above the din, Connie Mack shouted at me to wave. I did, once, and the crowd roared back. Whoever I was to them, I had to be important, seated between such major sports idols at the head of a procession. Somewhere in old newspaper files or in a dusty Japanese amateur photographer's album, there must be at least one picture of a small, completely overawed boy, dwarfed between two baseball giants in the back of an open touring car, on his way to his own version of glory."

Meiji Stadium was filled to capacity, all eager to see the sluggers hit home runs, a rarity in Japanese baseball. The visitors didn't disappoint them. Ruth and Foxx and Averill and Gehrig put on a show of power wherever they played. After the opening ceremonies, in which Marquis Okuma, president of the first Tokyo professional league, threw the first pitch and Connie Mack caught it, the fans enjoyed every minute of the 17–1 American victory. It may have been a form of hospitality that the crowds at the games rooted for the visitors to defeat the local teams. Or it may have been a matter of expectation; the Americans were the superior players and as such ought to win.

International News Service [INS] correspondent Jimmy Young was there. "I've been around the Far East a long time," he said later, "and I know that there's never been a demonstration and never a reception compared to the one the Japanese people gave those ballplayers."

Despite the talk of the likelihood of war between the two nations, politeness and reverence prevailed. "When we reached Japan," Mack said on his return, "the country was a hive of rumors of war with the U.S. But it soon was put under wraps while the team was there."

There were breakfast feasts and luncheon feasts and evening feasts at department stores, private clubs, and palatial homes of government officials, the American ambassador, and members of the emperor's family.

Presiding at an America-Japan Society lunch, Prince Iyesato Tokugawa said, "Many Japanese schoolboys do not know who is Premier but it is difficult to find a youth in Japan who does not know the names of Connie Mack and Babe Ruth."

Connie Mack received so many letters and notes, a professor of English from Meiji University was enlisted to translate for him.

At one dinner Mack made a speech explaining American baseball—the pennant races, World Series history and highlights, spring training, and the trading of players.

They saw the sights, catcher-spy Moe Berg from rooftops with his concealed camera. Berg said there was some suspicion that their telephones may have been tapped. Connie Mack took it all in with as much pep and enthusiasm as the youngest in the party. Standing on a street corner with *Cleveland Press* sports editor Stuart Bell, he was amazed at the sight of thousands of bicycles (many carrying huge bundles, even pieces of furniture), pedestrians (every woman seemed to have a baby on her back or in her arms), three-wheel delivery wagons and carts loaded down with everything imaginable, and taxis—somehow all maneuvering around each other without colliding.

"You could never touch one of those fellows sliding into second," Mack commented.

They didn't always avoid collisions. Jimmy Foxx said. "The first taxi I was in knocked over six men riding bicycles and instead of calling a cop and arresting the driver, the victims all politely bowed. You seem to be able to hit a Jap cyclist and he is seldom hurt."

The culture of politeness awed the Americans. One unidentified diarist wrote, "One thing that is so noticeable here is the extreme politeness which apparently exists not only to us visitors but amongst themselves. The men bow and scrape to each other in much the same manner as we do to our girls, but the woman of this country runs a mighty bad second. This is a man's country, every inch of it and it is just too bad if you are born a girl."

On Tuesday, November 6, the team left for an eight-hundred-mile trip to the far north. Mack stayed behind. That evening he wrote a long letter to his "girlies," Ruth, Rita, and Betty, describing the city and their reception, which "beat anything I have ever seen and never expect to see anything like it again." He missed "the papers very much—don't get any news to speak of." He urged them to write to their mother, who was in New York enjoying the Broadway shows with her old friend from Atlantic City, Ellen Burke, while Katherine's sister, Aunt Nan, stayed with the girls.

The players arrived in a town called Kokura in a downpour; twenty thousand showed up, so they put on boots and carried parasols and played in the steady rain. In Asahigawa, near Siberia, the accommodations were primitive. There was one old western-style bed and one bathtub in the whole town, Jimmy Young reported, and Babe Ruth was honored with those dubious comforts: "He got into the bathtub and darn near all the water went out of the tub in a big wave. The bed was a relic from the Russo-Japanese war. It had been captured off some Russian admiral's battleship and had gotten pretty lumpy in the meantime. Everybody darn near froze for it snowed out the first game. And there wasn't much to eat except raw fish and bean curds."

In Hakodate the players were taken aback when female members of the hotel staff entered their rooms and attempted to help them undress, stood discreetly aside while the men put on their pajamas, then reappeared in the morning to help them dress. How the polite Connie Mack would have dealt with this hospitality is difficult to envision.

The crowds were much smaller in these places, but as Mack explained in a letter to Earle, "They arranged a lot of games where the crowd would be small all due so they can increase the circulation of their paper."

The local players, mostly collegians, were small and lacked power, but Connie Mack was impressed by their speed and skillful defense. "Baseball in Japan has barely started," he said on his return home. "There'll be no stopping them once they get organized."

The all-stars left Japan on the *Empress of Canada* and stopped to refuel at Shanghai on December 6, where they beat a team of Marines and missionaries, 22–1. Some of the missionaries had walked for two or three days to watch Babe Ruth and Lou Gehrig loft and line long balls over the fence. Joe Cascarella, who pitched the game, remembered the missionaries embracing the players after the game. "I was embarrassed," he told his friend Richard Willing years later. "I felt like I hadn't done anything but pitch a ball game, and they were acting like I was bringing them the sacraments."

They gave two autographed balls to a Chinese fan who had learned the game at a seminary school in Shanghai. One of those balls survived the upheavals and revolutions in China and is now at the Hall of Fame in Cooperstown.

After stopping for three games in Manila, the party broke up, some heading for a grand tour of Europe, others changing ships at Honolulu to go to San Francisco. Mack and a half dozen others stayed on the *Empress of Canada* to return to Victoria. Mack celebrated his seventy-second birthday with a surprise party thrown by the players, who gave him two silver vases.

Arriving in Canada on January 2, 1935, Mack went to Portland to visit Roy's family. Tom Turner had sold his interest in the Portland club in December. Roy would resign as secretary of the Beavers and move to Philadelphia to join the front office at Shibe Park. While he was in Portland, Mack had to address the Babe Ruth rumors again. In a national radio interview he praised Ruth's play in Japan and his managing of the all-stars, then said, "I did not offer Ruth a job with the A's and know nothing of his future. I know he would like to be a manager."

Mack then stopped in Chicago to see league president Will Harridge. When he heard that both leagues had voted to ban future foreign excursions at their December meeting, claiming that too many postseason games might affect the players in the spring, Mack called it a mistake.

He arrived back at North Philadelphia station at 7:40 on the morning of Wednesday, January 9, and was greeted by Betty, Rita, and his daughter-in-law Sue. After a stop at home to freshen up, he headed to the office and confronted the stacks of mail and covey of news-starved reporters that awaited him.

What would become a three-hour session began with a recap of the trip and a prediction that there would be new pennant winners in both leagues. The day after the 1934 season had ended, Connie Mack had moved quickly to head off any prolonged bickering with Jimmy Foxx and nip any rumors about the sale of his star. He and Foxx agreed to a three-year contract at $18,000 a year. Mack also made the surprising announcement that Foxx would return to catching in 1935 and would replace Bing Miller as captain.

Expecting the questions to begin about Foxx and Miller, Mack was thrown for a loss when someone asked, "Is the deal for Higgins with New York definitely off?"

Unaware of the rumors that had circulated at the December meetings, Mack said, "There never was a deal for Higgins that I know of."

WRITER: Joe McCarthy told me he wanted Higgins.
MACK: He told you he wanted Higgins?
WRITER: Yes.
MACK: He told me he didn't.
WRITER: He said he offered a first baseman, a catcher, a third baseman, and money.
MACK, HEATEDLY: What did he call money?
WRITER: I understand that on January 11 we were to have something definite on the swap one way or the other.
MACK: There is no deal on for Higgins.

And there wasn't.

The questions then turned to Foxx's catching. Asked if it would slow him down, Mack said, "Why should it? Mickey has caught for nine years and nobody can say he has slowed up except naturally through age. Foxx will not get any faster. He will not improve any more at first base or third. His ability is in his power and I need him there. My success in '35 will depend on the pitching staff and 40 percent of the strength of any pitching staff is behind the plate. Young pitchers need a veteran catcher they have confidence in. I thought about it last year but his hitting fell off and I didn't want him thinking it was affected by catching."

As for the forty-year-old Bing Miller, Mack hedged his statement in October that Miller would not be back. "I can't answer that completely. Our plans are not settled. When a club loses as much money as we have lost during the last few seasons it often makes you so angry you make statements and snap conclusions that you often regret afterwards. But I can say Bing will have a job this year, and not as a scout. Bing has plenty of good baseball left in him. A place will be found for him."

Mr. Mack then went home and packed to go to Florida to play golf.

Anybody who knew Connie Mack knew what bunk the stories had been about Babe Ruth replacing Connie Mack. Even those who didn't know him but read the Philadelphia papers paid no attention to them.

During the 1934 season Roy Mack told Bob Ray of the *Los Angeles Times*, "I don't think he'll ever quit baseball. I get a letter from him every week. In his letters he writes about the 1935 and 1936 seasons and the players he's looking for."

Connie Jr. agreed; the word "retire" wasn't in their father's vocabulary.

Connie Mack's imminent retirement had been reported or predicted as long ago as 1911 and as far away as the Eureka, Utah, *Reporter*, which carried this story on October 27 of that year:

This season will probably be the last one for Connie Mack as manager of the Athletics.

If the Athletics win the American League pennant and the team is in good shape for next season Mack's retirement is almost certain.

Connie is a stockholder in the Athletic club and when he retires will become an officer of the club, probably president, in which capacity he would direct the club the same as Charley Comiskey directs the White Sox.

Mack is forty-nine and at times his health is not good. He has remained at home several times this season when the Athletics made short trips on the road. Another thing: Connie was married last fall and naturally prefers to remain at home instead of traveling over the country with his team.

Naturally.

The unknown source of this report, picked up by a weekly paper in a mining town in the middle of Utah, obviously did not know Connie Mack.

Mack never hinted at nor talked about retiring, and nobody expected him to do so. His answers to the perennial speculation contained too many "whens" to ever be convincing: "When I can no longer do the job" or "When my health will no longer permit it" or "When I'm eighty" or "When I find myself repeating the same stories" or other put-offs. Even the oft-quoted desire to "win just one more pennant" was never intended to lead to the inference of "then I'll retire."

Once he told Chicago *Daily News* columnist John Carmichael, "They keep asking me when am I going to quit? I always tell them 'After one more pennant. Just one more.' What I don't tell them is that after one more, there always is another and another for which to strive. They know and I know I'm never going to quit."

The truth was, as Mack said in a radio interview, "Baseball is my whole life and I wouldn't know what to do if I wasn't in the harness." On other occasions he put it, "If I stopped working, I would die in two weeks."

One day in 1939 Clark Griffith and Connie Mack were visiting in Griffith's office. Griffith was seventy, Mack seventy-six. Griffith had given up trying to both manage the Senators and run the business twenty years earlier. Griffith's nephew Calvin was there and later recalled the conversation.

"Give up the reins," Griffith urged Mack, "and let a younger fellow manage the club."

"Clark," said Mack, "the day I get off that bench I'm gonna become an old man and an old man dies. I'm gonna stay on the bench as long as I humanly can."

As for moving from the dugout to the office, he told Bob Paul in January 1938, "Do you think I could sit up here while the boys were trying to put over a run to beat, say, the Yankees or the Tigers? No, sir. I couldn't enjoy that. I want to be down there on the bench, fighting the battle with my boys."

Not even finishing last year after year would made him feel like chucking it all.

"Quit? Why should I quit? This will be my fifty-fifth season in baseball and I expect it to be as pleasant as all the others. That's right, every one has been pleasant." (Time had extracted the poison from the memory of the rancorous pennant-winning 1914 season.)

"Why, goodness gracious, I didn't have to win a pennant to enjoy myself. It's the game, the surroundings, the boys on the field and the friends you meet all over the circuit that keep me so enthused about baseball. If the days and nights throughout the season weren't so enjoyable, I'd quit. I stay on the bench because it's fun. Why, if someone asked me right now what I'd like most to do, I'd tell them I'd enjoy a ball game most of all."

Clearly, no man ever loved the life he led more than Connie Mack.

5 | BACK ON THE BOTTOM

At the New York writers' dinner on February 3, 1935, Will Rogers began his remarks by recognizing "dear old Connie Mack, young and keen as ever." Dizzy Dean was in the audience. Dean and Joe Medwick of the Cardinals were holding out for big raises after winning the World Series. Rogers drew laughs depicting Dean and Babe Ruth as downtrodden serfs of the niggardly magnates. Calling Dean "the best showman in baseball," Rogers concluded by saying, "The Cards should give him what he wants." Rogers drew a big ovation.

Connie Mack was not amused.

Heywood Broun, baseball writer turned general columnist, was the next speaker. Broun was a labor activist. He wasn't kidding when he said, "The players are underpaid, especially the showmen like Dean and Ruth who draw the crowds." The audience, few of them club owners, cheered.

Mack simmered.

Will Rogers had left when Mack stood up to speak. He began by describing the crowds and adulation that Babe Ruth had drawn in Japan. "Only Babe Ruth has the color today to draw such crowds," he said. "Players of today are much more skilled in all departments of the game. Why, catchers in a Class B league now are on a par with me when I was a major league player. But the present-day stars do not know how to put color into their work as did Honus Wagner, Ty Cobb, Eddie Collins, Rube Waddell, and some others I might mention. They are not showmen and for that reason they do not have the following that the greats I have mentioned and many others of the bygone days had."

He then blamed that lack of showmanship along with the Depression for the club owners' financial problems, likening the current situation to the days when he played for a team that was in such sad straits that "I felt ashamed to draw my pay on the first and fifteenth."

By now he had worked himself up to a fever of indignation. "It is an injustice," he all but shouted, "to say that ballplayers are treated unfairly in the matter of wages. The ballplayer of today is treated fairly and squarely by the owners. And anybody who says he isn't"—he fumbled for the right words—"doesn't know what he is talking about."

Sure, there had been tight-fisted club owners, but there were also men whose love affair with baseball had cost them more than if they'd married and divorced a half-dozen chorus girls: Emil Fuchs, Sidney Weill, John B. Day, Phil Ball, Charles Weeghman, Charles Somers, Chris von der Ahe, Bill Sharsig.

The crowd was on its feet cheering the seventy-two-year-old Mr. Mack, be it from sympathy, understanding, or just long-standing respect and admiration.

Mack concluded with the belief that baseball would prosper once again, and the players should be satisfied with what the club owners could pay under present conditions. As much as the criticism stung, it hurt Mack even more to be unable to pay his boys better. But he didn't have the income to do it. And most other clubs were in the same condition.

Lou Gehrig would be the highest paid player in 1935 at $31,000; Joe McCarthy, the highest paid manager at $35,000.

Eddie Collins had been after Mack to let Bing Miller go to Boston as a player-coach. Miller would see very little playing time with the A's and could make more money in Boston, so Mack released him with regret: "Ball clubs sometimes have to do the things they didn't want to do. In parting with Bing Miller I must say he is going with one of my dearest friends." On February 11 more than six hundred turned out for a farewell dinner for Miller.

Ever since 1929 John Shibe had been itching to raise the right-field fence to block the view from the rooftops on Twentieth Street. But the A's had begun to win, and their lineup of sluggers squawked at the idea. Even the right-handed swingers Foxx and Simmons hit enough to right to join the protestors. The A's had led the league in home runs again in 1934, but they were no longer winning. Rooftop seats were going for twenty-five cents, half the bleacher price. In 1934 there were days when the rooftops had more occupants than the bleachers. So a twenty-two-foot corrugated iron addition—the "spite fence," the neighbors called it—went up atop the old twelve-foot fence from the foul line to the center-field flagpole. Spectators would have to stand on tiptoes on the top row of the rooftop bleachers and then they could see only part of the infield, none of the outfield.

At the Philadelphia writers' dinner Mack said the only position that needed strengthening besides the pitching was behind the plate, and Foxx was the way to do it. "Foxx will be a great catcher. I used to say that Dykes was the greatest all-around player in baseball. Now it's Foxx. And I must say," Mack joked, "he'd be just as good [pitching] as much of the Athletics pitchers I've had of late."

Expecting Foxx to catch most every day, Mack had released Charlie Berry in January. He had second thoughts about that move and resigned Berry a few weeks later.

The Athletics' ten-year contract with the Fort Myers folks had expired. They returned on a year-to-year basis. On the first day of spring training, Mack made a point of letting everybody know that the title of captain he had given to Foxx carried some authority. Unlike last spring, Foxx was working hard. Mack liked what he saw with Fawksie behind the plate, throwing knee-high line drives to second. Sammy Dell Foxx was at spring training. He pitched one inning with his brother behind the plate.

Frank Hayes was sent down to Albany to gain much-needed experience.

Before his trip to Japan, Mack had been busy in the Texas League flesh mart. He paid Tulsa $7,000 for Alex Hooks (a .340 hitter, to play first base) and shortstop Lamar "Skeeter" Newsome. He bought the MVP second baseman Charlie English, infielder Buck Fausett, and outfielder Wally Moses, all conditionally, from Galveston. He shipped Fausett and English back and kept Moses, who cost him $8,200.

Moses was a bargain. His brush with John McGraw and the Giants sounds like one of those tall tales that ripen with repetition, but Moses always insisted it was true. In the fall of 1935, the Georgia native told a young aspiring baseball writer from Atlanta named W. E. "Ernie" Harwell, "I was with Augusta in the Palmetto League in 1931. This scout for the Giants came up to me and said John McGraw was looking for a Jewish player and he thought that I might make the grade. I told him my name gave him the wrong idea. I was not Jewish, but Scotch-Irish. My grandfathers came from Massachusetts and fought in the Confederate army."

The scout kept looking. Moses stuck to the story in an interview fifty years later.

Moses had a reputation as a straightaway hitter and a fleet-footed outfielder who did not consider fences an obstacle in going after fly balls. In spring training Mack cautioned him, "In Texas they have fences. Up here the walls are concrete. No matter how tough you are, you are bound to come out second best when you collide with them."

In August he went after a double in Comiskey Park, hit the wall, and broke his left arm. He was out for the rest of the year.

Moses was the fastest in the American League from home to first and an ideal leadoff man. He could have led the league in stolen bases, but Connie Mack reined him in. "Wally," Mack said, "I don't want you to run. You've got Cramer, Foxx, and Johnson batting behind you. They might hit one and you can walk around the bases."

It was the style of the times.

Bob Johnson reported overweight and nursing a sore wrist from a fall on his winter job in Hollywood. Connie Mack had become an ardent Bob Johnson booster, praising his team spirit and leadership as well as his ability. Johnson was a practical joker. It was the custom for outfielders to drop their gloves on the field in foul territory when they came in after the third out. Umpire Bill Summers recalled, "Johnson once hid a bird under the glove of his brother Roy, Red Sox left fielder. When Roy picked up the glove and the bird flew out, he ran to his position faster than Enos Slaughter."

(Ballplayers had more fun in those days than they do today. At the start of the eighth inning of a 15–4 New York win over the A's on September 29, 1937, at Yankee Stadium, Tony Lazzeri went to the mound and handed pitcher Kemp Wicker a soft, beat-up batting practice ball and slipped the game ball into his back pocket. Bob Johnson was the batter. The pitch came in; Johnson took a mighty cut and the ball "plunked" foul behind him.

"What was that I hit?" Johnson asked. The umps examined the ball, and somebody in the A's dugout hollered and pointed to Lazzeri, who was known as a quiet prankster. First base umpire Bill Summers went out to second base and found the game ball in Lazzeri's back pocket.)

Johnson in turn appreciated Mack's managing style and personality. But there was a problem: Johnson drank. It hadn't affected his performance, and he hadn't committed the unpardonable sin of taking younger players with him. But it was enough of a concern for Connie Mack to put this incentive in his $6,000 contract: "If in the opinion of the club the player shall have abstained from intoxicating liquors throughout the season, he shall receive additional sum of $1,500 at the close of the 1935 season."

There is no record of whether Johnson earned the sobriety bonus. The same clause was in his 1936 contract but not after that.

Eddie Rommel had departed to pitch and manage at Richmond. Lena Blackburne became the third base coach.

Somebody had the bright idea of putting Connie Jr. in the first base coaching box. Built like his father but three inches taller at 6-foot-5½, he had no place to hide from the raucous riders in the stands behind him.

A first base coach has little to do. The highlight of Connie Jr.'s brief coaching career came the day he picked up a Washington catcher's sign for a curve and alerted the batters. Otherwise he hated it.

"I had a very miserable year. The fans rode me incessantly: They called me 'Junior' when they got on me. It became a horrible word to me. Because I had married a senator's daughter, they considered that as high society. 'How's your bridge game? . . . What time is tea?' But the worst was when they mixed religion with it, stuff like 'Where's your rosaries? . . . Go get your beads.' I asked dad what to do about it. He said, 'Why don't you go after them?'

"I did, a few times. Chased into the stands after an abuser. Once I got the wrong fellow."

(When Earle was in the coach's box, opposing players rode him fiercely too. Ethan Allen of the Browns recalled, "We got on Earle and he burned between the ears. I later told Connie and he replied, 'He's been around long enough to take it.'")

Connie Jr. became the assistant treasurer and began to learn the concessions operation.

Connie Mack's brother Michael was still taking tickets at the gate. The seventy-year-old former pitcher Al Maul was still on the payroll, patrolling the grandstand entrances as he had for thirty years and would for another ten.

When Connie Mack promised somebody a job for life, he meant it.

None of the experts knew what to make of Mack's young team. All the regulars were under thirty, but they had some experience. The Athletics' powerful lineup lured three of the preseason guessers into picking them to win the pennant. The rest had them anywhere from second to last, the pitching being the big unknown.

An Australian sheepdog named Skipper was a regular at Terry Park. The players adopted him as a mascot, paid his owner twenty-five dollars, and took him north with them. They named him Rags; he slept in the berth with

Dib Williams. Rags developed an ear infection. Dib held him while Doc Ebling treated it. The lotion burned; the dog bit Williams. The bite became infected; Williams missed the first several games of the season. Rags was left with a vet in Atlanta.

The sidelining of Williams gave Rabbit Warstler a chance to play, and he made the most of it. He played in 138 games and put some pepper in the otherwise quiet infield with a voice that could be heard in New Jersey. Warstler and McNair were the top double play keystone duo in the league. Warstler started the year with a hot bat before tailing off. Near the end of the season Mack called him into his tower office. "Rabbit, you played great ball and hustled all the time. Take the rest of the year off." There were contradictory stories about whether Mack gave him a $1,000 bonus.

It just wasn't the same when the Yankees came to town for the first time in sixteen years without Babe Ruth, who had been released by the Yankees and signed with the Boston Braves. Some A's fans requested that a place be set aside on the scoreboard to post home runs hit by Ruth in that foreign land known as the National League. To the press, Ruth had become an old, tired story. A guy named Hitler, running around peddling phony peace pacts all over the place, was now making more headlines than the Bambino. Still, when word came over the tickers that Ruth had hit a home run against Carl Hubbell in the Braves' opener, more than one veteran writer was suspected of silently cheering in the press box.

Frank Navin's caution against expecting a sudden change in people's Sunday habits continued to be in evidence. On the first Sunday of the season it was so cold that only fourteen thousand showed up. At the end of May a Saturday doubleheader against Cleveland drew more than the next day's single game against Jimmie Dykes's White Sox.

Based on their late-September showing the previous year, Connie Mack was confident that his pitchers would keep them in the pennant race. It didn't take long for that thin zephyr of hope to die.

From the start the A's were never above .500. Although they were in almost every game to the last out, they started the year 2-11. Mike Higgins had sprained an ankle in the city series. Mack moved McNair to third and put the rookie Skeeter Newsome at short. But Newsome was jittery.

After they lost 5 in a row, Mack had had enough. "It is impossible to sit back and twiddle our thumbs," he said. "So something radical was imperative."

Mack moved Foxx to third and McNair back to short. First base was a problem. Hooks wasn't ready for the big league pace. Mack optioned him to

Atlanta and never brought him back. Lou Finney replaced him at first base. Mack tried and failed to buy Yankee farmhand George McQuinn, who was at Newark. He also tried to sign a big first baseman from Washington & Jefferson College named Al Helfer. Mack invited Helfer to a game at Shibe Park in which Jimmy Foxx played first and hit 2 home runs. After the game Mack said, "Well, Mr. Helfer, do you want to go to my office and sign a contract?"

"No," said Helfer.

"Why not?"

"I watched your first baseman hit two line drive homers. Besides, there's this radio thing I want to try."

Helfer began a forty-year sports broadcasting career; at one time he had broadcast more World Series and Rose Bowl games than anyone else in the business.

When Higgins returned, Foxx went back to first base; the catching experiment was over. Mack bought a weak-hitting second-string catcher, Paul Richards, from the Giants on May 25. Richards and Berry did most of the catching; four other catchers came and went.

For some reason Shibe Park fans had never taken to Dib Williams. They began riding him in his rookie year. The razzing got worse when he assumed the role of super utility infielder with the departure of Jimmie Dykes. Connie Mack decided that Williams would benefit from a change of scenery. At Bing Miller's urging, Eddie Collins asked for him. Mack sold him to Boston for $15,000 on May 1.

Ed Coleman was another target of the boo birds and couldn't buy a base hit. He had promised to reform his nocturnal habits but didn't.

Mack was shocked by his pitchers' turnaround. They looked nothing like they had last September. "You wouldn't think they were the same fellows," he told John Kieran. "Never again will I take any stock in what pitchers look like in the fall. We have a fine team. That's what makes the season so disappointing to me. I feel sorry for our players, too. It's discouraging to go out there and do your best and knock in a lot of runs, and then see a game absolutely given away by terrible pitching."

By the middle of May Sugar Cain was 0-5. Mack was puzzled; Cain had all the physical ability he needed to be a winner.

The team was in the west in early May when Mack learned that Cain was telling other players that other teams wanted him and Mack wouldn't trade him. That was news to Mack. Nobody had approached him about a deal for Cain.

When they returned home, Mack called Cain into his office. As he later told the story, "I tried to explain to Sugar how the rules prevented clubs from [publicly] expressing interest in other teams' players and no other club had approached me about him. He didn't seem to get it. So I said, 'You're going to sit right on that chair until you understand it, if it takes all day.' He sat there a long while, and finally he said, 'If you're going to trade me, go ahead and trade me.'"

Mack was stunned. "Dern it, I never had a thought of trading him."

The Browns had a veteran pitcher, George Blaeholder, whom Mack had been trying to pry from them for five years with no luck. So when the Browns came to town a few days later and manager Rogers Hornsby let Mack know that Blaeholder was available for Coleman and Cain, the deal was made.

Mack said that later that season Cain explained to him the real reason he had wanted out of Philadelphia: "Mrs. Cain was keeping the books for another player and his wife who were living with us, and there had been an argument about the bookkeeping. I didn't like that."

"Well, Sugar," said Mack, "I don't blame you. I can understand how that would kind of get under your skin."

Connie Mack's patience wasn't limitless. On May 29 in Boston Bill Dietrich had a 6–1 lead, but he had been erratic. Mack told Joe Cascarella to warm up and be ready to go against the second hitter if necessary. The Red Sox made 4 hits in a hurry before Earle said Cascarella was ready. The bases were loaded. Cascarella threw two quick strikes, then walked the batter. He walked the next one too, forcing in a second run. Mack yanked him. As Cascarella headed for the dugout, Mack said, "Joe, you can go right in and take off that uniform. You'll never pitch another ball for this club."

Mack optioned the dapper tenor to Syracuse. The Red Sox paid $5,000 for the option. Cascarella never won a game for them and not much for anyone else.

The departure of Cascarella left the A's with only seven pitchers.

Al Benton started 9 times without a win, averaging 2 base runners per inning. Mack believed he could be a successful pitcher but sent him to Williamsport without strings. Some of Benton's teammates were not sorry to see him go. Isaminger described him as an irrepressible practical joker. Nicknamed "Gink" by Flit Cramer, Benton's favorite pastime in the dugout was rolling up a thin scorecard and sticking the pointy end in the ear of whoever was sitting beside him. Benton eventually wound up in Detroit, where he had a few good years, his best for the 1945 pennant winners.

Bill Dietrich's erratic work as a starter and reliever was another puzzle for Mack. The local boy had been married for two years and had a baby. When Mack had a talk with him, Dietrich said, "Mr. Mack, I'll tell you what's the matter with me. I've got a wife and I've got a baby and I'm worried about my job."

"Well," said Mack, "if that's all that's worrying you, you can rest easy, for your job is safe for the next three years if I am here."

A few weeks later in Washington, Dietrich was battered for 5 runs in the first inning and 5 more in the second, though 3 errors behind him didn't help. As Mack told the story in a 1936 *Saturday Evening Post* article, a fan in a box seat next to the dugout started riding the pitcher something fierce. "The things he said to him would have curled your hair. . . . At the beginning of the third, I walked over to the place where the dugout met the tier of boxes, and I said, 'Young man, I'm going to keep Bill Dietrich in there until Washington gets twenty-one runs off of him.' His eyes bulged out and he collapsed like a balloon."

Dietrich gave up just one more run in the 11–2 loss.

Connie Mack was there for the next three years, but Bill Dietrich wasn't. The following July Mack put him up on waivers; Washington claimed him, and Mack let him go. A month later the Senators did the same, and the White Sox claimed him. Dietrich pitched for Chicago for ten years before Mack brought him back in 1947.

Vernon Wilshere started out 6-1 but finished 9-9. John Marcum became a one-man pitching staff. From the textile mills in the south to the oil fields of Oklahoma, Ira Thomas kept sending up semipro pitchers named Fink and Ferrazzi and Doyle and Turbeville and Lieber and Martini and Veach and Upchurch and Eaves—and Earl Huckleberry, who started and won his only big league appearance, 19–7, in which Charlie Berry caught and Fred "Firpo" Marberry was the umpire behind the plate. Their numbers in the record books were small in baseball terms but big in the lives of those who tasted those cups of coffee. Only Herman Fink left more than a toeprint in the diamond sand.

But it wasn't all the pitchers' fault. Sure, they averaged almost 5 walks a game and had an ERA of 5.12. Poor base running and too many infield errors added to their woes.

Mack now considered the pennant race to be a five-team chase. "There's such a thing in baseball as a team's year. Last season it seemed to me it was Detroit's year. I sort of sensed that. This season I think it's Cleveland's. Maybe I'm wrong. You can never count Mickey Cochrane out."

With it all, the A's were a semi-respectable 50-60 by August. They had the best outfield the veteran writers had seen in years—best in the league, said some of them. With Cramer's mentoring, the rookie Wally Moses was learning fast. They were all ball hawks; Moses was the fastest; Cramer had a rifle arm. There were no more clowns running into each other or letting balls drop between them. As of mid-July Bob Johnson was leading the league at .351; Cramer, who had a 6 for 6 day on July 13 (his second), was right behind him at .338. Moses was the best leadoff man in the league.

The A's then went 8-31 and fell into the basement when they lost 4 in a row to the equally pathetic Browns at home. Johnson hit only .242 in the second half, but Foxx and Cramer and Higgins kept hitting. Somehow a lineup headed by Moses, Cramer, Johnson, Foxx, and Higgins that led the league in home runs and was fourth in slugging average produced the fewest runs. Higgins hit his career power peak with 23; 3 of them came in a game on June 27 against Boston. He went down overswinging in an effort to hit a fourth.

Mack trotted out the semipros and minor leaguers to finish the season. Up until then attendance had been pretty good, but sieges of rain wiped out some potential big gates. Turned off by watching even the stars going through the motions, the fans stayed home in large numbers.

Connie Mack enjoyed going up against his former boys, swapping jibes and playing tricks. When they played the White Sox, Mack would sometimes use his old signs, faking out Jimmie Dykes playing third base, while somebody else on the bench was giving the real ones.

"When [Jimmie] went to the White Sox he sometimes caught my signs and foiled me," Mack said in a 1938 *Saturday Evening Post* article. "'Better change your signs,' he would say. So one day I told my team to ignore my signs. I would do a lot of exercise but mean nothing. A rookie at the other end was giving the real signs. Just to win Dykes's confidence I gave the same signals as the rookie early in the game. But in the sixth we had runners on second and first with none out. Herman Fink, the pitcher, was at bat. A bunt situation. I flashed the bunt sign, but the rookie signaled hit. Dykes came charging in to field the bunt and try for two. The ball whistled by Dykes's head into left field. Dykes was standing in the spot where the ball had passed him, hands on hips, feet wide apart. I had to laugh. 'Why don't you play the game right?' he called to me and laughed himself."

On July 27 Lefty Grove started for Boston at Shibe Park. In the second inning the Red Sox had men on second and third. Mack ordered Babe Dahlgren walked to pitch to Grove. Mose then hit a grand slam. Coming around third base, Lefty waved his finger at Mack and said, "Mr. Mack, you shouldn't have done that."

The thirty-five-year-old Grove proved his arm was sound as ever that day, working 15 innings, facing 69 batters, for a 7–6 win. Nobody counted pitches.

Deep in the second division by July 4 and just as deep in debt, Connie Mack decided it was time to do something about repairing his finances. (The Athletics were not alone in the red ink sea. Of the more than ten thousand amusement businesses in the country, only 40 percent showed any net income on their 1935 tax returns, and most of those were in the movie industry.)

The Red Sox were struggling to stay around .500. Mack conferred with Eddie Collins, who made no secret of his wish to buy Foxx.

"You can have more than Foxx," Mack said, "if I can get enough out of it to get out of debt." He jotted down a lineup that included several of his players. "That lineup will win for you," Mack said.

There were no pitchers on the list. Collins suggested adding Marcum, the A's only dependable starter. Mack was reluctant. They left it at that. By the end of the season only Jimmy Foxx had been told by Mack that he wouldn't be back. Foxx didn't know where he was headed.

Isaminger reported that Collins, Yawkey, and Mack met in New York on October 20, and Yawkey was willing to buy or trade for just about everybody Mack might part with. Mack asked for more time to consult with his partners, but that was a stall. The Yankees had expressed interest in Cramer and maybe Higgins. Mack wanted to see what Jake Ruppert would offer. Or so the story went.

Mack stayed home and listened to the Tigers-Cubs World Series on the radio, so there was no opportunity for the press to hound him at that time. But there was plenty of speculation as the December 10 league meetings approached. Chicago papers declared Foxx sold to the White Sox. Everybody wanted to be first with a scoop.

Philadelphia papers kept a headline in hot type: "MACK DENIES TRADE RUMORS."

Joe McCarthy dropped by Shibe Park and told reporters he had offered

$50,000 for Higgins a year ago, but Mack wanted $100,000. At that time Red Rolfe had just finished his rookie year as the Yankees' third baseman and had yet to prove he was major league caliber. His major fault was not getting enough on the ball when he threw to first because he didn't get set before throwing. By the end of the season that fault had been corrected. McCarthy was no longer interested in Higgins. (During the Yankees' powerful 1936–1939 era Connie Mack would say that Red Rolfe was the man who always seemed to make the key hit or defensive play that would beat the A's.)

McCarthy was told that Flit Cramer still belonged to the A's, a statement that was true but misleading; he was already promised to Boston.

When Connie Mack arrived at the Palmer House in Chicago on December 9, he was immediately surrounded by reporters. As always he played his cards not just close to his buttoned-up vest but inside it. He would deny what everybody knew until he chose the time to announce it. And when the time came, it was as undramatic as ordering dinner. That evening Mack sat in his suite and simply said, "Well, boys. Jimmy's gone."

As announced, it was Foxx and Marcum to the Red Sox for pitcher Gordon Rhodes, catcher George Savino, and a bundle of cash.

James Isaminger reported that as he and Tom Shibe walked together toward the elevators, they met Jake Ruppert. Even in those days the Yankees could afford to buy anybody and everybody they wanted. "Say, Mr. Shibe," said Ruppert, "when you have stars for sale why don't you give me a chance to bid for them? You have sold Simmons, Cochrane, Grove, and now some more players to other clubs, but forget completely that I am also in the market."

That wasn't likely to change. Connie Mack had made it clear many times that he would not sell stars to the top teams. Chicago, Detroit, and Boston had all been second division clubs when Mack sold to them. Boston had barely finished fourth in '35.

Although Jimmy Foxx had a radio program and a new house in Philadelphia, he was delighted at the prospect of a big raise, despite two years remaining on his contract. He said he had "reluctantly signed" and Connie Mack was "the only man in baseball" he would play for at the amount he had signed for. "I signed to help the A's out of financial trouble and never figured I was getting the dough to which I was entitled. I thought I owed Connie Mack something for bringing me up and giving me a chance in the American League."

Jimmy got his raise—to $25,000. He was now earning more than his former manager.

The rest of the deal—Eric McNair and Roger Cramer for right-hander Henry Johnson (an old nemesis while with the Yankees) and outfielder Al Niemic and more cash—was left unannounced until January, possibly to split the deals between two years for tax reasons. On Saturday, January 4, Eddie Collins learned that the *Inquirer* reported the deal would be announced the following Wednesday. On Saturday afternoon he called Mack and said, "Let's release the story tonight." They agreed on a 7 p.m. simultaneous release.

Tom Yawkey later said he had spent $350,000 for the four players. The A's books show $175,000 for Foxx and Marcum, and another $175,000 for Cramer and McNair on January 10. It was enough for the Athletics to pay off their debts with something left over.

His sale to Boston came as no surprise to Cramer: "At the start of the season Mack and I had squabbled about salary. [Cramer signed for $7,500.] He said to me, 'You sign this year and next year I'll trade you.'

"'You wouldn't trade me to St. Louis, would you?' I asked him.

"'No,' he said, 'I'll trade you to a good ball club.'

"You could depend on him doing anything he said he would."

(Cramer and McNair were happy they were still teammates. They had been roommates with the A's and were both avid hunters. Cramer boasted about how good a shot he was. One winter McNair invited him to go hunting in Mississippi. McNair bought a live turkey and took it out to the woods and tied it by a leg to a tree. Then he led Cramer to that spot. Cramer saw the bird and quickly aimed and fired. When he went to get his prize, he found a tag tied to it: "Nice shot Doc.")

Cramer's salary jumped from $7,500 to $12,500 at Boston. That put him near the top of the payroll; irs records showed general manager Eddie Collins, at $24,000, was the only person on the Boston payroll who had earned over $15,000 in 1934. McNair received a $500 raise to $8,000.

With these purchases ap estimated that Tom Yawkey had spent a total of $3.5 million for players since 1932.

In just a few years American League moguls had gone from welcoming Tom Yawkey's open bankroll to complaining that his big payouts were skewing the market and guaranteeing the 1936 pennant to Boston.

"If they can't win with that lineup," wrote Isaminger, "they ought to give up." The Red Sox would finish sixth. (Yawkey was still a long way from buying a pennant; he never did. When he finally won in 1946, it would be the Red Sox farm system that produced the talent.)

Detroit had to shell out $75,000 to the White Sox for Al Simmons, who had slid to a desultory .267 last year, to try to keep up. Jake Ruppert moaned that he had never had a chance to bid on any of the A's stars. But the Yankees probably wouldn't have matched Yawkey; Clark Griffith said they were so tough to deal with that "they always demanded your greatest stars for three aspirin tablets and four tickets to their opening game."

Connie Mack's perennial optimism had succumbed to reality. Just before celebrating his seventy-third birthday at home with his family, he said, "I feel good. I just go ahead and try not to worry, although sometimes the stimulus has been strong. I have had birthdays where the future was brighter . . . but perhaps next season won't be as bad as pictured."

The sale of the guts of his team was a source of great sadness in Connie Mack. Selling off players was not the reason he had devoted his life to baseball. He was at heart a builder, not a wrecker. All of these boys had started their big league careers with him, and he knew they had many more productive years ahead of them.

In a birthday interview a year later, he was still sick at heart over it. He told the AP man in Philadelphia, "If I could have but one wish, it would be a wish that never again would I have to sell another ball player. And, maybe, I'll get my wish. If I can help it, I'll never sell another first-class player to another club."

After dismissing any thoughts of retiring—"Dern it, I think I've got some of my best years left"—he returned to the effects of the criticism he had taken over the sales:

> You know, it hurt me more than anything else to have people think that I was something like a robber in selling players for big sums. . . . But it was a business deal. I didn't want to sell them—never wanted to sell any player—but I have to have money to go on with the game I've spent all these years with. It hurt me as much as it hurt Yawkey when the players I sold him failed to win the pennant. Most of all Marcum. I thought he'd win 20, 25 games for Tom and I was bitterly disappointed in him. [Marcum was 8-13.] But I'll tell you one thing. No one can buy those players from Tom today. I wish I had the money so I could buy all of them and release them.

Mack's patience with the press had worn thin, especially with writers' guessing games over player moves, trying to analyze Mack's motives, conflicts with players, anything that might be left unsaid when player trades were announced. But he managed a chuckle over rumors of a Philadelphia group making a bid for the entire club.

"So they're selling me out all the way now, are they? That's pretty good."

More than once he had told writers, "If you think you have a story, don't ask me about it first because I'll deny it and then you'll have nothing. Go ahead and write it, then if I deny it, you'll have a second story."

Just before the 1935 season ended, Cy Peterman of the *Inquirer*, not one of Mack's favorite writers, had shown him a story he had written for the next day's paper. In it he said, "If Connie Mack sells his star members of the 1935 team, he ought to get out of baseball."

Peterman asked if Mack had any comment.

"I've never told a sportswriter how to write his story yet and I'm not going to start now," Mack said.

(Peterman once savaged Mack for selling players, saying the manager might even sell his prized Bok Award, which he had been given in 1930. When Mack happened to meet Peterman on the street soon afterward, instead of cutting him short, he greeted the writer with great felicity. Asked by his companion why he did so, Mack said, "I got him guessing. Maybe he thinks I don't even read what he writes.")

When the January part of the deal was announced, Mack told a press conference, "As to why I made these deals, you can draw your own conclusions."

Well, that wasn't difficult. Mack later admitted he knew that if he hadn't sold the players, he would have had to get out of baseball. It was as simple as that. There were 233,173 reasons—the lowest number of people in fifteen years who had paid for the pleasure of watching the A's lose 42 games at home. (Only figures for the Browns, whose attendance total of 80,922 averaged fewer than fifteen hundred per date, were poorer. When the Athletics received a check for about $250 [based on twenty cents a head] after one series in St. Louis, Mack opined that the Browns would have to be moved, but he didn't know where.) The Athletics had finished last with Foxx et al.; they could do just as well without them.

Addressing a Penn Athletic Club dinner the following April, Mack said,

Owners of the Athletics, the Shibe and Mack families, never received a cent of the fortune paid by other clubs since 1932 for stars from the A's.

Every dollar received from sales was used to pay accumulated debts of the club. The club had no surplus in the banks. Our operating expenses are heavy. It was absolutely imperative that we sell our star performers, our only saleable assets. After the first sale to Chicago, we thought our club was out of the red. We stated then no more players would be sold. Conditions, however, forced the sale of the remaining players and it took a lot of money to clear our debts.

Connie Mack never laid the onus for his financial problems on the fans' lack of support: "We made a survey of conditions to find out why the fans were not coming out. Some did not have the money. The others had to attend to business every day in the week. They had no spare time. Our club had to act in accordance with the facts."

The Sporting News called it "tragic" to see Connie Mack deplete his team to an "unhealthy condition" and doubted that Mack could ever last long enough to make a comeback: "Assuming that Mack foresees his own retirement in the not distant future, who is available to take up the stupendous burden of rebuilding the Athletics? It is not likely that another Yawkey can be found who would be able or willing to pour millions into the reconstruction of the team. The gravity of the situation is easy to recognize. . . . It is easy to conceive that the already-dwindling following of the Athletics might be diminished to a point where the club would become a genuine White Elephant upon the hands of the league."

Damon Runyon didn't so deplore. He understood Mack's actions:

Baseball is a sport and it is a great sport, but it is also a business. It is a business of a most unusual nature. It has the element of gamble in it more than any other business of similar proportions in the world. . . .

Of all the men in baseball, I think that old Mr. Cornelius McGillicuddy of Philadelphia has the keenest understanding of the game both as a business and as a sport. If he didn't understand it as a business, old Mr. McGillicuddy would long ago have been sent to the cleaners financially. If he didn't understand it as a sport he would not have had the courage to make the business moves he has [made]. . . .

Mr. McGillicuddy could have taken the Philadelphia fans into his confidence and said, "These players I am selling haven't many years of service left in them. They may be good players this year but another year will make a difference in the price that I can get for them now. The time to sell a pig is when the pig is fat. . . ."

But not everyone recognizes Mr. McGillicuddy for the businessman he is, and while we are willing to mingle our tears with those of the bereaved Philadelphia baseball fan over the loss of their vaunted players, we must at the same time give a few oohs and aahs for Mr. McGillicuddy's financial genius.

Fifty years ago Connie Mack had learned that wisdom and genius didn't count for much with fans when it came to the sale of their favorite players. Hartford fans had complained when Mack had been one of the players sold to Washington by the Hartford club's manager to pay off the club's debts and keep the team alive.

At a time when club owners had respect for each other, Connie Mack was the most respected of all. He usually did more listening than talking in league meetings, but when he had a firm position—and sometimes when he didn't—he would enjoy a lengthy discussion. One phenomenon of baseball in the mid-1930s that would never be seen again was the presence of four former players who were also past or present managers representing their clubs at American League meetings: Mickey Cochrane, Eddie Collins, Clark Griffith, and Connie Mack. Two of the four had played for Mack. It sometimes brought a unique perspective to the business at hand, as, for example, a December 10, 1935, discussion of games in which managers and players had stalled when the clouds were black and it was about to rain. Trailing teams did it to prevent a legal game going into the books, leading teams to prevent the other team from catching up after five innings. Or a team in the lead might try to go out as quickly as possible to get a legal game in before the cloudburst. The subject at hand was how to stop these practices.

Here's the way it went:

TOM YAWKEY: Have the games suspended and continued the next day.
ALVA BRADLEY [PRESIDENT OF THE INDIANS]: Hold the managers responsible.
COCHRANE: Forfeit the game if it happens; that will stop it.
GRIFFITH: Suspend the manager thirty days if he allows stalling.
HARRIDGE: It's up to owners to control their managers.

MACK: We have to admit the manager doesn't like to lose that ball game and if he thinks the clouds are pretty heavy there, why naturally he's going to say, well, now, don't be in a hurry, just take your time going up there and you know you might accidentally unlace a shoe and tie it up. Naturally there is that in our game.

HARRIDGE: That isn't so bad. In this case the players refuse to run the bases and be tagged out and throw the ball to the wrong spot.

MACK: I have seen men deliberately strike out and also attempt to steal a base and not run very hard either to be thrown out. And you look through all of these things, no doubt, and it is hard on the club that is in the lead, but it is all right for the club that is behind."

COLLINS: I have no suggestions for correcting it. The only thing I can see is the players know the game would be completed at some future date.

MACK: In other words, Eddie, you feel if there was what appeared like stalling in the game, the umpire could use his judgment and say, well now, I will call this game and we will play this game off tomorrow at two o'clock.

COLLINS: I don't think there would be anything to encourage players not to play their best if they knew it would be completed eventually.

COCHRANE: Why not give the ump the power to remove the first player that stalls and fine him?

COLLINS: You are defrauding your public whenever you are not playing baseball to the best of your ability. I think there will be odd instances where your manager won't be to blame. I've heard it mentioned any number of times where somebody, maybe an individual on the coaching lines, where it will not be the manager, say go on down and get out in a hurry and hurry this thing up. The first thing you know this man goes down and it probably wouldn't meet with the approval of the manager. I know it didn't in this particular case, and Connie didn't know anything about it. The players have been known to do that. In instances like that it is an injustice to have the manager blamed, because he wouldn't be responsible at all.

[Collins then changed the subject, stating his belief that visiting clubs should have some say in deciding whether to postpone a game before it started. Connie Mack agreed.]

MACK: Of course I will admit frankly that last year our club probably called off a number of games that we probably could have played.

But as a rule we called up the visiting manager. We may not have always done so. There might have been occasions when we didn't even do that. But on the whole I think as a rule we did tell them what we wanted to do. We didn't think we would have anyone where it was a bad day and looked like rain, and yet I will admit that the sun did come out and we probably could have played two or three games we didn't play. I suggest we set a time, say around ten o'clock to call the visiting manager or business manager and say, we would like to call the game off today. How do you feel about it? If they feel the same as we do, all right. If they don't why then we would have to go on with the game. We ought to set something like a time to call the game off. A lot of people come in probably from a hundred miles to see a ball game. A good many didn't come this year in Philadelphia, but they might come. If we could call that off at ten-thirty because it was going to be a bad day, we would like to call that game off. If we got in touch with the visiting manager and he was willing to have the game called off, it is off, and those people who are coming one hundred miles, why they wouldn't have to come because they would be notified of it.

ALVA BRADLEY: Of course, Mr. Mack, isn't there another side to that question? Sometimes if your ball club is up and your grounds are wet, you want to play it.

MACK: Of course, if you are the home club in that case you would play it. If you were the visiting club you wouldn't. That's why I say we ought to give the visiting club an opportunity to say whether they would play or not. Or if you felt you wanted the club to play, instead of calling it off at ten we would wait and let the umpires decide in the afternoon. I know if any visiting club wanted our club to play that ball game, we would play it. But I have, as I said before, called off a game without even asking the visiting club about it. I think something should be done in regard to it.

By the end of the meeting, Mack concluded that if the two clubs couldn't agree on postponing a game, the umpires should decide. They came to no conclusion on the stalling issue.

6 | WAIT 'TIL NEXT YEAR

On October 1, 1935, Connie Mack wrote to Sr. Florence: "Our season closed yesterday. Am not at all sorry for the reason that our club has had a very bad year not only from a playing standpoint but from a financial standpoint as well, but there is another year coming and we hope to do much better."

He would be repeating similar sentiments every year for the next ten years, bumping along in seventh or eighth place, except for one wartime rise to a tie for fifth—while the Tigers and Yankees were winning every pennant but one—while undergoing the severest long-running siege of criticism of his life, especially from one Philadelphia columnist.

Connie Mack was clearly peeved at all the digging for details and motives surrounding the unloading of his stars in December and January. Near the conclusion of his January 7, 1936, press conference concerning the blockbuster deals, he was asked if he intended to sell or trade Mike Higgins or Bob Johnson.

Tapping his fingers on his desktop, he paused, then said, "I won't answer that, but I could if I cared to. I might sell or trade anybody I have for that matter."

"Then you won't say anything about the kind of team you will have at Shibe Park next season?"

"Not a word," he said. "For the rest of the off-season I am not going to tell anybody what players I will have in action next season. The only way you will know about any of my prospective players is when you see them working out in uniform at the training camp next March. If we have any item of news about the club or any player change we will duly announce it to newspapers but we won't comment on it or issue any interviews about our prospects,"

Coming from the cooperative, public-relations-savvy Connie Mack, always ready to pose for a foolish photo or help a writer feed a hungry column, this was a startling statement. It was said without anger but firmly. What he meant was that he wouldn't seek any publicity unless he had something to announce. But that's not the way it was taken.

A disbelieving James Isaminger gave Mack a chance to clarify his remarks. "In other words, the Athletics club does not care to have any publicity?"

"No," said Mack without hesitation.

(A few months later Mack said he'd been misquoted; he was "referring to another matter at the time." According to Bob Paul, when Mack was asked why he didn't complain to the misquoting writer's boss, he replied, "I can stand to take that misstatement better than the reporter. If I complained to his publisher, he might lose his job. No one will fire me for that lie. Besides, I can take it and come back for more.")

Being the Grand Old Man of baseball did not immunize Connie Mack from criticism. He took the most withering barrage of fire since his arrival in Philadelphia thirty-five years ago. Stung by the threat of a two-month blackout of news from half the Philadelphia baseball beat, the press struck back. Calling it "a revolutionary attitude for a major league club to take regarding publicity," Isaminger wrote, "Mr. Mack, your judgment is to be questioned when you decide not to announce any of your plans for 1936. In giving the pffftt to the press you are also giving it to the fans and no city in the circuit is in greater need of baseball revival meetings than Philadelphia. We fear that the good Mr. Mack furnishes the spectacle of a man who kicked HIMSELF when he was down."

Perry Lewis in the *Inquirer* wrote, "It's probably true that Connie Mack needed the money but what he needs even more is some PR advice. It would seem to the Old Sport that a man who has spent his life in an amusement enterprise that depends upon public patronage for its existence would realize that when he talks to the press he is talking to the public. In any business, sports or otherwise, telling the buyer in effect to mind his own business is not wise."

When asked whether Mike Higgins would be back, Mack had said, "My partners and I have agreed we won't say a word on the kind of team we will have next season. We are going to keep you all guessing."

Connie Mack and his partners were guessing too. They had no way of knowing what kind of team they would have.

The writers were guessing the A's would have a lousy team. They turned out to be right. Mack had Higgins and Moses and Johnson and Hayes and one thirty-year-old career minor league pitcher, Harry Kelley, drafted from Atlanta.

Connie Mack had cut his own salary to $17,000, lower than that of several other managers and club executives. Mickey Cochrane became the highest-paid man in baseball at $45,000 after his two pennants. Lou Gehrig, at $31,000, was the highest paid player in the AL; in the NL it was Dizzy Dean, at just over $21,000. Jake Ruppert, disappointed that the Yankees had gone three years without winning a pennant, cut Joe McCarthy's salary by $7,500 to $27,500, and Ed Barrow's by $5,000 to $20,000.

Connie Mack and Tom Shibe headed to Mount Plymouth, Florida, in January for a month of golf. Ben Shibe's eldest son had been president of the A's since his father's death in 1922. For the past eight years Shibe, now seventy, had been slowed by thrombosis. Many of his duties in the business office had been shifted to John Shibe, while Tom devoted most of his time to the A. J. Reach Company, where he had invented much of the machinery used in manufacturing baseball equipment.

While in Florida, Tom caught a cold and on February 2 decided to return home. Two weeks later he was dead.

For Connie Mack it was like losing a brother. He and Tom had been frequent traveling companions to league meetings, on spring training scouting trips, and at many sporting events. Mack returned to Philadelphia for the private funeral.

Tom had been instrumental in the negotiation of the terms for the hiring of Judge Landis as the first commissioner and was a trusted adviser to league president Will Harridge, who postponed his trip south to attend the funeral. Landis was in Florida recovering from surgery.

Tom and his brother John were as avid rooters for their team as any fan. They would rather win before a hundred people than lose in front of a full house. Tom and his wife Ida sat behind the A's dugout while John watched every game pacing nervously on a catwalk between the seats and the tower office.

In the past five years Connie Mack had seen several of his contemporaries in the founding of the American League and the end of the war between the leagues pass from the scene: Charles Comiskey; Pirates owner Barney Dreyfuss; Frank Navin; Ban Johnson; August A. "Garry" Herrmann, Cincinnati Reds president and chairman of the National Commission (baseball's governing body, 1903–1920)—all of them at a younger age than his seventy-three.

Tom and Ida Shibe had no children. Tom's estate, valued at $325,552, included 141 shares of the Athletics, valued at $24,675, and a note for $96,000 due from the A's, an indication that he had probably loaned the club money to help pay the bills. All but $2,000 was left in trust for Ida. On Ida's death the trust was to be divided between their nephews, Franklin and Ben Macfarland. (Ida Shibe died on May 13, 1952.)

A week later the board of directors named Tom's brother John president. Roy Mack became vice-president. John would represent the club at a league meeting on July 6, but his health was already deteriorating. A few weeks after that meeting he was found unconscious in bed one morning. His doctors sent him to Beeches Sanitarium. He resigned as president of the A's but hoped to recover and return to work.

Six more Class D leagues were set to open the 1936 season, bringing the number of minor leagues to twenty-seven. But the extent of the Athletics' farm expansion was a working agreement with the Class A Williamsport club and a promise to provide some players for the Cleveland (MS) Bengals in the Cotton States League.

Spring training camps were flooded with hopeful unemployed young men who wanted a crack at professional baseball. They wore sneakers and street shoes; spiked shoes cost $16.50, an outlay that many of them couldn't afford. They carried more dime store gloves than seven dollar professional models. A very few came by train, a few more drove; most hitchhiked or rode the freight cars with the hope of catching on with some minor league club. Part of the lure was their love of baseball. Part of it was a chance to earn a hundred dollars a month for five months. Hordes of kids showed up who couldn't even make a Class D team. Managers gave them a quick morning tryout before scooting them off to other camps until they gave up and went home.

Of the forty-six players who reported to Connie Mack in Fort Myers on March 1, only six—Higgins, Finney, Berry, Johnson, Warstler, and Dietrich—had been with the A's for more than one full season. There were so many newcomers, Earle Mack had to clip the list from a local paper and carry it around to help him tell his dad who was who. Away from Terry Park, said Earle, "We spoke to every young fellow we saw because we didn't know for sure if he was one of our boys."

Frank Hayes had benefited from a year in the minors. For a change, Mack's pitchers wouldn't have to wonder what stranger might be doing the catching when they started; the twenty-one-year-old Hayes caught 143 games.

Wearing a gray three-piece suit and gray fedora, Connie Mack said, "I feel twenty years younger just to see those boys out there trying so hard on the first day. This is going to be a happy spring training period for me."

On March 10 Jimmy Foxx, Roger Cramer, and Eric McNair drove down from Sarasota to visit with Mack at Richards' Royal Palm drugstore. That may have been the happiest highlight of the spring for Mack, if the writers watching his boys summed up his prospects accurately.

The A's lost their first six spring games. They finally won one against the House of David before fewer than a hundred onlookers. After watching them lose 3 to the Reds, New York–based columnist Hugh Bradley wrote:

> They are the most tragic thing that has ever happened to baseball. Unless Judge Landis does something about it, Philadelphia, the third largest city in the nation and with more than three million potential fans within its metropolitan area, may be represented by an AL team that would be booted off any suburban sandlot. . . . The players seem wholly inadequate. Even if they tried, most of them could be arrested for attempting to pass themselves off in baseball company two or three classes too good for them. The painful truth is that even this early in the training season they gave little indication of trying. . . . Meanwhile those few A's who seem to want to do something never seem to have more than the faintest idea of what to do.

Bradley called Philadelphia "the Devil's Island of baseball."

When Bradley asserted that Connie Mack had made several millions of dollars out of baseball, Mack probably laughed and wished he could get his hands on it.

Syndicated columnist Harry Grayson spouted more nonsense: "One also hears that Moses and other young Apathetics of last spring and this were forced into signing contracts calling for no more than $2,000 for the season." (Moses's salary had been doubled to $5,500. Johnson made $6,000, Finney and Warstler $5,000, Dietrich $4,000, Newsome $3,500, and Hayes $2,500.)

Grayson suggested a sign for Shibe Park: "Abandon hope all ye who enter here.

Even syndicated columnist Henry McLemore, a staunch Connie Mack admirer, couldn't resist giving the A's the needle. His preseason predictions listed only seven teams in the American League. "The Athletics, according to my calculations, will withdraw from the American League late in April as a protest against president William Harridge's sale of the moving picture rights to Mack Sennett's Keystone Comedy Company, and replace Burlington in whatever league Burlington is in."

The A's were tagged "the Pagliacci-letics."

When Isaminger, watching the rookies work out, was asked whom he liked, he replied, "My wife."

Joe Williams of the *New York World-Telegram* joined the chorus. He likened a game at Sarasota between the A's and Red Sox to "the soda jerkers from the Five-and-Ten" versus "the board of directors of J. P. Morgan & Co." Unlike the eager bunches of youngsters Mack had brought up in the past, he wrote, this group "all move around as if they are on relief. I'm afraid the great Connie Mack has played his last heroic role in baseball, and nobody will know until he tells the story himself why he persisted in carrying on. You can't rewrite Shakespeare, and even Mack can't improve on himself."

Mack was undaunted but made no bones about the state of his team. Speaking before the Fort Myers Rotary Club on March 17, he said, "I'm trying to mold another winner. It's no fun to pilot a losing team and I'm old enough to want to enjoy my job. We have a young and hustling club. It can hit and with some experience some of the rookies will turn into winning pitchers. It can't be done in a year, but given a couple of years, any manager can build a winning club out of ambitious material."

Ninety percent of the experts picked the A's to finish last (70 percent picked Detroit to repeat).

Mack may have resented writers' comments that "[the A's] aren't in the league any longer," but according to Stuart Cameron of the *Record*, he seemed to confirm their opinions while watching batting practice before a game in Tampa: "I came down south with twenty-three pitchers. [One of them was Walter Johnson Jr. at Mack's invitation—"Unsolicited by me," said Walter Sr.] I let Blaeholder [on waivers to Cleveland] and Mahaffey [on waivers to St. Louis] go because they are veterans on the way out. But out of the rest I couldn't pick a starting four or even name anyone definitely due to stay with us. I expect to take an awful beating. None of the new pitchers has shown what we expected. We have had a lot of injuries. My goodness, I don't ever remember so many injuries."

Harry Kelley was likely to be the so-called ace, although not much was really expected of him. At least he knew his way around on the mound, having won 20 or more for the last three years at Atlanta. Kelley's hands were so strong he could loosen the cover on a ball, a treatment that took some of the rabbit out of it.

Quoted once on what he thought of his club, Mack sounded like Casey Stengel's tutor: "Well, we might not do bad if we had somebody there instead of the man who is there."

Confused, the reporter asked him whom he was talking about. Mack pointed to the man throwing batting practice.

What did he have against him?

"Oh, nothing at all. I don't even know his name. But what I mean, if I must diagram it, is that I shall have a few good pitchers instead of the ones I have got. Since you ask, I admit my infield is all right insofar as infielding is concerned, but they can't hit. The outfield is all right insofar as catching fly balls is concerned, but my goodness I'm afraid they can't hit. And when you have players who can't hit or with pitchers who aren't established, you are ready for a great deal of beating. And that is the story of my ball club. But," he added, "we shall be in there trying, at least. The 'Athaletics' will fool many of the wise boys who already have counted them out."

Mack was unduly harsh on his outfield. Moses and Johnson could hit. Wally Moses blossomed in a hitters' season, batting .345, and dispelled any fears that his bone-breaking encounters with outfield walls might make him "brakey" by turning in spectacular acrobatic catches. Johnson would drive in 121 runs. Lou Finney had his best year splitting time between first base and the outfield. The farmer from Buffalo, Alabama, an avid reader of Rudyard Kipling and Zane Grey, batted .302 and led the league with 653 at bats.

The unknown was George Puccinelli, drafted from Baltimore, where he had won the International League triple crown, batting .350 with 53 home runs and 173 RBIs. Puccinelli was twenty-eight. Called up from Class B Danville late in 1930 by the Cardinals, he had pinch-hit against Grove in the first game of the World Series. In two other shots in the big leagues he had shown some power—8 of his 45 hits were home runs—but he was sent back to the minors when he struggled at the start of each season.

Sensing a need for some confidence-building, Mack told Puccinelli—probably calling him "son" rather than tripping over his name—"You're my right fielder. Even if you don't hit for a month, you'll still be in there. You'll get every chance in the world."

Spring tryouts continued in the opener at Boston; Mack used sixteen players—including four pitchers and three pinch hitters—in the 9–4 loss.

Three days later they opened at home on an overcoat day before a cavern of empty seats. The band practically outnumbered the shivering faithful, estimated at about fifteen hundred. The flag on the center-field pole drooped at half staff for the late Tom Shibe. It could have been a symbol for the season. But for their first Sunday game of the year, more than ten thousand showed up to see them lose their fifth in a row. Mack had put Puccinelli in the cleanup spot behind Bob Johnson and kept him there while he went 1 for 17. Mack assured him, "Don't worry. The job is yours."

The next day the Yankees came to town, usually a big draw. Only a handful—about a thousand—turned out to see the home team win its first, 12–11. Puccinelli was 2 for 3, including a 2-run home run in a seventh inning rally that scored 4 runs and tied the game, 11–11. The A's won it in the ninth.

Will Harridge viewed with alarm the meager turnouts in St. Louis and Philadelphia "That can't continue indefinitely," he said. "But in the meantime we will have to await developments. Certainly there is no immediate action contemplated."

Translation: major league baseball will continue its tradition of deploring while doing nothing.

From then through May 8 the A's were 8-8. During that stretch Puccinelli hit .483 and had 9 RBIs. Eleven of his 28 hits were for extra bases. (Puccinelli tailed off to finish at .278 with 11 home runs. The next year he was back in Baltimore, unfairly perhaps, and never batted in the big leagues again.) The A's hustled and scrapped and endeared themselves to the fans who came to see them. When Mike Higgins was sidelined by an injury, Russ Peters filled in and quickly became such a favorite that Mack left him in even when Higgins was ready to return—until they lost 3 in a row.

Mack was so exuberant he told AP writer Paul Mickelson, "The fans . . . who once bombarded us and called us names for selling Foxx and the other fellas are for us. The crowds are better than they were when we were champions. People are writing in and encouraging us. I'm getting a thrill myself."

If he didn't have a fighting chance to finish first, Mack was content to experiment all year, no matter where the A's finished. And he did: he wound up using 39 players—19 of them pitchers—the most since 1919.

Fifteen years ago Connie Mack had failed to sign Ted Lyons because Lyons didn't want to join a last-place team. Alfred "Chubby" Dean (5-foot-11 and 180 pounds) saw things differently. Dean was one of the uncounted athletes whose education Mack financed at Duke with no obligation to ever sign with the Athletics. A sophomore left-handed pitcher for Jack Coombs, Dean figured that since the Athletics had sold all their stars, he had a better chance to make the team than if he signed with the Yankees, who were interested in him. He wrote to Mack and said he wanted to leave school and join the A's. Mack urged him to stay in school and graduate. But Dean couldn't wait. He left Duke in January to go to spring training. When the handsome, carefree nineteen-year-old arrived in Fort Myers, everybody took a liking to him. He informed Mack that he didn't want to be a pitcher; he wanted to be a first baseman. After Jim Oglesby lasted only three games at first, Mack brought in Lou Finney, but he preferred Finney in the outfield.

In the early going, Mack used the rookie to pinch-hit. Dean was loose as a goose. He felt no more pressure pinch-hitting with the bases loaded than he did taking his cuts in batting practice. He was hitting .400 in that role in June, including 2 pinch hits in the A's 8-run seventh inning in Chicago on June 21, so Mack gave him a chance at first base. He hit .287 for the year but had zero power and a lot to learn. It took him all year to figure out when to go after a ball hit to his right or leave it for the second baseman. But learn he did and improved enough to claim the job.

Some rough diamonds got away. A nineteen-year-old track and pitching star from Trenton High School was invited to a tryout at Shibe Park. Mack looked him over, decided the youngster was too fast and too good a hitter to be a pitcher, and advised George Case to become an outfielder. That was one position where the A's didn't need any help. Mack offered Case a chance to play in Texas. That didn't appeal to Case. Mack recommended him to Clark Griffith, who signed him. Case finished the season with his hometown Trenton Senators, leading to a long, productive career with Washington.

On a rainy May 18 in St. Louis, Mack was all smiles despite his team's seventh-place berth. He kidded the local writers and the lone Philadelphia writer on the trip, James Isaminger, about their calling his team "a bush league" ball club. "I'm enjoying myself this spring," he said. "The boys are giving me everything. With a few breaks in our favor, we'll be up in the first division. Eight of our seventeen defeats have been by one run. We should have beaten the Tigers in the four games we've played them this season. As it is we won only one."

Back home against the Yankees reality set in by scores of 12–6 and 15–1 in a Saturday doubleheader. In the eighth inning of the second game the crowd of twenty-eight thousand, biggest in two years, bombarded the home team dugout with cushions, pop bottles, and torn-up scorecards and newspapers. The next day, a Sunday gathering of eight thousand watched Tony Lazzeri hit 3 home runs—two of them grand slams—and drive in 11 in a 25–2 massacre. (Connie Mack missed the carnage. He was in Bridgeport attending a memorial service for an old friend, Mike Flanagan.)

But on most days the young A's were giving a good account of themselves, hustling more than at any time the previous year. Without Jimmy Foxx, they were practically powerless, falling to seventh in the league with 72 home runs (the Yankees led the league with 182). Skeeter Newsome couldn't hit a lick; he was helpless against a low curve or outside pitch. At .225 he would have the lowest batting average among regulars in the league. But he was doing the slickest shortstopping the scribes had seen in a long time. He was the holler guy of the infield.

Bill Dooly, who had thrown his share of barbs at the team all spring, now conceded that "a spirit of verve and hustle has pervaded the entire team. It is a more interesting tribe to watch than was the star-spangled but dead-ended team of 1935."

"We've got a hustling team that is anxious to get somewhere," Mack told Mike Devitt of the *Record*. He continued:

Fans realize this group isn't like last year's team that played indifferent ball and cared little whether they won or lost. The present team has something to aim for. It is coming up. The teams we've had the past couple of years were composed mostly of players who had been with us when we won the league pennants. They had reached their goal and did not have the incentive these youngsters have. Thus the fans got indifferent ball. Now that our club is showing plenty of fight and hustle the fans are talking. Get the fans talking and you will draw them into the park.

Mack admitted that he was sleeping better than he had at any time last year.

Weekday crowds were thin, but weekend and holiday doubleheaders drew bigger turnouts than they had seen for a few years. They were drawing better on the road too, where they picked up twenty cents a head. A crowd of fifty thousand for a Sunday doubleheader at Yankee Stadium would pay a few salaries for the year. Despite the Yankees' runaway in the AL pennant race, the A's home attendance wound up jumping by more than fifty thousand, but it was still far below break-even levels, and a loss of more than $50,000 went into the books.

Eager to see what his young infielders could do, Mack put Rabbit Warstler on waivers and sold him to the Boston Bees on July 6. He saw what they could do: the infield fell apart. To boost the hitting Mack put Bob Johnson at second base for 22 games. But he was too heavy for a second baseman. His legs couldn't perform the infield acrobatics.

Losing streaks of 12 and 9 games between June 17 and July 22 sank them into the basement. His boys may have had the last-place blues, but Connie Mack at seventy-three had lost none of his enthusiasm or acuity. He missed nothing on the field. On July 14 he arrived in the dugout earlier than usual and watched the Tigers take infield practice. Out of the blue he said to the writers around him, "Well, we'll win today. Granger [Gehringer] will make about three errors to do it for us."

Gehringer made two errors in the A's 10–2 win. Asked what had tipped him off, Mack said, "He didn't have rhythm when he was fielding the ball. He seemed to miss that perfect beat when heading for the ball. He wasn't himself."

The pitching woes grew worse. Vernon Wilshere, the star southpaw from Indiana University who had looked promising in his 9-9 rookie year, relieved one day against Washington, threw 8 straight balls, and walked himself out of the big leagues. Mack resurrected thirty-seven-year-old Hod Lisenbee from St. Paul, who turned in a record-tying effort on September 11 at Comiskey Park, giving up 26 hits in a 17–2 loss. Lisenbee would pitch in the minors until he was fifty and never have another day like that one.

Mack signed right-hander Stu Flythe out of North Carolina State. Flythe walked 61 and managed to lead the league with 16 wild pitches in only 39 innings. Flythe had his most impressive line against the White Sox: 10 innings pitched, 20 runs, 12 hits, 24 walks, 4 wild pitches, and 1 hit batter.

Then came a Biloxi semipro named Red Bullock, who pitched 16⅔ innings and walked 37 and went back to Mississippi to become a high school coach and principal. The pipeline from Duke sent southpaw Pete Naktenis, who walked 27 and gave up 24 hits in 18⅔ innings. On July 1 Mack gave up on Bill Dietrich, who went to Washington for the waiver price. Washington sent him on to Chicago, where coach Muddy Ruel worked on some flaws in his delivery and Dietrich lasted eleven years.

Randy Gumpert, a tall, thin right-hander out of Monocacy, Pennsylvania, had been Mack's latest unpaid part-time home batting-practice pitcher for two years, beginning in 1934, when Gumpert was sixteen.

"My dad wrote to Mr. Mack and arranged a tryout for me. I was invited to pitch BP when they were home. We had a Model A Ford and I'd take some of my buddies and go down and throw BP, then we'd stay for the game. My dad was making about twenty-five dollars a week but Connie Mack never gave me any transportation money."

Gumpert signed after graduating and made his debut at eighteen. Over the next three years, he won 1 and lost 4 for the A's. His most memorable game occurred on September 13 in Cleveland. He started against seventeen-year-old Bob Feller.

"[Feller] struck out 17 and walked 9," Gumpert said. "I struck out 2—Feller twice. I lost, 5–2. A few days later after a game Mr. Mack was in the dining room and he waved me over and asked me to join him. He said, 'Rand'—he always called me Rand—'you weren't throwing as hard today as I've seen you throw before.'

"I said, 'Maybe not, but I felt all right.' But I was thinking: Feller struck out 17 and you're comparing *me* with *his* fastball?"

Looking back fifty years later, Gumpert said of the Athletics' young pitchers, "We were in the big league, but we weren't big leaguers. I know I was overmatched. All I learned from Connie Mack was how to keep my temper under control. Losing a hundred games a year, you just try not to lose too badly."

After bouncing around the minor leagues for ten years, Gumpert made it back up with the Yankees. He had his best year—11-3—in 1946 and stayed for the next six years.

Harry Kelley was a surprising 15-12, starting and relieving, with a remarkable 3.86 ERA, which put him in the top ten in a hitters' year in which the league ERA was over 5.00. On August 22 he was rushed to the hospital with appendicitis that ended his year.

Gordon Rhodes led the league with 20 losses. Twenty-four-year-old Herman Fink, a farm boy from North Carolina with a live fastball but no curve, lost 16.

To one new writer in town, Connie Mack was still the venerated Grand Old Man of baseball.

Columnist Red Smith joined the *Philadelphia Record* in 1936. His byline first appeared in mid-July, filling in for Bill Dooly at Shibe Park. His inimitable style was already in evidence, as in this lead: "Mr. Ben Chapman tried the novel but not notably successful experiment of fielding a ground ball in his teeth yesterday, and as a result the Athletics scampered out of the

Shibe baseball emporium with a 3–2 victory over the Washington Senators clutched in their hot, chubby little fists."

Smith's first interview with Connie Mack appeared on August 14. The A's had just come home from a 9-15 trip, a good two weeks for the last-place team. Mack probably greeted him as he usually did all new writers: "Hello, young fellow."

Smith wrote:

The gaunt gray gentleman with the incredibly tall collar sat, neat and prim, in his office at Shibe Park, and resolutely looked on the bright side of things.

When you're considering the Athletics, finding a bright side to look at is no task for a weakling. But Connie Mack is a silver-lining finder of vast experience.

"I'm not disappointed with this year's team," he insisted. "In fact, I'm pleased. Yes, I really believe I'm pleased.

"Last winter no one gave us a chance to win a game. We're winning about one out of three. So, you see, that's pretty good. As a matter of fact, the team isn't as bad as it looks. It's better than I expected."

After citing several players for their showing, Mack predicted, "I will have a better team next year, maybe not a first division club but I know we'll take some pot shots at the first division."

Smith asked him if he'd ever promised himself he'd have another championship in, say, four or five years.

"No, I may never have another championship. I don't as a matter of fact plan for a championship team as such. What I like is a team that has a chance. I build for that. Then when I have that, if everything breaks right, maybe we win a pennant. If not, I'm not disappointed."

As for his plans for retirement, "None at all," he told Smith. "I'll go along from year to year just as I always have done. Age cuts no figure, you know, except to those who are old at forty and think that everyone else should be, too."

Smith asked, "When and if the day of retirement comes, will the A's go on under the Mack dynasty?"

"I haven't the faintest idea," Mack replied. There was no mention of Earle as his automatic successor, as was widely assumed.

Later Red Smith wrote:

When I first got to know him in Philadelphia, he called me Mr. Smith and I called him Mr. Mack. I asked him finally to call me by my nickname and he said. "All right, and you call me Connie."

I said, "Look, Mr. Mack. I can't do that."

He said, "All right, I'll call you Mr. Smith."

But he broke down and I didn't because somehow I never felt old enough to call Connie Connie. You'd call him Connie in the paper but he was always Mr. Mack in personal address, though I noticed his old ballplayers like Al Simmons and Mickey Cochrane and Lefty Grove called him Connie. The younger players in my time there all called him Mr. Mack.

Connie Mack had become resigned to the ups and downs of the business he had made his life's work. "There is but one rule for a manager," he told *Baseball Magazine* editor F. C. Lane. "Just let him do his best and take the consequences. I have had too many players go wrong, too many players that I banked on fail to come through. I have seen too much of the uncertainties of baseball to be particularly surprised at anything that can happen now. It seems to me that the wise manager should work hard, use all the judgment he has, and then learn to take things as they come."

A realistic look at his club's finances—and Connie Mack was a realist despite his perennial show of optimism—told him that he could not compete with the deep pockets of such as New York and Boston for the top minor leaguers, nor could he build champions from the scratch of sandlots and campuses as he had done in the past.

Times had changed. "My players are good boys but they don't take baseball quite as seriously as I do," he told Lane. "You can't expect it and frankly I don't want them to. They'll be disillusioned soon enough. Of course we differ sometimes. A young man is inclined to look at things through rose-colored glasses. Young ballplayers make more money and seldom realize the owner's problems. To them every year is a prosperous year."

Tom Yawkey had lost close to $2 million on the Red Sox over the past three years. According to an AP story out of Boston, he had spent $738,549 on twenty-nine players since acquiring the team. He had the highest payroll in the league and a sixth-place finish, 20 games ahead of the A's. Lefty Grove and Wes Ferrell were his only reliable pitchers.

By midseason Mack had tagged the Yankees as "a great team." Joe DiMaggio lived up to his minor league reputation, and the Yankees made a shambles of the pennant race, finishing 19½ games ahead of Detroit. (On May 10 A's pitcher George Turbeville had given up DiMaggio's first big league home run. An A's pitcher, Luther Thomas, would provide the same service for Ted Williams three years later.)

"He had a big handicap to overcome right from the start," Mack said of DiMaggio, "and don't think it isn't a handicap stepping into the majors from the minors heralded as another Ruth. He showed us he had no weaknesses and he merits the rating of the outstanding player in our league."

Connie Mack was never stuck in the past. "He's good, but you should have seen so-and-so" was not his style. Asked a few years later by New York writer Jimmy Cannon to compare DiMaggio with Cobb and Speaker, Mack called DiMag "the greatest of them all. I mean, as the one man you want on your team. He never plays for himself."

Looking up from the basement, Mack was pleased to see Jimmie Dykes bring the low-rated White Sox in third, just a half game behind Mickey Cochrane's Tigers. He took pride in the success of his boys, who in turn acknowledged how much they had learned from him. Asked by Bob Paul to define Mack's system of managing, Cochrane said, "It's difficult to express in a few words, but you can come pretty close by saying it's the remarkable way in which the Old Man gets every player to not only give his best, but that extra something in the pinch. He sort of makes you feel you owe it to yourself to do it."

Mack appreciated perseverance, even when he was the object of the pursuit. He was always patient and gracious with autograph seekers as he walked through the Shibe Park concourse toward the clubhouse before a game. But after the game he kept on walking as he left the park. Usually his daughter or someone else was waiting in the car to take him home. A's fan Joe Nolan was sixteen when he went to a game one day with his father. After the game, he recalled seventy years later, "The players came out in twos and threes, and most of them stopped to sign autograph books for the young fans. Then out came Connie Mack and he walked right past the crowd. I decided to follow Mr. Mack down the street. After we had gone two or three blocks, I got up my courage to approach him.

"'Ordinarily,' he said, 'I don't stop to sign autographs. But you have followed me for quite a while so I'll make an exception in your case.' I thanked him profusely. He kept on walking and I headed back to meet my father outside the ballpark."

For the first time in his thirty-six years in Philadelphia, Connie Mack had a surprise party for his birthday, organized by Roy. He was in his office around noon on December 23 when a secretary told him that groundskeeper Bill McCalley had a problem in the clubhouse. Mack put on his overcoat and walked down to the clubhouse. McCalley met him at the door and opened it for him.

About fifty writers, radio announcers, photographers, club officials, and close friends yelled, "Surprise." An array of hot food and a big cake filled long tables. The writers gave him a pen and pencil set.

The slings and arrows fired at Mack after the sales of his stars appeared to have been forgotten, except that Mack acknowledged them in his remarks to the group.

Isaminger summarized his comments:

In the long number of years I have been manager of the Athletics, my relations with the press have always been cordial. I would like to say that you sports editors and baseball writers have always been fair to me both in success and adversity.

In such a long number of years it would have been impossible if at some time there was not some misunderstanding. But I realize that sometimes I have made mistakes and I know that the duty of a baseball writer is in the interests of his reader, even against his own personal wishes.

The more I live, the more I think of the big responsibilities of the baseball writer and marvel at the way they day by day produce attractive reading for the baseball fans.

He concluded with regrets that John Shibe's illness had prevented him from being there.

Bob Paul went further. Never on the same friendly terms with Mack as some other writers, Paul was present at the party, and what he wrote about Connie Mack's remarks to the writers describes the respect even Mack's sometime critics shared for the man:

As he talked, as though to a small group of close friends, he reached the heights of sincerity with a simplicity I'm certain has influenced many of his "boys" in this very dressing room.

Connie hasn't been treated well by sports scribes in general the past two or three years. The hard knocks and sharp criticisms cut deeply into the attendance. Away from Shibe Park as well as at home—for scribes have a way of passing personal opinions and desires to their brethren of the typewriter in other cities. Some of the printed thrusts the reporters honestly believed Connie had coming to him. I know that's how I feel about the caustic barbs I hurled Connie's way.

Misunderstandings between Shibe Park and the press brought rebukes from scribes and photographers. Frequently Connie was the victim of another Shibe Park executive's [John Shibe] improper treatment to newspapermen. He didn't complain.

Connie might have taken advantage of the joyful circumstances, combining birthday and Yuletide greetings, to rebuke the scribes for unmerited attacks. He might have gone so far as to publicly state that he never made that now notorious remark, "The A's are not looking for newspaper publicity," which led sports editors all over the country to order "no publicity for the A's." Connie made no such denial yesterday. It would have been exceedingly embarrassing to the man, sitting nearby, who burst into headline with the false quotation.

Instead, Connie explained his viewpoint of the recent campaigns—and his reaction to the attacks he suffered in the sports sections. He admitted he had placed himself open to attack by courageous scribes. He went further. He said if local writers hadn't taken him to task after certain transactions, like tearing apart a good ball club, the scribe wouldn't have been playing fair with his paper's readers.

As Connie revealed that promises given to other club owners regarding the secrecy of completed deals forced him to deny rumors of such trades, you saw the director of the A's in a different light. You recalled denials he'd made of deals when you knew he couldn't be telling the truth. The fault wasn't Connie's. He was keeping faith with a promise.

Now and then Connie interjected a touch of humor. For instance, he expressed amazement at the deals "concocted" during the winter months by baseball writers. And he wondered how some writers "arranged" summer trades and had the audacity to publish the same. I caught Connie's twinkling eyes gazing at me. I didn't blush. For if the truth must be told, it was Connie himself who first took me aside one winter in Fort Myers and said, "Paul, too many sports writers spoil a good story by first trying to have it verified. Go ahead and publish your yarn—then have it verified or denied later. Either way you have two good stories instead of none at all."

Frankly, I can't recall where I picked up some of the information that led me to dash into print with yarns that Al Simmons was on the block or Lefty Grove sold. I broke such stories because at the time I trusted my informant and realized all parties concerned had to deny the report. I do remember distinctly who told me Foxx and Cramer had been promised to the Red Sox. That was the August before the deal was announced. I couldn't disclose my source of information then. And I can't now, for the man still is in baseball.

Connie wasn't making a plea for unqualified newspaper support. He wanted the scribes to know he understood their job—and he hoped they'd gain a better insight on his. And if the time ever comes when he does something for which he should be rebuked—he expects the writers to do their duty. That's the Connie Mack of today.

Connie Mack was in good health. He could eat anything but blackberries and sweet potatoes. With Tom Shibe gone and John Shibe mortally ill, he was still his own general manager and was now acting club president too. He had no thought of vacating the dugout, however dim the prospects for success. During the 1936–1937 winter he took no vacation. He gave up golf, unable to shoot in the low 80s anymore.

"I'm too busy these days to have much fun," he said.

7 | WELL, THEN, WAIT 'TIL *NEXT* YEAR

John Shibe never left the Beeches Sanitarium after being admitted in July 1936. He died on July 11, 1937, of pneumonia. John and Ethyl Shibe had no children. His estate, valued at the time at about $200,000, was left to his widow. In 1940 Connie Mack would buy Ethyl's shares in the club for $42,000. John Shibe's executor, Stoughton Sterling, said the rest of the estate was "probably insufficient for the payment of debts," which amounted to $121,280. Fifteen years later, a destitute Ethyl Shibe would petition the American League for financial aid.

The private side of the ill-tempered John Shibe was unknown to the public. Behind his gruff veneer dwelt a generosity that he would have denied rather than let it be known. In 1933 Detroit rookie first baseman Hank Greenberg went out early every day to take extra batting practice. One day at Shibe Park, after a half-hour of practice, a groundskeeper told him he had to leave the field. As Greenberg told it, "An elderly gentleman sitting in the stands called to me. I went up to see what he wanted and he said, 'I very much admire what you are doing, young man. You tell that groundskeeper to assist you in every way possible. Tell him that those are John Shibe's instructions. And if he doesn't like it, send him right up here to see me.'"

A fight fan like Connie Mack, Shibe once heard about a prelim fighter who had been blinded by blows taken in the ring. Shibe arranged for an operation and a long recovery at a resort hotel—and paid for all of it. Nobody knew about it until after his death, when the fighter, sworn to secrecy by Shibe, told his story.

After baseball, John Shibe's enthusiasm was speedboat racing. It was an expensive hobby, and Shibe had gone at it in a first-class way. He equipped a complete machine shop under the left-field stands and employed a full-time driver, Armand DuPugh, and a German mechanic to maintain his fleet of racing boats. Al Ruggieri, the "Little Man" who did odd jobs around the ballpark, ran errands for them.

"Every morning before school I swept the shop. It must have been 150 feet long," Ruggieri said. "Then I went back after school."

In 1930 Shibe had bought a top-of-the-line V-16 Miller Gold Cup racing engine for his *Miss Philadelphia*, which finished second in the 1931 race. Two years later he hired the premier naval architect John L. Hacker to build him a President's Gold Cup winner. An entire Hacker construction crew moved in and built a twenty-seven-foot hydroplane of Honduras mahogany in the shop under the left-field stands. *Power Boating* magazine described it as "an exceptionally beautiful craft, probably the finest looking boat in the Gold Cup class." Its V-16 engine could hit eighty miles an hour. Named the *Ethyl-Ruth IV*, it cost $33,000.

Shibe entered it in the 1934 Gold Cup race at Lake George. His driver got a late start and drove it wide open for two laps to catch up, and the engine blew up. The boat had to be towed. John never tried again. The boat still exists in private hands. After John's death the engine was sold. Rebuilt, it powered three future Gold Cup winners.

There were rumors that John Shibe had been skimming gate receipts for several years to support his pursuit of the Gold Cup. According to Al Ruggieri, Howard "Yitz" Crompton, who was Shibe's chauffeur when he wasn't working in the clubhouse, knew of it "but did not turn him in." Ruggieri believed it was another employee, Yitz Krieger, who tipped off Roy Mack. It's likely that Connie Mack was also aware of it, but nothing was said.

When John Shibe died, Al Ruggieri left the A's and never went back.

The rumors may have been the basis for a telegram dated October 9, 1935, from someone named D. J. Walsh, apparently connected with a New York newspaper or wire service, to Bob Paul, sports editor of the *Philadelphia Daily News*. "Have tip Mack and Shibe are about to split out. With Mack selling stock and retiring as manager. If you get story, give us break. Will you? Regards."

When it had become likely that John Shibe would not return to work, Connie Mack was elected the Athletics' president on January 11, 1937. Suddenly he found himself alone at the top, without a Shibe partner after thirty-six years in which, he said, "not one bitter word ever passed between us."

One reason there had been no bitter words was that the Shibes had always been consulted by Mack, even though they left all the player decisions to him. "When I had decided to buy a player and obtained the details for the transaction," Mack told Bob Paul, "I went to my partners and told them I'd like to obtain the player in question. I told them the terms and explained why I thought the deal would benefit us. I did this whether the amount of cash involved was $10,000 or $100,000. And the Shibes so respected my judgment that not once did they object."

Mack in turn had left all the other decisions to the Shibes. That didn't mean he always agreed with John; he just didn't argue with him.

John had opposed the selling of advance box seats at the ballpark, insisting they be sold only at the downtown ticket outlet. When John resigned in August, Mack immediately opened an advance sale ticket office at Shibe Park. John had also been against Ladies' Days, which the club had instituted when it had opened for business at Columbia Park in 1901 but abandoned when the crowds became too big for the ten-thousand-seat ballpark. Mack reinstated them for the 1937 season.

"I have had it in mind for a number of years," Mack said. "Times have changed and we thought it would be nice for the ladies to go home and talk about the A's with their hubbies at the supper table."

The Athletics put numbers on the home uniforms for the first time and sold scorecards instead of giving them away, a change probably initiated by Connie Jr., who was now running the concessions operation under Bob Schroeder's guidance, bringing much-needed improvements to the variety and quality of the ballpark fare, which had been rated by well-traveled visitors as the worst in baseball. In 1939 they opened an in-house restaurant, the Café Shibe.

John Shibe had resisted the sportswriters' pleas to install an elevator to the press box, which hung suspended from the roof. Connie Mack made no immediate move to change that. The portly James Isaminger and the others would still have to climb the steps for a few more years.

The employee whose job was most affected by the departure of John Shibe was Bill McCalley. An avid home gardener, McCalley had been a local semipro pitcher scouted by Mike Drennan in 1924. When the A's needed some help with maintaining the turf at the ballpark, Drennan asked him to help out. McCalley stayed and the next year became the head groundskeeper. John Shibe had been fanatical about maintaining the grass and the drainage system and improving the grandstand facilities. Writers and players throughout the league had high praise for the cleanliness of the facilities and the condition of the field. If an A's player had a request or complaint about the field, it was immediately dealt with. Now McCalley took on all of John Shibe's responsibilities as superintendent of the entire grounds and grandstand operation, including ticket takers and clean-up squads. He and his seven assistants maintained Shibe's standards. There was still no advertising on the outfield walls. After fall football action tore up the playing field, McCalley and a crew of twenty men worked all winter resodding the entire surface with grass from Kentucky and scraping and painting the seats. An expert woodworker, McCalley made all of Bob Johnson's bats and salvaged broken bats for fungo use.

For the first time in years, major league baseball clubs felt optimistic enough to schedule four trips to their farthest rivals instead of three for the 1937 season. Baseball was firmly implanted in the national psyche. Its followers remained devoted to its doings through good times and bad, if only by radio and the newspapers, which reported no diminution of calls to their switchboards asking for the final scores of the day's games. Besides, baseball was the biggest entertainment bargain, whether the home team was winning or losing. If you didn't have $1.10 for a grandstand ticket, you could spend half that for a bleachers seat and enjoy four or five hours in the open air watching a doubleheader. Movie tickets ranged from about thirty cents in the neighborhoods to two dollars or more at the downtown palaces. Stage shows cost $6.60, college football games $4 or more. Headline championship fights were for the well-heeled, at $50 and up.

Although unemployment was still at 14 percent, the country was swept by strikes demanding union recognition and higher wages. Auto workers staged sit-down strikes; department store workers, steelworkers, and typewriter makers walked off the job. Minimum-wage laws went into effect, promising $750 annual incomes for six-day work weeks for hotel maids. Streetcar operators who took the fans to the ballparks earned $1,500 a year for a six-day week. A Phi Beta Kappa graduate engineer might be offered the same amount.

Strikes against General Motors inspired a union organizer to approach Detroit players to unionize them against the capitalists who were getting rich on their underpaid backs. The idea went nowhere. As *Detroit News* sports editor H. G. Salsinger pointed out at great length, "How can anyone unionize a profession where no two workers are of equal value to their employers and where salaries range from $4,000 to $48,000 a year?"

He went on to say that the unnamed organizer had chosen the wrong team: "Detroit is the highest salaried team in baseball and has been for two years. The New York Yankees are the next highest salaried. Besides drawing the highest salaries in the game, each Detroit player received a bonus check representing ten percent of his salary for 1936 and another check of more than $1,000 representing second-place money. What union organizer could get the Detroit players larger returns for their services than Walter O. Briggs is paying them? No wonder the self-appointed Messiah's proposal was received with loud guffaws."

Referring to the "enormous earnings" allegedly reaped by ball clubs, Salsinger wrote:

What did the owners of the Brooklyn club say while reflecting how deeply they are in debt to the banks; or the owners of the two clubs in Philadelphia, where one club had to sell all its star players to keep the banks from foreclosing; or in Boston where the American League club was nearly $500,000 in debt when Thomas A. Yawkey rescued it and where only financial wizardry is keeping the National League club afloat; or in St. Louis, where a public sale of stock last winter was used as a solution to the Browns' problems; or in Cincinnati, where the banks took over the club; or in Cleveland, where they had to discharge their general manager [Billy Evans, whose salary had gone from $30,000 in 1931 to $12,500 in '34 and '35 and was cut again in '36, moving Evans to quit and join the Red Sox] because they could not afford a general manager's salary; or in Washington, where only the sale of Joe Cronin for $250,000 cash kept the club going? Enormous earnings, huh?

AP writer Bill King put the Red Sox losses at more than $1.5 million over the past three years. But that was relative too. Tom Yawkey lost more money every year than Connie Mack's entire budget.

When Dizzy Dean was suspended in June for criticizing an umpire's balk call, leading to a brawl with the Giants, an AFL-CIO operative sought to capitalize on the diamond workers' unrest by sending a mimeographed letter to all players, urging them to organize. Nobody responded.

Half the Yankees' pennant winners were holding out—"raiding my bankroll," said Jake Ruppert. The attitude Ruppert expressed to AP sportswriter James Reston prevailed throughout baseball, rich clubs and poor alike, when he said that 20-game winner Red Ruffing "won't get more than $15,000 and he can sit in Chicago if he wants to."

In January the *New York Times* estimated that major league payrolls would top $3 million, the highest since 1930. Mickey Cochrane would be the highest paid manager in baseball in 1937: $36,000 plus a $9,000 bonus. Giants manager Bill Terry and Joe McCarthy topped Connie Mack's $20,000, which was less than the salary of George Weiss, vice-president of the Yankees' Newark farm club. The highest paid players in the American League were Lou Gehrig, who had to fight to get a raise to $36,000, and Hank Greenberg at $35,000, and in the National League, it was Carl Hubbell at $22,500.

Mack had cut his salary at a time when his family expenses were rising. He bought a house for his daughter Ruth and her family and helped support them.

Connie Mack's most obstinate holdout was Wally Moses. He had outhit Joe DiMaggio by 20 points, but his demands were far more modest. Among the best outfielders in the league, Moses believed he deserved a substantial raise from the $5,500 of last year. Mack agreed but said the contract he had sent was as big a raise as he could pay. "If he doesn't sign in ten days," Mack said, "I'll send him another one for last year's salary."

Moses worked out at Hot Springs at his own expense while negotiations continued. Two weeks into spring training he signed for $7,500, and Mack reimbursed him for his Hot Springs expenses.

"That's good enough for a man starting his third season in the fast set," Isaminger declared.

The Athletics were a quiet team, too quiet for their manager. His 1933–1936 teams, he said, were "about as combative as Aunt Maria's old tabby cat." He missed the boisterous, bantering loudmouths of his winning teams— Dykes, Haas, Simmons, Cochrane, and the rest. Since the departure of Rabbit Warstler, there was no fire, no chatter in the infield. He decided to do something about it.

One of Jack Coombs's players who had not gone to Duke on Connie Mack's dime was Red Sox third baseman Bill Werber. Duke's first All-American basketball player and an outstanding student, Werber was as much of an anomaly among ballplayers as Connie Mack had been in the nineteenth century. He had graduated with the school's highest honor, the Robert E. Lee Award. After his freshman year in June 1927 he had committed to signing with the Yankees, who paid for his last three years at Duke and invited him to travel with them that summer. The Yankees sold him to Tom Yawkey after a brief look in 1933 along with George Pipgras for $100,000. With the Red Sox Werber had led the league in stolen bases in '34 and '35.

Werber and Boston manager Joe Cronin had begun a feud when Cronin managed the Senators. At best they tolerated each other now, but Werber and general manager Eddie Collins didn't like each other at all.

It's unknown who first proposed an even swap of Pinky Higgins for Werber. Higgins, a year younger than Werber, was a better hitter; on defense they were rated about even. Higgins was quiet. Werber was a holler guy.

Higgins had given Mack four solid years. The two had established a bond; Higgins lived near Mack's home during the season, and they often discussed personal financial planning. Higgins had married in 1935. He sold insurance during the off-season and was investing a significant slice of his $10,000 income from the A's in annuities. According to *Dallas Journal* sports editor Flint Dupre, Mike had sought a raise from Mack in the spring of '36 that he didn't get.

Like most players, Higgins yearned to go to a team that could pay more and had a chance for a World Series berth. The Red Sox "Millionaires" and Detroit met those standards, despite Boston's sixth-place finish with six ex-A's on the roster in '36. Mack sympathized with Higgins's situation, and it's possible that was the primary reason he made the trade on Wednesday, December 9, at the league meetings in New York. Except first, both sides wanted to be sure their new men would agree to terms. (Higgins received no raise in Boston until 1938. He made it to the World Series with Detroit in 1940 and back with the Red Sox in '46.)

Mack called Werber at home in College Park, Maryland, explained the deal, and asked what it would take to sign him.

Werber hesitated. One of his Boston teammates was former A's infielder Eric McNair. He had seen McNair's routine imitating Connie Mack crying into an Irish lace curtain when a player asked for more money, and he had listened to McNair tell the probably fictitious story of how he had gone in to get a raise from Mr. Mack and heard such a hard luck story that he took out a fifty-cent piece and flipped it on the desk and said, "Here, get yourself something to eat," and walked out.

After an off-year in 1935, Werber had taken a cut from $11,000 to $8,500 from Yawkey. He wasn't about to take another one. Whatever numbers were discussed, Werber was satisfied when Mack offered him $9,000.

The deal went through.

Werber attended the Philadelphia writers' winter dinner and promised the audience that the A's would have a hustling team. That was the only way he knew how to play the game.

Mack wanted an experienced catcher to mentor Frank Hayes and work with his young pitchers. He drafted Earle Brucker from Portland. A career .300 hitter in the minors, Brucker was a thirty-four-year-old rookie whose chances of ever seeing the big leagues had seemed remote. As a student at USC in 1923, he had been given a brief look by the Yankees. He had suffered a sore arm and a fractured skull and was out of baseball for three years. After years in the low minors, he had helped the Beavers win the 1936 PCL pennant, coaching George Caster to develop the sinker he needed to win in the big leagues.

Brucker was a wise choice. He showed more hustle in spring training than most of the teenagers. He had a good arm, quick feet, and a fearless approach to blocking the plate. He became a valued catcher and pitching coach, remaining with the A's for ten years. Brucker preached to the young pitchers, "Changing speeds is the key to success, and throwing strikes."

Mack had used four second basemen in 1936. They all flivvered. They had big league mechanical ability but minor league mentalities and couldn't keep up the pace. Drafting thirty-three-year-old Bill Cissell from Baltimore, where he had hit .349 in '36, showed how desperate Mack was for an experienced infielder. Charles Comiskey had paid Portland $75,000 and five players valued at $48,000 for Cissell in 1927, and he had never lived up to the burden of the expectations that went with his price tag. His reputation as a drinker was widely known, and he made no attempt to conceal it. After a year in Chicago his 1929 contract for $6,000 included this clause: "If player saves the proper amount of money from his salary and refrains from using cigarettes and intoxicating liquor, an additional $1,500 will be paid at the close of the 1929 season if the player is a member of the Chicago club in good standing at that time."

The same clause was there in 1930. It's doubtful he collected it either year. By 1935 he was back in the minors.

It's hard to say why Connie Mack picked him up. It couldn't have been for a veteran to solidify a young infield of great potential because his infield had none. Maybe an experienced man would enable him to put off further experimenting for a year. After all, he had heard that Cissell, after two years in the minors, had reformed, meaning he had quit drinking in the daytime.

The only thing Mack asked of the veteran was, "When you go out drinking, don't take any other players with you."

Since the land speculation bubble had burst in Florida—and the Athletics were no longer the world's greatest baseball team—spring training in Fort Myers had become more expensive as attendance at the training games evaporated. It had become more difficult to entice other clubs to travel there for exhibition games. In the fall of 1935 Earle Mack had taken a troupe of barnstormers, including Foxx, Cramer, McNair, Higgins, and Berry, to Mexico City. The trip almost didn't happen. After getting Will Harridge's okay to proceed with the planning, Earle had signed up players, received an $800 deposit from each of them, and sent the money to his agent in Mexico to make the arrangements. At a league meeting in August, the other club owners prohibited their players from going. It took the intervention of Commissioner Landis, who ruled that the contracts must be honored, to enable Earle to make the trip.

Earle came back full of enthusiasm for Mexico's potential as a spring training base. Many pesos awaited them.

Urged on by Earle, Connie Mack decided to go. Why he did so is a mystery. Years later Connie Jr. said he never understood why the team went there. Writers speculated that Mack wanted to treat his boys to some exotic foreign travel. But it was completely contrary to his oft-stated preference for a shorter trip to a training site. The journey would take three days and nights, with changes in St. Louis and San Antonio, and require visas for everybody. There were no other big league clubs anywhere close.

Connie Mack sent his business manager, Bob Schroeder, to Mexico City to make the arrangements. Schroeder reserved rooms for the club to stay at a small hotel, L'Escargot, outside the capital city—way outside the capital city. A local resident, Fred Merando, agreed to arrange games against local semipro teams. But Schroeder could not raise any financial guarantees.

The A's were looking more than ever like a Duke alumni team. In addition to Bill Werber, the early arrivals included All-American fullback Clarence "Ace" Parker, who had interrupted his senior year to try to make the team, promising Mack he would go back and finish in the fall. On April 30 Parker pinch-hit a 2-run home run in the ninth inning against Wes Ferrell in his first big league at bat. But he was clearly overmatched. Mack sent him to Atlanta.

Mack expected big things from Luther "Bud" Thomas, an 18-game winner at Atlanta; a rejuvenated George Caster; the veteran workhorse Harry Kelley; and rookie left-hander Edgar Smith.

This was Red Smith's first spring training with the Athletics; thirty years later the experience was still being mined by Smith and other writers for story material. Connie Mack was not on the first train that took the pitchers and catchers out of Philadelphia. But the dense crowds who gathered at the stations in Monterey and San Luis Potosi and Mexico City didn't know that. Art Morrow wrote about the day the team's train stopped at a station and Smith got off to stretch his legs. The locals, who had never seen Connie Mack, took Smith for the lean leader, though he was much shorter and had red hair. A band struck up a march and a dignitary draped a horseshoe of flowers around Smith's neck. Smith accepted the flowers with dignity and got back on the train.

Perhaps the highlight of the trip for Smith was an opportunity to interview Leon Trotsky, the Russian revolutionary leader in exile in Mexico City.

The Hotel L'Escargot was way out in the sticks, miles away from Mexico City. The food was poor and foreign to the players and their innards. Nobody could read the Spanish menu. They didn't know what they were eating and probably didn't want to know. They had to bring in bottled water.

Connie Mack didn't know any Spanish either. One evening he decided to go to a show in Mexico City. He saw nineteen-year-old Randy Gumpert in the hotel lobby and invited him to go along. The show was in Spanish, and neither one of them knew what was happening.

"We got into a cab to go back to the hotel," Gumpert recalled, "and we couldn't make the driver understand where we wanted to go. Mr. Mack became a little frustrated, the only time I saw him really get excited. Eventually we got back."

Always the good sport, Mack posed for photos leading a donkey, then wearing a big sombrero and holding a lariat, with a senorita in high heels bending back in admiration in front of him.

The crowds at Delta Park were large for the first few games against local semipro teams that had more Cubans than Mexicans; as many as three thousand paid 50 centavos (fourteen cents). Then they stopped coming. The locals, who had been playing all winter, were no match for the big leaguers, and the games were so one-sided everybody lost interest. There were more spectators watching through holes in the fence than there were in the seats. Even the local teams stopped showing up. The A's appealed to a nearby Ford Motor plant to send a factory team. Otherwise they settled for intra-squad games.

"Strictly for their own amusement," wrote Red Smith, "the Athletics played a ball game here today and beat the daylights out of themselves, 17–6."

To avoid schedule conflicts with the two o'clock bullfights, Sunday games were played in the morning. Then they went to the bullfights. The first time they went, rain stopped the action after the second bull was dispatched. The next time they went, a matador was dispatched to torero heaven. They didn't go again. One Sunday morning Mack scheduled an early double-header, a practice game followed by one against the locals. Bill Cissell was so aggravated at the idea of playing two games in the morning, he went out Saturday night and got drunk and slept in Sunday morning. That evening he told Mack what he had done while assuring the boss that "I didn't take anybody with me."

The boss laughed it off.

The nights were cool, but the blazing sun seemed hotter than in Florida. Despite the occasional sandstorm, the Athletics lost only one day to the weather. Flies attacked like Ty Cobb sliding into home. There was no grass on the infield, and sheep stolidly grazed to create the same condition in the outfield. The clubhouse was cramped. The seven-thousand-foot altitude had everybody gasping. Mack heard the complaints but shrugged them off. "Everybody who makes a mistake or a bad pitch or an error blames it on the altitude," he said. "I'll still be hearing about the altitude on July Fourth."

But Mack did admit that the hotel was a mistake. "If we return," he said, "we will stay in the city center and the players can eat at Sanborn's," a restaurant that offered American food.

One day Mack called on Mexican president Lazaro Cardenas at the palace in Mexico City. What did they talk about? A Mexican newspaper ran a translated quote from Mack: "No importa de que empiece hablando; siempre termino hablando de beisbol" (It doesn't matter what you are talking about; you always end up talking baseball).

The thin air made bruises and abrasions and split fingers almost impossible to heal. Doc Ebling was busy day and night sticking adhesive on hands, legs, and faces. A line drive split a finger on Al Benton's pitching hand. It wouldn't heal. Lou Finney picked up a sinus infection, couldn't shake it, and went home. He also had a hernia and chronic appendicitis and would struggle through a miserable season splitting his time between first base and the outfield and the hospital. In October he would undergo surgeries to repair all three conditions.

And Doc Ebling wasn't feeling so well either. He had undergone surgery during the winter to remove part of his stomach. He was overworked, on a strict diet, and hardly slept. By the time they left Mexico, he was worn out. He never fully recovered and was back in the hospital in September. When it looked as if he would not recover in time to go to spring training in 1938, the A's brought in Racquet Club and Davis Cup team trainer James C. Tadley to fill in. Doc Ebling never came back. He died February 11, 1938.

Connie Mack became a casualty too. On Thursday, March 18, he was sitting on the bench when a wild throw got past the first baseman and bounced up and hit him on the shinbone. Lena Blackburne rushed over. "Are you hurt, boss?"

"No," Mack waved him off.

The next day he still felt no pain, but the abrasion looked nasty. The players gathered around while Doc Ebling tended to it and put gauze on it. "Well, Doc," said Mack, "I don't often bother you, do I?"

Mack paid no further mind to it. He had no temperature and said he felt fine. But the abrasion wasn't healing. A week later he intended to go to Good Friday Mass in Mexico City, but he stayed in bed instead. To Lena Blackburne that was a bad omen. He called Doc Ebling, who took one look and said, "Mr. Mack, you're going to the hospital."

They took him to the American Hospital, where a Dr. Garnett diagnosed a strep infection that had spread from the shinbone into his blood. Sulfa drugs, then in the early stages of development, went to work on him. It was the first time the seventy-four-year-old Mack had ever been a patient in a hospital. The players were allowed to visit him only after passing close scrutiny by a no-nonsense Irish nurse who watched over him.

The team was due to break camp the following Sunday night. After the day's game the players whooped it up, singing and joking like paroled prisoners as they packed up. They would split up into two teams and barnstorm their way home.

There was no way Connie Mack could go with them. Leaning on Lena Blackburne to put no weight on the leg, Mack was tucked into a compartment on a train to San Antonio. Arriving Tuesday morning, he was carried on a stretcher to a waiting ambulance and taken to the Medical and Surgical Hospital. Dr. John. W. Goode found no trace of infection. Mack was alert, peppy, eating and sleeping well, and couldn't wait to be back in the dugout.

He was discharged on Thursday, April 8, and joined one of his squads working its way home.

At a stop in Memphis Mack watched a thirty-two-year-old pitcher, Lynn Nelson, mow down his team for 3 innings without a hit. Plagued by frequent sore arms, Nelson had been up and down a few times with the Cubs, the first time in 1930, when he reported with an ailing flipper. "From the start I couldn't pitch," he told Cy Peterman. "At Catalina [spring training] they hit line drives. They still hit 'em off me in Chicago, and by May 1 the Chicago writers had dubbed me Line Drive Nelson."

Nelson was used to being hit—in a different way. He had won 19 consecutive amateur fights at 160 pounds in Fargo, North Dakota, before giving up the ring for the diamond.

Cubs infielders weren't used to dodging so many drives. One was quoted as saying, "I'd like to catch just one pop fly when he pitches. If he lives to be a thousand years he'll never be a pitcher."

In Seattle in 1932 the trainer had nursed Nelson's arm to occasional soundness, enough for him to work 295 innings and be drafted by the Cubs again. He wasn't much better this time and spent the next three years in the Southern Association. That's where Harry Kelley had seen him and recommended him to Connie Mack.

Nelson had been 14–16 with the last-place Memphis Chicks last year, but Mack was more interested in his 260 innings pitched and only 52 walks. He decided to jettison some youth for the veteran, leaving two infielders and two pitchers in Memphis and taking Nelson with him. Of the players he gave up on, only Al Benton was a mistake. Fifteen years later he was still pitching in the big leagues.

The still achy Nelson appeared in more games—a league-leading 38—as a pinch hitter and occasional outfielder than a relief pitcher and with more success, batting .354 overall with 29 RBIS.

The Athletics were traveling on April 14 when Connie Mack learned of the passing of Ned Hanlon. Mack had played under him at Pittsburgh in 1891 before Hanlon went to Baltimore and developed the colorful Orioles' championship teams of McGraw and Keeler and Jennings and Kelley and the rest. Mack sent a telegram to the family but could not attend the funeral in Baltimore. He acknowledged that he had learned more from Hanlon during that one half-season in Pittsburgh than from anyone else.

"I always rated Ned Hanlon as the greatest leader baseball ever had," he said. "I don't believe that any man lived who knew as much baseball as he did. He saw more under the surface than anybody else. He could size up opponents better than all others. He lived and talked baseball every minute when he was in the saddle. He was one of the first leaders to get away from the policy of holding on to slipping veterans to give youngsters a chance, and when he had a good youngster he knew what to do with him."

Connie Mack appreciated the value of the unquantifiable aspects of morale and the mental and emotional parts of baseball that elude the sabermetric formulae for rating players.

There was new pepper and patter in the infield. Bill Werber was a non-stop chirruper. The day before opening day Mack said, "Werber is an inspiring player. He's the type who can lead and lift a team. Think back over the clubs which have suddenly hopped away up. They always had a firebrand. Bill has made 'Leaping Lenas' out of everybody. I never had a team that hustled more."

Werber was also a scrapper, a fighter who believed he was paid to win, not just to play the game. He described his attitude as "mean": "If you were in my way you might get hurt. I might get hurt myself." He expected as much intensity from his teammates and wasn't shy about letting them know. It was that intensity that led to the injury that had plagued him in Boston and would for the rest of his career. About two weeks before the close of the 1934 season, he had walked back to the dugout fuming over his failure to deliver in a pinch and kicked a bucket of ice, breaking the big toe on his right foot.

Werber played in pain through the end of the season without telling anybody—and never did tell anybody. A bone spur developed in the toe that winter, leading to a disappointing '35 season. "The backs of both legs were continually painful," he said, "as was my right foot. However, even on two bad legs, I led in stolen bases again."

He went to Johns Hopkins, where Dr. George Bennett removed the spur and rebuilt the joint. "I kept my mouth shut about the whole business and played reasonably decent major league ball for seven more years, but I was in pain all the time," he said. "Even hurting, I could run faster than most in the league."

Werber was cocky and outspoken—to some players and writers, too full of himself. He was intelligent and displayed it. An infielder who camped under a pop-up and hollered, "I got it" might be advised that the correct grammar was "I have it."

Mack's friends, like the Pearlstones and Jacobys, who sometimes traveled with the team, left him alone when he was eating lunch in the hotel unless they had been invited to join him. "He wants to be alone to think about the game," Hyman Pearlstone explained to his eight-year-old grandson, Larry Budner, once when they were staying with the team at the Del Prado in Chicago. Sometimes when Katherine accompanied Mack on a road trip, even she ate at a separate table in the dining room. Occasionally Mack might invite a player to join him if he had something particular to discuss. But no player would dare approach Mr. Mack and ask to sit with him.

Bill Werber didn't hesitate. "Whenever Mr. Mack was alone in the dining room, I would go over to him and ask him, 'May I join you?' I wanted to listen to him. One morning I was having breakfast with him in Detroit and I asked him who were some of his favorite players from the old days. He said, 'Well, I guess I'd have to say Rube Waddell.' He told me of his antics and what a great pitcher he was."

Some of his teammates felt that Werber played for himself, an attitude common among ballplayers on last-place teams. The A's and Phillies finished last so often that such players were called "Philadelphia players." Werber's goals included leading the league in stolen bases. Sometimes he tried stealing a base when it didn't seem appropriate. Once in a home game in 1938 the A's had the bases full with 1 out in the ninth of a 6–6 game against Washington. Werber was on third. He got a jump on rookie pitcher Bill Phebus and broke for home. The throw was high, and he made it safely to win the game. He was criticized for taking a chance on the daring play with only 1 out. It would have been worse if he had been caught.

Red Smith of the *Record* and Shirley Povich of the *Washington Post* didn't like Werber, and they let it show in print. Whenever either of them was in the dugout and Werber saw them, words were exchanged that were not friendly. In 1960 twenty-seven-year American League umpire Bill Summers picked his All-Boor Nine, based on six factors: a conviction that no umpire was ever right on a close decision; refusal to accept contrary testimony from catcher, grandmother, or godfather; better knowledge of the rule book than the umpire or the people who wrote it; natural professional orneriness; an explosive temper; and a strong vocabulary.

Summers picked Bill Werber as his "All-Boor" third baseman: "Billy Werber is elected because of his profound knowledge of the rules and his unselfishness in sharing it with the umpires. His seriousness of purpose also was laudable."

(Two other past or future A's made the list: Paul Richards and Charles

"Greek" George. But, Summers added, they were perfect gentlemen off the field "in most cases.")

Werber was married and was not a night owl or drinker. A movie, a milkshake, and in bed by 10:30 was a typical evening. Fifty years later he called the 1937 A's "the worst behaved ball club I was ever on, . . . a badly behaved group of young men that had their minds on things other than baseball."

Connie Mack knew who they were. The coaches, Lena Blackburne and Charlie Berry, knew who they were. As long as a player produced on the field, nothing was said. If he didn't, he was gone. Mack sometimes saved their necks. Werber recalled that several of the better players on the team picked up a painful venereal disease. Mack paid for their medical treatment and explained away their absences from the lineup to the public and their wives.

"He earned the players' gratitude and appreciation," Werber said. But they paid for it another way. "Those players whose marriages had been saved by Mr. Mack found it difficult to argue with him over salary when contract time came around."

Werber was working in his father's insurance agency, where, he boasted, he made more money than he did in baseball. He didn't need the money, but he was like every other player in one respect: he needed baseball. He loved the game.

While holdouts and salary squabbles are part of baseball, this shouldn't leave the impression that—at least in a bygone era—the game was all about money. Fifty years later Bill Werber summed it up: "I think the attitude of pretty much all the guys I played with was, 'Can you imagine getting paid for playing ball?' They all loved baseball and were really playing it more for fun than for money. They felt they should be paid and they argued for money, but money wasn't the great objective."

Whenever NL or AL officials talked about the coming season, they were always looking forward to gains at the gate and several contending teams—always "except in Philadelphia."

At the National League's insistence the season started a week later to escape the early April weather. It didn't work. The A's had six rainouts before they played six games. Sitting in his Brunswick Hotel suite in Boston on a wet April 28, Mack said, "I have kept close tabs on the weather and in the week before we could have played every afternoon. The National's idea to start the season later is out of line. It can be mild in April, cold and rainy in May. Starting late doesn't guarantee anything."

Bill Werber got off to a slow start, causing the Shibe Park faithful to yearn for the return of the steady Pinky Higgins. But the Athletics came out fighting. Although he dropped two foul pop-ups on opening day in Washington, Earle Brucker put the A's in first place by driving in the winning run in the tenth inning. (There were no other AL games that day.) They hadn't been on top of the standings since a one-day perch in 1932.

The old jokes were resurrected in the press boxes: "You can tell what month it is by looking at the AL standings. If the A's are in the first division it must be April."

To everyone's surprise, Mack's boys stayed near the top. Beginning on May 8, they won 4 straight in the West and found themselves in first place with a 10–5 record on May 11. Five of their 10 wins came from the seventh inning on. George Caster had won three starts and lost one.

It seemed like old times for Connie Mack when the Yankees came to town on Saturday, May 15. And it seemed that way to Philadelphia fans too. On Saturday more than seventeen thousand turned out to see the Yankees beat them, 6–5. Reminiscent of the good old days, the crowd began to fill the streets outside Shibe Park hours before the gates opened at noon on Sunday. A record 38,738 sat, stood, climbed on the girders, and hung from the rafters to watch the Yankees win, 8–4, knocking the Athletics out of first. New York's rookie right fielder, Tommy Henrich, was a former Cleveland farmhand whom Connie Mack had tried to sign when Judge Landis freed him because the Indians ordered the New Orleans club to transfer him to Milwaukee to avoid his being drafted after he hit .346 in '36. But Henrich's asking price of $40,000 was too steep for Mack. Henrich practically single-handedly wrecked them, driving in 3 runs on Saturday and 4 on Sunday. But the A's came back on Monday before 7,860, the largest Monday crowd in seven years. Lynn Nelson relieved Thomas in the first and shut out the Bronx Bombers the rest of the way, fanning Lazzeri, Gomez, and Crosetti on 10 pitches in the sixth en route to a 3–2 win.

The following Thursday a Ladies' Day crowd of over thirteen thousand, half of it women who paid only a fifteen-cent tax, saw them lose to Detroit and fall into a three-way tie with Cleveland and New York.

New York oddsmaker John Doyle told Grantland Rice of the *New York Tribune* that the A's had been picked to finish last. "A month's play is a pretty good test. The odds should have been about 50–1. Mack's campaign has been so far the outstanding feature in 1937 sports. When you come back that fast at the age of seventy-four you must have more than a hat full of stuff."

Were they playing over their heads? Probably. Did Connie Mack know it? Probably.

Mack believed the Yankees had the best pitching in the league and would repeat. He didn't expect his club's prosperity to last. But he wasn't prepared for the bottom to drop out. His boys remained on top until May 24. From then on, they didn't exactly skid; they free-fell without a parachute, losing 10 in a row to start a 5-41 collapse that sent them tumbling through the standings like a dropped brick, landing in the basement by July 1. Their hitting disappeared as suddenly and permanently as aviatrix Amelia Earhart. So did their brains.

After showing some promise in 1936, Herman Fink was of little use. Fink was a big Laurel and Hardy fan. But he didn't enjoy some of the Laurel and Hardy routines of the A's, which cost him a chance to pick up a win in relief on June 6 in Chicago. The visitors trailed, 6–4, in the ninth. Dean led off with a single. Lynn Nelson batted for Fink and walked. Jack Rothrock singled, scoring Dean and sending Nelson to third. Now it was 6–5, men on first and third, no outs. Wally Moses popped to second. Brucker hit a grounder to Zeke Bonura at first. Instead of starting a 3-6-3 double play, Bonura stepped on first, then threw to Luke Appling at second. Nelson was dawdling toward home. Rothrock, instead of pulling up and getting caught in a rundown to give Nelson time to score, raced headlong toward Appling and was tagged out before the nonchalant Nelson got anywhere near home plate.

After the game Jimmie Dykes said, "We played it terrible but they played it worse."

Suddenly Bill Werber's enthusiasm seemed to wilt, or maybe it was his secretly pain-weary legs that were wilting. In the first game of a Sunday doubleheader at Yankee Stadium on May 29 he half-heartedly waved at a grounder that went by him to keep a New York rally going. In the eighth inning Frank Crosetti pulled the old hidden ball trick on him as he led off second base.

Connie Mack benched him in the second game; no matter who you were, if you didn't hustle, you didn't play.

Grantland Rice called the collapse of the A's "startling" though not unexpected:

Somehow I don't think Connie was as surprised as most of the onlookers. Maybe rapidly he was reaching a state where he believed what he saw, too. But I gathered a little earlier in the campaign that he didn't have any great hope of this year's team, which isn't strange. He was disappointed in last year's team. I saw his '36 array in training and couldn't give it anything. I thought it found its level very shortly after the season opened and was somewhat amazed when on talking with Connie, I discovered he was shocked and hurt by the fact that his young men had wasted so little time before plunging into the second division. This year in spite of some improvement in the team, so few of the players have advanced, he apparently had no hope or prayer of getting anywhere.

The A's hit bottom and stayed there, finally finishing seventh because the Browns were so much worse. Mack's boys tried, but they were simply not major league caliber. The infield was shot, the outfield depleted. Two days after the All-Star Game, Skeeter Newsome was beaned by a spitball pitcher in a game in Bridgeton, New Jersey, and was out until mid-August. Mack recalled Ace Parker and tried out a Springfield College student at short. Frank Hayes had a broken finger. Bob Johnson was hurt. Jack Rothrock was ailing. Lynn Nelson patrolled the outfield until Mack claimed Jess Hill off waivers from Washington. Hill was a brief sensation, hitting over .400 for a few weeks before regressing to his norm.

The pitchers could go only so far before blowing up. A few times Mack used three pitchers, three innings each.

They were swept in 13 of the 32 doubleheaders they played and won only 3. Philly papers kept a headline in hot type: "A'S LOSE TWO."

Through it all, Connie Mack maintained his sense of humor. Bill Werber recalled, "One day Foxx was up for Boston and I expected a bunt in that situation and played in at third base and Foxx hit a line drive that went between my legs and tore the glove off my hand. It landed back on the dirt behind third base. I looked over at the bench and Mr. Mack was laughing."

At a time when cigarettes were jokingly called "coffin nails" but nobody really knew why (it would be another twenty years before the first reports linking smoking to lung cancer), Mack apparently tolerated players' smoking. On August 9 he wrote Sr. Florence:

Yours of August 3rd containing two large packages of cigarettes for our baseball boys received. One and all of them desire me to thank you greatly for the favor.

Yesterday our club surprised themselves by winning a doubleheader from St. Louis. When winning those two games, it must have come about by your having the packages of cigarettes on the way to our boys.

Earl and his family join with me in wishing you the very best of health, but don't get to high up in the clouds for the present at least. Wait for a few years longer, before going so high up that you will reach heaven, as I feel sure you will get there when your time comes.

Season highlights? Mighty few. August 13–15 the Athletics handed the Yankees their only 3-game sweep all year. On the fifteenth a Sunday single game drew an astounding crowd of 32,346 who witnessed one of the rarest events ever seen on a major league field: Joe DiMaggio made 2 errors in one game, responsible for 2 runs in the 5–4 loss. In the second, with Bob Johnson heading for third, DiMaggio wound up and threw the ball into the seats. In the third he dropped an easy fly ball off Johnson's bat, enabling Bill Werber to score. For the Yankees it was like the day a bar of Ivory soap sank at Procter & Gamble. For the Shibe Park fans it was the biggest opportunity to cheer all season, and they made the most of it.

The beneficiary was rookie lefty Edgar Smith, who won his first game of the year after 11 losses.

Mack believed his team had improved over last year—and it had—but at a pace that would take him ten years to be back in a pennant race. What did improve was home attendance, up a whopping 50 percent, the highest since 1931, despite the seventh-place finish and no real pennant race. The biggest boost came through large Sunday turnouts, half the fans coming from out of town.

There was money in the bank again for Connie Mack to spend. Baseball still belonged to the hitters. Mack's best pitcher, Edgar Smith, had the team's worst record. His ERA was below the 4.62 league average. He was third in fewest hits allowed per 9 innings. But he was 4-17 in the won-lost column. Harry Kelley had gone backward; his ERA soared 1.50 above last year. "He didn't look like the Kelley of '36," said Mack. "But he can pitch. And I expect him to be a winner in '38."

The A's showed a little more speed, actually leading the league with 95 stolen bases. Bill Werber tied Ben Chapman for the lead with 35.

And Wally Moses suddenly became a power hitter. He had 208 hits and scored 113 runs, with a career-high 48 doubles (only 3 behind the leader), 13 triples, and 25 home runs. How did that happen?

"When I reported late to spring training, Mack put two rookies, Luther Thomas and Al[mon] Williams, to pitching to me. I was a lowball hitter, but they were pitching me high and tight. I had to choke up on the bat about three inches, but I found I could pull the ball."

Chubby Dean started the season at first base. The improvement he had made in the field last year stalled at an inadequate level. His disposition never faded, but his hitting did. Toward the end of the season Mack suggested he go back to pitching and pinch-hitting. He made his first start on September 19, held Cleveland to 1 run and 2 hits for 6 innings before tiring in the seventh, and earned the 8–4 win over eighteen-year-old Bob Feller.

Mack had used four second basemen in 1936. The will and the effort had been there, but the results had fallen short. He would use four more in 1937 with the same results. One of them was Wayne Ambler, one of the athletes for whom Connie Mack paid his way through four years at Duke with no obligation to ever sign with him. Jack Coombs called Ambler the best college second baseman he had ever seen. Turning down a $5,000 bonus offer from a National League club, Ambler joined the A's after graduation and made his debut on June 4. Sixty years later Ambler told interviewer Jim Sargent, "Bill Cissell's idea of fun when he was on the road was to get with the cops and ride around to the bars and see what was going on. A couple days before I joined the club, Cissell took a knife away from some guy, blade-first. His hand was bandaged up. He was a tough guy and he was going to play. But Connie Mack started me."

Ambler hit well and fielded sensationally. His fancy glove work impressed old-timers Joe Tinker and Johnny Evers when they saw him in Chicago. Cissell became expendable and was returned to Baltimore a week later. (In the January 1937 balloting for the Hall of Fame, Cissell received one vote, a commentary more on the people doing the voting than on Cissell.) But Ambler was hampered first by a jammed thumb, then by a broken jaw in a collision at home plate. He returned to action in September, probably too soon, and didn't hit.

Mr. Mack remained calm and even-tempered. His approach to correcting mistakes never included a bawling out in the dugout. Instead the next day the trainer or a clubhouse man might ask the player, "If you have a minute, would you go up and see Mr. Mack?" Always a request, never an order or a demand.

In his office Mack would go over the play in question and the way it had been mishandled. He then suggested how it might have been better executed, ending with, "If that situation comes up again, would you have any objection to doing it my way?"

Mack was still searching for a first baseman. He had taken twenty-one-year-old Gene Hasson to Mexico City, but Hasson belonged to Williamsport. He was bought by the A's in September and joined the list of players who homered in their first big league at bat (on September 9 against Washington). Hasson batted .306 and played errorless ball in 28 games. Maybe the tall two-hundred-pound left-hander was the answer.

Connie Mack had acquired the stature that inspired older fans to recall when they had seen him play. One day an elderly man approached him in a Boston hotel lobby and said, "I remember seeing you play first base in Pittsburgh when you were 5 for 5 in a game the Pirates beat Washington, 17–0. Four of the hits were off Win Mercer and the fifth off Billy Lush."

"By golly," said the tickled Mack, "you should tell my boys what a good hitter I was."

(After forty years the man had it pretty close. The date was July 8, 1896; the score, 19–0. Mack was 4 for 6 off Mercer and Charlie Abbey, an outfielder like Lush, who replaced Mercer in the seventh Inning.)

Mack was also being increasingly mentioned in the obituary of anyone who had ever had any contact with him. However tenuous the connection or however acclaimed the deceased was in other fields, lines like "He once played for Connie Mack" or "He was a friend of Connie Mack" were often included.

A lengthy obituary in the *New York Times* of October 20, 1936, for Dr. Daniel A. Jones, a New Haven dentist and eminent singer, composer, and voice coach at Yale for fifty years who had pitched briefly in the American Association in 1886, devoted as much space to his friendship with Mack as it did to his extensive musical accomplishments:

Dr. Jones was graduated from Yale as Connie Mack began his professional career with the Meriden (Conn) club and was Mack's catcher [*sic*] for several amateur games. A friendship began that never ended.

The Athletics have always been Dr. Jones's patron team. He sat on the bench with Connie Mack whenever he visited Philadelphia or any city where they were playing, and he and Mack visited each other repeatedly.

Mack valued highly his judgment on the pitchers the Athletics developed.

A nineteenth-century ballplayer, Joseph V. Battin, who died December 10, 1937, claimed two distinctions: as the highest paid player of his time at $700 a month and as the man who "discovered" Connie Mack and recommended him to Washington.

The first claim may be true; the second is dubious. Battin did play against Mack in the Eastern League in 1886 and may well have had good things to say about him, but he certainly didn't discover him, and it's a stretch to say he "recommended" Mack to the son of the owner of the Washington club, who had gone to Hartford to buy some players and was subjected to a little arm-twisting to agree to take Mack along with three others.

Connie Mack's stomach bothered him during the Red Sox series August 17–19 at home. Perhaps the thrill of sweeping the Yankees' three-game series just before that was too much for him. The A's then went to New York to start a lengthy road trip. Mack wasn't well, but he fought it as they headed west. He didn't realize—or wouldn't give in to—how run down he really was.

On Sunday, August 29, at Chicago he enjoyed watching his boys set league records, scoring 12 runs in the first inning, in which Bob Johnson had 6 RBIs; he finished with 12 total bases. Bill Werber recalled Mr. Mack smiling and chortling as his boys circled the bases. "My goodness gracious," Mack said, "isn't this a wonderful game? My boys teach me something new every day."

Two days later they were in St. Louis.

Mack's St. Louis friend Parker Woods had a grandson, Randolph S. Lyon Jr., whose mother had remarried. Randolph's stepfather was George Jacoby, president of the Jacoby Marble Company in Philadelphia and a longtime friend of the Macks. The two connections provided Lyons with many opportunities to visit the Macks and be in the presence of Connie Mack in both places.

"We lived just three houses from the Macks," Lyon recalled. "When I was twelve and thirteen I spent many hours in his den on his leather ottoman. He talked baseball in his huge matching leather chair."

The fifteen-year-old Randolph was spending the summer with his grandfather. Whenever the A's were in St. Louis, they entertained "Uncle Connie," as Randolph called him. On one trip in July when Katherine Mack accompanied the team, Woods took them to a St. Louis Municipal Opera performance in Forest Park. It wasn't exactly Connie Mack's cup of tea, but he went along without complaint.

On Thursday, September 2, Woods, Jacoby, and Randolph went to the Park Plaza Hotel for lunch with Connie Mack. They were sitting at a table waiting for him when Doc Ebling came over and asked them to come up to Mr. Mack's room. They found Mack in bed, not moving, his face white as snow. "He lay almost like a skeleton under the sheets," recalled Randolph. "He looked like he wouldn't live out the day."

Mack rallied enough to get on a train and go home. Earle managed the team that afternoon and for the rest of the season. Reluctantly—"I didn't want to desert the team in the last month"—Mack acceded to his doctor's orders and his family's pleadings to stay home the rest of the year and listen to the games on the radio. "I guess I didn't realize how run down my condition had become," he told Bob Paul.

Mack was at Shibe Park for the Labor Day doubleheader against the Yankees but did not manage the team. Despite the pennant race being over and the A's being in seventh place, another throng of 38,183 turned out, the biggest crowd in the league that day. (Cleveland's total for the day was higher but for a morning-afternoon doubleheader.) The concession stands closed early when they ran out of everything. The A's lost both games, but they had the satisfaction of twice taking 3 in a row from the Yankees, first in August at Shibe Park and then in the last week of the season at Yankee Stadium, where Edgar Smith threw a 1-hitter in a 7-inning game.

In mid-September Roy said the family was not concerned about Connie Mack's health and he was not being attended by a doctor. On October 5 Mack went to a hospital for X-rays; nothing worrisome was found. He was suffering from what was called "a disorder of the stomach," which might have been a gall bladder attack.

Mack wanted to go to the all–New York World Series but was advised not to take on the chilly autumn weather. He stayed home, sunning himself on warm days on the porch. Will Harridge came to visit, as did Mack's longtime friend Bob Quinn, now running the Boston Bees. He did not resume work until October 26, and then not regularly until after a stay in Atlantic City in early November.

Mack passed up the minor league meetings in Milwaukee, which would have been a nostalgic visit for him. He had managed there for four years beginning in 1897. But he went to the league meeting in the first week of December, where, in a discussion of whether players optioned out and recalled at the end of the season should receive the major league salary they had signed for, Mack had not forgotten his days as a player:

I would like to have a little discussion of this with the members here. The way I feel about it is that any man who signs a contract, whether he signs for $1,000 or $5,000—and I do not care who the player is—I have been a player and we have some other members here who have been baseball players [Cochrane, Collins, and Griffith] and I doubt if anyone who signs a contract for $1,000 or $5,000 for the season of '38, he signs that contract in good faith. The player does and he expects that at the end of the year if he is playing ball to get that $1,000 or $5,000. That is what he is working for, and if he doesn't get it the club that is handling him is going to get a black eye. I say a black eye and that is one way of putting it. It doesn't just seem fair to the player.

On December 23 Mack was driven to Shibe Park by Connie Jr., accompanied by two doctors, and led to the visitors' dressing room, where the writers had laid out an elaborate buffet luncheon, complete with a big cake decorated with bats and balls made of sugar. A few days earlier Mack had learned from a distant relative who had dug into the family records that he had really been born on December 22, not 23. When asked about it, he chuckled and said, "I'll continue to call it the twenty-third. It makes me feel younger."

Mack's remarks at the party were briefer than usual. "Since my illness I have received hundreds of comforting letters from friends and strangers and I want to take this opportunity to thank them as it would be impossible for me to send a personal reply to all. I hope my Athletics team will reward the fans for their wonderful support last season by finishing higher in the race next year."

The event was broadcast on Stoney McLinn's one-hour *Hot Stove League on the Air* over WIP with Judge Harry S. McDevitt the emcee. Several hundred friends, newspapermen, and former players—including Harry Davis, Howard Ehmke, Rube Oldring, Jimmie Dykes, Lawton "Whitey" Witt, Chief Bender, Frank "Home Run" Baker, Amos Strunk, Bing Miller, Herb Pennock, and Rube Walberg—were present. Mack, wearing a sweater beneath his suit coat, lit up at the sight of so many reminders of his glory days.

Mack's brother Michael, eighty-three, was there. Friends he had known since his arrival in Philadelphia thirty-seven years ago were there. Managements of the Phillies and NFL Eagles were there. Among the telegrams awaiting him were greetings from President Roosevelt and Vice-President Garner. It was as if they had all come to say goodbye—a living wake. His pale face and evident frailty gave credence to the belief of many present that Connie Mack would not survive another season.

In fact he had had his own doubts about seeing another season when he had come home in September.

"I think I may die," he told Connie Jr. from his sickbed.

"And indeed," his son recalled, "he looked like a skeleton."

Family members urged him to cut back, maybe manage the team just at home and let Earle take over for the grueling road trips.

But one of Connie Mack's dominant traits was stubbornness. All his life he had refused to budge in defense of a principle. He had been that way over a $75 difference with Pete Husting in Milwaukee in 1900, with Frank Baker in 1915, and in the Scott Perry case in 1918. Now he dug in his heels against time and infirmity.

When President Roosevelt had tried to make over the Supreme Court to his liking by imposing a retirement age of seventy, Connie Mack was asked what he thought of that. It might apply to an average for a group of men, he said, where some might start to slip at sixty-five and others not until they're in their eighties. But it didn't mean all men should retire at seventy, and it certainly didn't apply to him. He was looking forward to building another pennant winner. "Shucks," he said, "I don't feel old."

That was back in February. Now he told Red Smith:

I'm seventy-five because the calendar says so. If there weren't any calendars I'd be twenty-five or fifty. I don't feel any different than I did then and it's such a little time I've been around.

It's only when a man gets sick and down that his age counts. I've been sick and I realize that now. For the first time in my life I show my age, but I don't feel it. My goodness, it would go hard with me if anything happened and I couldn't be at the park every day. I doubt that I could take that.

You know, I still get the same kick out of baseball that I did as a boy up in East Brookfield. I still like to travel. Why, if we're only going to a nearby town for a little exhibition game, I want to go along.

In the July 1932 issue of the *Rotarian* Mack had said, "I will retire when my health demands it." With the past season bracketed by hospitalization in the spring and a lengthy convalescence from a stomach disorder in the fall, his health seemed to be demanding it.

He wasn't listening.

8 | THE ROOTS OF FAILURE

At seventy-five, Connie Mack could talk all he wanted about being young in spirit, but his body was old—the life expectancy in 1937 was fifty-eight for white males—and it was giving him a warning: slow down. But those who urged him to leave the dugout and stick to office duties were missing the point of Connie Mack's life: the game itself; the challenge of judging players' abilities and putting together the pieces of the jigsaw puzzle of a championship club; directing the action on the field; the company of younger men; the travel.

Mack still believed he was learning and improving as a manager with each year's experience. He wasn't stuck in the mode of how the game was played twenty years ago. Younger managers weren't outsmarting him. He was still an acute observer and strategist and knew the rules better than some umpires. His kindness and patience still earned him the respect of his players, who were young enough to be his grandsons. He enjoyed the challenge of working with them, counseling, teaching, and rooting for them to succeed.

The fact is that no man ever enjoyed his life's work more than Mr. Mack day in and day out: the annual cycle of league meetings; spring training; Pullman cars and hotel rooms and interviews and recognition and applause wherever he went; the World Series; and friends everywhere. No way was he going to give that up.

But Connie Mack and the Athletics had two weaknesses that together marked the beginning of the end of the business he had founded thirty-seven years ago. One lay in Mack's reluctance to get on board baseball's train to the future because he didn't like the direction it was going: the farm system. The other was that the Athletics' operation was a one-man band.

Over the years Mack had relied on informal agreements under which he would send a few players to a minor league club in exchange for a promise that he would be given first pick of one or two men from the club's roster at the end of the season. That's how he had bought Frank Baker from Reading in 1908. He had strong ties with Jack Dunn in Baltimore and Charlie Frank, first in New Orleans, then Atlanta, resulting in plenty of player traffic in both directions. That hardly made those clubs Athletics' farm teams.

There was a risk in optioning players to minor league clubs that the A's didn't control: managers could use them as little or as much as they wanted, sometimes giving more playing time to players the club owned and hoped to sell.

But Mack was trapped in his long-standing belief that the farm system was detrimental to minor league clubs, a sentiment shared by Ban Johnson, Clark Griffith, and Commissioner Landis: "I fought against other than hometown ownership of minor league clubs for years," Mack told Bob Paul. "I was of the opinion that absent ownership ruined interest in any team and robbed the town of civic pride in the success of its players. But it looks now as though fans in most minor league cities want a connection with a big league club."

In 1933 the Atlanta Crackers were considering hooking up with a major league team after suffering through a few second-division seasons. The Crackers' chairman, Hughes Spalding, had sought out Connie Mack's advice at the 1933 World Series in Washington. Mack told him it would not be to the club's advantage to do so. Spalding took his advice, and the Atlanta club operated independently, winning pennants while developing and selling players, with great success for another sixteen years.

A few years later the management of Coca-Cola, which owned the Crackers, was interested in selling the team. Correspondence indicates it may have offered it to Mack for $500,000. He had neither the money nor the inclination to buy it.

In fact Mack had once bought a minor league club, in 1929. As a favor to a longtime friend connected with the Martinsburg, West Virginia, team in the Blue Ridge League, he had agreed to take over the team when it was about to fold. Mack had chosen a veteran minor league manager he respected as a teacher and developer of young players, Dan O'Leary, and sent a rookie outfielder, Roger Cramer, to him. (The club folded after the season; the league followed a year later.)

Mack was also hesitant because he recognized the peril of conflicting priorities for minor league managers in pennant-chasing versus player development:

Minor league fans now have the idea that a parent club can rush needed playing strength in an emergency or send a couple of men to keep the team in the thick of the pennant race. The desire for a winner has surpassed the old urge for the development of hometown talent.

There's one danger that must be avoided in a farm system. You must select a manager of a Class C, D, or E team who is capable of patiently developing youngsters. Every manager likes to be a winner. And every fan, no matter where he lives, wants his hometown team to be a champion. But this often leads to managers overworking or rushing their young players when they should be brought along slowly in order that all faults may be corrected.

Minor league managers are partly to blame. They feel their future depends on winning a pennant so they refuse to spend much time developing youngsters who have enough natural ability to win for him. They're satisfied so long as they deliver. They send youngsters up to the majors who can hit or pitch but are totally lacking in a knowledge of the game's fundamentals. They come to us without having learned the value of reasoning out in advance what to do with the ball if hit to them.

In 1939 Mack pointed out this conflict in priorities as a reason the Yankees were en route to their fourth consecutive world championship: "With the Yankees it's different. Their minor league managers know they're expected to develop players. They can afford to go along with a promising boy, teaching him the things which will enable him to step right into the Yankees' lineup once he's called to New York. You don't see Keller, Gordon, Rosar, and others pulling dumb plays. They know what to do with the ball every time it comes to them, and they've even figured out what to do if they fumble it. That's why the Yanks are marching on to another pennant."

Mack had felt the effects of the change in the map of player control while seeking help during the past season. It used to be that when he needed replacements, he could turn to his friends throughout the minors for help. Now many of those friends had been absorbed into major league organizations. In building his last great team, Mack had paid big prices for minor league stars: Simmons, Bishop, Boley, Cochrane, Grove, Walberg, Earnshaw. Now the best of the minor leaguers were no longer available to him; they were being promoted to play against him. His shopping was limited to the shrinking number of independent clubs and prospecting among the college and semipro ranks. Mack's college boys gave him all they had, but they lacked the experience to cope with pitchers who had spent several years learning their craft in the minors. In August he had sent Earle on a two-week scouting trip that turned up nobody who could help them. It wasn't a lack of money or willingness to spend it. The A's were finally showing a profit. Over the next two years Mack would spend more than $200,000 for a dozen or so players. Philadelphia fans caught a brief glimpse of some of them. The rest never made it into a big league box score.

Even Earle Mack, filling in as manager during his father's illness in 1939, would be frustrated by the meager returns on the outlay. One afternoon after a 9-run ninth-inning uprising by the Indians had beaten him, 12–8, Earle indirectly and uncharacteristically criticized his father to Frank Yeutter of the *Bulletin* by ticking off the amounts paid for players. "All for what? To stay in the class with the St. Louis Browns and the Washington Senators. . . . We're still tail enders."

Connie Mack finally conceded, "For a club like the A's to obtain young players in the coming years it looks as though we'll have to follow the farm-system policy of the others."

Everybody in the league had a head start. In 1935 the Yankees had six farm clubs, four of them owned or controlled. The Athletics had none. Two years later the rest of the AL clubs' affiliates ranged from Chicago's six to the Yankees' fifteen or sixteen. Even the lowly St. Louis Browns had fourteen. The Cardinals were far ahead of everybody with thirty in 1937, twelve of them owned outright. The Athletics had just three working agreements—Class A Williamsport and Class D Federalsburg and Lexington.

Mack was enthusiastic about the expansion of the minor leagues, which gave him plenty of opportunities to get into the farming business. A record 3,490 players, 50 percent more than a year ago, had been reserved by minor league clubs for 1938. Mack said, "I don't know how many boys I had to turn aside since 1932 because there was no place for them to develop. Good boys, too; boys who today might have been in the majors had they been given the proper training and coaching. Gosh, it certainly was a pity that so many minor leagues folded up during the Depression. . . . The splendid comeback of older minor leagues and the rapid expansion of Class D and Class E [created but never used] leagues creates a healthy condition all down the baseball line."

Mack had a sterling reputation among minor league operators, providing uniforms and equipment when asked, visiting them to play exhibition games, and charging nothing but his travel costs. He would have had no difficulty forming solid working agreements or buying into clubs. There were plenty of Mack's former players who would have eagerly signed on to manage minor league teams, understanding that their job was to teach the "Connie Mack Way" at every level and only secondarily to win pennants.

But to build a formidable farm system, Mack needed a farm director, backed by a commitment to invest what it would take to operate minor league clubs—seldom profitably—and build a scouting staff adequate to supply them. Once upon a time he had been noted for the number of players he had "strings on," but those were the days when a dozen was a lot. The concept of keeping track of hundreds of players being taught by dozens of managers—the farm system on the Branch Rickey or George Weiss scale—was beyond Mack's imagination or desire or physical capacity. Besides, Rickey and Weiss had no on-field duties. Rickey was fifty-six; Weiss was forty-two. As for a scouting department, the A's had a few bird dogs but only two scouts—Phil Haggerty and Ira Thomas, and only Haggerty went on the road; Thomas spent most of his time helping to run Mack's baseball schools. Mack would sometimes press Earle or Lena Blackburne or an injured player into scouting duties. There was no way they could adequately cover the expanding minor leagues. Mack acknowledged in a letter to a man in Columbus who wrote to him about a teenage prospect that "it is very difficult to have our scouts contact all the players recommended to us."

Connie Mack needed a Billy Evans (Eddie Collins had snagged him to be the Red Sox farm director in 1936) or a Clarence "Pants" Rowland— the kind of men who were experienced in every aspect of the game, were well known throughout baseball, and had enormous respect for him. After Mickey Cochrane was fired as the Detroit manager in 1938, he would be out of baseball for ten years. He would have been happy to return to the A's in a front office capacity. Even the threadbare Phillies were ahead of Mack, hiring veteran pitcher and Baltimore general manager John Ogden as their farm director in 1940.

But Mack did nothing. For the next two years he stayed with the same three working agreements. And for the next ten years he relied primarily on two scouts (when Phil Haggerty died in 1941, Harry O'Donnell, a Baltimore scout for nine years, replaced him), sometimes augmented by Chief Bender and Eddie McLaughlin and a few part-timers; his volunteer bird dogs; and college coaches Jack Coombs at Duke, Chick Galloway at Presbyterian College, and Jack Barry at Holy Cross, who steered their best players to him.

It took Mack until the fall of 1939 to concede that he had to join the farm movement in earnest. "We can't win otherwise," he told Cy Peterman. "We can no longer develop those young players on a small club because we can't find [minor league operators]—to put it bluntly—who are willing to lose money in our behalf. By this I simply mean the major club sooner or later will own one AA, one A, one B, and several Class D clubs, and no longer depend on others to shoulder these minor league risks."

On October 17, 1939, the A's joined local backers to buy the Wilmington franchise in the newly reorganized Class B Interstate League. Chief Bender managed the Blue Rocks until June, when Charlie Berry took over. Mack expanded his working agreements to Class C Saginaw and AA Toronto.

(In November 1944 Mack negotiated to buy the American Association Minneapolis franchise from longtime owner Mike Kelley. They agreed on the price, but according to Kelley, "The terms of payment I insisted on were not agreeable to Mack." The A's would never own a minor league club above Class A.)

It would take until 1947 for the Athletics to hire a farm director and 1950 before they had a general manager.

The Athletics' other weakness was the front office—or lack of one. The deaths of Tom and John Shibe left a void that remained unfilled. Tom had been influential in American League matters for decades and had been Mack's closest and most trusted confidant since the death of Ben Shibe fifteen years ago. John had been well connected in state political circles and was responsible for the care and maintenance of Shibe Park and the operation of the concessions. Now all of the increasingly more complex aspects of the business of baseball—installation of lights for night games, negotiation of radio contracts, dealing with league and legal and political matters, making spring training arrangements, Shibe Park renovations—fell on Mack's self-described "hatrack shoulders" in addition to the drafting, acquiring, and signing of players; making too many appearances at lunches, dinners, award ceremonies, and the like; and all while managing the team through a 154-game season—at a time in his life when he had missed the last month of the 1937 season owing to a serious illness that was begging him to cut back.

"I don't know how one man could run the park and the club all by himself," Mack's daughter Ruth said. "I loved my dad very much and as close as I was to him I could never understand how he accepted all that psychological weight of responsibility and constant work and worry without ever a complaint. He was very human and like us all not perfect all the time, but he did a better job of it than anyone I ever knew."

But Mack didn't see it as a burden. It was his life. He had been doing it all since his days in Milwaukee forty years ago. He enjoyed being immersed in every aspect of the business that had to do with the players. He couldn't do all the scouting himself, but he could tell his scouts what he wanted them to look for and where to look.

Year after year into the 1940s, the Athletics were the only team with just two names listed in the league's official management directories: Connie Mack and Roy Mack.

In effect, Connie Mack was solely responsible for everything that Jake Ruppert, Ed Barrow, George Weiss, and Joe McCarthy combined did for the Yankees or Tom Yawkey, Eddie Collins, Billy Evans, and Joe Cronin did in Boston.

He filled every one of these roles full-time as if each were his only job.

Here he is as farm director:

The Athletics took over the Newport News franchise in the Class C Virginia League in 1941. Chief Bender managed the club that year. There was a twenty-six-year-old catcher at Williamsport in the Eastern League named Harry Chozen, who wanted to be a manager. He wrote to Connie Mack and, with a boost from the league president, Tommy Richardson, got the Newport News job for '42. It paid $400 a month.

On December 31 Connie Mack wrote Chozen a letter, listing the players on the Newport News roster and others who might come from Wilmington or Federalsburg. The letter reminded Chozen of the league's salary limit ($1,300 a month, equal to $85 per player). The A's minor league players would train at Rock Hill, South Carolina. Chozen recalled:

Mr. Mack wrote to me once or twice a week during the entire season. He wanted our daily attendance figures and reports on my players and others in the league. He told me about players he was sending me, who to suspend to make room on the roster to give somebody a look, commented on how we were doing in the standings, apologized for having no pitching help to send me—no detail was too small for his attention. He'd tell me he was sending me a second baseman from Lancaster and to play my present second baseman at shortstop. He'd send me a pitcher and say, "He needs some money so take care of him," stuff like that, sometimes two or three letters in as many days, with his team at home or on the road.

Chozen went to spring training with the A's in Anaheim in 1942. Along with his other activities, Mack found time to give him some advice on managing: "When there's 10,000 people in the stands and you go out to take a pitcher out and they start booing, remember, 300 people can boo you. The other 9,700 people can be for you, but you'll only hear the 300 booing you. Isn't that a good percentage that are for you?"

And "You're always going to be short of pitching. I want you to try to win whenever you can, but don't sacrifice tomorrow's game to keep the fans off you today. Don't use a good pitcher that you need tomorrow in a lost game today. Leave the pitcher in there. Whether you get beat 1–0 or 18–0, it only counts as one loss. The fans are entitled to as good as you can give them."

And "Every player is a different person. Some need to be patted, some kicked in the pants, and some need to be left alone. As you get more experienced, you'll know. Usually your first guess is the best one. Don't second-guess yourself. You'll make a lot of mistakes but you'll know it quicker than the people who will criticize you."

Harry Chozen's brother Bobby, an infielder, was invited to spring training for a tryout. Mack signed Bobby and suggested he go to Newport News. It was a mistake, recalled Harry. "Bobby played shortstop and the fans rode him terribly. One day I was coaching third base and the fans got on him so bad I went over to the stands and blew my top. Mr. Mack called me. 'Harry, we're more interested in your career. I don't believe Bobby's ever going to be a major league player. For your good, wait a week then release him. I'll send him a check for a full year's salary.'"

Mack followed that with a letter the next day:

At times we all make mistakes, and also get pretty sore when fans go out of their way to ride us. But don't worry on that score. Have arranged to have a player named Harry Eischen join you this week. He can play the infield, shortstop is his position, and would first play him in that position. Don't pay any further attention to some knockers. Just get the team back on its feet. Would advise getting the boys together and give them a real talk. Would advise under the circumstances to release your brother and send him home, pay his transportation. In doing this you will satisfy some of the knockers. Will give you the salary and bonus you will pay Eischen in a day or two.

Mack kept track of everything and overlooked nothing. On the road in Boston, he wrote to Chozen: "Be sure and call in Weaver [and] also the other boy you have out [on option]. While they may go into the army, will return some day at least hope so. One hundred won't break us. [It cost $100 to exercise an option to recall a player.]"

Chozen was trying to make the playoffs by finishing fourth (he did). On August 19 the A's were in Washington, and Mack was taking care of minor league business. He sent Chozen a telegram: "Will try to get player. Until then do best you can. Best wishes."

Mack brought his team to Newport News for an exhibition game. The ballpark was sold out. "Mr. Mack said he needed the money and took all the receipts," said Chozen. Using an old trick he'd learned from minor league manager Blackie O'Rourke, two weeks before the game Chozen put three dozen baseballs in an icehouse. "A week before, I took them out and let them thaw. It loosened the yarn. The A's hit a bunch of fly balls to the outfield and complained that the ball didn't carry in Newport News. They beat us, 3–2."

On September 30 Mack wrote to him:

Dear Harry:

Suppose you will be listening in on the World Series today. Would like your opinion of the players in the Virginia League. How do you like Fagan of Pulaski [a 20-12 pitcher]? How does he compare with [Don] Black of Petersburg [15-11]? Are they the outstanding pitchers in the league? Was in hope I could hear of some prospect as an infielder. How about outfielder and catcher? Am giving you quite a job in answering about players. Not easy to recommend players. The war makes quite a difference as to what we want and what we must take in order to have a team. Would like to get a team of young players but know this will be impossible. Hope you will have a fine winter.

Best wishes.

The Virginia League disbanded after the 1942 season, and Connie Mack never employed Harry Chozen again. But he kept in touch with him. In 1944

Chosen asked Mack to help his brother get into the navy's V-12 training program. Mack took the time on opening day to write him a note:

Dear Harry:

You can be assured I will do all that is necessary for your brother when called upon. Starting our season about one hour from now. As the day is pretty chilly am waiting for last minute in going out. Will no doubt be an odd year. Team looks better but so much depends on what can happen in a few days.

Mack contacted the secretary of the navy, and Bobby was accepted for the program.

"I never was an important person in baseball," Harry Chozen recalled, "but here was Connie Mack writing to me during the season about different players, expressing interest in the daily attendance figures—a major league manager writing regularly to a Class C manager. He was truly his own farm director."

Even when he was past eighty, Connie Mack was still trying to handle four full-time jobs. He needed help. He didn't seek it.

There were two reasons. He was stubborn, refusing to concede that time would or could erode his capabilities. His attitude continued to be: I'm a year older. I learn something every year. Therefore, I am better at my job than I was a year ago. And he still thought of the Athletics as a family business—the Shibes and the McGillicuddys. The idea of bringing in anyone from outside the family was anathema to him. For all his public statements of confidence in Roy and Earle, in the privacy of his mental scale they didn't measure up.

Earle was a baseball lifer, at home in the dugout or the bullpen or the coach's box. The players didn't pay much attention to him. When he would go to the mound and the infielders gathered around and he told the pitcher, "Daddy thinks we should make a change," sometimes the pitcher would tell him, "Go back and tell Daddy to go to hell," knowing full well he'd go back to the dugout and say only, "He won't come out." And Connie Mack would say, "Then leave him in."

Wartime shortstop Irv Hall put it more bluntly: "We always thought that Earle didn't know what town he was in."

The press didn't have a high regard for Earle. Al Horwits's son Skip related this story, indicative even if apocryphal:

> The writers were gagsters. They knew that Earle was a fidgety, nervous person. The A's were on their way back from spring training in California and they stopped in Kansas City for a game. That night my dad and a few others found a shop that printed newspaper headlines to order on a Kansas City newspaper format. They had a headline made that said: "Earthquake Expected" and put the paper in front of Earle's door. He was up early, opened the door, and picked up the paper. He packed his stuff and was on his way out of town when Mr. Mack stopped him and said, "Earle, they're playing a joke on you again."

Roy, forty-nine, now vice-president and secretary, had never been more than a minor league functionary, a back office man, with no vision or experience when it came to players or scouting.

Neither of the sons enjoyed anything close to the respect and devotion the players and club employees and sportswriters had for their father. In a later candid interview with historian William Marshall, columnist Red Smith said of Roy and Earle, "They were really stupid guys."

Connie Jr., twenty-five, was the assistant concessions director, still too young and inexperienced to take a leading role (and Roy would, to put it mildly, have been no ally of his "little half-brother"). Young Connie was the best and the brightest of the new blood and the most popular among the park employees.

Ed "Dutch" Doyle, a scorecard vendor in his youth, explained:

> Connie Jr. looked out for his boys. For doubleheaders they had to put on extra help in the concession stands between games. Where did they get the help? Connie always gave the jobs to the cushion boys because he knew they didn't make much money. For twenty minutes in the concession stands we got three dollars, a lot of money. If it rained, they gave us three dollars to help pull the tarp on the field.
>
> Everybody who worked there got a five dollar bonus at Christmastime. This was before people ever heard of bonuses. [Bob Schroeder and young Connie] did anything they could for the little guys. They were great guys.

Connie Jr. would have done well starting out under an experienced baseball person creating a farm system and working his way up. He never got the chance.

The Shibe side was pretty thin. Ben Shibe's grandson, Frank Macfarland, had a job in the office. Frank's younger brother, Benny, was being groomed to replace Rudy Ohl as traveling secretary. No presidential or general manager or farm director material there.

The sons of the founders could handle some of the business side—the concessions and stadium maintenance and travel arrangements and the like. But nothing to do with the baseball side.

New York columnist Jimmy Cannon once wrote, "Is a man fortunate who lives so long that the years make him a stranger in the time of his life?"

At seventy-five, Connie Mack remained a one-man show—a one-old-man show—in a business that was rapidly becoming corporate.

9 | THUNDER IN THE PRESS

In the spring of 1938 there were rumbles of thunder in the distance. Germany claimed Czechoslovakia and picked up its option on the city of Danzig. Austria was in the process of forfeiting to Hitler. The Japanese overran China, and they weren't scouting for baseball players.

Heartened by a pickup in the American economy, President Roosevelt had cut back on stimulus measures. This move proved to be premature; the economy went into a tailspin in 1938. Unemployment went back up to 19 percent, and factory output dropped back to 1934 levels.

With it all, the feds estimated that $600 million would be spent on sporting events and movies for the year, two-thirds of it on tickets selling for forty cents or less, with the government reaping about $18 million from its 10 percent tax on tickets over forty cents.

When the Athletics advertised for a trainer to replace Doc Ebling, they received more than one thousand applications, a number of physicians among them. Jim Tadley, who had intended to fill in just during spring training, took on the full-time duties. The club also enlisted a new team physician who became Connie Mack's personal doctor.

Born in Russia in 1899, Dr. Ilarion I. Gopadze was an officer on a White Russian military mission to Ankara, Turkey, when the Bolsheviks gained control of his hometown, Tiflis, Georgia, in 1921. He never returned and made his way to America, interning in Philadelphia in 1930. Two years later he joined the student health service at Penn and became the football team doctor. He was a sturdy six feet tall with a robust mustache, a formal but friendly "all-business" bearing, and an accent he never lost. He would remain the Athletics' doctor for seventeen years.

In 1936, 226 members of the Baseball Writers Association had cast the first ballots for players to be honored in a new baseball hall of fame to be built in Cooperstown, New York. Five players picked up the required 75 percent vote: Babe Ruth, Honus Wagner, Ty Cobb, Christy Mathewson, and Walter Johnson. No vote was unanimous.

A year later three more were added: Napoleon Lajoie, Tris Speaker, and Cy Young. Grover Alexander was elected in 1938, George Sisler, Eddie Collins, and Willie Keeler in 1939. The Hall would be dedicated on June 12, 1939.

The magnates meeting in Chicago on December 7, 1937, decided that this kind of recognition should not be limited to players. So at the same time that they voted to spend $100,000 to commemorate the 1939 spurious but convenient one hundredth anniversary of baseball's creation in Cooperstown, the two leagues added five of their pioneers "for their inspiration to baseball in its early years": George Wright, last survivor of the first professional team, the Cincinnati Red Stockings of 1869; Morgan G. Bulkeley, first president of the National League; Ban Johnson, founder of the American League; John McGraw; and Connie Mack. (Why George Wright and not his brother Harry, who had organized and managed the Red Stockings and managed in the National League during its first eighteen years of existence, they didn't say. Harry had to wait until 1953.)

In other AL business, only Ruppert and Mack favored lifting the player limit from twenty-three to twenty-five. A motion to raise visiting clubs' batting practice time from twenty to thirty minutes followed by ten minutes of fielding practice was defeated, 5–3.

In the middle of January 1938 Mack felt well enough to begin going to the office every day, but he didn't have to climb the two flights of stairs to get to the tower. A temporary office was set up on the ground floor for him. The need for an elevator to the tower was obvious; within a few months it was installed.

One month after his December birthday party Connie Mack astonished those who had been there and were among the thousand attending the baseball writers' dinner on January 25. (Since the economy had gone south, these dinners no longer began with oysters and ended with champagne.) Mack's stamina—he spoke for forty-five minutes—memory, and enthusiasm showed no hint of how ill he had been. Looking forward to spring training was apparently some kind of tonic, a magic bullet, for Mack. But he paid a price. The evening took a lot out of him.

After calling the guest of honor, Joe DiMaggio, the best young player to come along in many years, Mack recognized several members of his 1910 champions in the audience and spun yarns of their long-ago triumph over the Cubs in the World Series.

Perhaps Mack's praise of DiMaggio went to the young star's head. Soon he would draw boos from all over the country for demanding a $40,000 salary. So what if he had led the league in home runs and slugging and driven in 167 runs in his second year? It had taken Lou Gehrig a dozen outstanding years to reach $36,000. Lou was still the team leader. Who did the uppity kid from San Francisco think he was?

DiMaggio held out until after opening day, then signed for $25,000.

Although Mexican officials urged Connie Mack to return for spring training, he said adios to south of the border and headed back to familiar grounds: Lake Charles, Louisiana. The A's had trained there in 1920 and '21 and had drawn well. The bass fishing was good. The Giants, always a good attraction, would be nearby in Baton Rouge. The first game against the Giants on March 5, a homer-rife 11–10 game played in a gale that ended in a downpour, drew an overflow crowd of 3,500.

With his traveling partner Tom Shibe gone and still not up to full strength himself, Mack sent Earle, Lena Blackburne, Charlie Berry, and Bill McCalley to Lake Charles to take care of hotel and playing field arrangements. McCalley scattered grass seed over the dirt infield at American Legion Park and had it ready to mow when the pitchers and catchers and Connie Mack, accompanied by Mrs. Mack and their eighteen-month-old grandson, Frank Cunningham, arrived on Monday, February 21.

Looking frail and gaunt when he left Philadelphia, bundled in a heavy overcoat against the damp cold air, Mack was uncertain if he would feel strong enough to direct the practices when he arrived. But during the forty-hour train ride, he was his usual optimistic self. He had won a bidding war for Oakland second baseman Dario Lodigiani and hoped that would solve one of his major problems. A sandlot teammate of Joe DiMaggio in San Francisco, Lodigiani was twenty-one, had hit .325, and had been sought by several clubs. Mack sent outright and by option five players and $10,000 to the Oaks.

Mack served the traveling writers what had become his annual mix of spring greens: 40 percent hope, 40 percent hype, 20 percent reality:

I'm going to try to put a team on the field that will fight in every game. The fans gave us wonderful support last year and I'm going to see if I can't get a team that has a chance to win every game we might play. I base my claim for improvement on a much tighter infield. This year we'll have the services of first baseman Gene Hasson from the start. If there is a better fielder at that position in the majors I have never heard of him. Second base was a sieve all last season. I think we will be far stronger there with Dario Lodigiani. With Bill Werber at third and either Newsome or [Irv] Bartling at short, the infield ought to be fifty percent better than last year. My outfield is already set. The pitching should be stronger than last year.

A few days in the sun seemed to revitalize Mack. He even gained a few pounds. "Just to be with the young ballplayers again and watch them perform has been a help and a cure," he said.

He abandoned full-day workouts and split the players into two groups. One practiced in the morning, the other in the afternoon. Only Mack and the coaches were on the field all day.

His illness had not sapped his spirit. He bantered with the press, posed for hokey photos, put on a lively demonstration of a first baseman's fielding faults. Nor had he lost a step mentally. In an exhibition game against Cleveland, with writers and visitors sharing the bench with the team, Lynn Nelson was pitching. A ball was hit back to him on the mound. Nelson bobbled it and couldn't make the play. The writers speculated about how and why he had messed up the play. Mack said quietly, "That ball was hit harder than Nelson thought."

When the inning was over, an embarrassed Nelson came to the bench and said, "That ball was hit harder than I thought it was."

In Biloxi, where the A's beat the Phillies, 21–8, in a game described as the kind "the leans and fats play at the boilermakers' picnic," writers covering both teams gathered around Connie Mack that evening in the hotel lobby. Like children begging to be told the same story they'd heard a thousand times, the writers urged Mack to tell them about George Edward "Rube" Waddell. Mack told the stories so many times, it's no wonder the details varied over the years. When Lena Blackburne asked for the Punxsatawney story—the trip to that Pennsylvania town to bring Rube to Milwaukee, paying off Rube's debts, getting him on the train—Mack apologized for repeating the much-told tale but clearly enjoyed the telling as much as his audience lapped up the listening.

This was the first year that Lena Blackburne provided the solution to the slick surface of brand new baseballs. He lived in Riverside, New Jersey; the river beside the town was the Delaware. Blackburne decided the gooey stuff on the muddy river bottom near its shores would make an ideal replacement for the dirt and tobacco juice mix used by umpires to take the shine off the balls. He scooped out some of the mud, cleaned out the pebbles and shells, added a secret ingredient to smooth it out, and sold it to each club. The same substance is still used by umpires (or the custodian of the umpires' dressing room) to rub up a few dozen balls before every game.

Mule Haas, released by the White Sox, rejoined the A's family as a player/coach for his last active season. He was still spry and mouthy, but his batting eye was gone. Used primarily as a pinch hitter, he was 1 for 20 in that role. Haas would do more coaching at third base than Earle Mack, who sometimes confused base runners. Earle was "very excitable," they complained. "You never knew where he was when he was waving you home." Earle took the lineup to home plate and went to the mound when a pitching change was ordered; otherwise he sat in the dugout, chewing on a toothpick or match, drawing his $5,000 a year. The players liked him; he'd have a beer with them and didn't act like the boss's son. But they never saw him as managerial material. Still, Earle did have his supporters. Bob Paul believed he had done a good job in the closing weeks of the '37 season and deserved the chance to succeed his father—if that day ever came.

As the weeks went by, Connie Mack didn't like what he saw at Lake Charles. Too many players were showing up late for breakfast. None of the rookies in camp impressed Mack. At least one of them tried. One night a recruit pitcher spotted Mack and Lena Blackburne in conversation in the hotel lobby. He sat down beside Mack and said, "You don't mind if I help you think, do you?"

Mack said, "You better think about getting in shape."

Bill Dooly reported that early in the season the same rookie told Mack, "I haven't been able to do much pitching lately, but I think I'm ready to go now." To which Mack replied, "Yes, I think you are. You're going to Trenton."

The pitcher was probably lefty Bill Kalfass, a twenty-one-year-old from New York City who had won his first start at the end of last season and never won another.

Every spring training produces its positive and negative surprises. The positives were scarce this spring. Harry Kelley pitched 5 complete games in March and figured to be the ace of the staff. Lou Finney had been surgically renovated over the winter, gained weight, and looked fit. Dividing his time between first base and the outfield, he would pop a surprising 10 home runs.

On the minus side, Frank Hayes seemed to have gone backward as a catcher. He no longer welcomed advice. And he had become a boozer. Some of the pitchers preferred working with the veteran Earle Brucker. Gene Hasson turned out to be Mack's latest late-season call-up who sizzled in the fall and fizzled in the spring. He had impressed Mack with his flawless fielding and 3 home runs in 28 games in September. Now he reported overweight and seemed to have grown surplus thumbs over the winter. He had apparently succumbed to the "I've got it made" nonchalance induced by his impressive debut. He made 5 errors in the first 18 games, went three days without an error because it rained, then made 2 more in a 9–5 loss to the Browns on May 11. Mack gave up on him; at twenty-two Hasson was gone from the bigs, never to return. Dario Lodigiani was nervous and lacked confidence; the fear of failure seemed to hang over his every time at bat.

Raw as they were, Mack expected they would have shaped up by the time they broke camp and headed for New Orleans. But they hadn't.

"If they have anything," he said, "I have still to find it."

He did see one player he liked—on another team. The A's played several games against Beaumont, a Detroit farm club, whose twenty-one-year-old outfielder Barney McCosky wore out Mack's pitchers. Mack asked Tigers scout Wish Egan, who had signed McCosky, to name his price. Egan said, "No way. He's a Detroit boy and he's going to play for us."

Wally Moses didn't draw the attention that beleaguered Joe DiMaggio. But he was just as adamant a holdout in the spring of 1938. He had become a home run threat in '37, outhit Bob Johnson, and tied him for team leadership in home runs. He covered more ground than Johnson but didn't have the arm. He believed his third-year performance entitled him to a big boost in pay. Last year he had gone from $5,500 to $7,500. He may not have known what Johnson was making ($10,000) but he could guess, and he thought he deserved more. The papers reported him asking for $15,000 and Mack offering $10,000. During the standoff, with Moses working out on his own in Hot Springs, Red Smith quoted Mack: "He's a good player but he thinks he's a hell of a player and he's not. He's got too strong a weakness." Mack was referring to Wally's adventures in fielding ground balls hit to the outfield.

"We doubled his salary his second season," Mack told Bob Paul, "and last year not only gave him a substantial increase but also handed him a bonus at the end of the race. Then we advanced his salary further for 1938. We simply can't stand paying unreasonable salaries. I had to sell stars in the past because they drew too much money and I'm never going to get in that fix again. I won't make any further concessions to Moses of any kind. He will make the first move."

Mack needed Moses the way he had needed Frank Baker back in 1915, but he was prepared to do without him if he had to, just as he had done without Baker that awful season twenty-three years ago. "And if he doesn't sign, I will not sell or trade him," Mack said, as he had said about Baker.

Moses and his wife showed up in Lake Charles, but as a holdout, Moses couldn't practice with the team. Red Smith, who allowed the outfielder and his wife to present their case through his column, quoted Moses as asking for $12,500.

Mack gave it to him. At twenty-seven, Wally Moses was a star, the highest paid man on the team, the best leadoff man in the league since Max Bishop. But he never acted the part. He remained the country boy from Uvalda, Georgia. Bill Werber recalled a hot day in Cleveland when they lost a game before a big Ladies' Day crowd. "When we came out after the game there were women waiting for autographs, so we stood there signing for a long time. Then, as we were walking back to the hotel, Wally said to me, 'What's the matter with those people? They're trying to make celebrities out of us, and we're just like anybody else.'. . . That night we went to a stage show and saw Zasu Pitts and Rufe Hamilton. After the show we stopped in a drugstore for a chocolate milk shake and in walked Pitts and Hamilton. Moses grabbed my arm and said, 'I want to see them up close,' and went over to them, just as star struck as those women had been about him."

Sam Chapman roomed with Moses one year. "He was a quiet guy, fun loving, but could be gruff with anybody he didn't like. In his case, though, that was mighty few."

In his first spring game, Moses had 6 hits at Clinton, South Carolina, where the A's played Presbyterian College as a favor to the coach, Chick Galloway, Mack's shortstop for a decade in the 1920s. The game drew a large crowd; Mack gave his share of the receipts to the school. Then they went on to visit with Jack Coombs at Duke. The A's had five of Coombs's alumni: Hal Wagner, Bill Werber, Ace Parker, Chubby Dean, and Wayne Ambler.

On April 9 in a game with the Portsmouth Cubs of the Piedmont League, the Portsmouth catcher fell on Moses in a play at the plate and hurt Wally's shoulder. It affected his swing, and he never hit more than 9 home runs thereafter.

In the fifth inning of that same game Mack lost his starting shortstop when Skeeter Newsome was hit on the left side of his head near the ear by a pitch thrown by Erwin Sheren. Jim Tadley took Skeeter to a hospital. Newsome was incoherent for several days. It was his second beaning in less than a year. He told players who visited him that he would be back by opening day. But Dr. Duval Jones told Mack that Newsome was finished for the season. It would be 1941 before he stopped having dizzy spells.

That morning Mack had sent Wayne Ambler to Williamsport. Mack brought him back before he had time to unpack. "Boys," Ambler said when he rejoined the team the next day, "there's nothing like that minor league experience."

In 1936 Moe Annenberg, who controlled horse racing publications and wire services and had many dealings with prominent racketeers of the '20s and '30s and would go to jail for tax evasion in 1940, bought the *Philadelphia Inquirer*. Connie Mack Jr. always believed that for some reason Annenberg was out to get Connie Mack and that he had assigned sportswriter Perry Lewis "to run him out of town." Lewis wrote primarily about boxing and football and was never a beat writer for the Phillies or Athletics. He shared the duty of turning out the daily "Old Sport's Musing" column with Isaminger. Lewis lived and died by the bottle; other reporters often had to cover for him. But none of the others wrote the vicious attacks that enraged Mack's children, who beseeched their father to retaliate or they would do it for him.

"It really made me so sad as he loved the game so much," Ruth recalled. "I wanted to write to the papers that criticized him so much. He told me, 'Girlie, that's not a good idea.'"

The opening salvo had appeared on Monday, July 12, 1937:

We see in the Sunday *Inquirer* that since May 23 the Athletics had lost 38 out of 43 games and wonder how much longer such comedy baseball will be inflicted on the fans of Philadelphia. There can be no such thing as an empty cellar in baseball. Some team must occupy eighth place. But when the thing threatens to become a habit with a club and that club representing the third largest city in the United States, something should be done about it. Two more were dropped yesterday so it becomes 40 lost out of the last 45 played. The record of the Athletics to date is as follows: won 20 lost 47 percent .299. And had it not been for that mysterious winning streak early in the season which carried the Mackmen to the top of the standings, Connie's team would be entirely submerged at this writing.

That was just a warmup. The real campaign began in the spring of 1938. Although the Athletics drew the most consistent barrage, Lewis didn't spare Phillies' owner Gerry Nugent, who everybody knew didn't even have the proverbial shoestring to operate on. When Nugent sold his star slugger, first baseman Dolf Camilli, to Brooklyn in March 1938 to pay the spring training bills, Lewis wrote, "Year after year patrons of baseball go out to the two local parks hoping for the best and usually getting the worst. Things have come to such a bad pass that they give three cheers when the home club gets a man out. After all, a baseball fan must root for something. When a Quaker City diamond devotee visits another city he avoids mentioning baseball, thus hoping to avoid the ribald derision of his fellow man. But the poor sap keeps right on hoping, certain that prosperity is just around the corner."

The bashing of Mack and Nugent got under way in earnest on April 11 with a series of salvos originally announced as seven but which ran to fourteen.

"Without malice," the salvo began, "but the sincere hope that by debunking major league baseball as it is conducted in Philadelphia, the veil will be lifted from the abyss into which it has fallen or been pushed." The series was dedicated "to everyone whose civic pride is stung when he beholds the two teams representing this city in the national game be made the doormats of baseball with those responsible for this sad state of affairs conquered but content."

Lewis then offered a peculiar premise: it was a club owner's civic duty to field a winning team:

Owners of major league clubs playing the national game are not, in effect, owners of private businesses. They use the names of various cities and their clubs are more or less official representatives of the community in which they play their home games. [This is the kind of reasoning, turned on its head, that clubs use to get taxpayers to pay for their places of business.]

This being the case, a club owner is falling short of his duty if the city which has adopted his club fails to at least temper commercialism with some degree of civic pride and patriotism. For five straight years at least both local owners have lamentably failed to do this.

Over the next week, at lengths measured in column feet, not inches, Lewis harped on the unloading of stars by both teams, going all the way back to Mack's post-1914 sales, then the 1932–1934 sales, culminating in the December 1935 sales of Foxx and Marcum: "Philadelphia fans had become, by reason of the commercial instincts of local owners, gluttons for punishment, but this slap in the face just about floored them."

Lewis then lamented the failure to replace the departed stars except with minor leaguers who have made "our Athletics the joke club of the American League."

The bitter attack was confined to the sports pages until opening day, Monday, April 18, when it dominated the front page with a banner headline: "PHILS AND ATHLETICS STILL IN CELLAR CLASS ON THE EVE OF THE SEASON."

Another fresh baseball season on our hands, but nothing fresh for the fans of Philadelphia. Practically the same two groups of misfits that inflicted the same number of seventh places on Quaker City patrons last year; no new stars transplanted from other major league teams; nothing to enthuse over; nothing to hope for; nothing to do but take it on the chin as we have been doing for four straight years.

Fans of Philadelphia will be asked to support two teams that have already been consigned to lowly positions by their managers and owners. At the close of last season they knew they had nothing; throughout the winter they realized that with the coming of the Easter season, they would again be attempting to sell their customers minor league baseball for major league prices—but they have done nothing about it.

It didn't help when the A's lost the first three at Washington and the Phils blew up in the eighth inning of their home opener against Brooklyn.

At the opener in Washington, Connie Mack had a visitor: Daniel Casey, the same age as Mack, who had pitched against him when Mack was a rookie catcher for Washington fifty-one years ago. Then Clark Griffith went to the A's dugout and took Mack to meet President Roosevelt. Mack and FDR chatted a few minutes; the president asked him about his health and got the "never felt better" response. Roosevelt sat through the rain showers and enjoyed the Senators' victory thoroughly. Kelley, Williams, and Smith were hit hard in the 12–8 loss, and that's the way it was going to be.

Isaminger wrote, "If there is any improvement made in the Athletics over last year there was no indication of it today. They looked like the same old combine of 1937 when they helped share with the Browns the honor of being the football of the league."

Raking Mack and Nugent over the coals for not spending large sums for established stars, Perry Lewis cited the Browns' $150,000 offer for Joe DiMaggio (probably a publicity gimmick) and Philip Wrigley's paying $185,000 for a dead-armed Dizzy Dean (not mentioning that Wrigley had been widely called a fool for doing it).

Wrote Lewis: "Being beaten by Washington in the season's opener was no part of a shock to Quaker City fans who have become accustomed to defeat, but reading of club owners willing to part with such substantial sums in order to give their supporters better baseball is not a very nourishing way for the betrayed fans of Philadelphia to start the day right. It has been many years since Connie Mack spent important money for a ball player and as for the Phillies, well, not even the oldest inhabitant can remember when that club dug deep in an effort to strengthen its playing power."

Mack received letters from fans taking him to task for not buying some high-priced players like Phil Wrigley did. He started to reply to one: "I will give you $50,000 if you can find me a good ballplayer . . . ," then thought, "That's ridiculous," and tore it up.

The rest of the *Inquirer* series consisted primarily of letters from readers, some agreeing with Lewis, others defending Connie Mack. Some pointed out that the players Mack sold in the early '30s had most of their careers behind them or, like Foxx, were just going through the motions during their last few years in Philadelphia. The Red Sox, who had done most of the buying, had not won anything either.

At one point Gerry Nugent responded, "I can't afford to buy players to improve the team unless I get more attendance, and I can't get more attendance with a poor team. Otherwise I'd have to dig into my own pockets to buy better players." He envied the Cincinnati Reds, who had drawn twice as many through the gates as the Phillies while finishing behind them in last place. And of course he could dig into his own pockets all the way to China and not come up with enough yuan to buy a Class D rookie.

To which Lewis replied, "If he hasn't the capital to finance a major league club, let him give someone else a chance to save National League baseball for this city."

In another broadside, Lewis criticized both teams for refusing fresh capital: "We were surprised to learn recently that about twelve months ago a group of wealthy Philadelphia citizens attempted in vain to invest money in either the Phillies or the A's at a time when both teams were at as low playing strength as they are at present. They were not given the chance, however, to take the gamble. The present owners did not care to dispose of any part of their holdings."

No evidence has been found to identify those would-be investors or to link Annenberg to them. We don't know if the campaign was an effort to pressure either Mack or Nugent to sell or just a civic-minded publisher carrying the banner on behalf of the city's suffering baseball fans.

Connie Mack did not respond. He had built winning teams in the past, and he hadn't begun by spending big money for a star who would be surrounded by mediocrity. He did that only after he had built a solid supporting cast. He intended to build his next winner the same way. But how long would it take? His way wasn't working any better than it had during his seven years in the wilderness after 1914, and he had taken plenty of criticism in the years that followed until he regained the top.

But now there were better builders, using modern tools, in the game.

With Skeeter Newsome out, Mack tried four shortstops. None was big league caliber. One was the erstwhile Duke football star Ace Parker, who couldn't hit a curve if you mailed it to him. Parker parlayed that weakness into a brief, war-interrupted but spectacular career as a pro quarterback that took him into the NFL Hall of Fame.

Connie Mack patiently watched as one hopeful after another tried and failed. What they lacked could not be taught. His patience, thought some observers, was a weakness; he would sometimes go too long with a rookie who demonstrated that he was not big league caliber before giving up on him. Other players—especially the pitchers—started muttering as the losses mounted, "What's he thinking about? What's he got that guy in there for?"

Of course many of those same pitchers would have been back in the minors in a hurry if Mack hadn't shown the same patience with them, sending them to the mound year after year, hoping they would finally "get it."

One thing Mack had no patience with was lack of hustle—"soldiering" in the lingo of the time. Russ Peters had the first shot at the shortstop position. In the opener at Washington, Peters made one error and was hitless. The next day in the fourth inning the Senators' Mel Almada was on second with nobody out. He headed for third when Buddy Lewis hit a grounder to short. Peters dropped it. Dejection paralyzed him. He stood there looking down at the ball as it lay near his feet, while third base coach Clyde Milan waved Almada to keep on going. Almada slid home safely. There was no throw.

Connie Mack immediately turned to Wayne Ambler and said, "Go down and warm up in the bullpen."

Ambler replaced Peters in the fifth. Peters never played for Mack again. Three weeks later Connie Mack gave him the choice of being sold to Columbus of the AA American Association or to Atlanta of the 1-A Southern Association. Russ picked Atlanta, where he revitalized his career.

Wayne Ambler got the most playing time at short, but he was a second baseman and didn't have a strong enough arm for the position. He made up for it as best he could by getting rid of the ball quickly. Except for one big 5-hit day at Yankee Stadium in May, he swung a featherweight bat. Mack would sometimes use a pitcher, Lynn Nelson, to pinch-hit for him.

Dario Lodigiani shared second base duties with Stan Sperry, who'd been unable to make the Phillies two years earlier. They were capable at the plate, but they couldn't carry Wayne Ambler's glove. It didn't take long for Mack to conclude that Lodigiani would never be the kind of second baseman he was looking for. He was too slow. He'd do better at third—maybe.

These days Mack had to do most of his scorecard waving at his clueless infielders, not his veteran outfield. One day Lodigiani was playing third when Jimmy Foxx came to bat. Mack kept waving Lodi back, back, onto the grass. Foxx hit a line drive that tore the glove off his hand and carried it into left field. If he'd been playing in closer, it could have killed him. When the inning ended and Lodigiani came back to the bench, Mack chuckled and said, "I told you."

The A's got off to a 5-12 start. The big guns in the middle of the lineup weren't firing with men on base. In 11 of their losses they scored 4 or fewer runs. Bill Werber and Frank Hayes were hitting better than the outfielders. Connie Mack was still a hunch player. He pulled his number one, three, and four hitters—Moses, Finney, and Johnson—and dropped them to sixth, seventh, and eighth in the batting order. It was, Mack said, the first time he had put three outfielders batting just ahead of the pitcher. "But dammit, they were just not hitting," he explained, "We'll go along this way for a few days. By that time I hope they'll snap out of it."

It was an infielder, Werber, who drove in 5 runs in their 7–6 10-inning win that day.

The next day Mack replaced Finney in center field. They scored 13 runs in the next 2 games before resuming their skimpy scoring.

The A's played hard, and the fans appreciated their efforts. But when they blew a lead, the rough riders got on them. Sometimes the razzing was aimed at players getting drunk in some tavern the night before.

Connie Mack heard it as well as the fans in the stands. Early in the year he walked into the clubhouse one day before a game. "We're gonna have a meeting," he announced. Lena Blackburne set a chair in the middle of the room. Mack sat down. The players stood or sat by their lockers. (A photo of that meeting accompanied a 1938 *Saturday Evening Post* article.)

Mack asked each man about his drinking habits, then concluded with, "If you go to a tavern, have a drink and get out. Don't sit around. Don't give the fans something to talk about."

Bob Johnson was a quiet, solitary drinker. Nobody ever saw him drunk. As long as he produced on the field, Mack said nothing. Sometimes it seemed as if Johnson was carrying the entire team. On June 12 he did just that, driving in all 8 runs of an 8–3 win with a grand slam in the first, an RBI single in the third, and a 3-run homer in the eighth. He played every day, hit 30 home runs, drove in 113—44 more than anybody else in the lineup—and was fourth in the league in total bases.

When Gene Hasson failed, Lou Finney filled in at first base, but he wasn't the answer.

At twenty-six, Dick Siebert had been toiling in the minor leagues as a consistent .300 hitter and efficient first baseman for eight years. After brief trials with Brooklyn, he had landed in the Cardinals' chain gang with no hope of moving up to replace Johnny Mize. He started the '38 season on the bench. Every time a club claimed him on waivers, Branch Rickey withdrew them and sent Siebert back to Columbus in the American Association.

A college graduate, Siebert appealed to Commissioner Landis to spring him. Landis, no fan of the farm system and of the Cardinals and Branch Rickey in particular, said he would investigate.

The squabble made the news, and Connie Mack contacted Rickey, who may have sensed free agency for Siebert in the works, which would cost him a possible sale. On May 14 the Athletics bought Siebert for $7,500 and Gene Hasson, outfielder Paul Easterling, and pitcher George Turbeville, none of whom ever played in the big leagues again.

Dick Siebert made his debut for the A's in Cleveland on May 16 and had 2 hits batting fourth.

Another rookie broke in that day and was hitless batting seventh. Sam Chapman was a football and baseball star at the University of California in Berkeley. He had made national headlines as an All-American fullback and had led Cal to a 13–0 win over Alabama in the Rose Bowl on January 1. In the spring he was a shortstop or third baseman. Scouts for the Cincinnati Reds and the Yankees each offered him $9,000 to sign.

Somebody else was interested in him too.

Ty Cobb had a home in nearby Menlo Park and went to the Cal games. He wrote to Connie Mack and recommended Chapman to him. Cobb also wrote to Chapman: "The best thing you can do is to sign with Connie Mack. I played twenty-five years in the big leagues and in the last two years I learned more about the game from Mr. Mack than in all the other years I played."

The Athletics offered Chapman a $6,000 bonus and $500 a month for five months.

Looking back fifty years later, Chapman said, "I would have signed with the Yankees if it hadn't been for the letter from Cobb. With either Cincinnati or New York I would have been in the World Series and made more money. I also might have been hurt or stuck in the minor leagues. Who knows? I have no regrets. Wouldn't do any good if I did. And $6,000 was big money in those days."

Chapman was really more interested in football at Cal. But three years of colliding with linemen made a baseball career seem easier on the body. The Washington Redskins had drafted him as their number two pick in December 1937. Pro football was still a shaky proposition; the Redskins had just been relocated from Boston. (Washington later traded the rights to him to Detroit, where he would have played baseball for the Tigers and football for the Lions, but Connie Mack wouldn't part with him.)

Connie Mack sought playing talent first, but he was enough of a showman to appreciate that signing a nationally known football star would reap publicity and bring in the curious as well as the diehard fans. Mack didn't want Sam Chapman to get mixed up with his "badly behaved boys." A few weeks before Chapman reported, Mack said to Bill Werber, "Bill, we've got a promising young player arriving in a few weeks and I'd appreciate it if you would let me room him with you. I would like to see him get started in the right way."

That impressed Werber. "Mr. Mack asked my permission," he said. "He did not tell me I was to have a new roommate. The man showed a lot of innate psychology. For this, you don't need a university education."

Chapman didn't wait for graduation. He got on a train and joined the A's in Cleveland the night of May 15. He slept late the next morning and was awakened by the ringing telephone. It was Connie Mack, asking him to come to Mack's room.

Mack looked over his six-foot, 188-pound newcomer and said, "You're my new left-handed outfielder from California, aren't you? You're nice and big."

Chapman said, "No sir. I'm your right-handed infielder from California."

Mack thought a minute, then said, "You're starting in center field today."

That shook up Chapman. But he said nothing. "I was twenty-two and he was seventy-five. I was lost and in awe." He had played a few games in the outfield that spring but had mostly been at third base. Here he was making his big league debut in center field. He had forgotten to pack his glove and shoes and a sweatshirt. When he left Mack, he went shopping. "I was so nervous I didn't realize they furnished sweatshirts," he said. "So I came in the clubhouse with my red sleeves and they're all wearing blue."

Clubhouse man Yitz Crompton took him in tow and fixed him up with the number 14 uniform worn briefly by the departed 210-pound Babe Barna.

Chapman's debut that afternoon was memorable, much as Sam preferred to forget it. The Cleveland pitcher was the terrible-tempered Johnny Allen.

"My first time at bat I hit a line drive that hit him in the shin. The ball bounced to the second baseman who threw me out. But every time I faced Allen after that he knocked me down first pitch."

Before Chapman went out to center field, somebody handed him a pair of flip-down sunglasses. He had never seen anything like them. The A's, behind the even-tempered, hard-working Luther "Bud" Thomas, led, 3–2, in the seventh. With one out, the Indians' Earl Averill hit a routine fly to center. Chapman fiddled with the sunglasses, flipped them up and down, then threw them off. The ball landed in his glove and fell out. By the time Sam picked up the ball, Averill was heading for second. Chapman heaved it over the infielders' heads. A pair of infield hits scored Averill with the tying run.

When the inning ended, Bud Thomas reached the dugout first. He threw his glove against the back wall, loudly cursing bush leaguers in the outfield.

"Mr. Mack just sat there quietly, never responded," said Bill Werber. "If that was Joe McCarthy, he'd have jumped up and punched the man."

The embarrassed Sam Chapman headed for the farthest corner of the dugout away from Connie Mack. Mack leaned forward and pointed a long index finger at him and said, "Chappy, I want to talk to you." Chapman walked the length of the dugout to the other end, where Mack was sitting. "Chappy," Mack said, "don't worry about that. You showed that you have a strong arm."

The Indians won the game, 4–3, in the last of the tenth. Chapman lingered in the dugout, waiting for everybody to leave before he took a shower. While he sat there, he could hear Bud Thomas yelling, "If that college so and so does that to me again, I'll brain him." Sam felt sure he was headed for the minor leagues.

It's unknown whether James Isaminger was ordered to join Perry Lewis's firing squad or just agreed with its aims. Either way, shortly after Sam Chapman's disastrous debut, he let Mack have it: "Fans are tired of the influx of ill-suited collegians, pitchers who do not know how to stand on the rubber and others who do not have the slightest grasp of fielding and batting. Why such hopeless material should be foisted on a major league team only a scout hiring a player of that kind can explain. There have been some brilliant exceptions out of Duke, but some in the past three years should make the guilty scouts blush with shame. Fans will not be satisfied until Connie Mack makes a shake up of his scouting system."

Since his "scouting system" consisted primarily of Ira Thomas and Earle Mack and college coaches like Jack Coombs, Jack Barry, and Chick Galloway, that wasn't likely to happen. Mack was no longer free on Sundays to check out nearby minor leagues or leave the team for week-long forays as he had done in his younger days.

Chapman was lucky to break in between Wally Moses and Bob Johnson. Moses taught him how to get a jump on a fly ball and throw to the right base. Johnson was more of a hitting coach, teaching him what to expect from different pitchers. He began to enjoy playing center field. He liked to run and covered a lot of ground. He was the kind of gentle giant who would knock a guy down at second base to break up a double play, then help him up. In the clubhouse he moved like a fullback going through the line. The other players learned to pull in their bare toes to avoid being trampled.

Chapman quickly learned one of the same lessons that Ty Cobb had learned: Connie Mack was a great outfielder. "He knew what each pitch was going to be, and moved the fielders. He would sometimes wave me over toward right, for example, and I would shake my head—no way—to myself and the guy would hit the ball right to me."

Connie Mack taught patience by example. He was patient with his boys and wanted them to be patient with themselves. Slumps were part of the game. "Be patient," he'd tell an anxious hitter. "It'll come."

Ty Cobb had tried to see Sam before he left to join the A's but didn't get the chance. So on May 18 he wrote a letter saying what he would have told him if they'd met: "You will be bothered for a while by tall stands and shadows, also sun fields, and backgrounds when batting. Get lots of fielding practice with glasses and you will be OK in a short time. You are with the best man to break in under. He is very patient and kindly. Get your advice from him. You will have several that will want to help you and they are sincere but different minds sometimes muddle things. Relative to batting listen to no one except Mr. Mack or who he delegates to advise you. Get out early and get some extra batting practice, etc."

After warning him against listening to anybody except Mr. Mack, Cobb wrote, "Now, Sam, I am taking the liberty to tell you a few fine points and try them out at practice and I believe you will profit, for I do believe I have learned some batting fundamentals in the years I have been in baseball."

Cobb then proceeded to fill six pages in green ink with advice on how to stand, where to stand, where to keep his hands and elbows, how to adjust to inside and outside pitches, how to read pitchers, how to swing the bat—all this from the man who said he did all his thinking before he got up to bat, leaving his mind clear to react. And he was confirming what players of his time had complained about: that he was always trying to get them to hit like he did.

Whether or not it was with Cobb's help, Chapman became a deadly curve ball hitter. His teammates claimed he could see the ball twice, hitch his swing, and come back and wait on the pitch until it broke.

Chapman also learned a lesson that Lefty Grove had learned the hard way: be careful what you say to writers. When one of them asked Sam how the big leagues compared to college ball, he took it to mean the playing and living conditions and said something like, "They're fine; it's so easy."

The way it came out was, "Chapman says the big leagues are easy." According to Philadelphia writer Stan Baumgartner, who told the story ten years later in *Sport* magazine (with some of the details wrong), the next day in New York the A's lost a doubleheader, 10–0 and 13–1. Chapman was 0 for 7 with 5 strikeouts and 1 walk. When he reached first base on the base on balls, Lou Gehrig said to him, "So you think the big leagues are easy. You'll learn, sonny, you'll learn."

Chapman learned in a hurry; hits became scarce—5 in his next 30 at bats.

Ty Cobb was reading the box scores. He felt a personal responsibility, having recommended Chapman to Connie Mack. On August 19 he wrote a two-page letter giving Chapman more to think about:

> I hope you will pardon my writing you and any suggestion is merely my interest in your work. You have over a considerable period proven you can hit, and from 350-odd down to present average shows something rather than lack of hitting ability. Now too much hitting can be bad when you are meeting the ball good one after another. Stop.
>
> Don't take strikes. Ask Mr. Mack to let you hit first good one for a while. You may unconsciously be using a system of taking first strike and they know that. Never let them figure you out. Cross them up. Always stay in an offensive state of mind.
>
> One other very important thing. Don't guess what the next ball will be. You will sort of know what is coming by figuring your pitcher and balls and strikes on you but never guess.
>
> In your practice try a little more weight on your forward foot than back foot, also keep back leg straight. Now if you try this I'm sure you will get results, and weight on forward foot will make you step in correctly. Also not stride too long and keep your power in hand at all times. I mean be ready for any kind of pitch and you won't pull away with any part of body. Decoy the pitcher by trying to convey him your aim to take the next pitch and remember the catcher is watching you and gives his signals. So start your decoy work for his benefit and as pitcher starts get ready to take your crack at ball. Keep your elbows away from body.
>
> Best of luck. Forget yesterdays. Don't worry. Just do your best. You have already made good.

It was signed "T.R.C."

Chapman slid to around .250 and stayed there the rest of the season. He showed some power with 17 home runs, second on the team to Johnson's 30.

Dick Siebert was sidelined for two weeks after a collision with Detroit outfielder Pete Fox, and in July he was out for six weeks with a knee injury. When he came back, he wore a brace on his right knee. He struggled at the plate and in the field for the rest of the year. Surgery repaired the knee, but he would wear a brace for several years.

Both Siebert and Chapman took their share of baptismal riding from the raucous Shibe Park chorus, but they overcame it to become fan favorites during their lengthy careers in an A's uniform.

Bill Werber's hitting was off, and he was no longer a contender for base-stealing laurels. His legs and back ached much of the time. He took to giving a how-de-do swipe at hard-hit balls that got by him instead of getting in front of them and blocking them.

New York writer Dan Daniel characterized Werber as someone with too much culture and imagination for the game who played as though it was beneath him. "In his first year anywhere he goes great then seems to brood about his fate."

Dario Lodigiani said, "Werber was a scrapper, good base runner, got the big hit, but when we were losing bad he wouldn't do anything to hurt himself. One day after one was ripped at him and he sideswiped it a little and it got by him, he came into the dugout and Connie Mack said, 'Mr. Werber, now see that you don't get hurt out there.'

"Werber said, 'You ain't kidding. I'm not getting hurt.'

"Mack said, 'Chances are you may be in greener pastures next year.'

"Werber said, 'I don't know how green it'll be, but I know I'll be in a different pasture next year.'

"It was getting a little heated. Everything got quiet in the dugout."

The A's lost 8 in a row in early July, won a few, then lost another 9 in a row. They were in most of them, but a lack of timely hits and too many untimely errors doomed them. Braven Dyer of the *Los Angeles Times* reported that no Philly writers were accompanying the A's on the road. In an unguarded moment, Mack admitted to the press that most of his players weren't big league material and never would be what it took to make a winning team. He didn't go into details. He didn't have to. The only prospects available to his scouts were the leftovers that other organizations were willing to sell or unwilling to sign. He liked his outfield and catching, but the infield and pitching were weak. And that, as Mack had said of Wally Moses, was a "strong weakness."

Later Mack told Bob Paul that he had probably talked too much. But that's when the truth is most likely to escape.

Jokes about the A's popped up again, and maybe Connie Mack contributed to them. Maybe. Probably not, but there *was* a real Judge John P. Scallen presiding in Detroit at the time. Anyhow, this is the story the UP sent out, datelined Detroit, July 29.

Connie Mack sat on the bench with Judge John P. Scallen, his old friend, listening to police cases and occasionally was asked to sentence a few.

Mack listened to Jack Berry, 33, found on a park bench with a bottle of rum.

"I know you, Mr. McGillicuddy," the defendant said. "I used to be a bat boy for Ty Cobb." The judge interrupted a long baseball chat between Mack and Berry with a demand for sentence.

"Make him see my team play," Mack suggested. "That's the worst sentence that could be imposed by any man."

Justice was done. The next day the Tigers took two from the A's, 10–7 and 8–7.

The Phillies had a long-standing invitation from Connie Mack to share Shibe Park, and they were eager to accept. Baker Bowl had been built in 1895. With fewer than twenty thousand seats, it was the smallest ballpark in the major leagues. As far back as 1926 John Shibe, anticipating the Phillies' moving, had built a large clubhouse for them under the left-field stands and an office opening off Lehigh Avenue. But the Phillies had been locked in a ninety-nine-year lease since 1912, and it was a question of which would come first, a successful negotiation to end the lease or the city's condemning the decrepit old firetrap. The lease-breaking won.

The move figured to benefit both teams, giving the Phils a larger, more attractive playground and the A's some additional revenue.

A one-page document dated 1949 in the files of the American League outlined the rental agreement:

Philadelphia Athletics have as tenants the Philadelphia Phillies under the following arrangement:

Phillies to pay Athletics 10 cents on each paid admission. The Phillies also pay to the Athletics $500.00 for each night game in addition.

The Athletics pay all the maintenance for complete light bill, etc.

The Athletics operate the concessions when the Phillies occupy the ball park and turn over to the Phillies 50% of the net profit for the period the park is occupied by the Phillies.

Phillies are permitted to sell their own scorecards and retain the revenue and also the advertising on the scoreboard.

The Phils played their last game at Baker Bowl on June 30, 1938. Gerry Nugent declared that he expected his last-place minions to play better ball at Shibe Park.

They didn't.

In August an epidemic of sore arms among star pitchers—Carl Hubbell, Dizzy Dean, and Lefty Grove among them—prompted Ford Frick to blame the lively ball that made pitchers work harder. Most managers agreed with Connie Mack, who said, "I can't see any differences from five years ago. It's just one of those things. Happened more than usual, that's all. If you get right down to cases, you'll see it's the older pitchers whose arms are hurt."

When Dick Siebert's bum knee needed resting, Mack bought left-hand-hitting first baseman Nick Etten from Atlanta, which had farmed him out to Jacksonville, where he was hitting .370. Etten joined the A's in Washington on September 8. He took a cab to the Shoreham Hotel but was so nervous he left his bag with his baseball gear in the cab. When he introduced himself to Mr. Mack and told him what had happened, Mack said they'd track it down, then added, "Maybe it's just as well it happened. The Senators have a real tough lefthander pitching today."

The pitcher was a wild southpaw, Ken Chase, but Etten played that day anyhow. And what a bang-up debut it turned out to be.

Rookie catcher Hal Wagner, twenty-three, had been recalled by the A's from Spartanburg. Wagner was what veterans called a fresh busher. He was mouthy but not in the way the old catcher Connie Mack had distracted batters with genial chatter. Wagner complained about the umpires' calls and heckled batters.

Washington second baseman Buddy Myer had been in the league for fourteen years and had won a batting championship in 1935. His first encounter with the young catcher came in a game at Philadelphia on September 3. Every time Myer came to bat, Wagner rode him. Finally Myer told him off.

Five days later in Washington, Myer was up in the sixth inning. Wagner complained about a call by umpire Bill Grieve. Myer told him to shut up and let the umpires run the game. Wagner gave him a smart-alecky comeback. Myer fumed. He reached first on a walk. Max West doubled down the left-field line. Myer rounded third and headed for home. Sam Chapman's throw had him beaten by six feet. But Wagner made a rookie mistake. He crouched directly in Myer's path, holding the ball. Doing a perfect Ty Cobb imitation, Myer leaped in the air, knees bent, spikes aimed right at Wagner's chest. The ball flew one way. The catcher flew another, out cold. Myer got up and walked right past him.

The Washington fans booed their own man. Earle Mack led the rush out of the A's dugout as if to challenge Myer, who snarled at him, "Teach that guy how to catch," and kept on going. A few pushes were all the contact that was made.

The Senators' doctor tended to Wagner's cuts and bruises and led him off the field. Coach Charlie Berry, who hadn't played in two years, was hurriedly put on the active list to replace Wagner behind the plate.

That wasn't the end of it. As Nick Etten remembered it, Connie Mack was furious. When the inning was over, Mack told Bud Thomas the next time Myer came up to bat, "I want you to knock the button off his cap." Myer batted again in the eighth, and Thomas wasted no time obeying orders. Down went Myer, the pitch nicking his cap and knocking it off his head.

This time the hundreds in the stands sounded like thousands as they booed the pitcher. Myer calmly got up and trotted to first base. But he was boiling. He reached second on a ground out and set out to steal third as Rick Ferrell struck out. Berry's throw to Bill Werber was in time. Werber held onto the ball as Myer slid in, spikes high, and grazed Werber's arm. It was shades of Cobb sliding into Baker thirty years ago. But unlike Baker, Bill Werber thought it was intentional. He whirled and socked Myer on the cheekbone, the ball still in his hand.

In an instant third base coach Clyde Milan was on Werber's back. The brawl was on. This time there was no mere pushing and shoving. Charlie Berry, a former football star, ran down the baseline and lit into Myer, then decked six-foot, two-hundred-pound pitcher Joe Krakauskas, who claimed he was just standing there minding his own business and not swinging at anybody. The men in white were swinging at anybody and everybody in a gray uniform. Genuine blows were struck in encounters all over the field.

It took five minutes for police and umpires to break it up. Werber and Myer were suspended for three days, but Connie Mack didn't learn about it until after Werber's home run beat the Red Sox in Boston the next day. Werber shouldn't have played, but the Red Sox didn't protest. They had climbed to second place but had no chance to overtake the Yankees.

The Washington fracas was Charlie Berry's last game. He remained a coach until 1940 and two years later, with Connie Mack's sponsorship, began a twenty-year career as an AL umpire.

Connie Mack was not one to ease up when somebody was going for a hitting record. The A's were in Detroit for two days September 20–21. The Tigers' big first baseman, Hank Greenberg, was the latest aspirant to Babe Ruth's 60 home runs mark. He had hit 53. The first game was rained out. They played two on September 21. Mack told his pitchers, "Greenberg will try to pull every pitch to left field. Throw everything outside."

In the first inning Randy Gumpert didn't get it far enough outside, resulting in number 54. (Greenberg was stopped at 58.)

It had been a long hot summer. The A's lost 99 games, 16 of them by 1 run. They played 13 doubleheaders during the dog days of August, including 7 in 8 days at Shibe Park. Somewhere along the way, Mack made an offhand comment that when a player went stale, it was a good idea to let him rest for a day or two. Nothing revolutionary about that. But when one writer quoted him as suggesting that players be given a vacation during the season—a week or so off to go to the beach or the mountains—Mack was ridiculed by writers around the country.

"Baseball men must have thought I was in my second childhood," an irate Mack said. "I made no such statement."

Once again, the pitching was poor. Not wild—the pitchers walked fewer than the league average and only 33 more than the pennant-winning Yankees. But opponents' hits rained steadily and runs were rampant. Besides that, the A's were the worst in the league defensively, making more errors and fewer double plays than anybody else.

Mack had expected big things from the veteran right-hander Harry Kelley. On opening day Kelley didn't get out of the first inning. That evening he got word that his son was ill, and he flew home to Arkansas. He came back a week later; in two starts he didn't get past the second inning. His next start was for Washington, which claimed him on waivers.

George Caster was the workhorse, pitching 281 innings, leading the league with 40 starts, and completing half of them. Maybe his sleepwalking kept him in shape. His 16 wins were 30 percent of the team's 53 for the year.

Line Drive Nelson pitched with a chronic sore arm, but suddenly the line drives were going right at somebody wearing a glove—for a while. On June

23 he was 8-1, and the A's were 26-30, just 9½ games behind the Yankees. From then until the end of the season Nelson was 2-10 and the A's were 27-69, dropping to 46 games out of first place.

Between illness and injuries, Chubby Dean was of no use, pitching only 23 innings and pinch-hitting 9 times all year.

Mack had drafted right-handers Nelson Potter from Columbus and Ralph Buxton from Oklahoma City. Buxton didn't last, but Potter did. He was twenty-six with plenty of minor league experience and not much stuff except for a screwball that gave left-handed batters fits. He worked mostly in relief but was hit hard and had 2 wins and 12 losses and a 6.47 ERA to show for it.

Earle Brucker had an astounding year at the plate, hitting .374 with a .561 slugging average, before blood poisoning ended his season in mid-August. His hitting earned him a raise to $6,000.

Connie Mack's desperation and threadbare, haphazard scouting system—a staff of one—with which he was trying to compete for talent provided an example of why he was losing that competition when he pressed Earle Brucker and Lena Blackburne into going on the road in September to find somebody "who can help us right now."

The result: Mack sent $20,000 and Ace Parker to Baltimore for twenty-three-year-old Jim Reninger, a right-handed pitcher who was 6-8 with the Orioles. Reninger never won a game, allowing 78 base runners in 39 innings over two years.

When you lose 99 games, highlights are scarce. Perhaps sensing that Connie Mack's days of managing were nearing the end, the Cleveland Indians decided to honor him at Municipal Stadium on June 19. Mack was in his glory at a pregame luncheon, working the room, chatting animatedly with everyone. A crowd of twenty thousand gave him a two-minute ovation when he was introduced and walked to the mound wearing a brown suit, his scorecard sticking out of his coat pocket. Players from both teams formed a semicircle around him. Cleveland baseball writers gave him a gold pencil. The Indians presented him with a leather-bound book containing the signatures of everybody—*everybody*—in organized baseball: every league and club official, manager, coach, and player down to the youngest rookie on the smallest Class D team. Commissioner Landis led it off with the inscription: "Do you know anyone entitled to have his name mentioned ahead of Connie Mack? I don't."

Then the first-place Indians defeated the A's, 5–4. Meanwhile, at Fairmount Park race track outside St. Louis, a four-year-old, Mr. Mack, came in second in the eighth race.

Otherwise for Connie Mack a good day was any time the A's didn't have to bat in the last of the ninth against the Yankees. It happened three times. They were 5-16 against them for the year. (When the Yankees won their third straight World Series, Mack proclaimed them the greatest team ever, surpassing his own 1910–1914 and 1929–1931 A's, the Cubs of 1906–1910, and the Orioles of the 1890s. He singled out Bill Dickey as the most valuable Yankee for the 1938 season.)

The A's and White Sox saw the biggest declines in attendance. The A's drew 385,000 and lost $48,000. The Phillies drew only 166,000.

After Mickey Cochrane was hit in the head and nearly killed by a pitch thrown by Bump Hadley on May 25, 1937, he never played again. When he recovered, he was not the same man. All the fight and fire he had poured out on the field remained inside him, but now he had no outlet for it except his own players. They had finished second that year but were struggling in fifth place on August 6, 1938, when club owner Walter O. Briggs, an auto body manufacturer, fired him.

The firing of one of Mack's boys provoked the resentment that the old-timers like Mack and Clark Griffith had for the "bushwhackers," who had not grown up in the game. Mack considered it "bunk" that managers were responsible for winning or losing pennants. "Winning a pennant depends 95 percent on the players," he told Bob Paul. "The other 5 percent is relatively so unimportant that it can be forgotten. Men on a winning club know what to do. A manager's big job under such circumstances is handling his men. He has to keep them satisfied, prevent the formation of cliques, and see that the fun-loving players don't wander too far after they leave the ballpark. One baseball man told me he thought a manager of a real good ball club could sit in the grandstand and be just as useful as on the bench. In other words, he meant the players could win just as easily without the manager as with him."

Mack cited his 1912 team, which he considered his best after the A's had won the previous two years:

I was confident this 1912 team would make it three pennants in a row. Well, it didn't. We finished in third place. Gosh, it was awful sitting there on the bench day after day watching my boys lose crucial games and being powerless to do anything about it. I just had to take it.

When we started the next season, I estimated our strength as 30 percent less than that of 1912. Some of my players were passing the peak of their game, one or two suffered from an overdose of the pennant gout, and I couldn't see how we'd come through. But win we did. Frankly, I directed the team the same way as in 1912. The victory, therefore, wasn't due to new strategy or so-called masterminding. The players had decided to win the pennant so I sat back and enjoyed watching them do it.

Mack believed that managers of losing teams often turned in a better job than those with pennant winners. "It's a more difficult job managing players who need hours of coaching. They lack polish as well as experience. You'd be surprised the number of flaws the average youngster breaking into the big leagues has. Sometimes I wonder how their managers in the minors put in their time to earn their salaries."

Mack wrote to Sr. Florence: "Don't blame you for feeling as you do about the way they treated Mickey Cochrane. It's always the men who have not been in baseball very long that hurts our game. They overlooked the part that real sports plays in our game[;] just too bad that Mickey was tied up to a man who knows so little about baseball. If Frank Navin had lived it would not have taken place, therefore don't want you to lose all your interest in the game just because one man treated Mickey as he did."

Whether it was the A's dismal showings or the firing of Cochrane or both, Sr. Florence declared herself no longer a baseball fan. On September 28 Mack wrote to her: "Don't know what to say about your giving up your love for baseball[;] don't like to think of your doing so but you know best. Our season here this year was not so good[;] am in hopes to have a better one next season[;] will keep trying doing the best always."

Sr. Florence's disavowal of baseball didn't last. Her prayers continued to rise, but the Athletics didn't.

BASEBALL FIGHTS
THE FUTURE

If fellows like Thomas Edison and Guglielmo Marconi hadn't been so good at inventing things, the 1930s moguls of major league baseball might have been spared the pain of wrestling with the forces of modern times, specifically the electric light and the radio. When confronted by these high-tech wonders, the magnates didn't know what to do with them. They recoiled at the idea of innovation like seventeenth-century bishops.

Temporary and portable lighting systems had been used sporadically since the nineteenth century by company and semipro and black baseball teams. Connie Mack's 1902 pro football team once played a night game in Elmira. He described the setup as "kind of a searchlight trained on the ball. I stood in an aisle near the front and couldn't see the ball." In 1910 Charles Comiskey had tried out a lighting system for a game between two city teams. The lights proved inadequate. On June 23, 1927, General Electric staged a demonstration game on a floodlit field in Lynn, Massachusetts, that impressed players from the Red Sox and Senators who saw it. To counter the effects of the Depression and stay in business, minor league clubs began putting up permanent light poles. Independence, Kansas, of the Western Association was the first to turn on the lights, for an exhibition game against the House of David on April 17, 1930. Two weeks later the first league game under the lights took place at Des Moines. Despite a cold, wet May, the first six night games in Des Moines averaged over 2,300 fans per night. A Monday Ladies' Night drew a record two thousand women, admitted free, plus over fourteen hundred paid.

Other minor league clubs took notice and installed lights that players of the time denigrated as "candles." By the end of 1934 sixty-seven minor league clubs were drawing big crowds to night games. About that time Powel Crosley bought the moribund Cincinnati Reds and brought in a redheaded dyna-mo named Larry MacPhail to run the club. Urged on by MacPhail, Crosley went into the NL meeting in December 1934 to ask for permission to play seven night games in 1935. Crosley argued that the last-place Reds had drawn barely over two hundred thousand in each of the past two years, and 70 per-cent of that had come on Sundays and holidays. Night games would provide another "special occasion" kind of attraction. The NL voted, 5–3, to allow any club to play up to seven night games. Only the Reds installed the lights.

The American League brushed off the "bush-league" idea. One AL official (not Connie Mack, who was in Japan) called it a "burlesque" of the game.

On May 24, 1935, President Roosevelt pressed a button in Washington, and (thanks to more of Edison's inventions) the lights went on at Crosley Field. The Reds climbed to sixth; attendance more than doubled. NL presi-dent Ford Frick, trying to catch up with what the minor leagues had already learned, saw it as an aid in attracting women and families who could not go to games during the day. The American League still scoffed. "A passing fad," said Clark Griffith. In December the AL chorused a unanimous "no" to the idea.

Nobody in the National League followed MacPhail's lead either until he followed himself, installing lights at Ebbets Field when he moved to Brook-lyn in 1938.

Although Connie Mack had gone along with his colleagues in vetoing night games in December 1935, he agreed to play a game under temporary lights against the Penn Athletic Club (PAC) at a YMCA field on July 6, 1936, to raise money for the PAC team to go to the Olympics to demonstrate the game. When the 1936 season was over and Mack looked back at how the Reds had benefited and how night ball had saved minor league clubs from bankruptcy and entire leagues from folding—and the sky hadn't fallen—he saw the light.

Since the 1933 death of Browns owner Phil Ball, the executors of his es-tate had run the struggling franchise. The heirs were eager to be rid of it. Ball had had many other profitable businesses. For him a baseball club was more of a hobby. The Browns had made a profit only once, in 1922. More than half the big league teams had reported a profit in 1936; the Browns were not among them. They drew 93,267 and lost $159,000. No visiting club had taken away enough to pay its expenses. Lawyers for the estate asked Branch Rickey, then vice-president of the Cardinals, to help them find a buyer. He didn't have to look farther than the office next to his. Cardinal official Bill

DeWitt had a friend, Donald L. Barnes, a successful St. Louis businessman and a baseball fan. Rickey received what the *Reach Guide* called "a commensurate commission" for his efforts.

Barnes headed a group that included DeWitt and nine hundred public stockholders. But Barnes had a condition before completing the deal. He wanted approval to play night games. At a special league meeting on November 12, 1936, to approve the sale, Barnes indicated that the Browns and Cardinals, who were tenants of the Browns at Sportsman's Park, would share the cost of installing the lights. Jake Ruppert moved, and Detroit owner Walter O. Briggs seconded, that night games be prohibited except by majority vote of the league and, if approved, that no more than seven could be scheduled in a season. Both said their teams would not play any night games anywhere, but they reserved the right to change their minds. Lou Comiskey of Chicago moved to allow the Browns to play seven night games. The league gave Barnes a tentative go-ahead, which was ratified on December 8. The Yankees and Tigers refused to play any after-dark games.

When Connie Mack then asked for the same right to play seven night games, he gave his dear friend Clark Griffith fits. Griffith was firmly, loudly opposed to night ball, but it was clear from the minutes of the meeting that he was very uneasy about disagreeing with his closest friend in baseball. It was also apparent that the oldest man at the table had the most progressive outlook. Here's how it went:

MACK: If we allow St. Louis to play seven night games, I would like to see how the clubs feel about Philadelphia if we decide to put in the lights. I am thinking seriously about it. I may not want to. I have just an idea that possibly we would like to put the lights in over there. I'm not positive we're going to do it, now, but I have been giving it some thought. I think our town is on the same lines as St. Louis. I have an idea we would do pretty well with those lights, and if we decide we will make our decision probably in the next six weeks. I understand we can get them in in about thirty days. We will make our decision in about six weeks whether we want those lights in or not. And if we decide to go on with them why, of course I would like to have some clubs to play with. I want to find out which clubs will play a second night game in Philadelphia. Will Chicago?

GRABINER: No. One is all we want.

Detroit, represented by Mickey Cochrane, said no. St. Louis and Cleveland agreed to play one or two. When it came to Washington, Clark Griffith squirmed: "I am not going to turn Connie down, but I think it is setting a bad precedent."

MACK: I believe it isn't going to do any harm whatsoever to go in there and play seven games in towns like, well, in any town. I think it would do you a lot of good, too. I do not believe in standing still. I believe in moving on. If it is going to pay us to play night ball, why, I say let us play night ball.

GRIFFITH: If you have to have it, I will play you every night in the week. But if you can go without it, I say no. You know I would like to see you do better than anybody in the world.

MACK: We wouldn't spend sixty or seventy thousand dollars if we didn't think we needed them.

GRIFFITH: I am against night baseball.

MACK: You probably have the right idea. Probably we never should have played a doubleheader from the time we started baseball up to the present time. But we know what it means now to play a Sunday doubleheader. We know we can hardly live without doing it at the present time. [Clark Griffith had proposed no Sunday doubleheaders until a team's last visit of the season. It was voted down.] I believe it would be a benefit to us all if we played night baseball. If we decide to put them in, see, I would be perfectly willing to try it for a year, stop right there and take our loss.

GRIFFITH: You will never stop once you start.

MACK: Then it will be a benefit.

GRIFFITH: You will take us all to night baseball.

MACK: I do not want to take anyone in that doesn't want to go in. But I would like to take all in that want to go in. If the majority feels Philadelphia should not adopt it this year, it is all right.

GRIFFITH: I wish you would try it another year without it.

MACK: What we want to do is make some money.

GRIFFITH: I may be in the same boat in another year, too. But I am firmly convinced we shouldn't go to this thing until we are forced to it.

MACK: How do other clubs feel about it?

GRIFFITH: I do not want to vote against Connie Mack.
MACK: I want you to vote how you feel.

League president Will Harridge then called the question of giving Philadelphia permission to play up to seven night games in 1937. Boston, Chicago, and St. Louis voted yes; the motion lost.

(This seemed counter to the other clubs' complaints about the meager attendance at Shibe Park. It made no sense that St. Louis should be given the okay to try night games to improve its finances but Philadelphia should not. The most likely explanation is that the opponents of night ball were afraid the sale of the Browns would have fallen through if Donald Barnes had been turned down.)

Tom Yawkey explained his vote. "I voted yes because I think that way. If he knows his town and knows his own situation and feels that seven night games in there would help him to make money he has not been making otherwise with a club that unluckily has been down or close to the bottom or on the bottom, why I think we ought to give him permission to do it. And if I felt that way I'd hope the league would give it to me."

MACK: That's awful nice of you, Mr. Yawkey, but if the league as a whole thinks it would be better to wait another year and see how this lighting proposition is going to turn out, why it is all right with Philadelphia.

At this point Jake Ruppert seemed confused. "As I understand it, Mr. Chairman, the motion we voted on was whether we would play night games. We didn't refuse Mr. Mack the right to put in the lights."

But that's exactly what Ruppert's vote *had* done.

Harridge explained that the question was in fact whether to give Mr. Mack permission to install lights for night games. He said that if there was any misunderstanding of the request, they would vote again.

That might have produced a different result, but Connie Mack could see that even if his request was approved, there were at least four clubs who would refuse to play any night games at Shibe Park.

To make himself feel better if not Connie Mack, Clark Griffith suggested that if the Phillies put in lights, then the A's should have the same privilege. The foxy Griffith knew that Phillies' owner Gerry Nugent didn't have enough money to buy a light bulb.

"I would just as soon withdraw [the request]," Mack said. "We will go along this year without them."

A year later a majority of the American League owners still saw no future in night baseball except as an emergency measure for a club that might be in desperate financial shape. And they didn't believe any club was that bad off. Even if a club could persuade them it faced imminent bankruptcy, the sunshine-only boys maintained that any emergency approval would be good for one year. And who was going to make the necessary investment to install lights for what might be only one year?

Nonetheless, Cleveland owner Alva Bradley sought permission to play seven night games in 1938. Bradley admitted that his club did not face a financial emergency. That killed his chances. With the opposition led by Clark Griffith, he found only two supporters. Inexplicably Connie Mack was not one of them.

After Larry MacPhail's introduction of lights at Ebbets Field in 1938 helped the seventh-place Dodgers' attendance leap to the highest since 1932 (almost 30 percent of it coming in their seven night games, including a record 38,748 who saw Johnny Vander Meer's second consecutive no-hitter on June 15), Mack renewed his determination to gain the league's approval.

He invited Westinghouse executives to come to Shibe Park and lay out how they would light the field. They assured him that technical advances had been made that would provide better results than those in Cincinnati or Brooklyn. The cost would be around $100,000. With the Phillies now tenants at Shibe Park, Gerry Nugent would be asked to put up some of the cost. But regardless of what the Phillies' owner did, Mack was intent on moving ahead, borrowing the money if necessary.

Before heading for the December 1938 meetings, Mack told reporters, "I'm going to do a bit of lobbying, feel my way around, and try to get the rest of the magnates to see it my way."

Asked what night of the week he thought might be best for night games, Mack harkened back to his days as a single young blade in East Brookfield in the 1880s. "Date night—Wednesday—would be a good spot. I remember the days when I was doing a bit of courting. If I could have gone to the baseball game it would have solved quite a few problems of entertainment."

Mack went into the meeting expecting that New York, Chicago, Detroit, and Washington would be opposed. "We must progress the same as any other sport," he pleaded, "and night baseball is one of the steps forward that baseball has taken. Night baseball has its place in the scheme of baseball as much as day games. We cannot dictate to the public. Those who work during the day want night games."

His argument failed to sway the reluctant foursome, but according to H. G. Salsinger of the *Detroit News*, a little old-fashioned horse trading succeeded. Wrote Salsinger: "Clark Griffith wanted to sell Zeke Bonura to the Giants [for $20,000 and two players] but needed waivers. Connie Mack refused to waive on him. Griffith appealed to Mack and Mack told Griffith that if he voted for night ball, Mack would waive on Bonura."

Griffith switched his vote. Bonura went to the Giants.

The Cleveland Indians then expressed their intention to install lights.

(Indians manager Oscar Vitt looked forward to pitching Bob Feller at every nocturnal opportunity. In Cleveland's inaugural night game on June 27 Feller gave up 1 hit and struck out 13 in a 5–0 win over Detroit. In Chicago on August 18 he gave up 3 hits and fanned 8 but lost an old-fashioned 11-inning duel with Edgar Smith, 1–0. He split two other night decisions.)

The approvals came with these conditions: no Saturday, Sunday, or holiday nights; no inning may start after 11:50 p.m.; no more than two night games may be played by any visiting team; authorization was good for one year only.

Mack was undaunted by the one-year limit, believing that was just a bluff to try to deter any club from tiptoeing into the future.

By January 1939 General Electric was able to advertise, "Baseball at night has proved profitable to the approximately 150 professional clubs [all but two in the minor leagues] which are playing at least a portion of their games under the lights. They have thrown over the tradition that baseball is a daylight game, to take advantage of the additional profits from games at night. You, too, can gain those added profits playing under the lights."

The Athletics played the first night game in the American League at Shibe Park on Tuesday, May 16, 1939. Cleveland and Chicago also turned on the lights that year. The Browns, the Giants, and Pittsburgh installed lights in 1940.

"The Giants are making a mistake," said Ed Barrow. "The thing will die out. Night ball is not baseball. . . . The stunt will wear out its welcome. As long as I have anything to say about the running of the Yankees, they will not play night ball in the Stadium."

The Yankees didn't, until Larry MacPhail and two partners bought control of the club in 1945 and Barrow no longer had anything to say about it. In 1946 the Yankees were the last in the American League to put up the lights.

The writers had as much adjusting to do as the players, given the deadlines for the several editions of metropolitan dailies. Red Smith, conceding that "at night there are at least five times more people free to attend games than in the afternoon," complained in an October 1947 article, "Has Baseball Forgotten the Fan?": "Baseball at night is strictly a theatrical spectacle. It brings the game into competition with wrestling, leg shows, and dog racing. . . . It is vain to argue that night baseball bears scarcely any recognizable resemblance to the pleasant game of hot, lazy afternoons which Americans grew up loving, for owners are in business for a profit. But night baseball is all business. What is all business is not in any degree a sport."

At seventy-eight, Connie Mack was still more farsighted than his contemporaries. In the spring of 1941, a young Atlanta sports broadcaster, Ernie Harwell, asked Mack about the changes that had taken place in baseball in his lifetime.

MACK: Night baseball. The night baseball has been a wonderful thing for the minor leagues. Up to the present time the major leagues most of the clubs are rather opposed to playing night baseball. But I believe they all eventually will come to it. To my way of thinking the club owners should be very open-minded in regards the future of baseball.

HARWELL: Mr. Mack, do you think any of the major league ball clubs will get to the point where they play more than seven or fourteen [night] games in a season?

MACK: Well, that's where I feel the club owners should be open-minded. Now, for instance, this coming year—uh—they're going to find that most people today who have positions and have jobs that now, due to the fact that there isn't a great deal of business, there hasn't been a great deal of business, that they're coming to it. And we've lost those fans that we used to have that used to take a day off to come out to see our games. Now you take the laboring man of today. If he gets the position he's going to hang to it and it's my thoughts that run to we should play more night games in order to . . . if we want to succeed financially in baseball.

Like the automobile, radio was a game changer in American life. In the beginning there were no networks. (The NBC network opened in 1926, CBS the following year.) The limited time that stations were on the air was filled by speeches, roundtable discussions of weighty subjects, and studio musicians and singers. It didn't matter what was on: more and more people were staying home in the evenings to listen to sounds and voices from far away. When the 1928 political conventions were broadcast, movie houses were empty. As new shows became popular, theaters went out of business.

In 1934 songwriter Irving Caesar testified before the FCC that radio was crippling the recovery of employment: "For 2½ hours each day 40 million people are busy at their dials and while thus engaged they cannot walk down the shop-lined streets, wear out their shoes or their wearing apparel, nor can they ride the highways in their automobiles with the attendant consumption of gasoline, tires, and wear in engine. It was a paradox wherein the auto industry spent nearly two million dollars on one network to advertise motor cars and yet further habituates the public to disuse of the automobile."

As with any new technology, there were angle-seekers, pirates, hijackers. Given the high interest in baseball, pioneering stations looked for ways to bootleg play-by-play broadcasts of the games.

According to Harold C. Burr, writing in *Baseball Magazine* in 1937, in 1921 a powerful radio station in Schenectady, New York, sought out sportswriters covering the New York games to transmit the action via Western Union to the station, where an announcer would report it on the air. The station offered W. O. McGeehan $1,000 for the season. That wasn't enough for McGeehan, who turned it over to a younger colleague, Dan Daniel. Grantland Rice took the job in 1922.

Other stations used messengers who relayed information by telephone or by signals to a confederate outside the park.

The World Series was first broadcast in 1922—an all-New York event—to a limited area in the northeast.

Baseball's owners didn't know what to make of it. Those who feared the effects of game broadcasts on attendance were further cemented in their beliefs when fight promoter Tex Rickard staged Gene Tunney's last fight in July 1928 and sold the radio rights to NBC for $15,000. As a result, Rickard said, he lost $150,000 on the fight and vowed never to broadcast again. What's more, he predicted, some day that new-fangled invention, television, would "take big sports events further away from the men who foot the bills to promote them."

Cubs owner William Wrigley Jr. was way ahead of his fellow club owners. He knew that advertising paid. It worked for him in peddling chewing gum. Broadcasting the action of the games was free advertising. It aroused a curiosity and interest in the players as personalities, especially among housewives listening to the games while they ironed or cooked. That led to a desire to go out and see them in person. In 1924 Wrigley threw Cubs games open to any and all stations who wanted to carry them—free. At one point Chicago games were aired over five different stations.

Hal Totten, a desk man at the *Chicago Daily News,* was the first, broadcasting on the newspaper's station, wmaq. "But Wrigley wanted an old-time player doing the talking into the mike," Totten recalled, "so they hired Circus Solly Hoffman. Hoffman lasted one day. He wasn't wordy enough, didn't let his voice rise and fall, never got excited, lacked what we call radio presence." Players on the sidelines with injuries sometimes joined the broadcaster and picked up a fee.

One Chicago station, wjjd, brought in what it called a "Parade of Immortals" as color commentators alongside announcer John Harrington. The visitors included actor Joe E. Brown and former stars Tris Speaker, Johnny Evers, Joe Tinker, Walter Johnson, and Mordecai "Three Finger" Brown.

Wrigley also sponsored an hour-long summary of the highlights of the day's game from 7 to 8 p.m.

When a game was rained out, some stations carried recreations of out-of-town games. (When the A's 1935 opener at Washington was snowed out, the players listened to an account of the Boston at New York opener—but not over a New York station; all three New York teams still spurned radio.)

The American League was all over the place on the issue. On February 4, 1924, fearing that Wrigley's wild ideas would result in empty ballparks, Ernest Barnard of Cleveland moved that it be the sense of the al that radio broadcasting outfits be barred from all league parks during the progress of a game. Connie Mack seconded it, and it passed, 8–0.

But radio men didn't have to be in the ballpark; using Western Union reports, a Washington station, wrc, aired the Senators' road games in 1926.

On December 14, 1926, the al voted to leave radio decisions to individual clubs. The White Sox joined with Wrigley in allowing game broadcasts. Only two Chicago stations carried the Sox games. White Sox management found the publicity boosted attendance and became staunch believers. Ty Tyson began broadcasting Tigers' games.

Meanwhile, a few minor league clubs were experimenting with the idea. On July 3, 1928, a new station in Salisbury, Maryland, carried the first broadcast of a Class D game between Salisbury and Northampton, with broadcasts to continue unless they detracted from attendance. The league disbanded on July 10, so the clubs never really determined radio's effect.

Over the next several years the issue was discussed at length at just about every major league meeting. Year after year the American League was stalemated. Every vote—to leave it to individual clubs or to ban broadcasts entirely—seemed to run into a 4–4 vote.

At the December 1933 meetings Landis and the league presidents received telegrams from Robert B. Irwin, executive director of the American Federation for the Blind: "In behalf of the 114,000 blind people of this country we earnestly urge continuance broadcasts of major league baseball games. Thousands of sightless people who will never see a baseball game follow the broadcasts with intense interest."

The whole business was complicated by Western Union contracts, which gave the company the exclusive right to distribute play-by-play details to subscribers. Western Union said it wouldn't object if clubs wanted to have their games broadcast as long as the stations received their information from Western Union. That would seem to allow recreations of road games. But broadcasters sitting in radio booths at the games didn't need Western Union.

So when the Tigers' play-by-play caller Ty Tyson appeared before the AL owners in December 1935 and asked for approval to broadcast Detroit road games live from the other ballparks in the league, Western Union said this would violate its contracts. Tyson was turned down.

Some players found radio a lucrative sideline. In St. Louis Bobo Newsom and Dizzy Dean had contracts for a program sponsored by a furniture store. Mel Harder did a program in Cleveland for thirteen weeks. In 1937 Bob Feller and Carl Hubbell had radio deals.

A fifteen-minute pregame interview might earn a player a new pair of shoes or a hat.

Former players were already making their way into the business: Harry Heilmann in Detroit, Jack Graney in Cleveland. Jack Onslow in Boston hosted a baseball school of the air, on which he analyzed the day's action, pointing out good plays and bad.

By 1937 more than two hundred stations carried some kind of baseball programming. A year later the number exceeded three hundred. The biggest beneficiaries of radio's appetite for nightly programs on the day's scores and highlights were veteran sportswriters, who knew the game and the players and had instant name recognition among their listeners.

Game broadcasts were wildly popular everywhere. In small towns and rural areas men gathered at filling stations and railroad depots and wherever there was a radio, or ran down batteries listening on parked car radios, or pressed their ears against crackling homemade crystal sets. Radio stores put up loudspeakers outside to let passersby know what they were missing by not buying a radio and listening at home. But not in the nation's biggest city, where the three big league teams had a no-radio pact. They also banned recreations of games by stations in, say, Chicago when the Cubs played in their ballparks.

According to Harold C. Burr, in order to keep radio stations from bothering them, the Yankees asked an outrageous $100,000 for the rights. So games were bootlegged from Yankee Stadium by a man with a concealed, battery-powered shortwave unit whispering into the transmitter to a truck parked outside, where his voice was relayed to the station. Later wires were set up from the park to a hotel and from there to a studio control room, and spectators phoned in each play.

The New York agreement to ban baseball broadcasts blew up in 1939, when Larry MacPhail brought Red Barber with him from Cincinnati to Brooklyn.

At the same time the lights were saving minor league ball, major league radio came along to kill it, especially in the Midwest, where Chicago and St. Louis stations covered wide areas of prairie. Fans in small towns stayed home to listen to big league games. In 1935 the minor leagues petitioned Judge Landis for relief: "Continue major league radio and we perish."

Landis said it must be dealt with but didn't say how.

In 1941 Lee MacPhail, business manager of the Reading, Pennsylvania, Brooks in the Interstate League, complained about the A's broadcasts to Commissioner Landis, who ordered them stopped.

"The A's ceased to broadcast and also came to Reading to play us an exhibition game to defray any damages that we might have suffered," MacPhail wrote in *My Nine Innings*. "Connie Mack could not have been more gracious."

Eventually the major leagues passed a rule forbidding teams from broadcasting games into minor league territory when the minor league team was playing.

The minors would fight the same losing battle against televised big league games twenty years later.

Meanwhile, more and more minor league clubs were selling the rights to their games and expanding road game broadcasts. But not everybody in the minors saw game broadcasts as a boon. In May 1935, after ten years on the air, officials of the Los Angeles Angels, owned by Wrigley, canceled their broadcasts because of falling attendance. A poll revealed a prevalent attitude among listeners: "Why go way out [to Wrigley Field] when we can sit back and listen to Oscar Reichow announce the games?"

Where was Connie Mack in all this? It's hard to say. He enjoyed listening to the radio, and by 1933 there was plenty to listen to. On March 2, 1933, Franklin D. Roosevelt's inauguration was the first to be broadcast. By then the air waves were full of speeches, eyewitness accounts of earthquakes in California, remote interviews with round-the-world aviators, pickups from golf tournaments, even take-at-home IQ tests offered by a University of Chicago professor. Many world figures from Hitler to George Bernard Shaw could be heard. Commencements at military academies were aired. Amelia Earhart's voice was heard as she flew over New York City.

In 1934 Ford bought the network rights to the World Series, which could be carried by any network, for $50,000. For the next three years Ford paid $100,000 a year, which went into the players' pool, adding $588 to each winner's share in 1937. In 1938 there were no sponsors.

On August 17, 1939, Landis completed a deal giving exclusive broadcast rights to Mutual Broadcasting, sponsored by Gillette Safety Razor, for $100,000. The marriage of Gillette and the World Series would last almost twenty years.

During those years Connie Mack was also a frequent guest at the microphone, not just on sports programs and preseason roundups, but also on other shows, local and national. His life story and longevity made good radio fare. His "Day" in Brookfield in 1934 had been covered by a network. He appeared on a popular network program, "The Inside Story," which interviewed celebrities from sports and the theater, and on dramatic programs.

As for game broadcasts, Mack didn't believe that radio would help contending teams' attendance, but it might help trailers like the A's. Yet he had sat on the sidelines while other clubs had rushed in. At times he voted with the Yankees, Browns, and Senators against leaving the matter to the individual clubs. At other times he seemed to oppose an outright ban. It's likely that he didn't really know which way to turn—until 1935, when on December 11 he announced that the A's and Phillies would broadcast their home games in 1936. Mack had been quoted in November as asking for $25,000 for the rights; the Phillies probably received the same. Dolly Stark, an AL umpire looking for an easier, better-paying way of life, would announce the home games of both teams for the Atlantic Refining Company on WIP, and Bill Dyer would do the same on WCAU for General Mills, whose Wheaties were everywhere on baseball broadcasts.

In 1937 Dyer and Roger Griswold broadcast A's and Phillies' games for General Mills and Socony-Vacuum gasoline. The next year Bill Dyer did the Phillies' games on WCAU; New York newspaperman Stan Lomax broadcast A's home games on WFIL for Kellogg's corn flakes, and Byrum Saam did the same on WIP for Atlantic Refining.

Listeners quickly formed a fond but critical bond with their favorite announcers. One day in 1938 a policeman caught a foul ball and tossed it back onto the field. Byrum Saam said, "His conscience must have hurt him; he must have gotten in on a pass." Station WIP was flooded with complaints from policemen and fans. The next day Saam apologized on the air, while fans at the game aimed catcalls at one of the radio booths, not realizing that their wrath was being fired at the WFIL booth, whose occupant hung out a sign: "My name is Stan Lomax." (Saam was elected to the broadcasters' wing of the Hall of Fame in 1990.)

During the 1936 season New York station WMCA was pirating A's game broadcasts from WCAU and Red Sox games from WICC in Bridgeport and using the information to recreate the games in New York while the Yankees were playing at home. General Mills was the sponsor in both cases. Jake Ruppert asked the American League to do something to stop it.

That was the situation when the American League met to discuss the problem on July 6 in Boston. John Shibe represented the Athletics at the meeting. Bear in mind that his health had been deteriorating; he was days away from collapsing, forcing his resignation as club president. The discussion that took place, at times reading like an Abbott and Costello routine or a Marx Brothers script, is taken from the minutes of the meeting. It shows baseball wrestling with how to deal with the new technology that was beyond its comprehension or control. It also displays the cantankerous side of John Shibe that the press had endured for years.

JOSEPH C. HOSTETLER [AL ATTORNEY]: General Mills is your sponsor in Philadelphia?

JOHN SHIBE: No, we don't pay any attention to them.

JH: But you sold the games to station WIP and WIP sold it to General Mills. [It was WCAU.]

JS: Well, we didn't give them any rights to anything. If they send me any letters, I just throw them back at them. I don't answer them.

JH: I understand you don't give them any right to broadcast in New York but on the other hand they are taking that right. Your contract—or in none of the contracts as far as that is concerned—limits the fellow who has the program from any reuse of it. One way to broadcast a game is by listening to somebody else's broadcast. Another is to have somebody in the ballpark go out after every half inning and telephone what happened.

JS: How are they going to get back into the field after they go out? They can't come back.

JH: Don't you give them return checks?

JS: Give them, hell no we don't.

EDDIE COLLINS: There are plenty of pay stations in your park.

JS: Not in our park. We don't broadcast on Sunday.

JH: I can't tell you from Mr. Shibe's contract with WCAU whether they have the right to broadcast only over one station or if anyone else has the right to broadcast shortwave.

JS: Well, they have got the right from Gimbel's and WCAU.

JH: To broadcast shortwave?

JS: I don't know whether it is shortwave, but WCAU agreed to answer questions. When they send them in to me I just take them and throw them back into the mail. I don't give a God damn where they go. You say they have got the right from Gimbel's? The same crowd General Mills? I don't know. General Mills only with WCAU I think.

JH: Who has WIP?

JS: That is the one that Dolly Stark has. He is all right. I don't know the sponsor but this fellow Dyer with his Wheaties, he has started to branch out now and answer baseball questions. And Christ, they deluge the office. I just take them and throw them back into the mail.

JH: Do they advertise any product over WIP?

JS: Wheaties I think. Yes, it is General Mills I'm sure. [It was Atlantic Refining.] They have two broadcasts. Dolly Stark doesn't mention it. They only get that with Dyer. Stark doesn't mention anything. That WCAU fellow does that. Stark's man doesn't. Stark never says anything that is advertising. Dyer does.

JH: Not in between the innings?

JS: Not between the innings. Stark's man between the innings doesn't say a word about it. The other crowd, this fellow Dyer, he does mention it. That one station WCAU. I listen just as consistently as you do and have people doing it.

CLARK GRIFFITH: I don't see how Stark can support the program.

JS: Do you remember the time I told you they were reporting it in Maryland and you went and got the accounts and said, "I'm going to stamp it right out?" They were all crooked. The Western Union man was taking in Philadelphia.

CG: Stark would give the play by play descriptions and the other fellow would do the advertising?

JS: No, he would not. I just got through telling you. We've got one right in our clubhouse, a radio. We put it on. And we have got one up in the tower.

CG: Who is sponsoring it?

JS: The whole crowd. I don't know.

CG: Well, there is some advertising in there or they wouldn't be doing it.

JS: We have got one there in the refreshment stand and Stark doesn't mention anything about advertising.

[John Shibe then got started on the announcers.]

JS: They make mistakes. Your announcers are rotten. They will say a pop fly. Christ, it hits the fence. Is that a pop fly?

JH: You mean the authorized announcer?

JS: Why, right there in our own grounds. He says a pop fly and a Texas Leaguer. Christ, it bounces off the fence and they get two bases on it. And then he can correct himself. See, your announcers are not so God damn good. None of them.

[WIP was apparently picking up games involving the Red Sox and Yankees and broadcasting them.]

JS: People would rather listen to Boston and New York games than ours.

JH: I was surprised at what Mr. Shibe said because this study that Wheaties sent out to us, they claimed, Mr. Shibe, that they saved you in Philadelphia.

JS: They are God damned liars and I will tell them. They are nothing but Goddamned lying bastards. Save us? Christ, they didn't save us. They kept them away from the park. I know what they are after me for and you don't know. They are begging me, and you know what they want? They want me to give them all our data from the time we opened our grounds. That is what General Mills wants. Let them try to get it. God damn it, they ought to be ashamed of themselves. Give them all our data, what we took in, what we paid out, players and everything? Not by a damn sight. They are God damned liars and I told you that before. Didn't I tell you that right in this room but it didn't seem to register. They claim they saved me, that they helped me. I told you that before, but you couldn't see it. You are getting it now, right from me.

JH: Wait a minute.

JS: Wait a minute. What the hell is the waiting? I come in here and it is brought up again. I don't want to wait. I spoke my piece.

JH: What I mean is the thing that they want, they sent out to all the presidents of each league team, that advertising study. Now that was made, they claim, by some group of specialists, and I said I was surprised when you said you weren't going to broadcast. That would indicate that their report isn't so.

JS: That would indicate that what isn't so?

JH: This study, the one they sent to the presidents.

JS: That is all right. But I was told to sign that by Mr. Harridge, that it wouldn't affect my standing with them.

WILL HARRIDGE: You haven't lost a thing. You helped yourself by signing it.

JS: Well, that is all. I acted under your advice. Now when a company comes into my office and wants all my business data, which I give to this man here [pointing to Harridge] which they want for outside use, why God damn it they want it for a dishonest purpose. And don't you think they're honest, because they will trim you any time they can.

The league's attorneys, trying to find out how New York station WMCA got its information, set a trap. They planted misinformation in the original game broadcasts and different errors in the Western Union reports and heard the errors from both sources repeated on WMCA's bootlegged recreations. The station said its broadcasts were based on wire reports from International News Service. The AL then filed a complaint with the FCC.

Between July 1936 and a November 12, 1936, league meeting, with John Shibe now in a sanitarium, Connie Mack found himself in the middle of the controversy. He had renewed the team's radio contract and apparently approved General Mills as the sponsor. That caused Hostetler to have a fit at the meeting. He directed his comments at Mr. Mack:

HOSTETLER: The only way we could do this thing that was bothering Mr. Ruppert was to do it on behalf of Boston and Philadelphia because when Cleveland plays Boston in Boston and Philadelphia plays St. Louis in Philadelphia, Mr. Ruppert in New York has no special interest in those two meetings. And of course he has no financial interest in the proceeds of the two games. These complaints were filed in the name of the league and the Philadelphia and Boston teams. Renewal of the Philadelphia contract in the face of it, if they approve the same sponsor is, as I told you, Mr. Mack, just as though a woman sued a man for rape and then married him before the trial. It would take the sting out of it.
MACK: I have not approved of the sponsor yet.

Hostetler then urged Mack to tell General Mills that he would not approve them unless they agreed not to sponsor the bootleg broadcasts in New York.

MACK: Suppose I wait to hear from you before I say anything to the station.
HOSTETLER: All right. I'll write you a letter Monday.

In March 1937 the FCC warned that stations rebroadcasting games without permission of the league or the originating stations could lose their license.

The quality of the announcers varied widely. Some of them didn't know what they were watching. Umpires George Moriarty and Bill Dinneen, working the 1932 Boston at Washington opener, complained to Will Harridge about

Ted Husing's call of the game, specifically his charge that the umpires were changing their decisions too often. The umps started their calls with the right hand flat at the left knee, then made a sweeping gesture thumb up over the right shoulder if the runner was out. Husing was prematurely calling base runners safe as the umps began their gestures, then covering himself by blaming the umpires for changing their calls when their thumbs went up.

In 1932 *The Sporting News* asked its readers to vote for their favorite game broadcasters and what kind of broadcaster they preferred. The surprise winner was Arch McDonald in Chattanooga, with 57,000 votes. (The majority of fans wanted colorful, dramatic presentations, which were not Arch McDonald's forte, as anyone who heard him for many years in Washington can verify.)

At the 1936 All-Star Game, Commissioner Landis appeared before a meeting of baseball play-by-play announcers and outlined his guidelines for this new, fast-growing business.

If you see men putting up a gallows in center field and then see them lead me out to it and hang me on it, why, go on and describe it into the microphone. But don't you question the justice of the hanging, understand?

When you broadcast baseball, let your hearers have it just as it is, but don't umpire the game. Don't decide controversies. It's different with the baseball writers. They're privileged to have their opinions. They can criticize an umpire. Don't give a reproachful name to an umpire over the air. And don't say anything that would indicate you favor either team. Your medium is different from the newspaper writers'. I'm not saying which is best, not making any comparisons. It's just a different medium, that's all.

When Leo McEvoy was vice-president of the Browns in 1934, he had advocated a ban on all game broadcasts. Now employed by the American League, McEvoy was appointed director of radio in December 1936, assigned to work in the league office in Chicago and monitor all broadcasts of AL games—thirteen of them at the same time—including the five Chicago stations.

What was he listening for? On November 12 the AL had passed a resolution saying each club had the right to pick the announcers for its games and to censor what went out over the air. But the clubs had to use a uniform league contract that said stations broadcasting from AL parks may not let announcers criticize umpires or managers or official scorers' decisions. No second-guessing. Contracts had to include this wording: "An announcer must not injure the good name or reputation of baseball."

McEvoy's job was to listen for violations of these regulations.

The entire business was prompted by an incident that took place on Sunday, July 26, 1936. The day before, a Chicago announcer had criticized umpire Charles Johnston, calling him "incompetent" after he had ejected Jimmie Dykes, Luke Sewell, and Mervyn Shea in a game against the Yankees. The next day a full house of fifty thousand turned out for a doubleheader. From the minute Johnston appeared on the field, the crowd was on his back, the boos punctuated by an occasional glass or tin missile. The hostilities reached a climax in the bottom of the eighth of the second game, when Johnston called a Sox batter out at first base despite the fact that the pitcher covering first dropped the ball after the tag. When third base umpire Bill Summers upheld the call, bottles, beer cans, and fruit showered down on Summers. While the field was being cleared, Jimmie Dykes got on the PA system and asked the crowd to calm down or the game would be forfeited to New York. That quieted things until the last of the ninth, when a bottle flew out of the stands and struck Summers in the groin, forcing him to leave the game. Commissioner Landis, who was present, ordered the field announcer to inform the spectators that a $5,000 reward would be paid for the arrest and conviction of the guilty party. That brought on more boos.

The future of baseball and every other sport began on October 10, 1931, when W2XAB, an experimental CBS television station in New York, broadcast the first in an eleven-game schedule of football games, Notre Dame vs. Northwestern. Viewers saw a white tin football with the team name on it being moved on a black field with white stripes, while wires and magnets were used to depict the movement of the ball as an announcer at the game described the action. When the ball changed hands, the tin device was flipped over with the other team's name on it.

On February 11, 1937, in Philadelphia, Connie Mack participated in a Philco demonstration of its new improved TV transmission with a leading news commentator of the time, Boake Carter. The picture was transmitted three miles away to a group of invited publishers and editors sitting at the Germantown Cricket Club.

It was the first televised baseball interview.

11 | A VERY SICK MAN

On his seventy-sixth birthday in 1938, Connie Mack entertained the writers with tales of the old days that were not so good that he wanted to see them return. He talked about the time he and Tom Shibe had put together a professional football team in 1902 and the day he had refused to put his team on the field in Pittsburgh until the home team delivered the guarantee money. Then, speaking of the upcoming 1939 season, he said, "We have a hard row to hoe. We need a few more players to fill out our team, but it's harder to find them than it was to get that guarantee money in Pittsburgh."

In the old days Mack's looking for a few good men had consisted of sifting through trainloads of collegians and semipros. Now he was buying them by the bushel, mostly seasoned minor leaguers, mostly flops. Sorting through the scraps left available in the 1938 draft, the A's were the most active club, taking six: veteran pitcher Roy Parmelee from Minneapolis; Henry "Cotton" Pippen from Sacramento; Joe Gantenbein from Toronto; Bill Nagel from Baltimore; Leon Kyle from Pensacola; and Bill Beckmann, a thirty-one-year-old right-hander, from Atlanta. Parmelee was thirty-two; Pippen, a twenty-eight-year-old right-hander; Gantenbein, a twenty-two-year-old infielder who would play two years for the A's. Mack also bought pitchers Bob Joyce from Oakland and Sam Page from Spartanburg. He would take eighteen pitchers to spring training. Only Beckmann lasted as long as three years and was 20-25 in that time.

Mack's highest-priced player—$35,000—was Bill Lillard, twenty, touted by San Francisco Seals manager/salesman Lefty O'Doul as "the greatest shortstop prospect and the fastest player on handling balls I ever watched. His speed in double plays . . . and in whipping the ball to first is uncanny." Mack took O'Doul's word; neither Ira Thomas nor scout Phil Haggerty saw Lillard, called by O'Doul a surefire star—if he could hit. "The pitchers may or may not stop him," O'Doul shrewdly hedged. "Time will tell. But he hit .335 for us in 81 games last year, before he pulled up with a bad knee."

As it turned out, the pitchers did stop Lillard. Mack optioned him to Baltimore for 1939. In 1940 he would hit .238 and never play in the big leagues again.

Mack signed more college stars, some of them before they graduated, a move that brought a storm of protests to Judge Landis's desk from coaches. Landis ignored them, and that irked the coaches even more.

(Landis was more intent on fighting gambling. Somebody wrote to him complaining about the gamblers in the stands at Shibe Park. On June 19, 1939, Landis wrote to Mack, urging him and other owners to do what they could to "keep after these vermin" by "throwing them out of the parks on their heads." In 1940 he sent Mack a list of the gambling activities observed in the right-field stands at Shibe Park on April 16 and said, "I wish you would get to work on this thing, and let me have a report of your progress at the end of your series with Cleveland May 2," repeating his advice on how to dispose of "these rats" when caught in the act during a game. Landis had a better chance of getting the moon to lay off the tides. Landis was also a hawk on players fraternizing with friends on other teams, on or off the field. Umpires were stationed in the stands before games to report untoward friendliness, which brought an automatic fine. The first time Dario Lodigiani, a rookie from San Francisco who had played alongside Joe DiMaggio in junior high, was at Yankee Stadium, he approached DiMaggio during practice, stuck out his hand, and said, "Hi Joe, how you doing?" DiMaggio said, "Dario, no talking. We'll both get fined," and walked away.)

Most of the collegians that Mack signed fizzled. One was Eric Tipton, Duke's star halfback on the 1938 unscored-on team that went to the Rose Bowl. Tipton couldn't hit except for one wartime season in Cincinnati.

One who didn't fail was a left-hand-hitting outfielder with a sweet swing at Washington College in Chestertown, Maryland. In 1936 Ira Thomas had offered Bill Nicholson a thousand dollar bonus. Nobody else had shown any interest in him, so Nicholson took it. A few weeks later Yankee scout Gene McCann saw him and offered him $5,000, but he had already signed with the A's. He was hitless in 10 pinch-hitting appearances that year. Nicholson spent 1937 at Portsmouth and '38 at Williamsport. He hit over .300 and 42 home runs in two years. But Mack didn't think he was ready yet. He had his eye on Dee Miles, a thirty-year-old outfielder with the Chattanooga Lookouts, a consistent .300 hitter with 9-home-run power. On August 8, 1938, he offered Lookouts' general manager Joe Engel $25,000 plus a player of his choice for Miles. Engel chose Bill Nicholson.

Dee Miles was a jovial, happy-go-lucky part-time outfielder and full-time pinch-hitter for the next four years, hitting close to .300 in both roles, with only 2 home runs. In 1939 Joe Engel sold Nicholson for $35,000 to the Cubs, where he reigned for ten years as the Wrigley Field fans' all-time favorite right fielder.

One day in December Mack telephoned Bill Werber and asked him to make the short drive from his home in College Park, Maryland, to Shibe Park to talk contract. Werber was set on getting a $1,500 raise to $11,500. There flashed in Werber's mind a scene from a few years ago. During a pregame chinfest in the Red Sox dugout, ex-Athletics Lefty Grove and Max Bishop were discussing their days with the A's. Werber remembered Grove saying, "Don't ever let Mr. Mack get you up in his cupola office. You'll wind up wanting to pay him to play for the A's."

Werber found an excuse not to go.

It wasn't that Mack acted intimidating. Most players, especially the younger ones, just felt intimidated in his presence when they were in his office.

"When you opened the door and saw him sitting there in that high-backed chair taller than you were standing up," said utility infielder Al Brancato, "he was such an impressive figure, you forgot what you were going to say to him."

Unlike some club owners and general managers, Mack did not demean his players to get them as cheaply as he could. He just didn't have the money, and they knew it.

Later that month Mack was in Washington visiting Clark Griffith, and he asked Werber to meet him at Griffith Stadium. Again Werber found an excuse to avoid him.

So Mack gave up and mailed him a contract in January 1939 that called for a $2,000 cut, along with a long letter detailing the reasons he could not afford to pay him more: attendance had been down 10 percent at Shibe Park in '38 and almost as much throughout the league. The club had lost $48,000, and the outlook for the new year was no brighter. Unemployment was still above 17.2 percent. And, incidentally, Werber's batting average had dipped to .259 and his stolen bases to 19.

The thirty-year-old third baseman returned the unsigned contract with a letter that displayed the attributes some players and writers found insufferable in him. Trampling all over his respect and admiration for the Old Man, Werber conceded all of Mr. Mack's financial troubles and sarcastically advised him to sell the Athletics and find a more profitable investment.

Nearly sixty years later Bill Werber admitted, "That was an error on my part and I've always regretted it. It was an insolent letter. I should have handled it differently. Despite my salary differences with him, he was a thoroughly nice, kindly man."

Like in the stalemate between Connie Mack and Frank Baker in 1915, both men dug in. Neither budged. Spring training began without Bill Werber.

Connie Mack set out to dispose of Werber. He suggested a swap with Cleveland for holdout Earl Averill but was turned down. Eventually he agreed on a $25,000 price with the Cincinnati Reds. But when Reds general manager Warren Giles offered Werber no more than Mack had paid him, Werber still insisted on the $1,500 increase. Giles said no, the Reds couldn't afford to pay him any more than Connie Mack had. Several phone calls from both clubs failed to move Werber. The deal was dead.

Connie Mack didn't want a disgruntled, mouthy, sore-legged player on his team. The fire Werber brought to the game wasn't worth the smoke. But he had no other offers. He called Werber and told him the Athletics would send him a check for the $1,500 difference if he'd sign the Reds' contract.

Werber said no. He wanted it as part of his salary from Cincinnati. It had become a matter of principle to him, and no amount of reasoning can break down a brick wall of principle. Werber was prepared to stay home and sell insurance if he didn't get what he wanted.

The Reds wanted Werber for the same reason that Mack had wanted him. They were a club on the rise, with good pitching, finishing just 6 games behind the pennant-winning Cubs in '38. They had an efficient but quiet infield whose weakest spot was third base. Just before the season started, Warren Giles surrendered and agreed to Werber's terms.

(Later Werber said, "It was the principle of the thing. At the end of the season I actually returned the [$1,500] to the Reds' front office. That's probably another first.")

And that's how Bill Werber made it to the World Series in 1939 and a world championship in 1940, beating Detroit, which had obtained an over-the-hill shortstop, Dick Bartell, for the same reason the Reds had bought Werber.

First baseman Nick Etten was late reporting to Lake Charles. Not exactly a holdout, he had received a contract for $1,750. He wrote to Mr. Mack that he didn't think that was big league money. Mack sent him a new contract for $2,500 and told him that was the best he could do, adding. "We feel the Athletics can finish last with or without you."

Etten signed and was optioned to Baltimore.

During spring training Dick Siebert was bothered by a sore left arm, injured in a game on March 23. He said nothing and kept on playing and hurting. By opening day he couldn't take the pain any more and told Mack he was unable to play. Mack was furious with the collegian for saying nothing about his condition.

Siebert's reasoning was a sign of the times; it didn't pay to let on you were hurting, lest it gain you a reputation for being injury-prone and send you back to the bushes: "Last year when I was brought down with that injured knee cap, they said I was too brittle to play major league ball. So when my throwing arm began bothering me this year I just kept quiet because I didn't want to be known as a putty player."

Mack didn't want to move Lou Finney to first. Judge Landis came to his rescue, ruling that Nick Etten had been optioned out the maximum three times and returning him to the A's. When Siebert recovered from his injuries, Mack sold Etten outright to the Orioles. Etten eventually wound up with a World Series ring as the Yankees' wartime first baseman.

Lynn Nelson had picked up the nickname "Line Drive" because so many of them were hit off him. But last year they had usually gone right at somebody, and he had managed to win 10 games. Nelson thought he was underpaid at $5,000. Nick Etten recalled: "There wasn't much to do at night in Lake Charles. One night we were at this place for dinner, about ten of us, and Nelson got a little high. Connie Mack Jr. and his wife and another couple came in and sat down at a table behind us. Nelson was complaining about how little he was being paid by 'that old turkey neck' and young Connie leaned over and said, 'I don't think you should be talking about him that way.' Nelson said, 'I don't care. It still goes. He's an old turkey neck so-and-so.'"

Connie Mack had more "badly behaved boys" to deal with. He had drafted a twenty-two-year-old infielder, Bill Nagel, from Baltimore. He had to get Nagel out of jail to report to spring training. It seems the night before he was to leave his hometown, Memphis, for Lake Charles, Nagel and his girl were at the Peabody Hotel dancing. The bandleader was giving his girl the eye. Nagel told him, "If you do it again, I'm going to come up there and knock you off that bandstand." And he did just that. Connie Mack bailed him out.

According to Nick Etten, Nagel got Mack's attention again when it came time to leave Lake Charles: "Come time to get on the train and his radio was with his luggage and he couldn't find it and was raising a howl. Lena Blackburne tried to quiet him down but he said he wasn't going anywhere until he got his radio. The noise brought Connie Mack out to see what was going on."

Nagel was good for 12 home runs but little else.

Throughout their travels through Texas and on to North Carolina, the Macks and the team were treated like royalty, feted at breakfasts and barbecues, led by police escorts from town to town. In Dallas Mr. and Mrs. Mack were joined by their friends, Mr. and Mrs. Parker Woods from St. Louis and the Pearlstones. It was as though the South was bidding farewell to Mr. Mack, suspecting that it might not see him in its midst again. The A's never returned for spring training to Lake Charles or Texas.

In a preseason radio roundup, Mack was frank in his assessment of the A's: "Our club is—uh—better but—uh—if good enough to win over other clubs—uh—I don't know. It will be a hard task—uh—for us to overcome these clubs. I wouldn't—uh—tell Joe McCarthy to look out for our club."

In the spring of 1939 Connie Mack had a rigorous schedule of speaking engagements: luncheons, dinners, special events. The night before opening day he was in Easton, Pennsylvania, to speak at a dinner honoring Lafayette baseball coach Bill Coughlin's twenty years there before seven hundred alumni.

On Saturday, May 13, one day after returning from a western trip, Mack went up to New York with Mrs. Mack to appear at a Saturday morning sports class for 250 youngsters at the New York World's Fair, where he was introduced by former syndicator Christy Walsh, the fair's director of sports. Then he took a train back home, but rain washed out the day's game against the Yankees.

Rudy Ohl had worked for Connie Mack for almost forty years, the last twenty-five as Mack's traveling secretary and golfing partner and closest companion on the road. The pipe-smoking Ohl was also a breeder and trainer of champion hunting dogs, a judge at dog shows, a driver and official at harness race tracks, an owner and trainer of game-cock fighters, a student and hunter of small game birds, and an expert fly fisherman.

Mack, seventy-six, decided that Ohl, seventy-five, was too old for the arduous demands of a ball club's travel schedule. Benny Macfarland took his place. Ohl continued to show up at Shibe Park and check the turnstile counts at every home game until shortly before he died in 1946.

Chicago policeman Cornelius McGillicuddy, identified as "a cousin" of Connie Mack, retired at sixty-three after thirty-three years on the beat.

But the Athletics' manager kept rolling along as sprightly as a young colt. On April 26 in New York some of his boys were chatting in the hotel lobby. As Mack walked by, a writer commented that he looked fit enough to do better than Tony Galento against heavyweight champion Joe Louis in their upcoming fight. Mack laughed, "Gosh I don't know about that. I might hop around faster but I'm not very good at bending any more. I don't think I could get low enough." Galento didn't survive the fourth round.

Before the work could begin on installing the lights at Shibe Park, seventeen homeowners in the adjacent block of Twentieth Street asked the zoning commission to ban the lights. The A's countered with a neighborhood canvass of their own that produced 150 signatures in support of the night games. The protesters lost, and Westinghouse began putting up eight 147-foot towers holding a total of 750 fifteen-hundred-watt floodlights at a cost of $105,000.

The A's didn't stop there. New lights brightened the dingy ground floor concourse in the main grandstand. Under Connie Jr.'s direction, all the concession stands were renovated, some turned into clean, spacious cafes with tables and chairs, an innovation far ahead of the facilities at most other ballparks. The menu included soup, hot or cold platters, and drinks; sixty cents would buy a full meal.

The Athletics lost the first American League night game on May 16 at Shibe Park, 8–3, to Cleveland in 10 innings before fifteen thousand on a cold night. Roy Parmelee catered the Indians' 5-run tenth and was soon handed a one-way ticket to Louisville.

Clark Griffith was at the game. He didn't like it. "This game wasn't meant to be played at night," he told Shirley Povich. "It was meant to be played in the Lord's broad sunlight. There's more to a ball game than just a ball game. There's fresh air and sunshine and everything that goes to make up a fine afternoon. I don't want night baseball at Griffith Stadium. I won't put it in unless I have to, at least. Not unless I'm driven to it."

In addition to the installation cost, the electric bills would come to about

$1,000 a game. Griffith believed it would take many years for Connie Mack to recoup his investment. It took one season.

On May 24 the White Sox were at Philadelphia for the second night game. Jimmie Dykes went home and told Sox owner Lou Comiskey how great the lights were. When the A's were in Chicago, Comiskey asked Mack about the details of installing lights and decided to put them in. The White Sox played five night games in two weeks in August, with a crowd of thirty-five thousand on a Monday night against the last-place Browns, a match that might have—*might have*—drawn a thousand in the afternoon. No more convincing argument could be made for the economic benefits of night ball.

Possibly surrendering to Connie Mack's pleas, Ed Barrow agreed to switch the Yankees' Monday, June 26, game to a night game. A Monday afternoon game at Shibe Park in May, when there was still a pennant race, had drawn five thousand. Now with the Yankees ahead by 13 games, they'd have been lucky to attract three thousand. The Yankees were 8-0 against the A's so far. The result: the biggest turnout of the year—33,075—watched Cotton Pippen beat Bump Hadley, 3–2. The next day the Yankees were not enthused about eating supper at 1 a.m., breakfast at noon. (Connie Mack had adjusted by eating dinner at four o'clock on the afternoons of night games.) The Yankees' only observation about playing under the lights was that ground balls appeared to move more quickly.

The 1939 A's had an outstanding outfield in Chapman, Johnson, and Moses; a decent first baseman in Siebert, when he could play; and a catcher, Frank Hayes, who could hit but had none of the fire of a Cochrane or the rapport with the pitchers of Earle Brucker. The rest were holes in the batting order. The long-legged Chapman led all AL outfielders in total chances per game. When he got off to a slow start in the spring, the only person who smiled over that was Washington Redskins owner George P. Marshall, who wanted Chapman to flop as a baseball player so he'd join the Redskins' backfield.

Clark Griffith was one who thought it might happen. "Football players are too muscle bound in the shoulders," he said. "They can't get the bat around quick enough on high inside pitches."

On May 5 Chapman hit for the cycle. He would still be in the A's outfield ten years later, an unsung, all-around outstanding outfielder.

Bob Johnson was another who started slowly, almost lethargically. The hecklers were riding him fiercely. Broadcaster Taylor Grant said, "Our broadcast booth was on the first base side and we could hear the leather lungs in the stands. They got on Johnson a lot. One day he was on first base. He looked up at one of the hecklers who was right near our booth. The crowd was so small you could look him right in the eye and you could tell Johnson was gesturing, pointing. His message was clear: 'You—right after the game—if I see you.' He swung his fist; I think the guy left."

Connie Mack thought Johnson's slump was more a case of alcohol, not attitude. One rainy day some of the players were standing in the grandstand looking out at the field. Mack stood near Johnson.

"Your legs are starting to go," Mack said to the thirty-two-year-old outfielder, "and you are going faster than your legs. You'd better mend your ways."

Johnson, who had tremendous respect for Mr. Mack, took it to heart and went on to a career-high .338 with 114 RBIs. He even stole 15 bases, close to the top ten in a year of the sluggers. Johnson finished eighth in the MVP voting.

When Eddie Collins Jr. graduated from Yale, there was never any question of his signing with anybody but Mr. Mack. He made his debut on July 4 and saw mostly pinch-hitting duty.

The A's pitchers weren't any wilder than the rest of the league, but they were exceedingly hittable. Bud Thomas started in Boston on April 23. Mack's advice on pitching to Red Sox rookie Ted Williams was, "No fastballs." In the first inning Thomas threw Williams a change-up. Williams walloped it for his first big league home run. Exit Thomas.

George Caster had started 40 games last year. He started 17, won 7 of them, this year.

From the time Nelson Potter had joined the A's in 1938, there seemed to be a sort of frayed selvage in his relationship with Connie Mack. Playing high school basketball, Potter had torn a cartilage in his right knee. Once in a while it would lock, and he'd have to knock it back into place. It happened one day in 1938 while he was at bat. Mack told him if he had trouble with it, let Dr. Gopadze take care of it.

Potter recalled, "Dr. Gopadze operated but he took out the other cartilage, not the torn one. Connie Mack wanted me to go back to him but I said no. I had it done in Chicago and the A's paid for it."

One day Potter was pitching against the Yankees. Sitting beside Mack in the dugout, he said, "You know, Mr. Mack, I think there's something a little unfair about this game of baseball that some people haven't considered. There's Joe DiMaggio out there. I think he's making about [$]40 or [$]45,000 a year, and they expect me to go out at my salary and get the guy out. If I can get him out, I ought to be worth [$]45,000."

Potter later mused, "I don't think he liked that very much."

When the Yankees came to Shibe Park in August for a weekend series, Connie Mack was ill and Earle was managing the team. The Athletics were nestled in seventh place. The Yankees' lead had shrunk to 5½ games over the Red Sox. Potter started the Friday game and blanked the Bronx Bombers until a 6-run fifth finished him. On Saturday the Yankees exhausted the A's bullpen in an 18–4 barrage; Potter gave up 6 runs in 3 innings.

The Sunday doubleheader drew the biggest crowd of the year—34,570. In the first game Earle left Lee Ross in to take an 8-run battering over 8 innings, but the A's won it with 3 in the eighth and a 3-run home run by Frank Hayes in the ninth. The crowd was wild with joy. The mood quickly turned ugly when Cotton Pippen was battered for 5 runs in the second inning of the nightcap. Nelson Potter picked up the story:

The place was packed, sold out an hour before the first game. A lot of tomato growers from New Jersey were there that day. They used to bring newspaper and tear it up in little pieces and put it in a sack and when something happened they didn't like, they would grab a handful of that confetti and throw it in the air. It was a mess.

After the second inning Earle started looking for a relief pitcher. No one was in the bullpen; they were all worn out. I'm sitting on the bench and he comes down and looks at me. He's almost crying. New York is beating our brains out and he's got over thirty thousand people booing him, raising the dickens and throwing that confetti in the air. He says to me, "I'm in a predicament. You suppose you could go out there and just get the ball up there?"

Like a fool I said, "Well, I'll try."

They beat my brains out, too. I pitched the last 6 innings and gave up 15 runs in the 21–0 rout. Course the fans didn't care that I'd pitched the two days before. I took plenty of booing.

I decided that the end of this season I'm going to go up and talk to Mr. Mack and tell him I think I'm entitled to a bonus, if for nothing more than that one particular game.

[Potter worked 196 innings in 41 games with an 8-12 record and a league-high 6.60 ERA.]

So I did. I went up there and said, "Mr. Mack, I believe I'm justified in asking you for a bonus this year. I pitched some pretty good ball for you and this one occasion when Earle was managing and I'd pitched the two days before, I helped him out, and my salary isn't very big."

Mr. Mack said, "Yes, I believe you deserve one, and nothing would make me happier than to give you one. But it has to come in through the gate before I can give it to you. You know, if I hadn't held back on a few things, I couldn't have met our last salary."

I was flabbergasted. I just left.

Chubby Dean was Mack's bullpen. He relieved 53 times and was usually up throwing to Charlie Berry on the other days. His arm felt like lead, and he yearned to be a starter on a regular schedule. But he never complained, nor lost his smile. And he hit .351.

The defense made the most errors and fewest double plays—despite numerous opportunities—in the league. The gap between runs scored and runs given up widened to 2 per game. The Yankees romped again, and only the Browns, losers of 111, propped up the A's in seventh place. Earle Mack's lengthiest audition as the A's manager was not auspicious. The team was 25-37 when he took over and 30-60 the rest of the way. They won two more games and drew ten thousand more customers and lost $2,500 less than last year.

Did night and Sunday baseball keep the Athletics in business? Of the 395,000 total home attendance, almost one-third—120,922—came from the seven night games. Eleven Sundays brought out more than 161,000. Together they accounted for more than 70 percent of the total. That left about 112,000 for the other forty-five dates—an average of less than 2,500 per game.

Without night and Sunday games the A's would have lost a lot more than their reported $45,500.

In the past Connie Mack had been reluctant to publicly praise players on other teams. In a 1941 interview with Ernie Harwell he explained that "often times it makes a lot of trouble for the other clubs when you commence to boost your opponent's players. It means that the players sometimes take advantage of that and they say well, Mr. Mack says I'm so and so, Mr. Dykes says I'm so and so or Mr. Baker says I'm so and so, and so the player tries, would demand something exorbitant in the way of his salary and so I dislike very much to say it."

But Mack was so impressed by what the Yankees had achieved, he did not hesitate to go public with his admiration for individual members of the 1936–1939 world champions.

Asked by Bob Considine in May to name the greatest player in the game at the time, Mack didn't hesitate: "Joe DiMaggio. Don't let anyone kid you. DiMaggio's one of the greatest players who ever lived. He'll go down in baseball history. I should know. I've been looking at ballplayers for sixty years. I'll tell you what makes him great. He does the hard things gracefully and often. He'll be good until the '50s."

He told New York writer Jimmy Cannon, "He's the greatest team player I've ever seen."

(Ty Cobb agreed with Mack, predicting that DiMaggio would someday rate a place in the all-time greatest outfield.)

Mack also lauded Bill Dickey, calling him the most vital cog in the Yankees' machine, and conceded that he would now rate the Yankees' catcher above Mickey Cochrane as the best ever. (Dickey seemed to have a book in his head on every hitter—*every* hitter—he ever saw. Joe Gantenbein, a part-time infielder with the A's in 1939–1940, was a low-ball hitter, and the Yankees pitched him high outside. Three years later Gantenbein was in the army at Ft. Riley, Kansas, and he and Pete Reiser went to St. Louis to see a game in the Yankees-Cardinals World Series: "We were in the hotel coming down the stairs and Dickey was going up. He says, 'I know that sergeant there. We used to pitch him high outside.' I said, 'Hi Bill' and we shook hands. He did not remember my name but he recalled how they pitched to me.")

Two years later Mack would be singing the praises of the Yankees' new double play combination of Joe Gordon and rookie shortstop "Phil Rizz-two."

He also had high praise for Joe McCarthy. Accepting an award from the Sportsmanship Brotherhood in 1941, he said, "I used to think—and say—that John McGraw was the greatest manager of all time. But I think I have to change that now and put Joe McCarthy at the head of my list. He has earned first place."

When veteran baseball writer Fred Lieb passed that along to McCarthy, the Yankees' manager said, "Connie was very kind to say that. But let's not kid each other. There is one man who is baseball's greatest manager, and no one else can be spoken of in the same breath with him. The name is Connie Mack."

Mack's admiration for the Yankees didn't prevent him from joining Clark

Griffith in putting through a "break up the Yankees" rule banning any player transactions with a defending pennant winner. The rule was approved in December 1939 but would be repealed at the 1941 All-Star Game meeting.

On June 12 the sleepy town of three thousand souls in Cooperstown, New York, celebrated the opening of the National Baseball Hall of Fame. Commissioner Landis cut the ribbon. On the steps were gathered the living among the first twenty-five inductees. The emcee, Pittsburgh writer Charles "Chilly" Doyle, president of the Baseball Writers Association, first read off the names of the thirteen pioneers. Connie Mack was the only survivor.

After a nod to the recently adopted myth about Abner Doubleday's invention of the game in the town, Mack said, "My sincere thanks for having my name enrolled with these great stars who have taken part in promoting the game for the past one hundred years. And I am quite certain in the years to come of the game progressing due to the fact we have the honorable William G. Bramham as head of the National Association, Ford Frick of the National League, and Will Harridge of the American League, and above all we have that great and honorable Kenesaw M. Landis, the commissioner of baseball, who is the real commissioner. Thank you very much."

The twelve players were then introduced.

Connie Mack had become an institution. Everybody—even non-baseball fans—knew the name. It didn't matter that his team had been last or next to last for the past five years and could well be for the next five. Advertising agencies believed his endorsement of a product carried weight, even if, like non-smoking players in cigarette ads, he knew nothing about the product. An ad in *Collier's* September 16 issue showed Mack, the non-driver, pitching Veedol motor oil.

Lou Gehrig had taken himself out of the lineup on May 2 in Detroit after 2,130 consecutive games. The mortally stricken Iron Horse never played again. That afternoon before the game a photographer asked Gehrig to pose with Tigers rookie Barney McCosky. "I was uncomfortable, didn't think they should bother him," McCosky said, "but he agreed. He put his arm around my shoulders. It felt like he was leaning on me for support." After a few weeks of taking the lineup to home plate before games, the Yankee captain found it too difficult to walk and remained in the dugout. Players who saw him during that time remember him struggling to climb stairs or go up a ramp to the clubhouse, pulling himself up with both hands on the railing. When the Yankees arrived in Philadelphia on June 26, Connie Mack asked Joe McCarthy for a favor: please ask "Mr. Gehridge" if he would take the lineup card to home plate before the second game of the June 28 doubleheader to give Philadelphia fans a chance to show their appreciation of him. Gehrig agreed. When he emerged from the dugout and the 21,612 onlookers spotted him, the eight-minute ovation shook the thirty-year-old ballpark. Connie Mack strode out to home plate in his blue suit and shook hands with the hero of millions.

For the A's fans, it was the only bright spot on a day the Yankees hit 13 home runs, 3 by DiMaggio, and destroyed the A's, 23–2 and 10–0. For Connie Mack it was the last day he managed for the year. If it wasn't something he ate, it might have been something he saw—the Yankees' feasting on his pitchers—that made him ill that night on the train to Boston.

Actually Mack had been feeling poorly for the past month. When John Henry, a pitcher who had been one of the players sold with Mack by Hartford to Washington in 1886, died in Hartford on June 11, Mack wanted to go to the funeral. The A's had just returned from a lengthy road trip. Dr. Gopadze ordered him to stay home.

On Mack's arrival in Boston, the Red Sox doctor, E. J. O'Brien, checked him over and advised him to stay in bed that day. Earle became the acting manager. Mack's daughter Mary was visiting in New Hampshire and hurried to Boston. Mrs. Mack came up from Philadelphia and took charge. It was probably a gall bladder attack, similar to one he had had in 1937. Doctors wanted to operate and remove the gall bladder—a far more risky procedure in those days than it is today, especially for a seventy-six-year-old in Mack's condition—but Katherine wouldn't let them. She put him on a train and took him home. Mack later said the only thing he recalled about the train ride was arriving in Philadelphia and vaguely hearing a conversation between the Pullman porters and an ambulance driver. "I heard one say, 'Shall we take him out the window or the door?'"

They had to remove some panels from the Pullman car to carry him off on a stretcher.

Dr. Gopadze took one look at him and held out no hope for his recovery. Nor did Mack himself, who, according to Red Smith, said he was so sick he tried to die and couldn't.

The newspapers assigned reporters to the Mack death watch. Joe Tumelty recalled sitting at the kitchen table with Mack's daughter Mary—"She liked her Irish whiskey. I stuck to ginger ale"—while the doctor was upstairs.

On July 3 Roy said, "Dad's still a very sick man. He's still running a little temperature but he has shown a slight improvement over last night. All in all, we are very much pleased with his condition. His recovery will be slow. The main thing is to conserve his energy. No visitors are allowed. Mrs. Mack and a special nurse are with him constantly."

Mack was confined to his bed on a liquid diet until July 16. He was forbidden to listen to the games on the radio. On July 7, when Earle stopped by to tell him they had beaten the Senators the night before, Earle told reporters, "He's still seriously ill. It'll be a long time before he pulls out of this one."

On July 23 in Detroit the Tigers led, 15–3, after the top of the eighth. Earle decided on a mass substitution: he replaced seven men, sending Sam Chapman out to play first base and Eddie Collins Jr. to right field. The A's had a Gettysburg College catcher traveling with them named Harry O'Neill. Earle sent him in to replace Frank Hayes. O'Neill caught one inning, didn't bat in the ninth, never appeared in another major league game, and was killed on Iwo Jima March 6, 1945, one of two major league players killed in the war.

By the end of July Connie Mack was sitting up, dictating a few letters. He didn't leave his bedroom until August 23.

"Am starting to feel better," he wrote to Sr. Florence the next day, thanking her for her prayers in a hand "not very steady so please excuse."

Mack gave his first interview that day and as usual claimed he wasn't "really sick." He'd just eaten too much. According to Roy, "Somebody once told Dad if he began to lose weight at his age with his height and active way of life, he'd be in trouble. So he started eating extra portions, stuffing himself as he wasn't used to doing, and I guess that brought it on."

"The doctor says I'm good for many more years," said Mr. Mack.

Connie Mack was either selectively deaf or acutely stubborn. His body was yelling at him to quit trying to do the work of four men. But it was speaking a foreign language.

On his bedside table was a book on the philosophy of life, *Time Out to Live*, by William West Tomlinson. For Connie Mack, his life was the Philadelphia Athletics.

Nothing could keep him from joining 23,285 at the Sunday, September 10, doubleheader against the Red Sox. Between games his 1910–1914 champions played a 2½-inning game against his 1929–1931 champs, winning 6–4. More than forty players from both eras were there. Mack was in his glory, greeting each of his former stars, posing for countless photos, signing scorecards, commenting into the radio mike. Mack bought special uniforms and a gold ring for each of the old-timers. The event was his contribution to baseball's so-called centennial celebration. That evening they gathered for a reunion dinner put on by Mr. Mack, but their host was home in bed; the day's activities had taken too much out of him.

Less than two weeks later he was back in the office every day, seeking trades. On October 31 Mack said his entire team except for Hayes and Johnson were "on the auction block." (Whether their exclusion from the sale counter was viewed by Hayes and Johnson as good news or bad is not known.)

Mack went to the December meetings in Cincinnati, where he ran into Al Simmons looking for a job. After bouncing among the Tigers, Senators, Bees, and Reds (where he made his final World Series appearance), the thirty-seven-year-old Simmons had been handed his release. It didn't take much persuasion for Mack to rehire his favorite player for pinch-hitting and coaching duties; Simmons was happy to be back with the A's, even for $6,000.

The only thing Mack cut back was his speaking appearances. He posed for a pencil portrait by S. J. Woolf, reminiscing about all the changes he had seen in the game and the players—but not hankering for the old days—in response to Woolf's questions.

"A lot of people like to hark back to the good old days," he mused, eyes closed envisioning them, "but if baseball fans of today had a chance to see an old-fashioned game, they'd give it a grand laugh."

When Woolf asked, "What makes a pennant-winning team?" Mack smiled and said, "Having a bunch of players like the Yankees. Seriously, the most necessary thing is a good pitching staff."

He then went on to add that a great catcher and other first-class players helped.

"In addition, all these men have to know how to play together. This is where the manager comes in. He must see that there is team play, that each one supports the weakness of the others. For no matter how good a player is, he isn't as strong in some respects as the others. It's all a game, a great game for those who watch it, even greater for those who play it."

Anyone who had seen the skeletal Connie Mack "trying to die" in the fall of 1939 was amazed to see him back on the banquet circuit four months later. In February 1940 he accepted an invitation from veteran New Haven sportswriter Hubert Sedgwick to attend a writers' dinner, where he enjoyed his first meeting with golf legend Bobby Jones.

"What a splendid fellow!" he wrote to Sedgwick a few days later, beginning a ten-year correspondence and friendship, during which Mack would often lunch with Sedgwick and his friends at the Yale Club in New York and leave box seat tickets for them whenever the A's were at Yankee Stadium.

Mack was an avid football fan all his life. Once at the Yale Club Mack was thrilled to meet a man whose name he could never pronounce, the greatest football player of the early days of the game, Pudge Heffelfinger. Former NFL star end Bill Hewitt, who played offense and defense for the Bears and Eagles in the 1930s without a helmet until league rules required it, lived in an apartment on the third floor of Mack's daughter Ruth's house for a year after his wife died. To Ruth's children he was like part of the family. Ruth recalled him fondly: "We called him Uncle Bill. He and Pop-Pop listened to the football games on the radio on Sundays. Connie Mack loved kids and they loved him, but when the game came on, forget it. Everybody out."

(Hewitt died at thirty-seven when his car skidded off an icy road on January 14, 1947.)

Connie Mack had his first dealings with the Carpenters of Delaware when duPont executive Robert R. M. Carpenter and his son, Bob Jr., led a movement to return a minor league club to Wilmington after a twenty-six-year absence. With community support they built a new ballpark and approached

Mack to join them in operating a franchise in the recently expanded Class B Interstate League. Mack acquired a half-interest, with Carpenter taking the other half, bringing the A's fledgling farm system up to five. He staffed the front office and sent Chief Bender to manage the club. Bender didn't like managing; Mack replaced him with Charlie Berry halfway through the season. The franchise was a great success, drawing almost twice the anticipated attendance. During the season Mack brought the A's to Wilmington to play the local team.

In June 1939 Mack had decided to hold his next spring training in California; he didn't know where at the time, just somewhere between San Francisco and Los Angeles. He settled on Anaheim in Orange County, amid the Valencia orange orchards. The facilities, the playing field, and the weather suited him perfectly. The Portland Beavers' camp was just three miles away, with other teams in San Diego, Hollywood, and Los Angeles, and the Pirates were nearby in San Bernardino. The railroad fare across the country was over $11,000, but the exhibition game crowds were the biggest the A's had seen in years.

Frank Hayes was the only late arrival, ending a holdout by showing up March 17 and signing for a $1,500 raise to $8,000.

Connie Mack may have felt as if he was in some kind of time warp as he watched Eddie Collins Jr. and Al Simmons playing alongside each other in the outfield. Collins lacked a big league arm and was optioned to Baltimore for the season.

Mack had become old news in Florida and Lake Charles. In Anaheim he was the new celebrity in town. Veteran Los Angeles sportswriters Bob Ray, Paul Zimmerman, and Richard Hyland kept him busy with interviews. A local De Soto dealer provided him with transportation. Connie Mack Day in Los Angeles drew ten thousand people. The movie crowd went gaga over him.

Broadway columnist and former sportswriter Ed Sullivan filed this report for "Everyday Magazine" in the *St. Louis Post-Dispatch*:

HOLLYWOOD, Cal., March 9.
YESTERDAY a crowd of us from Hollywood motored out to Anaheim, a pretty little town about 30 miles away, to see Connie Mack, because Mr. Mack is a famous personage in sport and well beloved by all professionals, whether they are in show business or in sport.
We found him seated on a camp chair near the bench of his Philadelphia Athletics. . . . I think that you kids should know about him because

in a disordered world, here is a gentleman of the old school who tells you that the homely virtues are the substantial ones.

He is starting his fifty-seventh season as a professional showman, is Mr. Mack. In more than half a century of active life, he has handled thousands of men from every section of the country. His teams have played before millions of fans. He has known every shading of success and failure. He has met men of every faith and every color and every temperament. He has had in his employ men who were sulkers, men who were alibiers, men who were honest, men who were dishonest, men who were loyal and men who were disloyal. He has seen every facet of the ring of emotions which makes up everyday life.

At 77, CONNIE MACK'S message to the kids of the country is that the best things in life are free, and additionally, that the solid virtues are the only permanent things. He means honesty, decency, self respect, integrity, kindness. He tells you kids that some of the greatest players he's ever had failed because they had no sense of discipline and refused to obey orders. In other words, he says that talent without discipline and training is worth nothing.

Sitting with him, and listening to him, the thing that strikes you most forcibly is the veteran's fine face. . . . The lines criss-crossing it form the highway of a great life. . . . At 77, Connie Mack can look every man straight in the face because he's always played the game that way.

Hollywood celebs, enormously successful, are apt to become a trifle bored and blasé. They've seen everything, or pretty nearly everything. They've got everything, or nearly everything and under those circumstances, life is likely to lose some of its flavor. And people so situated are apt to lose a sense of appreciation. . . . At 77, Connie Mack finds life a lively affair, and his enthusiasm and his sense of appreciation and gratitude are things to arouse you. "Watch that boy playing third base," he said. "I think he's going to be a great ball player." He said it just as enthusiastically as he said it in his first season in baseball, back in 1883. He was enthusiastic about the baseball park layout at Anaheim. He was enthusiastic about the bright sunny day and the crowd of townspeople who had turned out for the afternoon.

IT'S SO EASY to lose your enthusiasm. You can so easily become sour and cynical and half-smart. Mack, at 77, gets as much kick out of commonplace things as though they had been created for his particular benefit. On the way back from the ball park, one of the Hollywood crowd mused: "I learned a tremendous lesson watching that man today. I'll never again be bored with my work or with everyday things. I'm going to try to look at life as he looks at it. He has the right viewpoint; we have the wrong viewpoint."

THERE ARE a lot of things that are wrong in the world, but when you meet Connie Mack, and are inspired by meeting him, you become convinced of the truth of something that Raymond Massey said in "Lincoln in Illinois" and something that we should not lose sight of. Massey, as Lincoln, recalled that once a great ruler asked his wise men to coin one sentence which would apply equally to everything. The wise men returned in some weeks with the sentence, "This too shall pass."

When you are confounded by things that are evil and vicious, remember that line: "This too shall pass," because time and years cure pretty nearly everything and restore all things to focus. At 77, Connie Mack agrees with this, I imagine, but amends it to read that the permanent values never alter. They may be bruised or postponed or deflected, but eventually everything adjusts itself to the yardstick of centuries. I'm glad that we went out to see Connie Mack, because Mr. McGillicuddy is proof that this is a pretty nice sort of world if we have nice people like Mr. McGillicuddy.

And Connie Mack ate up all the attention, hobnobbing with movie stars, many of whom were avid and knowledgeable fans: Joe E. Brown, the Three Stooges, Bob Hope, Bing Crosby, Gene Autry, Roy Rogers, Leo Carillo. Mack was feted at numerous sports dinners and didn't hesitate to take a bow at every opportunity.

Red Smith described Mack being introduced before a fight at Hollywood Legion Stadium: "He would spring through the ropes nimbly and draw erect, hands clasped overhead, acknowledging the spontaneous cheers."

Late one Friday night Mack and some players went into the hotel coffee shop for a snack. Mack ordered a ham sandwich. One of the players said to him, "Mr. Mack, don't you know today is Friday and you're eating a ham sandwich?"

Mack said, "It's all right. I'm eating it on Philadelphia time."

For the players Anaheim was a far more lively scene than Lake Charles or Fort Myers. They visited the movie studios—"watched a rehearsal where one of the Barrymores complained that he couldn't see the sign to read his lines," rookie Les McCrabb remembered. They all went to Leo Carrillo's ranch north of San Diego for a barbecue and some bobcat hunting. Mack donned a huge cowboy hat for photographers. He and Carrillo, who later gained worldwide fame as TV's Cisco Kid's sidekick Pancho, became close friends; in the following years, whenever Carrillo was in the East, he would visit Mack at Shibe Park. In November 1945 Mack reminded him, "Remember when I posed in that oversized hat? If I can get you in a baseball uniform we'll be even."

When the A's and Pirates went up to San Francisco for a weekend, it was the first time Mack had been in that city in thirty years. One morning local writers trying to interview him in the hotel lobby were constantly left looking at each other while Mack answered one page after another to go to a phone booth and take a call. To Dick Friendlich of the *San Francisco Chronicle*, "It seemed as if everyone he had met there in 1909 called him that morning. Those who didn't call came by with some semipro in tow seeking tryouts."

One evening Mack spoke at an Elks Club father-and-son dinner. Another evening the mayor hosted a banquet for him. Some of the writers accompanied Mack but were ignored by the big shots surrounding Mack, who spotted one of the writers standing alone by the wall. Wishing to include him, Mack waved the writer over, saying, "I want you to meet these people."

Red Smith, Stan Baumgartner, and a few other writers rode with him in a limo from San Francisco to San Quentin for a game against the prison team. Considering how ill Connie Mack had been just five months earlier, it was natural for his friends to be solicitous about his well-being, although they knew he hated being fussed over as if he were an old man. The window was open. The morning fog chilled the air. Somebody asked Mr. Mack if he wanted the window rolled up.

According to all accounts of those present, Mack exploded: "Damn it to hell. I'm all right. Everybody's always worried about me. Mrs. Mack says, 'Con, wear your rubbers. Con, put on your overcoat. So I put on my damn rubbers and I put on my damn overcoat and I walk to the drug store to get medicine for her. . . . And that Lena Blackburne. It's always 'Boss, can I get you something' or 'Boss, do you need something' and where is he? Back in Anaheim laid up with a sore back."

The window stayed open.

It was as if Connie Mack was determined to dispel any suggestions that his health was an issue. One day early in the season, Detroit catcher Billy

Sullivan Jr. said hello to him on the field. "He slapped me on the back," Sullivan recalled, "and almost knocked me into the dugout."

But Al Simmons and Lena Blackburne noticed that his hand shook a little more when he waved that scorecard.

As a concession to comfort, Mack allowed a square hole to be cut in the center of the wooden bench in the Shibe Park dugout and a sponge rubber cushion inserted for him to sit on. Taylor Grant worked with the game broadcasters doing pregame dugout interviews with the players. Grant was built like Mack: six feet tall and 126 pounds.

"I would be in the dugout with the players before the interviews," Grant said. "[Mack] didn't arrive until just before game time so I would sit on his cushion. One day he came in early and I was still sitting there. I apologized and got up. He said, 'That's all right, Taylor. You're the only one can fit there. Better you than some of these lard-asses around here.' . . . People may question that he said that, because he was a very dignified man. But I can still hear the words ringing in my ear [over fifty years later]."

The A's traveled east with the Pirates for over three weeks, dipping into Mexico along the way. Wherever the train stopped, regardless of the time of day, Connie Mack would appear on the rear platform of the last car like a presidential candidate on a whistle-stop campaign He greeted people— cowboys, Indians, cattle and railroad workers, soldiers—some of whom had driven a long distance in hopes of seeing the man who was truly a legend in his own time. Sometimes Mack would climb down and stretch his legs, answering questions and shaking hands until the train was ready to depart. Once a fan asked him who was the greatest player, Joe DiMaggio or Ty Cobb.

"That's a great question," Mack said. "Joe DiMaggio is the greatest player in the game today. Cobb could hit with him, was a better base runner, as fine a fielder and thrower, but most of all he had that fighting spirit. He fought with anyone any time and kept fighting til he was done."

Jeane Hoffman, a pioneer woman sportswriter and cartoonist in Los Angeles, moved to the *Philadelphia Evening Bulletin* at the age of twenty-one and became the first woman to join the men in the Shibe Park press box. The world did not end as a result.

In his constant search for pitchers, Mack took a liking to a Yankee farmhand, Joe Beggs, a twenty-nine-year-old right-hander who had been a winner at Newark for three years, and therein lay a lesson in how the baseball business worked at the time. Prior to the recent winter meetings, a team could put a player on its waiver list and withdraw the name if any other club in the league claimed him—once. If it circulated the name again and a club claimed him a second time, it had to let him go for the waiver price. The previous December the rule had been changed; now a player on the list could be withdrawn any number of times if claimed.

One use of the waiver list was to go fishing for nibbles of interest in a player. A team claiming him might be willing to pay more than the waiver price. Another was to try to slip a player through unclaimed in order to trade him to a club in the other league or send him to the minors.

Every club did it, but the Yankees were the most industrious at it. "Each time the Yankees ask waivers," Connie Mack explained to Frank Yeutter of the *Bulletin*, "they send out forty or fifty names."

Whenever Joe Beggs was on the list, Mack and Cleveland business manager Cy Slapnicka claimed him. Every time he was withdrawn.

"You get tired claiming players you know you can't get," Mack said. "So I finally let him go. I guess that was the case in Cleveland too."

When nobody claimed Beggs, the Yankees were free to trade him to Cincinnati for veteran lefty Lee Grissom.

"I guess maybe the Yankees did put one over on us," said Mack.

(The Yankees may have put one over on themselves too. They sold Grissom to Brooklyn in May. Beggs had a 12-3 season relieving for the pennant-winning Reds. The Yankees lost the pennant by 2 games.)

Mack proposed that clubs be required to state the purpose of securing waivers for each player: to option him to the minors or sell him for a specified price to a specific club. Clark Griffith favored abolishing the right to withdraw a waiver request if a player was claimed. Neither idea went anywhere.

Mack waded through the minor league merchandise mart, checkbook in hand. He gave Memphis $15,000, pitchers Bob Joyce and Sam Page, and outfielder Babe Barna for a 6-foot-2 left-hander, Herman Besse. The twenty-eight-year-old Besse had won 17 with 6 shutouts. He'd win 5 in five years for the A's. Mack spent $7,500 for thirty-year-old right-hander Ed Heusser, $15,000 for Atlanta third baseman Al Rubeling, and another $15,000 drafting pitchers Elon Hogsett from Minneapolis and Johnny Babich from Kansas City. (Hogsett was thirty-six; Mack sold him back to Minneapolis in April for $5,500.)

Grantland Rice observed, "Mack has paid out as much money this season as any other owner has paid out—possibly more."

Mack wasn't done.

The Tigers, who had finished fifth, needed an outfielder. Mack needed a second baseman. In December he had traded Wally Moses to Detroit for promising second baseman Benny McCoy, twenty-four, who had hit .302 in 55 games but was not regarded as a great glove man. A month later Judge Landis, blasting the entire farm concept with its options, cover-ups, and phantom transactions as "evil because such ownerships are operated to control great numbers of players, imperiling their essential rights," emancipated McCoy and ninety other Detroit farmhands, thus canceling the trade. (Moses was stuck back with the last place A's while the Tigers won the 1940 pennant.)

Shortly after freeing the Detroit farmhands, Landis sent out a three-thousand-word proposal that would eliminate farm systems and replace them with some form of baseball schooling system and a general subsidizing of Class B, C, and D leagues. There would be no optioning of players, and nobody would control hundreds of them. After a collective spasm— Connie Mack was one of the few who said it was a good idea—the owners ignored the suggestion.

McCoy was now a free agent, and a bidding war began. Twelve clubs pursued him. A young free agent with big league experience was a rarity in those days. Connie Mack let McCoy know the Athletics were prepared to give him $5,000 over the highest bid. When Pittsburgh's offer of $40,000 ended the bidding, McCoy called the A's. Connie Mack was in California. McCoy told Earle, "If your offer is still good, it'll cost you $45,000. Earle said yes. He took the check, signed by Bob Schroeder and Roy, to McCoy's home in Grand Rapids and handed it to him on January 29. McCoy put the money into an annuity. The Athletics also gave him a two-year contract for $10,000 a year.

Where did the money come from? Rumors that Tigers owner Walter O. Briggs had loaned Mack the money to pay McCoy in hopes of obtaining Moses went unanswered by Mack. The A's ledgers show that the club borrowed $50,000 from the American League on February 1 and repaid it in two installments on July 22 and November 1.

Mack gave $7,000 to another Tiger farmhand set free by Landis—twenty-nine-year-old right-hander Pat McLaughlin—but received no return on this investment.

Earle now declared that McCoy, Rubeling, Lillard, and Siebert gave the club "a grand young infield, and we certainly should be pennant contenders by 1941."

The Yankees had recalled seven players from their Kansas City farm club but left Blues' right-hander Johnny Babich exposed to the draft, and Connie Mack snapped him up. Babich, twenty-seven, had been pitching for nine years, including two in Brooklyn and a brief stay with the Braves. He had been 19-6 in 1939.

Babich balked at the $4,000 contract sent him by Roy Mack, who was now handling the routine contract negotiations.

"When you went up from the minors, you were supposed to get at least a 10 percent increase," Babich said. "I got a letter from Roy telling me the raise was in there and it wasn't. They were offering me the same as I had earned in Kansas City."

When Babich arrived in Anaheim, Connie Mack asked him why he hadn't signed.

"The money your son is offering me is Coast League, not big league money. I can't live on what you're paying me. I need more money."

Mack said, "I'll give you a bonus at the end of the year."

Babich left it at that; he had been out of the big leagues for four years. He didn't know how his thirty-seven-year-old arm would hold up. He would pitch "for coffee and hot cakes," he said, and see what happened.

For all that, Babich said, it was no different in Brooklyn or Boston, and the Yankees were "just as cheap. All the years I was in baseball I heard complaints from players about how terrible the Yankees treated them. When we were in New York I'd visit with [fellow Bay Area residents] Gomez and DiMaggio and the rest and they'd complain about how they were paid."

(One day in 1949 the A's were playing the Yankees. New York outfielder Hank Bauer was on third base. During a lull in the game, the A's third baseman, Hank Majeski, asked Bauer how much he made. "Twelve thousand," said Bauer. "I make more than that," said Majeski, who was earning $15,000.)

Chubby Dean still yearned to be a starter. Unfortunately he showed no reason he deserved the role, being belted freely in spring training. When a strained back muscle sidelined him for a while, he thought about it—"brooded" would be too strong a word for the cheerful Chubby—and got up the nerve to ask Connie Mack for a chance to start a game. Mack gave him his chance, and the young southpaw responded with the best pitching Mack had seen so far that spring.

On a hunch Mack bypassed his veteran starters and handed Dean the ball for the opener against the Yankees. There was naught but grim determination in the playful Chubby's face as he bore down, gave up 1 unearned run and 6 hits, and beat the defending champs, 2–1, on his own tenth-inning sacrifice fly. Then he relaxed and laughed for the first time all day.

A week later he shut out the Bronx Bombers, 3–0, on 4 hits.

Had Connie Mack found another star lefty?

The A's got off to a good start, breaking even in 6 games against the Yankees and Red Sox; then they were devastated in Washington by blowing a 6–1 lead in the last of the ninth with 2 out and nobody on base. But they bounced back with two rallies of their own. On May 20 they were fourth with a 12-14 record. Dean and Babich were each 4-1.

Then they began to sink.

Benny McCoy knew that Philadelphia fans were not an easy bunch to play before. The big money and the publicity he had received made it even tougher, although the players never expressed any resentment over his good fortune. McCoy told Bob Considine in late April: "Their attitude is, 'The more you can get, the more power to you. That's true of the fellows on other teams, too. They've come to me and said they're glad I got that dough."

Connie Mack wasn't putting any pressure on him. When he met McCoy at the Philadelphia writers' dinner in January, Mack told him, "Benny, I don't expect you to be another Collins. Just go out there and play your game and we'll go along with you."

But the fans made him feel like they expected him to get a hit every time he batted.

And he didn't. He had 2 hits in the first week, both doubles, and made 4 errors.

"I'm no great star," he told Considine. "Never was and maybe never will be. But I know I can play better ball than I've played so far. The trouble with me is I'm pressing. I'm not loose out there. . . . I'm tight. Trying too hard."

The general thinking in sports pages was that the Athletics were going nowhere, that Connie Mack was over the hill, that the game had passed him by. But some of those who had played for him knew better than to count him out. The Athletics were in eighth place when they came to Boston July 1. Ed Rowe of the *Christian Science Monitor* was sitting in the Red Sox dugout with Lefty Grove and Jimmy Foxx, silently watching the A's take batting practice. Rowe asked them if they were remembering their days with the A's.

"No, I don't often go back over what has already happened," said Foxx. "I was thinking that Connie might have another real good team in a year or two. You wouldn't suspect it now after glancing at the standings but I like the way some of his young players move around on the field. He spent a lot of money on new men last winter and expects to be in the race again in '41."

Grove spoke up. "That's right. Connie will win another pennant before he's through. He's on the road back again."

Later Rowe was interviewing Mack at the hotel when Foxx walked in. "I was speaking at a men's club the other night," Foxx said. "When I predicted that [Mack] was on his way to the top again, they laughed. I suppose they thought I was fooling because this is one of his leaner years, but I wasn't. They'll be up there next year. One good pitcher and another outfielder could make the difference."

Foxx's hitting was better than his predicting: the A's lost 100 games and finished last, then lost 90 in 1941.

As usual, it was the pitching. After his 4-1 start, Dean won 2 and lost 12 with a 6.61 ERA—highest in the league (he still batted .321 as a pinch hitter). Herman Besse was a bust, allowing 104 base runners in 53 innings.

George Caster, the sleepwalker, was 4-19 with a 6.56 ERA. On September 24 Caster must have felt like the flag waving over Ft. McKinley the night the bombs were bursting in air around it. In the sixth inning the Red Sox launched 22 total bases off him, including home runs by Williams, Foxx (his 500th), Cronin, and Jim Tabor. In November Caster was cast off to the Browns for $8,000. Well, hardly cast off. He wound up on two consecutive pennant winners: St. Louis in '44 and Detroit in '45.

In his frustration Mack had begun to equate a pitcher's ineffectiveness with lack of effort rather than lack of ability. Right-hander Les McCrabb had been a semipro shortstop and pitcher in Quarryville in the Pennsylvania Amish country when a local catcher recommended him to Connie Mack. Invited to a tryout in 1936, McCrabb threw to Earle for fifteen minutes, then said, "I'd like to try out as a shortstop."

"You're a pitcher," said Connie Mack, and sent him a Williamsport contract. Called up at the end of the 1939 season, McCrabb started 1940 throwing batting practice. On April 26 in Washington he relieved in the seventh inning. "All the catcher, Frank Hayes, was calling for was curves," he said. McCrabb walked 2, hit a batter, and lost a double play when the third baseman dropped his throw. For the next two days he was back to throwing batting practice. Then he relieved in the seventh against Boston and gave up 3 runs on 5 hits. At the end of the inning, Connie Mack said to him, "You're not trying."

McCrabb snapped, "I can't throw batting practice and pitch too."

The next morning the still angry rookie went up to Mack's office. "Mr. Mack, you accused me of not trying yesterday."

"I thought it over," said Mack, "and I talked it over with [bullpen coach] Charlie Berry. You're gonna be with us all year."

"If you're going to use me that way I don't care if I'm with you all year or not."

Years later McCrabb admitted, "I should have kept my mouth shut." Three days later he was in Toronto.

Ed Heusser worked in 41 games—35 in relief—only 2 behind the league leader, Bob Feller. He was 6-13. He told Red Smith:

I pitched relief pretty near every day. One day Connie Mack said to me, "I don't think you're trying." I said, "If it was anybody but you said that or if you were younger, I'd climb your frame."

That night he called me to his hotel room. He said, "When I was playing, if anybody told me what I told you today, I'd have been a lot rougher than you were."

I said, "Mr. Mack, nobody ever accused me of not trying. But I worked five innings and four the day before and two a couple days before that."

He asked me how much money I was getting and I told him [$3,000]. "Well," he said, "I don't think that's enough for a man working as often as you." And he sat right down and wrote me a check for a thousand dollars.

Heusser had more success with Cincinnati during the war.

One of Mack's new pitchers was Cecil Porter Vaughan out of the University of Richmond. Given an $8,000 signing bonus, the 6-foot-1 blond left-hander had a dazzling smile and world-conquering confidence. He made his debut June 16 in Cleveland against Bob Feller, giving up 2 runs on 2 hits until he was removed for a pinch hitter in the eighth and had no decision.

Vaughan surpassed even the handsome Chubby Dean as a matinee idol. Connie Mack decided to promote him as his Sunday pitcher to draw the ladies. Vaughan pitched 6 Sunday games, not very well. He threw a total of 12 wild pitches in 99 innings, won 2 and lost 9, and never won again.

Few people remember Porter Vaughan; umpire George Pipgras was one of them. Forty-five years later he recalled a game at Yankee Stadium on August 11. In the fourth inning, with Charlie Keller on third and Babe Dahlgren on first, Dahlgren broke for second. Vaughan turned and threw to second. Pipgras, umpiring at third base, immediately called a balk on Vaughan.

Pipgras recalled, "Connie Mack came into our clubhouse after the game and asked me to show him the rule on that balk call. The pitcher had stood back of the rubber and motioned like he was going to throw a pitch and turned and threw to second and caught the runner off by fifteen feet. I showed him in the rule book—'There it is, Mr. Mack'—and he walked out. Lena Blackburne was with him and said, 'I don't see that in my rule book.' He had an old book."

Nelson Potter, 9-14, worked 200 innings with a 4.44 ERA. Potter was the best fielding pitcher Mack had seen for some time. On June 13 at home against Chicago he had 4 putouts covering first base and started a double play in a 3–2 win.

Johnny Babich was the ace of the staff at 14-13 with a 3.73 ERA. Four of his losses came in a one-month span beginning July 12: a Bob Feller 1-hitter beat him, 1–0; an Al Milnar 6-hitter beat him in Cleveland, 1–0; he lost a 4-hitter in St. Louis, 5–0; and he lost, 2–0, in New York to a combined 2-hitter by Red Ruffing and Steve Sundra. After that one, he told his wife, "There goes my bonus."

But that was the only time the Yankees beat him; he was 4-1 against them when Connie Mack asked him to come up to the office on Tuesday, September 24, and handed him a check for $1,000.

The Yankees, Tigers, and Indians were fighting for the pennant. Mack called the Cleveland middle infield of Ray Mack and Lou "Boordeer" (Boudreau) the best keystone combo he'd seen in a long time. The previous winter, anticipating a decline by Bill Dickey, Mack had predicted the Yankees, after a run of four straight world championships, would finish third in 1940. Babich was eager to do his part in making the prediction look good.

"You're pitching against the Yankees on Friday," Mack said. "I hope you knock them off."

"Mr. Mack," said Babich, "you know when I go out there to pitch, I mean business."

"I know. You showed me that," said Mack.

Babich pitched a shutout until the ninth, Sam Chapman drove in 3 runs with a home run and double, and the A's eliminated the Yankees, 6–2, while Detroit was clinching the title with a 2–0 win over Cleveland. It was a most satisfactory way to cap off a 100-loss season.

Frank Hayes caught almost every day and filled in twice at first base, hitting .308 with 16 home runs, behind Johnson's 31 and Chapman's 23. Wally Moses was still the premier lead-off man in the league with a .394 OBP. They may not have hit when Babich was pitching, but they were no slouches at the plate, scoring only 7 fewer runs than second-place Cleveland. But it was all done by the catcher and the outfield. McCoy wound up hitting .251. Mack considered him a disappointment but believed he would do better in '41 without the pressure that had accompanied his high price tag. McCoy improved to .271 the next year, then four years in the navy cut short his career. Bill Lillard and Al Rubeling turned out to be first-class lemons. Mack had signed a local boy, Al Brancato, and optioned him to Williamsport, where he led the league with 98 RBIs in 1939. But Al couldn't solve big league pitching no matter how hard he worked at it. Mack turned him over to Al Simmons, who soon gave up on him and let him know it. Except for Dick Siebert, who twice broke up Bob Feller's bids for no-hitters with eighth-inning singles, the infield was so weak at the plate that Mack often used pinch hitters for them—and then pinch-hit for their replacements.

Al Simmons played occasionally in left field and hit .500 as a pinch hitter, reaching base seven consecutive times in one stretch.

Recruits from Duke continued to arrive. After his first year at the school, infielder Lawrence "Crash" Davis had had his expenses paid by the Athletics. As was true of others, there was no commitment to sign with the A's, but the feeling of obligation was hard to duck. After graduating, he took a train to Philadelphia and went up to Mack's office in the Shibe Park tower. Mack offered him a contract for $2,500, the standard rate for rookies.

"Mr. Mack, there's no way I'll sign for that. I can make that much back home playing ball."

Mack's back stiffened. "Young man," he said sternly, "you can go back home."

Davis gulped. "I'll sign," he said.

Years later Davis admitted, "Just reporting to a major league club was the greatest thrill I ever had, not even being on the field. Why, the guy at the gate even knew my name. That was so important to me, a fresh, frightened kid out of North Carolina."

On June 5 the A's were losing to Detroit, 9–1. Sam Chapman led off the ninth against Schoolboy Rowe. Mack called out, "Davie."

"Yes, sir, Mr. Mack."

"I want you to pinch-hit."

Davis jumped up, grabbed some bats, and charged up to home plate. Chapman was still in the batter's box. The umpire, George Pipgras, called time. "Wait a minute," he told Davis. "This guy's still hitting."

"Take it easy," the Tigers' catcher, Birdie Tebbetts, said to the nervous Davis, who fouled out to third after Chapman reached base.

Davis, slowed by an old ankle injury, was a holler guy in the infield, full of pepper, always hustling—sometimes too much. He would charge into right field after a short fly ball, sometimes interfering with a catch the right fielder could have made, until Mack pointed out that right field was not his territory. He didn't hit in his three seasons with the A's and gained more fame as the basis of the character bearing his name in the movie *Bull Durham*.

Under a new working agreement with Toronto, the Athletics had the right to buy any two players for $7,500 each. They took just one, a right-handed pitcher, Phil Marchildon, who said he was twenty-four but was really twenty-seven. A tightly wired, nervous native of Penetangqushene, Ontario, Marchildon had done more skiing than pitching in his life, with only two years' professional experience after pitching for a nickel mining company team. Marchildon, though labeled French-Canadian, had no French accent; Ontario was 80 percent English-speaking. He was not tall—5-foot-10—but muscular, with "arms like an ape," remembered Taylor Grant. Lena Blackburne looked him over and reported he had a big league curve.

Marchildon joined the A's in Cleveland on September 15. Mack intended to take a look at him the next day, but with a three-way battle for the pennant among the Indians, Tigers, and Yankees, the other two teams squawked about Mack's using a brand new recruit against the Indians. So Mack started second-year man Bill Beckmann instead. Beckmann beat Cleveland, 4–3, but the A's were equal opportunity losers in the last two weeks: 2-3 against Cleveland, 1-2 against New York, and 1-3 against the pennant-winning Tigers.

So Marchildon sat until Washington came to town, then demonstrated that the complainants had a point: he gave up 6 hits, 3 walks, and 2 wild pitches in 3 innings. Pitching coach Earle Brucker saw him tipping his pitches, landing off balance—doing everything wrong. When the Red Sox beat him, 4–1, in the last game of the season, they ran wild on him with 8 of their year's total of 55 stolen bases.

"We'll work on everything in the spring," Brucker told him.

The Athletics were headed for the train after the last game in Cleveland when *Inquirer* sports editor James Isaminger was felled by a near-fatal stroke.

He had covered the A's for thirty-five years and was Connie Mack's frequent ghost writer. Isaminger lived another six years but never wrote again.

In the end the Athletics recorded the league's highest errors and ERA, which combined to let in almost 2 more runs per game than the second-place Indians.

Attendance was up 10 percent; income from the Phillies fell as their gate dropped 25 percent. For the decade 1931–1940, only the St. Louis Browns had lower attendance in the American League. With no more stars to sell, the club had a net outlay of $109,800 for players, resulting in a loss of $57,622 for the year. It would have been more, but that fall the Philadelphia Eagles of the NFL began playing their home games at Shibe Park. Those five dates and the St. Joe's Prep School games at Shibe Park added $21,000 to the year's income.

On June 23 Mack left the team in Chicago and went home for his daughter Betty's June 27 wedding to Jim Nolen. The only big wedding for Mack's four daughters, it was a swanky affair at the country club where Connie Jr. belonged.

Twenty-three years after the drafting of young men to fight a war had ransacked Connie Mack's Athletics, the world was fighting again, and a new draft began. For Connie Mack this time it started closer to home. On November 7, nine days after his son Connie III was born, Connie Jr.'s draft number, 177, became the 3,019th number drawn.

During the December league meetings in Chicago, a group of forty—players and their wives, politicians, writers, businessmen, and lawyers—attended a dinner for Mack. When introduced, Mack stood erect behind his chair at the head table. His eyes glowed with happiness.

"Sometimes it pays to grow old," he said.

He and his brother Michael, eighty-four, were the last of the brothers and sisters born to Michael and Mary McGillicuddy. Michael still worked directing traffic outside the reserved seat windows at Shibe Park.

On December 20 Connie Mack bought himself a birthday present: the 141 shares held by John Shibe's widow, Ethyl. The stock had been valued at $300 a share in 1938. Total cost would be $42,300 at that price. Mack now owned a majority interest for the first time. The sons of one of Ben Shibe's daughters, Elfrida Macfarland, worked for the club, Ben as traveling secretary and Franklin as assistant treasurer. Elfrida would be on the club's payroll beginning in 1941 at amounts varying from $200 to $400 a month until January 1950.

Connie Mack readily admitted the role his ownership in the club had on his longevity in the dugout. "I'm satisfied I would have been looking for a new position very often," he said. "I guess too much stress is put on the manager, but that's the game I suppose."

The writers gave him a birthday luncheon at the Warwick Hotel, at which he said, "I know no manager likes to finish last, and even at seventy-eight I'm looking for the day when I can be hanging around the top again. It's much nicer up there."

Then Connie Mack went back on the hectic rubber chicken circuit just as if he hadn't been at death's door a year ago.

13 | THE "MINOR LEAGUE" A'S

After another last-place finish, Connie Mack no longer wished for one more pennant before he retired. "I am not as interested now in that as I am in having a fighting chance." He called the Yankees the team to beat in '41, adding, "I'd like to finish right next to them."

In his annual hunt for pitching, Connie Mack did business with Jimmie Dykes, trading Dario Lodigiani to Chicago for a dependable starter, thirty-four-year-old right-hander Jack Knott. The A's were now employing more attendance bonuses in salary negotiations. Knott signed for $7,500 with a $1,500 bonus if he won 12 games (he did) or attendance reached six hundred thousand (it didn't). In April the Yankees were trying to unload thirty-seven-year-old Bump Hadley. The Giants took him on a trial basis and quickly returned him. Mack paid $2,500 for him and assumed his $7,500 contract. It was an odd purchase. Hadley was the kind of veteran a contending club might pick up for a year—clearly not the Athletics' situation.

Persuaded by Earle Brucker, Mack spent an extra $2,500 for his pitchers and catchers to report two weeks early at Carlsbad, California, near San Diego. Most of the time was spent soaking in the mineral baths and hiking in the mountains. The tennis courts were off limits in the belief that playing tennis affected a pitcher's delivery. There were seminars on pitching but no throwing.

Brucker worked with Chubby Dean, Nelson Potter, and Porter Vaughan on their tendencies to tip their pitches. Johnny Babich taught the rookies how to work a batter, using their stuff to the best advantage. But he developed a lame wing and was of little use during the season. In October he would be released to Newark in exchange for third baseman Lou Blair.

At the time of Phil Marchildon's sale to the Athletics, Toronto general manager Dan Howley had cautioned him, "Getting to the major leagues isn't half as tough as staying there."

Earle Brucker set to work to ensure that Marchildon stayed there, changing his delivery, his landing, his concealment of the ball before he threw it. The rookie threw with a stiff wrist and gripped the ball too tightly. Knott and Babich taught him how to work the hitters. Marchildon had some control problems, but he won 10 games and had the lowest ERA on the club, well below the league average.

Mack's pep talks concentrated on attitude. "I tried to make the pitchers realize that they can win, get them out of the defeatist frame of mind which has handicapped our staff the past few years," he told Stan Baumgartner. "We can win if the hurlers will put their shoulders to the wheel. The difference between a winning and losing team in our league is entirely mental. If the boys have the will to win, they can win, and that is what I hope to instill in them."

Connie Mack enjoyed another hearty welcome in Anaheim, though Katherine was confined to the hotel with the flu. Still thinking like a ballplayer, the first thing he did on reaching the playing field was check the wind. Before a game against the White Sox one day he told a visitor on the bench, "This will be a high-scoring game." In the first inning two Sox outfielders misjudged fly balls, leading to 5 runs. When the visitor looked inquiringly at Mack, he smiled and said, "There was a strong wind blowing and I thought the outfielders would have trouble."

Mack did not invite any youngster to a spring training camp for a look unless a scout had recommended him. One day he received a letter at the Angelina Hotel from a local lad, Donald L. Douglas, seeking a tryout. Mack replied:

My dear Mr. Douglas:

Am going to advise that you write Joseph O'Rourke, manager Federalsburg club, address Shibe Park Philadelphia Pa of position you play, age and etc.

Sincerely,
Connie Mack

Douglas never played pro ball. More than fifty years later the framed letter still hung on the wall of his office at D. L. Douglas Associates.

Of the team's prospects, Mack wrote his daughter Ruth on March 8, "Cannot say much for the new men though I like the looks of pitchers Harris, Johnson and Ferrick."

Mack had traded Ed Heusser for Luman Harris, twenty-five, who had studied pitching under Paul Richards at Atlanta. Harris worked mostly in relief but would become a steady wartime starter for the A's.

Rankin Johnson Jr. came up from Class D and soon went back down.

Tom Ferrick was a twenty-six-year-old former minor league pitcher who had torn a shoulder muscle and been released. The muscle tear eventually healed, and he was working at the Brooklyn navy yard and pitching for the semipro Bushwicks when A's scout Eddie McLaughlin recommended him to Mack, who invited him to spring training without a contract. "I never asked how much I was going to get," Ferrick said. "I just wanted to make the team and have a chance to pitch in the big leagues."

About three weeks into the season he had pitched several times and still hadn't signed a contract. Ferrick said, "That's the kind of shape the [A's] office was in. Nobody questioned it in the league. One day Connie Mack called me to his office and said, 'We forgot to sign a contract. I think we better do it.'"

He signed for $3,000.

With plenty of new faces in the crowd, Mack acquainted them with his policy on drinking and late-night activities: "I know some of you fellows like to go out and have a drink or a beer after a workout. I only have one rule about that. I don't want any more than two people to go together. If three or more go together, each one will buy a round. They do it again and that's six beers. The temptation is there. With only two, the most you have is four between you. But three of you leads to six or nine."

Mack came back to the subject again during the season, reprimanding one of his coaches in front of the team for his nightly jaunts accompanied by a player. "I don't mind you staying out late at night," Mack told the coach, "but I don't want you taking another fellow with you. Let him go home and get his rest."

That may have taken place at the Del Prado Hotel in Chicago, where some airline stewardesses stayed at a nearby hotel and plenty of partying went on.

There were no curfews, no bed checks. "If you're going to be late, let one of the coaches know," Mack told them. "And if you can't do what you want by 12:30, forget it."

The dress code on the road was coat and tie, no matter how hot it was in those days when air conditioning was a luxury. "You're in the major leagues and you should look like it."

Mack talked about looking for an edge against their opponents, something about a batter or pitcher they could use to their advantage. There were no videotapes to study. They had to stay alert on the bench, looking for a sign, a batter's weakness, a pitcher's tipoff.

Pete Suder, twenty-four, had been a third baseman in the Yankees' system since 1935. The son of a Serbian steel mill worker in Aliquippa in western Pennsylvania, Pete was a .300 hitter at the Class A level. In the fall of 1940 the A's had drafted him from Binghamton. Suder had started out at $65 a month in '35 and equated the big leagues with big money. The first contract he received from the A's was for a disappointing $2,500. He sent it back with a note: "I'd rather work in the steel mill. I made that much in Binghamton."

Connie Mack wrote him back and reminded him that he had made only $250 a month in Binghamton.

"You can't lie to those people," Suder concluded. "He told me if I was still there after June 1 he'd give me another [$]500. I signed but I thought if he's got somebody else better than me he'll send me away to save that [$]500. But he didn't."

The chipper, effervescent Suder stayed thirteen years and became one of Philadelphia's most popular players.

The A's opened the 1941 season with 2 wins in New York (and who could remember the last time *that* had happened?). Nelson Potter went the distance in winning the second game, 10–7. But he was shelled for 26 runs in the 23 innings he worked in the first two months of the season. Despite lamenting his lack of pitching, Mack sold him to the Red Sox for $6,000 on June 30.

Some of Connie Mack's player purchases seem odd, almost quirky. A 6-foot-3 right-handed pitcher named Orge "Pat" Cooper was twenty-three. He had pitched almost entirely in Class D—without phenomenal success—in 1936–1937, then was out of baseball until he won 3 games for Class D Lynchburg at the start of 1941. Now he was in the army, and Mack gave Lynchburg $500 for the rights to him whenever he was discharged. In 1946 Cooper pitched 1 inning for the A's and in '47 played first base in one game and pinch-hit in twelve others.

The 1941 season was a roller coaster ride for the Athletics. The team's fortunes—and the fans' enthusiasm—rose and fell like the tides at the Bay of Fundy. In May they won 7 of 8 to finish a home stand, went on the road and won 7 of 10, and were only 4 games behind the first-place Indians. Connie Mack's wish to be in the thick of a pennant race again seemed to be coming true. Back home the fans couldn't wait for the team's return. Then they lost 6 in a row in Cleveland and Detroit, and the elation deflated like a harpooned blimp. Dick Siebert's bum knee was swollen, filled with fluid. Bob Johnson moved to first base, weakening both the infield and outfield. Benny McCoy was fretting, expecting to be drafted any day (he didn't go into the service until February 1942) and wasn't hitting. Well-pitched games were rare. While on the road, they were spared the scathing press they were getting back home—until they walked into Shibe Park on Saturday, June 14.

Somebody had made a collage of headlines and clippings from the local papers ripping the team and had printed across the top: "To the minor league A's—the boys who couldn't take it."

If it was intended to make them angry, it worked. But it didn't faze Connie Mack. When he saw it, he said, "I got a long telegram too, but I could tell after the first line that it came from a gambler who had lost money, so I threw it in the waste paper basket. But maybe it's all for the best, I mean the clippings. The boys will learn not to believe either good or bad comments. It's life."

The best they could do was 9-9 at home and dropped to sixth.

On the way home from a 5-10 road trip, the A's stopped at Williamsport for an exhibition game on July 21. Eastern League president Tommy Richardson presented Mack with a bench made from bats, some of them replicas of the models used by the 1929–1931 A's. The bench had red, white, and blue cushions. It sat in Connie Mack's office for the next ten years.

The next day Mack called a brief meeting in the clubhouse. "We've had a bad road trip," he said. "If we don't win a few games, I don't know how I'm going to meet the payroll."

For whatever reason, the bats came alive and the tide rose. They went 9-4 and edged into the first division, just 3 games behind the third-place Red Sox

It wasn't exactly pennant fever—more like first-division frenzy. The biggest crowd ever to see the A's at Shibe Park—39,618 paid and another 600 freebies—turned out for a Sunday, August 3, doubleheader against second-place Cleveland. Bob Feller won his twentieth in the opener, but the A's took the second game. During the following week the ticket office was deluged with the biggest advance reserved seat sales ever for a Friday night game, single game Saturday, and Sunday doubleheader against the Yankees, a weekend that drew almost seventy-five thousand—15 percent of the year's total attendance.

Then the tide went out again—in a hurry. The Athletics were 16-39 the rest of the way and another season passed away—literally for the Athletics, interred in the basement.

The A's average game time for the year was two hours and 4 minutes, but once the skid began, they seemed to want to get each game over as quickly as possible. The two fastest games were 1:29 for a 2–1 win on September 11 and 1:28 for a 1–0 loss at Washington in which two knuckleballers, Emil "Dutch" Leonard and Roger Wolff, walked only 1 batter between them on September 20.

The A's could score runs, but the pitching was the worst in the league, and the infield defense was ragged. By now Sam Chapman was covering more ground than his outfield companions. Not that Moses or Johnson had slowed, but Chapman was six years younger than Moses and ten years younger than Johnson and had more range than either. So it was, "Hey, Sam, it's all yours," on anything he had a chance to reach. As a result, Chapman led AL outfielders in putouts, total chances per game, assists, and errors. His hitting had improved in each of his four years, and he had power—fifth in slugging average. All three outfielders had strong arms, leading the league in assists.

Tom Ferrick was Mack's main relief man, compiling an 8-10 record. He didn't start a game until September 14 and won only one of his four starts, a 4-hit shutout in St. Louis. In October his name was on the Athletics' waiver list, although Connie Mack had no intention of letting him go. When Cleveland claimed him, somebody in the A's office slipped up and failed to withdraw his name.

Ferrick said, "After the season I stayed in Philly working at a factory making batteries for submarines. One day I got a call that Mr. Mack wanted to see me. I went to his office on a Saturday. 'Young man,' he said to me, 'when we signed you we didn't give you any money. We made $7,500 from Cleveland for you. I want to give you something for yourself. I think you can use it.' He gave me a check for a thousand dollars. He didn't have to do that. I really loved Connie Mack. He was a very compassionate human being, very kind and gentlemanly."

Al Simmons never stopped hating pitchers. Now that he was in the third base coach's box instead of the dugout, he could ride enemy pitchers up close and personal. On July 29 Edgar Smith of the White Sox had been unperturbed by Simmons's razzing, outpitching Phil Marchildon, 1–0, into the ninth at Shibe Park. The umpires had been more upset than Smith, warning Al several times to shut up. With Pete Suder on first and 2 out in the ninth, Mack called on Simmons to pinch-hit for Marchildon.

Broadcaster Taylor Grant was in the wcau booth. "You could see the way he walked up to the plate; he was determined to hit a home run and win the game."

Simmons took a big cut but lifted a fly ball to center field. As Smith walked off the field, their paths crossed at the first base line. Simmons, probably more angry at himself than Smith, snarled, "This must be a hell of a league when a *** like you can pitch a 1–0 shutout." Fists flew; hard blows were landed before Simmons's old pal Jimmie Dykes and the umpires could break it up.

After the game Grant went into the clubhouse. He asked Dick Siebert, "What was that all about?"

"Search me," Siebert said. "Ask Al. Go ahead, I dare you to ask him."

Grant took the dare. "What did you hit him for, Al?"

"What did I hit him for?" Simmons snapped. "He got me out, for Cris-sake."

By August 1 there was no more pennant race in the American League—the Yankees were 12 games in front of the pack—but there was still some excitement. From the middle of May until July 16 Joe DiMaggio's 56-game hitting streak electrified the nation. In its wake and sometimes in its shadow, Ted Williams flirted with .400 at the same time and continued after DiMaggio's streak ended. The Athletics didn't gain much at the gate during DiMaggio's run, hosting the Yankees for games number 39 and 40 of the streak, still short of the old record. But they figured prominently in the climax of the Williams saga.

Ted Williams had always murdered A's pitching in Philadelphia. In his rookie year, 1939, he had batted .432 with 3 home runs, 5 doubles, and 2 triples at Shibe Park. Connie Mack was impressed.

One day in May 1940 the Red Sox were in Philadelphia. Williams arrived at Shibe Park a little early. Earle Mack went over to him and said, "Ted, my dad would like to meet you."

Williams was getting a bad press for popping off and acting like a temperamental ingenue. Al Simmons and other jockeys were blistering him. He didn't know what to expect from Connie Mack:

So I went up to the tower office, and there he was—stiff collar, turkey neck, tall skinny guy in this little bitty office. He let me talk and we were there fifteen-twenty minutes, then he said to me, "Ted, you're going to be one of the greatest hitters ever." I never forgot it. That's the only time I ever talked to him.

But my most vivid memory of him is when I would come to bat, and he had that scorecard in his hand and he'd stretch up about five inches and lean forward and he'd be moving that scorecard. They would do some things to me at the plate that were not in any way percentage baseball, like walking me and moving the winning run to second base.

Williams had been batting over .400 since July 24, reaching .406 at the start of the last week. But he fell off in three games in Washington before the final weekend in Philadelphia. Connie Mack had rescheduled the Friday game to create a season-ending Sunday doubleheader, which attracted a turnout of 10,268. So Williams had to wait two days, during which he took coach Tom Daly to Shibe Park to throw batting practice for him.

Williams didn't like facing pitchers he had never seen. It took at least one time at bat for him to read them. In this series he would face only pitchers new to him.

On Saturday it was Roger Wolff, a knuckleball pitcher recently recalled from Wilmington. Williams was 1 for 4; his average fell to .39955. If he sat out Sunday's doubleheader, he would qualify for .400. Williams never considered it. He would play both games, come what may.

Sunday morning Mack called a team meeting. Although he had ordered his pitchers to walk Williams three or four times in four games during the season, he told his pitchers and catchers, "We are going to pitch to Williams today. But we're not going to make it easy for him. If you let up on him, you'll never pitch for me again."

Years later Harrington Crissey Jr. interviewed several of the A's who had played that day. They recalled that Mr. Mack asked them how they wanted to play Williams. Pitcher Tex Shirley said, "We told him we preferred to play Williams as a dead pull hitter: the first baseman close to the line, second baseman in the hole between first and second, shortstop close to second but still on the shortstop side of the bag. The outfielders did not shift, but played straight away."

Plate umpire Bill McGowan remembered Frank Hayes telling Williams the first time he stepped into the batter's box, "I wish you all the luck in the world today, but we're not giving you a damn thing."

The way Williams remembered it, Hayes said, "Mr. Mack says we're not going to make it easy for you, Ted. But we are going to pitch to you."

Williams later expressed his appreciation for Mack's pitching to him; he walked only once.

Dick Fowler, plucked from Toronto under the terms of a working agreement, started the first game. New to Williams? Didn't seem to matter. First time up, line drive single to right.

Long home run in the fifth. Curve-balling left-hander Porter Vaughan on in the sixth? Bounder over his head to the right of second into center field, then a bullet over first base. (Twenty-five years later Williams recognized Vaughan, a man he had batted against twice and never seen since, at a banquet and boomed, "Where have you been?")

On Williams's last time up, Crash Davis booted his grounder at second. Williams had reached base five times, 4 for 5. The Red Sox won, 12–11.

Fred Caligiuri, another rookie just up from Wilmington, pitched the second game. By now they all looked like batting practice throwers to Williams: single through the infield, double that tore through a loudspeaker horn on the right-field fence and bounced back onto the field, finally a routine fly ball to left, to finish at .4057.

Lefty Grove started that second game for Boston. Having won his three hundredth (and last) on July 25, he had already announced his retirement. Only Bob Johnson and Al Simmons remained of his former A's teammates. Neither was in the lineup that scored 3 runs on 4 hits in the first inning, the last that Lefty ever pitched.

To the end, said Ted Williams, "Lefty Grove had that competitive edge every great success in sports or business has, that absolute determination and 'win-the-game' attitude. He was the smoothest pitcher I ever saw."

Although 14 percent national unemployment crimped many household incomes, the Athletics' early flights into the first division enabled the club to reap the highest receipts—and visiting clubs their biggest Shibe Park paydays—in ten years. Bolstered by the sales of Potter to Boston for $6,000, Ross to the White Sox for $8,500, Dean and Ferrick to Cleveland for $15,000, Nagel to the Phillies and Lillard to San Francisco for $5,000 each, and $50,000 for the radio rights, the net profit was close to $100,000.

"We are much pleased with the attendance for a last-place ball club," Mack said. "Philadelphia fans have been kind to us and we certainly appreciate it."

An additional scoreboard was erected at the base of the right-field wall. Although electric scoreboards were in wide use by then, this one was still manually operated.

Mack bought a green Buick—his last new car until 1947—a special job with dual carburetors. But he never drove it. Ruth or Frank Cunningham or sometimes Earle did the driving.

At the instigation of Mack's longtime friend, Judge Harry S. McDevitt, the state legislature had unanimously declared May 17 as Connie Mack Day, the first time the state had accorded such an honor to a sports figure. For a story to run that day, the *Record* asked Mack if a reporter and photographer could spend a day with him beginning at his home. "We'll start at eight in the morning," Mack told them.

That was a little early for reporter Bill McGaw and photographer Marty Hyman; they arrived late but were warmly greeted. Asked how many rooms there were in the house, Mack said, "Too many. I think it's twenty, maybe twenty-one counting a nook or two. Golly, it's too big. Mrs. Mack wants to go into an apartment so we're going to sell the house."

McGaw asked him why he still wore the old-fashioned high collars.

"Because my neck's too long," Mack said. He then showed them his closet, filled with boxes of the collars, new and old. "I buy them by the dozen, have them laundered and put them back in the original boxes. Get 'em straight from the manufacturer. They're hard to get any place but at a factory. Buy 'em out in St. Louis. Cost me $3.50 a dozen."

Connie Jr. picked him up at nine and took him to Shibe Park. There he read his mail, dictated letters, and received visitors, Hyman taking photos of it all, until about one o'clock, when he went into a small bathroom and came out with a towel, which he spread on a chair and pulled up another chair, announcing, "I'm going to have lunch now."

McGaw wrote, "Then he pulled out a little wicker basket filled with sandwiches, a thermos bottle full of steaming soup and a spoon and platter."

By now the constant entreaties to "hold it" from the photographer were beginning to irritate Mr. Mack. "Please," he said, "I usually take a nap at two—it's two now."

So Hyman snapped photos of him napping.

After the game Hyman said, "Now all we need is to go home and get a picture of you and Mrs. Mack eating dinner."

"Ah," said Mack, "we are eating out tonight."

"Swell," said Hyman, "We'll go along, too. That's a better picture anyway. Where you going?"

"I am not going to tell you," said Mack.

They didn't get any more pictures.

The May 17 events began at noon at the mayor's office and continued at Shibe Park. In addition to politicians, Commissioner Landis, club owners, and officials from both leagues, several of Mack's former players were present. Jimmie Dykes left his White Sox in New York to be there. Lefty Grove came down from Boston.

Judge McDevitt had begun a campaign to rename Shibe Park as Connie Mack Stadium. He had a metal sign made and installed over the main entrance, but as long as Mack was in charge, it would remain Shibe Park. (The sign never came down. On February 13, 1953, when Mack was in St. Petersburg, the club's directors officially changed the name.)

Morning showers kept the crowd down to 12,361, but the sun came out for the ceremonies.

Connie Mack fidgeted while the speeches and gifts were being presented, and George M. Cohan sang a song he had written for the occasion.

Mack briefly thanked the speakers for their kind words. "And to you fans, you loyal supporters of our club, win or lose, I want to express my thanks for helping make baseball what it is to me—my life."

Then the Tigers scored 5 in the eighth and won, 8–3.

Among the many letters Mack received was one from President Roosevelt, written two days later:

Dear Connie Mack:

As an old friend and sincere admirer I want to join, even though belatedly, the legion of devoted followers who have been paying tribute to you. As sportsman and as citizen you richly deserve the honors that are heaped upon you and I gladly join in the accolade of felicitations and good wishes.

At the suggestion of a teacher, Ben Lewis, the administration of the Murrell Dobbins Vocational School across the street from Shibe Park invited

Mack to an assembly on May 21 to honor their famous neighbor. Mack not only accepted the invitation, but he also brought several players with him and told stories of his great teams and players of the past, then invited the entire school to the afternoon game against the White Sox. This became an annual event for several years.

Chick Galloway was one of Connie Mack's former players who was now part of Mack's network of college coaches/scouts. He worked at Presbyterian College in Clinton, South Carolina, and scouted the area's many textile leagues. There he saw two tall, husky teenagers, right-handed pitcher Tom Clyde and lefty pitcher/first baseman Leland "Lou" Brissie.

Scouts were as thick as stands of pine trees in the South. At least a dozen of them were following the pair. Some who visited the Brissie home received a cool reception from Lou's father, who wanted two things for his son: a college education and to play for Connie Mack.

"My dad admired and respected Connie Mack for his reputation and his character," Lou said. "He thought the world of him. But he told me it was my decision who to sign with. When the Dodgers offered a $25,000 bonus, he said, 'Connie Mack has been around a long time and is highly thought of. Let's see what he says.'"

The Athletics were on the road, due to return home on July 21. So Chick Galloway got in his car and drove the two boys to Philadelphia. They arrived on the twenty-first and were treated to seats in the press box that night for a lightweight fight between Sugar Ray Robinson and Sammy Angott. The next day they worked out for Mack, scout Harry O'Donnell, and Ira Thomas. Earle Brucker caught them. When Brissie said he was more of a first baseman, Brucker told him, "Concentrate on pitching, Lefty. You have what it takes."

They went up to the office, where Mr. Mack told them, "You can choose to play for Jack Coombs at Duke, Jack Barry at Holy Cross, or Chick Galloway at Presbyterian. I will pay your tuition and expenses for three years, then you'll report to the Athletics."

Mack gave them agreements to that effect to take home and have their parents sign.

On the way home they stopped to take a look at Duke. Blue Devils baseball and basketball star Bill McCahan, pitcher Lee Griffith, and who knows how many others who never made it to the A's were already there on Mr. Mack's dime. "It was too big for a small town kid like me," Brissie said. "And

Holy Cross was too far away. Presbyterian was only about thirty miles from home, so I told Chick that's where I'd go."

They arrived back in Clinton around midnight. Lou's father met them, and they sat in a hotel lobby and signed the agreement.

Tom Clyde pitched briefly for the A's in 1943, went into the service, and never made it back to the big leagues.

Lou Brissie enlisted in December 1942. He pitched at Camp Croft in the spring, then went overseas. Baseball would have to wait.

Donald Barnes had purchased the St. Louis Browns in 1936. During the next five years he had lost about $500,000. His pleas to allow the Browns to play fourteen night games instead of seven in 1941 had been turned down; the Browns had drawn 193,000 for the year. They had no working capital. In November 1941 Barnes and the league office made inquiries about buying the Los Angeles territory from P. K. Wrigley, who owned the Pacific Coast League franchise, in order to move the Browns to California.

Connie Mack was visiting his friend, Walter Grier, in Milford, Delaware, when he received a telephone call from league president Will Harridge, who told him that the Browns were interested in moving to California. The league would prefer that two teams move there. Would Mr. Mack be interested in moving the Athletics to San Francisco or Los Angeles at the same time?

The call was not prompted by concern over the Athletics being a drag on the rest of the league. They had just shown their first profit in nine years with attendance up almost one hundred thousand. The A's were usually sixth in home attendance, some years topping the White Sox.

Mr. Mack said no.

Whether Mack's refusal would have had any effect on the proposal is unknown; events at Pearl Harbor while the league was meeting in Chicago ended the California discussion.

14 | ANOTHER WAR

For the second time Connie Mack had the uncertainties of wartime to deal with. Indeed the overture to "The Great War: Part Two" had been playing itself out for several years, but it had been "theirs"–over there in Europe and Asia—not "ours." Now the United States was on the stage.

Just as baseball had looked to Washington for clues to its continuance twenty-five years ago, it again awaited a green light from the White House. It wasn't long in coming. On January 14 Judge Landis wrote to President Roosevelt asking for an okay to open the season. The next day Roosevelt replied, assuring Landis that he considered the game a vital factor in the nation's morale: "I honestly feel that it would be best for the country to keep baseball going." He even requested that more night games be scheduled to enable day-shift defense plant workers to enjoy more of them. The major leagues "patriotically" agreed; clubs with lights scheduled two night games with each visiting team.

The war went badly for the United States and its allies in the first six months after the attack on Pearl Harbor. Casualties had been heavy, especially in the Pacific. The United States had been caught unprepared in every way. There were German U-boats off the East Coast and Japanese submarines off the West Coast. Judge Harry McDevitt was appointed the civil defense chairman for Philadelphia. Whenever he was at a game in the summer of 1942, if there were reports of a potential attack of any kind, he would take charge, and the public address announcer would relay his orders to the crowd.

Centers called "Stage Door Canteens" opened all across the country as places for servicemen far from home to relax and enjoy some entertainment. Movie stars, musicians, and athletes volunteered their time and talents. In Philadelphia the canteen was set up in an Academy of Music rehearsal room.

Taylor Grant volunteered to ask Philadelphia ballplayers to appear one evening a week. On the night the draft age was expanded, Connie Mack and a few of his players showed up. Grant introduced them, saying, "Mr. Mack, is it true that you were classified 1-A today?"

The crowd laughed.

When Mack said, "If they want me, I'm ready," the room shook with applause and cheers.

Mack appeared at war bond rallies along with movie stars and entertainers and delivered a rousing pep talk: "We gave those Japanese some beating in baseball when we went over there in 1934, but that was nothing compared to the beating our boys are going to give them now."

A second All-Star Game, matching AL stars against a team of major leaguers in the service, raised $160,000 for military relief organizations. Clubs offered to deduct 10 percent of consenting players' salaries to buy war bonds. The Athletics, along with other clubs, devoted gate receipts to army and navy relief funds. The players and club employees were among the 26,514 paid attendance at a Sunday doubleheader on August 23 that raised $35,000.

Writers covering the major league meetings held during the days immediately after December 7, 1941, were too distracted to make a big deal out of swaps of veteran outfielders like Wally Moses and Mike Kreevich.

It's not clear why Mack traded Moses, thirty-one, to Chicago for Kreevich, thirty-three, and a pitcher who never appeared in an A's uniform. Moses was still an effective leadoff man and a .300 hitter. Moses had fought Mack over money just about every year, but contracts hadn't even gone out yet. (Moses would make the same $12,500 in Chicago as he had with the A's.) Kreevich signed for $8,000 with an attendance bonus he didn't collect on.

Was the trade made just to shave $4,500 off the payroll? Not likely. Could Mack have seen something that told him that Moses would never bat .300 again? Nobody offered any explanations, but Mack and Moses remained on good terms; Mack brought him back to the A's six years later.

Despite the war jitters among residents of the West Coast, Connie Mack did not hesitate to return to California for spring training. At some time during his stay there, somebody at one of the movie studios proposed making a film based on his life. The idea was mentioned to Mack, who asked a cousin, Ralph Gutzsell, a Chicago attorney, to represent him in the negotiations. There was speculation over who would play the leading role. Mr. Mack's physical structure limited the possibilities; Fred MacMurray was one name frequently mentioned. Connie Jr. was asked to jot down notes about incidents that might be useful to the story. The discussions continued over the next ten years. But it never happened.

Anticipating higher transportation expenses (they didn't go up) and hotel and meal costs (up about 5 percent) and lower attendance (down 20 percent), Mack believed the players should share any financial sacrifices brought on by the war. If he was gambling on the unknown gate receipts, they should too. Many contracts went out with bonuses based on attendance.

Through all the losing years Bob Johnson had never let up. He had hit at least 20 home runs nine years in a row, driven in over 100 runs for seven. He did his drinking discreetly, often hosted parties for the players at his home, but nobody ever saw him drunk. In 1985 the Society for American Baseball Research (SABR) would rate him forty-seventh on the all-time players list.

Johnson had been routinely rejecting the first contract he received each year and usually wound up with a better one. He was now the club's highest paid player at $15,000. Mack sent him a contract for $10,000 with a scale of $2,500 in attendance bonuses beginning at a gate of 450,000.

Johnson sent it back. The standoff continued into the middle of March. Mack wouldn't budge on the salary figure. He finally agreed to lower the first bonus level to attendance of 400,000, with another $2,500 at 450,000. Johnson earned the first bonus but not the second.

Frank Hayes waged a similar battle before agreeing to a scale of bonuses that would result in a total of $9,000. Jack Knott's attendance bonus enabled him to match his '41 salary.

Not everybody took a cut.

Dick Siebert wrangled all spring before squeezing out a $1,000 raise with attendance bonuses that would pay him another $1,500. Phil Marchildon fought for and received a $2,000 boost to $5,000.

For the year, Mack shaved about 10 percent ($18,000) off his player payroll.

Mack's three sons also took $2,000 pay cuts, to $5,500. Connie Mack's salary remained at $20,000 until 1943, when he would cut it to $14,000.

One day a one-armed man appeared in the offices at Shibe Park. His name was Pete Gray. He had lost his right arm in a childhood accident and had learned to throw and swing a bat with his left hand. A fast runner, he was twenty-seven and had been playing semipro ball in the coal country north of Philadelphia. Somebody had suggested the A's give him a tryout, without telling them anything about him.

Gray asked to see Mr. Mack. While he was waiting, Roy Mack saw him. "Where's the kid we're supposed to look at?" asked Roy.

Gray said he was the one. As Gray related the story to John Steadman of the *Baltimore Sun,* "I was told then that Connie was busy and couldn't waste his time seeing me."

Mack was quoted as saying he had enough trouble finding capable players with two arms and didn't see any future for a one-armed player.

Gray wound up playing for Three Rivers in the Canadian-American League, then starred for Memphis for two years before the Browns picked him up in 1945. Gray was honored as the most courageous athlete of the year at the 1944 Philadelphia writers' dinner. Mack met him there and said, "There was a one-armed fellow one time who wanted a tryout. Are you the same boy?"

Gray said he was. Later he said his most enjoyable day in baseball came on July 4, 1945, when he had three hits against the A's, the last a ninth-inning single that drove in the tying and winning runs.

Based on their late fall showing, Mack looked to Fowler, Marchildon, Caligiuri, and Wolff for his pitching. He had drafted a tall, lanky right-hander, Russ Christopher, from Newark. The twenty-four-year-old overhand sinker ball specialist was like a fifth infielder. He had won 16 games but, more important, had demonstrated enough stamina to pitch 13 complete games and 185 innings. Christopher had a leaky heart, first diagnosed when he was in high school. His lungs received less oxygen than they needed. He was unable to sprint with the other pitchers. When he warmed up and came back to sit down before a game, the other players could see his heartbeat moving his shirt. He had rejected medical advice to give up baseball for his health and would almost certainly be exempt from military service.

In Taylor Grant's words, Russ was "polite, intelligent, a nice kid," among the quieter members of Mack's teams, who, winners or losers, were usually a boisterous, fun-loving bunch.

Sam Chapman enlisted in the navy. Benny McCoy and Al Brancato were early draftees. What remained of the infield was scraggly, erratic, and near-ranging, the outfield weakened by the loss of Chapman and Moses. The most optimistic comment that Connie Mack could come up with was, "We won't be all that bad."

They had no power and no speed. As usual, most of the blossoms that bloomed in the spring—tra-la—had nothing to do with the summer.

The Athletics barnstormed east with the Pittsburgh Pirates. When they arrived in Big Spring, Texas, Mack agreed to spend an hour talking to an Abilene team of youngsters, the Andrews Aces. He saw these requests not as an intrusion but as an opportunity to enjoy what had always been closest to his heart: teaching.

Howard Green, manager of the Aces, reported in the *Abilene Reporter-News* that Mack's most fervent advice to them was to correct their weaknesses: "Good hitters always like to hit. . . . Throw away that bat and learn to field. . . . Watch every good player you can. The semi-pros will help you. Take their advice and correct your weaknesses. . . . Learn to throw and to throw to the right base. There has been many a boy who failed to stick in the majors because he threw to third with no chance at all for the runners and permitted the man on first to advance to second. The chance for the double play is lost. Hold that runner on first."

Mack told them the difference between an ordinary player and a great one was that "the great one rises to heights at important moments." He cited Jack Barry and Al Simmons as examples. Simmons was no longer on the active list, but, said Mack, "He's only a coach, but he works harder than anybody on this club."

He then posed for pictures with the young ballplayers.

When the *Philadelphia Public Ledger* folded in 1941, Al Horwits was out of a job. Mack was fond of the young writer. They sometimes collaborated on magazine stories that appeared under Mack's byline. According to Horwits in *No Cheering in the Press Box*, he received a check payable to Connie Mack from the *Saturday Evening Post* for a 1936 article, "Winning Them in the Clubhouse." Horwits took the check to Mack. "We sold this article on the strength of your name," he told Mack. "You're entitled to the major portion of it. You tell me what."

Mack said, "Who's it made out to?"

"Connie Mack."

Mack took it, endorsed it, and handed it back. "It's all yours. All I did was spend a few mornings with you and tell you what you wanted to know. It's good for baseball. The check is yours."

Now Horwits was unemployed. Connie Mack offered him a job with the A's as director of public relations. But there was strong opposition from the board of directors. It's unknown if they objected to creating the position or to Horwits personally. Connie Mack told them, "If you don't want him, then you can have my resignation," and walked out of the board meeting.

Mack had already announced the hiring of Horwits; the next day Roy denied it.

According to Horwits, Connie Mack told him that Roy and Earle opposed his being hired. "But I want you and I'm going to pay you out of my own pocket. I'm not going to let the club spend this money. My sons want to run it this way—fine. As a matter of fact, I've resigned over this but they won't accept my resignation. I've told them I'll manage the club but that's all I'll do. I've resigned everything else. I'm going to hire you for this year and give you a chance to find something because it wouldn't be good for you to be involved in this atmosphere. I gave you my word that you had this job and you do. And when you file your income tax, I'm your employer, not the Philadelphia Athletics."

No wonder Al's widow, Claire, said forty years later, "My husband adored Mr. Mack."

Horwits stayed a year, then went to Hollywood and became a publicist for movie studios.

The Cleveland Indians had known nothing but turmoil for the past few years. In 1940 they had revolted against their manager, Oscar Vitt. Their whining about his public criticism of them probably distracted them enough to cost them the pennant. The club had brought back former manager Roger Peckinpaugh in '41, but the team sank to fourth. Now, hoping to emulate Clark Griffith's success with his "boy wonder" managers Bucky Harris and Joe Cronin, the Indians appointed their twenty-four-year-old shortstop, Lou Boudreau.

Asked about the wisdom of such a move, Connie Mack said, "His youth makes no difference to me. I don't care whether he is twenty-four or forty-four. Either he can or he can't. In any case, they've tried everything else at Cleveland and 'Boordeer' is worth the gamble."

A year of facing major league pitching had persuaded Pete Suder that he would be a .250 hitter at best. He decided that in order to stay in the big leagues, he'd better make himself more valuable by learning to play every infield position. Beginning in spring training and throughout the season whenever the club was at home, he was out early with somebody to hit him grounders at every position. It worked; he lasted thirteen years, only once playing a full season at one position.

Connie Mack called him Sude; the players called him Ben Blue because he resembled the long-faced, dour-looking movie character actor.

Mack signed a tall, rangy, lefty first baseman, Bruce Konopka, who could hit but was a tanglefoot in the field. Mr. Mack put on a glove and players watched in awe while the seventy-nine-year-old one-time catcher demonstrated the proper footwork around the bag.

The most promising rookie in camp was Elmer Valo. Christened as Imrich when he was born in Ribnik, Czechoslovakia, Valo was six when his family arrived in Palmerton, Pennsylvania. His father worked in a zinc mill. Elmer took to baseball and played high school and semipro ball. In 1938 a local teacher had tipped off Connie Mack about him. Earle Mack and Ira Thomas took a look at him and invited him to a tryout at Shibe Park.

"I was still in high school," Valo said. "The teacher, Edgar Polsen, and my father went with me. Mr. Mack sat in the stands while Dave Keefe pitched to me, then hit some balls to me in the outfield. Then we all went up to Mr. Mack's office. When I saw the polished wood floor in the office I started to take my cleats off, but he told me not to worry about it."

Mack offered to pay Valo's way through Duke, but Elmer turned him down. He was ready to sign, but he wanted to play his last year of high school basketball. They didn't talk about money. Mack put a blank, undated Williamsport contract before Elmer's father, who signed it. Connie Mack then "desked" it.

Elmer and his father and Mr. Polsen stayed for the game. When Elmer saw players who were smaller than he was and pitchers who didn't throw any harder than the semipros he hit against, he left full of confidence.

According to league records, Mack apparently sent the contract—for 1939—to the league in October 1938, followed by a notice optioning Valo to Federalsburg.

In the spring of '39 Mack arranged for Valo to play on semipro teams in the city and work out with the A's when they were home. After he graduated, Valo finished the season at Federalsburg, hitting .374. Recalled by Williamsport in October 1939, his contract was assigned in February 1940 to Wilmington, where Valo led the Interstate League, hitting .364. In the fall he was recalled and hit .348 in 8 games. Mack optioned him to Wilmington again in 1941, and he had another good year, then batted .420 in 13 games for the A's.

(The story later promulgated by Red Smith that Valo was a four-decades player, having appeared in one game late in 1939 and been purposely left out of the box score by the official scorer because he wasn't on the roster, was made up by Smith, who said he was that official scorer. It never happened.)

Pete Suder and Elmer Valo had a ball in the big leagues. They stuck together like wet hairs, sharing a room two blocks from Shibe Park in the home of the Chisholm family for the next thirteen seasons, except for time in the army and a few years when their families were with them. They paid thirty dollars a month for room and laundry but no meals, except, recalled Suder, "After a night game [the landlady] put out a real fancy spread for us." Otherwise they went to Sam Framo's, an Italian joint a block away, for a round loaf of Italian bread cut in half and stuffed with steak and peppers for fifty cents.

On the Pullmans they rode over the wheels or in the upper berths until they gained some seniority. In New York they rode the subway to Yankee Stadium. They stayed at the best hotels, their eyes bugging out in the fancy dining rooms like the Del Prado in Chicago, where the waiters wore white coats and the service was what they imagined it would be in some fancy hotel in Europe and the kitchen saved the scarce prime steaks for ballplayers.

The players had some favorite restaurants in cities like New York, and Connie Mack agreed to give them meal money in those cities. In others they signed the checks at the hotels and ate well, knowing that if they went a few dollars over the daily limit, nothing would be said. And they learned something about tipping waiters. According to Valo:

We stayed at the Copley-Plaza in Boston. Signed the checks in the dining room—no limit—steak and eggs for breakfast if you wanted it. Mr. Mack never said anything. One Sunday morning Suder and I and a few others were there for breakfast. The day before we had given the waiter a quarter tip and he said, "You better keep this. You need it more than I do." Now we're at the same table and we're sitting there a long time and nobody is waiting on us. Connie Mack came in and one of us waved him over and said, "Mr. Mack, it's almost time to go to the ballpark and we've been waiting here and nobody will serve us."

He said, "Why not?"

One guy said, "Well, we gave him a quarter tip yesterday and we thought that was all right."

So Connie Mack went to the head waiter and they started moving. I think he gave them tips to give us better service.

Suder was a practical joker. In those days infielders threw their gloves on the grass behind the infield after the third out. Suder enjoyed pranks like slipping a little rubber snake under Phil Rizzuto's glove.

"When Phil picked up his glove he jumped up and started stomping on that little rubber thing," Valo said.

On the trains and in the hotel rooms Pete Suder was in the middle of the card players. Poker games were nickel and dime, three raise limit. Dick Siebert and Jack Knott were bridge players. The coaches played hearts and pinochle.

In spring training Mack did more watching than teaching. He let his coaches know what he wanted them to impart to individual players. But Mack missed nothing. When Valo was struggling at the plate, he said, "Val, put a little more weight on the balls of your feet."

"It helped," Valo recalled.

Valo was not a great outfielder, but he was an energetic one. If a game— or, in one case, a no-hitter—was on the line, he wouldn't let a railing or wall stand in his way. Playing right field, he also quickly learned that Mack, at seventy-nine, was still a great outfielder: "I remember him one time moving me over close to the right field line and Bob Kennedy, a right-hand hitter with the White Sox, was hitting and I think a lefty was pitching and he kept moving me over and I thought, 'Well, I should be able to cover to the line now,' and he brought me in a little bit and the ball was hit right to me and I was amazed. It taught me to study the pitchers more."

One time Valo made a base running mistake. "You're running with your head down," Mack said. Another time he was looking somewhere else when Mack was trying to move him in the outfield. Mack spoke to him about it.

"He was teaching me," Valo said later, "but I thought he was getting on me. I said to him, 'Mr. Mack, get off my back. If you don't like me, trade me or give me my release.'

"He said to me, 'Young man, if I didn't like you, you wouldn't be here.'

"I kept my mouth shut after that."

Valo hit only .251 in his rookie year, but he would still be with the Athletics long after Mr. Mack was gone.

Another highly touted Wilmington grad, Jack Wallaesa, was a 6-foot-3½-inch shortstop. After he graduated at Easton (PA) high school in 1939, his coach sent him to Shibe Park for a tryout. Mack watched as Charlie Berry put the teenager through his paces. "I was nervous," Wallaesa told Stan Baumgartner, "but I remember my junior high coach saying no athlete would ever be great unless he felt that same nervousness before the start of any game."

Mack remarked that he had never seen so tall a shortstop, but Wallaesa reminded him of one named Williams, who wasn't as tall but was built like a heavyweight (he was probably thinking of Ned Williamson, whom he had last seen over fifty years ago).

The A's signed Wallaesa for $150 a month and sent him to Class D Federalsburg.

At the time Wallaesa was a right-handed batter. In 1940 Mack had sent him to Wilmington with orders to learn to bat lefty as well. "It was hard to learn," Wallaesa said. "I seemed so clumsy."

But he stuck to it, hitting .252 in '41. Now Mack saw him as the A's shortstop of the future. When he reported, he had a sore throat that lingered for two weeks. He lost twenty pounds. The clubhouse man gave him Al Brancato's old uniform. Brancato was six inches shorter; the pants barely reached his knees. Weak and unsteady in the field, Wallaesa looked more like a clown act than a big league shortstop.

Stan Baumgartner said to Mack, "Wallaesa wouldn't look so bad if he had a uniform that fit him."

Mack agreed and ordered a new uniform for him.

When they traveled to San Francisco, Mack asked Seals' manager Lefty O'Doul to work with Wallaesa. After a few minutes observing the rookie, O'Doul said, "You're swinging off-balance. You're an easy mark for a change-up or a slow curve."

The next day Babe Ruth was at the ballpark. Mack asked the Babe to look at Wallaesa's swing.

"I was so excited I didn't know what to do," Wallaesa told Baumgartner. "He showed me how he put his right foot in front of his left and took a big stride. I tried it and it felt great so I started to bat that way."

Wallaesa hit .300 during the first two weeks of May, but one day he had a bad day in the field and the wolves got on him. "The more they howled the more I pressed. Eventually they had me missing balls I should have put in my hip pocket, or throwing them into the stands. Almost any rookie is bound to crack under such heckling."

He made 12 errors in 36 games and was batting .256 when the army rescued him.

Mack doubted that Crash Davis would ever hit big league pitching. In April he paid the White Sox $6,500 for thirty-year-old second baseman Bill Knickerbocker, a .250-hitting stopgap, not a building block.

With the Athletics the batter was free to call for a hit and run with a man on first, a strategy that sometimes caused confusion. Spitting toward third was Suder's sign. Knickerbocker had five different signs.

"I couldn't follow them," Valo said. "I had to watch Earle Mack coaching at third, too, and I couldn't watch both. I'd have to call time and get the sign straight."

It was Knickerbocker's last year.

When Wallaesa went into the army, Mack put Pete Suder at shortstop, but he wasn't satisfied with Sude's play there. In July he brought back the shortstop he had sold to Boston in 1936, Eric McNair, and therein lay a story. In 1938 McNair's wife had died in childbirth. His world fell apart. The Red Sox traded him to Chicago, where his old teammate, Jimmie Dykes, helped him come out of his depression. McNair batted .324, and the Sox finished fourth. Now thirty-three, McNair was hanging on with Detroit when the Tigers sold him on waivers to Washington. McNair refused to report. "I'll play for anybody but Griffith," he was quoted. Connie Mack paid $4,000 for him on July 25.

Nobody who had played for the Athletics enjoyed telling stories about Connie Mack's alleged tightness more than McNair. His imitation of Mack crying into a lace curtain over his financial woes, his yarn about flipping a quarter onto Mack's desk after hearing the Old Man's tale of woe and saying, "Here, you need this more than I do," were well known by his Boston teammates.

Like most exaggerations, there was a kernel of truth in McNair's routines, though this truth was wrapped in contradictions. Art Morrow, who knew Mack as well as any of the A's beat writers, said that Mack would "argue, even quibble, over a few dollars in a player's contract, yet think nothing of giving him a $1,000 bonus—as he once did—because by winning the final game the A's had been saved from a fate worse than 99 defeats." (This happened twice, in 1938 and again in 1942, but the records did not reveal whether George Caster in '38 or Luman Harris in '42—or both—received the bonus.)

Connie Mack lent himself to caricature, but in fact haggling over relatively small financial differences is as much a baseball tradition as the seventh-inning stretch. Thirty years later, in an era of six-figure salaries, future Hall of

Fame third baseman Brooks Robinson said he would go back and forth for months over a $500 difference with Orioles general manager Harry Dalton.

Anyhow, here was Eric McNair agreeing—eagerly, according to Stan Baumgartner—to return to the Athletics.

"It has been McNair's one ambition to return to Mack," wrote Baumgartner, probably overstating it. "He feels happy with the Old Man, who understands his sorrows, allows him to play in his own way, and never upbraids him for anything."

McNair's arrival enabled Suder to move to third and tightened the infield. But the A's had already taken up residence in the basement for the third year in a row.

Joe Coleman was a pitcher at a Catholic high school in Malden, Massachusetts, in 1940. The school principal was Brother Gilbert, the same priest who had launched Babe Ruth as a ballplayer at St. Mary's in Baltimore. One day Ruth visited his old friend at the school. The principal sent for Coleman and introduced him to Ruth, saying, "This kid looks like a pretty good prospect, but he doesn't know how to throw a curve."

Ruth picked up a few erasers and went out to the hall and taught the young pitcher the proper wrist action by throwing the erasers through the corridor.

"He actually made them curve," Coleman said.

When the two Boston clubs showed no interest in the senior, Br. Gilbert sent him to see Connie Mack, who offered to pay his tuition and expenses to go to college. Coleman said he didn't want to leave home. Fine, said Mack. Go to a school in Boston.

"All the bills went to Mr. Mack," Coleman said. "But after a half year I quit and was ready to play ball."

Mack sent him to Newport News, where the eighteen-year-old was 15-12 and learned from another pitching immortal, Chief Bender. "Bender was the greatest teacher I ever had. He taught me, 'Think, and know what you're doing with every pitch. Never waste a pitch. Even on an o and 2 count, do something to try to make the hitter chase it.' And he taught me how to throw a nickel curve."

Promoted to Wilmington, Coleman won 18 and was called up in September 1942. On September 19 he pitched 6 innings in relief and took the 11–9 loss to Washington.

After the season Mack told him, "I look forward to having you with me next year." By then the navy had him, instead.

Once school was out, Roy's son, Cornelius McGillicuddy III (not to be confused with Connie Jr.'s son, also Connie Mack III), joined the club as a batboy. He made his first trip with the A's when they headed west on July 21. His parents went along, but his grandfather—"Pa-Pa"—and Lena Blackburne looked after the youngster. On future trips he roomed with his grandfather.

"All the players were swell fellows," young Connie said. "They took me with them to the movies. Every now and then my grandfather [possibly remembering his days as a rookie with a big league team when he had decided the time had come for him to buy a round of beer] would hand me $5 and say, 'It's your turn to take them to the movies.'"

Connie III remained an A's batboy until 1948.

Ruth's son, Frank Cunningham Jr., was six when he joined the team as a gofer, then became the ballboy who sat beside the screen behind home plate and supplied the home plate umpire when necessary.

"I knew my place," Frank said. "It was my grandfather's business place and I couldn't go up to him and talk about other things when he was busy. He sat in the middle of the dugout. I sat at one end. During the games it was serious. If there was a dispute on the field he would say to Earle, 'Find out what's going on out there,' and Earle would go."

The A's were never at .500 and sank slowly and steadily until they crashed deep into the basement with a 2-15 record beginning August 21. They weren't the worst team in the league in any single department—just bad enough to lose 10 more games than anybody else and finish 48 games out of first place.

Fred Caligiuri couldn't get anybody out before he was shipped back to Wilmington. Jack Knott couldn't get anybody out though he tried all year. The only lefty, Herman Besse, started 14 times and won 2 of them.

Looking for pitching, Mack cast a covetous eye on Bob Harris of the Browns, a workhorse who won almost as often as he lost for the second-division Browns. Frank Hayes wasn't hitting and was unhappy with his contract, and Mack was unhappy with his unhappy catcher. With Hal Wagner, signed out of Duke in 1937, doing most of the catching, Hayes's weight went up as his batting average went down. Mack thought a change of scenery would be good for him. At twenty-six, Harris was ripe for the military draft, but Mack was undeterred. On June 1 he sent Hayes to St. Louis for Harris and catcher Bob Swift, another light man with the bat.

Harris pitched well but had no support; on June 9 he shut out Chicago, 2–0, for his only win before going into the army. He never returned to the major leagues.

Dick Fowler was 4-9 in 17 starts, 2-2 in relief.

Phil Marchildon shouldered the biggest load: among the top five in innings pitched, starts, complete games, and wins (17) and at the top in walks. But he was not satisfied. He had been 6-3 in May, when he stepped in a hole running in the outfield and twisted his back. He said nothing and lost his next four starts before Mack benched him for a week. He picked up his seventeenth win on September 9 with 5 innings of shutout relief in a 13-inning 5–4 win at Cleveland and was hoping for three more starts to try to reach 20 wins. But the A's season had only eleven more days to go; he lost four days later and, on the last day, had a 9–4 lead against Washington when the Senators scored 7 in the ninth. Mack gave him every chance for the win, leaving him in until Washington took the lead. It was one of nine games the A's lost when leading after 8 innings.

Marchildon was also unhappy that Canadian laws required the salaries of athletes playing in the United States to be directly deposited in Canadian banks, except for $35 a week to live on. And he carried a grudge against Mack for years because the manager didn't give him a bonus for his performance or wish him luck as he went off to war after the season.

Roger Wolff and Washington's Dutch Leonard were the top knuckleball pitchers in the league. Wolff threw the widest-breaking knuckler in baseball, yet his strikeouts always exceeded his walks.

"Wolff's knuckler was by far the best I ever saw, bar none," said Elmer Valo. "Most of them wobble a little bit, then drop. His jumped all over like a butterfly. Nobody could catch him." He was 12-15 for the year with a 3.32 era, the only pitcher on the staff with an era lower than the league average.

Infielder Irv Hall was Wolff's roommate in '43. "He'd lie in bed filing his fingernails and tossing the ball into the air. When he got to where the ball wouldn't rotate at all, he'd quit filing his nails."

Hard-working Russ Christopher started 18 games, completed 10, and won only 4 of them. At one point he lost 11 in a row; the A's scored 3 or fewer runs in 9 of them.

Mack kept signing young players even though he expected to lose them to the service. On Ira Thomas's recommendation he gave a 6-foot-2 right-hander, Bob Savage, a $1,250 bonus to sign upon graduating at Staunton Military Academy. The twenty-one-year-old New Hampshire native was wild, walking 31 in 31 innings; he was charged with 1 loss in his 3 starts and was in the army six months later.

The A's had lost 98 games prior to the season-ending doubleheader against Washington. Connie Mack was determined to avoid losing 100 games. That morning Dick Siebert went to Mack and asked to be excused from the second game. He had made an early train reservation home. Mack said he could go if the A's won the first game. Siebert hustled more than at any time all year, but Phil Marchildon blew the 9–4 lead in the ninth and lost.

Siebert was fuming; his disposition went south while the second game went into the tenth inning before the A's won, 2–1, dodging the ugly 100-loss smudge.

In the clubhouse cleaning out his locker, Siebert fretted about missing his train. But Bob Johnson, having been refused an attendance bonus he thought he had coming, was in a fouler mood. "I'm never coming back to this club," he snarled as he packed up.

Summing up the season, Connie Mack said, "We lost twelve good men to the army. We'll be better next year. In fact I think we'll finish in the first division."

He didn't say how.

On September 18 the Macks sold their home at 604 W. Cliveden for $9,975. (In 1950 the house, advertised as "formerly occupied by Connie Mack," was offered at $28,500. It has since been partitioned into several apartments.) Shortly after the season ended, they moved into an apartment about two miles away, at 620 West Phil-Ellena Street. Mack liked the neighborhood. It was an easy walk to the drugstore to pick up the evening papers and a short drive to a few movie theaters, which he enjoyed two or three nights a week.

Word quickly spread among the kids in the area. One of them was John J. Kenney Jr. "Sometimes we would stop in the entrance of the apartment and look at the names on the mailboxes. There it was, Cornelius McGillicuddy."

But they had never seen him up close until one day a few years later. They had been playing ball on the nearby school grounds, and when it got too dark, they gathered on the steps of Swank's corner drugstore, drinking sodas and talking.

"I had my Bob Feller model glove I had received for my birthday," said Kenney. "A tall older gentleman came up to us on his way into the drugstore and stopped. He asked to see my glove.

"'Boy, that's a nice glove,' he said. 'When I played ball we wore leather gloves that you would wear in the winter to keep your hands warm.'

"After he went into the store a man said to me, 'Do you know who that is?'

"I said, 'No.'

"He said, 'That's Connie Mack.'"

The autumn of 1942 was not a pleasant time for Connie Mack. The trouble began in the clubhouse after the team's closing doubleheader September 20. (The A's season finished a week earlier than the rest of the league.) Bob Johnson's contract had called for a bonus of $2,500 if attendance reached 400,000 and another $2,500 if it reached 450,000. While packing up his gear to head home to Tacoma, Johnson, who had received the first bonus check, asked about the second one. Mack said there wouldn't be a second check; they hadn't come close to 450,000. Johnson didn't believe him. According to Stan Baumgartner, "Hot words passed between them. The fine feelings of ten years were smashed in five minutes."

Johnson may have been so adamant because of the evidence of his eyes. Or perhaps he was keeping score at home, noting the reported attendance figures in the box scores. Despite its lowly position, the team had temporarily sparked the interest of the fans. In the last week of May, a Monday night game against Washington, Friday night and Saturday Memorial Day games against Boston, and a Sunday doubleheader with the Yankees had drawn over eighty-five thousand. The papers projected a total of six hundred thousand for the year, which would be the highest in a decade and a record for a last-place team.

The official final count was 423,487, although an unofficial Retrosheet.org count of daily attendance as reported in the newspapers—sometimes using an obvious round number estimate—adds up to 546,141. Attendance bonus clauses always specified "paid home attendance." What was reported was the turnstile count, which would have included servicemen, kids, and other non-paying pass holders, for whom the home team did not owe anything to the visiting club or the league—or a player's bonus.

The club's books seem to support Mack. In the closest comparable year, 1940, official attendance was 432,145 for fifty-seven home dates; admissions totaled $552,542, compared to $522,926 for 1942. Visiting clubs' shares totaled $120,135 in 1940, compared to $118,616 in '42. The league's share of receipts was $21,607 in '40 and $21,174 in '42. Had the actual paid attendance exceeded 500,000, as it did in 1941, the amounts paid to visiting clubs and the league in 1942 would have been closer to the 1941 figures: $148,148 to visiting clubs and $26,455 to the league.

The war of words grew more heated through the winter. Mack had met his match in stubbornness. Johnson wrote to Mack asking to be traded "even if you pay me the second bonus."

Mack huffed, "I don't owe him a second bonus and he knows it."

When Johnson was put on the trading block, several clubs expressed interest. None of them had any players to spare and offered only cash, which Mack rejected. Clark Griffith won the raffle in exchange for infielder Jimmy Pofahl (who refused to leave his defense job, the A's receiving $6,250 compensation) and Cuban outfielder Roberto Estalella.

Johnson was happy to be away from the left-field wolves at Shibe Park: "I never could understand why they booed me. I batted in over a hundred runs for seven straight years, but I was a bum when I struck out."

But he was not happy about his part in the argument that had led to his departure. His respect for Mr. Mack was undiminished. The first time the Senators and A's met in 1943, Johnson walked across the field and shook hands with Mack. "Wasn't that nice of Bob?" said Mack. "He didn't have to do that."

It was a bad deal for Connie Mack. Estalella could hit, but he turned easy fly balls into spectacular catches and had no idea of where to throw the ball after he caught it. Bobo Newsom, who had been with him in Washington, said, "Bobby's a 4-to-1 shot to throw to the wrong base, and if there were five bases instead of four, he'd be 5 to 1."

To replace Johnson, Mack sent $5,000 and Dee Miles to Seattle for veteran outfielder Jo-Jo White, who had played for Mickey Cochrane on Detroit's pennant-winning teams in '34 and '35.

In November Mack lost another longtime friend when George M. Cohan died. Mack and several other baseball men were honorary pallbearers at the funeral in New York.

On December 23 Mack took time out from a busy day at the office to attend an eightieth birthday luncheon hosted by the local sportswriters. (A citywide gala celebration would take place in February.) Mack spoke for an hour, retracing his life and career as he was wont to do on such occasions. He concluded with a prediction that the St. Louis Browns would win the 1943 pennant. He called that one a year too early.

15 | NEW KID ON THE BLOCK

Gerry Nugent and the Phillies were flat broke. Worse than that: they were *concave* broke. Not only were they penniless, but they were also in debt to the National League. NL president Ford Frick went looking for somebody to rescue the franchise. Bob Paul, sports editor of the *Philadelphia Daily News*, was approached by local sports promoter and professional basketball pioneer Eddie Gottlieb, acting on behalf of Leon Levy, president of WCAU and one of the backers of the new CBS network. This is Paul's story:

> Gottlieb came to me and asked a favor: "I understand the Phillies are for sale. I want you to find out if they can be sold to a Jewish person. The owner of WCAU wants to buy the club but he's been told that because he's Jewish he didn't have a chance. The only person that can answer that question is Ford Frick. As a sportswriter you can ask questions that we can't. I'd like you to ask him."
> I said, "What's in it for you?"
> He said, "I would be general manager. We would have enough money to have a winning club."
> I called Frick and put the question to him: "Will the National League or baseball accept a Jewish owner?"
> He said, "Of course I wouldn't say to you they won't accept a Jewish owner. I would never say a thing like that. I cannot tell Nugent what to do with his ball club. I'm not going to tell Nugent to talk to that man or listen to him or take his money. The answer to your question is yes, a Jewish man can buy a ball club."
> I relayed that answer to Gottlieb. It turned out that his group said that wasn't a definite enough answer. They were not going to be put on the spot of having their religion being the main issue in buying a

ball club. They wouldn't go to Nugent unless Frick assured them they would be accepted if their finances were in order.

So they didn't buy the Phillies.

In February Frick found a buyer in William D. Cox, a New York lumberman. That would lead to monumental consequences for the Athletics.

On February 5 more than 850 civic, business, and baseball people turned out at the Bellevue-Stratford Hotel for the delayed celebration of Connie Mack's eightieth birthday. In speeches of the kind usually heard at a funeral, he was lauded by old friends Clark Griffith, Bob Quinn, and Branch Rickey, among others.

Quinn spoke of Mack's generosity to the needy and to young men trying to go to college: "I know because I handled the money on many such occasions. And I want to add that Mr. Mack accorded me the same courtesy and consideration on our first meeting forty-seven years ago as he does now. That is one of the beacon lights of a great man."

Rickey said, "I went to him with my first problems and he gave me sage counsel and encouraging advice. We don't just admire Mr. Mack, we love him."

Judge McDevitt quoted former A's outfielder Walter French, who at a similar gathering a decade ago had said, "On December 23, 1862, our Lord created Connie Mack, was satisfied, and rested for the remainder of the day."

Jack Kelly, Olympic oarsman and longtime friend, called him "an oasis of peace in a world torn by strife, a man of understanding in a world of misunderstanding."

Mack's longtime friend and protégé Tommy Richardson, president of the Eastern League, who had organized the event, presented Mack with a unique tribute, described by Stan Baumgartner in *The Sporting News* as "a plaque of 92 autographed balls containing the signatures of every man connected with the organized game in 1942."

Mack was brighter of eye and keener of mind than many younger men in the room as he rose near midnight and once again recounted his beginnings in baseball, touched on highlights of his career, and thanked the newspapermen for their support. Then, showing that he was not stuck in the good old days, but was still more forward-thinking than anyone else in the room, he suggested that the practice of selecting all-time all-star teams was obsolete. Citing the many changes the game had undergone over the years, he said, "There were great ball teams in the '80s. There were good teams in the '90s. Then came the beginning of this century, and every 10 or 15 years there comes a new crop of great players. But when you look at all-time all-star teams no matter when they are picked, the same three names are in the outfield—Cobb, Speaker, and Ruth. The infield never changes. That isn't right. I think the all-star teams should be selected by the baseball writers every fifteen years. That is fair to every player for the game changes and new players ought not to be compared with old-timers. There are a great number of star players today who should be given proper place in all-star selection."

Al Simmons had watched the caliber of pitching all last season and decided he could hit it. Besides, he had begun to brood over the fact that he was 103 hits shy of 3,000. That hadn't meant much to him during his heyday—there were only six who had reached 3,000 at the time, and nobody made a big deal about it. But now as he neared forty, he began to mentally kick himself for all the times at bat he had wasted during his peevish periods and the days off he had taken. He hadn't batted once in 1942. When he told Mr. Mack he wanted to go back on the active list, Mack thought it was a bad idea to try to come back after a year off, especially at the age of forty. "But if you want to do this and can hook on with somebody else, you have your release. And when you're ready to come back, your job will still be here."

On February 3 Eddie Collins agreed to take him on the Red Sox. Simmons found his eyes and legs were as good as ever, but his reflexes weren't. The wrist action required to get around on a fastball was gone. He collected 27 hits and batted .209. After the season he admitted it had been foolish. "No man worked harder or was in better physical condition for a comeback. But I couldn't make the grade."

Connie Mack had made a December trip to Savannah and a few spots in Florida in search of a new training site. Then the government announced restrictions on travel that threw baseball for a loop. Commissioner Landis ordered all clubs to set up camp some place close to home. All plans to head for their usual sunny climes went out the window. Teams arranged with private schools, colleges, resorts—any place that had some indoor facilities as well as a diamond. No club went farther than 450 miles from its home ballpark. The Washington Senators just stayed home.

The Athletics went thirty-five miles to Wilmington, Delaware. They stayed at the Hotel duPont, three miles from the ballpark where their farm team played. Connie Mack usually walked to the park; while most of the players went by bus. One cold day the players were waiting for the bus. Mack came out of the hotel and walked briskly by them, waving to them, "Come on boys, the walk will be good for all of us."

Bobby Estalella asked the man next to him, "How old he?"

"Eighty."

"He eighty?" Estalella said. "He live to be a hundred. We win the pennant, he live to two hundred."

Estalella decided if the Old Man could walk the three miles, he would too.

The Athletics' training camp was as much of a novelty to the local residents as it had been on the team's first spring in California in 1940, especially to the youngsters in the small town. Charlie Lucas, fifteen, was one of them: "Kids would come up to Mr. Mack for autographs. He was very patient and always obliged them. He sat in a box with Mr. Carpenter [Wilmington Blue Rocks co-owner with Mack] in a gray wool overcoat on cold days. Kids gathered around him and he would talk to them like a grandpa: 'Are you playing ball in school? . . . How's your grades?'"

Was Connie Mack fifty years ahead of his time? Or do we just imagine that men were men and pitchers finished everything they started in those days? On March 27 he was quoted in the *Washington Post:* "Pitchers ought to get themselves in shape. Nobody should have to tell them to work every day, but dammit they want to take a day off now before they throw batting practice. And in a game if somebody hits a home run, they suddenly get an ingrown toenail and have to be taken out."

Maybe he was just fed up with one complainer and let off some steam. At eighty, his fire clearly had not gone out.

Over the winter Mack watched more of his players go into the service, bringing the total to twenty (by the end of the year it would be twenty-nine). Dick Fowler and Phil Marchildon reported for duty with the Canadian armed forces.

Mack's daughter Mary had left the convent to marry Francis X. O'Reilly in 1932; by 1935 she had separated from her husband and later moved in with her parents in their apartment. She was a social service worker at Temple University Medical School when she decided to join the WACs and went off for motor corps training.

Connie Jr. went to work for Bendix Corporation, then the Third Service Command while occasionally helping out Bob Schroeder in the A's concessions business.

Mack's grandson Connie McCambridge was attached to an engineers'

(LEFT) Connie Mack and his daughter Ruth pose with Mr. and Mrs. Dick Bircher before Bircher took them up for Mack's first airplane ride for his birthday in 1933. *Courtesy of Alice Cunningham.*

(BELOW) Dib Williams, Doc Cramer, Bob Johnson, and Eric McNair relax before a game. *Courtesy of the author.*

(ABOVE) Businessman Henry J. Heesch, Babe Ruth, Japanese promoter Sotoru Suzuki, and Connie Mack, Yokohama, 1934. *Courtesy of Alice Cunningham.*

(OPPOSITE) East Brookfield resident Jean Rooney presents greetings to Connie Mack at Mack's 1934 return to his hometown as Mack's longtime pal George M. Cohan looks on. *Courtesy of East Brookfield Historical Society.*

(ABOVE) Ben Shibe's son Tom succeeded his father as president of the A's in 1922. He and Connie Mack, shown here at an AL meeting in 1935, were as close as brothers. *Courtesy of Robert Warrington.*

(OPPOSITE TOP) Spring training in Mexico in 1937 was a disaster. Front row from left: Lena Blackburne, Skeeter Newsome, unk, Lynn Nelson, George Custer, Bill Werber, Bill Cissell, Ace Parker, Charlie Berry, Earle Brucker. On horseback: Lou Finney and Frank Hayes. *Courtesy of Bill Werber.*

(OPPOSITE BOTTOM) Mack was always available to writers and photographers. Here he poses with coach Charlie Berry and photographers covering 1938 spring training in Lake Charles. *Courtesy of Robert Warrington.*

(OPPOSITE TOP) The first Hall of Fame induction class. Standing from left: Honus Wagner, Grover Alexander, Tris Speaker, Nap Lajoie, George Sisler, Walter Johnson. Seated from left: Eddie Collins, Babe Ruth, Connie Mack, Cy Young. Ty Cobb arrived too late for the photo. *Courtesy of the author.*

(OPPOSITE BOTTOM) Despite his public image as a staid old man in a high stiff collar, Connie Mack was a ham at heart. Here he clowns with the Three Stooges during a trip to California. *Courtesy of Dennis Nolen.*

(ABOVE) Connie Mack loved the movie folks, and they loved him. When the A's trained in California in 1940, veteran actor Leo Carrillo (pictured here with Mack), best known for his role as Pancho on the Cisco Kid television series, invited the entire team for a day at his ranch. *Courtesy of the author.*

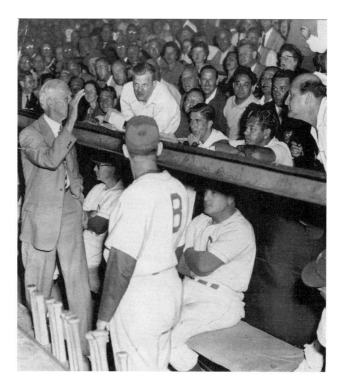

(ABOVE) Connie Mack admonishes fans for setting off fireworks
when Joe DiMaggio came to bat on July 7, 1949, at Shibe Park.
*Courtesy of Special Collections Research Center, Temple University,
Philadelphia* PA.

(OPPOSITE) Connie Mack and Phillies' manager Bucky Harris chat
before a city series game in 1943. Harris was starting his twentieth
year as a manager, Mack his forty-fifth. *Courtesy of the author.*

(OPPOSITE) Still going strong at eighty-one, Mr. Mack had no thought of retiring. *Courtesy of Robert Warrington.*

(ABOVE) There was more publicity than pitching tips involved when Mack struck a pose while his young pitchers looked on at spring training in Fredericksburg, Maryland, in 1944. *Courtesy of Robert Warrington.*

(ABOVE) Mr. and Mrs. Mack with friends (probably Mr. and Mrs. Parker Woods at left) at the 1944 World Series in St. Louis. *Courtesy of Connie Mack III.*

(OPPOSITE) Connie Mack does not appear pleased by the weather or what he sees on the field. *Courtesy of the author.*

(OPPOSITE) Mack poses as if he's "on the job." In fact, he seldom moved from his seat on the bench during a game. *Courtesy of Robert Warrington.*

(ABOVE) Bob Schroeder checks out vendors at Shibe Park. Until his death in 1950, Schroeder worked for the A's for forty-eight years, rising to concessions manager, secretary, and a member of the board of directors. *Courtesy of Robert Warrington.*

(LEFT) Connie Mack holds pitcher Bob Savage's daughter Bobbie on his knee during spring training 1947. *Courtesy of Rita Savage.*

(BELOW) Mickey Cochrane, Jimmy Foxx, Lefty Grove, and Bobo Newsom at an old-timers' game. In his later years, Connie Mack sometimes had trouble recognizing his old stars. *Courtesy of Gil Dunn.*

In 1947 Mack returned to Meriden, Connecticut, where his professional baseball career had begun in 1884. He is greeted by Patrick Carter, a teammate on the East Brookfield town team of his youth. At left is Danny Murray, Meriden's 1884 batboy. In the center is Charlie McGrath, mascot of the 1884 team. *Courtesy of Joe Budwitz.*

(ABOVE) Mack's grandchildren Connie III, Michael, Susan, and Dennis Mack visit Pop-Pop before a game at Shibe Park. *Courtesy of Connie Mack III.*

(OPPOSITE) Connie Mack never gave up on Lou Brissie, whose war wounds made it unlikely he would ever pitch in the big leagues. *Courtesy of Lou Brissie.*

(OPPOSITE TOP) Connie Mack's three sons put aside their feuding long enough to pose with their father for this display of fraternal harmony in July 1950. *Courtesy of Special Collections Research Center, Temple University Libraries, Philadelphia* PA.

(OPPOSITE BOTTOM) Mack was always game for a gag shot, like this one dreamed up by PR director Dick Armstrong announcing the signing of "a new catcher" in 1950. *Courtesy of Dick Armstrong.*

(ABOVE) Connie Mack tries to explain baseball to the Duke of Windsor at spring training in West Palm Beach, 1950. Notice how straight the old catcher's fingers are, despite arthritic knuckles. *Courtesy of Connie Mack III.*

(ABOVE) Connie Mack writes a letter, ca. 1950. *Courtesy of Alice Cunningham.*

(OPPOSITE TOP) The Cornelius McGillicuddy clan gathered on Christmas Day 1951. Back row from left: Mary's husband Albert Schurr, Ruth's husband Frank Cunningham, Connie Mack, Connie Jr., Betty's husband Jim Nolen, Ruth. Frank Cunningham Jr. is in front of Connie Jr. Seated from left: Mary, Katherine, Katherine's sister Margaret, Betty, Connie Jr.'s wife Sue. Front row from left: Susan, Dennis, and Connie Mack III; Kathy Cunningham, Jimmy Nolen, Alice, Connie and Bill Cunningham; Michael Nolen, and Michael Mack. *Courtesy of Connie Mack III.*

(OPPOSITE BOTTOM) Mack offers batting advice to Connie III while Michael and Dennis look on. *Courtesy of Susan McGillicudy.*

(OPPOSITE TOP) Connie Mack on his ninety-first birthday with his grandson Michael Mack in Fort Myers. *Courtesy of Susan McGillicuddy.*

(OPPOSITE BOTTOM) Tris Speaker and Ty Cobb visit with Mr. Mack at the Philadelphia writers' dinner in January 1954. *Courtesy of Robert Warrington.*

(ABOVE) The Macks and the Philadelphia Eight congratulate each other on their agreement to save the A's for Philadelphia, October 17, 1954. Roy Mack later regretted the deal and scuttled it. *Courtesy of Special Collections Research Center, Temple University Libraries, Philadelphia PA.*

Connie Mack looks closer to tears than smiles when he turned ninety-two a month after his Athletics moved to Kansas City. *Courtesy of Robert Warrington.*

division from Michigan waiting at Fort Dix, New Jersey, to go overseas. When he asked for a pass to say goodbye to his grandfather, Connie Mack, two officers decided they had to go with him.

"They were all ice skaters," McCambridge said, "and they wanted me to ask Dad if he could get them in to use the hockey arena. Dad picked up the phone and it was all set, just like that, and on a Saturday afternoon they went to play hockey and skate—all free—and I stayed in camp because I had duty."

Only ten minor leagues opened for business; all but one completed the season. When the draft age was raised to thirty-eight and the list of departing big league players grew longer, the key of all of baseball shifted from major to minor. Every big league team had a minor league caste to it, be it AAA or AA, or, as in the case of the Athletics, somewhere around Class B. Clubs were permitted up to forty players on their reserve rosters; nobody had that many. The A's had twenty-nine. Except for four pitchers, Mack's only major league players were Suder, Siebert, Valo, Swift, and Wagner. After a few days of practice Roberto Estalella said to him, "Mr. Mack, you one of the greatest managers but if you do something with these bums, you the greatest manager in whole world."

Connie Mack knew full well what he had to work with. He didn't need the garrulous, fun-loving, overweight Bobby Estalella to remind him. His thoughts may have resembled those of George Washington on first inspecting the rebel rabble he was asked to command or the Duke of Wellington surveying the troops pressed into His Majesty's service: "I don't know what effect these men will have upon the enemy, but, by God, they terrify me."

Mack had bought pitcher Jesse Flores, listed at twenty-four but really twenty-eight, on a trial basis from Los Angeles for $1,000 in September. Flores had been 14-5 with the Angels. Mack liked what he saw and paid the $9,000 balance on April 27. Flores was a heady pitcher, threw several pitches including the most effective screwball in the league, and was sneaky fast. Midway through the season he added a knuckleball. He pitched 230 innings and was 12-14 with the only ERA on the staff lower than the league average.

Don Black was another old-for-a-rookie pitcher—twenty-six. Mack paid $5,000 for him after he'd won 18 for Petersburg in the Class C Virginia League. Black worked over 200 innings for a 6-16 record.

Under a working agreement with Williamsport, Mack had his pick of up to three players. He had taken just one, twenty-four-year-old infielder Irv Hall, who had spent six undistinguished years in the lower minors. The 5-foot-10, 150-pound Baltimore resident was tickled to death to be in a major league spring training camp. Strictly a singles hitter, he not only became the everyday shortstop, but he also survived the return of the servicemen and lasted until 1947.

When Hall signed his 1943 contract for $2,500, he told Mack, "My father wants to be a farmer and I want to borrow $1,800 to buy a farm for him."

Mack agreed. "We'll take so much out of your salary until you pay it back."

At the end of the year there was still $600 due. Mack called Hall to his office, canceled the rest of the debt, added a $1,200 bonus, and gave him a '44 contract for $4,000.

With an eye as much on their military draft status as ability, Mack had drafted two men with enough big league experience to demonstrate they were not big league caliber: outfielder John Welaj, twenty-nine, from Buffalo, and infielder Eddie Mayo, thirty-three, from Los Angeles. But they hustled, gave it all they had, and never complained, grateful to be back in the big leagues. Mayo won the third base job, but in a spring game a throw ricocheted and hit him in the left eye, which developed a blind spot. He said nothing, but dealt with it and batted .219. During the following winter Mayo's eye cleared up. The Tigers picked him up, and he had five productive years with them.

(Twenty-seven years later, Mayo attended a ceremony dedicating a monument in front of Connie Mack's birthplace in East Brookfield, Massachusetts. At a dinner that followed, Mayo said, "I once asked [Mr. Mack] about what was the hardest thing in managing a ball club, expecting he would answer about strategy or player relations. 'Telling a player you have to release him,' said Mr. Mack. It was a classic remark and a lesson that has helped me greatly in my business career.")

Like many who played for Connie Mack, what John Welaj remembered most was what he learned from sitting beside him on the bench. "I heard him tell pitchers how to pitch to certain batters, and hitters what to do at the plate in certain situations. And, of course, his moving the outfielders."

But now there was less of that moving of the outfielders than there had been in the past. "You need real pitching to move your men around," Mack said. "You've got to know that your pitcher knows where and how he's going to throw the ball. . . . But my pitching now is so uncertain it's not worthwhile to try and play that style."

Connie Mack still promulgated the illusion that Earle would succeed him, with a cryptic qualification. He told reporters on May 11, "Earle is going to be the next manager of the Athletics, if they ever have one, and he'll probably do a better job than his dad."

The A's opened in Washington in a wartime atmosphere that prevented President Roosevelt from being there. War Manpower chief Paul McNutt, whose ball-playing days went as far as Indiana University, filled in for him. Before the first pitch, Clark Griffith walked toward the A's bench and gestured for Connie Mack to come over to the VIP box. Mr. Mack's emergence from the dugout evoked a standing ovation from the twenty-five thousand, and he ate it up. He took off his hat and clasped his hands above his head, grinning broadly as he strode rapidly across the field. On his way back he waved to the fans in the bleachers.

The war affected the game in another way besides the loss of players. There was a shortage of rubber to go around the core of the baseballs, so Spalding experimented with something called balata, which was similar to golf ball cover material. The result was a dead ball. The balata balls were identified with a star and were used only until May 9, when synthetic rubber replaced the balata. The new synthetic rubber balls resulted in Mr. Mack's being accused of cheating.

The A's were in third place, only 2 games behind the Yankees, when Detroit came to town for a May 31 doubleheader. Hal Newhouser shut out the A's in the first game. Roger Wolff had a 4–2 lead in the top of the sixth of game 2 when Rudy York hit a long drive that looked like it was headed for the bleachers until it died like a plugged quail and was caught.

York and Tigers manager Steve O'Neill demanded to see the ball. It was one of the discontinued dead balata balls. O'Neill filed a protest with the league.

"Some old balls had come in from the factory along with the fresh supply," Mack explained to Dan Daniel of the *New York World-Telegram* on June 11, "and if they got into the game the umpires were at fault." The protest was rejected.

The A's had no hitting or pitching, just a pretty good defense. By July 4 they were in the cellar to stay. They lost 105 games and were swept in 18 doubleheaders. The old baseball gallows humor set in: "Somebody's always saying we got to have harmony on this team. When we going to get that guy harmony?"

In some ways they matched the futility of the 1916 A's, Mack's worst team, losers of 117. The '43 version batted 10 points lower than the 1916 outfit and was shut out 24 times. They finished 49 games behind the Yankees but only 20 games below seventh, two-thirds the gap of the 1916 team.

Through it all Connie Mack shivered in the cold wet spring, rode the patched-together antique railroad cars through the hot summer, watching, missing nothing on the field, knowing this would not be his year—there may never be another "his year"—but never surrendering hope.

On July 6 in Cleveland Mack demonstrated that his mind was still sharp. Oris Hockett led off and singled for the Indians. Lou Boudreau walked. Roy Cullenbine sacrificed them to third and second. Ken Keltner hit back to the pitcher, Orie Arntzen, who threw to catcher Bob Swift. Hockett danced between third and home without drawing a throw while Keltner made it to second and Boudreau, head down, raced for third and arrived while Swift was chasing Hockett toward the base. Apparently thinking that Boudreau was entitled to third, Hockett kept on going into left field. Swift instinctively tagged Boudreau, who was standing on the bag, and caught up with Hockett. Third base umpire Joe Rue called Hockett out.

Two outs, men on second and third.

Connie Mack called time and beckoned for the umpire.

"Mr. Grieve," he addressed Joe Rue, "don't you think that, since Hockett had regained third base before Boordeer was tagged, Hockett was entitled to the base and Boordeer was tagged for the second out? Hockett was then tagged for the third out [or, under the rules, for going out of the base path], making it a double play."

Rue pondered that while the press box crowd and the fans wondered what the discussion was about. "You're right," he said.

Red Smith commented, "Only Connie could get the play right and the umpire's name wrong."

A rookie umpire, Hal Weafer, was the first base umpire. A few innings later Bobby Estalella hit a ground ball that an infielder picked up and threw wild past first. After crossing the bag, Estalella turned to the left and walked back. First baseman Mickey Rocco had recovered the ball and routinely tagged him. Weafer called Estalella out for turning to the left after crossing the bag. Connie Mack knew the umpire had blown the call; the old rules had required a turn to the right, but they had been changed to allow the base runner to turn either way with impunity as long as he didn't make a break for second. Mack said nothing at the time.

When he wanted an explanation for a controversial call, or, as some umpires put it, "to berate us about something," Mack would sometimes send

Earle out between innings to tell the umps, "Dad wants to know after the game why you made that call," and the umpires would go over to the dugout after the game. This time, reported Red Smith, the wily Mack said to Weafer, "Ah, on that play at first, Estalella turned the wrong way, didn't he?"

"No," said Weafer, "I thought he made a break for second."

"So," wrote Smith, "he avoided the trap which Connie, two jumps ahead of everyone, was laying for him."

The A's wound up losing the game, 2–0. That evening Mack admitted he hadn't been all that smart. "If I had known we were going to lose, I would have kept quiet about that play at third and let them call it wrong. Then I could have protested the game and it would have had to be replayed."

On August 8 Elmer Valo went into the army just as the Athletics were beginning a record-tying 20-game losing streak, the last 17 mercifully on the road. They didn't see themselves as that bad and in fact were in most of the games right up to the last out. Mack juggled the lineup like W. C. Fields, but there wasn't much to juggle; most of them were batting .220 to .240. Roger Wolff won the last before the swan dive, 4–0, over New York on August 6. Eighteen days later the A's were in Chicago for a doubleheader, their fourth twin bill in four days. The White Sox scored 2 in the ninth to win the first game, 6–5. Between games Connie Mack said to Wolff, "You can either set a record or break this string." The A's scored 8 runs in the third, and Wolff cruised to an 8–1 win.

Mack didn't hesitate to use Wolff in relief, especially for Jesse Flores, who tired in the late innings. Wolff's knuckler would get by a catcher, but Mack seemed to sense when it would be most effective. In a game in Boston he sent Wolff in to pitch the ninth with an 8–7 lead. With two out and the tying run on base, Mack ordered Bobby Doerr intentionally walked, causing gasps of disbelief among the by-the-book grandstand managers for his putting the winning run on base. The next batter was Babe Barna, who had played for Mack five years earlier. Mack didn't believe Barna could hit a knuckleball. He was right.

During the season a variety of exhibition games was played to sell war bonds: old-timers' games, service teams playing major league all-star clubs, doubleheaders involving three teams. On August 26 Mack was present at the Polo Grounds along with a group of old-timers including Babe Ruth, Eddie Collins, Honus Wagner, Tris Speaker, and Walter Johnson. As the oldsters fell down attempting to catch pop flies and sixty-four-year-old Roger

Bresnahan tried to hold on to Johnson's pitches while Ruth tried at length before finally hitting one into the upper deck in right field, Connie Mack "almost cried. I wanted to remember them as they were in their prime," he told Stan Baumgartner.

The All-Star Game played in Shibe Park on July 13 was the first one played at night. Dick Siebert was the only A's representative. The Yankees had six men on the AL roster, but manager Joe McCarthy chose not to use any of them and still won, 5–3.

The story of Carl Scheib is illustrative of how Connie Mack dealt with young players at that time. In 1942 Carl was a fifteen-year-old pitcher in Gratz, Pennsylvania, north of Philadelphia in the coal country. The town of eight hundred people was not on any scouts' itinerary. But it was on a traveling salesman's route. One day the salesman called on the general store in town, and the woman behind the counter told him about the star pitcher for the local high school. The salesman saw him pitch and wrote to Connie Mack about him.

Next thing Carl knew, he had a letter asking him to come to Philadelphia for a tryout.

On Saturday, August 29, his brother Paul, a catcher, drove him to Shibe Park. The game was rained out, but the rain had let up by the time they arrived. Scheib recalled:

I had no glove or shoes or uniform, so they had to go around the clubhouse and collect them for me. I went down to the bullpen and all the coaches and big wheels were there. I threw to Earle Brucker and Mr. Mack said, "You hurry back next year as fast as you can."

I had two years to go in high school but didn't finish. The only thing for me in Gratz was the farm or the coal mine so I left quick as I could. My dad was a coal miner and died at fifty-seven. The next year I quit school and became the regular batting practice pitcher, traveled with the team, got into a few exhibition games. In August we had a four-week road trip. On the train coming home Mr. Mack said to me, "It's time for you to pitch."

I said, "I'm ready."

The Yankees were in town for the Labor Day doubleheader. That morning Carl and his parents went up to Mr. Mack's office. His dad, Oliver, signed the contract for $300 for the rest of the season. Mack gave him $500 for signing and handed Oliver Scheib a check for $1,000.

"Now you go down to the clubhouse," Mack told Carl, "and get a uniform with a shirt number so you can be identified."

The A's won the first game, 11–2. Earle Brucker, the bullpen coach, took Scheib to the bullpen for the second game. He was sitting beside Orie Arntzen, who was old enough to be his father. Scheib was amazed that an old man like Brucker could still crouch and warm up a pitcher; Brucker was forty-two.

The Yankees led, 5–2, when the A's rallied for 2 runs in the last of the eighth. Johnny Welaj had pinch-hit for the starter, Don Black. Orie Arntzen started the ninth and quickly gave up a few hits and walks. Earle Mack emerged and rapped the Shibe Park wall by the dugout with his hand, the signal for Scheib to warm up. Carl started throwing. More Yankees scored. Earle went out to the mound.

"You're in there," Brucker told Carl.

The first man Scheib faced was Nick Etten, who tripled and scored when Joe Gordon grounded out. Carl, called "Charlie" in the *Times* account, then gave up a single to Hemsley, and Crosetti flied out.

The Yankees won, 11–4.

At sixteen years, eight months, and six days, Carl Scheib became the youngest pitcher in American League history. He worked in five more games, pitching the last 4 innings of the season and taking the loss when Cleveland scored 4 runs in the top of the eleventh to break a 4–4 tie.

Under the new management of William Cox and Bucky Harris, the Phillies had turned over almost the entire roster. The new faces brought out the crowds. Although the Phillies finished seventh, they won 22 more games than the year before. Attendance doubled; they outdrew the Athletics, 466,975 to 376,735, for the first time in twenty-three years.

But the Athletics benefited by it; the rental income from the Phillies almost doubled, to $57,997, which included back rent owed at the time of the sale of the club to Cox. With $37,000 from the NFL Eagles, $7,681 from two prize fights, and a payroll of only $131,952, the Athletics managed to show a profit of $17,697.

In the fall of 1943 Mack spent that much and more trolling in minor league waters. Then the Macks went for a rest to Atlantic City, where he visited a military hospital and umpired a softball game for the walking wounded.

While termites were eating away the foundation of the Athletics from within, another turn of events ultimately contributed to bringing down the house of McGillicuddy. On November 23, 1943, Commissioner Landis banned Phils' president Bill Cox from baseball for betting on games. Robert Carpenter Sr. of the duPont dynasty, a minority stockholder, bought control of the team from Cox and installed his twenty-eight-year-old son, Bob Jr., as president.

"The closest I'd ever been to a major league team was to watch a game from the stands," Bob Carpenter said. "It was all a new experience to me. I got a lot of help from Connie Mack. I would visit him in his office at Shibe Park and he was most gracious." With millions at his disposal and about to go into the army, the young Carpenter quickly hired Red Sox farm director Herb Pennock as his general manager and farm director. Major league rules forbade two clubs from sharing ownership of a minor league club, so Connie Mack sold his interest in the Wilmington Blue Rocks to Carpenter.

The resurrection of the perennial National League doormats began. The impact wasn't felt immediately. The Phillies remained in last place during the war, then built a farm system and a pennant winner.

How the battle for survival in what was destined to become a one-team city would have turned out if William Cox had kept his nose clean and run a threadbare operation while the A's became pennant contenders in 1948, or if Connie Mack Jr. had bought out his brothers and competed with Bob Carpenter Jr. on an equally funded basis, must be left to the realm of the what-ifs. Since the Athletics owned the ballpark, it might have been easier and more attractive for the tenants to move out to the greener pastures beckoning in the west.

16 | ENTER BOBO

The war had been going better since victories in crucial Pacific battles in mid-1942, but it continued to grind its way slowly through thousands of casualties with no end in sight. In February 1943 Connie Mack wrote to the wife of a distant cousin, Madeline Kittredge, who had written to tell him of the death of another relative, Julietta O'Keefe, bringing her up to date on the activities of his family:

Connie Jr. now thirty years old has joined the army has a wonderful wife with four children the oldest not five years old. Connie was anxious to join when the war started but I couldn't see him going and leave that young family. [He had been drafted in January and was slated for overseas duty in the field artillery.] Earle's boy is in the Navy has seen plenty of action so far has escaped without being injured. Roy has four children. Our new family consists of Connie Jr. and four girls. Mary has no family. Ruth has three boys and a little girl. Rita has no children her husband now at sea gone only recently. Betty our baby has only a James Jr. her husband is on his way over as a contract instructor no telling when he will come back. . . . At eighty-one am going pretty strong health wonderful. Michael the oldest brother only one living 86 but not in good health.

Michael died at ninety-four in 1952.

As he had done more than twenty-five years ago, Connie Mack was corresponding with his players in the service. He wrote to Bob Savage in April 1943, listing his likely lineup for the coming season: "Was pleased to hear from you. Hope everything will work out for you as you would like."

Things didn't work out so well for Savage. After six months in North Africa, he was involved in the Allied landing at Anzio and was wounded in the assault on Monte Cassino in February 1944. While in a hospital in Africa, he wrote that he had taken shrapnel in back of his right shoulder: "I hope they will be able to dig it out because more than anything else I want to be able to pitch for you again." The doctors were unable to remove it, and it remained there the rest of his life. When he recovered, they sent him back to Anzio, where Savage found to his relief that his pitching ability was unaffected by the metal lodged in his back. "We played another army team at Anzio," he wrote. "My co was the catcher. I pitched a no-hitter and he assigned me to jeep driving. No more carrying a heavy machine gun."

Savage was wounded again on December 1 in France. When the war in Europe ended, he thought he was headed for Japan but instead wound up in Austria, where he did some pitching for the Third Division team.

In February 1944 Phil Marchildon wrote Mack a cheery letter from England, where he was stationed as a rear turret gunner on a Lancaster bomber in the RCAF. Marchildon wrote that he hoped to hook up with B-17 pilot Billy Southworth Jr., son of the Cardinals' manager, a teammate at Toronto in 1940. Six months later Marchildon bailed out over Denmark and wound up in a German POW camp.

Connie Mack first heard from Lou Brissie in a letter sent from Italy on November 7, 1944, just before Brissie's 351st Regiment headed for the Appenine Mountains and a forty-four-day stalemate against dug-in German forces in snow, freezing rain, and foot-deep mud. Five days before Mack replied to the letter on December 12, Corporal Brissie's battalion had been destroyed by a day-long barrage of German shellfire, and he was in a field hospital begging the doctors not to amputate what was left of his shattered left leg. He was transported to Naples, where a Cleveland Indians fan, Dr. Wilbur J. Brubaker, did the first of twenty-three operations to wire together what little bone was left and sew up the torn muscles and tendons.

No longer an owner of the Wilmington franchise, Connie Mack had to look elsewhere for a training site. He considered Atlantic City but settled on Frederick, a town in western Maryland. Although he spoke as if nobody would ever have to return to the South for spring training again, he couldn't mean it, not when six inches of snow covered Frederick on March 6 and two weeks later cold rains flooded the field for five days.

The A's stayed at the Francis Scott Key Hotel, which had a large lobby filled with deep chairs and sofas. On those idle days the place was filled with players smoking and talking. There were always several gathered around Mr. Mack, eager to hear stories of the old days.

A men's clothing store occupied space off the lobby, and fourteen-year-old Ken Shook worked there, pressing suits and running errands. When things were slow, he would sit on the floor among the lobby sitters and listen to the conversations. One day he was sitting beside Mr. Mack's chair. "He was talking and he looked down at me and smiled," Shook said. "He looked frail but he wasn't. He started to get out of this deep chair and I put out my hand to help him and he squeezed it with a strong grip as if he was making fun of my thinking he was too feeble to get up by himself."

Holdouts were rare, with millions of GIs making $21 a day—once a month—and even the highest-ranking generals earning $8,000.

Mack had two minor squabbles. Outfielder Bill Burgo, up from Wilmington, had hit .371 in 17 games in 1943. He thought he was worth more than $3,000. Mack said of him, "I don't care much if he stays out. He's a funny man. Every time he has a good day he lets you know what he's getting, just as if I didn't know."

In 27 games Burgo would have few good days to talk about.

More interested in draft-proof respectability than the future, Mack paid $10,000 to Toronto for Luke Hamlin, thirty-nine, who had won 20 for Brooklyn in 1939 and gone back to the minors in 1943. Hamlin balked at a $4,500 contract; Mack eventually raised it to $6,000. He reaped 6 wins, including 2 shutouts, from Luke's last year.

Hal Wagner wanted to continue to work at a war plant and catch on weekends only. Mack brought back Frank Hayes, who had had a miserable year in St. Louis, batting .188. Mack sent the Browns $10,000 and two pickups from Elmira, Sam Zoldak and Bernie Lutz. Hayes caught every game—not every inning—but all 155 games. (The next year he caught 151.)

The oldest players in Frederick were Hamlin and another thirty-nine-year-old right-hander, Joe Berry, who, in addition to a 2-inning demitasse with the Cubs in '42, had appeared in 740 games in seventeen years in the minor leagues. Connie Mack wanted experience in the bullpen and he got it, giving Milwaukee $10,000 for their 18-game winner. Berry was worth it. He worked in 53 games, all in relief, and picked up 10 wins against 8 losses, with a 1.94 ERA. Mack rewarded him with a $2,000 bonus at the end of the year. Berry would be just as effective in '45, leading the league with 52 appearances.

The youngest in camp was a sixteen-year-old first baseman, Jacob Nelson

Fox (who never used the Jacob). Fox lived about fifty miles from Frederick in St. Thomas, Pennsylvania. When he learned the A's would be training nearby, he pestered his parents to take him to meet Connie Mack. Maybe he'd get a tryout. He had no interest in school, just baseball. In December his mother wrote to Mr. Mack, telling him of her baseball-crazy son, who had just turned sixteen on Christmas Day. Ordinarily Mack would not invite a youngster to spring training without a recommendation from somebody. But these were difficult times and sixteen-year-olds weren't being drafted, and besides, the letter from a proud but concerned mother moved him. Perhaps it reminded him of himself at that age, an eighth-grade dropout who would rather play baseball than eat.

So on Saturday, January 8, he sat at his desk and wrote:

My Dear Mrs. Fox

Am pleased to hear from you. Also pleased to know that you are interested in baseball. Note what you say about the young sixteen year old boy who thinks of nothing but baseball. How big a boy is he, what does he weigh and how tall. I may one of these days be able to help him. Yes I do think he could go into baseball without being in High School. If he was good enough player at present time to make one hundred & fifty dollars per month he would receive quite an education by traveling around the country. Has he had at least one year in high school. Suppose you have him drop me a line at Shibe Park.

Sincerely yours,
Connie Mack

Mack had not invited Nellie Fox to camp. And the youngster didn't bother to write. He just showed up, persuading his parents to drive him to Frederick in their 1937 Chevy on Saturday morning, March 18. Accounts vary as to his introduction to Mr. Mack, but there was something about the little guy—who was probably no more than 5-foot-6 and 140 pounds—clutching his first baseman's mitt that appealed to Mack. Somebody located a uniform not too much too big for him, and he found himself working out at first base with his idol, Dick Siebert, who did not brush him off but gave him pointers. It didn't matter that some of the other players were as unknown as he was and would quickly disappear or that some of them were old enough to be his father. As a fan, he knew the names of the returning players. He watched and listened, gulping in the whole experience.

Some of the veterans laughed at him. "I don't think my son Earle took the boy seriously at first," Mack said. "When Fox went home after his first day in camp, one of the sports writers asked Earle if the boy would be back. Earle said, 'I hope so. He wore one of our suits home.'"

But what impressed Connie Mack was what he most wanted to see in a young player: enthusiasm, a palpable love for the game. You couldn't teach that. It was something Mack had seen in another youngster who had tried out more than twenty-five years ago: Jimmie Dykes.

Nellie demonstrated that he knew how to handle himself taking throws at first base, though Connie Mack quickly decided that was not the right position for him. The youngster looked confident at the plate, rapping a single on his first time up in a practice game. Mack offered him a Lancaster contract, which his father signed. But the youngster needed a work permit, so the Foxes went home to obtain the necessary documents and returned their son to Mr. Mack's care. His roommate was pitcher Carl Scheib, also at his first spring training. Scheib was a year older than Fox.

During the next few days Fox replaced Dick Siebert at first in the late innings of exhibition games. Then Mack turned him over to Lena Blackburne at Lancaster, where he hit .325, spending part of the season at Class D Jamestown, playing first base and the outfield.

The recruits at Frederick included three rookies bought after the '43 season from the Class B Lancaster Red Roses for a total of $20,000: outfielder Lew Flick, pitcher-outfielder—and manager—Woody Wheaton, and third baseman George Kell. Flick and Wheaton left few traces. Flick spent the season awaiting induction into the navy that never came. Wheaton, 4-F due to high blood pressure, a career minor leaguer who had once had a trial with the A's in 1936, was soon back in Lancaster.

George Kell was another story.

Born in Swifton, Arkansas, Kell was a freshman at Arkansas State when he was signed by Brooklyn Dodgers' scout Tom Greenwade in 1940. In 1941 at Newport in the Class D Northeast Arkansas League, he managed to hit .310 in a home park with lights so dim they relied on automobile headlights during the games. The next spring the hefty 5-foot-9 Kell reported to Durham for spring training. Brooklyn general manager Larry MacPhail thought he was too fat and ordered him released.

"There I was, nineteen years old, without a job," said Kell. "They didn't pay your way home. I stayed in the hotel a few days, signed meal checks, while they kept trying to get me out of there. The Lancaster club of the Interstate League came to town for a game and somebody told me they needed a ballplayer. I signed with them, hit .299, and in 1943 led all baseball, hitting .396."

That attracted bevies of scouts. Kell knew that Yankees scout Paul Krichell was eager to buy him, and "I wanted to go to the Yankees like everybody else." The Cubs were also interested.

In 1943 the A's still had a half interest in Wilmington in the same league. They had no working agreement with Lancaster like the one they had with Elmira in the Eastern League, which they paid $3,000 a year for the right to first choice of players. But Connie Mack had friends in Lancaster. Jim Peterson, a former pitcher for the A's, was listed as the club's treasurer and one of the three owners. Another was Norman McClain, a Philadelphia contractor.

On Sunday, August 6, Connie Mack left Earle in charge of the A's doubleheader loss to the Yankees and went to Stumpf Field in Lancaster, where the Wilmington Blue Rocks were playing a pair. But he wasn't there to scout his own farmhands. Kell recalled:

I didn't know he was there, but my mother and father had come up to see me play and recognized him. Just before the game my father called me over and said, "They're not going to tell you that Connie Mack is here. They thought it might worry you. I want you to know he's here and he's going to be looking at you."

Mr. Mack stayed for the doubleheader and I hit a home run and after the game he came down to the clubhouse and shook hands with everybody and said to me, "Young man, how would you like to play in Philadelphia?"

"I'd love it, Mr. Mack."

He said, "I'm going to buy your contract and when this season is over you report to me in Philadelphia."

I was startled. I figured Mr. Mack must have had some understanding that gave him first choice on our players. [He didn't.] Still, I can't say I was disappointed. I was going to the big leagues and two years earlier I had been released outright.

Kell broke in with the A's on September 28, part of a lineup of nine rookies who beat St. Louis, 8–3, before 1,450 of the curious. He had one hit, a triple, off Al Milnar in his first time at bat, then signed for $3,000 for '44, "and was tickled to get it."

When he received a train ticket to Frederick in February 1944, Kell wanted to bring his wife with him, but he didn't have the money. He wrote to Mr. Mack, "Would you be willing to send me a train ticket for her, let her stay in the hotel and sign meal checks, then take it out of my pay a little at a time?"

Mack agreed. He always encouraged players to bring their wives to spring training.

"The total cost for her came to maybe $500," Kell said. "First pay check, nothing was taken out. Second, same thing. I went up to see him and told him I was worried that he would take it all out of one check and leave me with nothing. He said, 'No, son, you play hard and give me a day's work for your salary and you don't owe me anything.' And he never took a penny out. He could be generous in this way and nobody would ever know it."

Kell had impressed Mack with his glove at Frederick. The only question was whether he could handle the jump from Class B to big league pitching. If Kell had any doubts, Mack quickly boosted his confidence.

"Son," he told Kell, "you're going to be my third baseman this year. You'll have some good days and some very bad days, but the job is yours."

Mack had chosen Ed Busch, twenty-six, from Elmira, where he had hit .303, and installed him as the regular shortstop. Busch did a decent job— for the times, a singles-hitting .271 hitter who made 49 errors was not the worst of the wartime shortstops. He kept the job for two years, until the big leaguers returned.

Irv Hall had a sore arm all spring and couldn't throw until opening day. He got off to a slow start but wound up playing every game. "Mr. Mack always impressed me that if he thought you had ability, he would play the string out on you until you showed that you didn't have it. He stayed with you."

Exhibition games were mostly with service teams, although the spring training locations enabled the A's to play the Yankees a few times, in Atlantic City and Frederick, where the whole town shut down for the event on April 5. On days off during the season the A's played exhibition games at service camps and Eastern League towns. The players didn't mind; in the minor league towns the A's charged a fixed fee, which Mack divided among the players.

There was one conspicuous absentee at Frederick.

At the December 1943 major league meetings Connie Mack had traded Roger Wolff, thirty-two, his most dependable pitcher (and the club's loudest bench jockey), to Washington for pitcher Bobo Newsom, thirty-six. Why? Newsom had been 13-13 for three teams in '43, ending the year back in Washington for the third time. Wolff was 4-F due to bad teeth. Newsom was 3-A. (It was a busy month for Newsom; he completed six weeks' residence in Las Vegas to obtain a divorce from his first wife, was reclassified 1-A and ordered to report for a physical—which he flunked due to an old knee injury—and married Ruth Griffiths.)

The trade was not a cost-cutting move for Mack, just the opposite. Wolff had earned $6,000, Newsom $15,000, and that's what Connie Mack paid him.

There are two possible explanations for the trade. None of the catchers wanted to catch the knuckleball pitcher; Hal Wagner had been charged with 13 passed balls. And Mack knew he had a colorless collection of nobodies to present to the public.

Connie Mack was as much of a promoter as Bill Veeck, in a far more subdued style. He understood the relation of baseball to show business, the attraction of stars, not just on his own team, but throughout the league. Attendance had fallen by half in Boston and by a third in New York with the absence of Ted Williams and Joe DiMaggio in 1943.

Bobo (or Buck—the two names supposedly came from his use of them for everybody else) was a showboat. Newsom was good copy: garrulous, self-promoting, full of bluster and stories and mimicry—a 6-foot-2, 200-pound thirty-six-year-old, "just a boy at heart," said Mack. To which Newsom reportedly replied, "Maybe so, but this boy wants a grown-up man's wages." Connie Mack hadn't had a character like Bobo for thirty-seven years. It was as if he missed Rube Waddell, and if he couldn't have another winning team, he could at least have one that was more fun. To Mack a so-called "hard-to-handle" fun-loving extrovert was more of a joy than a challenge.

Ray Kelly of the *Evening Bulletin* wrote of Newsom, "Connie Mack found him irresistible. He assigned a coach to act as a bodyguard against Newsom whenever he heard Bobo was available." And Bobo was often available, changing teams fifteen times in twenty years.

Kelly quoted Mack: "If I hear Bobo is coming this way and if he sees me I'm afraid he will talk me into a job. I can't resist the man."

Newsom was also a workhorse, good for 250 innings; he walked a lot of batters and struck out a lot of them and probably threw 150 pitches a game.

He threw hard and high; the infield had less to do on the days he pitched. You couldn't drive Buck Newsom out of a game with a bat or a ball—literally. On May 28, 1935, in the third inning, Cleveland outfielder Earl Averill had hit a line drive that caromed off Newsom's left knee into foul territory. After a few minutes, Newsom tested his weight on it and stayed in the game. Between innings the trainer put ice packs on it. Newsom weakened in the eighth; the Indians scored 3 runs and won, 5–4. After the game he went to a hospital, where they found his kneecap had been broken. He was out for six weeks.

Newsom started for Washington on opening day in 1936. In the fifth inning his third baseman fielded a bunt and threw toward first. The ball struck Newsom behind and below the right ear. Down he went like a felled ox. Time was called while he staggered to the dugout and rested. Seven minutes later he emerged and went on to outpitch Lefty Gomez, 1–0. Said the *New York Times*, "The imprint of the ball was on his neck and right ear through the rest of the game as conspicuous as a birthmark."

A three-time 20-game winner, Newsom had pitched the 1940 Tigers to the pennant with a vicious sidearm fastball, giving up only 4 runs in 3 complete games in the World Series. He would have been the Cy Young Award winner if that prize had existed.

Newsom made more preseason copy for what he didn't do than most players earned for their deeds. Mack invited him to come up to Philadelphia from his home in Hartsville, South Carolina, to sign a contract with the press on hand, then be introduced at the writers' dinner on January 27, as Mack had done with Benny McCoy in 1940. Bobo was a no-show.

Mack heard nothing from him until he showed up in Philadelphia on March 1. Mack hurriedly alerted the press. The next day the tower office was crowded when Newsom breezed—make that blew—in. Mack stood up and extended his hand. "Hello, Buck."

"Hello, Bo," said Newsom, who immediately occupied Mack's black, high-backed chair and conducted his own press conference, while Mack, reported Kelly, "sat on whatever was handy" and watched like a youngster being entertained by a clown.

Red Smith reported that when Newsom left the office to take a phone call, Mack "dropped absent-mindedly into the boss's seat. As the door opened for his employee's return, Connie sprang up in mock alarm, re-installing the great man with exaggerated humility. Bobo was quite nice about it."

"All he did was talk baseball," Mack said later. "I couldn't get a word in edgewise."

Newsom wasn't sure if he'd play at all "until I see if I can get in shape." It wasn't about money, he said. "If I play at all it will be for Mr. Mack. I'm sure I'd like it here. If everybody who's booed me turned out to cheer me, we'd fill the stands every day."

After Newsom left—without signing a contract—Mack said, "Well, I guess we'll just have to wait until he makes up his mind."

A month went by, during which Mack heard nothing from Buck. When Mack told the press he intended for Newsom to pitch the opener in Washington but he hadn't heard from the "peculiar fellow," he got a collect call from Buck, who'd been in Florida and assured the manager that he would be there, ready to pitch the opener.

"There was none of that old bragadoo that sometimes gets into his talk," Mack told the writers. "He's gotta act right when he's with us. He's a good businessman and he can be a good pitcher again. I'm counting on his bride to keep him in order."

Bobo didn't want to spend any time up in freezing Frederick, Maryland. He told Mack he would work out at home, or maybe at White Sulphur Springs, West Virginia, or maybe in Florida. Oh, and please send some bats and balls and uniforms to his home in Hartsville. Mack told him whatever he did was okay, take his wife along, the club would pay all his expenses. Mrs. Newsom traveled with him throughout the season.

Newsom finally showed up at Frederick on April 14. According to Kelly, he and his wife arrived in a taxi from Hartsville, about a five-hundred-mile ride. Mack paid the fare, then signed Newsom and gave him the ball to pitch against the Curtis Bay Coast Guard team. Mack said his "indifferent" work in that game cost him the opening day assignment in Washington. Maybe so; it's more likely that Mack wanted to use him in the home opener four days later, when Newsom shut out the Red Sox, 5–0.

Buck Newsom liked the high mound at Shibe Park, which reached the allowed limit of fifteen inches, and he gave Mack his money's worth, working 265 innings with a 13-15 record and 2.82 ERA, plus many hours of amusement. Between the practical jokes of Bobo and the garrulous Bobby Estalella with his white suits and big black cigars chattering away in an accent that few of them could decipher, the A's clubhouse was no place to take a nap. On the train rides Newsom would stand on a chair in the club car, holding a Bible he had borrowed from a hotel room, glasses perched on the end of his nose, and imitate a preacher from his native South Carolina delivering a sermon.

Irv Hall recalled one evening when Mr. Mack and most of the players were sitting in a hotel lobby, chinning. "Bobo Newsom was the center of attention, telling us how when he was with Detroit he made this much money in salary and this much in bonuses and this much in World Series money and we're all adding it up in our heads and it's up around $50,000 and nobody in those days was making that kind of money and Mr. Mack was sitting there doing the same and when Bobo walked away, Mr. Mack said to the rest of us, 'You know, he is real interesting, but he is a real liar,' and we all laughed."

When he wasn't pitching, Bobo might be in the bullpen or the clubhouse or on the bench joking around. But on the mound—"in my office"—Newsom was all business. "Dead serious on every pitch," said George Kell. "You better bear down or he'd get on you. Didn't want anybody on the bench talking or joking or laughing. I was almost afraid of him at first."

Newsom had little regard for Bobby Estalella's defensive abilities, although the Cuban had improved since the previous year, maybe because Mack had sent him to Indianapolis at the end of the '43 season in exchange for the veteran Joe Moore. When Moore went into the army, the deal was canceled, and Estalella had a reprieve from the minor leagues.

Newsom was pitching one day when Estalella missed a catchable ball and a few runs scored. At the end of the inning Newsom went down to the water cooler at the end of the dugout and jumped all over Estalella. Mr. Mack stood up and said, "Leave him alone. You do the pitching and he'll do the outfielding and I'll do the managing." Bobo barked back at him, "Bullshit, Mr. Mack," and Mr. Mack said, "Well, horsefeathers to you, Mr. Newsom."

The swashbuckling champion A's of fifteen years ago would have laughed; the youngsters who were overwhelmed at being in the big leagues sat there aghast that anyone would talk back to the venerable Mr. Mack.

Sometimes when Earle went out to the mound to take Bobo out of a game, Newsom told him, "Get your ass out of here."

Earle went back to the dugout and told his father, "Daddy, he won't come out."

Daddy said, "Well, leave him in."

Buck Newsom knew how to pitch, and Connie Mack knew how to manage pitchers. Newsom appreciated that. When he had worked for Rogers Hornsby in St. Louis, Hornsby had a standing fine for any pitcher who threw a strike on an 0 and 2 count, regardless of the outcome. Newsom considered that absurd. "It handicapped a pitcher who knows what he's doing," he told Shirley Povich. "It isn't always necessary to waste a pitch. Mr. Mack lets us throw the ball we think we can get the hitter out with."

Russ Christopher appreciated it too, throwing his sinker on a two-strike count and challenging the batter to do anything but pound it into the ground, if he could hit it at all.

Newsom may have been all business on the mound, but the fans loved the way he conducted his business. He strutted around the mound and barked at umpires with broad gestures and windmilling arms when he didn't like their calls. One day he was sounding off so enthusiastically that Mack was afraid the umpire would throw him out. He said to Al Simmons, "Go out there and do the arguing."

"But they'll run me out of the game."

"So what? We can spare you more than Bobo."

Umpire Ernie Stewart described two episodes involving Newsom to Larry Gerlach in *The Men in Blue.*

The first occurred September 16, 1944, at Yankee Stadium. In the second inning Frank Crosetti hit a ball down the left-field line. Stewart was umpiring at third base. The ball curved around the foul pole fair but was in foul territory when it landed. George Pipgras, the first base umpire, thought it was foul and indicated as much to Crosetti. Newsom thought Stewart had called it foul at first, then signaled fair:

> Out came the A's [Stewart said]. Their dugout was on the first base side so they had a good view of the left field foul line. Earle was stomping around and Mr. Mack was standing up in the dugout waving his lineup card. Newsom came over. "Bobo," he said, "you haven't called one right all year." I said, "Bobo, you just got that backward. You mean I haven't missed one all year." "Well," he said, "you might be right at that."
>
> After the inning George Kell, playing third for the A's, went into the dugout. I saw Connie Mack talking to him. Then the bench quieted down. Al Simmons, who was coaching at third, stayed to listen to it. When he came out, he said, "Ernie, you ought to know what George Kell said about that home run of Crosetti's. He told Mr. Mack that you called it right. It was a fair ball." I said, "I appreciate that, Al, but it was a fair ball even if he said it was foul."

The way Stewart told it, Newsom had a trick play where he would straddle the rubber and throw to pick off a baserunner. One day a runner slid into third and stood up to dust himself off, apparently calling time. Kell sneaked in behind him. Newsom, straddling the rubber, threw and Kell tagged the runner. "Out," said third base umpire Passarella.

The other team argued that the ball was not in play. Stewart, the home plate umpire, agreed with them and overruled Passarella.

"Mr. Mack was furious. He sent Earle—the little weasel, we called him. Earle said, 'We're going to protest this game.' I said, 'Great, Earle. Let Dad protest this game, but he ain't going to win it.' Mack did protest but it was disallowed."

Newsom never went after the fans, but he traded barbs with dugout hecklers. On June 16 at Yankee Stadium, the Yankees bunted successfully against him three times in a 5-run sixth. Wrote Lou Effrat of the *Times*, "Newsom, with gestures that could not be mistaken, turned toward the Yankee dugout and demanded to know why the Yankees didn't get up there and hit like men, instead of bunting and forcing him to run himself dizzy in the heat."

There's a story, illustrative even if apocryphal, of the day Newsom was pitching against the Senators, and two Washington pitchers, Sid Hudson and Ray Scarborough, were riding him about his age. Scarborough had a big nose; Hudson was a 6-foot-4 string bean. Bobo walked over to the Washington dugout and said, "Well, well, if you two don't remind me of a fire truck—hook and ladder."

In a late-season, meaningless game Newsom might deliver a balloon (a.k.a. eephus), a slow, high, arcing pitch.

Newsom wasn't the only cutup on the team. The quiet, reserved Russ Christopher startled everybody one day in Washington when he went out to warm up before the second game of a doubleheader wearing a zoot suit—baggy peg pants, big hat, three-foot watch chain looped at his side. Red Smith reported that Mayo Smith had been in on it, but Russ told his brother Lloyd that nobody else was involved. "He had on his regular uniform," Lloyd said, "but the rest was added. It was out of character for him, but he never said anybody else put him up to it. When Connie Mack saw it he sat bolt upright and leaned a little forward, but never said a word."

After removing the costume, Russ pitched a complete-game 4–3 win.

Al Simmons was still itching to add to his hits total. Mack tried to talk him out of it, then reluctantly put him on the active list: "I watched him in practice, heard him growl and snarl when he failed to meet squarely with the ball, watched his lips draw tight when the fans chided him at failures in practice games."

On June 13 in Boston Simmons pinch-hit and grounded into a double play. When he came back to the bench, one of the young players said, "What's the matter with you? You're white as a sheet."

"Don't worry about me," Al snapped.

Later he told Red Smith, "All my life I've always turned pale in the clutch. I don't know what it is. Nervous energy or something. I've never been scared."

Simmons added 3 more hits in 6 at bats, the last on July 1, when he played left field and was 2 for 4. He finished with 2,927.

Connie Mack used subtraction, not addition, to believe his team had a shot at the 1944 pennant. The departure of so many top players brought other teams down closer to the level of his "too lame, too old, or too young" Athletics.

When they opened at Washington on April 18, the A's had only three major leaguers on the field behind Luman Harris: Siebert, Hayes, and Jo-Jo White. Two from Lancaster (Kell and Wheaton), Irv Hall, Ed Busch, and Bill Burgo finished the lineup. But they fought back with a game-tying ninth-inning rally and a game-winning run in the twelfth, sending Connie Mack happily striding up the runway to the clubhouse, waving his hat to reporters and fans lining the way.

"I wouldn't want to say how far we'll go," he told a reporter, "but we beat a good ball club."

Asked if he thought the league would finish out the season, he said, "Not a doubt in my mind that we'll finish the season and be ready for the next one."

But the A's seemed headed for the cellar again in the early going. Mack traded Hal Wagner to the Red Sox for outfielder Ford Garrison, a twenty-nine-year-old career minor leaguer who was 1-a in the draft. The trade was small news but had a big immediate impact.

According to Ed Pollock, Connie Mack had learned from the Red Sox that there had been sickness in the outfielder's family, resulting in big doctor and hospital bills. Garrison had drawn an advance against his salary. When he reported to Shibe Park, Mack sent for him. Assured that everyone in Garrison's family was well again, Mack said to him, "Mr. Garrison, we think you can help us now that you have nothing to worry about," and handed Garrison an envelope containing a check for $1,500. Mack had also paid off Garrison's debt to the Red Sox.

Garrison responded by hustling like a reincarnation of Ty Cobb. He broke in with 14 hits in his first five games, including 2 home runs, and became the talk of the town. The A's won seven of his first eight games, pulled in over one hundred thousand fans—a full 20 percent of the year's total—and climbed into fourth place. Garrison inevitably cooled off, but he gave the A's everything he had in his only full season in the major leagues. The navy took him after the first week of the 1945 season.

George Kell got off to a slow start. A right-handed batter, he had always been an opposite-field hitter with no power. It was tough making the jump from Class B to the big leagues, even against wartime pitching. And not all the first-class pitchers were gone; the likes of Hal Newhouser, Dizzy Trout, Early Wynn, and Tex Hughson were still around. Despite being the batting king of the minors, Kell was willing to listen to advice. The trouble was that there were too many people willing to offer him tips: Try this. Try that.

Connie Mack noticed. He told Al Simmons, "Tell everybody to leave him alone, and tell him to ignore them all. If you have any advice for him, give it to him, then you leave him alone."

Simmons delivered the message, then told the rookie, "I'm just going to give you a couple words of advice and we'll let it go at that. You'll never be a good hitter til you learn to pull the ball."

Kell said, "How do I do that?"

Simmons said, "Move up on top of the plate and look for the fastball. You may get hit a few times, but you've got to be aggressive and start pulling the ball or you're going to get hit in the face."

Kell took his advice. He never became a home run hitter, but he went on to twice lead the league in doubles.

It was a year when nobody had a good team. In May Connie Mack said that every team would be in first place at some time during the season. On June 11, when the last-place Senators were only 4½ games out of first place, Clark Griffith said every team would be in *last* place at some time before the year ended.

"It's the only eight-team race I've ever seen," Griffith said. "Eight second-division teams."

The war was a true leveler. At the end only 25 games would separate the first- and last-place teams, the narrowest gap since the war year of 1918.

With the pennant up for grabs, Connie Mack set out to buy the best of the mediocre draft-proof gap stoppers available. On June 17 he gave the Browns $12,500 for thirty-year-old outfielder Hal Epps. Another $4,000 went to Buffalo for thirty-four-year-old catcher Bob Garbark. Dick Siebert was leading the league at .330 in August when he was accidently spiked by

Lou Boudreau and was out for several weeks. Mack bought Bill McGhee, thirty-five, from Little Rock to play first. Siebert moved to left field when he returned. His hitting fell off; he finished at .306.

Mack brought back Chief Bender to spell Dave Keefe in pitching batting practice and to tutor the youngsters on the art of bunting.

On the train rides Mack noticed the stakes in the poker games getting too high for his comfort and banned the games. When he found a game going on in a hotel room, he let the participants know he was not pleased. The players stuck to pinochle and gin rummy and bridge.

The Athletics family lost another longtime fixture at Shibe Park when PA announcer Babe O'Rourke had a stroke on July 14, 1944. The rotund announcer, who once led an hour-long sing-a-long for eight thousand fans when the lights failed during a game in 1943, had been on the job for thirty years.

The A's had lost eight in a row, scoring a total of 18 runs, and were in Detroit on July 23 for a Sunday doubleheader when the new and short-term Athletics saw an example of Connie Mack the hunch-player that his older hands were used to: he started the first game with a pinch hitter. Mack listed Jo-Jo White, who in nine years had never played anywhere but the outfield, as his shortstop leading off. White was surprised but realized he was just pinch-hitting. He led off the game with a single, scored a run, and headed for the showers. A few minutes later, one of the players came into the clubhouse and said, "You better hustle back out there. It looks like you're going to hit again."

The A's had batted around, and White came up again and made an out that scored the sixth run. Then he went in and took his shower.

In early August the A's were seventh, 10 games under .500 but only 5 games out of the first division. After a terrible '43, fourth place was a goal worth aiming for, if only to give the boys a small slice of the World Series melon. Mack set out to improve the team. Siebert was playing left field and not too well. The Tigers had released .192-hitting outfielder Charlie Metro. Mack gave him $2,500 to sign and $2,000 for the rest of the season. "I had been making $3,800 at Detroit," Metro said. "He didn't ask me what they were paying me and I didn't tell him. I hit only .100 for the A's but the next year he gave me a raise to $5,400. I have no complaints about money with him."

Metro was a typical wartime big leaguer. He had never shown much in the minors, couldn't hit, and couldn't run. But Mack liked him because, at twenty-six, his head was always in the game.

"On the bench during games," Metro said, "I would get a scorecard and write the lineups and keep track of the number of pitches our pitchers threw to each batter. I was at one end of the dugout and Mack was at the other end. One day he looked down and called me over. 'Son, what are you doing? Why don't you pay attention to the game?' I said, 'I am.' I showed him what I was doing. He said, 'By golly, that's a good idea. You keep doing that.'"

Mack apparently saw managerial material in Metro, who said, "During a game he might call me over when a pitcher was in trouble and say, 'What do you think?' I might say, 'He's done,' and he'd say, 'Why, thank you, son.' But he'd already made up his own mind."

Metro went on to a long career as a manager in the minors with two stints in the majors. Six years later he was managing at Montgomery when the A's played a spring game there.

"Connie Mack was sitting in the grandstand near the dugout. He called me over and said, 'Son, I see you're doing well. I've followed you as a manager. Are you still marking the pitches on your scorecard?' He was very gracious."

At eighty-one, Connie Mack was still playing the outfield, as Metro recalled.

"My first game with the A's I played left field. Detroit was in town. Eddie Mayo was up. I was shading him toward the line a little. Don Black was pitching. Connie Mack is waving me more toward the line. I moved four or five steps. He kept waving that scorecard at me. I kept moving, thinking to myself, 'What is this old man doing?' Now I'm maybe twenty feet from the line. Mayo hit a line drive right at me on the first pitch. I was impressed. I came in and he said, 'Nice catch,' with a little smile."

Most of these fill-ins knew they were enjoying a taste of the big league life they had once dreamed of but had become reconciled to the likelihood that they would never see. And they made the most of it, gathering in hotel lobbies in the evenings and listening to Connie Mack and Al Simmons talk about the A's great teams and players of the past. It didn't take much prompting for either one to reminisce about Bender, Waddell, Collins, or Grove, Dykes, Foxx, and the rest of the 1929–1931 champions.

George Kell had been a Cardinals fan growing up. One evening he told Mr. Mack he had been rooting against him in the 1930 and '31 World Series. Mack chuckled. "Ah, that fella [Pepper] Martin," he sighed.

One Sunday the game was rained out, and Irv Hall and Ed Busch rode the subway downtown. They went into Bookbinder's seafood restaurant and saw Al Simmons sitting with another man. They were just about to order when Simmons came over and said, "Order whatever you want. It's on me. I just won a five hundred dollar bet with that guy who didn't believe that Eddie Rommel won 27 games for the seventh-place A's in 1922."

Irv Hall said, "I ordered the biggest lobster they had. Weighed about five pounds. It was so big the claws were on one platter and the rest on another."

Judge Landis was still out to wipe out gambling at ballparks. He considered Shibe Park the worst in the country and wrote to Mack and Phillies' general manager Herb Pennock for the state of the situation there. He then asked the Philly police department to conduct a raid. They chose Labor Day, September 4, when the Giants were playing the Phillies to conduct the raid. Twenty gamblers were arrested. Landis might as well have raided the U.S. Supreme Court, where small-stakes World Series betting pools were a tradition among the eminent justices.

Maybe one reason Mack and Pennock weren't too stirred up over it was expressed by Red Smith in an interview with historian William Marshall: "If they had tried to clean out the gamblers from the Phillies and A's games, I think both of the clubs would have gone bankrupt . . . because [the gamblers] were the few who paid their way in every day."

The parade of premature wakes for Mr. Mack, which had begun back in 1938, continued. It seemed as though everybody wanted Connie Mack to enjoy the eulogies while he could still hear them. Despite his constant reiterations that he felt fine and had no intention of retiring, those who wanted to honor him feared that another siege of ill health such as he had undergone in 1937 and 1939 might trump his intentions. It had begun to take on the appearance of more farewell tours than actress Sarah Bernhardt had had, starting in 1941 with a "Day" for him in every city in the league. Ed Pollock of the *Bulletin* was behind the latest, billed as Connie Mack's fiftieth year of major league baseball management. It was the fiftieth anniversary of his start at Pittsburgh in 1894, but four of those years had been spent in Milwaukee, then in the Western Association. No matter; it was an occasion to celebrate longevity. On August 4 a night game was scheduled against the Yankees. The A's didn't need any outside promotions when New York was in town, but that's the date the committee chose. Unfortunately a transit strike had shut down all public transport in the city, but somehow 29,166 of the faithful found a way to be there for the big night. Even members of the press paid their way in to the tune of $2. A ninety-four-page program was filled with the kind of tributes usually reserved for cathedral memorials.

A big screen covered the scoreboard and a film of highlights of Mack's career was shown. There were gifts and speeches. Abbott and Costello did their "Who's on First" routine. Most of an all-time team selected by Mack was on hand: Bill Dickey, George Sisler, Eddie Collins, Honus Wagner, Tris Speaker, Babe Ruth, Walter Johnson, Lefty Grove, Frank Baker. Mickey Cochrane was in the navy. Ty Cobb was home with poison ivy.

The Yankees spoiled the party, Hank Borowy beating Bobo Newsom, 1–0.

Three days later Mack went to New York to manage one of the two teams in *Esquire* magazine's first East-West Boys' All-Star Game in the Polo Grounds.

And then he rested. Maybe it had all been too much for him. Maybe he felt the 95-degree heat more than usual. Or maybe it was Dr. Gopadze's orders that he take some time off. He took a rare midseason vacation, managing the second games of doubleheaders and turning the rest over to Earle. Asked why he worked the late games of twi-night doubleheaders, he said, "I don't go to bed early, anyhow." He denied that he was ill: "It's only when we lose that I don't feel well."

He may have been tired, but he didn't shy away from commitments he'd made. He had promised to bring his team to play against the naval base team at Bainbridge, Maryland. In an August 28 letter, a young officer stationed at Bainbridge wrote to a pal back home in Wellsboro, PA: "Connie came along with his club, the Athletics. He has been sick for the past week or two but he came along today because he didn't want to disappoint the boys, who are in their training for a crack at the Axis."

The A's won 6 of 8 against the west during Mack's vacation, prompting him to suggest that maybe he should stay away longer and resurrecting speculation that he was ready to step aside and let Earle take over, a notion that Mack quickly squelched, sounding like Queen Elizabeth II on Prince Charles: "He'll get his chance but not for a while."

On September 13 an exhibition football game was played in pouring rain at Shibe Park. The next day the field was so torn up that Mack had to call off the last home game against the Yankees. The Phillies were in town on the fifteenth, so the A's game had to be moved to New York to be played on September 17. To the grateful Yankees it meant another home game; they had played much better at home than on the road. But to Ed Barrow it was an outrage. It didn't mean an extra home date; it turned a single game into a doubleheader. No football games should be allowed until the season was over, Barrow declared, and intended to take it up at the next league meeting.

At the time the Yankees had a half-game lead over the Tigers, who led the Browns by a half game. The Red Sox were only 3 games behind. The Yankees were accepting orders for World Series tickets.

At Yankee Stadium on Saturday afternoon, September 16, Mack asked Lena Blackburne to call a pregame meeting. Sitting on a stool in the middle of the room, he said, "Gentlemen, I hate to think that the Yankees will win a pennant because of the Philadelphia Athletics. You know, we haven't beaten that club very much. [They were 6-13 against them so far.] Now all I'd like for you to do is for everybody to try to play a little bit better than the way you've been playing."

The A's swept the three games in New York, much to Connie Mack's great glee. So far that year, George Stirnweiss, the league's stolen base leader, had nabbed 9 out of 10 with Frank Hayes catching. He was 0 for 2 in the series. On Saturday Bobo Newsom won, 6–3. In the first game on Sunday, before a crowd of fifty-six thousand, ex-Yankee Larry Rosenthal hit his only home run of the year, a ninth-inning, pinch-hit, 2-run shot off Ernie Bonham, to win it, 5–4. Don Black won the second game, 2–1. When the A's headed west, the Yankees were third, 2 games back of Detroit, 1½ behind St. Louis, where the A's then lost 3 in a row to help the Browns win their first and only AL pennant.

Russ Christopher's year had begun with a sore arm. He was hit hard and had won one game in the first two months. Earle Brucker persuaded him to relieve his arm stress by going to a deep sidearm delivery. If he threw it off his shoe tops, it was impossible to hit. If he let it go a little higher and it came in waist high, batters would waste it. To conserve his energy Christopher also began a no-windup delivery. He reversed his midseason record of 4-10, going 10-4 the rest of the way.

One of those 10 wins was bittersweet. Many of the A's players were rooting for Detroit, their next opponent. When Christopher beat the Tigers, 2–1, on 4 hits, Red Smith reported that the pitcher said he was sorry he had won that day. "But I couldn't let up, could I?" he asked.

Earle Brucker lit into him. "Don't ever let me hear you say a thing like that again. There's only one way to play this game, Christy, and you know it."

The A's finished the season with five games in Cleveland, trailing the fifth-place Indians by 4 games. They held Cleveland to 6 runs while winning 4 with 1 tie to finish tied for fifth, their highest finish in ten years. In the closing doubleheader Joe Berry won both in relief, pitching the last 2 innings of the first game while the A's came up with 4 in the ninth to win, 5–2, and the last 4 innings of the second game, a 0–0 tie until the A's scored 5 in the tenth to win, 5–0.

Much to Mack's gratification, they did it with markedly improved pitching, giving up the fewest walks in the league and the third fewest runs.

Connie Mack believed he had reason to be optimistic. Sure, wartime baseball may have been like the land of the blind, but why couldn't the Athletics be the ruling one-eyed team?

Mack went to the all–St. Louis World Series, in which only 28 runs were scored in the six games. Cardinals shortstop Marty Marion might have been considered the Series MVP (he batted only .227 but hit some key doubles and was outstanding in the field), but Mack dissented from some of the accolades. In a letter to Lou Brissie, he wrote, "The games were well played and the best team won although they had to work hard in every game played. Marion was the real star of both teams. The newspapers are now classifying him with Honus Wagner, as a matter of fact, some feel that he is even better, however, I doubt this due to Wagner being a great batsman as well as base runner."

Despite a rebound of over 25 percent in attendance, the Athletics had become dependent on rental income: $48,259 from the Phillies, almost $43,000 from the Eagles (when the New York Giants won the NFL East, the Eagles' loss cost the A's an additional $22,000 from the championship game). Another $19,000 came from promoter Eddie Gottlieb's black baseball games and two prize fights. That's what gave Mack the capital he had spent for his mostly stopgap players—of them all, only George Kell would have a lasting impact—and still show a net profit of $17,899.

For many people, their lasting image of Connie Mack had nothing to do with winning or losing but with small acts of kindness.

One-time pitcher Tommy Thomas was the manager of the Baltimore Orioles. He had played for the late Orioles owner Jack Dunn in the 1920s. In 1944 he was in a pennant race and needed some players. As minor league managers had done for forty years, he turned to Connie Mack.

"Mack sold me what I needed, cheap. He sent me Felix Mankiewicz, pitcher Sam Lowry, and third baseman Frank Skaff, all for $6,000. They helped me win the pennant and little world series."

One day in the spring Frank Baker saw a student named Bill Hill playing for Washington College. He gave Hill a letter of introduction to Connie Mack. Hill went to Shibe Park and handed the letter to Mack, who watched him work out. The Lancaster business manager, Al Cartwright, was sitting with Mack. After watching Hill, Mack called him over and told Cartwright to sign him for Lancaster.

Cartwright said to Hill, "I'll give you $100 a month."

Mack said, "Give the boy $125."

While this may sound like testimony to Mack's alleged cheapness, it was more than the going rate for a rookie in the lower minors at a time when a player could get a room in a private home for $3 a week and show a profit on the $2 meal money on the road.

Taylor Grant was now with the ABC radio network in New York. When the A's were in town, he would go to their hotel to see players and coaches he had been close to. On one occasion, after visiting with Earle Brucker, he got off the elevator in the lobby and met Mr. Mack getting on. They shook hands.

"Are you going to the game?" Mack said.

"Sure."

"Do you have your ticket?"

"Yes, Earle Brucker said he'd leave something at the gate for me."

"Fine. Good for Earle."

When Grant arrived at Yankee Stadium and asked for the tickets he was told, "Oh, yes, Mr. Mack left these for you."

"The Yankees were tough about that," Grant said. "Maybe Mr. Mack knew that Earle might have trouble with them. He wanted to be sure. That kindness was always there."

One day in November Connie Mack had a visitor named Joe Budwitz. They had been scheduled to get together on Connie Mack Day on August 4, but Mack's schedule had become too crowded, and he had left a ticket for Budwitz that night for a seat behind the A's dugout and invited him to return another day.

For three hours Mack entertained his visitor and a newspaper photographer who accompanied him. After lunch in his office, they toured the press box, the club house, and the dugout.

Who was Joe Budwitz? He was a high school janitor and sports enthusiast from Meriden, Connecticut, the town where Connie Mack had begun his baseball career in 1884. Mack enjoyed reminiscing about old acquaintances, including former pitcher Ed Walsh, now a Meriden resident.

"He made me feel right at home," Budwitz said. "It was as though I'd known him for years. He was a friendly man. The thing that impressed me the most, I guess, was the fact that I didn't feel nervous. They say Mack had a way of making people feel at ease. That's how he gains their respect and confidence so quickly. When he talked to you, he had his eyes glued to you. He never shied away. He wanted you to know you were his center of attention. I told him I walked a lot, didn't smoke or drink. He said, 'Same as me. I hope you live a long time. Stay out of the rocking chair as much as possible.'"

In a *Sporting News* poll of 129 press box tenants rating managers, Connie Mack was far ahead of the rest in two categories: best liked by players and by writers.

In truth not everybody in baseball liked Connie Mack. They respected him and called him "Mister," but they didn't all like him. Umpire Ernie Stewart (1941–1945) said:

The only club I didn't care for was the Athletics. The team was good, but the management wasn't. Mr. Mack was a nice gentleman, but he was not the saint that everyone has painted him to be. The umpires didn't like Mr. Mack or his son Earle, the messenger boy. Mr. Mack was instrumental in getting [Will] Harridge his job, so he had a lot of influence on the [league] president. Mack would call the front office any time he felt he didn't get the best of something. . . .

Most clubs provide beer, soft drinks, and sandwiches for the umpires and between games of doubleheaders the concessionaires would bring in lunch. They catered to us pretty good because they knew an extra three or four minutes between games could bring them in a lot of additional sales. We always ate slow, gave them thirty minutes instead of twenty-five. But in Philadelphia we wouldn't give them an extra minute. Mr. Mack never sent a hot dog into an umpire's dressing room in his life. So, baby, we'd ring the bell right on twenty-five minutes in Philadelphia.

Nevertheless, on Connie Mack Day in 1941, the American League umpires had given him a Hamilton wristwatch. (It's unknown if Stewart chipped in.) The watch, proudly worn by Mack's grandson Connie III, was still running seventy years later.

Kenesaw Mountain Landis died on November 25, 1944, at seventy-eight, ending twenty-four years on the job. He had been hospitalized since October 2 but was expected to go home soon and to be offered a seven-year extension as commissioner. Two weeks after his death he was elected to the Hall of Fame by a veterans committee he had appointed on August 4: the founder of the Hall, Stephen S. Clark, Connie Mack, Ed Barrow, Bob Quinn, and writers Sid Mercer and Mel Webb. (In April the committee met again and added ten more players.)

Landis and Connie Mack admired each other, despite an occasional censure by Landis, who had nullified some of Mack's player transactions that ran outside the base paths of the rules. And the judge had been on Mack's back for not doing enough to stop the gamblers in Shibe Park. But Mack had remained as firm a backer of the judge as he had been of Ban Johnson, sharing Landis's disdain for the farm system.

Neither man was inclined to idle chitchat during a game. Both watched everything on the field intently, Landis in his usual position, chin resting on the rail.

Chicago writer John P. Carmichael in the March 1956 *Baseball Digest* described Mack's once sharing a box with Landis at a World Series game, probably in the 1930s, when the Cubs made three postseason appearances. Carmichael reported that Landis said, "Why aren't you in this thing?" To which Mack replied, "We had some unfortunate afternoons, mostly in the ninth inning. I'm coming to believe that the fans would appreciate a shorter game, say eight innings."

The major leagues put off appointing a successor to Landis, naming the two league presidents and Landis's longtime secretary, Leslie O'Connor, to run things while a committee came up with a list of candidates. The next meeting was called for April 24 in Cleveland. Believing that no action would be taken at that time, Connie Mack sent Roy to represent the club. When a few owners pushed to settle the matter, the list of seven finalists was quickly whittled down. At Larry MacPhail's urging, Senator A. B. "Happy" Chandler of Kentucky became the unanimous choice.

Essentially a back-slapping politician, Chandler hadn't a clue as to what the job entailed or what his responsibilities and authority were—or weren't. Within six months there were quiet calls for buying out his contract and sending him on his way. In October Mack commented on it in a letter to New Haven newspaperman Hubert Sedgwick: "Everything has been straightened out pertaining to the Commissioner. Due to the number of errors he made there was quite a little ill feeling at one time against him, however, all this has been corrected and am sure that he will do a very good job from now on. It is also his intention to place an experienced baseball man in his office which will be of great help to him."

It was the owners' decision to hire veteran baseball man Muddy Ruel to teach Chandler the ropes.

Mack became a firm supporter of Chandler, considered by many players as a players' commissioner. His road remained rocky throughout his tenure.

Mr. and Mrs. Connie Mack arrived at the Town House Hotel in Los Angeles on December 7, 1944, to stay until February. Mack was deluged with speaking engagements. At one dinner he sat beside football coach Amos Alonzo Stagg and Mrs. Stagg. Mack and Stagg had not seen each other since 1888, when Stagg had pitched for Yale in a spring game against Washington, where Mack was the catcher.

"Was really a great treat in meeting Lonny Stagg," Mack wrote to Sedgwick on January 25. "Mrs. Stagg is a lovely women [sic] and was delighted in having a long talk with her during the evening as we sat side of each other."

The Macks were entertained by George Murphy, a leading song-and-dance man in movie musicals, whose father, Mike, a noted football and track coach and trainer at Yale and Penn in the early 1900s, had been a great friend of Mack's.

At the December minor league meetings in Buffalo the A's were represented by Roy and Earle, PR director Jim Peterson, Roy's assistant and ticket manager Peter J. "Jimmy" Flood, Chief Bender, Lena Blackburne, and Ira

Thomas. It's unclear why so many of them were there. The brothers, vowing to match other clubs' outlays, were looking to expand their farm system by buying the Scranton franchise, but they were outbid. They left with working agreements with Toronto (AA), Lancaster (B), and Lexington (D) and control of the Martinsville (D) club.

Baseball received some good news in March. The head of the War Manpower Commission announced that ballplayers working in defense plants during the off-season would be allowed to leave their jobs and play ball without repercussions.

In 1942 Bill Veeck owned the Milwaukee club in the American Association. He had a swift young outfielder named Hal Peck. He was about to sell the twenty-five-year-old Peck to the White Sox when the outfielder tripped carrying a shotgun and dispatched two toes on his left foot. Peck missed most of the 1943 season but came back and was hitting .375 by midseason 1944. (He wound up at .345 and led the league with 282 total bases.) By now Veeck was a Marine in the South Pacific. He had given his vice-president, Mickey Heath, full authority to make player deals in his absence. In July the Yankees wanted Peck for immediate delivery. Heath said they couldn't have him until after the season. The deal fell through.

Connie Mack then bought Peck for $20,000 and four players, despite Heath's insistence that he couldn't have Peck until the '44 season ended. Peck would hit a respectable .276 for the A's but had no power.

Between September 1944 and the end of the '45 season the A's would spend another $80,000 on players who never became household names except in their own households.

By now Roy and Earle were handling most of the salary negotiations.

Dick Siebert had earned $10,000 in '44. He was holding out for $13,000. The Macks offered $12,000. Holdouts were often fought over differences of $500 or $1,000. It was a time when an annual income of $1,700 supported a family of four very comfortably. New York hotel rooms went for $3; you could buy a big breakfast for under 35 cents. A year at Harvard cost $1,000 tuition. Red Smith was earning $90 for writing six columns a week and covering baseball and other assignments for the *Record*.

Radio announcer Taylor Grant's closest friend on the A's was Dick Siebert. While he was in Philadelphia, Grant had lined up a house for Siebert and his wife, Marie, to rent each season. The Mack brothers knew of that friendship.

One Sunday morning in the spring of 1945 Grant received a call from Roy and Earle. They described the Siebert salary standoff to Grant, then said, "You want to see [Siebert] play, don't you?"

"Sure."

"Well, see what you can do to get him to sign."

Grant thought, "This is not terribly businesslike. And they are really vesting in me more power than I have."

But he made the call to Siebert. "We laughed a little over the Macks' assumption that I would be on their side in this dispute," Grant said. "He told me, 'The last offer they made me was $12,000. It's a fair enough compromise. You can call them and tell them the contract is in the mail.'"

Siebert also gained a rare concession for the times: a single room on the road.

Russ Christopher rejected a $6,000 offer, which Connie Mack raised to $8,000.

The Athletics returned to Frederick for spring training. Mack had a fit when George Kell showed up about twenty pounds overweight. "Young man," he would have yelled if Mr. Mack ever yelled, "are you trying to eat your way out of baseball?"

Mack put him on a diet in the dining room and on the field: no batting practice. "You will run in the outfield and that's all until you lose that weight." Ten days passed before Kell could pick up a bat.

It didn't take Mack long to realize his team would need "a lot more batting power to hope to win a pennant." He predicted, "Detroit will win this year. The return from the navy of Al Benton, along with Trucks and Newhouser, gives them the pitching edge."

After a 6-2 start, the Athletics sank slowly and steadily into the cellar and remained there, losing 98 games. They were 13-63 away from Shibe Park. In the middle of June they went on the road and lost 20 out of 22. Newsom and Flores were pitching well, but when a team scores 21 runs in 15 games, it doesn't win a lot. Nobody hit .300; they were last in runs scored.

The previous fall Mack had drafted a thirty-year-old career minor leaguer from Buffalo, Mayo Smith, who had led the International League at .341. But in February Smith came down with rheumatic fever and was bedridden for three months. Desperate for an outfielder who could hit, Mack asked him to report in June. Smith was still going for regular heart checkups and hardly had the strength to round the bases, but he did what he could, hitting .212 in 73 games.

In May Mack brought up tall, thin right-hander Steve Gerkin, twenty-nine, from Lancaster. Gerkin didn't pitch that badly; the A's were shut out in 3 of his starts, and he lost 3 in relief. By mid-August he was 0-12. It was enough to drive a man to drink. He started a night game in St. Louis on August 10 and lasted 2 innings. George Kell recalled: "He went back to the Chase Hotel and went up to the rooftop night club and got pickled, ordered a big dinner and champagne, cost 75 or 100 dollars, and the next morning we had a meeting and Mr. Mack let him know in a nice way it was coming out of his paycheck."

A week later Gerkin was back in Lancaster, 0 for his big league career.

Back in the cellar again, Connie Mack concentrated on teaching. As always he let his men know how he wanted the game played and turned them loose. Possibly no other manager ever held a lighter rein on things like stealing bases and hit-and-run plays. He let them use their own initiative, but they better use their heads or they'd hear about it.

Irv Hall said, "Connie Mack loved a running game. I hit ahead of Ed Busch. Busch had a hit and run sign with me: plucking at his shirt. One time he did something with his hand near his shirt and I couldn't tell if it was on his shirt or a little away from it. So I ran and he took the pitch and I'm out at second base. I came into the dugout and said, 'I'm not taking any more hit and run signs.' The Old Man jumped on me real quick. He was mad. He said, 'You take hit and run signs when they're given to you.' I sat down, didn't say a word."

And, as always, Mack was in touch with what they did off the field too. He looked at their canceled paychecks to see where his boys were cashing them, and in too many cases, he didn't like what he saw.

"Cash your checks in banks, not bars," he told them. "A lot of these bar owners are gangsters. That guy on the corner of Broad and Lehigh where some of you cash your checks is a known gambler."

Connie Mack's occasional garbled pronunciation of players' names brought only silent smiles from his boys. Washington outfielder George Case was a perennial stolen base leader. To Mack he was always Chase, as in: "Kell, this Chase fellow is a fast runner and good bunter. I want you to play in so close he can't bunt."

Sometimes Mr. Mack would say something that made them laugh out loud—with him, not at him. By the end of June the A's were deep in the cellar, while everybody else was within range of the first-place Tigers. In Detroit for a weekend series, Mack led off the Saturday morning meeting at the hotel: "Now, fellows, I want you to hustle and bear down and give it all you got. Everybody in the league has a chance to win it [pause] except us. Let's make 'em pay for it." Everybody laughed with him.

Their "all" wasn't enough. The Tigers swept the series.

Mack gave the team occasional pep talks. "He was afraid we would embarrass ourselves," said Charlie Metro. On the road they always met in a conference room or mezzanine area, never in the clubhouse. "He didn't trust the clubhouses, with good reason. You could hear through the walls. He never trusted Cleveland. The story was they listened through a heating vent. He was justified; I learned that when I managed [Kansas City in 1970]."

After losing 14 in a row, the A's finally won one, the first game of a July 4 doubleheader at St. Louis. But they lost the second game when the one-armed Pete Gray drove in the winning runs in the ninth. Connie Mack was as upset over that loss as if it had cost him the pennant—beaten by the one-armed guy the Athletics had brushed off. How humiliating.

The next morning in the mezzanine of the Chase Hotel they were all sitting around a big table, with Al Simmons and Earle Brucker flanking Mack.

"He was still fuming," recalled Metro fifty years later. "There were ash trays on the table. 'I'm disappointed,' says Mack, 'and not only that, but I'm damn mad, damn mad,' and he slapped his hand down on the table and I can still see those ash trays jumping up in the air. Al Simmons says, 'Calm down, Mr. Mack,' and Mr. Mack says, 'You shut up Al.'"

They lost that afternoon too, but Pete Gray didn't beat them.

In July a young catcher named Joe Astroth was discharged from the Coast Guard. Astroth had played on service teams and drawn attention from several scouts, including Harry O'Donnell of the A's. The St. Louis Browns offered him a $10,000 bonus but wanted to start him in the minor leagues. The twenty-two-year-old Illinois resident said no; he wanted a big league contract. In July he worked out with the Dodgers at Wrigley Field. They wouldn't go as high as the Browns and wanted to send him to Montreal. He received a call from Connie Mack inviting him to Philadelphia for a tryout. When he arrived, the team was in New York. Bob Schroeder put him on a train to New York, where he worked out with the A's, then checked into the team hotel, the New Yorker.

The next morning at nine o'clock the phone rang. It was Mr. Mack: "Young man, I'd like to come down and talk to you."

The meeting took about three minutes and went like this:

CM: How would you like to be with my ball club?

JA: I'd like that. I don't want to start out in the minors.

CM: Okay, you won't have to. That's all settled.

JA: Mr. Mack, how about the money?

CM: Oh, the same as the other fellow [outfielder Ernie Kish, a Coast Guard teammate of Astroth's, who appeared in 43 games in 1945 and was gone], $500 to sign and $500 a month.

JA: Oh, no, Mr. Mack.

CM: What do you want?

JA: I want $10,000 to sign and $500 a month.

CM: Good luck, young man. We don't pay that kind of money. If we owe you anything for your travel, tell the secretary and he'll pay you.

And out he went.

Astroth had a long train ride to his home near St. Louis to think things over. He wanted the money, but he also wanted to start out in the big leagues. When the A's were in St. Louis on August 8, he called Mr. Mack and accepted his offer.

The A's beat the Browns that day, then lost 19 of the next 22.

"When a team is going bad like that," Astroth said, "you see a lot of little huddles of players during batting practice talking about why they should not be the ones to blame or be released."

Connie Mack knew what the players were buzzing about. On their return to Shibe Park, one of the coaches announced a pregame meeting in the clubhouse. Astroth said:

In walked Connie Mack in his suit and straw hat. We're sitting in front of our lockers. His false teeth slipped a little and clattered when he talked, and he gestured with his right hand. This is what he said:

"Young men, we have lost 19 out of 22 games. I just have one thing to say. If you can say in your heart that you have given a hundred percent on that field, I can't and nobody in Philadelphia can fault you."

And he turned and walked out. It's quiet. We look at each other, each one thinking it was aimed at somebody else. What I got out of it was, it doesn't make any difference how you do, if you give a hundred percent nobody can fault you.

The A's benefited at the gate when 47,729 Detroit fans turned out at Briggs Stadium on July 1 to welcome back the first of the stars to return from the service, Hank Greenberg. The Tigers took 2; Greenberg homered in the first game off Charlie Gassaway, and the Tigers maintained their slim lead in the five-team pennant chase.

Wet weather had resulted in the A's playing 42 doubleheaders, including 11 in 17 days from August 26 through September 12. They had some good runs, winning 8 of 11 with two ties in a July home stand against the west before losing 10 in a row.

After beating New York lefty Joe Page, 4–2, before 34,716 at Shibe Park on June 17, Russ Christopher had 11 of the team's 20 victories. Then his sinker and slow curve went out of control, and he lost 7 in a row before they came back. He finished 13-13, working a career-high 227 innings, more than many a stronger man. (Looking back, he told his brother Lloyd, a cup-of-coffee wartime outfielder, "You know, I was never really a major leaguer, but neither were three-fourths of those other guys.")

Mack rewarded him with a year-end bonus of $2,000 and a '46 contract for $10,000.

Bobo Newsom beat Boston on April 21, then lost 12 in a row, taking some fearful beatings along the way. He had finished only one of his starts by June 24, when Mack left him in to take a 13–5 licking from the Yankees in which he gave up 15 hits good for 30 total bases. He lost two in two days, trailing 2-1 after 7 innings on June 30, and taking the loss in relief the next day when he retired only 1 of the 5 he faced in a 6-run seventh inning in Detroit.

Jimmie Dykes and Mule Haas of the White Sox were the most effective—and therefore most hated—bench jockeys in the league. They had given Ted Williams fits when he once suggested he'd as soon be a fireman as a ballplayer. In 1940 they had driven the Cleveland club up the wall and contributed to the Indians' loss of the pennant with a merciless riding of them as "Crybabies" for their complaining about manager Oscar Vitt.

Now they turned their attention to Bobo Newsom.

Jack Ryan of the *Chicago Daily News* reported (or made up) that Haas wrote a letter to Newsom:

We've all known for quite some time that your pitching equipment would be incomplete until you acquired a balloon. A newspaper item about the sale of surplus government barrage balloons suggests how this need can now be filled.

The newspaper account says that the Reconstruction Finance Corp. has offered 234 surplus barrage balloons for sale. They're priced from $50 to $721 for a deluxe job.

With your waistline you might be on the reckless side going up in one of those 50 buck numbers.

Why not spend a few extra bucks and make your ascension in safety?

Incidentally, Bobo, the RFC guarantees these balloons will rise to 6,500 feet. Just for the record, how high do you go when you blow up?

Newsom finished 8-20.

Twi-night doubleheaders became popular with club owners and fans. On Monday, July 16, the Browns played two at Washington before 26,120. A Monday afternoon doubleheader might have drawn a quarter of that. Meanwhile the A's were sweeping a twi-nighter from Chicago before 14,223. On Friday, July 20, a twi-nighter in Washington drew 20,528, who saw the Senators win 2 from the Tigers to move within 3 games of the league leaders. It was 2 a.m. before the Tigers got to bed. They were up at seven, took a train to Philadelphia, and went directly to Shibe Park for the three o'clock game.

On that same Friday night at Shibe Park 15,731 saw the A's take two from Cleveland. Irv Hall was due to report for his draft physical at six Saturday morning. After the games he went out drinking. He flunked the physical and got to Shibe Park thirty minutes before the Saturday game, which went 24 innings until darkness ended the 1–1 tie after four hours and forty-eight minutes. (League rules prohibited turning on lights to finish a day game.) Only four pitchers worked: Les Mueller pitched 19⅔ innings for Detroit; Dizzy Trout finished. For the A's Russ Christopher, weak heart and all, went 13 innings. Forty-year-old Joe Berry, who had worked 4 innings on Wednesday and 3 on Friday, pitched the last 11.

Neither team scored after the seventh. The A's had 3 singles in the tenth, but outfielder Jimmy Outlaw cut down the winning run at the plate. In the top of the twenty-fourth, the Tigers loaded the bases with 1 out. A snappy Busch-Hall-Siebert double play ended the threat. With 2 out in the bottom of the twenty-fourth, Mack sent Joe Burns up to pinch-hit. Then he called him back and sent up Charlie Metro.

Metro hit a long ball down the line and thought he had won the game, but it curved foul. Then he singled. Irv Hall grounded out to second, and umpire Bill Summers said it was too dark; he could no longer see Dizzy Trout's fastball.

The game tied the league record set by the Athletics and Red Sox in 1906. It was 9:20 before the Tigers finally reached their hotel. A's catcher Warren "Buddy" Rosar could hardly walk. Left fielder Bill McGhee complained that his feet were sore, to which Earle Brucker replied, "What are you kicking about? Yesterday you were complaining about sitting on the bench."

The two men who had the most to complain about were George Kell, who went 0 for 10, and press box attendant Otto "Smitty" Susneck. Part of his job was to take the elevator down to the ground level in the eighth inning and hold it there until he took Connie Mack up to his tower office after the game. He held his post from 4:30 until almost 8.

In three previous shots in the big leagues, thirty-two-year-old catcher Charles "Greek" George had never hit above his 200-pound bulk. On May 27 Mack paid Toronto $6,000 for him and traded Frank Hayes to Cleveland for catcher Buddy Rosar. In a visit to Walter Reed Hospital to talk baseball with wounded servicemen, Mack was asked why he had made the trade. "Hayes could catch every day," he said, "but he didn't talk it up much and the A's needed a catcher with lots of chatter."

Greek George was good at talking it up all right, but most of his chatter was belligerent, not inspirational. He had what is called in the trade "a reputation," gained in his many years in the minors. More than once he had gotten on his teammates about their professional prowess in a way that led to invitations to fisticuffs. According to Bill Veeck, who had had him at Milwaukee, George loved amusement parks, was unpredictable, and once started a near-riot on a Ferris wheel.

Sam Levy of the *Milwaukee Journal* described a 1943 game at Toledo when George was catching for the Brewers. The game was tied in the last of the ninth. The Mud Hens loaded the bases. When a pinch hitter, Footsy Marcum, walked to force in the winning run, George was so mad that he fired the ball at Marcum and hit him in the back. Out rushed the Mud Hens, armed with bats. Milwaukee manager Charlie Grimm quickly got his men off the field, then chewed out the Greek for almost getting his whole team killed.

In a game in June George and Buck Newsom stood on the mound and argued about what pitches to throw, illustrating with clenched-fist gestures, to the delight of the crowd.

On Labor Day, September 3, the Yankees drew the biggest crowd of the year—36,021—to Shibe Park. The visitors won both games. The second game went into the tenth inning tied, 6–6. Greek George and plate umpire Joe Rue had been bickering about Rue's ball and strike calls the whole game. When the New York pitcher, Ken Holcombe, was called out on strikes to end the top of the inning, the catcher started to walk toward the dugout. Suddenly he stopped, turned, and said a few words to the umpire. In a flash he leaped toward the ump, swung, and hit him, opening a cut over his right eye. Rue raised his mask ready to strike back when the other umpires, Cal Hubbard and Charlie Berry, both former football players, wrapped their arms around the combatants. Hubbard threw George out of the game, yelling, "You'll never play another game in the big leagues."

In the dugout George told Mack what had passed between him and Joe Rue and what Hubbard had said. Mack was fuming. After the A's failed to score, he said to George Kell, "Tell Cal Hubbard I want to see him."

Kell went out to third base. He could see how angry the umpire was. "Mr. Mack wants to see you," he said.

"No, I'm not going over there."

"He told me to tell you he wants to see you."

"You tell that old [so-and-so] if he wants to see me, come out here."

Connie Mack was standing waving at the umpire. Kell went back to the dugout and said, "Mr. Mack, he said to tell you he's not coming over here."

Mr. Mack's stubbornness took hold. "You go back and tell him I want to see him."

Kell, helpless in the middle, pleaded, "Mr. Mack, he's not coming."

"What did he say?"

Kell swallowed hard. "I'll tell you what he said. He said, 'You tell that old [so-and-so] if he wants to see me to come out here.'"

Years later Kell could still see Mack bristling with fury. "Nobody had ever called him what Hubbard did. But Hubbard was mad, too, because one of his partners had been hit by a player. Hubbard didn't budge."

After the game Stan Baumgartner asked George what had happened.

"Rue called me a name that no man will stand for. I turned and asked him if I heard correctly. He said yes. No man where I come from will take that so I hit him with the flat of my hand."

League president Will Harridge suspended George pending a hearing. Connie Mack defended his catcher.

So did Red Smith of the *Record*—sort of. Conceding that George was a pop-off and Joe Rue was friendly, patient, and not bellicose, he went on to say that umpires sometimes did say things that were uncalled for and perhaps should not be treated with the fragility of a Ming dynasty vase. He would await the outcome of the hearing before judging the catcher's actions.

Harridge and umpire-in-chief Tom Connolly interviewed George and Rue. The catcher was suspended indefinitely. His big league days were over, but he played another seven years in the minors.

In August Mack told Charlie Metro, "I am sending you to Oakland for a shortstop, John Caulfield."

Metro said, "Jesus Christ, Mr. Mack, you couldn't send me any farther."

"Now, now," said Mack, "don't swear, son. You go out there and when you get there, wire me and I'll send you $2,500."

"And he did," Metro said. "And paid me for the whole year. I have no quarrel with Connie Mack about money. He was not the tightwad he has been made out to be."

Don Black was a good pitcher when he felt like it. Unfortunately, too often hung over is what he felt like. It didn't escape Mr. Mack. In the second inning in Chicago on May 31, Black ran to back up a play at third and collided with umpire Charlie Berry, a large target. Black had to leave the game, and Joe Berry came in cold to finish it. Black's record was 1-3 when the A's boarded the overnight train to Boston on June 4. It was raining when they arrived the next morning and headed to the Somerset Hotel for breakfast. They were all in the dining room when Black staggered in. He joined Dick Siebert, Charlie Metro, and Al Simmons at a table and ordered a bowl of split pea soup.

Metro said, "We're eating our eggs and he's fumbling with the spoon to eat his soup and Simmons moves over a little to block Mr. Mack's view of what's going on, and the guy leans over to spoon up some soup and falls face down right into the bowl. We're all moving in close to try to cover it up and Connie Mack says, 'You don't have to do that. I've seen it.'"

After three years of trying to drive his pitcher from drink, Mack finally gave up. He suspended Black without pay—something he rarely did—for thirty days. Black went home to Petersburg, Virginia, and pumped gas until July 6, when he returned with Mack's warning, "This is your last chance." He next won on July 22, a 6-inning game shortened by rain, but his days with the A's were over. Five days after the season ended, Mack sold him to Cleveland for $7,500. On July 10, 1947, Black no-hit the Athletics at Municipal Stadium. On September 13, 1948 Black suffered a cerebral hemorrhage while at bat. He recovered but never pitched again.

Pitcher Phil Marchildon was the first of Mack's servicemen to return from the war. A Lancaster tail gunner in the Royal Canadian Air Force, Marchildon had been shot down on August 17, 1944, during a mine-laying run near the Kiel Canal. He bailed out and was captured in Denmark and interned at a POW camp in Germany. As the Allied armies advanced in April '45, the Germans emptied the prison camps and force-marched the prisoners away from their liberators until the Allies caught up with them and rescued the survivors of the march.

Two weeks after he arrived home, Marchildon began receiving telegrams from Connie Mack urging him to rejoin the team. Suffering from shredded nerves and shrieking nightmares, Marchildon ignored them. Mack called him and said, "Maybe you can't pitch, but getting back with your teammates and into training will be good for you."

Marchildon thought, "Maybe he's right."

He joined the team at the Del Prado in Chicago on July 6 and was warmly greeted. He hadn't pitched for almost three years. His legs were weak. His hands shook so much he could hardly light a cigarette. His stomach knotted when he heard a loud noise—or for no reason at all. He was wound up like an eight-day clock.

About three weeks later Mack said, "We're going to have a day for you. I'd like you to start that day."

Marchildon was angry. He believed that Mack was using him to draw a good day at the box office. "I'm not ready," he said. Al Simmons told Mack he wasn't ready. Mack didn't listen. On August 17 in Cleveland he decided to see what Marchildon could do and sent him in to start the fifth inning of a 1–1 game. Phil gave up 4 runs on 2 hits and 4 walks in 2 innings and took the loss.

Almost twenty thousand Shibe Park fans welcomed Marchildon home on August 29. He started the second game of the twi-night doubleheader and had his fastball, screwball, and curve all working. He had pitched 5 innings of 2-hit ball; reaching for a ground ball that got by him, he pulled a muscle from his groin to his right knee and had to leave the game. Still hobbling, he started four days later but didn't have the strength to make it past 2 innings.

Dick Fowler came back from the army with an entirely different story from Marchildon's. Stationed in Canada throughout the war, he had been given permission to pitch every Sunday for Hamilton in the Niagara League. It wasn't the big leagues, but it was baseball. The 6-foot-4 right-hander, who was "Mr. Flowers" to Connie Mack, rejoined the A's in August. After a few relief outings, including a 7-inning workout against the White Sox on September 5 in which he gave up 8 runs and 13 hits, he made his first start four days later against the Browns. His change of pace and assortment of curves produced a 1–0 no-hitter, ended in a no-hitter-record seventy-five minutes on a ninth-inning triple by Hal Peck and single by Irv Hall.

Toward the end of the season Sam Chapman and Al Brancato returned. They weren't ready to play regularly, but they were back.

One of the returning servicemen Mack signed was pitcher Bill Connelly. Connelly had no pro baseball experience but plenty of another kind. He had been wounded on Iwo Jima by a Japanese sniper, who shot him through the mouth, knocking out three teeth. He was not yet twenty. Discharged from the Marines in August, he signed with the A's for a $5,000 bonus.

Mack handed him the ball to start in Detroit two days later. The six-foot right-hander lasted 1 inning: 3 runs, 3 walks, 2 hits and a 4–1 loss.

Maybe I rushed the lad, thought Mack. He waited until September 7 to use him again, this time in relief at home against the White Sox. Connelly gave up 1 run on 5 hits and 5 walks over 7 innings for his first victory. The next year he was in Savannah and never pitched again for the A's. After brief trials with Chicago and Detroit, he resurfaced again when the Giants bought him from Toledo in August 1952 and was 5-0 for them.

George Kell had a satisfactory second year; he hit .272, his doubles doubled, and he led all third basemen in putouts and assists. One day in September Earle Mack said to him, "George, you have improved so much this year and played so hard, Dad appreciates it and is going to give you $1,000 at the end of the season."

The season ended and nothing happened. Kell hung around for a few days. Somebody had told him that Earle didn't have the authority to say anything about anything, but Kell decided he'd go up and see Mr. Mack. He had nothing to lose.

In the tower office Kell said, "Earle told me you were going to give me a thousand dollar bonus after the season."

Mack was shocked. "I didn't know about that."

Kell could see that he was telling the truth. "Well that's what he told me."

Mack said, "Well, son, I might have discussed with Earle that I do appreciate what you've done for this ball club, but I don't remember promising you a thousand dollars. You come back in the morning. I'll talk to Earle."

Kell returned the next morning and Mack handed him a check for $1,000.

Philadelphia was still the third-largest city in the country, a center for publishing and radio and phonograph manufacturing. In addition to the 2 million in the city, another 3 million lived in the surrounding area. But its two baseball teams were asleep in the deep. They both needed binoculars—and a clear day—to see seventh place. A league-wide attendance boost sparked by another close pennant race—the Tigers nosing out a Washington team that had finished last in 1944—went unnoticed in Philadelphia. The A's and Phillies' *combined* attendance was less than that of five other major league teams. Still, the cash flow was more than enough to cover expenses, though the Athletics posted a $19,023 loss on the books.

At eighty-two Connie Mack was entitled to be set in his ways. He ate breakfast every morning at eight, had lunch and a nap in his office when the club was home, and showed up in the dugout about five minutes before the first pitch. He often watched batting practice and infield practice from somewhere in the stands, far enough back to be as unnoticed as possible. But his physical appearance was too recognizable for him to remain anonymous for long.

Dick Fitzgerald, later a sportswriter for the *Inquirer,* recalled:

I was ten in 1945. My dad and I went to a game at Shibe Park. It was early; the A's were taking batting practice, and we had a ball and our rain checks and we saw Connie Mack sitting in a dark suit in the upper deck behind home plate watching batting practice very intently. Nobody was around him.

My dad said, "Let's go up and ask him for his autograph" and we did and my dad said, "Mr. Mack, would you sign this" and handed him the ball. Connie Mack began to write and I was standing there and all I could think was how long it was taking him to sign his name, and then he signed the rain checks. And my dad thanked him and we left and then I saw that he had signed them "Cornelius McGillicuddy" and I knew why it had taken so long.

Mack's entrance into the dugout was choreographed. At home there was a coat hook on the wall behind his place. Earle would be at home plate with the umpires when he arrived. He would take off his coat and very meticulously hang it on the hook and sit down just in time for the first pitch.

Sometimes if the A's fell hopelessly behind in a game at home, he would stand up, remove the coat from the hook, put it on, and leave. Nobody said anything.

By now it was becoming clear to everybody in the dugout that Mr. Mack was slipping. Players who had been away for a few years were shocked by the change. Observant players on other teams noticed it too.

"There was a marked deterioration in his condition," said Ted Williams, who returned from the Marines in 1946. "I'd say Connie Mack really hurt the club from then on."

Since Williams was not privy to what went on in the A's dugout, his observations must have been based on examples of Mack's strategy in games against the Red Sox and what Williams, who enjoyed visiting with opposing players, may have picked up.

Mack's symptoms over the next several years would be consistent with a series of mini-strokes, which went undiagnosed or, if suspected, untreated. He kept moving his defense with his scorecard, but now Al Simmons was telling the outfielders, "If Mr. Mack moves you, move over, but before the pitcher throws, move back where you were." Mack became more nearsighted, unable to see the infield clearly. Yet it was uncanny to Pete Suder how he seemed to know just where the edge of the infield grass was, even though it wasn't visible from a seat in the depressed dugout. "When you looked out from the bench, nobody could see the infielders' feet. But if he wanted me to play in, somehow he'd move me until I reached the edge, then he'd stop me."

"He made plenty of mistakes managing on the bench," said Kell, "but usually nobody questioned it. He had such complete control of the situation and himself."

Mack sometimes lost his place in a game situation, like a man reading a book who dozes and drops it and can't find the page he was on. Al Simmons was the Old Man's chief corrector and protector. Once in a while Al would gently suggest that he might want to rethink something. One day they had the tying run on second in the ninth inning, and Mack told his best pinch hitter to go in as a pinch runner. Simmons stopped the player and said, "Mr. Mack, the pitcher is the next batter after the man at the plate and you'll want to use this man to hit for him."

Mr. Mack said, "Oh, that's right, my goodness, my goodness, that's right."

When he wanted a pinch hitter but couldn't think of the man's name, he would say, "I want . . . I want . . . I want . . . ," and one of the coaches would give him the name he was looking for. "Yes, that's right, I want him to pinch-hit."

Batboy Scott Irwin remembered a time when Mack called on Elmer Valo to pinch-hit. Valo was already in the lineup playing right field.

Mack was not at all embarrassed or self-conscious about his lapses. He never took offense or became upset when someone corrected him. One day he sent a slow runner in to run for someone. The man was picked off first. The next morning in the meeting Mack said, "I shouldn't have sent you out there in the first place cause you can't run a lick."

Nobody ridiculed him—even privately. The respect was palpable. Bobo Newsom was the most likely to make fun of anybody, but, said George Kell, "Bobo loved him like a father."

One day in Detroit the A's had the lead when the Tigers threatened in the ninth. Newsom, who rarely relieved, was sitting next to Mr. Mack in the dugout. As the score got closer, Mack got excited and slapped Bobo on the arm. "Tell Newsom to get ready in the bullpen."

Newsom got up and went to the telephone and said, "Tell Newsom to get ready," and came back and sat down. Whoever was in the bullpen got up and started throwing.

Mack's memory lapses extended to not recognizing his players. He'd seen so many come and go, it became harder for him to keep them straight. Carl Scheib said, "I'd been with him for two years and I met him in the elevator one day and he said, "Haven't I seen you some place before?"

Mack's handwriting became more quivery as the years passed. He retained his routine for making out the lineup—writing, not printing, the names. One day it led to a dilly of a rhubarb.

George Kell began the year batting eighth, then moved up to seventh in May. Irv Hall batted sixth most of the time. Opening a home stand against Detroit on May 23, Mack wrote in Kell batting fifth ahead of Hall for the first time. The next day the public address announcer and the scoreboard had Kell fifth and Hall sixth again. But to home plate umpire Ed Rommel and Detroit manager Steve O'Neill, it looked like Mack had written Hall batting fifth, followed by Kell, on the lineup cards Earle gave them before the game.

Batting fourth, Joe Burns led off the second and struck out. Kell then went up to bat and struck out. O'Neill, the only one who could lodge a complaint, said nothing. Hall then singled. Before the next batter, Dick Siebert, stepped in, O'Neill claimed that Hall had batted out of turn. Rommel looked at his lineup card and agreed. He ruled that this negated Hall's hit, and under rule

44 he called Hall out for batting out of turn, ending the inning. When this was pointed out to Mack, he said to Kell, "My, my, George, I wrote your name down wrong."

Earle later took the blame for the mixup. But the incident wasn't over.

In the third inning, Rommel decreed that Kell, not Siebert, should lead off. Confusion ensued. Mack called Rommel, his one-time 27-game winner, to the dugout for a lengthy confab that changed nothing. Both managers disagreed with Rommel's decision and filed protests, although Connie Mack withdrew his after the A's won, 7–2.

After the game Rommel admitted, "I thought I was right out there, but I may be wrong."

He was. (The fact that rule 44 read as if it had been written by a couple of old ballplayers named Pickles and Pretzels after a few drinks didn't help.)

According to Retrosheet, Rommel made two mistakes: declaring Hall out for batting out of turn and ordering Kell to lead off the third. Dick Siebert, who followed Kell in the lineup in the seventh spot, should have been declared out (and Hall's time at bat voided), and the number eight batter, Frank Hayes, should have led off the third inning.

Since it was a question of interpretation of the rules and not judgment, O'Neill's protest seemed valid, but it was denied by league president Will Harridge (whose decision read like it *too* had been written by Pickles and Pretzels). Maybe Harridge didn't have the heart to nullify one of Connie Mack's rare wins that year. The Tigers won the pennant by 1½ game; had they lost by a half game, Harridge might have had some explaining to do.

At times Connie Mack seemed preoccupied—or his mind a blank (how do you tell the difference?). One day thirteen-year-old Tom McCauley stood on the catwalk outside Mack's office, hoping to get an autograph. When Mack came out, Tom stepped forward and asked for his autograph. Mack, usually very gracious with youngsters, stared at him, started to walk away, then stopped and came back and signed for him.

How did Mr. Mack deal with these messengers of decline? He didn't. That is, he accepted them when they appeared, then shrugged them off or quickly forgot them. Senility is as forgetful of having forgotten something as it is of the original something forgotten.

As far back as 1933 Mack had said, "When my players can't get any more help from me; when I give them the wrong answers; and when my mentality is questioned—then I'll realize the time has come to say goodbye to the dugout."

The thousands of ballplayers who had come and gone during Connie Mack's lifetime could sympathize with his desire to put off the agony of saying goodbye to the dugout for as long as he could. They had all gone through it to some degree when their diminished skills were no longer marketable. Baseball was a tough, challenging profession. Connie Mack had devoted all his energies, his brain, his soul to it year-round for more than fifty years. To him it was more appropriate to say "Happy New Year" on opening day than on January 1. For anyone to suggest he retire from managing was tantamount to suggesting he retire from living.

Who, then, dared to be the executioner?

Not Earle, the submissive servant of his father. Earle might have feared the backlash if he was the one prodding Dad to quit so that he could take over. Or maybe he had finally realized that he was never going to succeed to the job, even if Roy was still being quoted that Earle would succeed their father when the time came. The players had no respect for him, and his father knew it. Al Simmons, not Earle, was the one advising the players to disregard the scorecard-waving and the inappropriate signs. Simmons was the one most often correcting Mr. Mack and suggesting he do something different.

It would not be Roy, who lacked the guts and the closeness and personal rapport with his dad. Roy's family was never present at the Sunday dinners hosted by Ruth. (Neither was Earle's, come to that.) Earle and Roy were already reported to be "squabbling." Squabbling over what was never said.

Connie Jr.? He was in the army; besides, he knew better than any of them that telling Dad to quit was the same as telling him to die. What loving son could do that?

Among the coaches, Al Simmons could have suggested it and gotten away with it. He wasn't worried about Mack firing him over it or of getting another job, as he later proved. But he had been with Mack for most of the past twenty years and loved the Old Man. He would do everything he could to protect him, cover for him, before he'd ever come right out and suggest it was time for him to go.

(In November 1951 the city of Milwaukee honored its all-time sports heroes. Connie Mack made the trip to sit at the Simmons family table. He held Al's mother's hand and said, "Mrs. Simmons, I also love Al like a son." That, said Simmons, "was my greatest thrill.")

Ira Thomas had been with the A's for thirty-five years. He had once been offered a chance to manage the Browns, but, the family story went, Mack talked him out of it. He and Mack were as close as brothers. When Thomas's nephew was to be married, Mack attended the bride's shower arranged by Mrs. Thomas.

Thomas was now primarily a scout and PR man, no longer in the clubhouse or the dugout. If he heard anything, he probably discounted it. During the off-season Mack seldom went to a speaking engagement or a dinner without him, and he saw no signs of Mack's slowing down in that department.

There was a time when Harry Davis, Mack's closest associate for twenty-five years, could have told him and, maybe, persuaded him. But Davis had been away from baseball for almost twenty years.

At the heart of it was that Connie Mack was Mr. Baseball, and baseball defined Connie Mack.

BACK TO NORMAL
105 LOSSES

At the age of eighty-three, Connie Mack had marital problems. As is often the case, it was about money and property. Not the spending but the giving of it.

Mack's goal was to leave his wife and children a solvent family business that the sons would carry on in harmony. In 1945, possibly based on some estate-planning advice, he decided to sign over half his shares to his sons and pay whatever gift taxes this incurred. He turned in stock certificate number 56 for 747 shares in exchange for

#64–373 shares in his name
#65–149 shares for Roy
#66–112 shares for Earle
#67–113 shares for Connie Jr.

Including shares they had received over the years, each of his three sons now held 163. Together the Mack family owned 891 shares; the descendants of Ben Shibe held the other 609.

Mr. Mack didn't consult Mrs. Mack. When she found out about it, she was not pleased. And she let him know it.

Why she went public about the squabble is unknown. Maybe a reporter learned of it and called her. In any event, on April 22, 1946, she told the world, "I learned in October about the transfer of the stock. I went to St. Petersburg in December and asked him about it. He said it would all be straightened out in two or three years. He is 83 and life is too uncertain to anticipate what may happen in the next two or three years. The point is there are eight persons to be considered in this: his seven children and myself. And it didn't sound very good when he gave more than half the stock to three of them."

(Between this transaction and 1950 Connie Mack's interest in the A's would be reduced from 373 to 302 shares. In 1950 Katherine owned 100 shares. It's possible that she had held 29 shares and Mack gave her an additional 71 to placate her and pave the way for a reconciliation.)

Katherine never spelled out what she considered fair; she was just looking out for her four daughters. It had nothing to do with who ran the business. The girls weren't interested.

But she did have a point. What could happen to "straighten it out" in two or three years? Mack could die; in that case she would be entitled to at least one-third of his property, will or no will. Why would he apply a time frame to such an eventuality? He was certainly not contemplating selling his remaining shares, which represented almost all his net worth. That would be tantamount to retiring.

Connie Mack never intended to cut out his four "girlies" or his wife. He probably had in mind creating a trust for them similar to the one he had made in 1928 and later revoked. He eventually did so when the team was sold eight years later.

In her April 22 statement, Katherine also said they were now living apart. How that happened depends on whom you believe.

She said, "I returned to Philadelphia the first of January and later he sent word that he was not returning and that he was sending for his clothes."

Mack's chauffeur, Chuck Roberts, said, "I took him home after an afternoon game in April and left and about nine o'clock she called me and said, 'Chuck, I put him out. You better come and get him.' They'd been arguing and when I got Mr. Mack and put him in the car I asked him, 'Mr. Mack, what happened?' and he said, 'She put me out.'"

Mack moved into an apartment at the Mayfair House, an elegant fourteen-story Regency style building just behind the family's former home at 604 W. Cliveden. He took some of his meals in the building's restaurant.

The Athletics were in New York when the story broke. As always, Mack was reluctant to talk about his private affairs. They were, in his opinion, nobody's business. "I would just rather not talk about it at all," he said when asked by reporters. "It would be so much better if people would just attend to their own business. I'm sorry, but I've had to hang up on several people who have telephoned me about it. All I can say is that Mrs. McGillicuddy and I have been married for thirty-five years and in that time I have never spoken one harsh word to her."

This was a time before the media considered it an obligation to act as the public's snooper. The matter disappeared from view until Connie Mack moved back to the apartment at 620 W. Phil-Ellena and the Macks hosted a dinner party to celebrate their reconciliation on October 22.

"We're very happy about it," said Mrs. Mack that evening.

"Don't care to talk about it," said Mr. Mack.

While they were in California for the winter, Connie Mack wrote "84" on a baseball on his birthday and signed it "Con to Katharine" [sic].

In 1944 Connie Mack had said, "When the war is over, I look for better, more exciting baseball played by more skillful men before greater crowds than we have ever known. Attendance should soar after the war. Even now baseball is making millions of new fans, young fans and women fans. Night games have done much to popularize baseball. Whether night games will increase after the war I don't know. I feel that no team should play more than fourteen home night games. Nevertheless I believe that baseball will give the fans what they want."

He was right. Attendance soared. The boon of night baseball had convinced Clark Griffith to see the light in Washington, and he now led the movement to allow unlimited night ball.

Those "more skillful men" Mack referred to did not include all the returning stars, for in truth Connie Mack did not expect much from the returning players, his own or those on other teams—unless they had been lucky enough to play plenty of baseball while in the service. In his view even a one-year layoff diminished a player's skills. Baseball required the loose, flexible, supple muscles of the young. The requirements of war were just the opposite.

"I don't believe DiMaggio, Keller, 'Rizz-two,' Henrich or any of the Yankees will be as good ball players when they come out as they were when they went in," he had been quoted in *Esquire*. "If the war continues a year longer we can count all the stars who see overseas action out as stars in post-war baseball."

Some players would have lost a step going to first that they would never regain. The timing, reflexes, batting eye, and muscle memories could return, but it would take a while, especially for those who hadn't touched a ball for two or three years. Mack also foresaw a change in the mental attitude of the men coming back from war. A man who had faced death in battle was less likely to get excited by a base hit with the bases loaded. "He is going to lack the springboard of ambition."

Mack's thinking was based on his experience following World War I, when many of his young hopefuls had left their baseball futures on the battlefield, and his recollections of old-timers like Amos Rusie and Frank Baker, who had lost something after one-year layoffs. He may have been preparing himself for similar disappointments this time around.

His outlook would turn out to be true of some, but by no means all, of the returning players.

The war's end touched off a wave of activity in the trading market as clubs sought to replace wartime fill-ins. Connie Mack looked forward to the return of the men he had lost, despite his uncertainty over how their military service had affected them. His pitching looked promising, but his outfield and infield needed improving, except for George Kell, who had blossomed into the best third baseman in the league. The catcher, Buddy Rosar, needed a backup.

For the past ten years, while his competitors had been raising young players on their farms, Mack had been browsing the bazaars for baseball bric-a-brac, like a tourist in the Paris flea market collecting *objets d'art* that might look handsome on the mantel, only to find that once one brought them home, they wouldn't do at all.

Now he was like a shopper at a Goodwill secondhand store, picking up the castoffs of clubs cleaning out their closets to make room for the return of their first-class goods.

In October Mack traded Dick Siebert to the Browns for first baseman George McQuinn. Mack had tried to obtain McQuinn in the past—the distant past. McQuinn would be thirty-six in May. Siebert was thirty-four. The swap didn't do much for either team. Siebert, incensed when the Browns tried to cut his salary, quit and went into broadcasting in St. Paul. The Browns demanded that the deal be nullified, but Commissioner Chandler refused, citing the Browns' attempt to cut Siebert's salary as a factor in Siebert's quitting.

Mack gave McQuinn a raise to what Siebert had been making. So there was no cost-cutting involved. The trade was a sign that the A's had no first base prospects coming back from the war or up from the minors. McQuinn did little for the A's, posting the lowest batting average of any regular in the league: .225. Released at the end of the year, he signed with the Yankees and earned a World Series ring in '47.

Mack picked up catcher Gene Desautels on waivers from Cleveland and drafted infielder Gene Handley from Sacramento and outfielder Frank Demaree from Portland. Desautels was thirty-eight, Demaree thirty-five, Handley thirty-one—hardly building blocks.

Although Buddy Rosar caught 116 games and made no errors, the pitchers didn't think highly of him. Bob Savage called him "a terrible catcher. His head wasn't in the game." Desautels hit .215 backing up Rosar, then retired.

Demaree didn't report.

Handley shouldn't have bothered.

The A's returned to Florida for spring training but deserted Fort Myers for West Palm Beach on the other coast, where there were more big league teams available for practice games. Toronto also trained there. The move paid off: exhibition game net receipts topped $16,000, the highest ever for the A's. Mack quickly signed a three-year agreement.

The Macks left Philadelphia on December 15, 1945, and went to St. Petersburg until checking into the Hotel George Washington in West Palm Beach in March 1946. Once again the Athletics were a new show in town. In the evenings an orchestra played in the hotel lobby. Whenever Connie Mack walked through on his way to the dining room, the band played "Take Me Out to the Ball Game," and everybody stood up and applauded.

Connie Mack was an anachronism to the new generation of ballplayers. Those young enough to be his great-grandsons could do nothing but stare at the sight of the tall, thin old man wearing a dark business suit in the A's dugout. Jerry Witte, a thirty-year-old rookie with the Browns, said the first time he saw Connie Mack in Sportsman's Park, it was like "staring at a statue that moved from one ballpark to another."

Gene Woodling was a rookie outfielder with the Indians. Fifty years later the picture of Mr. Mack entering the A's dugout remained vivid in his memory: "He usually appeared during infield practice about ten minutes before game time. We'd be looking for him and when he came in everything sort of stopped. In our dugout we all stood up. It was the same when I went to the Yankees, for as long as he managed. It was a sign of respect, and one of the nicest things I ever saw in baseball."

Even players' wives were flustered in Mack's presence, as if they were approaching someone out of a history book. Once in a hotel lobby Mrs. Joe

Coleman was introduced to him. "I was so nervous, meeting the great Connie Mack for the first time. I was so in awe of him I was afraid I'd say the wrong thing. I shook hands with him and said, 'How do you do, Mr. Mack. It's nice to meet you. How are you feeling?' For the next fifteen minutes he proceeded to tell me how he felt, which put me at ease."

Spring training camps were crowded with returning servicemen. Eight second basemen and more than twenty pitchers reported to the A's in West Palm Beach. During the year Mack would use forty-one men, eighteen of them identified as pitchers, to lose 105 games.

The veterans were shocked by the inflation in everyday prices. A haircut now cost a dollar, a shave fifty cents. Prices in fancy Worth Avenue shops in Palm Beach knocked their eyes out. Higher prices also hit Philadelphia baseball fans; a new city amusement tax ratcheted up ticket prices to $3.25 for reserved seats, $1.30 for the grandstand, 75 cents for the bleachers and children.

Baseball faced another dilemma with its returning servicemen. The Selective Service Act guaranteed a veteran his old job at the same or higher salary, with a guarantee against being fired or demoted without cause for a year after his return. What did that mean? If, in the judgment of a manager, a player had lost his prewar major league skills, would that be considered legitimate "cause" for release or demotion?

Club owners thought so; players whose years away from baseball had sapped their abilities were being released by the trainload. Some of them did not go quietly.

When pitcher Bob Harris strained his shoulder, Mack gave up on him in March. Harris signed with Milwaukee. Second baseman Benny McCoy, the high-priced free agent of 1940, had been away for four years, although he had played some for the Subic Bay Naval team in the Philippines. McCoy had always been slow getting started in the spring, but he no longer had the agility the position required. Mack asked him to switch to the outfield. McCoy said no. Mack released him on March 30. McCoy tried out with Detroit, didn't make it, and went home and managed a semipro team.

Harris and McCoy took the A's to court, claiming their prewar pay for a year: $5,500 for Harris, $10,000 for McCoy. After a year of legal back and forth, they settled for 75 percent.

Jack Knott, nearing forty, returned with nothing left and was released in May. He didn't sue.

Jack Wallaesa came back amid high expectations. Fear of failure rides on the shoulders of every ballplayer. It's heavy; in Wallaesa's case it was too heavy. The 6-foot-3, 190-pound shortstop barely hit his weight and made 22 errors in 59 games. Mack optioned him to Toronto. At the end of the year Jimmie Dykes gambled $15,000 of White Sox money on him in hopes of some improvement. It never came.

Connie Mack looked forward to the return to normal. "Baseball is a better game than it was ten years ago," he said, "and it will be an even better game ten years hence."

Forty-three minor leagues would open the season, another "back-to-normal" sign, giving Mack's three scouts—Harry O'Donnell, Ira Thomas, and Tom Turner—plenty of miles to cover.

Hoping to glean some talent from the hosts of returning young men, the Connie Mack Baseball School invited players sixteen to twenty-six to try out in the spring, and in June it became a traveling audition with Ira Thomas and Jack Coombs in charge. It lasted for four years.

Bobo Newsom remained the highest paid on the Athletics at $15,000; Sam Chapman was next at $12,000.

Hal Peck and Phil Marchildon were Mack's only two holdouts.

Peck received a raise to $7,500, didn't earn it, and was sold in June to the Yankees for $10,000.

Mack sent Marchildon a contract for $7,500. Marchildon asked for $12,000, based on the 17 games he had won in 1942. "That was a long time ago," said Mack. "Show me what you can do now and I'll make it up to you. Otherwise, stay home."

Cheapskate, Marchildon muttered, and grudgingly settled for the $7,500. "I almost hated him," Marchildon said in his 1993 autobiography. He still resented that Connie Mack had not given him a bonus when he had won those 17, nor wished him well when he went off to war.

Marchildon cut his hand in spring training, didn't start until May 6, and didn't win a game until June 7. But he pitched well; the A's weren't hitting.

Marchildon was still a nervous wreck. He had not completely recovered from the effects of his wartime experiences. On a ball hit back to him, his first impulse was to shy away from it. His hands shook. He broke out in sweats. Suddenly on the mound his nerves would blow like a shorted-out socket, his stomach knot up. Some nights on the road he would walk the streets restlessly.

Through it all, his legs were gradually regaining their strength, and he took his regular turn and relieved 7 times. When he won his eighth game on August 11, Connie Mack gave him a check for $1,200. When the season ended, he was 13-16 with 16 complete games. Connie Mack handed him another check for $2,500.

At twenty-four, it didn't take Bob Savage long to get back into condition— or back into the pitching groove he'd started in 1942: losing. The A's scored a total of 8 runs in his first 6 losses, 3 runs or fewer in 12 of his 15 losses. He earned 3 wins, twice beating the Yankees. When he didn't start, he was in the bullpen. "I could pitch every day," he said. "I had a rubber arm, and it took me only eight or nine pitches to be ready." Savage needed a change-up pitch and toyed with the idea of a knuckleball, but Earle Brucker talked him out of it, so he developed a palm ball. He started 19 games; another 21 times Al Simmons came out of the dugout and waved his arms and jumped around like a wild man, the signal for Savage to warm up for relief duty. Savage had the league's highest ERA among starting pitchers at 4.06.

The Toronto club needed a catcher and appealed to Mack. One day the manager saw Joe Astroth in the elevator. The conversation went something like this:

CM: Young man, Toronto needs a catcher. I want you to go there.
JA: Mr. Mack, we had a deal. I was to stay in the major leagues.
CM: Young man, you should be happy to go to triple A.
JA: I'm not going.
CM: You should be happy to go to triple A.
JA: I'm not going.
CM: Young man, I don't care where you go.

Astroth went to Toronto. He played in one game and was sent down to Class B Lancaster for the season. He spent '47 in Savannah and '48 in Memphis before he became a big league catcher.

In April Mack said he lacked hitting and fielding, and his pitching was uncertain. Outside of that, he was optimistic.

Mack was relying in the outfield on such as Hal Peck, Tuck Stainback, Ford Garrison, and Russ Derry alongside Sam Chapman, who had lost the ability to pickle curve balls the way he had three years ago, and Elmer Valo, whose delayed release from the service led to a slow start.

Valo had agreed to a $5,000 salary on March 26 but did not come off the

National Defense Service list until April 23. Nevertheless, he pinch-hit on April 18 and started in left field on the twenty-first. Then he pinch-hit a few more times. On April 30 somebody in the A's office noticed that Valo still hadn't signed a contract. Connie Mack called him in and gave him a $1,000 bonus to sign.

When his pal Pete Suder heard about it, he told Valo, "Why didn't you tell me you hadn't signed? Don't you know you could have become a free agent?"

"I don't know," said Elmer. "It didn't make any difference. I knew Mr. Mack was going to sign me sometime."

Mack knew he couldn't buy a quality outfielder. He'd have to give up something of value, and he didn't have much to offer.

The Tigers, meanwhile, were desperately in need of a third baseman. They were loaded with first-rate outfielders: Hank Greenberg, Jimmy Outlaw (who was playing third because all they had behind him was the spavined Pinky Higgins), Pat Mullin, Doc Cramer, and Roy Cullenbine from the '45 world champions; returning veteran Dick Wakefield; and prized rookie Hoot Evers, in addition to Barney McCosky, a former Detroit sandlotter and a fan favorite.

The Tigers had inquired about George Kell two years earlier but were turned down by Mack, who considered the then rookie a key part of his rebuilding plan.

Just as Detroit's head scout Wish Egan had George Kell in mind, Connie Mack knew which Detroit outfielder he wanted and, more important, which one he didn't want.

Dick Wakefield had signed out of the University of Michigan for a then record $52,000 bonus in 1941, led the league with 200 hits and 38 doubles in his rookie 1943 season, and was hitting .355 in '44, when he went into the navy. When he came back, he was not the same. He seemed lackadaisical, going through the motions.

One day Jimmy Cannon of the *New York Post* read a wire report that Connie Mack was attempting to buy Wakefield. Cannon wrote:

I mentioned this to [Mack].
"I don't want him," he said crankily. "I don't want him at all."
He glared at me, still proud of his knowledge of the league.
"Why do you say that?" he demanded.
I told him a press association had disseminated the rumor.
"He's half a ballplayer," Mack said. "I don't want half a ballplayer."

(In 1948 the Tigers were again trying to peddle Wakefield. Mack's opinion hadn't changed; he didn't want a high-priced player "who won't hustle for the team he is with.")

Mack had a long fixation on Barney McCosky. Back in 1937 and '38 the A's had trained at Lake Charles. McCosky was with Detroit's farm club, Beaumont, which played several spring games against the A's.

"I killed them with my hitting and fielding," McCosky said, "and Connie Mack wanted me then. But Wish Egan, who had signed me, said no way. I was a hometown boy and they wanted me in Detroit."

Detroit writer Watson Spoelstra reported that Mack walked into the Briggs Stadium office when the A's were in town on May 17 and said something like, "I need an outfielder and you seem to have plenty of them. I'm willing to consider a deal for George Kell."

Detroit head scout Wish Egan, assigned to do whatever it took to get Kell, told a different version of what happened. When he inquired about Kell, Mack told him, "Oh, my, George is a fine ballplayer. I couldn't let him go for anyone less than Barney McCosky."

According to sportswriter Art Hill, Egan later described what happened next: "I was stunned but not for the reason he thought. We were quite prepared to give him McCosky and another good player for Kell. But I had to make a show of resistance. I pointed out that McCosky was one of my boys. I had signed him for the Tigers. But Mr. Mack was determined to have him, and I finally let myself be talked into an even trade. I didn't know how he felt about it. I was delighted with the deal, but at the same time I was a little ashamed of myself for taking advantage of the Old Man."

Maybe. This sounds like a yarn spun years later by a storyteller looking in a distorted rear view mirror. At the time nobody panned the deal or suggested that Connie Mack had been taken. Frank Yeutter of the *Evening Bulletin* wrote, "Connie believes he outsmarted Detroit in making the deal."

If you look at the record books as of May 17, 1946, you see a promising third baseman with two years' experience and a twenty-eight-year-old outfielder who had what some players called "the sweetest swing in baseball," with a four-year batting average of .316, a league-leading 19 triples and 200 hits in 1940, and a .304 average in the World Series. McCosky missed three years in the navy, but he had been playing ball, facing big league pitching in Hawaii, where he managed the navy team in the island world series.

Two years later a 1948 baseball annual publication would have this to say: "If the Tigers thought they made a smart deal, they have only to inspect the

Philadelphia outfielder's record for the last two seasons to realize it was a fairly even swap."

Both Kell and McCosky fulfilled what was expected of them, though neither had an immediate impact on his new team's fortunes. Kell hit .327, and the Tigers finished second (they never won a pennant during Kell's six years in Detroit). McCosky, a line drive hitter and the best bunter in the league, was an ideal number two or three hitter. He batted .354 and gave the A's an outstanding outfield with Valo in right and Chapman in left.

At the time of the trade McCosky was hampered by sore leg muscles and a sprained ankle and was hitting just .196. George Kell was batting .299 and had been 7 for 16 against Tigers pitching so far in '46.

The next morning the Tigers called Mack at his hotel and closed the deal. Due to an impending railroad strike, the A's had chartered a plane to fly to St. Louis after the game that afternoon. The players had a big discussion about flying and took a vote on who was willing to fly. (The team flew; the strike didn't happen; Mack and Al Simmons and Bobo Newsom took the train.)

George Kell was on the elevator on his way to breakfast when Connie Mack got on. "Young man, I need to see you in my suite," said Mack.

Kell's first thought was that the manager was concerned because there weren't enough players willing to fly to justify the charter. "Mr. Mack," he said, "I voted to fly, if that's what you want to talk about."

"No, I have something important to talk to you about."

They went up to Mack's suite. "I have traded you to Detroit for Barney McCosky," Mack said.

Kell was stunned. "Why? I've played hard for you, Mr. Mack. I'm having a good year."

"You don't understand, son," Mack said. "This is a great city and great ball club. You're going to do well in this game. You're going to make a lot more money here than I can afford to pay you, and you'll love it in Detroit."

Looking back, Kell reflected, "I felt rejected at the time. I was really shocked and it showed. I'm sure what he said was to make me feel better about being traded, but Mr. Mack was that way. Two years later he said I was one of the five best players in the game and he knew I would be when he traded me away."

(All his life George Kell referred to him as Mr. Mack. "Even to this day I'll meet people who say, 'Did you know Connie Mack?' and there's something about it that grates me. It's like saying something derogatory about my father. He's sacred to me.")

As for making more money in Detroit, Mack was right about that. Kell had asked for $7,500 in the spring, and Mack had said $6,500 was the most he could pay, "but if you have a good year I'll give you the $1,000."

When Kell reported at Briggs Stadium that afternoon, the general manager, George Trautman, asked him, "How much are you making?"

"Mr. Trautman, I'm making $6,500 and Mr. Mack has promised me $7,500 if I have a good year."

Trautman said, "Son, when Detroit trades for you, you've had a good year already. We'll give you $8,500."

At the end of the season Kell received a $2,500 bonus. By 1948 he was up to $20,000.

Barney McCosky was even more shocked than Kell by the trade. He had missed several games with a sprained ankle. He was taped up and putting on his shoes in the clubhouse when one of the coaches came over to him and said, "You just been traded."

"What? To who?"

"Philadelphia."

He sat there thinking: Mr. Mack finally got me.

When he reported to the A's in Chicago four days later, McCosky told his new boss, "Mr. Mack, you finally got me."

"Yes, McCusky, I finally got you," said Mack.

The trade raised Mack's payroll; McCosky was earning $14,000.

There was little reaction to the trade in Philadelphia, partly because the club was firmly lodged in the cellar and none of the writers was traveling with the team. The story was that McCosky had been dissatisfied with his limited playing time in Detroit and was assured by Mack that he would play every day.

George Kell received a big round of applause from the 19,981 on hand on his first appearance as a visitor to Shibe Park on June 4. But McCosky had quickly become a fan favorite in Philadelphia. When the A's returned home on June 1, McCosky had 4 hits in a 10–4 win that broke a 9-game losing streak and in the next game had 3 more. The Athletics' first venture into public relations beyond Mr. Mack's personal appearances was a fans' newsletter called *Along the Elephant Trail*. The June issue featured a photo of Barney McCosky.

To replace Kell, Mack switched Pete Suder to third until he could land a third baseman. Hank Majeski had come up in 1939 with the Boston Bees as a second baseman. Bees manager Casey Stengel switched him to third, a position that suited him better. He loved the action and had a strong arm. The Yankees bought him in 1941 and sent him to Newark, where he led the International League at .345 in '42 before going into the Coast Guard for three years. When he came out, he was twenty-nine and third in line in New York behind Billy Johnson and bonus baby Bobby Brown.

Mack may have seen him play at Newark or sent someone to look him over. He remembered him and bought him for $10,000 on June 14.

Frustration or the erosion of the tarp on Mack's once volcanic temper sometimes allowed it to erupt.

On May 19 in St. Louis, Elmer Valo was playing near the line in right field for a right-handed batter who hit a pop fly back of second. Chapman in center field was nowhere near it. Second baseman Irv Hall didn't go back for it. Valo, hustling all the way, got within ten feet of it when it dropped. Somebody—Earle or Simmons—yelled from the dugout, "Jesus Christ, where were you playing him, Elmer?"

Connie Mack jumped up, called time, and waved for Valo to come in. He sent Hal Peck out to right field.

"Elmer," Mack said, "you're going to Toronto tomorrow."

All Valo said was, "That's all right, Mr. Mack."

Valo cleared waivers but didn't go anywhere. He didn't play for almost two weeks, never quit hustling, and hit .307 for the year.

Robert L. Burnes of the *St. Louis Globe-Democrat* reported an incident in a game against the Browns when the first base umpire called an A's batter out at first base even though it was clear to everyone watching that the first baseman's foot was not on the base when he took the throw. The runner screamed at the umpire. Earle Mack, coaching at first, joined in. Caps and towels flew out of the A's dugout.

Burnes wrote, "Suddenly a towel flew out of the left-hand corner of the dugout where Mr. Mack habitually sat. Somebody in the press box said, 'Either the Old Man threw that himself or had to duck to get out of the way.'"

Connie Mack sat in silence for a full minute after the call, then said, "That's the worst decision I have seen in all my baseball life." He stood up, called and waved for the umpire to come over, then began to walk out onto the field. A few of his boys, assisted by the home plate umpire, gently urged him to go back and sit down. The umpire admitted, "I couldn't see the play from where I stood. The runner was in my way. But I know we must have missed it. All I can say is I'm sorry."

The much-traveled Bobo Newsom was restless again. He had started in grand style, holding the Yankees to 3 hits in the season's second game, a 7–1 win in which Connie Mack reverted back to his 1910 strategy in a 5-run seventh inning. The A's literally bunted Randy Gumpert out of the game, putting down 4 of them, including a squeeze play by Kell that went for a hit, and a 2-strike bunt by Newsom that scored another run. Newsom unveiled his new knuckleball, which the Yankees refused to swing at or dodge, resulting in 3 hit batters. In his next start he shut out the Red Sox.

After Newsom had won three of his first four starts, the A's quit hitting behind him. They scored a total of 1 run in three of his starts and 3 in his fifth loss on May 30 in New York—the eighth loss in a row for the A's. After the game Newsom stormed around the clubhouse yelling, "I want my release."

It was a typical Bobo show and everybody laughed.

"I'll bet anybody a hundred dollars I'll get my release," he shouted.

Pete Suder said, "Just buy us all a beer if you get it."

"I'll buy you a case," Bo announced.

Two days later the A's were back in Philadelphia, and Newsom went up to Mr. Mack's office. "I want my release," he said.

Mack said he was satisfied with Newsom's work and would even give him a contract for next year at the same money right then and there.

Newsom said no, he wanted to go somewhere else where he could make more money.

Although Newsom was thirty-eight, he seldom needed a trainer's attention and was still good for over 200 innings a year. He had some market value, but Mack just let him go.

"When he kept on insisting on his release I was happy to give him a break," Mack said. "He gave me his best for two years and I felt the least that I could do was reciprocate in this way."

Two days later Newsom signed with Washington for the fourth time (at the same salary). A year later he was pitching for the Yankees in the World Series.

Connie Mack urged his players to ignore what they read in the newspapers. On August 1 in Chicago Pete Suder hit a grand slam off Gordon Maltzberger in the third inning of a game the A's eventually lost, 7–6. By the time they got on the train to St. Louis the afternoon papers were out. Suder picked one up and read this: "Pete Suder earned his entire $2,500 salary all in one day." He showed it to Mr. Mack in the dining car and said, "Mr.

Mack, we've got to do something about this. I make more than that [he made $5,000]."

Mack's advice: "Don't say anything to them. Let them write what they want."

From August 15 to September 15 the A's were 17-16. The offense was still light, but the pitching improved. Then they lost the last ten with a lineup of players most of whom would soon be gone.

Connie Mack had seen enough autumn glories turn into spring flops to vow not to get his hopes up by September performances. Nevertheless, the lure of that siren once again proved irresistible to him. Joe Coleman and Bill McCahan came up from Toronto in September. McCahan, a nephew of Danny Hoffman, an outfielder on Mack's 1905 pennant winners, made his first start in the second game of a Sunday doubleheader at Cleveland on September 15, opposing Bob Feller, who had already won 24 games and passed 300 strikeouts.

Joe Astroth had also been recalled. He was getting his first look at Feller and was awed by what he saw. Sitting beside Russ Christopher, he whispered, "Boy, that guy is some kind of pitcher."

Connie Mack heard it. He leaned forward, looked at Astroth, and said, "But he can be beat, young man."

And McCahan beat him, 2–0, in a 7-inning game.

Why did the A's finish so deep in the cellar? They weren't the worst pitching staff, giving up fewer runs than fourth-place Washington, despite the second-highest ERA at 3.90. Marchildon and Fowler each lost 16 games with lower ERAs than the league average. (Luther Knerr lost 16 also, but with a 5.40 ERA, he deserved it.) The infield was a quartet of banjo hitters, the outfield pretty powerless. Sam Chapman hit half their 40 home runs. Irv Hall left the big leagues as the player with the second-most at bats without hitting a home run. Still, they scored only 8 fewer runs than the sixth-place Indians they trailed by 19 games.

An unsettled, porous infield—a dozen different second base–shortstop combinations took the field—gave Mack's pitchers a handicap every time out. When Washington manager Ossie Bluege was asked why he traded outfielder George Binks to the Athletics for pitchers Luther Knerr and Luman Harris, who had been 6-30 between them in 1946, Bluege said, "We never pay any attention to a pitcher's record with the Athletics."

Harris and Knerr pitched a total of 15 innings for Washington; neither ever won another game.

Connie Mack sort of shrugged it off; it was just one of those years. After Allie Reynolds and Bob Feller threw back-to-back 3-hitters at them in July, he wrote to his friend Donald McComas, "Our boys don't seem able to place the ball where the player is not playing in other words when one of our players hits the ball hard its right at someone."

There were some who blamed Connie Mack for the team's woeful standing. Milton Gross of the *New York Post* wrote that the fans of Philadelphia were clamoring for Mack to step aside in favor of "an enlightened, live-wire, free-spending ownership."

Connie Mack had to be paying no attention or—more likely—was just too almighty gracious to object to a story broadcast by sportscaster Bill Stern, a renowned peddler of preposterous fiction posing as dramatic fact. On Friday, October 4, the night before Stern would be calling the Columbia-Navy football game in his usual imaginary style, Mack was the guest on his weekly program. Stern narrated a fanciful tale about how the young Connie Mack, working as a janitor in the town jail, had been given a diamond by a murderer about to be hanged and how Connie had sold the diamond for $2,000 to Diamond Jim Brady and used that money to buy "his first interest in a baseball team, a team later to be called the Philadelphia Athletics."

It got weirder. Years later, Stern related, Mack received a letter from Lillian Russell, the most famous actress-singer of her time, who said she remembered how Brady had bought the diamond from Mack and given it to her, and now she was broke and would he like to buy it back, and Mack did, then sold it and used the money to free another murderer, a former ballplayer named Sam Crane (for whom Mack had really gained a parole with the promise of a job—the only truth in the whole tale).

The sad part was that Connie Mack went along with this melodrivel. When Stern introduced him, Mack, probably reading from a script that had just been handed to him, said, "Good evening, Bill. I'd like to add one thing to that story you've just told. I am glad I was able to help Sam Crane gain his freedom from the Eastern [State] Penitentiary for I believe he's learned his lesson."

The banter then went into the upcoming World Series, Mack picking the Red Sox over the Cardinals in six games, and the naming of his all-time team.

Stern then asked, "What about the future, Mr. Mack? What are your plans?"

"I'm an old man, Bill. I have only one ambition left, and that is to have one more great team for Philadelphia before I die."

That part was true. But it didn't look likely, not even to the eternal optimist. In December he wrote to his grandson Connie McCambridge, "Our team will be about the same [next year], will have to hope for the best. I'd like to get out of that last place position thou don't look too encouraging."

Two movements that shook up baseball in 1946 had little effect on the Athletics. The wealthy Pasquel brothers in Mexico raided the major leagues for players to stock a new Mexican League. Several front-line players took the money and jumped. The ensuing legal battles when the players sought to return lasted longer than the Pasquels' league. The only player the Athletics lost was Roberto Estalella, whose departure was cheered by American League pitchers. Line drives off his bat had broken Ed Lopat's arm in 1943 and Al Benton's leg in '45.

Robert Murphy, a labor relations lawyer, formed the American Baseball Guild and set out to persuade players to join. On June 7 he held a pregame meeting in Pittsburgh, urging the Pirates to go out on strike to gain recognition of the guild. The players voted, 20–16, to strike, falling short of the two-thirds majority Murphy needed to act. Murphy planned to go next to Philadelphia. When Connie Mack heard about it, he closed the clubhouse to all visitors, Murphy kept going to New York. The guild died. But some of Murphy's rumored objectives were accomplished: $25 a week "Murphy money" for spring training expenses and a $5,000 minimum salary. In 1947 the players' pension plan began; players had to put in $250 to be eligible. Not all of them did.

A different kind of tremor was felt in Shibe Park, one that would have a stronger impact on Mr. Mack and the Athletics.

From 1935 through 1945 the A's and Phillies had competed to see who could bore the most fans. Except for the war year 1944, both teams had finished seventh or eighth every year. A's supporters, either through habit or residual loyalty—the Athletics had been great in most fans' lifetimes; the Phillies had finished as high as fourth only once since 1917—or to give out-of-town friends and relatives a chance to glimpse that eighth wonder of the world, Connie Mack, had turned out in slightly larger groups than the Phillies attracted.

In 1946 both teams rode the postwar boom, but the times they were achangin' in Philadelphia. The rejuvenated Phillies under Bob Carpenter and general manager Herb Pennock improved by 23 wins over their '45 record and rose to fifth with only one returning regular—catcher Andy Seminick. Among the new faces was a hometown rookie outfielder, Del Ennis, who hit .313 and gave the "phanatic" boo-birds a new favorite target, because . . . because . . . well, just because he was a local boy. Phillies' attendance soared to over a million, a startling gain of 750,000, and a record for the city.

The A's, meanwhile, were offering many of the same old last-place bunch. The wave of prosperity was strong enough to lift the A's attendance by 150,000 despite their finishing 17 games beneath seventh place. They were still dependent on their tenants to help pay the bills. More than $113,000 came from the Phillies and $68,719 from the Eagles. Without those additions the bottom line would have been $100,000 in the red.

For the first time in thirty years the A's faced serious competition for Philadelphia baseball fans' devotion and dollars.

19 | CONNIE MACK AND THE INTEGRATION OF BASEBALL

Major league baseball has always been part of—and reflected—an American culture in which, until the middle of the twentieth century, the conventional wisdom held that blacks were inherently inferior to whites. The separation of the races in the workplace, marriage, housing, public facilities, and recreation was the custom and, in many states, the law. Ideas like civil rights and equal opportunity were absent from the public agenda or most of the public's conscience.

Connie Mack, along with the other baseball club owners of his time—and the fans of their teams—grew up in that society and absorbed its mores.

In an attempt to—not exonerate—but understand the events and the people of the time, it is essential that readers check their twenty-first century standards and attitudes at a mental baggage depot. Looking back invites the abuse of hindsight by applying retroactively the values and culture of a future time as though they were eternal, which they are not. Most Americans today are strangers to the United States of the 1920s, '30s, and '40s, as well as to its earlier existence. They never lived there.

Years later black writer Brent Staples recognized that when he summed up Connie Mack: "He's from a different era and it would be ungracious, unwise, narrow-minded to begrudge a man his era, for how can they live outside that time?"

For much of his career Connie Mack was ahead of his time in many ways. But by the time America's values and ethos began to evolve in racial matters, he was no longer the firebrand who had helped lead the players' rebellion of 1890 and the American League's breaking of the National's big league monopoly ten years later. Now, in his eighties, he was neither physically nor mentally fit to lead either the charge for change or the opposition to it—or, for that matter, even to comprehend it. That parade had passed him by.

The Athletics had been playing postseason games against colored teams and had made their ballpark available to them as far back as 1902. Like other club owners, Mack admired Negro Leagues players and was widely quoted as telling one or another that they could "name their own price" if only they were white. Club owners admitted them free to their ballparks (except, said Negro Leagues star Judy Johnson, Branch Rickey's St. Louis Cardinals).

Some northern sportswriters campaigned for baseball to be a pioneer of integration in the 1930s (although the press boxes were still not friendly toward Negro writers even after 1947). In May 1940 the *Philadelphia Record* announced that it would start a campaign urging the A's and Phillies to sign Negro players. The sports staff tried to squelch the scheme, but an editor overruled them. One month later in *The Sporting News* "Press Box" column, there appeared this item: "That Philadelphia a.m. sheet has stopped its agitation to get Negro players in the majors because of the reactions of its white readers."

Because of his stature in the game, Mack was often asked for comment by the Negro press. He bridled at being—as he saw it—ambushed by the issue.

Al Monroe, sports editor of the weekly *Chicago Defender* in the early 1930s, reported that he once called Mack and asked him to pose for a picture with White Sox trainer Bill Buckner, a Negro. Mack said, "Why should I pose with him? He's no ballplayer."

"For my paper," Monroe said.

Mack consented. When Monroe showed up with Buckner and saw Mack in the lobby, he introduced himself and extended his hand. Mack stared at him. "I'm the newspaperman who called you about that picture with Bill Buckner."

"What paper did you say?"

"The *Defender*, the nation's greatest Negro weekly."

Mack turned and walked away without a word.

"No written law has ever been more binding than unwritten custom supported by public opinion," wrote feminist Carrie Chapman Catt.

Custom, tradition—baseball was always slow to abandon these, especially when they were supported by public opinion. The new, the unpredictable, panicked the club owners. They knew that change was coming, was inevitable, but they were not inclined to get out in front of the parade any more than the department store managers and restaurant owners and innkeepers and theater owners who feared a white backlash if they served Negro customers alongside whites

In 1937 Clark Griffith told *Baltimore Afro-American* sports editor Sam Lacy, "I know the time will come, but the climate isn't right. We wouldn't have the support of society."

Lacy conceded that it was an unrealistic goal at that time. Negro Leagues star Leon Day said later, "They couldn't have signed any black players in the 1930s even if they wanted to. It would have been suicide for the club owners and murder for the players."

But it has become de rigueur in the baseball/sociology genre to brand Commissioner Kenesaw Landis and major league club owners of the 1930s and '40s as racists. Landis, it is claimed, could have pressured club owners into signing Negro Leagues players. One writer went so far as to cite Landis's being "circumspect" enough never to admit to being a racist as proof that he was. (The same writer quoted Mack as saying he "could not cross the well-known prejudice of Kenesaw Landis," thus in one sentence transforming the speculative into the "well known" and attributing to Mack a wholly implausible utterance.)

On July 25, 1942, the *Afro-American* headlined: "Landis Clears Way for Owners to Hire Colored." Sports editor Art Carter made it clear that it was up to any owner "willing to blaze the trail in breaking down the bar against colored players."

After Paul Robeson appeared by invitation at a major league meeting in 1943, Landis reiterated that "each club is entirely free to employ Negro players to any extent it pleases and the matter is solely for each club's decision without any restrictions whatsoever."

Fay Young wrote in the *Chicago Defender*, "The Negro knows Landis is right, but Landis can't spend a club owner's money."

Those who choose to disbelieve the record cannot be persuaded otherwise.

Connie Mack respected and admired successful businessmen. He was impressed by wealth and by educated men. He had felt his lack of education keenly throughout his life. Talking baseball, he could more than hold his own. But talking sociology and economics, he couldn't. When men like Tom Yawkey and P. K. Wrigley put their names to a report in 1946 warning that integration "of any one club may exert tremendous pressure upon the whole structure of Professional Baseball, and could conceivably result in lessening the value of several major league franchises," Connie Mack listened and nodded.

Years later Connie Jr. explained to his son Dennis, "Connie Mack was the least wealthy of the owners and wealth impressed him. If no blacks was what they wanted, he'd go along with it. It wasn't that he himself was bigoted but that he wasn't willing to stand up to the principle that that's the wrong thing to do. That's the way it was and he would go along."

Fear was a factor in Connie Mack's thinking. His business was his life, his only source of income. Everything he owned was invested in the Athletics. Fresh in his memory were the wartime race riots in Philadelphia, New York, and Detroit—where a game had to be postponed because of violence near Briggs Stadium that left 34 dead and 670 injured—and the August 1944 week-long transit strike in Philadelphia. Three hundred storefronts were smashed in the black North Philadelphia neighborhood. What was the strike and the violence about? The upgrading of eight Negroes to jobs formerly held exclusively by whites. Ten thousand union members shut down the city, the nation's third-largest war production center, because they didn't want blacks taking white drivers' jobs. (At the same time organized labor was berating Clark Griffith and Connie Mack for not signing black players to take white players' jobs.)

If Negroes flocked to the games to see Negro players, would white attendance drop? Fights on the field were part of the game. What would happen if white and colored players started swinging at each other? Would a racial brawl break out in the stands? Race riots were raging in cities all over the country as the debate went on.

It doesn't matter that these fears later proved to be groundless. That was later. This was now. It's easy to look back and see how it all turned out. But the men making the decisions at the time were looking around them, at the society in which they lived and worked and invested in their ball clubs.

Connie Mack's first reaction to Branch Rickey's signing of Jackie Robinson was to duck the issue. "I'm not familiar with the move and don't know Robinson," he said. "I wouldn't care to comment."

Mack and Branch Rickey had been friends and mutual admirers for more than a quarter century, so close that members of Rickey's family could recall no one other than Mr. Mack ever addressing the imposing Mr. Rickey as "Branch." Robinson was in Florida with the Montreal club in March 1946. Some Florida cities canceled Montreal's exhibition games because local ordinances prohibited whites and Negroes from playing together on the same field.

Montreal players—though not Robinson—had appeared in some Dodgers exhibition games. The Dodgers were due in West Palm Beach to play the A's on March 9.

The day before, A's beat writers Stan Baumgartner and Don Donaghey were culling the usual spring training chaff with Connie Mack in his hotel room. Red Smith, who had moved to the *New York Herald Tribune* a year ago after ten years in Philadelphia, was also in the room. In interviews with several writers and historians years later, Smith described what happened when one of the Philadelphia writers asked Mack what he would do if the Dodgers brought Robinson with them.

Mack snapped, "I wouldn't play them. I used to have respect for Rickey. I don't anymore." He ranted on in what used to be uncharacteristic fashion for him, but the filter between Mack's mind and mouth had begun to fray. At any time he might come out with comments that shocked those who had known him for decades, words they knew would have been embarrassing if they appeared in print. So they didn't print them.

Baumgartner, who had pitched for Mack twenty years earlier, said, "You wouldn't want that in the paper, would you, Connie?"

"I don't give a goddamn what you write. Yes, publish it," said Mack.

According to Smith, Baumgartner wanted to run the story, but Donaghey persuaded Mack to take his comments off the record.

Nobody, including Smith, wrote the story. "I decided," Smith later said, "that I'd forgive old Connie for his ignorance."

Katherine Mack had always forbidden any baseball talk at the dinner table, a taboo that annoyed Mack's grandson Connie McCambridge, who remembered breaking it during Thanksgiving dinner that year at Connie Jr.'s house: "I asked Dad what he thought about Jackie Robinson and there was a colored maid waiting on us at the time and afterward I bit my tongue, because Dad made it very plain he didn't like it. He was very emphatic in his disapproval. 'No, no, no,' he said."

Robinson's sensational 1946 season in Montreal produced plenty of crude riding from players and fans but no riots, no desertion of the games by white fans. Apparently Connie Mack noticed and changed his views—at least in public. At the December league meeting in Los Angeles, John R. Williams of the *Pittsburgh Courier* reported, "Evidence that the question of Negro players in major league baseball is no longer a 'behind the scenes' topic was obvious when Connie Mack, venerable owner of the Philadelphia Athletics, heretofore silent on the subject, willingly gave his views:

> "This is a new day," Connie Mack stated, "and I see no reason why Negroes should not be accepted in organized baseball. I hope to see Jackie Robinson with Brooklyn and sincerely hope that he makes good."
>
> Mr. Mack made this statement before his son, Roy Mack, and Jack Zeller, former general manager of the Detroit Tigers.
>
> There is a new attitude among the owners and officials relative to the Negro player. There was a time when they refused to discuss the issue. It was considered dynamite and they stayed away from it. Thanks to Branch Rickey and Jackie Robinson, however, they are no longer dodging the subject.

This statement by Connie Mack welcoming the integration of baseball has been obscured by the fact that he was still among the majority of club owners who had not signed a Negro player by 1950. But much of what has been written about his failure to sign black players is a result of faulty memory or shoddy research.

In *Dollar Sign on the Muscle,* Kevin Kerrane wrote: "After WWII [Judy Johnson] scouted for the A's. He spent most of his scouting energy trying to persuade his boss, Connie Mack, to sign players like Larry Doby, Minnie Minoso and Hank Aaron. 'I wound up giving tips on all those players to scouts from other teams. I just wanted to make sure the kids got a chance, because I could see that Mr. Mack was gonna pass them by.'"

Johnson was not signed as a scout for the A's until February 1951. Doby had been with Cleveland since 1947, Minoso since 1949. The Boston Braves and several other teams had been scouting Aaron for several years without the need for any "tips" from Judy Johnson.

Johnson's story about trying to get the A's to buy Hank Aaron in 1952 [from whom isn't clear] for $3,500 has been widely repeated and embellished. Whoever his "boss" was that he supposedly called at one o'clock in the morning and was told, "The price is too high for a man like that," it was not Connie Mack. By then Mack was no longer making any player decisions. He was certainly not dealing with scouting reports. Jimmie Dykes was the manager, Arthur Ehlers the general manager and farm director. Roy and Earle Mack were running things.

Mack's debilitated ability to express himself clearly at this stage of his life made him uncomfortable being put on the defensive by writers who continued to target him about not signing Negro players.

On September 1, 1949, *Cleveland Call & Post* writer John E. Fuster called Mack at the Cleveland Hotel looking for an interview. "Try me after four," said Mack. Fuster went to the hotel, couldn't find him, and decided to wait until after the game that night. After Larry Doby drove in the winning run in the eleventh inning, Fuster figured that Mack wouldn't feel like talking to a reporter, but he took a chance and caught up with Mack walking out of the stadium. This is what he wrote:

> "Mr. Mack, I am the reporter who called you earlier today with some questions about Negroes in baseball."
> "I cannot talk now."
> He kept walking looking straight ahead.
> "But all I want to know is whether or not you would consider playing Negroes on your team."
> "I have nothing to say."
> Perhaps Connie Mack had answered my question after all.

Unlike more militant writers, Fuster understood that for the better part of Connie Mack's life the black man had been regarded by the entire society as a second class person:

> When [Mack] was born Abraham Lincoln had not yet signed the Emancipation Proclamation. There were still 3,000 slaves in Washington, D. C. It might be hard for Mr. Mack to entrust a position on his team to a Negro—harder than you think.
> But how grand it would have been if this highly respected "Old Man of Baseball" could have told me Thursday night before he quick-stepped away into the crowd, "This is America, and I believe a man deserves a chance whatever his race, creed or nationality."

Fuster was looking for an eloquence and vision and clarity of thought that this most respected of men no longer had at the age of eighty-seven.

20 | THE GLEANER

In the middle of the 1946 season Connie Mack surveyed the forty-three active minor leagues and reflected on how few of them had an Athletics presence. The A's owned clubs in Savannah (Class A), Martinsville (C), Federalsburg (D), and Lexington (D) and had working agreements with Toronto (AAA) and Lancaster (B). That was it. He decided the time had come for him to relinquish the burden of acting as his own farm director and bring in somebody from outside the family. (The time had really come ten years ago.)

The man Mack chose to build a farm system was no stranger to him. Arthur Ehlers had been a young pitching prospect from Maryland whose big league dreams had been shattered along with an arm and a leg in France in World War I. Turning to the business end of the game, he had been president of the Interstate League for seven years and was now promotion director for all the minor leagues. Mack approached him in August. Ehlers took until December to accept the challenge.

In a comment that seemed to imply their father's lack of confidence in the abilities of Roy and Earle to carry on the business, Ehlers told Frank Yeutter of the *Evening Bulletin*, "Mr. Mack told me he can't go on forever and he didn't want the whole thing to go 'boom' when he decided to relax a little. He said money will be no object. He wants a strong organization with no thought of cost."

Ehlers conceded that the A's were eight to ten years behind everybody else. "We have to inaugurate a million dollar business and it isn't going to be child's play."

With the minor leagues expanded to fifty-two for 1947, there were plenty of clubs looking for major league partners. The Athletics dropped Toronto— "We don't need a AAA club," said Ehlers—and added outright ownership of Lincoln (A), Moline (C), and Red Springs (D) and working agreements with

358

Birmingham (AA), Vicksburg (B), Niagara Falls (C), Nyack (D), and Welch (D), bringing the total to thirteen. (The Yankees had twenty-five.) Facilities needed to be rebuilt, lights improved, staffs hired. The scouting roster expanded to six, with expenses not including salaries rising to $24,560, more than double the year before. Operating losses for the A's minor league clubs would exceed $150,000 in the first year.

Connie Mack had the bifurcated memory that comes with age. He might not recognize one of his players in an elevator, but events from the ancient past still registered. One day in West Palm Beach Mack was encircled by reporters when a man walked up and introduced himself as "Hank O'Donnell of the *Waterbury Republican*." Mack immediately broke off what he was saying and declared, "Waterbury? Why, I made my first five dollars playing baseball in Waterbury. One day our East Brookfield team played a game there. After our game there was a semipro game and we stayed to watch it. One team was short a catcher and they offered me five dollars to catch."

Mack's mental card catalog on players was still clear. In the spring of 1948 the A's were at Vero Beach to play the Dodgers. Most of the Brooklyn players had never met Connie Mack. A young pitcher, Rex Barney, had signed with Brooklyn in 1943. Someone introduced him to Mack, who said, "I know who you are. You're from Creighton Prep in Omaha. We scouted you too."

There was a small stand at the Dodgers' Vero Beach training center where players could get a fresh-squeezed glass of orange juice during the day. Mack recognized the man who ran it as a nineteenth-century player.

Mack was still a master teacher. In spring training or during a game, he might tell a young player quietly, patiently, "Young man, I saw you do this out there. I think you should be doing it this way." If they repeated a mistake, he'd remind them, gently. They never took it as criticism. "We knew he was doing it for our own good, to build up our confidence," said Joe Coleman. "We all looked up to him."

With no farm crop of his own to harvest, Connie Mack picked his way through the produce of others and gleaned some remarkable results.

Eddie Joost was a thirty-year-old journeyman shortstop who had more of a reputation for what he did with his mouth than his bat or glove.

"I was hard to get along with," Joost admitted. "If I thought somebody was giving me the business, I would sound off."

Born in San Francisco, Joost broke in with the hometown Missions at seventeen while dodging the truant officer as a high school dropout. It was 1933. His $150-a-month salary supported his unemployed parents and his three brothers.

In '35 and '36 Joost played two full seasons at third and short, learning from master third baseman Willie Kamm in '36. He was a .280s hitter with some doubles power. Cincinnati scout Bobby Wallace recommended him, and the Reds bought him. He reported in New York on September 9, 1936. On his first day he took some infield practice and a few swings in the batting cage. Reds manager Chuck Dressen watched him and took him aside.

"Kid," he said, "you look pretty good. You've got ability, but you'll never be a major league player."

"Why do you say that?"

"I can tell by your mannerisms, how you do things, you'll never progress enough. You'll be a utility player, that's all."

(Sixty years later Joost said, "Anybody who ever played for Dressen or knew him can hear him talking like that.")

Joost stewed about that all winter. When he arrived in Tampa for spring training in 1937, he was assigned to work out with the minor leaguers. The twenty-year-old hothead fumed for a few days, then confronted Dressen.

"Charlie, I don't understand this. You paid a lot of money for me, then you told me I'd never be a major league player, and now you won't even give me a chance to make the big club. I don't like it."

Joost had a hard time absorbing the lesson that managers wanted things done *their* way, not his.

During a practice game he booted a ball at third. Dressen, who had been a third baseman for the Reds in the 1920s, said to him, "You played that ball wrong. When I played third I knew how to make that play. Here's how you should have done it."

Joost watched him go through the motions of how a "good third baseman" would do it. The next time Dressen offered him some advice, Joost said, "Don't tell me how to play third. I looked up your record. You weren't so great."

That earned him a ticket to Syracuse.

In '38 Dressen had moved on, and Bill McKechnie headed the Reds. But Dressen's rap on Joost was in his file, and he spent the year in Kansas City. The next two years he stuck with the Reds but went nuts riding the bench wearing his "utility player" tag while the Reds won the pennant in '39 and '40. Reds third baseman Bill Werber remembered Joost, called "Dapper" by teammates, as "a griper, always bitching but never quitting. He was sour most of the 1940 season, thought he was better than others and should be playing, but he never quit on himself. When the lid of a water cooler fell on our regular second baseman Linus Frey's toe and broke it, Joost was ready and helped us materially in the World Series," which the Reds won.

That earned him a regular spot in the lineup for the next two years. He led the league in errors both years (including one on May 7, 1941, at New York when he tied a record of 19 total chances in a game), but it was a small bat and big mouth that wore out his welcome.

One day Joost was playing shortstop, and Frey was playing second. There was a runner on first. Joost signaled for Frey to cover second on a steal. The runner took off. The catcher threw. Nobody covered second, and the ball went into center field.

After the inning, McKechnie told Joost, "That was your fault."

"Wait a minute," said Joost. "Yeah, it was a mistake, but I'm pretty sure I gave Lonnie the sign to cover. Lonnie, do you remember me giving you the sign?"

Frey said, "I think so."

McKechnie didn't buy it. "If you gave Lonnie the sign, he'd have been there. You were wrong."

That's the way it went. "There was one confrontation after another," Joost said. "If I thought I was right, I said so. I told him what I thought. If he didn't like it, there was nothing more I could do."

The Reds sent him to Boston with Nate Andrews and $25,000 for All-Star shortstop Eddie Miller. It was the same story with Braves manager Casey Stengel. Joost split his time between second and third—neither his best position—and slumped to .185.

For several years Joost had worked for a meatpacker cutting meat and playing in a winter league. There was a manpower shortage in 1944. Joost sat out the season and worked as a driver for the meatpacker. That meant he did the loading. Lifting whole lambs and sides of beef built his strength. When his draft status was up for review, he passed the physical but was never called.

In 1945 Joost broke a toe early in the year, then in June suffered a broken left wrist when the Giants' Billy Jurges slid into him. He tried to come back a month later but couldn't swing a bat or catch a ball. On September 1 the Braves had a three-week road trip coming up. He met with general manager John Quinn, manager Del Bissonette, and coach Bob Coleman.

"I can't play," Joost told them. "You can save some money if you don't take me on the trip. Just send me home for the rest of the year."

Quinn agreed to let him go home and pay him through the end of the season. Or so he thought.

Ten days later Joost received a special delivery letter: for jumping the club, you are hereby suspended without pay.

Joost appealed to Commissioner Chandler, but nothing happened.

No longer welcome in Boston, Joost was traded to the Cardinals with $40,000 for outfielder Johnny Hopp. For the Cards, he was just minor league fodder; they assigned him to the Rochester Red Wings. Eddie being Eddie, he didn't go quietly. If he had to go back to the minors, he wanted it to be close to home in the PCL or he'd quit. But he needed the money, with his third son on the way. He held out until April, when Rochester general manager Joe Ziegler gave him "one of the best contracts in the minors."

Several factors came together that year. During the winter Joost had visited often with Ty Cobb, who lived not far from him in the Bay Area. Cobb was always full of advice on hitting, and Joost soaked it up: "Be absolutely relaxed at the plate. . . . Just meet the ball, don't pull it. . . . Study the pitchers."

Add to that his built-up muscles and an easygoing manager in Burleigh Grimes, who left him alone to play his game, and Joost thrived. Playing the entire season at shortstop alongside Danny Murtaugh, he led the Red Wings with a career-high 19 home runs (at a time when 23 led the National League) and 101 RBIs.

One day during the '46 season Connie Mack and Earle Brucker had been talking about how to improve their pitching. According to Stan Baumgartner, Brucker said, "Your pitchers are okay. What you need is a shortstop, somebody who will turn slow rollers through the infield into outs and double plays. When you get a shortstop, you'll have a real pitching staff."

Mack agreed. He wound up using six different shortstops and four second basemen that year. "Our infielders never had time even to rig up a set of signals," he said. He wanted a dependable veteran shortstop. When he discussed it with his scouts, Eddie Joost's name came up. The report on him was that he was a good fielder, strong arm, fair hitter. There were two raps against him: he had trouble getting along with management, and he was a drinker.

That didn't faze Mack. He had dealt with both types plenty of times. Besides, he knew that if some fans or a reporter saw a player having a beer in a bar and the next day the player made an error, he'd be tabbed unfairly as a drunkard. Maybe that was the story with Eddie Joost. Mack wanted to find out for himself.

He sent his top scout, Harry O'Donnell, to follow Joost for the last month of the '46 season. "Watch Joost on and off the field," he said. "Does he drink in public? Does he take anybody with him? Does it affect his play?"

Joost vehemently denied he was a drinker when O'Donnell put it to him:

I heard that story when I got to Rochester. It's a lie and I know who spread it. Here's how it began. One night in Boston pitcher Danny MacFayden and I had a beer in a nightclub and when we went outside we met a politician who was a friend of Danny's. They got to arguing about politics for about forty-five minutes and then he drove us home. The next day we were called in by John Quinn, who had a report that we were drunk and disorderly outside the club. It wasn't true but it stuck and gathered momentum. I wasn't playing so it got around that I drank too much.

O'Donnell turned in a thumbs-up report: nothing wrong with Joost. Has one beer now and then. Covers the ground. Great arm. A leader. Get him.

Mack sent Russ Derry, John Caulfield, and Vern Benson with $10,000 to Rochester for the big-mouth shortstop. The first time Mack spoke to him, Joost acknowledged his truculent reputation.

"Boy," said Mack, "I know you've had a lot of problems."

"Yes, Mr. Mack, and a lot of them have been created by myself. I'm a different person now."

"I know all about it. And I know you can play better than you showed in the National League. That's all I care about."

Grateful to Connie Mack for giving him another shot at the big leagues, Joost vowed to shed his clubhouse lawyer behavior, a promise he kept.

But he hadn't changed completely, not when it came to money. With Connie Mack in California for the winter, Earle and Roy were in charge of mailing out contracts. They sent Joost one for $7,500. He sent it back with a letter demanding $15,000. Whoa, said Earle. This is a case for Daddy.

Connie Mack called Joost and raised the offer to $9,000. Not enough, said an angry Joost. "If you give me a chance, I bet I can get $15,000 from some other club."

"Go ahead," said an equally angry Mack. "I'll give you twenty-four hours to make a deal for yourself."

Joost made a few calls, got no bites, gave up, and signed.

In West Palm Beach Joost quickly showed Mack he had made no mistake in acquiring him. "He makes plays for us no shortstop has made since Joe Boley," Mack said. "He hustles and he's quick. He's my shortstop."

Disappointed by George McQuinn's 1946 performance, Mack was in the market for a first baseman. At the major league draft meeting on November 1 the Athletics had the second pick, after the New York Giants. Mack had in mind Dick Adams on the Sacramento roster, who had driven in 155 runs at Wenatchee.

There was another first baseman considered by scouts the best in the Pacific Coast League.

Ferris Fain had played four full years in the PCL and was eligible for the draft for the first time. A resident of Oakland, Fain began working out with the San Francisco Seals when he was a high school lad of seventeen, getting into a few games at the end of 1939. The Seals paid him $200 a month, which came in handy; Fain's father, a jockey who had finished second in the 1912 Kentucky Derby, had died when Ferris was a child. In 1940 the left-hander batted .238 and had a lot to learn. He had the best teacher in the business in Seals manager Lefty O'Doul.

O'Doul (and Connie Mack) believed the best hitters used a short stride before they swung. Fain was the worst kind of overstrider. To cure him O'Doul started by putting a rope through the batting cage, tying one end to Fain's right ankle, and holding the other end. "He couldn't move more than a few inches," said O'Doul. "At first he felt he would fall or get killed by a pitch." O'Doul later tied the rope to Fain's belt loop. They kept at it until Fain was cured. The next year he batted .310.

But the lessons weren't over. In '42 Fain adopted the O'Doul swing, shortening up on the bat handle and sighting the pitch over his right elbow. But he wasn't comfortable doing it; a season-long slump kept him below .200 much of the year. O'Doul benched him in September.

Fain spent the next three years in the U.S. Army Air Forces, playing ball on service teams in California and the Pacific, picking up tips from teammates like Joe DiMaggio and Joe Gordon. He rejoined the Seals in '46 and sprayed line drives to all fields for a .301 mark, leading the league with 112 RBIs and 117 runs scored.

Fain's hustle and enthusiasm on the field had been noticed by Connie Mack back in 1942, when the A's had trained in California and played the

Seals. He had been impressed by the stocky 5-foot-10 first baseman's agility with the glove and remembered it.

Seals owner Paul Fagan considered the twenty-five-year-old Fain a $100,000 prize, worth maybe more after another year. He wasn't about to let Fain be drafted for $10,000. (The entire draft system was a canker in the mouths of minor league moguls.)

The Seals had had a working agreement with the New York Giants in 1945 and maintained close though informal ties with Giants owner Horace Stoneham. According to Ed Pollock of the *Evening Bulletin*, Fagan thought he had a gentlemen's agreement with Stoneham: since only one player could be drafted from a AAA team, the Giants would use their first pick to choose somebody else from the Seals, taking Fain out of the draft pool. In exchange, the Giants would have first right of refusal when the Seals were ready to sell Fain.

It happened that there dwelt on the San Diego roster a third baseman named Jack "Lucky" Lohrke. The "Lucky" referred to his narrowly having escaped injury or death three times, once when he survived a train wreck, once when he missed an army flight that crashed and burned, and most recently on June 24, 1946, when he was recalled by San Diego from the Spokane club. Notified to report to San Diego while Spokane was on the road, he got off the team bus at a rest stop in the Cascade Mountains minutes before the bus went off the road, killing nine of his teammates. Lohrke's .345 average at Spokane and his story attracted the interest of first-year Boston Braves owner Lou Perini, who was unfamiliar with the intricacies of baseball's administrative rules. On August 30 Perini obtained an option on Lohrke for $7,500 or a player with another $25,000 and a player or $7,500 more due if the Braves kept him for thirty days after the '47 season started—a potential total of $40,000.

Under the rules the option had to be exercised and the initial $7,500 paid before October 1, or the player would be eligible for the draft. The day before the draft meeting in Commissioner Happy Chandler's office in the Carew Tower in Cincinnati, the balloon went up when Chandler announced that Lohrke was eligible for the draft.

Lou Perini yelled, "No fair. We already own Lohrke. We sent the check and the papers."

Chandler said, "If you did, nobody ever told our office."

For a half hour Perini appealed to his fellow owners' sportsmanship, exhorting the commissioner to give him a break and the other clubs to lay off drafting Lohrke ahead of the Braves, who had the ninth pick. Happy Chandler was unmoved. So was Horace Stoneham, who recalled a similar situation back in 1925, when somebody in the Giants' office had neglected to recall a player they had optioned to Toledo and the Cubs had drafted him—an outfielder named Hack Wilson. Stoneham saw an opportunity to grab a real bargain and used his first pick to claim Lohrke for $10,000.

That left Ferris Fain hanging from a low branch, and Connie Mack plucked him. (Mack also drafted Dick Adams, who hit .202 filling in for Fain for one year.)

Like Eddie Joost, Fain expected a big league jump in salary. He dealt with Earle and finally squeezed out a $500 raise to $8,000, but Earle pleaded with him, "Don't tell Dad."

The Athletics' payroll reflected the postwar times, topping that of the 1929–1931 pennant winners for the first time, at $302,389.

At West Palm Beach, Connie Mack had the best-looking pitching staff he'd seen in years. At thirty-two, Jesse Flores was the oldest. The returning servicemen—Fowler, Marchildon, McCahan, Savage—had a year of derusting behind them. They were young—twenty-three to twenty-six—strong, and healthy. Marchildon had the most stuff, but his control was still shaky. He fooled around with a forkball, but it put a strain on his forearm and sabotaged his other pitches. Earle Brucker told him to forget it. Russ Christopher, the most experienced at twenty-nine, had completed only one of his thirteen starts last year. Given his heart condition and lack of stamina, even one complete game was a miracle. As soon as he threw a few pitches, his lips would turn purple. The other players were afraid he'd have a heart attack and die on the mound. Mack and Brucker decided that Christopher would be most effective working frequent short stints out of the bullpen.

The pitchers were aided by the groundskeeper's adjusting the mound to the specs of each starter, causing Bob Feller to complain that the Shibe Park mound was "built differently for every game."

Buddy Rosar, at thirty-three, had done plenty of crouching behind the plate over the years. His legs were more autumnal than springy. Mack told him to quit running to back up first base on every ground ball hit to the infield. "Half the time you won't do any good. A wild throw will probably wind up in right field." Rosar could no longer catch every day. To back him up Mack paid Washington $7,500 for Fermin "Mike" Guerra, a thirty-four-year-old light-hitting third-string wartime catcher with the Senators—hardly an impressive resume. But Guerra was a heady catcher, capable of managing a team in the Cuban winter league.

Nobody has ever gone through as much hell to fulfill a dream of being a big league pitcher as Lou Brissie. Since being wounded in Italy in December 1944, he had undergone twenty-three operations, which he could have avoided by having his left leg amputated below the knee.

Throughout 1945, as Brissie underwent operations in Europe, then back home in hospitals in Georgia and Alabama, Lou and Mr. Mack kept up a steady correspondence that created a lifelong bond between them. Even though Brissie had never signed a contract and the outlook for his ever pitching again seemed remote, Mack assured him that his college education would be taken care of and there would be a place on the A's roster whenever he was ready to pitch, however long it took. Mack's letters were sometimes addressed to "Cpl. Brissie" and other times to "Lefty." Whatever doubts he may have had during this time, Mack never stopped encouraging the 6-foot-4 southpaw from the day he received word from Brissie of his wounds and the first attempts to save his leg.

"Connie Mack never gave up on me," Lou Brissie said. "He gave me an opportunity when nobody else would have."

On January 16, 1945, Mack wrote:

"Pleased to receive your letters of December 23rd and 28th, however, regret exceedingly to hear that you met with such a serious injury and am glad that you are getting along so well. Am in hopes you will be ready, if necessary, to continue your baseball and basketball playing this summer. The doctors can do great things today as they have already proven by their work in helping some of our boys."

Two weeks later Mack wrote:

Was very much pleased to hear of your improvement and from what your doctor states, your recovery is going along very satisfactorily. Am always pleased to hear from you, more so now than ever, so please keep on writing as I am interested in your condition.

Can understand your longing to play baseball, just keep up this feeling as it will go a long way in helping your present condition. You can be assured of our looking after your schooling. Would want you to finish and receive your College diploma before joining our club, therefore, do not worry about the future as you will be well cared for after leaving the Army.

In April Brissie was back home in Ware Shoals, South Carolina, between hospital stays. Mack expressed the hope that he would be able to "join the club in another year or two at the most" and invited him to come to Shibe Park when the club was home for a long stay.

Brissie made the trip to Philadelphia in midseason, using crutches. Mack arranged a room for him with a family two blocks away where other players stayed. One day Lou put down the crutches and tried to throw to Earle Brucker. Mack cringed, expecting Lou to fall on every pitch.

"Poor boy," Mack thought. "He'll never be able to pitch."

But Mack kept up the encouragement. On September 5 he wrote, "Was pleased to hear from you and to know that you are doing a little limbering up. No doubt, you will be able to throw that ball by the batters in due time."

Two months later Brissie was in an Alabama hospital for another operation.

In the spring of 1946 Brissie requested some equipment and a warmup jacket, which Mack sent, and began working out with the nearby Spartanburg club.

On April 26, 1946, Mack congratulated Lou on the birth of a daughter, then wrote: "Note what you say at this time that you are not in the very best of condition, that is as far as your running is concerned. Our club will be at home for some time starting July 1st and am going to suggest that you come up here at that time. Sincerely hope you will be able to join our club at least in another year."

Between operations Brissie visited Mack in July and tried to throw. This time the effort led to an infection, and Brissie wound up in Valley Forge military hospital outside of Philadelphia for three weeks. None of the players who saw him gave him any chance of ever pitching again.

Nevertheless, Mack promised to send him a contract and did, in December, for $400 a month. Mack's last letter, a handwritten note from Hollywood on February 6, 1947, was to "Dear Leland": "Have been thinking of you and would like to know how your leg feels after the winter. Would like you to answer just as soon as you receive this short letter."

Brissie replied that he was ready to report for duty.

Not that his determination needed any booster shots, but in September

1946 Brissie's father, who had urged him to sign with Connie Mack, died at forty-four.

"I've got to make good," Brissie swore. He showed up at West Palm Beach with a cut-down shin guard padded with sponge rubber for his leg and declared himself ready to pitch.

Mack told him, "I can send you to Buffalo, where you'd have a good teacher and manager in Paul Richards, but I can't tell you how often you might pitch. Or I can send you to Savannah, which we own, so I can guarantee you'll pitch regularly. Which would you prefer?"

Savannah was an easy choice for Lou. "I can't run in the outfield," he said. "I need to pitch often to stay in condition." It was also close to home.

Early in spring training Ferris Fain was doing calisthenics. He came down awkwardly, his right foot slid in the sand, and he felt pain in his knee. The next day trainer Jim Tadley was working on it when something popped out of place. Tadley diagnosed it as a loose cartilage that would require surgery. Fain didn't want to hear about any surgery. He wanted to play. Doc Tadley maneuvered the cartilage into place, put a tight bandage on it, and bought a steel brace for him, and that's the way Fain played all season.

WCAU sports editor Bill Campbell had joined the A's game broadcast crew. In an interview in West Palm Beach he asked Mack about his two new infielders, Fain and Joost. Mack replied:

I actually believe that Finn is going to help our ball club wonderful from San Francisco. Now of course he got hurt and we haven't seen a great deal of him, but we did see enough of him to know that we are going to have a first baseman.

Eddie Joost at shortstop is a real ballplayer. I'm really surprised and well satisfied with Joost as our shortstop. Last year we didn't have a man regular for the position. Now this year we have a man who knows what it's all about.

Campbell said, "The pitching staff is encouraged by the way Joost comes up with the balls that in previous years would go through for hits."

"Oh yes, there's no doubt about that, and he will come up with them and he'll make plays that will surprise our fans too."

Connie Mack was inspired by the hustle and fire he saw in his boys. But he no longer made his usual rosy predictions. Figuring he'd rather surprise than disappoint, he cagily said, "We can promise our patrons good baseball and nothing more. We cannot promise to win."

Players who had witnessed Connie Mack's decline in the past few years had gotten used to it. But it came as a shock to some of the newcomers.

Eddie Joost's first encounter with Mack's wayward memory came early in the season:

> The clubhouse was long and narrow, maybe five feet wide down the middle of the lockers to the showers. It got hot in there. The equipment trunks were up against the wall at one end. One day between games of a doubleheader I'm sitting on one of those trunks in a sweatshirt and uniform pants with a sandwich and a glass of milk and Connie Mack came in. He said to me, "Boy, what are you doing there?" I said, "Mr. Mack, it's hot in there. I thought I'd sit out here and eat my sandwich." He said, "This is for the players. You better not be here when I get back." He didn't know who I was.

Ferris Fain was a rookie who considered himself a seasoned, knowledge-able ballplayer. He knew how to draw a walk but didn't go up to bat looking for one. It didn't take him long to conclude that "something was screwed up" with the Athletics. In a game early in the season he was at bat with two strikes on him. "I look up and I'm getting the take sign from the kindly old gentleman in the straw hat, and I've got to figure somebody is not with it."

This went on for a while, Fain getting take signs on all kinds of counts. It came to a head one day in New York:

> I had as good an eye as anybody in the game. [Fain struck out only 34 times and drew 95 walks for the year. His on-base percentage of .414 was then the fourth highest for a rookie in the twentieth century.] I watched that ball up to the plate. I was a cripple shooter. If I got a guy 2–0 or 3–1 I'm looking for a pitch and if I get it somebody's hopefully gonna suffer. But I'm getting take signs and when you take on those counts that ball looks like a basketball. I'm hitting fourth and with a man on second they want me to drive the guy in with a walk?

Frustrated, Fain twice chased pitches he would ordinarily let go by, striking out the second time.

Now I am pissed. I had done too much taking of good pitches. I went back to the dugout and threw the bat down on the ground and it quivered like an arrow. I'm pacing back and forth in the dugout and I stop in front of Connie Mack. I said, "Take, take, take. You can take that take sign of yours and stick it up your ass." I said that to Mr. Mack, the legend. Holy Christ. I thought I was on my way back to San Francisco.

After the game Earle Brucker told me, "You better go apologize." I said, "I'm not apologizing to anybody. That guy's taking the bat out of my hands and I meant just exactly what I said."

There was a lot of good night life in New York. That evening I'm partaking of it. When I get back to the hotel I'm starting to think, "These steaks up here are beautiful. Maybe I better reconsider."

I hadn't totally convinced myself when I went to the ballpark the next day. Connie Mack never got to the dugout until ten minutes before game time. I come down the runway and go to get a bat out of the bat rack for batting practice and who do I have to go by? Connie Mack. Two hours before game time and there he sits. I tried to sneak by so maybe he won't know me when I hear, "Boy—boy—boy." I'm ready to plead for leniency. I said, "Mr. Mack, yesterday I. . . ."

He interrupted. "Yes young man—uh—uh. I know young man—uh—uh. I just wanted to tell you that you've shown me that you play a decent game of baseball—uh—and from here on you don't have to look for any signs."

He was not so senile or so proud that he couldn't see what he was doing wrong and admit it, even to a rookie. He was a gracious, kindly, wonderful old man, but the key word there is *old*.

Some of Mack's foibles drew a laugh. One day he wanted a pinch runner. He had two rookies on the bench, Bill Hockenbury and Austin Knickerbocker. Mack called for "Hockenbocker." Both players jumped up and started onto the field. Al Simmons, coaching at third, stopped them and, figuring that the call was for the faster runner, Knickerbocker, sent Hockenbury back. Even Mr. Mack chuckled. It was the closest Bill Hockenbury ever got to a big league box score.

Connie Mack was no fool. He knew himself as well as he knew his players. If he had a blind spot, it was his refusal to concede that his decline might be harming the team. Some of the players thought so. Sometimes moves that should have been made weren't because, by the time somebody spoke up or a mix-up was straightened out, it was too late.

On August 24 in Detroit, the score was 4–4 in the last of the ninth. With 2 out, the Tigers had men on first and second. Vic Wertz, who had 3 hits, was up. Mack ordered Carl Scheib to walk him, moving the winning run to third base. Whether this against-the-book move was considered one of Mack's characteristic gambles or an unintentional lapse in judgment, nobody questioned it. Scheib followed orders. The next batter, Pat Mullin, hit a shot that Fain fielded back of first but had no play, and the winning run scored.

Never was Connie Mack's innate grace and kindness more evident than in the way he coped with the erosion of his mind. Had he been defensive, petty, or peevish; had he alibied, denied, or shifted the blame; had he kenneled the player who spoke up, his boys might have been more rebellious, although they had no owner to cry to—he was sitting in the dugout. But he wasn't, and they weren't. His sincere, soft-spoken admissions of his failings disarmed his players.

Al Simmons had assured Ferris Fain that it was okay to ignore the signs when he was at bat, but Fain figured that other players on the club were obeying them and that hurt the team. One day with a man on first and one out, Mack surprised Hank Majeski by ordering him to bunt. Majeski did as he was told and moved the runner down to second. The next batter popped up. Before he left the dugout, Majeski said, "That was lousy baseball, Mr. Mack."

"Yes, it was, Mr. Majestic," said Mack.

With it all, his boys marveled at how well he was doing for his age, mentally and physically. Major League game times were moving up; the A's now started on weekdays at two-thirty, Saturdays at two. (Night games began at nine.) Earlier starting times meant more exposure to the peak heat of the day. On sweltering afternoons the young men would crouch in the tunnel, sponging ammonia water over their heads, while Mack sat calmly in high-collared shirt and tie, broiling under the corrugated tin roof through the whole nine innings.

(A year later Mack made news by surrendering to the heat for the first time in living memory, taking off his stiff collar and tie between games of a doubleheader.)

Mack didn't know the hitting tendencies of the newer players in the league or the strengths and weaknesses of his young pitchers, so he didn't do much positioning of his outfielders any more. But his mental file on how to play the old-timers like Luke Appling (a right-handed batter who hit to right) remained sharp, to the amazement of his youngsters.

Connie Mack was still the boss, but he gave Al Simmons plenty of leeway. Later Simmons wrote, "In 1947 I started to call the plays from third base. However, [Mr. Mack] told me that whenever I was in doubt to put my left hand to my collar and he would help me. Occasionally, I had to walk to the dugout to ask him if he was going to use a pinch hitter since that would alter my strategy. He was the manager until his last day on the bench."

Simmons was glossing over his more active role. There were times when he ignored Mack's signs and made his own decisions. Mack knew what was going on. That was one aspect of his leadership style that remained intact: he had always valued individual initiative in his players. Simmons would come back to the bench and Mack might say, "You used better judgment than I did."

Poor umpiring—or what he considered poor umpiring—had always exasperated Mack. Unable to go out on the field to argue a call, he would send Earle out to summon the umpire or wave for the umpire to come over to him. When the ump came over, the conversation might go like this:

"You missed that one."

"I don't think so, Mr. Mack."

"Oh yes, you missed it."

After the ump left, said Pete Suder, "Mr. Mack would smile a little at us on the bench."

Other times he would confine his complaints to those around him. Eddie Joost remembered a time when home plate umpire Bill McGowan called a few strikes that Mack disagreed with. He said to Earle, "Run out and tell Mr. McGowan I wish he'd dust off the plate."

Mack always backed his players when they had a complaint about an umpire. In an April home game against Washington, the Senators' Joe Grace hit a ball to right that George Binks misplayed. Grace headed for second, where Eddie Joost was waiting for the throw. The ball beat the base runner by three feet, and Joost tagged him sliding in. The umpire, Charlie Berry, was standing behind the play. Joost came up from the tag and almost bumped into him.

"What did you call it?" Joost asked.

"Safe," said Berry.

"No way," yelled Joost. "He didn't even get to the base. You guys have to make that call right."

"That's enough out of you," said Berry.

"What do you mean?"

"Let me tell you something. You're new to this league. You keep this up, you'll never get a close call at second again."

"You mean that?"

"I sure do."

Joost said, "When I go in, I'm going to tell Mr. Mack exactly what you said, so if he says anything to you, you'll know I told him."

When the inning was over, Joost sat down next to Mack and related the conversation.

"He said that to you, boy?" asked Mack.

"Yes, he did."

When the game ended, Mack said to Joost, "Stay right here with me, boy."

The umpires had to go through the A's dugout to get to their dressing room. Mack stopped Berry: "I want to talk to you. My player says you said something to him on that play at second base."

Berry looked at Joost. "You told him what I said?"

"I told you I would."

Berry said, "Well, he came up out of the play and pushed me back. I guess I got a little out of hand. I did say what he told you and I apologize to both of you. It wasn't intentional."

Mack said, "I'm glad you said that, Charlie. If you didn't apologize, your job was gone."

In one of his early starts, rookie Joe Coleman didn't think he was getting a fair shake on the ball and strike calls from umpire Bill McGowan. He was kicking up a fuss on the mound. McGowan called time and walked out to him. It was evident to everybody in the park that the umpire was reading him the riot act.

After the inning Connie Mack asked him, "What was that all about?"

Coleman said, "He called me everything under the sun. I didn't answer back, didn't want to be thrown out of the game. But I don't think I'm getting a fair call on the pitches."

Mack sent Earle out to home plate with a message: "My father wants to talk to you."

McGowan came over, and he and Mack huddled in a corner of the dugout for a few minutes.

The next time McGowan worked an A's series, he sought out Coleman. "We had a long talk," Coleman said, "and I told him I didn't appreciate the language he'd used with me. He told me he'd had a bad night the night before. From that day on I never got a bad call from him."

When Phil Marchildon's 6–1 opening day win in New York (in which a rookie, Yogi Berra, played right field for the Yankees) was followed by the A's losing the next six, the press consensus sang the "same old A's" tune: The Old Man was content to ride along on the high tide of national prosperity, spending as little as possible to field nondescript, uninspiring teams until the time came when they would have to carry him off and his equally nondescript, uninspiring offspring, Earle, would take over.

The obituary was premature. The Athletics were no longer a go-through-the-motions bunch. Their spirit reminded Mack of his championship teams. One day in Detroit they came from behind three times, the last with home runs by Valo and Majeski in the seventh inning for a 9–8 win. Except for the easygoing Sam Chapman, still struggling to regain his prewar form, and the placid Barney McCosky, this was a fired-up mix of veterans and newcomers who enjoyed playing the game and let it show. Spare outfielder George Binks, of whom little was expected, reeled off a 17-game hitting streak. When he cooled off, somebody else got hot, then somebody else.

The Athletics reached .500 on June 5 and were in third place, only 5 games behind the Yankees, on June 23, the first time in fifteen years they had been that high that far into the season. "I never thought they had it in them," said Mack.

But in the end the A's were no match for the Yankees—nobody was that year, not after the New Yorkers began a 19-game winning streak on June 29.

In 1945 Lena Blackburne had made Nelson Fox into a second baseman at Lancaster. Fox hit .314 and was second in the MVP voting. In '46 he was drafted into the army for a year and returned in May 1947. The teenager hung around with the A's for two months, making occasional pinch-hitting and pinch-running appearances, and got to make one play in the field, but the inactivity made him restless. His roommate, Carl Scheib, had also returned from a year in the service, where he had learned the value of changing speeds and throwing to spots from the catcher on his army team, Bobby Bragan. Scheib was itching to pitch. The roomies decided to go up to Connie Mack's office and ask to be sent to the minor leagues, where they could play. Halfway up the stairs to the tower they chickened out and retreated. It finally dawned on somebody that Fox would benefit by playing every day, and back he went to Lancaster.

Mack had signed free agent Bill Dietrich, a local boy he had given up on eleven years ago. Dietrich pitched well, winning 5 games before arm problems sidelined him in June. That gave Carl Scheib a chance. He made his first start on June 11, shutting out Detroit, 4–0. Six days later he beat Detroit again, 5–2, and followed that with a 3–0 win over Chicago. Suddenly Scheib was the new "boy wonder." Then the Yankees came to town for a night game on June 27. Nine of the Yankees were headed for the All-Star Game. Before the biggest crowd of the year—38,529—the boy wonder was hit for three doubles, a triple, and a home run in the 7–1 loss. On July 6 New York teed off on him again for 12 hits in 3 innings.

Whenever great pitching coaches are discussed, nobody ever mentions Earle Brucker. But in the days before the title was even used, Brucker was the best. Drafted by Mack in 1936, he made his big league debut at the age of thirty-five. Five years later he became a coach, and he had become the closest to his pitchers of any coach in the league. He sat in the bullpen during the games and never stopped teaching, pointing out how pitchers were setting up hitters, quizzing them on what they would throw in certain situations. When the old catcher talked, they listened. Years later many pitchers testified that "I learned more from Earle Brucker than anybody else as long as I was in the game."

In those two Yankee games that Scheib pitched, Brucker saw some things he didn't like. He thought Scheib was tipping his pitches. He also thought the youngster was throwing with a stiff wrist and, with no windup, leveraging too little of the power his 205-pound build could generate. With Mack's concurrence, Brucker worked with Scheib to relax his wrist and bring his arm back more before throwing. The change affected his control, and he finished the year with a 4-6 record. Brucker assured him he would see the benefits of the changes next year.

When Mack's boys had stumbled at the start of the season and were written off, the hecklers got on them so fiercely that the players couldn't wait to get out of town. Former hero Sam Chapman became the number one target. As the team fought its way back, the tide turned among the fickle fans. They appreciated the fighting attitude of the new A's, something they hadn't seen in years, and the noisy infield chatter.

Once, after the A's had lost a few in a row, Mack called a meeting in the clubhouse. He didn't chew them out. Joe Coleman said, "He tried to instill in us that our abilities were better than we were showing. Not that he thought we weren't trying or hustling, because he knew we were. He cast it from the fans' viewpoint: 'The people of Philadelphia are supporting us and we should do better for them.'"

The A's returned home on June 13, and 28,628 turned out for a night game against Cleveland. Banners reading "Hammering Hank" and "Battering Barney" hung from the upper-deck railings. When rowdy fans rode the team, where before others would join in, now those sitting nearby would turn on the hecklers, shouting them down. All the players were popular. They chatted with the ushers and fans, who were now turning out early to watch batting and infield practice. Tom Shibe's widow, "Aunt Ida" Shibe, had been at every Athletics spring training but one since 1910 and seldom missed a home game. When reporters had interviewed her in recent years, she would tell them, "Don't you dare say I'm a grand old lady. I'm not old. I'm very young in spirit."

Over the years Ida Shibe had had many favorite players, but Eddie Joost became her all-time favorite, not only for his spirited play, but also, she said, because "He's always just so nice to me and to everybody that I call him my boy friend."

Hank Majeski became the favorite of Ruth Cunningham's family and was a frequent dinner guest at her home. Elmer Valo was cheered as he ran over anybody and anything that got in his way of a base or a fly ball. "But," he said, "I didn't crash into walls all the time, just when it meant something in the game."

Connie Mack still saw Pete Suder as another Jimmie Dykes, capable of filling in anywhere in the infield without weakening the team. "I'd like to have an infield that you can't break into," Mack had told him when he returned in 1946. "If I have a third baseman, second baseman, and shortstop who can beat you out, I'll have an infield I don't have to worry about." Sude had played every infield position and two games in the outfield in '46.

Mack wanted a solid-hitting second baseman with a good glove to complete his infield. Gene Handley was a disappointment. The Yankees were shopping Joe Gordon, who had missed forty games due to injuries and slumped to .210, but was still the best defensive second baseman in the league. Mack offered a bundle of cash. The Yankees needed a pitcher more than they needed money.

"Give us Marchildon for Gordon," said George Weiss

"No way," said Mack.

So Gordon went to Cleveland for Allie Reynolds.

Handley injured his knee in late May and was out for two months, and Suder stepped in and became the other half of the best 4–6 duo in the league. When Handley came back, Majeski was beaned and missed ten days, and Handley played third. He never got back to second base.

Pete Suder and Eddie Joost were like Eddie Collins and Jack Barry: each made the other better. They anticipated where a ball might be hit by watching the catcher. "If you see where the catcher is setting up," Suder said, "you can tell where a guy's likely to hit the ball. Your instincts pull you that way and give you a little better start toward the ball."

With his quick read off the bat Suder assisted Elmer Valo in getting a jump on bloop hits to right field, yelling, "In-in-in" as soon as contact was made.

Suder perfected the phantom tag on double plays. He had the maneuver down to a science, crossing the bag and coming off it a split-second before the throw from Joost or Majeski reached him. "I was the biggest cheat you ever saw," Suder said. "I got to the ball quicker that way and got it away quicker." Another benefit was that he got out of the way of the base runner sliding into the bag.

The entire infield had rifle arms, firing bullets right at the chest—no rainbows. Unlike most infielders, Joost held the ball with his whole hand wrapped around it, but his throws were always right on the mark. And they loved what they were doing. Once in a while, when a ground ball was hit to third with nobody on base, Majeski would throw to Suder who came across second and threw to first, making a pseudo double play, and they'd laugh about it. But opposing managers didn't always laugh. "One time Lou Boudreau came out of the dugout arguing with the umpire that I had missed second base on the pivot," Suder said. "*With nobody on first*. We weren't making a joke of the game. Majeski was just used to throwing to me first."

The A's went every year to the maximum-security Grateford Penitentiary to play the prison team. When they pulled the nobody-on-first double play there, Suder said, "The guy who hit the ball let us know he didn't like it, so we decided never to do it there again."

While the other infielders were chirpers, Majeski joked around in the clubhouse but was serious on the field. In conferences on the mound, he was the most encouraging and upbeat.

A fierce, sometimes belligerent competitor and quick tempered on or off the field, Ferris Fain had no use for what he called "milk shake drinkers," who didn't fight for every hit, every game, every cause. If a base runner ran over his second baseman, Fain would be down there flinging fists at the enemy. He sat on the top step of the dugout during a game, ready to lead the charge if the occasion arose. He would fight at the drop of a hat or even if the hat didn't drop. He fought with opponents, teammates, strangers in bars. It seemed as if everybody who knew him had a favorite Fain fight story. In some of them, the Burrhead was on the losing end.

One night during a poker game Fain popped off about something, and one of his drinking buddies, Allie Clark, reached across the cards and bopped him on the nose.

Sam Chapman roomed with Fain on the road. "We were walking back from a movie in Detroit one night and went through a park and there was a guy on a stage making a speech beating down the United States. I looked around and Ferris was missing. Then I saw him up on the stage pounding this guy. The cops came and took Ferris away. I had to go down and get him out of jail."

In 1951 the A's had an obscure relief pitcher named Johnny Kucab. One night on the train Fain was looking for him with fire in his eye. The players hid the 6-foot-2 Kucab and watched with amusement as Fain stormed around. Fain turned on Carl Scheib. "What's so funny?"

"Not a damned thing," said Scheib.

Fain never found Kucab that night.

On the night of September 5, 1947, at Shibe Park against Boston, Fain walked to lead off the seventh. Buddy Rosar hit a long double. Fain rounded third before the ball was picked up. As he did so, third baseman Eddie Pellagrini backed into him and sent his cap flying. Fain scored standing up, then turned and raced back down the third base line—to retrieve his cap, thought the onlookers. Instead he headed for Pellagrini, pushed him, and started swinging. Fists flew in usual baseball-fight futility before Al Simmons and the umpires broke it up. There was nothing personal in it, Fain said afterward. He just thought Pellagrini tried to trip him, that's all. And that was enough flint to light his fuse. Fain was ejected and suspended indefinitely, a penalty that turned into three days. Pellagrini was not ejected, prompting a tantrum by Connie Mack, who argued—accurately but extraneously—that the third baseman would have been guilty of interference if Fain hadn't scored since he did not have the ball at the time of the contact.

To Ferris Fain everything hit on the first base side of the mound belonged to him. If a slow roller was hit down the line and the pitcher came over to field it, the pitcher might take a thump to his back and go sprawling while Fain picked up the ball and threw to Suder covering first. Then Fain would help the pitcher up while reminding him, "I'll take care of these. I've handled a lot more of them than you have."

Fain kept the rest of the infield alert because he sometimes threw to a base without looking. He loved nothing more than charging in for a sacrifice bunt, sometimes cutting in front of the pitcher, and throwing to second or third to catch the lead runner. Most of the time. Whenever they played the Red Sox and left-handed swinger Ted Williams was up with a man on first and nobody out, Pete Suder would kid Fain. The banter went something like this:

"Go on in and charge that bunt. I'll back you up."

"You want it, you go in and get it."

"Don't worry, he's not going to swing."

"Williams never bunted against us," Suder said. "With the shift on against him, he would've hit .500 if he did."

Sometimes Fain's haste and enthusiasm trumped his foot-planting for balance, and he bounced a throw off the mound or threw a souvenir into the seats. That never stopped him from trying it again at the next opportunity. It's one reason he led AL first basemen in assists four times and in errors five times, sometimes both in the same year.

Sam Chapman remembered an incident that couldn't be verified but illustrates the team's hold-your-breath attitude whenever Fain embarked on his favorite fielding adventure. In Shibe Park the A's dugout was on the third base side. Everybody on the bench was alert to the possible need to duck if there was a man on second and a bunt was expected. One day Chapman told broadcaster Chuck Thompson, "When a base runner was heading for third and Fain picked up the ball, Mr. Mack hollered, 'Look out, he's got it again.'"

Connie Mack overlooked the times the play didn't work. He didn't want to squelch Fain's aggressiveness.

Connie Mack had achieved his prized team harmony. His boys were having fun. Mike Guerra was as much a prankster as Joost and Suder, who both made Phil Rizzuto's life miserable when they played the Yankees, putting rubber snakes and frogs in his glove where it lay on the outfield grass when the Yanks were at bat. Russ Christopher was the clubhouse comedian. There was no dissension. The younger pitchers tended to hang out together, and groups of four or five went to shows together and had their regular card games, but it wasn't what you'd call cliques.

The routine morning meetings on the road were a thing of the past. Mack made out the lineup and named the starting pitcher and the long and short relievers for the day. Earle Brucker met with the pitchers before the game. Occasionally Mack called a clubhouse meeting, which few players took seriously. He might urge them to play harder for the sake of the fans who were so supportive of them. He talked about drinking, as he had been doing for fifty years, and about their after-hours conduct. Some of the meetings became indelible memories for the players.

One took place at the Del Prado Hotel in Chicago. It may have been triggered by the presence of a few women waiting for players on the train that left Philadelphia for a western trip or the conduct of two players who, the story went, had seen a silhouette of a woman undressing in a hotel room they could see from theirs and had called the room to invite her to a party. She turned out to be an elderly widow who reported them to Mr. Mack.

Or both.

Mack was furious. To some of the younger players, it seemed surreal to see this tall, thin, well-dressed, dignified old man shaking a long bony finger at them, his false teeth clicking, stammering, "G-g-goddammit. There was a time when I wasn't married for twenty years, and in that whole time I never had anything to do with a woman. But you fellows, you fellows— the train isn't even out of the depot and you're off looking for something."

He went from one to another, upbraiding them for chasing women and drinking and staying out late on the road.

Recalling the scene, Ferris Fain said, "Mr. Mack was right in everything he said." Fain should know. He was primarily a beer drinker, but he liked his "cc" and "vo."

"I drank too much when I was playing," he admitted. "You're on that field three or four hours a day, and it's where's the girls and booze the rest of the time. There was no drug use but tons of drinking. It didn't affect most players on the field, though. They were young and got plenty of sleep. By the time it took a toll they were out of the game. Maybe dead. . . . We had no bed checks. Just don't get caught in the elevator or the lobby late at night."

In August the A's were still tied with Detroit for third. Connie Mack put his hopes of finishing higher squarely on Phil Marchildon. "Our pitching is good and we're scoring runs," Mack said. "Our only weakness is we're slow on the bases. Marchildon is the key to our having a great chance to win."

Marchildon did his part, going 13-5 after a 6-4 start, despite recurrent bouts of intestinal flu. Eleven of his 19 wins were over first-division finishers. He must have thrown an enormous number of pitches—nobody was counting—in his 276⅔ innings; he walked a league-leading 141 and struck out 128.

Playing every day in August wilted the A's infield. Too many were playing sick or hurt. Joost had a fever, Suder a sprained ankle, Binks and Guerra broken fingers, McCosky a sore elbow, Fain wobbly knees. Marchildon pitched with boils under his left arm, and McCahan was weakened by a bout of grippe. Russ Christopher had a heavy cold. But they all played, sick or hurt. For reinforcement Mack bought veteran catcher Herman Franks from St. Paul (where he also managed the team) for $7,500. Elmer Valo was beaned on August 9 in Washington and sidelined for three weeks, prompting the A's to order metal pads to insert into their caps when batting. When George Binks was filling in at first or the outfield, the rest of the bench was pretty barren. The A's lost 7 in a row in the last week of August and fell to fifth.

About that time Connie Mack ran into a problem that took him back nearly twenty years, to the days of Lefty Grove. Mack, an early proponent of the designated hitter, didn't want his pitchers running the bases, especially on blazing hot days. He believed it took so much out of them, they wilted when they went back to the mound. "Strike out," he used to tell Grove. "Don't take the bat off your shoulder." Most of his current pitchers weren't any great shakes as hitters, although Carl Scheib was a wannabe outfielder who would be used as a pinch hitter in future years. But they weren't automatic outs either. In August the pitchers suddenly started hitting and scoring runs. Invariably they were kayoed in the next inning.

Mack and Brucker decided the remedy was more running in the outfield on days they didn't start.

Elmer Valo returned to action on September 3 in Washington and made a leaping catch against the fence to save a no-hitter for Bill McCahan. Only a wild throw by Fain on a ground ball back of first in the second inning marred McCahan's otherwise perfect game. (When the A's had been forced to sell their interest in the Wilmington club to the Phillies, McCahan had been the only player on the Blue Rocks roster who didn't go with the franchise.)

Mickey Rutner was a twenty-eight-year-old third baseman bought on a look from Birmingham in September. He had been at Wilmington with McCahan. He arrived just after the no-hitter.

"Bill thought it would be a good time to go up to the office and ask Mr. Mack for a raise," Rutner told interviewer Lou Jacobson. "When he came back to the clubhouse he said Mr. Mack had started shaking and he didn't want to be responsible for him dropping dead so he ran out of the office. Everybody laughed. One of the veterans said, 'That's his favorite trick.'"

True story or not, Mack did give McCahan a $1,000 bonus and a $3,000 raise to $8,000 for the following year. And Mack's hands had begun to shake, not just when money was being discussed.

The A's might have had two no-hitters in a week. On August 26 at Cleveland Phil Marchildon set down the first 23 batters. The A's led, 1–0, in the eighth inning, when umpire Bill McKinley called a 3–2 pitch ball 4 on Ken Keltner. Marchildon and catcher Buddy Rosar beefed so much about the call that they were fined $25 each, but McKinley was too wise to eject a pitcher with a no-hitter going. The Indians tied it in the ninth with their first 2 hits; Marchildon's double won it in the twelfth, a 2–1 5-hitter. Connie Mack didn't swear much in the dugout, but he tolerated it in his players. He understood the frustrations of the game. Rutner started out hot with 2 hits in each of his first three games. Then he tailed off. In a late-September game against Washington, he hit a line drive over first that looked good for extra bases. Mickey Vernon leaped up and caught it. Rutner walked back to the bench cussing and sat down next to Mr. Mack. When another batter hit one a few inches higher over Vernon's glove, Rutner muttered, "Catch that one you son of a bitch."

"Mr. Mack looked at me and smiled," he said. "He knew how I felt."

Mack returned Rutner to Birmingham the next spring. "They want a lot of money for you," he told the disappointed youngster, "more than I paid for my entire infield [which was $30,000]."

Connie Mack had started his baseball career in Meriden, Connecticut, in 1884. When he had left Meriden at the end of the season, the fans had given the popular slim catcher a gold watch. He vowed to return one day but had never gone back. The International Silver Company, makers of Rogers 1847 silverware, planned a centennial celebration marking one hundred years since its founding of the silverplate industry in Meriden, with a new Remembrance pattern. Somebody at the company was aware of Connie Mack's story and suggested inviting him for the occasion. The company turned to its advertising agency, Young & Rubicam, where the account executive was Bob Paul, former sports editor of the *Philadelphia Daily News*.

Paul went to Mack's office one Saturday morning in June and described the company's proposal. The conversation revealed some of the internal tug-of-war going on within the Athletics' family management.

"They sponsor a semipro team, the Insilcos," Paul said, "and they want you to bring the team and play a game at their Insilco Field."

Mack checked his schedule. "We're in Washington on June 30 and then Boston July 2. We could stop on the way and play July 1."

"That would work," said Paul. Knowing that Connie Mack often took his team to small towns to raise money for local causes, taking nothing but minor expenses, he was surprised when Mack said, "How much will they give us? I would do it for nothing, but my sons Roy and Earle insist we get some money every time we play an exhibition game. I don't want to fight my sons. I'll have to get something."

"Well," said Paul, "they only have fifteen hundred bleacher seats, and they don't usually charge any admission. But maybe they would for this game. If they charge a dollar, they could take in $1,500. Do you want it all? I can't make any deal without consulting with the company."

Paul suggested to Insilco sales manager John Shaw that the company offer $1,500 and not go over $3,000. Mack and Shaw agreed on $1,800. Any additional proceeds would go to the Meriden Boys' Club building fund.

When the event was announced, the demand for seats was so great the company rented ten thousand bleacher seats. The event raised over $5,000 for the Boys' Club.

The A's left Washington in the morning and arrived at 4:45 that afternoon. Thousands mobbed the railroad station and lined the parade route to where a turkey dinner for three hundred was held before the game. Connie Mack sat atop the back of the seat in an open car, clasping his hands over his head like a prize fight winner, enjoying every minute of it. From his arrival, he was the center of an eddy of activity. He barely ate anything at the dinner. His ice cream melted while he fielded introductions, photographers' requests, autograph seekers, and newsreel and radio interviews. At the ballpark International Silver presented Mack with a one-hundred-piece set of the new Remembrance pattern. The governor and mayor were there.

Mack chatted with Pat Carter, who had played against him in 1883 in North Brookfield. Batboy Daniel Murray and mascot Charles McGrath from the 1884 Meriden team were there. Local resident Ed Walsh and Meriden-born Jack Barry visited with Mack in the dugout while Mack's friend Joe Budwitz, the school janitor, looked on raptly. Of Walsh, Mack said, "I saw that great pitcher many times as an opponent and I saw him pitch in many games that I thought I would rather he didn't pitch."

The Mutual network broadcast the proceedings and arranged for Commissioner Happy Chandler to be present. Renowned radio commentator Lowell Thomas emceed the events and did his two nightly broadcasts from the site. At nine o'clock the game was stopped while Bill Stern interviewed Mack at home plate on his network program. The popular show "We the People" did a five-minute segment.

To the packed bleachers Mack said,

I've been around a long time and it's sixty-three years since Meriden. Now I'm eighty-four years old. Some people think I've been around too long. I hope to stay with them a little time to come.

I am not going to retire until I feel I am no longer a help to the team. That goes whether I win a pennant or not. Hank Greenberg, now with Pittsburgh, had made no offer for the team as has been rumored. If he did my answer would be the same as it would be to anyone else. The Philadelphia Athletics are not for sale. There is not enough money to buy my team.

He then announced that he would turn the team over to his sons when he retired and hoped it would remain in the Mack family.

The game was shortened to 5½ innings when a thunderstorm drenched the crowd.

Before the game Bob Paul had mentioned to Earle Mack that the company team had a seventeen-year-old outfielder from nearby Waterbury who wanted to be a ballplayer. "Look him over," Paul said. A few days later Paul asked Earle what he thought of the youngster, who had made two hits and one error.

"He'll never go anywhere. He doesn't have it," was Earle's assessment of Jimmy Piersall.

The management at International Silver was thrilled with the success of the day, as was Connie Mack, who wrote to Bob Paul: "You can be assured that I will never forget my visit to Meriden on July 1st and just want you to know that I greatly appreciate your cooperation in making the day such a memorable one for me."

Mack returned to Meriden four more times, twice with his team, to help raise money for little league and intermediate league fields.

Lou Brissie's remarkable season at Savannah was the inspirational story of the year. He fulfilled his seemingly impossible dream in spectacular style: 23-5, a 1.91 ERA, and a league-leading 289 strikeouts in 254 innings, including a record-tying 17 in a May 29 game against Macon.

Called up by the A's, Brissie made his major league debut starting the last game of the season in New York on Sunday, September 28. He was completely overshadowed by an old-timers' game that included several of Mack's former stars. The rookie was overwhelmed, surrounded by players from the past that he had read about in his youth: Ty Cobb, Tris Speaker, Lefty Grove, Home Run Baker, and a dozen more. Dizzy Dean came into the dugout and sat down beside him. "How ya doin?" said Diz. The awed Lou could mutter only a word or two in response. He was warming up along the third base line when the emcee introduced Babe Ruth. The ailing Babe, just out of the hospital, came out of a box seat hunched over, wrapped in an overcoat, and walked slowly by the nervous rookie. His voice reduced to a hoarse whisper, all the Babe could do was wave to the cheering crowd and shuffle back to his seat.

Brissie went 7 innings, gave up a double to Joe DiMaggio, a triple to Tommy Henrich, and a home run to Johnny Lindell; he walked 5, threw 2 wild pitches, and lost, 5–3. He demonstrated that his bum leg was no handicap in the field, handling 1 putout and 1 assist.

The Athletics finished at 78-76—a gain of 29 games over the year before—in fifth place, only 2 games out of the first division. They were no longer pushovers or the butt of jokes. For a change the pitching was not a problem. Mack had used eighteen pitchers in 1946; he used only nine in '47 until Lou Brissie pitched the last game. Last year forty-one players had made it into the lineup; this year only thirty-one did, including three called up in the last week.

The staff ERA was the third lowest in the league. Everybody started and relieved except Marchildon, who was 19-9 despite leading the league with 141 walks in 277 innings. McCahan won 10 and Fowler 12, with a 2.81 ERA. Jesse Flores pitched better than his 4-13 record indicated. Bob Savage and Russ

Christopher each worked in 44 games, fourth most in the league, and were probably warming up in another 30. Christopher's 10-7 record, all in relief, is indicative of the number of times the A's came from behind in late innings. His longest outing was 6 innings. In mid-July he pitched in three games in a row. Considering his physical condition, his record was remarkable.

(The Athletics still used hand signals to bring in a reliever: picking flowers for Dick Fowler, shoveling coal for Coleman, wild gesticulations for Savage, tall man for Christopher, banging on the wall for Scheib.)

Ferris Fain's heavy brace and bum knee affected his pivot when he swung and cost him maybe a dozen hits on ground balls he might have beaten out. A sudden turn or twist in the field made him wince. The only rest he had came when an unwelcome bruised thumb sidelined him for two weeks. With it all he still batted .291.

When the season ended Fain went on a thirty-day barnstorming tour with Bob Feller's All-Stars, then underwent two operations in which Dr. Gopadze removed some calcified bone chips from his knee.

Hank Majeski struggled at the plate until Earle Brucker, possibly at Connie Mack's direction, advised Majeski to get rid of all his unnecessary bat-wagging before the pitch was delivered and use his powerful wrists to pull the ball. Majeski became a .280 hitter with occasional power. He finished the year with the fewest errors—5—of any third baseman and was second to Ken Keltner's 29 double plays in 16 fewer games.

Eddie Joost's eyes had begun to bother him in Rochester, but he was concerned that scouts would pass him up if he wore glasses. He started the '47 season without them. His astigmatism got worse, especially under the lights. In a night game in Cleveland on July 10 Bob Feller fanned him three times in the first eight innings. As the ninth inning started, the A's were losing, 2–1. Mack said to him, "Boy, come here. How many times did you strike out so far?" Joost said, "Three." Mack said, "I'm going to put in a pinch hitter for you. I don't want you to break the record." Before Joost batted, the Indians replaced Feller with Ed Klieman. Mack let Joost bat. He struck out again.

Joost's batting average fell below .200 and hit bottom at .193 on August 15. Despite his struggles at the plate, Connie Mack recognized his value to the team. On August 5 Mack gave him a revised contract with a $3,000 raise to $12,000. That might have given Joost the confidence to confess to Mr. Mack, "I think I need glasses."

"So get them," was all Mack said.

It was too late to do much for his batting average, but in 31 night games so far, Joost had struck out 32 times. In the next 14 night games he struck out 8 times.

It took time for him to adjust to the glasses. The wire frames impeded his picking up the pitch, so he had to open his stance more. Somewhere along the line he had a chance to ask Ted Williams for advice. Williams told him, "You get out in front too much. Put your weight on your back foot. That way you won't stride too soon or overstride."

There is controversy over whether there is such a thing as a clutch hitter. Validly or not, observers at the time believed that Joost deserved the reputation. He batted only .206, but he drove in 51 runs in addition to his 13 home runs, both tops among leadoff batters in the league. (Lou Boudreau, batting fourth for Cleveland, hit a hundred points higher but had only 3 more RBIs.) Joost drew 114 walks, but he also struck out a league-leading 110 times.

To at least two baseball writers, leadership in lifting a team from last place to only 2 games out of the first division had value not reflected in the individual stats: Joost received two first-place votes in the MVP balloting, won by Joe DiMaggio with a one-point edge over Ted Williams, whose Red Sox finished third after winning in '46. (Three of the twenty-four voters failed to give DiMaggio even one point; one omitted Williams from his ballot. Joost was tied with Barney McCosky for eleventh, behind Phil Marchildon, who was ninth.)

It was a banner year for baseball at the gate. For the first time the A's home and road admissions topped $1 million. Home attendance of 911,566 beat the team record set in 1925. For a change, the A's didn't have to depend on the rent from the Phillies and Eagles; net income exceeded $200,000. (That included $5,000 from the N. W. Ayer advertising agency for the sale of the club's first television rights, a rich price considering there were only fourteen thousand TV sets in the entire country.)

Connie Mack was in a position to say, "Nobody is for sale." And he could be a buyer. When the broke Browns unloaded several of their top players, Mack said he offered a bundle of cash and a player for heavy-hitting shortstop Vern Stephens, who went to the Red Sox instead. What that would have meant for Eddie Joost's future is unclear.

The pace had worn on Mack more than in the past. Every team was playing night games now; the A's played twenty of them at Shibe Park. (Detroit,

New York, and Boston still refused to play more than two a year at any other park.) At home Mack would go home in the afternoon and take a long nap instead of his brief snooze in the office before day games. On those occasions Katherine usually went back to Shibe Park with him. Their social life had diminished primarily because, of the couples he and Katherine had been friendly with, the husband or wife or both had died. Going to movies and Sunday dinners at Ruth's house in the off-season was about it.

At the December meetings, the Pacific Coast League's bid for major league status was turned down, as was a proposal to add two teams to each major league, a move the National favored but the American turned down, 5–2, the A's being one of the five. Mack believed that eight teams was the right number for a league to contain and that expanding to the west coast would not be profitable.

At the writers' and broadcasters' birthday luncheon for him, Mack's vision of the future was clearer. He said that television would be as big a boon for baseball as radio had been; all records, including Babe Ruth's home run marks, would be broken by a new generation of great hitters; and there would be no third major league.

The Philadelphia Reciprocity Club threw an elegant eighty-fifth birthday party for Mack at the Union League. Connie McCambridge and his wife, Evelyn, were invited. The men wore black suits or tuxes, but Mack had on a gray suit with a bright tie. Mack was working the room when he came to his grandson's table.

"Dad, you sure look great," said McCambridge.

"Connie," said Mack, "I really wanted to wear my black suit, but your Aunt Katherine, you know, she wanted me to wear this one, and whatever you do, son, please the ladies."

By now Mack had become something of a rambler as a public speaker. In a long, stirring speech he had this to say about his future:

And I want in conclusion to say that I—uh—appreciate very much these gentlemen coming from, all the way from New York as well as our local players, our local broadcasters, who are here tonight and it's very nice and very kind of them to come here and I appreciate it and I appreciate above all the Reciprocity Club giving this dinner to me tonight. I realize that I have been around a long time and as the judge

[Harry McDevitt] said—uh—that he—uh—that he hoped that I would stay for the next fifteen years which will make it the hundredth year and—uh—if I do that I'd be well satisfied.

Had the Athletics improved so much in 1947 despite Connie Mack's managing—not because of it? Who knows how many people believed that? Few of them said it. Phil Marchildon was one who publicly complained that Mack had cost the A's twenty games.

Mack deserved the credit for the acquisitions of Joost and Fain and Majeski and for raising another crop of sturdy young pitchers. But few of the out-of-town writers were aware of the extent of the coaches' and players' gently nudging things in the right direction during the games or of the local writers' covering it up. When manager of the year speculation had begun in August, with the league-leading Dodgers' and Yankees' skippers the obvious choices, St. Louis writer Robert L. Burnes had suggested the honors should go to the eighty-four-year-old Mack: "We believe that Mack's ability to put an almost sure-shot last-place club in the first division is more of an achievement than moving a potentially 'top four' team into first place."

That winter in a lengthy interview with Ed Fitzgerald for *Sport* magazine, Mack said, "When the time comes when my players get to telling me how the game should be played, then I'll know I'm through."

That time had come. His watch had stopped.

Since Connie Jr's return from the army, the strained relations among the brothers had shredded further. Reports of the schism seeped into the newspapers, forcing Connie Mack to address them. Dan Daniel reported this comment by Mack in St. Petersburg in February 1948:

Philadelphia newspapers have been playing up rumors of dissension in the Mack family. They have gone so far as to say that the situation has become so serious that the control of the Athletics will have to be sold.

It is very important that you follow me closely. As to dissension, Connie Jr. and Roy had a tiff recently. Connie has charge of the concessions. They did not see eye to eye about certain things.

Whatever the tiff was, it no longer exists. There now is harmony among the Macks.

Mr. Mack was papering over the cracks. His innate optimism had evolved into an "everything will be all right" blindfold. It was more than a tiff, and it wasn't new, and there was no harmony. Roy was twenty-four years older than young Connie, had always considered him a pesky little brother, and had treated him that way ever since he had entered the family business in 1934. Roy and Earle had now assumed more of the contract dealings with players, but dissatisfied players had little use for them and took their cases to young Connie, a situation that irritated Roy. Connie had young ideas; Roy had old ones; Earle had none. Whatever Connie proposed, Roy's reaction was like that of Groucho Marx in *Horsefeathers*: "Whatever it is, I'm against it." Following the peaceful debuts of Jackie Robinson and Larry Doby, Connie wanted to sign Negro Leagues players; the others would have none of it. With the postwar boom in attendance, he wanted to add a grandstand in right field. Roy didn't want to spend the money. The situation was corroding the organization.

Of greater importance, Connie Jr. knew his father's leadership ability—if not his health—was declining. Some kind of preparation for the future was imperative. As things stood, his father's death or incapacity would result in chaos. No estate planning had been done since Mack had revoked a trust seventeen years ago. Two years had passed since Mr. Mack had assured his wife that things would be straightened out.

The way he put it, Connie Jr. was approached in December 1947 by Olympic sculling champion and wealthy construction contractor Jack Kelly, a longtime friend of the family, with an interest in investing in the Athletics and having his son take a role in the business. The two men negotiated a deal in which Kelly would buy the 628 shares held by Connie Mack, Roy, and Earle, for $2,500 a share, a total of $1.57 million. (The stock had been valued at $300 a share in 1938.)

As part of the agreement, Connie Mack would remain as president "at a high salary" for the duration of his life (no mention of his remaining as manager); Roy would receive a salary of $10,000 for life. There was no mention of Earle's remaining on the payroll.

Equally important to Connie Jr., Kelly had the resources to pour more capital into building a winner They may have had an eye on the Carpenters, whose Phillies had drawn almost as well as the A's with a seventh place team in '47 and who had the money to spend whatever it took to win the competition for the city's baseball dollars.

The deal would provide financial security for Connie's parents and sisters, as well as the ball club, and cure the chronic discord that infected the management of the business.

The offer was rejected by Connie Mack, Roy, and Earle, perhaps in part because Kelly made it known that he wanted his son, Jack Jr., to join the front office and learn the business. Roy and Earle then made a counterproposal to buy out Connie, which he rejected, believing that it would be disastrous if the business fell into Roy's control.

Describing the negotiations at a subsequent board meeting, where he put Kelly's offer on the record, Connie Jr. said, "I felt that my position in the family demanded that I stay and look out for the interests of my mother and sisters."

21 | "THEY SHOULDA WON IT"

It almost happened.

Seventeen years after he'd last won a pennant, nine years since he'd been so sick he tried to die, the eighty-five-year-old Connie Mack came *this close* to pulling off a miracle.

"They shoulda won it," said Ted Williams fifty years later.

Ironically Connie Mack may have been the reason they didn't.

Physically Mack was in excellent health. He was a man of moderate and regular habits. He walked briskly, straight and lean and hard as a railroad track. He routinely played catch with his grandsons in the yard at Ruth's house before Sunday dinner. They put two bases about thirty feet apart and played pickle, one person manning each base and one running between them. Pop-Pop wore a glove and made the throws and catches.

Ira Thomas lived with his nephew, Jim Morrow. One evening when Connie Mack arrived to take Thomas to a dinner, Mrs. Morrow decided to give her little boy the memory of being held by Connie Mack. "Jimmy Jr. was five. I picked him up and handed him to Mr. Mack," she said. "And he put Jimmy up on his shoulder."

His appetite was hearty, his sense of humor lively. His weight didn't vary any more than his wardrobe. Randolph Lyon, who had spent some summers with Mack's children at Atlantic City in the 1930s and called him Uncle Connie, wrote:

> I very well remember Uncle Connie, his sons and daughters, having dinner at Bookbinder's [one of Mack's favorite restaurants] in the late '40s. Uncle Connie must have polished off a couple buckets of steamed clams before he devoured a lobster that hung over the platter at least five inches on each end, all the while unhampered by his high starched

collar. Toward the end of the meal, my wife, Jane, asked Uncle Connie if she could ask him a personal question.

"Why sure," he said.

Jane asked, "Do people bother you for your autograph and, if so, what is your most memorable occasion?"

He said, "That's easy. The team, the coaches and I were gathered on the North Philadelphia station platform early on a Saturday morning on our way to New York. This beautiful young lady approached with an autograph book and brightly asked me for my autograph. In my best penmanship I scrawled best wishes, Connie Mack. After I returned the book, the young lady gave a big frown. When I asked her what was the matter, she said she thought I was Henry Ford."

One day in St. Louis an elderly man approached Mack in the hotel lobby. "I've been following your career for fifty years, Mr. Griffith," the man said, "and I've always wanted to shake your hand."

"Thank you, thank you," said Mack, "only I'm not Clark Griffith. I'm Connie Mack."

"Oh, but you look just like Mr. Griffith."

"That's right," said Mack, "we look exactly alike, only I'm six-two and he's five-two [actually five-six] and I'm like a rail and he's, uh, he's better built. But you're right, we could be mistaken for each other."

Connie Mack's memory had become more farsighted as his eyes became more nearsighted. Arthur Daley of the *New York Times* discovered that as Connie Mack's past became more distant, it became clearer in his mind than the present. Sitting with Mack in spring training, Daley asked him about his current team:

A troubled look came into his watery blue eyes.

"In right field," he said vaguely, "I'll have, er, what's his name? You know, the fellow who runs into walls."

"Elmer Valo," I said.

He nodded gratefully. I prompted him on every name. He knew his entire cast but just couldn't identify anyone. Then I asked him which team was his favorite.

"By golly," he said, using a favorite expletive, "it was the 1911 team. Danny Murphy was the leadoff hitter [he batted fifth] and he hit .329

[he did]." In sure and swift fashion he rattled off not only the batting order but all the batting averages.

But some of his old memories were foggy. Air-brushing his history of signing green youngsters off sandlots and college campuses and enrolling them in his Shibe Park baseball school, he told Daley, "In the old days we brought up only proven players. We didn't have boys in the majors learning what they should have learned in the minors. We have boys around now who don't know a thing about playing big league baseball. Some of them get a lot of money to get here, too."

In 1930 Grantland Rice had written, "It will be interesting to see how far this Athletics team can go [it was winning its second of three straight pennants] because it is almost certain that Connie Mack will never try to build another once this one slips. He has never tried to be a big money maker and he won't retire a wealthy man. But he will have enough to support him in the way he wants to live, which happens to be the simple life."

At that time Rice had known Connie Mack for twenty-five years. He didn't really know his man. Here was Mack, trying to build another winner.

What Connie Mack had achieved the previous year in bringing his expected last-place team just 2 games out of the first division had astounded the so-called seers and pundits. Now, armed with a strong young pitching staff, made younger by the sale of Jesse Flores to San Diego, and an infield he considered second to none defensively, he smelled another pennant.

Looking for bench strength, Mack drafted Billy DeMars from Mobile and signed veteran free agent Skeeter Webb. Webb was finished and DeMars never got started. Mack also drafted outfielder Don White from San Francisco in case Elmer Valo ran himself into a wall and a hospital. White was kept busy.

Sam Chapman could still do an outstanding job in the outfield, but it had taken him until the last two weeks of the '47 season for his bat to wake up.

"If Chapman doesn't snap back," said Mack, "we won't have much to bother anybody with except our pitching."

Mack also sought a backup first baseman in case Ferris Fain's knee acted up. His first choice was Hank Greenberg.

A Tiger regular since 1933, except for four years in the army, Greenberg had been sold to the Pirates for about $35,000 after the '46 season. Greenberg's year in Pittsburgh had not been particularly pleasant nor productive for him or the team, which finished tied with the Phillies for seventh place.

"Other players resented I was paid so much [$85,000 including bonuses, according to some stories, more according to others]," Greenberg told New York writer Joe Trimble. "When things went wrong, they didn't hesitate to gripe. I'm an outspoken guy and I lashed back."

At the end of the year the Pirates released him. Mack, as did everybody else in baseball except perhaps some of the Pirates, had the highest regard for Greenberg. When he had been sold to Pittsburgh, Mack had written to his friend Donald McComas, "Greenberg will help Pittsburg [the spelling of the city when Mack had played and managed there] and create new interest in baseball. He is one grand fellow."

According to a *Sporting News* editorial, the practice of polling players for their reaction to the possible signing of a new player had begun with Branch Rickey's introduction of Jackie Robinson to the Dodgers. Given the reports of dissension in Pittsburgh, Mack decided to poll his players regarding the possibility of signing Greenberg. They overwhelmingly said yes.

Greenberg said he would take less to play for the Athletics: "I would like to help Connie Mack win a pennant." But he was just being polite. Bill Veeck had been wooing him for months to join the Indians as a player or coach. Greenberg really wanted to move into the front office, and when Veeck gave him an opportunity to buy into the Indians in March and become a vice-president, Greenberg took it.

Mack next turned to the recently released Rudy York, who was a whole different story. Signed by the Tigers fifteen years ago, York was a 30-home run RBI machine who had paired with Greenberg to power the Tigers to the 1940 pennant with a combined runs scored and batted in of 239 for York and 279 for Greenberg. But York, now thirty-four, was a drinker—just beer, the story was, but a case at a time. In 1941 the Tigers had inserted in his contract perhaps the most detailed sobriety clause ever seen: "Shall be eligible to receive bonus check of $1,000 on last day of each month if during that particular month the player totally abstains from any drink or beverage containing alcohol in any form or quantity. Forfeiture of the above monthly check will result for any single infraction of the above agreement. Club further reserves the right to fine additionally and suspend the player without pay for more than one offense."

York didn't earn any bonuses and never again batted above .300, but he continued to be a run producer and played in two more World Series, in '45 and '46, the last with the Red Sox. The White Sox picked him up in '47 and released him at the end of the year. After polling his players and receiving a positive response, Mack signed York for $15,000.

Connie Mack didn't want Rudy York influencing any of his younger players; York was the A's only player who didn't have a roommate on the road.

Mack's temperance lecture had been modified over the years: "Limit your drinking to one beer a day with dinner. Too many players are afraid to drink in front of the manager, so they go to their room and have four or five. Or they go to a bar with two or three other players and each one has to buy a round and they drink too much."

In addition to his tippling, York had a reputation as a great curve ball hitter. Pitchers must not have thrown him any curves in '48; he was 2 for 18 as a pinch hitter and hit .157 with no home runs for the A's.

In 1939 the average worker's salary was about $1,300 a year. The average ballplayer ranked above the average worker in income and status, but just by a few steps. By 1948 the gap had widened a little: the national median income was $3,500 a year (a new car cost half that, a new home a little more than double that); most big league players earned around $8,000. (The owners agreed to a Major League salary minimum of $5,000, which gave plenty of young players a raise.) Players rode the subways and shared rides to the ballpark, and many still worked in the off-season.

But the growing presence among club owners of men with corporate backgrounds had brought a whole new view of paying big salaries to valuable executives and employees, including the stars who brought the fans through the turnstiles. Joe DiMaggio would become the first $100,000 player in 1949, bewildering the Macks and Griffiths and Rickeys, who went back to the neolithic days of the game.

The new age inspired Stan Baumgartner to reflect on a day in 1926 when he was a lame-armed lefty for the A's on his way out. Sitting with Mack reading the newspapers in the lobby of the Tuller Hotel in Detroit, he noticed an item that plasterers had been granted an hourly raise that would enable them to earn $12–$16 a day. He read the story to Mr. Mack, then said, "Gosh, plasterers can make more than ballplayers these days."

Without looking up, Mack replied, "Maybe you ought to take up plastering."

Nursing a cold in St. Petersburg in January 1948, Mack griped about his holdouts—Joost, Fain, McCosky, Valo, and Savage. "They can stay where they are. I wrote each of them, 'Don't you dare come to my training camp until you've signed. I don't even want you around town.'"

"I don't know what's come over these fellows," he told the AP. "They think I pick money off trees the way they pick oranges down here. We had a good year last year and I gave every player, even those who didn't do us much good, a nice increase in salary."

Mack expanded on the subject to Dan Daniel:

We at Shibe Park live off the club. Many of us. I have been able to live a fine life. I have no complaint. I owe everything to baseball. But I haven't any money.

The club owner who has to depend on what comes in at the gate now is confronted with the necessity of organizing a second business. The salary situation has become exceedingly rough on Griffith and me and a few others in the majors. You cannot imagine the impacts salaries such as those which are being paid to Ted Williams, Bob Feller, and Joe DiMaggio have on clubs like ours. . . .

Where does that leave me? In the position of being forced to enlarge my chain and develop our own talent more than ever before.

Precisely where Branch Rickey had been twenty-five years earlier in St. Louis.

So what did the Athletics do? Having lost $147,000 in the operation of their minor league clubs in '47, they cut the farm system from thirteen to ten, all but one owned or controlled. The lack of any immediate potential production out of the farms was reflected in their levels: eight were Class C or D; none was higher than Class A.

The Cardinals had a hundred scouts, from bird dogs to full-timers. The A's had about forty, mostly part-timers, none earning as much as $10,000.

Not all of Mack's holdout problems were serious. Bob Savage quibbled over expenses to bring his family to West Palm Beach and didn't get them. Ferris Fain didn't squawk about a $3,000 jump to $11,000; he just wanted some expenses paid. Valo received a 20 percent raise, Joost 25 percent. Mc-Cosky drew a $1,000 raise to $15,000, putting him at the top of the payroll with Joost.

Missing from the holdout ranks was the perennial malcontent Phil Marchildon. Determined to fight for a hefty raise to $17,500, he was the most surprised person in Canada when a contract arrived in the mail for that amount, so surprised that his resentment began to melt. Maybe the Old Man wasn't such a bad guy after all.

It was somewhere during a postseason barnstorming trek through the southwest and Mexico with Bob Feller's All-Stars that Marchildon had reportedly voiced what many of the A's thought but wouldn't say: that Connie Mack had cost them twenty games in '47.

Marchildon may have made the comment in the tradition of players who hoped to provoke a trade to a better team by badmouthing the manager. Perhaps his traveling teammates, maybe Feller himself, had persuaded him that the Indians or Yankees coveted him.

Gordon Cobbledick of the *Cleveland Plain Dealer* wrote, "It has been hinted that Phil Marchildon might be traded as the result of his alleged charge that Connie Mack cost the A's at least twenty victories last season."

If Connie Mack suspected that was Marchildon's motive, he dismissed it, telling Dan Daniel, "The pitcher may have been tired."

The reports were like catnip to the AL fat cats, who began to swarm like the sharks around the fisherman's prize giant marlin in *The Old Man and the Sea*. Bill Veeck, believing his Cleveland Indians were one pitcher short of overtaking the Yankees, was interested enough to leave his Arizona training camp for Florida to see Mr. Mack.

Russ Christopher was unhappy over his contract, which called for the same $10,000 he had made in '47. He knew that the starters were all getting raises. That's where the money was in the days before high-priced closers. He also realized that pitching with a leaky heart was taking a toll on his health and this would probably be his last season.

The story was that Russ Christopher told Mack he wanted to be a starter and to be paid accordingly and that somebody in the front office had promised Christopher that he would be a starter. Nobody in the A's office was in a position to make such a promise. It's more likely that Christopher just wanted the kind of money that veteran starters earned. In any event, he signed for the same $10,000.

Then in late March Christopher wound up in an Orlando hospital with pneumonia. It looked like he wouldn't be doing any pitching.

Commissioner Happy Chandler was in Orlando on April 4 to honor the two oldest and closest comrades in the American League, Clark Griffith and Connie Mack. The two had been instrumental in the launching of the new league in 1901 and had demonstrated that competition and friendship could coexist for almost fifty years.

Mack was always a good sport, willing to pose however he was asked and to join in a stunt for a laugh. Griffith, seventy-eight, and Mack were asked to race from third base to home before the game between their teams.

Mack said, "You ought to give me a handicap. I'm seven years older than you are." Griffith, eight inches shorter than Mack, said, "You ought to spot me a start because your legs are much longer."

The official starter was Washington's seventy-one-year-old coach, Nick Altrock. Altrock fired a cap pistol and kept shooting it behind them as Griffith walked at a spritely pace and Mack, arms flailing at his sides, strode alongside to the cheers of the 2,429 at Tinker Field. They finished together. Mack received two neckties, Griffith two boxes of cigars.

One of the spectators was Bill Veeck. He was there to buy Phil Marchildon.

"Name your price," Veeck said to Mack.

"Not for sale," said Mack.

Veeck then asked about Russ Christopher.

"I can't sell him," said Mack. "He has a bad heart."

By Veeck's account, he said, "I know about it. I'll give you $25,000 for him if you permit me to talk to him first."

"He's a sick man. He can't play."

"That's not your problem, Mr. Mack."

Mack gave his permission and said he would sell Christopher only if the pitcher agreed.

At the hospital Veeck found the thirty-year-old pitcher barely breathing. "Do you think you can pitch?" he asked.

"I don't know."

"Do you want to?"

"Sure I want to."

"I'm going to buy your contract. I'll do the best I can for you."

Christopher told Veeck that it would probably be his last year and that the Indians could use him however they thought best.

Mack's reaction: "I did not think that Christopher would consent to the sale."

Veeck gave Christopher a $2,500 raise to $12,500. Used primarily as a finisher, Christopher worked 59 innings in 45 appearances and helped himself and the Indians to a World Series winners' share. Then he retired. Six years later he died at thirty-seven.

On the first day of spring training Lou Brissie went out on the field. Dave Keefe said to him, "Mr. Mack wants to see you."

Brissie went into the clubhouse and saw Mack talking to the trainer, Doc Tadley. Mack asked Tadley to stand outside and keep everybody out. Then he said to Brissie, "Sit down here. You had a great year in Savannah and I don't want you to worry about making this ball club. However you pitch, you'll be with me all year. Take your time. Follow your own program getting into shape. We're expecting great things from you."

Years later Brissie reflected, "He gave me a chance when no other manager would have. When he said that, he took all the pressure off me."

Well, not all the pressure. Brissie knew he had to prove that he could pitch in the big leagues. He was a pretty good hitter, had no problems running the bases, but was sometimes awkward in fielding his position.

Connie Mack was in great demand as a civic club and after-dinner speaker. He knew the public relations value of those appearances and seldom turned them down. But it had become more difficult for him to express himself, and he had begun to take a player or coach with him to do most of the talking. He chose Lou Brissie to fill that role for him in Florida.

Connie Mack was so satisfied with the spring training facilities at West Palm Beach, he signed an eight-year contract. But a few months later he complained to Dan Daniel in a *Baseball Magazine* article that the contract forced the A's to play too many exhibition games. "When that contract expires [he would be ninety-three by then] I will start training this club my own way. We will play games only on weekends, perhaps on Wednesdays as well. But none of this seven-days-a-week stuff."

The Athletics astounded the baseball world by sweeping the opening 3-game series in Boston with three war-damaged pitchers picking up the wins. The A's hadn't opened 3-0 in eighteen years. After Phil Marchildon went 11 innings to win the Patriots' Day morning game, 5–4, Lou Brissie started the afternoon game. The A's led, 4–1, when Ted Williams came up to bat in the sixth and lined a drive up the middle that banged into Brissie's bad leg and felled him like an oak tree. Brissie lay on the mound in agony as the ball caromed away. Williams stopped at first and rushed to the mound. Brissie looked up at him and said, "Why didn't you pull the ball?" (The next time Williams faced Brissie, on May 31, Ted hit a home run off him in the fifth inning. As he reached second base, Brissie hollered at him, "I didn't mean pull it that far.")

After several minutes, Brissie stood up, took a few practice throws, and declared he was ready to continue. He not only finished the game but gave up no more hits and struck out Williams his next time up. His line for the day: 2 runs, 4 hits, 1 walk, 7 strikeouts.

When the game ended, the fans swarmed onto the field while Lou's teammates surrounded him with handshakes. Coach Dave Keefe said to Lou, "Mr. Mack's waiting to see you in the dugout." Brissie found him standing on the top step, his hand extended. "You pitched a great game, a great game," Mack said.

"He seemed a little choked up," Brissie recalled.

The A's took Brissie to a nearby hospital, where no damage was found. As for Connie Mack, he was quoted in *Time* magazine: "I never felt so tired in all my life."

In the third game Barney McCosky drove in 2 runs with a double to break a 3–3 tie in the ninth. Bob Savage, still housing shrapnel in his shoulder, relieved Joe Coleman and pitched the last 3 innings to gain the win.

The next ten days were here-we-go-again time; the A's were 1-5. Then Eddie Joost reeled off a 17-game hitting streak, and the A's won 10 in a row before the Yankees beat them, 3–0, on May 14. In the past Yankee Stadium had been a nightmare for Mack's teams. Undaunted, they swept the next day's doubleheader behind Coleman and Marchildon and led the league with a 16-6 record.

A's pitchers had thrown 14 complete games. Lou Brissie was doing double duty, starting 3 and finishing 3. Bob Savage had worked in 5. They were the bullpen, and they wouldn't last long at that rate.

In the first game of the May 15 doubleheader in New York, Connie Mack had two occasions to stand up, put out his hand, and say "Thank you" to a player who had made an outstanding play—and both times it was Elmer Valo, who made a leaping catch to rob George McQuinn of a 3-run home run in the sixth and another in the eighth (on a ball hit by Yogi Berra) when he leaned over the low railing to make the catch, then fell back onto the field with the wind knocked out of him. Pete Suder pried the ball out of his glove before the umpire would call the out. Valo limped off the field amid a deafening roar from the crowd of over sixty-nine thousand. He was out for a week.

When Valo came back, he ran into a wall chasing a long foul ball in St.

Louis on May 23. He kept playing and making diving catches until May 31, when he complained that he couldn't lift a bat and Dr. Gopadze discovered he had two broken ribs. This time he was out for 22 games; the A's won only 8 of them.

The paucity of talent in the farm system forced the desperate Mack to send $20,000 and George Binks to the Browns for a powerless .170-hitting outfielder, Ray Coleman. He also acted to bolster his bullpen.

The St. Louis Browns were looking to go young. They offered the thirty-six-year-old Nelson Potter around the league, looking for players in return. Since Mack had given up on him and sold him in 1941, Potter had become a mature, successful starting pitcher, winning 19 games and starting 2 World Series games for the 1944 AL champion Browns. He had been a starter and long reliever while the Browns rapidly returned to their habitual second-division haunts. When no satisfactory players were offered for him, the Browns sold Potter to Connie Mack for $17,500.

The thirty-eight-year-old Bill Dietrich had been nursing a sore arm since Mack had signed him in '47 after his release by the White Sox, twenty years after Mack had originally signed him out of high school. Mack had not given up on him, nor cut his salary. When Dietrich said his arm felt sound again, Mack gave him a start on May 19 at Cleveland. Nelson Potter arrived from St. Louis in time to relieve him in the sixth but not in time to avoid a 6–1 loss. Potter allowed 1 hit and 1 walk.

Two days later Potter pitched 2-hit ball for the last 3 innings to preserve a 9–6 win for Joe Coleman.

A week later he relieved Lou Brissie and pitched the last 5 innings against the Yankees, giving up 2 hits and 1 walk and earning the 5–3 win.

An 8-game winning streak in late May culminated in the Athletics' taking the first three games of a weekend series against the Yankees. After wins on Friday and Saturday, they won an exciting opener of a doubleheader on Sunday, May 30. Tommy Henrich's home run tied it in the ninth. Nelson Potter pitched the tenth. He was harassed by the umpires for supposedly throwing a spitter, a charge that Earle Mack protested fiercely. (Potter had once been ejected in 1944 for throwing a spitter, but he always denied having done so.) The furor didn't bother him; he set down the Yanks 1-2-3. Then Sam Chapman drove in Ferris Fain for the 7–6 win.

The second game began in a light rain. The A's scored 1 in the first. New York scored 2 in the fourth and had men on first and third with no outs in the sixth when the rain fell harder, the sky darkened, and umpire Art Passarella called the game, an act to which "Mr. Mack took violent exception," wrote James P. Dawson of the *New York Times.*

A's broadcaster Chuck Thompson said, "Mack waved for home plate umpire Art Passarella to come to the dugout. When Art leaned in, Mack grabbed him by the neck and shook vigorously. Art never flinched, just let him have his say."

At that point the A's were still in first place. Connie Mack had only good things to say about Nelson Potter.

On June 2 against the White Sox Potter had his first poor outing, giving up 3 runs on 4 hits in 2 innings of a 6–2 loss. Four days later against Cleveland he worked the last 2 innings of a 5–3 loss and gave up 1 hit and 2 walks.

His next game was his worst. On June 9 he relieved Carl Scheib in the sixth against Detroit with 1 out after George Kell's 3-run home run had tied it at 3–3. The A's took the lead in the last of the sixth. In the top of the seventh Potter gave up 3 runs on 4 hits and had to be rescued by Bob Savage.

In seven appearances (five of them scoreless) Potter's line was 2 wins, 1 loss, 17⅔ innings pitched, 6 runs, 14 hits, 4 walks, 13 strikeouts.

The A's had been in a virtual tie for first with Cleveland when Potter joined them. They were in second place, 3½ games back, when they faced the Browns in a doubleheader at home on Sunday, June 13.

The day began for Connie Mack with a run-in with Bill Dietrich, whose arm problems had been diagnosed as adhesions that could be broken by pitching. But he had started only twice, the last time on June 2, losing both times, and relieved twice, pitching a total of 15⅓ innings.

Mack was talking to someone in the clubhouse when Dietrich interrupted. "I want my release," he said. "If I can't pitch regularly with this club, I don't want to be here at all."

"Very well," said Mack. "You shall have it."

Mack was simmering, He may have been thinking what he voiced a few days later: "I am always making mistakes. I made one when I hired Dietrich. He cost me $35,000—$10,000 for signing and $12,500 each for last year and this. I paid him in full when I let him go."

He may also have been thinking that another of his mistakes had been turning down a reported $20,000 offer from the Dodgers late in the '47 season because Dietrich said he didn't want to leave the A's.

Mack was still on edge as Lou Brissie took a 5–1 lead into the eighth inning. Lou suddenly lost it. Three singles made it 5–2. Brissie then walked Andy Anderson to load the bases with nobody out.

The signal went out for Potter.

Potter walked the first batter he faced, forcing in a run. Mack fretted. It was the first time all year that an A's pitcher had committed the sin of walking in a run. Paul Lehner singled in 2 runs—the second scoring on a wild throw from Ray Coleman—to make it 5–5. Mack sizzled. Roy Partee popped out to the catcher, then George Binks singled to make it 6–5. When Eddie Pellagrini singled to reload the bases, Mack exploded. He was on his feet and sent Earle to the mound to get Potter.

It has been said that as men age, they revert to the ways of their youth. In recent years Connie Mack's hot temper had occasionally breached the barriers that time and experience had built. By now those barriers had eroded further, along with his memory and judgment. His legendary patience had worn thin. But how much patience can be asked of an eighty-five-year-old man for whom every loss pushed a little further away the realization of a dream that flirted so tantalizingly within his reach, then seemed to dance away? He was pressing, frustrated. He had waited for seventeen years—no, not waited, had worked, endured, suffered through a thousand exhibitions of bad baseball—to return to the top. For years he had said he just wanted one more contender. And now that he had it, it wasn't enough. He wanted a winner, for the Philadelphia fans as much as for himself.

When Potter reached the dugout, Mack was waiting for him at the entrance to the clubhouse tunnel. Their conversation was quiet—there was no shouting—and to the players on the bench it didn't look confrontational. But it was. "He was fuming," Potter recalled.

Mack said, "Is that the best you can do? It looked terrible."

The implication that he had not been trying infuriated Potter. "I was so mad at the time that if Mr. Mack had been younger, I would have slugged him." Instead he said, "Yes, It did look terrible, I agree, but it isn't true that I wasn't trying out there. It was just the best I could do."

Mack said, "You're through on this ball club."

Lou Brissie was sitting at the other end of the dugout. "I was shocked. I had never seen Connie Mack that way. He was visibly upset and angry. But I couldn't hear what they were saying."

After Charlie Harris retired the Browns with another run scoring, the players on the field came in and learned what had happened. Eddie Joost said, "We were all surprised. It wasn't warranted, but when Connie Mack made up his mind to anything, that was it."

Potter went into the clubhouse, got a box from clubhouse man Yitz

Crompton, and started to pack his personal things. Connie Jr. and Dr. Gopadze had watched the encounter and came into the clubhouse and asked him what had been said. When Potter told them, they said, "Oh now, don't get upset. He just flew off the handle. He'll forget about it. He didn't mean anything by it."

Potter said, "No, the way he told me I was through with the ball club it sounded to me like he meant it, and that's the way I took it."

When the players filed in after the game, several of them tried to persuade Potter to ignore it. The Old Man would get over it.

The Old Man might get over it, but Potter wouldn't. Besides, he saw it as an opportunity to better himself. At that time of year any club in the race was looking for a player who could help it. Mack was in his office between games. Potter went up and asked for his release.

"You'll get it," Mack said.

Some reports have Mack apologizing to Potter and asking him to reconsider. But Art Morrow quoted Mack, "I don't want a fellow like that around this ball club. He just doesn't fit into the picture."

Whatever that meant.

To some of the A's, Nelson Potter acted like he didn't care about anything. He was so calm and even-tempered, he seemed nonchalant on the mound. He really wasn't; he just *looked* like he wasn't trying. Potter's former St. Louis teammates were shocked by the events. The Nelson Potter they knew could never be accused of not doing his best. Browns manager Zack Taylor, who had been a coach for the '44 pennant winners, said, "He's one of the toughest competitors in the business. He throws his heart out with every pitch."

Potter told the AP, "Mr. Mack just got excited about losing a ball game and flew off the handle. It isn't true as Mr. Mack inferred that I wasn't trying my best. I told him I was doing the best I could but otherwise kept quiet. I have respect for his age."

Potter went home to Mt. Morris, Illinois, and waited. He had to clear waivers before pursuing any offers. He had calls from a half dozen clubs in both leagues. Potter threw a screwball and figured he'd bring a new look if he went to the National League, so he signed with the Boston Braves, got a bonus and a raise, and wound up with a full share of the losers' World Series pot—$4,651.51.

"Mr. Mack did me the greatest favor in the world," he said.

The night after Dietrich and Potter were fired, the A's boarded a train for the west, a journey on which, wrote Ed Pollock, "Mack locked himself into his drawing room and saw and talked to no one except the porter for almost twenty-four hours." They stopped in Pittsburgh for an exhibition game billed as a possible World Series preview. The Pirates were 1 game behind the Giants and Braves, tied for first in the NL. The A's picked up $11,217, the most from an in-season exhibition in twenty years.

Before the game, the AP reported, Mack bristled when asked what had happened between him and Potter: "I said, 'Were you doing your best out there?' I also said, 'I paid $20,000 for you and that was my mistake. I don't care how good any player ever was, has been, or could be. All I care about is how much good he is now. That is what I have been telling all of them ever since I have been in this business.'"

To say he had never cared how good a player "could be" was to deny all the years he had patiently developed so many raw youngsters from Eddie Collins to Eddie Collins Jr. until they starred or flopped. But that was buried in the lava of his anger.

Mack went on: "I admit I made a lot of bad talk in what I had to say to both Dietrich and Potter. But damn [the *New York Times* edited that to "darn"] it all, we're out to win, and when you don't win you don't play and you don't stay with my ball club. I am always making mistakes. I made a mistake in letting Russ Christopher go."

The irrationality in all this is further evidence of Mack's deterioration. Yes, he could have used Christopher, who had won 10 games for him last year. But Christopher had also *lost* 7—all in relief. He had obviously had some days when his best wasn't good enough. Mack had never questioned his effort. Now it was a year later, and Connie Mack was a year older and in the pressure cooker of a tight pennant race for the first time since he had been in his prime at sixty-five.

This was not the same Connie Mack who had played Rube Waddell like a game fish through six spectacular years, put up with the peripatetic Joe Dugan for five years before conceding defeat, and massaged the mercurial Lefty Grove to greatness and the moody Howard Ehmke to a one-game immortality. Sure, he had curtly dismissed assorted spear carriers over the years, when his team was going nowhere and he soured on a man, shaming him in front of his teammates by telling him to "go in the clubhouse and keep on going." More often he had been content to abide them until the end of the season, then send them on their way. But those were players he didn't need.

He needed Nelson Potter.

Asked what he intended to do with only five healthy pitchers (Fowler had bursitis, Marchildon a cold in his back, McCahan a stiff shoulder), he said he had several deals in mind but did not desire to discuss them since he wasn't sure they could be completed.

No deals were made.

Meanwhile, Bill Veeck was busy strengthening the Indians. He signed Satchel Paige, boosted his bench by trading for Chicago outfielder Bob Kennedy, and paid the Browns $100,000 for pitcher Sam Zoldak.

On the night of June 15 in Detroit, Dick Wakefield launched a home run to left field. McCosky went back and jumped, but the ball went over his glove. In the process he banged his back against the railing. Don White replaced him. McCosky was out for five days but played in pain the rest of the year. It didn't seem to affect his hitting. At the time he was hurt he was batting .265; he wound up at .326. The effects of the injury would come later.

In Cleveland on Sunday, June 20, a major league record 82,871 saw Feller and Bob Lemon sweep the A's, 4–3 and 10–0. Bill Veeck had tried to break the record in May, but rain had caused him to fall short. He wasn't aiming for it this day; the advance sale was small. But the A's had become a hot attraction. Veeck was happy to provide Mr. Mack with the biggest visitors' share he ever received.

Even without Nelson Potter, the A's finished the western trip winning the last 7 in a row, while the Indians were 3-5, and came home tied for first place.

A long-forgotten phenomenon called pennant fever swept Philadelphia. Advance sales set franchise records for the home stand beginning July 9. A doubleheader Thursday night, July 15, with the Indians drew a crowd of 37,684 that looked forward to taking the lead. They were disappointed when the Indians took two, 6–1 and 8–5. In the second game Satchel Paige earned his first major league victory in relief.

One thing that had kept the pennant race so tight was Bob Feller's erratic performance. Picked by Yankee manager Bucky Harris along with Bob Lemon for the All-Star Game despite a .500 record, Feller said he would skip the game and rest instead. There were conflicting stories about whether the decision was made by Bill Veeck (as Feller always maintained). But it was Feller out there on the mound, not Veeck, taking the heat from players and fans wherever he pitched. When Feller started at Philadelphia on the night of July 16, the 19,809 fans gave him a royal razzberry. The A's kayoed him in a 5-run first inning, and Lou Brissie won his ninth, 10–5.

(Feller was 9-11 at that point. It could be said that he kept Cleveland in the race in the second half; he went 10-4 the rest of the way.)

When Joe Coleman shut out the Indians, 5–0, the Athletics remained a half-game back.

Pete Adelis had become the latest in the long tradition of loud-mouthed hecklers at Shibe Park. The size 52-suited human foghorn had started out hawking newspapers on the street and now worked in the advertising department at Gimbel's department store. Sitting in the photographers' catwalk suspended in back of first base, he had nicknames for everybody and zeroed in on sore spots gleaned from keeping up with the news and gossip and box scores and how the players were doing before they arrived in town. For years, while working as an usher, he had ridden both home teams as well as the visitors in a voice that carried like a thunderclap. One of his favorite targets was the 6-foot-6 Brooklyn first baseman Howie Schultz. He kept it up even after the Phillies acquired Schultz in 1947. According to one story, Phillies owner Bob Carpenter suggested that as Pete was a park employee, it might be fitting for him to confine his heckling to the visiting teams. With that epiphany, Pete became a changed man. From then on, he targeted only visitors. Some players and managers just laughed it off. Others dreaded playing at Shibe Park, where they had to endure two hours or more of constant bellowing from one source.

Adelis relied on repetition to nettle players, especially pitchers. A's broadcaster Chuck Thompson recalled hearing him belt out, "Walk him, Walter" over and over when Washington pitcher Walt Masterson walked 3 in the second on August 10 and 3 more in the 4-run third that ended his day. When a target reacted with a gesture or hollered back, Adelis knew he had succeeded.

Connie Mack had no objections to Pete's carryings-on, which were never profane, never too personal. Adelis used a light touch on veteran stars such as DiMaggio, Musial, Williams, et al. The fans around him enjoyed the show. The Athletics treated him to a series in New York in May, where he sat in the Athletics' box seats and did his best to rattle the Yanks. Even in a record Saturday crowd of 69,416, Adelis could be heard unto the distant bleachers. The A's swept the doubleheader.

In 1947 Bill Veeck had signed Larry Doby as the first Negro player in the American League. Doby had pinch-hit a few times at Shibe Park. Now he was Cleveland's center fielder. Like many players around the league, some of the older Athletics did their share of riding him: "Hey, nigger, shine my shoes" and "Porter, carry my bags." They sat at the other end of the dugout from Mr. Mack, who either didn't hear the taunts or ignored them.

The fiction that Connie Mack hired Pete Adelis, characterized in some books as "a racist heckler," to follow Larry Doby around the American League during the '48 season gained traction by writers citing other writers, each adding a layer of exaggeration, until it has become one of the many taradiddles that infest Connie Mack's legacy like weevils. It never happened. What did happen was the Yankees, impressed by Pete's performance in New York in May, invited him to come and sit in their official box and ride the Indians during an August series. When someone objected to his sitting there, Adelis moved to a seat beside the Cleveland dugout. Cleveland writers commented that "our fellows never knew where the next yelp was coming from." The Yankees won 2 out of 3. That was the extent of Pete's travels.

On July 28 the A's were in Cleveland. Down 3–2 in the eighth, they had men on first and second with 1 out. Russ Christopher replaced Bob Lemon on the mound. After Rudy York popped up, Don White hit a fly ball to left-center field. Doby raced for it, raised his glove over his head, and lost it in the sun. The ball hit the tip of his mitt and bounced off his head. Two runs scored, and the A's held on to win, 4–3.

The Indians came to Shibe Park on August 31 for night games on Tuesday and Wednesday that drew a total of more than fifty thousand. Pete Adelis was ready for Doby. Wearing a World War I German spiked helmet with "Dopey" painted on it, Adelis was not going to let Doby forget about his fielding mishap of a month ago. Hollering, "Hey, Dopey," he held a little hammer above his head. Whenever Doby looked in his direction, Adelis banged the hammer on the helmet. Chuck Thompson was in the radio booth just above Adelis. "Everybody laughed," he said, "including Doby." The riding rolled off Doby; he made no errors, started a double play by snaring a Ferris Fain line drive and throwing to first to double up the base runner, and had a hit in each game.

On August 4 the American League race was the closest in history that late in the season:

Cleveland	56-38
New York	57-39
Philadelphia	59-41
Boston	58-41

While Babe Ruth was still strong enough to travel, Mack had asked him to appear at Shibe Park to give the fans a chance to cheer him one more time. Babe showed up at Mack's office, where Mack's daughter Ruth met him and escorted him down to the field. The Babe, thin and weak, said a few words in a hoarse whisper that held the moist-eyed crowd in complete silence until he finished. The Athletics went to New York for 4 games beginning August 13 with a half-game lead over Cleveland, 2 over Boston. That afternoon the Athletics' former public relations director Jim Peterson took Mack to see the Babe in the hospital.

From his hospital bed Ruth beckoned Mack close to him. "The termites have got me," he whispered.

On Friday night Lou Brissie took a 5–0 lead into the eighth. The Yankees exploded for 8 runs off Brissie, Harris, rookie Alex Kellner, and Scheib. The next day Mack left Dick Fowler in to take an 8-run beating in the second inning, abetted by errors by Fain and Suder. Staring at disaster, Mack sent Kellner out to start the third. He escaped damage until the fourth, when the lefty walked 3 and gave up 4 hits for 4 runs.

Now 1½ games back, the A's faced a hostile Sunday doubleheader crowd of 72,468 in the big stadium that had been a graveyard of hopes for so many Athletics teams over the years.

In the first game Phil Marchildon had a 2–0 lead when he walked leadoff man Bobby Brown in the ninth. Henrich popped out to Suder. Joe DiMaggio stepped in. Marchildon broke off two sharp curves for strikes. Then he called catcher Buddy Rosar out to the mound.

"What do you think about wasting a fastball, then coming back with the curve? That should throw him off."

"Okay," said Rosar, "but make sure you waste the fastball."

Marchildon wasted it up around the eyes; DiMaggio wasted it out of the park.

After an infield hit and another walk, Carl Scheib replaced Marchildon and closed out the inning with no further damage. Undaunted, the A's scored 3 in the tenth, and Lou Brissie came in after a DiMaggio triple had made it 5–3 and got Yogi Berra to ground out to end it.

His boys' gameness, their refusal to fold, moved Connie Mack to do something he had done in the past but had had few occasions to do in recent years. Between games he went into the clubhouse. The surprised players stopped what they were doing and stared at him. He raised his hands and applauded. "This is for you," he said softly and went out.

The A's won the second game, 5–3, and left town still just 1½ back of the Indians.

The Yankees' pennant hopes died that day. About eight o'clock the next evening, Babe Ruth died. Mack said, "We know he was the greatest home-run hitter the country has ever seen. What he has done for the youth of America could not be done by any other man. The youth of our country thought more of him than of any man living."

Mack attended the Funeral Mass at St. Patrick's in New York. Dan Daniel sat with him. When the service ended, it was raining. Daniel wrote: "It was hard to leave the church during the rainstorm. I told Connie I would lead him to the Madison Avenue side and there get him a cab to his hotel. In the sacristy we encountered a gathering of some forty priests. They gathered around Mack as if he had been the cardinal. . . . One priest said, 'Mr. Mack, we pray for you every day.' Another priest spoke up, 'Yes, especially with men on base.'"

The A's came home for a 17-game home stand on August 20, in second place, 2½ games behind Cleveland. They lost the first 5, won the next 5, then lost the last 7 and left town in fourth place, 8½ games out. During the slump a few of the players got to sniping at each other on the bench. After one of the losses, Connie Mack appeared in the clubhouse. They all stopped what they were doing, all eyes on him. He stood there, obviously disturbed and discouraged, for a full minute. "I want you all to remember," he said quietly, "in the heat of a pennant race things are said that are not true. That's understandable. Just remember to forgive each other. You're just going to have to do better than you're doing," and he turned and walked out.

Ferris Fain had gone 0 for 8 in the Labor Day doubleheader in New York. His average had slumped to .249. That didn't sit well with the burrhead. His knee was hurting—had been hurting all year. Two days later the A's were in Washington for a twi-night doubleheader. Taking a walk in the area around the Shoreham Hotel that afternoon, Fain and a few other players stopped to watch some youngsters in a pickup game. When the game ended and the boys left, Fain noticed a bat had been left behind. He picked it up and took a swing. It felt about the same weight as his regular model and was an inch or two longer. He carried it back to the hotel and, on a hunch, used it that night. He had 3 hits in the first game, a 10–7 win preserved when he leaped high in the air to grab a ninth-inning line drive by Mickey Vernon with 3 on and 1 out and turned it into a game-ending double play. In the second game Fain walked 3 times.

In another twi-night twin bill the next day, Fain had 2 hits in each game.

"Nobody could get that bat away from him now," Earle Brucker commented.

Fain said he'd like to find the kid who left the bat but not to give it back. "I'll give him three of mine."

In the days that followed Fain was 17 for 34. Then the bat split. When a representative of the bat maker dropped by Shibe Park one day, Fain showed it to him. "We haven't made that model in ten years," he said. But he took the remains and shortly thereafter six new bats of that model arrived at Shibe Park.

The A's won 5 in a row on the road in September and came into Cleveland with just a glimmer of hope left, trailing by 7½ games. In a tough Sunday doubleheader that epitomized their season against the Indians, Carl Scheib lost the first game when Larry Doby broke a 3–3 tie with a home run in the last of the ninth, a game in which Russ Christopher relieved Bob Lemon with the bases loaded and 2 out in the eighth and got Pete Suder to pop up to the catcher, then pitched a scoreless ninth.

In the second game Steve Gromek outpitched Dick Fowler, 2–0.

The next day Russ Christopher shut them down again after they had pulled to within 4–3 in the seventh. The sweep left the A's with a 6-16 record against the eventual pennant winners.

The Red Sox and Indians finished in a tie, broken by Cleveland's 8–4 one-game playoff win, with the Yankees 2½ games back and the Athletics 12½ back in fourth place. For the first time in fifteen years, the A's enjoyed a slice of the World Series melon, though it wasn't as big a slice as they had anticipated. The players voted thirty-three full shares, including the traveling secretary, clubhouse man, and coaches. Connie Mack's share, as in the past, went to the groundskeepers.

The what-iffers mused: if Marchildon and McCahan had repeated their '47 seasons, Mr. Mack would have had his "one more" pennant. Marchildon was the workhorse—226 innings—but he was wild all season, averaging over 5 walks per 9 innings; on June 24 at St. Louis he had given up 4 runs on 1 hit and 10 walks in 4⅔ innings. One day in Detroit he delivered a pitch ten rows up in the stands between home and third. He was plagued all year by bouts of a flu-like infection in his gut that he'd picked up as a POW. Dr. Gopadze tried penicillin and other wonder drugs to no avail. By mid-August he was worn out and went 1-6 the rest of the way, finishing at 9-15.

Bill McCahan had played pro basketball after the 1946 season, but Connie Mack frowned on that and gave him a $1,000 bonus to give it up for the winter of '47. Now a successful big league pitcher, McCahan took his bonus money and more and bought a big car and a new house. He needed a winter job and found one working for an oil company lifting heavy oil drums.

He reported to West Palm Beach with his formerly loose, flexible arm muscles stiff and hard. He needed painkilling shots every time he pitched.

After two starts in April, somebody suggested his problem stemmed from infected teeth. So he had them pulled. It didn't help.

McCahan started in Cleveland on June 19, gave up 6 hits and 8 walks, and lost, 4–0. He didn't start again until July 10 and lost again, 4–0, this time walking 11. On July 22 he didn't get out of the second inning, walking 5.

Bill McCahan won 4 games and lost 7. The promise of '47 was gone.

There were days when the pain in Lou Brissie's leg was so unbearable, he needed a shot of painkiller before he could walk. Sometimes Dr. Gopadze gave him penicillin shots to kill infections. When wounds opened, Lou applied sulfa powder. Every night he rubbed oil into the shattered area to prevent it from cracking and oozing. When more serious problems arose, he went back to the doctors who had operated on him, who were now in Cleveland and Washington.

The shortage of pitchers had put Carl Scheib in the bullpen after 11 consecutive starts. Scheib relieved 8 times and started 3 games during a six-week period beginning mid-July, before finishing September as a regular starter again. He finished with a 14-8 record (3-1 in relief).

Fowler, Brissie, Coleman, and Scheib each worked around 200 innings. The Athletics led both leagues in complete games because they had to; they had no Russ Christopher, no Nelson Potter after June 13, no bullpen.

And only the shell of the manager they used to have. Had the astute handler of pitchers and diverse personalities, the aggressive buyer of final vital pieces—the Connie Mack of twenty years ago—been in the dugout in 1948, Ted Williams's "shoulda won it" might well have been "won it."

In addition to pitchers' arms dropping off, there was one other factor that sank the A's: Overlooked by history but adored by A's fans of the time, Elmer Valo went all out all the time, but he had made one too many game-saving challenges of walls and railings. Valo missed 45 games. It was no coincidence that the Athletics were 17-28 when he didn't start. More than one win in a pitcher's column was due as much to his glove and hustle as the pitcher's arm.

The A's won 23 1-run games and actually gave up more runs than they scored while winning 14 more games than they lost. Connie Mack didn't have much power in his lineup. Eddie Joost led the team with 16 home runs. They were sixth in batting and slugging. With a weak-hitting lineup, Mack considered a walk as good as a hit in the manufacturing of runs. That's why he continued to flash take signs even on hitters' counts like 2-0 and 3-1. Plenty of times a pitcher bore down too much on those counts and the so-called cripple missed its mark. By now even Ferris Fain had bought into the strategy, which reached its apex on June 21 at St. Louis when the A's drew 16 walks, led by Joost's 4 and Fain's 3. Unfortunately A's pitchers gave up 18 hits, and they lost that day, 9–8.

The A's first four batters walked more than 400 times. Joost and Fain finished second and third to Ted Williams in drawing free passes. Fain batted .281 with 1.71 hits plus walks per game.

Eddie Joost won a television set given by restaurant owner Frank Palumbo as the A's MVP and $1,000 for winning the *Bulletin*'s fan voting for the team MVP, a tribute that irked Hank Majeski, who had hit .310 with 120 RBIs, fifth in the league. Joost, called the most underrated player in the league by Ted Williams, finished tenth in the MVP voting, which was dominated by Cleveland player-manager Lou Boudreau.

The most expensive base hit in Connie Mack's long career was made by Earle "Gidge" Brucker Jr. on October 3. The son of Mack's longtime pitching coach, Gidge was a strapping 6-foot-2, 210-pound catcher. As a teenager he had spent a summer traveling with the A's, catching batting practice. Put into the lineup in a game at Gatersford prison, he had hit a long drive over a high cell block. After a stint in the navy, Gidge attended San Diego State, where several scouts were watching. Connie Mack asked Brucker to give him a chance to match any offer made to his son. When one scout offered him a $30,000 bonus, Brucker Sr. said, "No kid is worth that much," but he would have to give Mack a chance to match it. Mack hesitated; sentiment may have overruled judgment. He matched the offer, giving Gidge $10,000 on June 17, with the rest payable by December 31, and signed him to a Lincoln contract. At Lincoln Gidge was in 12 games and hit .344, then was sent to Savannah, where he batted .238 for manager Eric McNair.

Brucker Jr. was strong but awkward. His throws to the pitcher, made from a squatting position, were often erratic. He was tried in the outfield and found wanting. Brought up by the A's at the end of the season, Gidge caught the last two games and had 1 hit, a double. The next spring he was sent down to Martinsville and never saw another big league pitch.

Tributes to Mack continued throughout the year, as though nobody wanted to be caught planning one and be too late.

In September there was an elegant dinner for Mack at the Union League. He was at the top of his social game, darting hither and yon among the guests, greeting old friends and strangers alike with a hearty "How are ya, young fella?" One of Mack's former players, Cy Perkins, now a coach for the Phillies, brought along a rookie pitcher named Robin Roberts. "I walked up to him and introduced myself," said Roberts, "and he said, 'You don't have to tell me your name. I've seen you pitch.'"

Mack followed Roberts's career. Four years later he wrote to the committee holding a testimonial dinner for Roberts: "You are paying tribute to a young man who is not only one of the greatest pitchers of his day, but who is a credit to the game of baseball in every way. Robin Roberts is the ideal American athlete—a real leader who possesses a perfect blend of the will to win and the spirit of fair play and good sportsmanship."

With their highest-ever attendance—945,076—the Athletics were back on top of the local scene as the sixth-place Phillies' gate dropped by 140,000. It wouldn't last.

By 1949 the Phillies' future would assume regular positions in the lineup: Richie Ashburn, Dick Sisler, Granny Hamner, Puddinhead Jones, Jim Konstanty, Robin Roberts—augmented by the acquisition of four popular players from the Cubs: Russ Meyer, Bill Nicholson, Hank Borowy, and Eddie Waitkus.

The Athletics' last hurrah had been sung.

22 | **THINGS FALL APART**

As far back as 1946 Connie Jr., anticipating a postwar pickup in attendance, had spent $1,250 on plans to expand Shibe Park that included lowering the field and installing new boxes along the first and third base lines and building a double-deck grandstand in right field to expand the capacity to about forty-five thousand. The distance down the right-field foul line would be shortened to 315 feet, and a screen would be put across the lower deck to prevent cheap home runs. Stairs would be replaced with ramps. The cost would be about $2 million.

Now, buoyed by the club's strong showing in the '48 pennant race and a $232,000 profit for the year, Connie persuaded his dad to try to buy the houses along Twentieth Street and get the city to close the street to accommodate the expansion. The back of the upper deck would extend over the sidewalk on Twentieth Street. The A's had enough political connections to achieve the latter. Buying up the houses would not be so easy. They called on Ted Gorsuch, longtime real estate broker and partner of Ira Thomas in the North Philadelphia Federal s&l, of which Mack was a board member. Gorsuch had represented both Mr. Mack and Earle in their real estate transactions.

Gorsuch reminded them of how they had used a front to buy up the property to build Shibe Park, to avoid word getting out and property prices soaring. "When you buy a few and they find out who's buying, the prices will double," he warned them.

Connie Mack told Gorsuch to go ahead and buy two or three and see what happens. The records show that Gorsuch bought two adjacent houses, numbers 2717 and 2719. It's unclear in whose name the houses were bought; Gorsuch held the mortgages, and the Athletics collected monthly rents of $45 and $36 on the two houses for at least the next three years.

In July 1948 Connie Jr. went to Detroit to get ideas on copying the right-field stands at Briggs Stadium, where the upper-deck pavilion projected out about ten feet over the playing field.

The city zoning board gave its approval for the plan in the fall.

Either Gorsuch was unable to buy any more houses, the word got out, and the asking prices went up, or Roy and Earle persuaded their father that this was just another of their half-brother's harebrained ideas—or all three. The only expansion that happened was the addition of 2,500 box seats. (This blocked the view between the dugout and the bullpen, so there was no more playing charades to bring in a reliever. A telephone was finally installed.)

In 1949 the minor leagues expanded to fifty-nine, but they were not prospering. Today minor league baseball is big business. In the 1940s and '50s, it was a dying business, surviving on civic pride and shoestring budgets, especially in the smaller towns. Three technological advances were contributory factors to the decline.

Minor league cities and towns were invaded by the expansion of major league radio broadcasts over independent networks that covered vast areas of the country and network-televised games on Saturdays. The minors campaigned to ban radio and television broadcasts of any game outside a fifty-mile radius of a club's home territory while an affected minor league team was at home. But big league baseball's saturation took a toll.

The other factors were a boom in home air conditioning and the novelty of television, enabling millions of people out in minor league land to stay home and enjoy new forms of entertainment without suffering the heat, humidity, and mosquitoes at the local ballpark.

Connie Mack considered buying the Minneapolis franchise, as he had come close to doing five years ago, but backed out at the last minute, saying only that the time was not ripe for such a commitment. He may have been referring to the dwindling attendance in the minor leagues and the cost of carrying a AAA club. Perhaps it was another example of the tug-of-war among his sons that increasingly stymied any progress. (Had the deal gone through, might the Athletics have wound up in Minneapolis instead of the Senators? We'll never know.)

Jimmie Dykes, fired in mid-1946 in Chicago, had gone to Hollywood to manage for two years but was let go after the '48 season. At the winter meetings in Chicago, Connie Mack asked him to come back to the A's as a coach. The voluble Dykes turned his meeting with Mack into good copy for the writers: "The first thing Mr. Mack said to me was, 'Jimmie, I'm afraid we can't pay you what you're worth.' I said, 'Cripes, Mr. Mack, do we have to start in where we left off sixteen years ago?'"

He signed for $10,000.

Speculation began immediately that Dykes had been brought in to succeed Mack as the A's manager.

Wally Moses had made it to a World Series with the Red Sox in 1946 in his fourteenth season, hitting .417 in four games. He just missed another Series by a playoff loss to Cleveland in 1948. Released after the '48 season, he was welcomed back to the Athletics as a player/coach. Despite their salary dispute of ten years ago, Mack had told him he would have a job with the Athletics for "as long as I am there." Moses remained on the active list through 1951 and stayed on as a coach.

With Chief Bender pitching batting practice and working with the pitchers, Mack enjoyed the comfort and security of being surrounded by men he admired who had played for him.

Spring training was a busy but harmonious time for Connie Mack. Although he had predicted the Indians would repeat in '49, he believed he had the makings of a contender. His worn-out and sore-armed pitchers had rested for six months. He had what he considered the best defensive infield in the league, a veteran outfield, and three dependable catchers in Joe Astroth, Buddy Rosar, and Mike Guerra—if Guerra ever showed up.

For the third year in a row, the Cuban was full of excuses for reporting late. "That 'Geera,'" Mack fumed. "He always has some story. Boston refused to pass [waivers] on him last year. Maybe they'll claim him this time."

Guerra had been managing and playing in the winter league. He didn't need weeks to get into shape. He was the fastest and smartest of Mack's catchers, the preferred battery mate for many of the pitchers, and Mack knew it.

Buddy Rosar tore up a knee in a collision at the plate on May 7; that and his sore right shoulder made Mike Guerra the number one catcher with rookie Joe Astroth the backup.

The back injury that Barney McCosky had suffered when he had run into a wall last June had given him fits all winter. Two vertebrae kept slipping and grating on a nerve. He never stopped hurting and would be out for the year. Not until December 1949 would he finally give in to an operation. That left Sam Chapman, thirty-three, who now wore glasses; Wally Moses, thirty-eight; and Elmer Valo, twenty-eight, in the outfield—the same outfield that had played together as far back as 1941. With the farm system still unproductive, Mack scrounged for bench strength and pinch-hitting duty by signing a career .311 hitter, Taft Wright, thirty-seven, who had played for Dykes at Chicago. Wright suddenly forgot how to hit: he was 3 for 19 off the bench.

On the first day in West Palm Beach Mack gathered his boys in the outfield and kept his remarks brief: "You can win if you just get in top condition and stay in condition."

No mention was made of rules or curfews or the evils of alcohol; by now Mack was limiting his lectures to one-on-one appeals to the heavy drinkers to consider the effects on their careers and families. In a few cases he sent players' semi-monthly paychecks to their wives.

The A's flew to Venezuela and Cuba for ten days and regretted it; the food and water gave them so many internal miseries that the trip wasn't worth it.

Connie Mack was no longer voicing objections to Jackie Robinson's being in the Brooklyn lineup. On March 15 Robinson helped attract a crowd of 3,868 to Wright Field, the biggest baseball crowd in the city's history. That was dwarfed five days later when a Sunday crowd of 6,988, including 2,000 Negroes in segregated bleacher sections, saw the A's win, 5–0.

At contract-mailing time Mack was still brooding over the late-season collapse of Phil Marchildon and its effect on the team. He had peevishly cut him the maximum 25 percent to $13,125.

Marchildon didn't sign. By the time Mack arrived in West Palm Beach, he had second thoughts. His veteran pitcher, if healthy, was the key to his pennant chances. When Marchildon showed up, Mack told him, "I think maybe we were a little too severe," and raised his offer to $15,000. Marchildon signed.

"Get back to where you were two years ago," Mack said, "and you may do better than that."

Marchildon didn't get back. He looked sharp for 8 innings against the Red Sox on April 21, matching Mel Parnell, 0–0, until the ninth, when he looked as if he had suddenly been attacked by internal butterflies. With 2 outs and 2 on, walk, walk, single, walk, and 3 runs were in, and the Shibe Park boo birds rode with him into the dugout. It didn't help Mr. Mack's disposition when Alex Kellner went in and walked in another run.

Five days later in New York Marchildon threw 2 pitches and grabbed his right shoulder in agony. Alex Kellner finished that one too, a 5–4 loss.

Marchildon tried again on May 21 and was bombed for 6 runs in 3 innings by the Tigers and never pitched at Shibe Park again. He worked a total of 4 innings the rest of the year. His last appearance for the A's came in Boston on September 2. Four walks and 2 hits, including a Bobby Doerr home run, finished him. The only man he retired was Ted Williams.

For the first time Connie Mack had three top-notch left-handers, from the 6-foot-5 Lou Brissie to the 5-foot-6¼ Bobby Shantz. In the middle was Alex Kellner.

Connie Mack was never keen on small pitchers. He preferred big men in the box. He would cite Dickie Kerr, who had won 2 games for the White Sox in the 1919 World Series, as the lone exception who came to mind. (His old pal Clark Griffith was another.)

So Mack had not been enthused when Harry O'Donnell signed a kid named Bobby Shantz from nearby Pottstown in 1948. Bobby had never played high school ball. He was working in a sawmill and pitching in the semipro ranks. Scouts admired his big league curve but passed him up because of his size. His catcher was Lou Parrise, the son of the owner of a butcher shop on Twenty-First Street near Shibe Park, where clubhouse boys had gone for bones to rub the bats of the likes of Jimmy Foxx and Al Simmons. Parrise had gotten into a few games with the A's during the war. He thought Bobby had a shot at the big leagues and persuaded O'Donnell to give him a chance.

When Shantz beat a team from Egypt, Pennsylvania, 4–1, outdueling Curt Simmons, who had just received a $65,000 bonus from the Phillies, O'Donnell signed him to a Lincoln contract for $300 a month. O'Donnell also signed Bobby's brother Bill, a 6-foot-1 catcher, to a Class C Moline contract.

"Bonus? Forget it," Shantz recalled. "I was happy to sign with anybody who would give me a chance."

Shantz's fastball and curves baffled the Western League's Class A hitters in 1948. He won 18 and struck out 212. That earned him an invitation to West Palm Beach and his first meeting with Connie Mack.

"I had never seen anybody that old," Shantz said. "He was very quiet, very nice to everybody. All the wives, including mine, liked him. The wives all sat together and he would buy them all Cokes."

Shantz was tutored by Earle Brucker and Chief Bender. Bender knew that Shantz would not survive trying to throw his fastball past big league hitters. He drummed it into the pint-sized southpaw: "Learn to change speeds or you won't last." It took Shantz two years to master changing speeds on both his fastball and curve and become a winning pitcher.

But nobody had to teach him how to field his position. His father, a semi-pro player, had drilled him in taking ground balls in the infield and outfield, and he worked out in pepper games. He was a Gold Glove fielder before the award was invented, and was the first pitcher to win it.

Some minor shoulder surgery kept Shantz out of action until a brief relief appearance on Sunday, May 1. The first batter he faced coming in against Washington in the fifth inning with 2 men on and 1 out was pitcher Joe Haynes, who rapped a single to drive in 2 runs. Shantz retired the next two batters. The next day he was in his car on his way to Buffalo. By whose orders? Nobody knows. Fowler and Coleman were hurting. Marchildon was useless. Shantz may have needed more experience, but the A's needed him now.

When Shantz arrived in Buffalo, he was told to leave his car under the stands and go to Detroit to join the A's. He reported on May 5 and pitched batting practice. The next day Detroit scored 3 in the third off Carl Scheib and had a runner on third with no outs in the fourth when the call went to the bullpen for Shantz. The rookie calmly left the runner stranded and went on to pitch 9 innings of no-hit ball, walking 7 and hitting 1 batter. Meanwhile, the A's tied the game in the eighth. In the top of the thirteenth pinch hitter Wally Moses hit a 2-run home run to make it 5-3. The no-hit string was cut when George Kell led off the bottom of the inning with a double. Vic Wertz singled him home. Then Shantz displayed his fielding ability. Hoot Evers popped up a bunt down the first base line. Catcher Buddy Rosar fell trying to field it. Shantz leaped over him, caught the ball in mid-air, and threw to first to double off Wertz. Then he calmly struck out Bob Swift.

Shantz never pitched in Buffalo. He remained with the A's, "where he'll learn more," said Mack, as a starter and reliever. He was 3-4 in each role.

"He astonished me," Mack admitted. "I never thought he'd win in the big leagues. But he showed me. I think he's going to be a great one."

Shantz also fit in with the card players on the team. Anyone looking for a low-stakes poker or hearts game knew to head for Suder's or Shantz's room.

Thirty-five years earlier Connie Mack had said, "You do not know if a young pitcher will be an asset or a liability until you start a season." He had never found a reason to change his mind. He didn't know what to expect from Alex Kellner when the pitchers gathered at West Palm Beach.

Kellner was sixteen when the Cincinnati Reds signed him after his graduation from a Tucson high school in 1941. The lanky lefty pitched one year in Class C before joining the navy. Somehow his contract wound up with Birmingham while he was in the service. By 1947 the Athletics had a working agreement with the Southern Association Barons. After his 11-9 season the A's claimed Kellner for $7,500.

He was twenty-three when he first met the eighty-five-year-old Mack in spring training in 1948. "It was exciting to me to meet him for the first time. We met on the field and he said, 'I'm glad you've joined our ball club. Do the best you can.'"

Earle Brucker thought Kellner needed another pitch and taught him the slider.

Kellner relieved in two games before Mack called him into his office and said, "I'm sending you to Savannah so you can work regularly. But we'll bring you back as soon as we can."

Kellner went down and was 9-3, including a no-hitter, when the A's recalled him in August. He was nervous and wild; in 16 innings he walked 13, hit 2, and threw 3 wild pitches.

On May 8, 1949, Kellner started in Chicago. He had worked 19 innings so far and walked 12. In the first inning leadoff man Gerry Scala singled. With 2 out, Gus Zernial tripled him home. With 1 out in the second, Floyd Baker singled. Kellner balked. Don Wheeler walked. The pitcher, Randy Gumpert, put down a bunt. Kellner picked it up and threw it into right field. A run scored. Scala singled in two more. The Sox led, 4–0. After the rattled Kellner walked Luke Appling, he walked to the dugout when Carl Scheib replaced him.

There are many painful experiences in life: root canals; sitting through twenty years' worth of somebody else's home movies; piano recitals of eight-year-olds, none of whom are yours; sitting through every minute, day and night, of a national political convention. None of these comes close to the agony of watching your pitcher miss the strike zone pitch after pitch: ball 1, ball 2, ball 3, ball 4; next batter, ball 1, ball 2, and so on: the groaning frustration of the players on the field, up on their toes and down on their heels with every errant effort; the tightening grip on the innards of the manager debating how long he should let it drag on. No man should voluntarily subject himself to as much of this torture as Connie Mack had endured over the years. Nothing but the mysteries of DNA can explain why he hadn't snapped like Inspector Clouseau's boss in *The Pink Panther*.

Now he did.

This is the way Alex Kellner remembered it:

When I got back to the dugout the Old Man was waiting for me on the steps. He was mad, red in the face. He said, "Young man, if I ever see you walk two men in a row again, it'll cost you a thousand dollars."

Being a rookie, I didn't know what to say or do. He turned around and went back to the bench and sat down. I sat at the far end of the bench and the more I thought about it the madder I got. I didn't know what to do. I got up and sat down next to him and said, "Mr. Mack, do you think I was walking those men on purpose?"

And he blew up again. "My god, all you do is walk, walk, walk 'em." How he hated those bases on balls. I got up and went down in the runway. Dykes followed me and said, "The Old Man just doesn't like walks. He doesn't have anything against you. Those walks have been killing us. Don't worry about the fine. That's just talk."

(Dykes later said walks cost the A's at least 40 games that year. "Standing on home plate was the safest place in the park when our guys were pitching.")

The next day they played a night game. Kellner arrived at Comiskey Park with Valo and Suder about the same time as Mr. Mack. "As we walked in Connie Mack saw us and came over and was very pleasant. 'Glad to see you boys,' he said. He asked me how I was. 'Fine,' I said. He said, 'Let's have a good game today,' and off he went. It was as if it had never happened."

Starting and relieving, Kellner worked 245 innings and won 20 games, Mack's first 20-game winner since Lefty Grove. He might walk 8 in a game, even 3 in an inning, but the A's usually did plenty of scoring behind him. He was 4-3 against the Yankees, and that made up for all the errant pitches with Mr. Mack.

Lou Brissie was hampered by circulation problems in his wounded leg that would require some kind of surgical repair before long if he was to continue pitching. The pounding a pitcher's legs take was magnified by his condition. But it didn't stop him from working 229 innings, including 18 complete games, and winning 16. Perhaps his best game came on May 28 in New York. The A's were in second place, 4½ games behind the Yankees. Starting against Vic Raschi, Lou led, 1–0, and had a 2-hitter going when Yogi Berra doubled home Tommy Henrich to tie it in the bottom of the ninth. Joe Page and Lou then matched zeroes until the fourteenth, when Billy Johnson's double scored Berra with the winning run.

Despite the loss, Connie Mack congratulated Lou on "a great game."

Jimmie Dykes was in an awkward position. He was the new man on the coaching staff, but he had been a manager for fifteen years. He had his own ideas on handling pitchers, even if that was Earle Brucker's domain. Dykes believed that pitchers—except the day's starter—should work at shagging fly balls in pregame exercises—none of that standing around and visiting stuff. "It's the only way you'll stay in condition," he told them. He had the uncanny ability to hit fungos just out of their reach, and whoever didn't hustle would be doing extra laps.

Dykes knew as well as the other coaches that Connie Mack was no longer the man he had played for. When Dykes was coaching at third, Simmons and Earle flanked Mack on the bench, but it was Simmons who did the reminding of who the next batter was and what the count was: "Con, if this next pitch is a ball, it'll be 3 and 1. What will you want to do?" Mack would tell him he wanted the batter to take or hit or hit and run or steal or whatever, and Simmons would pass it along to Dykes on the coaching line to give the signs. Dykes, like Simmons, didn't have the heart to tell the man he loved like a father that it would be best for the team if Mr. Mack stepped down.

In his seventieth birthday interview with the AP, way back in 1932, Mack had said, "When you handle a team of twenty-five men, you can't fool them. When my players begin to whisper among themselves that Mack is not what he used to be, I'm going to hear those whispers. Then I'll know it's time for me to consider getting into the background."

His players were whispering among themselves; he didn't hear them. The players didn't express any anger or resentment. They didn't rebel. They just dealt with it.

Occasionally one might voice his frustration. At one point during the season Elmer Valo was in a slump. Mack pulled him out of a game for a pinch hitter. As he walked by Mack, Valo said, "How do you expect me to come out of a slump sitting on the bench?"

Al Simmons told him to "sit down and relax."

Eddie Joost said, "[Mr. Mack] couldn't concentrate, didn't know what was going on. We all ran the club. The players, sometimes with the coaches, would decide what should be done and put it to Mr. Mack for his okay. He never objected, just said, 'Go ahead and do it.' We didn't go around him. We had too much respect for him to do that."

Joost said that when the infielders thought they needed a new pitcher, he would signal to Earle Brucker to make a change.

Other players thought that Mack was as alert as ever and knew exactly what was going on. The problem was that the mental highways connecting his seeing what was developing, making a decision, and expressing it had developed potholes. The journey took so long that it became too late to act.

Mack's grandson Frank Cunningham was the batboy. "There was a sparkle in his eyes," he recalled. "His countenance was alive. You could see the energy."

"His mind was keen," said Joe Astroth. "He knew what was happening. One cloudless day a high foul ball was hit down the first base line. Mike Guerra and Ferris Fain both charged for it, calling for it. Mr. Mack turned to Earle and said, 'They're not fooling me. On a high sky neither one of them wants it.'"

One day he observed a young left-handed batter taking batting practice, "That young fellow has a beautiful swing. He's going to be a great hitter someday, if he learns to hit the ball."

Sometimes Connie Mack would go home after the first game of a Sunday doubleheader and listen to the second on the radio, pacing nervously, impotently, silently, jingling the change in his pocket. Frank Cunningham sometimes went home and listened with him. "There was no talking during the game. You were in the room with him but he wasn't really aware of your being there."

On those occasions when Frank stayed while Mack went home, "Sometimes Earle and Al Simmons would sit me in Pop's place in the dugout in my uniform and tell me to twitch my nose or flick my ear. I was flashing the signs."

Connie Mack had always enjoyed the theater. Whenever the team was on the road and a theater owner gave him two tickets to a play, he would ask one of his players to go along with him. One night in Washington he received two tickets to the Rialto Theater. He saw Joe Astroth in the lobby and asked him to go along.

"We took a cab," Astroth said, "and when we got there he reached in his vest pocket and paid the driver with a few crisp new bills. The play was *A Streetcar Named Desire* with Judith Evelyn. It was a pretty steamy play for him. After the first act he wanted to leave. Before we left the manager asked him if he would like to go backstage and meet the cast, so we did. I trailed after him and they all made a big fuss over him."

The A's were 6 games back in sixth place when the Yankees came to town on Saturday, May 14. That day they rallied with 6 runs in the seventh and eighth for an 8–5 win. Kellner relieved McCahan in the sixth and walked 2, but one was intentional.

In the first game on Sunday before a full house of 35,004, Kellner relieved in the ninth inning with the Yankees leading, 7–5. The A's tied it in the bottom of the ninth on home runs by Joost and Chapman off Joe Page and won it in the eleventh. Kellner allowed 1 base runner in 3 innings to pick up his second win in two days.

In the second game, Allie Reynolds had a 6–0 lead when the A's woke up and drove him out with a 7-run explosion in the sixth inning, the last two scoring on a single by Elmer Valo off Page. The Sunday curfew ended it there.

Just like that they had cut 3 games off the Yankees' lead. A week later they were in second place, only 2 games back. That's as close as they got. On July 4 they were still hanging in there, 4½ games back. Then they sank like a lump of lead, battling for fourth instead of first behind New York, Boston, and Cleveland. They didn't make it, finishing fifth with an 81-73 record.

The pitching was thinner than Mr. Mack. Coming off three doubleheaders in five days, he had only two pitchers, Scheib and Charlie Harris, who didn't have sore arms.

On the night of July 22 in Chicago Carl Scheib started for the A's. The first six Sox batters singled. The seventh walked. The spectators kept looking to the bullpen, but nobody got up. Another single, double, and two walks followed, and 8 runs scored before the third out. As he walked off the field, Scheib received a big ovation from the twenty-two thousand in the stands. When he reached the dugout, Connie Mack asked him, "Can you finish the game?"

"Sure," said Scheib.

He blanked the Sox until the eighth, when they scored 4 more on 4 hits and 2 walks.

The A's weren't much healthier at the plate. Beginning July 30 they went through 36 innings without scoring a run, plus an added shutout at the hands of a Notre Dame junior named Art Wood in an exhibition game at Harrisburg. Mack was so desperate, he picked up sixteen-year veteran Augie Galan from the Giants for $100 (that's what the ledgers show) and signed Roberto Estalella, who had been playing in Venezuela after jumping to Mexico. Connie Mack's eyes weren't so good any more, so he might not notice Roberto's elephantine feats in the outfield. Estalella's hitting turned out to be barely visible too.

Jimmie Dykes toured the farm system looking for somebody worth promoting. He found nobody.

In Pete Suder's selective memory, "Nobody ever took me out pivoting on a double play."

He was not quite agile enough in a game against the Browns on June 17. Dick Kokos spiked him on the foot as Pete relayed the throw from Majeski to Fain. He was carried off the field. Expected to be out a week, he missed a month.

Given a chance to play, Nellie Fox made the most of it, buzzing around second base like a hungry mosquito in a bedroom at midnight. All the infielders but Joost were tobacco chewers. Fox's cheek full of chaw seemed to add 10 percent to his weight. He joined Jimmie Dykes and Joe Coleman in their preference for big black cigars. From June 22 to August 28 he would play 50 games without an error. His OBP stayed well above .400.

Connie Mack was still the Athletics' best public ambassador. The *Baltimore Afro-American* gave him expansive coverage when he visited a nineteen-year-old Negro patient at Freedmen's Hospital in Washington in late June.

The patient, George Bryant, had been bedridden for years with arthritis. An avid sports fan, he was an encyclopedia of stats and history. As a contributor to the hospital's mimeographed newspaper, he had predicted the A's would win the pennant. Somebody sent Mack a copy of the article.

Mack rounded up Nellie Fox and Earle Brucker and took them to see Bryant.

"It was quite a meeting," reported the *Afro-American*. "Young George, bubbling over with enthusiasm, swapped talk with Mack about the Athletics' 'million dollar' infield of the early 1900s. They talked about the powerhouse aggregation of the 1930s.

"Nellie Fox was amazed at Bryant's knowledge of A's history and asked him, 'Do you know my batting average?'

"'You were batting .419 before this current series started.'"

Fox was batting .417.

Hank Majeski was beaned by Early Wynn, hit behind the left ear on August 7 at Shibe Park. Carried off on a stretcher, he was out of the lineup for a month and still had dizzy spells from the concussion when he returned.

He slowed at bat and in the field; batting close to .300 before he was hit, he tailed off, hitless in the last three games, to .270.

With Pete Suder playing third, Nellie Fox picked up more playing time. On August 14 in the first game against the Yankees, Lou Brissie walked the bases loaded in the fourth, putting big John Lindell on first. Charlie Silvera hit a double-play embryo to Pete Suder at third. Sude threw to Fox, who skipped past the bag and turned to throw to first when 215 pounds of Mrs. Lindell's little boy barreled into him and landed on top of him. Two runs scored while Fox checked to see that no limbs had been detached.

The sight may have been enough to convince Connie Mack that Nellie Fox's life expectancy as a big league second baseman would not be long.

A more telling fact about Fox was that he not only stayed in the game after being run over by Lindell, but he played the second game too.

But Mack's opinion seemed confirmed when Fox struggled at the plate through late August and September, finishing at .255 with a .354 OBP.

New York City went all out with a three-day celebration of Connie Mack August 19–21. On Friday he was the hero of a ticker tape parade down Broadway, standing in an open car, waving to the crowd as schoolboy teams marched before and after him. At City Hall the mayor and Joe DiMaggio greeted him. At Yankee Stadium fifty-seven thousand gave him a standing ovation before the Yankees won. The next day Mack received another ovation from over sixty-three thousand before the Yankees won again.

On Sunday the nostalgia was thick as a London fog. The dugouts were filled with Yankee and Athletic stars of the past who would play a two-inning game. The old A's included Max Bishop, Mule Haas, Mickey Cochrane, Al Simmons, Jimmy Foxx, Home Run Baker, Jack Barry, and Lefty Grove. Some of them had to repeat their names when they greeted him before he recognized them. The ceremonies began with the two current teams gathered before a collection of microphones. Mack strode out briskly in his three-piece suit, scorecard in hand, to accept a plaque from AL president Will Harridge.

A bonfire of memories was kindled for Mack as he watched Lefty Grove throwing with the old form, if not the old speed, to Mike Cochrane, who looked lively enough to catch nine innings, "Camera Eye" Bishop drawing a leadoff walk, Al Simmons and Jimmy Foxx hitting line drives. Mack's old knuckleball ace, Eddie Rommel, umpired behind home plate.

"To see the old timers playing two innings was worth a great deal to me," Mack wrote to his Connecticut friend Hubert Sedgwick.

In the game that followed Ferris Fain hit a grand slam in the seventh, and the A's won, 8–7. Any victory over the Yankees was prized more by Mack than all the silver trays and trophies he received. The day ended with a dinner in the Stadium Club, at which all who took part in the day's activities received a watch.

"The Yankees have been wonderful to me," Mack told every writer who approached him." The visitors' share of the gate from the three-day series was also wonderful.

(While Connie Mack was being feted in New York on Sunday, the Giants were playing a doubleheader at Shibe Park. In the ninth inning of the second game, Phillies center fielder Richie Ashburn caught a fly ball near his shoes. At least he said he did; the umpire said he trapped it. A run scored. The Phillies argued vehemently. Fans showered the field with soda bottles, fruit, and other missiles. The umps forfeited the game to the Giants. Connie Jr., in charge of the concessions, announced that Shibe Park vendors would henceforth follow the practice of most other parks and serve all drinks in paper cups.)

Boston trailed New York by 1½ games when the Red Sox came to Shibe Park for a weekend series on September 10. On Saturday the Athletics handed the visitors the game, 9–1, in an exhibition reminiscent of Mack's last-place teams. Don White in right field was apparently mesmerized by anything hit by Ted Williams, misplaying a first-inning fly ball into a double and dropping a fly ball in the fifth. A 6-run first inning included one of Fain's 2 errors in the A's total of 4. (Fain led the league with 22 errors, most of them on hurried throws to second or third.) With plenty of opportunities, the A's made 5 double plays.

After the game Connie Mack went into the clubhouse and tore into them for their embarrassing performance.

Maybe it stung. Who knows? On Sunday they took 2 from Boston while the Yankees were sweeping the Senators, opening a 3-game lead. In the first game the A's turned 2 double plays, 1 the hard way. With DiMaggio on second and Pesky on first and no outs, Williams hit a grounder to Suder, who threw to Joost to get Pesky. DiMaggio tried to score on the throw to first. Fain cut him down at the plate.

Carl Scheib threw a 2-hitter in the 4–0 nightcap and went home with a prize. With 1 out in the ninth, Lou Stringer walked. Al Zarilla grounded to

Fain, who started a 3-6-1 double play that tied the 1945 Red Sox record of 198 double plays. Scheib put the ball in his pocket. In the clubhouse he asked all the infielders to sign it. He still has it.

The Athletics went on to set a still-standing record of 217 double plays. And, no, it wasn't just because they had so many opportunities. They had good hands and rifle arms and the wizard of the phantom tag, Pete Suder, at second base. Nellie Fox contributed, participating in 68 of them when Suder was out or played third. Fain's 194 is still the record for first basemen.

The 1949 season was a disaster only because it had begun with such great expectations. Attendance was good, especially on the road, until the A's played at home most of September. It fell by more than one hundred thousand, but another healthy profit went into the books, about $144,000. In just about every category on offense and defense they were in the middle of the pack, resulting in an 81-73 fifth-place finish. The team's most potent offensive weapon was once again the base on balls. The first four in the lineup—Joost, Valo, Fain, and Chapman—worked a total of 484 walks. Joost averaged more than a walk a game, something only Babe Ruth and Ted Williams had done before in the AL. Joost, Valo, and Fain had a combined OBP of .419.

Eddie Joost was second to Ted Williams in runs and walks and hit 23 home runs.

Sam Chapman continued to be Old Reliable, hitting 24 home runs—enough to tie for third in the league—and driving in 108—fifth in the league.

On November 20, 1949, the Washington Touchdown Club hosted an eightieth birthday luncheon for Clark Griffith. Connie Mack, a month away from turning eighty-seven, went down on the train.

"I may not be around much longer," he said. Immediately afterward he left and returned home. When Griffith realized what Mack had done, he choked up. "Imagine the old man traveling all that distance by himself in one day just to be with me. I hope Connie will live to be 120."

23 | WHO'S IN CHARGE?

At a winter meeting in Chicago a few years earlier, Al Simmons had traveled the ninety miles from his home in Milwaukee to ask Connie Mack if he would be retained as a coach for the next season. Red Smith reported the conversation:

> "Al," said Mr. Mack, "you have a job with the A's for as long as you want it."
> "That's great. Thanks. But, um," he stammered, "you're not getting any younger, Mr. Mack."
> "I see what you mean. I'm sure my sons know how I feel about it."
> "Maybe they do, but would you mind telling them?"
> "Don't worry, Al. I'll mention it."

After the last home game of the 1949 season, Simmons asked Mack if he could skip the remaining five games in New York and Washington. "I'm not feeling well."

> "Will you be at the World Series?" asked Mack.
> "No. I'm going to Hot Springs."
> "Well, Al, in that case I'll see you in Florida at spring training next year."

Before leaving for his home in San Diego after the last game of the season, Earle Brucker called Mr. Mack to say goodbye.

Mack told him, "Don't do anything unless something really big comes your way. In that case, I'll let you go. But if you leave, you'll be breaking up my plans."

Ten days later Connie Mack told the local beat writers that he would have an announcement to make in a few days.

"Good news, Mr. Mack?" asked one. "Maybe a trade?"

"No," said Mack. "At least in my opinion it is not good news. It's very bad news."

The writers had only one day to speculate. The next morning they were called to the tower office.

Art Morrow described Mack as sounding "disconsolate and tired when, in a voice choked with emotion," he announced: "Jimmie Dykes will be back with us next year, but Al Simmons and Earle Brucker have been released. They have both done good work for me, splendid work, and I am really sorry to see them go . . . but there was nothing I could do about it."

It was evident to everybody in the room that the ax had been wielded against Mack's wishes when he said, "[Simmons and Brucker] both are wonderful fellows and I thought they did a fine job for us. But the board of directors decided we could do without them and they have the final say in running the ball club."

You can almost hear the sigh.

Wrote Morrow, "The manager shook his head like a man crushed."

A few days later Mack tried to backtrack on the clear impression he had given that the coaches had been fired despite his objections. It was as if he had been chastised for revealing his displeasure and his extinguished authority and exposing the facade of unity within the family, as if the friction wasn't common knowledge already. "The board of directors knows what it's doing," he said

Asked to comment, Connie Jr. said, "It was done for the best interests of the club. We decided a change in our coaching setup would prove beneficial to the team. So we made the changes."

Clearly Connie Mack was no longer in control, not even part of the "we."

Ray Kelly of the *Bulletin* was one of the many mystified by the action: "There appears to be no forthright explanation for the abrupt firing. . . . At no time during the season did Connie Mack express any dissatisfaction with them. Al is as good a third base coach as any. Brucker is a great pitching coach."

Connie Mack called Al Simmons in Hot Springs and gave him the news. "He was bitterly disappointed," Mack said, "and asked if we couldn't hold up news of his release for a time. He said he'd like to resign. I told him it was too late."

Connie Jr. may have been covering for Dad when he said, "It was the original intent of the club to give them a chance to resign, but a slip-up in the front office let the story out prematurely."

Sounding like an admonished child, Mack apologized for giving out the story before the coaches had been notified. "The news was given out too soon, but that was my fault. I am responsible for that, not the directors. I wrote to Brucker about it, but I don't know whether they put an air mail stamp on the letter or not. I'm afraid that this will be the first he heard about it."

The first Earle Brucker heard about it was when someone at the *Inquirer* woke him with a phone call. He received the letter later that day. Brucker was disappointed but not angry. "None of this is easy to take. . . . I'm sorry I won't be with Mr. Mack next year."

That evening Simmons told Art Morrow, "What disturbs me so much is not entirely the dismissal. After all, that's within the club's rights. But the way the whole thing has been handled. I can't see how Mr. Mack can blame any of us for the club's poor showing this season. Why doesn't he go out and get some new players and get a new assistant manager to replace his son, Earle? The coaches weren't responsible for some of those terrible mistakes made this year. On coaching jobs you get blamed for so many things that aren't your fault."

Connie Mack had more trouble working with family than he ever had had with the Shibes. His three sons were on the board of directors. He no longer was, dropped in 1947 "to relieve him of some of the burdens of the office," though what burdens went with being on the board were unclear. His absence during the winter, either in California or Florida, when the board met, may have been a factor. Until then his sons had seldom questioned Dad's judgment when it came to players and coaches. The last time had been over the hiring of Al Horwits in a public relations position in 1941, when Mack threatened to resign as president and ended up paying Horwits out of his own pocket.

In addition to Roy, Earle, and Connie Jr., the board now consisted of Benny Macfarland, representing the Shibe interests, and club secretary Bob Schroeder.

It was, wrote H. G. Salsinger of the *Detroit News,* "a very odd cast of characters that had taken over control of the Athletics."

They didn't want to argue with Mr. Mack and didn't have the nerve to look at him across the table while taking actions they knew would upset him. And Connie Mack didn't want to argue with them, as he had told Bob Paul in 1947, "I don't want to fight my sons."

So what happened? With no minutes of the meeting, we can only speculate on who led the move to fire the coaches and who went along with it. At any other club a disappointing season often resulted in the firing of the manager, not just a couple of coaches. What did the board hope to accomplish? They knew the problem began at the top. Did they talk about Mr. Mack's senility? Did anyone suggest that he be asked to step down now, depriving him of the celebration of his fiftieth year as the club's first and only manager? Not likely. To some extent the human addiction to round numbers helped to seal the fate of the Philadelphia Athletics. We make a big deal out of a fiftieth milestone, a very small deal of a forty-ninth or fifty-first. The forty-ninth anniversary of some world event or disaster goes unnoticed, but milestones like the fiftieth and hundredth are highly marketable.

Nobody was going to deny Mr. Mack that big five-oh. Maybe the only thing they agreed on was that Connie Mack wasn't what he used to be and 1950 should be his last year in the dugout.

One unnamed board member, probably Bob Schroeder, hinted at the underlying problem: "You know there was some friction on our club this year. By this move we figured we could eliminate it."

Friction on the club? Not in the clubhouse. Sure, not everybody liked Al Simmons, whose garrulous, fiery personality grated at some of them. But young hitters still eagerly sought him out for batting tips. Simmons had never liked pitchers, even those on his own team. Red Smith remembered a night in 1947 in Washington when he had shared a postgame cab ride with a furious Simmons and listened to Al berate Jesse Flores for blowing a three-run lead: "Three *** runs and they blow it and that Flores just stands out there and throws and don't ever try anything. Never even tries to move a *** hitter back or loosen him up. Just stands out there and throws and lets 'em take a three-run lead away from him."

Simmons had nothing but disdain for Earle Mack and made no pretense of hiding it. But to Simmons, if they didn't come to blows, then it wasn't friction: "How can they say I caused any friction? There never was any as far as I was concerned. To make sure there wasn't, I avoided Earle Mack."

Nobody could associate Earle Brucker with friction. He was the coach the players aired their gripes to. Everybody liked him, especially the pitchers.

When he and the pitchers walked out to the bullpen before a game, somebody in the press box would invariably say, "There goes Mother Brucker and his chicks."

More than once Connie Mack had told reporters, "Brucker is the best coach of pitchers I have ever known."

Neither Simmons nor Brucker could be seen as a threat to undermine Connie Mack in the hope of replacing him, instead of Earle's inheriting the job. Neither one wanted it. (By now Earle probably didn't either.) After his dismissal Brucker turned down offers to manage in the Pacific Coast League, choosing instead to sign as a coach with the St. Louis Browns. It took him a while, but by September he would have the last-place Browns' pitching staff organized to where they won 10 of 11, including 4 straight over Cleveland that knocked the Indians out of the race. The A's were in Detroit at the time. Somebody in the press box wondered, "What made the Browns so hot?"

Art Morrow said, "Pitching."

"Why should the St. Louis pitching suddenly become so good?"

"Earle Brucker and nothing more."

No, the friction referred to by the unnamed board member was in the board room. Roy and Earle, though having little use for each other, were allied against Connie Jr., the only one with any rapport with the players and the Shibe Park employees. He had more ideas in a week than Roy or Earle had had in thirty years.

Al Simmons was probably the target. Earle must have burned with resentment and humiliation when first Simmons and now Dykes and Simmons were Dad's first lieutenants in the dugout. He was still "officially" the assistant manager, though he "assistant managed" mainly when his father was absent. He was still "officially" the heir to the manager's office, but that inheritance was unlikely as long as Roy and Connie Jr. had anything to say about it—and Earle knew it. The firing of Simmons alone might be seen as spite or jealousy on Earle's part. To blunt that perception, Brucker was sacrificed too.

Privately Connie Jr. said that his priority was to "protect Dad." He might have gone along with the firings, believing that Simmons and Brucker were taking advantage of his father's fondness for them and slacking off. Yet Red Smith wrote that just two years earlier Mack had told him, "I wish I had nine men named Simmons."

We don't know what Connie Jr. said in the meeting or how he voted. He and Benny Macfarland were allies. If they voted not to fire the coaches and

Roy and Earle voted yes, that left the mediation-minded Bob Schroeder in the middle. Maybe he cast the deciding vote in a futile quest for harmony.

Schroeder's health was failing; he would soon begin several stays at Temple University Hospital, where he died on February 5, 1950, at fifty-nine, ending more than forty years with the Athletics. He had started with the club as a peanut vendor in 1902, when his father, Joseph, was the head groundskeeper at Columbia Park. John Shibe had sent him to business school, and he had risen from Shibe's secretary to become concessions manager, club secretary, and a member of the board. Under his direction the concessions operation had become a very profitable enterprise for the stockholders. In 1939 he and Connie Jr. had modernized the food service at Shibe Park by opening several clean, bright eating areas resembling small neighborhood cafes, with tables and chairs. He was a soft-spoken peacemaker, respected by everyone, often trying to negotiate peace among the brothers, always with a smile.

Earle said of him, "Bob was a level-headed fellow, so easy to get along with. He never jumped at conclusions and whenever anybody in the organization had a problem, we took it to Bob and he thought it out clearly."

Connie Mack was in St. Petersburg when he heard the news of Schroeder's passing. "Oh my golly," he said. "This is a terrible shock. I find it hard to believe. This is a great blow to everybody. He was a wonderful boy."

The Athletics paid his $1,000 monthly salary to his widow, Madeleine, for five months.

The fact that Jimmie Dykes survived the shakeup reinforced the speculation that he was slated to succeed Mack. This was bolstered by a report that Dykes had turned down an offer to manage the Senators, and, it was said, he would not have done so unless he had some assurances from the Mack boys.

If the directors thought their actions would be docilely accepted by the public, they were not tuned in. They figured the firing of two coaches would be a one-day story. The deluge of unfavorable publicity and letters took them by surprise. The press fanned the fire and the public grew heated, believing the iconic Mr. Mack was being ill-treated by his ungrateful offspring.

Connie Jr. had become the club spokesman and drew the most "sharper-than-a-serpent's-tooth" arrows for plotting to undermine his father's authority by exiling his lieutenants. He had hoped to dodge the need for further explanations. Now he decided it was up to him to answer the criticism. Roy and Earle were incapable, and none of them could be sure of what

Dad might say. It was as if the sons knew the Old Man could no longer be depended on for the necessary hedging and dissembling that was part of the business.

On October 19 Connie Jr. was interviewed on wptz-tv and gave the impression that his father planned to step down after the 1950 season and that Earle would succeed him. He ended with this: "But we hope Dad will not go into total eclipse. We want always to be able to look to him for advice and his word then as now will be the real authority in the management of the club's affairs."

Hogwash. He must have choked on those words. If that were true, Al Simmons and Earle Brucker would not have been fired, and he knew it.

The next night on wcau Connie Jr. found himself in the uncomfortable position of contradicting his father's expressing surprise and displeasure at the "bad news" of the firing:

The board of directors believed that Brucker and Simmons were not doing a good job. The matter was discussed with Dad, who gave his approval before the two men were let go. The confusion was caused by the fact that Dad just hated to part with his two old friends. He knew, however, that it was for the club's best interest and went along.

After all, and let there be no mistake about this, Dad still is running this ball club. Many people don't believe that a man of eighty-six is capable of leading a big league club. But Connie Mack is and does. Simmons and Brucker undoubtedly believe they had done a good job. We didn't and dropped them.

[Connie Mack undoubtedly believed they had done a good job too, putting the lie to "Dad still is running this ball club."]

We want coaches who are full-time assistants, men who will come out to the ballpark in the morning and help a player in his work to shake a batting slump, men who'll take time to teach rookies, men who will generate a winning spirit [things that Earle Mack never did], and take a real interest in our ball club.

Understand we are not blaming Simmons and Brucker for our failure to live up to expectations in 1949. We fell because we didn't have the reserve strength to insert when our regulars slumped or were injured.

We don't intend to have this happen again. We are ready to spend big money if the other ball clubs will sell the players we are after.

Asked how long Connie Mack would manage the team, he said, "Dad recently said he would like to manage one more year. After next season he may step down. Earle will succeed Dad when the time comes."

Connie Mack had never said that publicly; he always hedged or quashed any retirement talk when the subject was raised. Either he was telling his sons one thing and the public something else, or the boys were signaling that *they* intended to retire him. Two months later the coverage of his annual birthday gathering with the press never mentioned the word "last" or "farewell" before the word "season" in a detailed discussion of the outlook for 1950. The writers asked him, "If you win the pennant in 1950, will you quit managing?" Mack's answer: "I don't think so. I'd probably want to win again the next year."

Prior to the 1950 season *Look* magazine sports editor Tim Cohane wrote that 1950 would be Mack's last year as manager; he would be forced out by his sons. Denials flew like home runs out of Shibe Park.

At West Palm Beach in the spring of 1950 every writer who asked the same question got the same answer from Mack:

To the AP: "Mark my word, I have no intention of retiring. It's the last thing I'll ever do."

Wrote Arthur Daley of the *New York Times:* "'No, sir,' he snorted indignantly, or at least as indignantly as this most remarkable old man ever can get. 'I hope to manage for many years to come.'"

Art Morrow wrote: "Baseball's Oldest Inhabitant has no intention of making this his last season in baseball."

Nobody else in the Athletics family said anything more about Connie Mack's last season.

In fact nobody else said anything more about anything. Except Al Simmons. He felt that he and Brucker had been made the goats for the A's having finished fifth. While acknowledging that he had no use for Earle Mack, Simmons burned over Connie Jr.'s comments that he had failed in his duties toward Mr. Mack, a man he loved and respected as much as any nonfamily member could.

Simmons wrote an open letter to the Philadelphia fans:

I dislike continuing the discussion, but feel I should reply to the charges of Connie Mack Jr. that I didn't do a good job, wasn't a full-time worker, didn't help players shake batting slumps, didn't take a real interest in the ball club.

These charges, if not denied by actual proof, give the fans a one-sided story.

In 1948, when Mr. Mack and I ran the club, I was given a $2,500 bonus at the end of the season, and a raise of $2,500 that put me in the five-figure class. Do ball clubs do that for a man who hasn't produced?

As for not being around earlier to teach rookies, I asked Mr. Mack many times about that and volunteered my services. He always replied there was no need for me earlier, since they had other coaches to look after the younger men.

I have no idea why they fired Earle Brucker, because he is one of the best coaches of pitchers in the country. I was fired for two reasons—because the club finished fifth when it was supposed to finish third, and a goat or goats had to be found; and because Earle Mack and I never got along. I am not a "yes man." I am not the quiet type. When I thought certain things should be done for the good of the club, I told Mr. Mack, whether or not he agreed.

I do not believe that Mr. Mack ever willingly agreed to fire Brucker and me. If he gave his consent it was under pressure by the directors—his sons—who owe all they are to Connie Mack. I want the fans of Philadelphia to know that I think as highly of Mr. Mack right now as I ever did. I respect and admire him more than I do any man in America. I considered it a privilege to play for him and to serve under him.

Simmons then thanked the writers and fans for their support over the years:

I am sorry that after nearly twenty years' association with the Athletics I had to leave under such circumstances. But the directors own the club now and can fire whom they please.

I hope to get another job as manager or coach in baseball to show whether I can hustle and instill in players the will to win.

Simmons signed as a third base coach for Cleveland, where his fire proved to be still alive. He was ejected four times, more than any other year as a coach. The Indians were in the pennant race until September, finishing fourth.

The Sporting News editorial writer was one of the few observers who applauded the changes, expressing more confidence in the three sons than the writers who knew them. The lengthy analysis actually wound up making a better case for firing Connie Mack than the coaches:

There should be no shedding of tears over the release by the Athletics of coaches Al Simmons and Earle Brucker—against the wishes of Connie Mack. The nationwide wail that went up over the action of the directors of the club was due to sentiment and without a common-sense view of what took place.

The announcement from the tower at Shibe Park boils down to this: the 86-year-old owner is no longer the supreme commander. The five-man board of directors has taken over, and because the board includes Connie's three sons . . . it has been accused of everything from atrocious taste to filial disloyalty.

If bad taste was involved in the incident, it could be found in Connie's own frank statement that he disapproved of the action of the board. It was Mr. Mack himself, and not his sons, who revealed that the house of McGillicuddy stands divided, although many in the American League were aware that in the past few years all has not been well. In being placed in an embarrassing position, it is a position in which his own hand lettered the directions. The general public would not have known of the situation if Mr. Mack had remained silent.

[In other words, the old man should keep his opinions to himself to preserve the appearance of harmony, even though anybody who could read knew there was none.]

As for disloyalty, those who know the Mack family dismiss this suggestion with a scornful laugh. Every one of Connie's sons would stand by their famous father in any real trouble and at whatever personal cost. But it is evident that the time has arrived when these same dutiful sons—Roy, 61, Earle, 57, and Connie Junior, 34—none of them kids either in years or in temperament, believe that in this day and age of keen competition which has narrowed down in some respects to a battle of dollars, they simply have to say, "Dad, you'd better let us handle this."

It is an attitude which the elder Mack should welcome. The years sit with incredible lightness on the shoulders of the Grand Old Man, but it isn't reasonable to believe that he can discharge all the duties of owning, operating, and managing a major league club without the assistance and the guidance of his younger associates.

It is not for *The Sporting News*, which has long admired Mack to a degree little short of idolatry, to say that he should turn over some real authority to his directors [although that is what the writer seems to be saying], but it is evident that he already has done so, whether by force or disregard of his wishes.

There is and always will be a place in Philadelphia and in baseball for Connie Mack, but that place is not necessarily in the front lines of the hurly-burly competition for success, traveling on trains, getting up early and going to bed late, matching energy and wits with rivals young enough to be his grandchildren. [In other words, the board should have fired the manager, not the coaches, but nobody was going to say that out loud or in print.]

Modern baseball is a young man's game, and other club owners who try to convince themselves to the contrary are kidding no one but themselves. There may be no substitute for experience, but neither is there a substitute for the physical and mental stamina needed to meet the challenge of the human dynamos who have moved into the business in the last 20 years.

Mr. Mack is fortunate. Most owners in his position would have to seek the help of outsiders. He can turn to his own flesh and blood. The parade never will pass him by because his sons will lift him up on their able shoulders and carry him along to watch it before they become old men, and perhaps some day once more to lead it.

Pity Connie Mack? *The Sporting News* feels more like congratulating him, and he should congratulate himself that he has three sons to carry on a name he devoted so many years to make famous.

In the long history of *The Sporting News*, its editorials were often proven by subsequent events to be way off the mark but never more so than in this one.

The Mack sons smiled over it. Earle said, "People are going out of their way to speak to me and shake hands. I never knew I had so many friends."

There was no comment from Roy.

On November 30, 1949, at the Bellevue-Stratford Hotel Connie Jr. introduced two new coaches, old A's teammates Bing Miller and Mickey Cochrane.

Miller's appointment had been expected; during the winter he worked at "The Tavern" in suburban Cynwyd, a place frequented by members of the A's front office. He had coached for both Dykes and Cochrane and jumped at the chance to be reunited with them and Mr. Mack.

Cochrane was a surprise. "I didn't know a thing about it until last weekend," he said. "I received a call from Mr. Mack in Detroit. He put the question to me."

It had been obvious to Bing Miller last August at the old-timers' game in New York that Mike was eager to be back in the game after thirteen years. Cochrane did not need the job. He had been a well-paid representative of a tire company in Detroit and owned a Lincoln-Mercury agency in Billings, Montana, where he was a partner in a dude ranch sixty-two miles out of town (it was not a success). The coaches earned $10,000. Despite speculation that he was brought in to succeed Connie Mack, Cochrane had no interest in managing again. After his near-fatal beaning in 1937, managing from the dugout had taken a severe toll on his health.

The idea was probably young Connie's, perhaps as a way to deflect criticism from the firing of Simmons and Brucker. If that was a factor, it worked. The reunion of the popular stars from the championship years delighted the fans as much as it did the old teammates.

Publicity and promotion had been farmed out to the Adelphia PR agency since 1948 at a cost of $15,000 a year. The public flap over the firing of Simmons and Brucker and the bungling efforts to overcome it convinced farm director Art Ehlers that the Athletics needed a bright, energetic, full-time, in-house public relations staff. He knew just the man for the job.

In 1947 Ehlers had signed Princeton graduate Dick Armstrong to a minor league contract. When the A's took over the new Portsmouth, Ohio, franchise in the Class D Ohio-Indiana League in 1948, Ehlers suggested that Armstrong might have a brighter future in the front office than on the field. Armstrong became the Portsmouth business manager and shone as a promoter, putting on a big Connie Mack Day in 1949. In October Ehlers asked him to apply for the new public relations position with the A's.

As part of his application, Armstrong outlined an ambitious series of events to celebrate Connie Mack's golden jubilee. He was hired, along with the PR director of the NFL Eagles, Ed Hogan, as a consultant.

Ed Pollock summed up the mood of the press as hopeful but skeptical:

"One thing is certain. With a comparatively new farm system, new coaches and a new public relations office, the A's are moving toward a new era. To make it a good era, there must be real cooperation between the various units of the organization and the full support of all of them must be directed toward winning new fans and holding the faithful."

24 | THE OLD OPTIMIST

Connie Mack's golden jubilee season was a disaster. Or was it a comedy, like when the family throws a big, expensive party for grandma and grandpa's golden wedding anniversary and most of the expected guests don't show up and the band can't play what anybody requests and the party blows up when old family feuds erupt?

Only nobody laughed.

The planning had begun in the middle of the '49 season. In August Mack had told his scout Harry O'Donnell, "Find me another pitcher who can win ten games. That's all I need to win the pennant."

O'Donnell came up with two: a twenty-seven-year-old Buffalo right-hander, Bob Hooper, who had finished the year with a 19-3 record working 175 innings split between 18 starts and 18 relief appearances, and a wartime 22-game winner for the Cubs, Hank Wyse, thirty-two. A lame wing had carried Wyse back to the minors. But he was sound enough to work 215 innings at Shreveport with an 18-8 record.

Mack bought Hooper conditionally before the draft and later finished the purchase for $15,000. Wyse was drafted for $7,500.

O'Donnell cautioned Mack, "Wyse may not be a good boy."

"Let me worry about that," said Mack, "as long as he can win ten games."

A few months after the draft Connie Mack was at a baseball meeting with O'Donnell when they were approached by Shreveport president Bonneau Peters.

PETERS: I'm surprised you drafted that fellow [Wyse].
MACK: Don't you think he can win ten games for us?
BP: Ten? He could win fifteen.

CM: Then what's the matter?

BP: He just got out of jail.

It seemed that Wyse had gotten into a fight with two other men after a car crash. They were all arrested and taken to the local jail, where the fight resumed. Wyse finished third in the fracas, taking a long gash in his left arm.

None of that bothered Mack, not if "he could win fifteen."

Adding to the optimistic outlook, Art Ehlers enthused over outfielder Ben Guintini, twenty-nine, drafted from Dallas: "Guintini found himself this year, hitting .307 with 32 home runs."

Guintini found himself back in Dallas after four hitless at bats.

Connie Mack had decided that Hank Majeski's best days were behind him. He had been in a slump before he was beaned the previous August and hit just .167 after July 30. When he came back in September, he had a few productive days, but Mack began looking for a replacement, seemingly looking here, there, and everywhere.

On September 14, 1949, the A's gave the Cubs $10,000 for infielder Frank Gustine, a ten-year National Leaguer at twenty-eight and over the hill at thirty. Ten days later they gave Montreal Bill McCahan and $25,000 for Kermit Wahl, twenty-six, a wartime utility infielder for the Reds who hadn't hit then and wouldn't hit now.

By this time it was hard to know who was making these decisions: Earle? Roy? Art Ehlers? Connie Mack? The board of directors?

On October 9 the A's traded the banged-up Buddy Rosar to Boston for thirty-three-year-old infielder Billy Hitchcock as a backup for Pete Suder, then sent twenty-one-year-old Nellie Fox to Chicago for catcher Joe Tipton.

According to White Sox president Chuck Comiskey, it was Earle who came looking for a catcher to replace Rosar. Comiskey asked for Pete Suder. Earle wasn't about to be responsible for trading Sude, one of his father's favorites. But he knew that Dad wasn't sold on Fox; indeed nobody, including the A's veteran infielders, foresaw anything but a utility role for the likable, hustling little fellow. (When Fox blossomed into a .300 hitter a few years later, Mack replaced his sale of Herb Pennock as his greatest baseball mistake with the trade of Fox, who lasted another fifteen years.)

The White Sox already had an all-star second baseman in Cass Michaels, only two years older than Fox. But Michaels had had some run-ins with White Sox manager Jack Onslow and in May would go to Washington for power-hitting first baseman Eddie Robinson and pitcher Ray Scarborough.

Tipton, a volatile, hard-drinking Georgian, had been touted as a slugger but had hit only .204 for the Sox with 3 home runs. With Cleveland in 1948 he had been one of the free-swinging participants in a brawl among the celebrating Indians in the Kenmore Hotel after their playoff win in Boston. Traded to Chicago, he had not impressed Jack Onslow, a one-time catcher. On May 1 the Sox almost blew a 14–3 lead when the Browns scored 8 runs in the ninth inning. After the game Onslow berated Tipton for his pitch calling during the horrendous inning. They almost came to blows. Onslow also believed Tipton was one of the clubhouse stool pigeons.

Connie Mack assigned Lou Brissie to room with Tipton, hoping that Lou might have a beneficial influence on him. It didn't work.

"I knew him but never really knew him," said Brissie.

Tipton brought to spring training a fondness for "On Top of Old Smokey," which he sang incessantly, and a footlocker full of mason jars filled with white lightning—the good stuff flavored with a stick from charred old whisky barrels in each jar. One evening he invited Ferris Fain and a few others up to the room to sample it. The tasting ended when Tipton fell in the bathroom and cut up his face. The next morning he went down to breakfast and Jimmie Dykes saw him. When Brissie appeared, Dykes said to him, "I'm disappointed in you."

"What for?" Lou asked.

"You were drinking and had a fight with Tipton and beat him up."

"Not me," said Brissie, and told him what had happened.

Athletics' pitchers preferred pitching to Mike Guerra or Joe Astroth. But Tipton became the number two catcher behind Guerra.

In the next few months somebody in the A's front office spent another $25,000 on an assortment of half a dozen guys nobody ever heard of and made an offer to a one-time military school star second baseman and all-around athlete, just out of the army after two years in Korea, but Dan Rostenkowski turned it down for a career in politics, which led to thirty-six years in Congress.

Dick Armstrong went to work as the A's public relations director in the wake of the brouhaha over the firing of Al Simmons and Earle Brucker. The first thing he did was ask a professor at Philadelphia Business College, John Bucci, to conduct a survey of the public's attitude toward the Athletics—not just the fans who had reacted so vehemently to the firing of the coaches, but also the general public. He wanted to know what those who didn't go to Shibe Park thought about the Athletics too. It might help explain why they didn't go.

When the results came in, they were devastating. The club's approval level was as low as Republican presidential candidate Alf Landon's numbers against FDR in the 1936 election. A negative image of Connie Mack for selling his stars was still resilient, even though that had been fifteen years ago in the middle of the Depression. Ten years ago, while recovering from his near-fatal illness, Mack had told Ed Pollock, "I'll never buy any high-priced players again. I don't want my family to inherit a debt-burdened club." And he hadn't. Now he was seen as a skinflint who wouldn't spend any real money to improve his team. The stars of the '48 and '49 teams—Joost and Fain and Majeski, Fowler and Brissie and Kellner—had been cut-rate bargains.

Armstrong showed the survey results to the club's directors. Roy shrugged them off; to him the word "promotion" meant a civil servant's rising from a G-3 to a G-4 position. But Connie Jr. saw the need to do something fast and dramatic to overcome the public's negative opinion of the club. The postwar boom that lifted all boats wouldn't last forever. The Phillies were on the rise, having finished third (with the same record as the A's) in '49. Bob Carpenter had given a $65,000 bonus to a young left-hander, Curt Simmons, in 1946. Their farm teams had produced new young stars.

For the A's the quickest way to make a splash was by spending big money for the best available players. Plans for the $400,000 construction of the two-tier grandstand in right field were shelved. The money would be used to "buy a pennant for Dad."

Roy and Earle were skittish about spending money for anything. But Roy trusted Art Ehlers's judgment. If Ehlers said they had to spend the money, he'd go along. And Art said it. Roy and Earle were probably quaking when they told reporters, "We are going all out. No limit on what we will spend."

So Connie Mack went to the New York meetings in December 1949 with a half million dollars to spend. But he didn't go alone. The whole family was there: the three sons and Benny Macfarland (four-fifths of the board of directors) and coaches Mickey Cochrane, Bing Miller, and Dave Keefe. They were there to keep Connie Mack on a short leash, to be able to confer and approve or turn down any deals on the spot, to represent the club to the press in the hope of avoiding the kind of mixed messages that had accompanied the firing of Simmons and Brucker. Connie Mack was still the face of the Philadelphia Athletics, but he was no longer the voice or the unquestioned brains.

Bill DeWitt was peddling flesh to raise money to keep his St. Louis Browns afloat. Roscoe McGowen of the *New York Times* asked DeWitt if he was selling off his entire roster before transferring the franchise.

"We're selling ballplayers but not clubs," DeWitt said with some asperity. "We're not broke and we're not considering moving the franchise to Los Angeles or anywhere else."

DeWitt said his reason for selling players was simply because "we couldn't make expenses by drawing only 270,000 fans last season and selling is the only way we can make up the deficit." In other words, the same thing Connie Mack had done seventeen years ago.

The prime ribs in DeWitt's showcase were second baseman Gerry Priddy, a .290 hitter with 11-home-run power, and third baseman Bob Dillinger, a fast, line-drive-hitting leadoff man. Dillinger, thirty-one, had come out of the army in 1946 on a wave of publicity after batting .406 in the high-octane Pacific service league. In '47 he had led both leagues in stolen bases with 34 and led the AL for the next two years, though his numbers declined to 20. His .324 had been third in the league in '49, aided by batting .420 against A's pitching.

The way Connie Mack told it a week later, he went after everybody in DeWitt's meat market and some who weren't. His first objective was outfielder Roy Sievers, a .306 hitter with 16 home runs and 75 RBIs in his rookie year. Mack offered DeWitt $200,000 for Sievers. DeWitt turned him down. (When Sievers read the story, he decided, "I'm worth at least 10 percent of that" and threatened DeWitt's health by asking for a raise to $20,000. DeWitt, described by Sievers as "the worst penny pincher," almost choked. Sievers settled for $9,000.)

Mack said he then offered DeWitt $300,000 and five players for Dillinger and Priddy. DeWitt thought he could do better in separate deals for each. So Mack offered him $150,000 and five players for Priddy. DeWitt said no. When DeWitt packaged speedy .229-hitting backup outfielder Paul Lehner with Dillinger, Connie Mack coughed up $100,000 plus Frank Gustine, Rocco Ippolito, Billy DeMars, and Ray Coleman. It was the Athletics' largest outlay ever of cash and players in one deal.

But that's not quite the way Connie Jr. described the negotiations at the time. He told Frank Yeutter of the *Bulletin*:

There was no exaggeration in the financial figure we talked about. We would have gone to half a million dollars to get the players we wanted from the Browns. But they wouldn't trade the two outfielders we asked for [Sievers and twenty-one-year-old Dick Kokos, who'd hit 23 home runs]. And we most assuredly would not pay the preposterous price they asked for Priddy. [The Browns sold Priddy to Detroit for Lou Kretlow and $100,000.]

The deal finally came down to Dillinger and Lehner. We would have paid cash for them but DeWitt insisted upon players. We're not sure how good Billy DeMars will be [not very] or how long Ray Coleman will last [three years]. We know Frank Gustine is finished. [He was, raising the question of who had paid $10,000 for him three months earlier?] But Ippy Ippolito is another story. He was with Lincoln last year and scouts who saw him say he will probably become an exceptionally fine player. [He didn't.] However, we want a pennant winner now. That's why we wanted Dillinger and Lehner. Lehner will let us start an outfield of Sam Chapman, Elmer Valo, and Lehner, which is better than any combination we've had for several years.

Lehner was a little guy—5-foot-9, 160 pounds—but he covered ground and had a good arm. Still, Connie Jr. had fogged out the '48 performance of Valo, Chapman, and Barney McCosky before McCosky hurt his back.

The next day the A's traded Hank Majeski to Chicago for right-handed reliever Ed Klieman, who would pitch under 6 innings for them.

The Connie Mack of five years ago would have spurned Bob Dillinger with the same label he had put on Dick Wakefield: "half a ballplayer, who wouldn't hustle for his own team." But the Connie Mack of 1950 was desperate or less discerning or not in control—or all three. He either couldn't see or didn't want to see what everybody else in the league saw. His board of directors and Art Ehlers saw even less.

Dillinger could hit all right, but he was more of a stationary infielder than Majeski, who had the best hands in the A's infield and a rifle arm. Dillinger didn't even have a popgun. He threw what Ferris Fain described as "four-hoppers" to first base. Everybody in the league knew he was a nonchalant infielder who waved at ground balls going by like country kids waving at freight train engineers rolling past their back yards. Clark Griffith called him "placid, careless, and lackadaisical. He tipped his hat to too many ground balls."

Dan Daniel put it more delicately: "Dillinger did not play challenging ball in the field."

"A .309 hitter, a .309 fielder," was the way some players described him.

Dillinger wasn't going to put his body in harm's way; he wore thick glasses and did not wear a protective cup. Ballplayers knew that wearing glasses made it a little more difficult to pick up a ball hit to one side, and Dillinger took plenty of riding about it. According to one account, when he answered back, "How can I get 'em when I can't see 'em?" DeWitt advised him to keep quiet. "Don't let that get around."

Had Mr. Mack polled his players on the deal, as he was said to have done several years ago for Hank Greenberg and Rudy York, they would have told him, "Don't buy him."

They knew something else about Bob Dillinger: he was an odd duck. His nickname among his teammates was "Goofy."

Tom Ferrick was a pitcher with the Browns in 1949:

We had a party one night in early August at Gerry Priddy's house, wives and all. Dillinger and George Kell were both hitting about .340, leading the league. We're in the kitchen having a drink and I said, "Bob, wouldn't it be great if you could lead the league this year?"

He said, "I'm not going to lead the league this year."

"What do you mean?"

"Hell, if I lead the league this year, I'll get a $5,000 raise. Next year if I don't lead the league I'll get a $5,000 cut."

I said, "So what are you going to do?"

"I'm going to hit about .323 this year, maybe .333 the next year, and I'll get the raises and won't take any cuts."

[He ended the year at .324; Kell won the title at .343.]

That's the way he thought. His batting average went up a little every year with the Browns. He was the best curve ball hitter in baseball. But he was no team player.

Joe DeMaestri, who would play alongside Dillinger in Chicago in 1952, concurred: "You wouldn't want nine guys like him on your team. He said some weird things, had his own ideas about everything. You didn't want to spend time with him. He had some grooved bats, and shaved them in such a way you couldn't tell the hitting surface was almost flat."

When players shagged flies in the outfield or ran, Dillinger always ran alone.

The writers speculated that Dillinger could steal 40 bases with the more aggressive A's attack, 4 more than the entire team had swiped in '49.

The A's had the best leadoff man in the league in Eddie Joost. Where would Dillinger fit in the batting order? Connie Mack said he would bat fifth, a strange spot for a man with no power. After a while Mack moved him up to third, then second, then first, dropping Joost down to sixth.

Paul Lehner had his own style of wackiness. Ray Kelly described him as "an in-and-outer chiefly because of his bizarre behavior." According to one story, the Browns were at Shibe Park one night in 1949 when Lehner showed up with a gimpy knee. He asked manager Muddy Ruel, "Am I playing?" Ruel said, "No." After the game the Browns headed for Detroit—without Lehner, who had disappeared. When he showed up at Briggs Stadium, Ruel asked him where he'd been. "Well, you said I wasn't playing so I went to Toledo to see my girl."

Connie Jr. told Yeutter, "Sure, I know they say Lehner is wacky, but Dad handled Rube Waddell and Osee Schreck and a lot of other strange fellows and I'm sure Lehner will not be any more difficult than those guys."

What he didn't say was that Dad had been forty years old, not eighty-seven, when he had handled Rube and Osee. He could no more handle them today than he could handle Kentucky Derby winner Middleground in May.

On his eighty-seventh birthday Mack's watery blue eyes reflected more hope than vision when he told the UP, "We have the best real chance to win the pennant that we've had in the past several years. We'll have a better in-field with Bob Dillinger at third base. [With Dillinger and Joost wearing glasses, the A's infield was said to lead the league with twelve eyes.] Our outfield is stronger. We expect 100 percent catching from Joe Tipton and Joe Astroth. Our pitching, particularly if Joe Coleman comes in at playing weight, will be excellent."

Coleman had tried to eat his way out of baseball when he was hurt in midseason in '49.

Dillinger had earned $18,000 at St. Louis. Connie Mack sent him a contract for $20,000. Dillinger showed up for the writers' dinner in late January and said he'd like a little more. "After all," he told the writers, "they paid $100,000 for me and Lehner." With Mack in Florida, Earle was in charge of contract negotiations. But this was out of his league. Dillinger didn't sign until March 6 and wrung $25,000 out of Mack, making him the highest paid on the team.

Mack sent Hank Wyse a contract for the minimum $5,000. Wyse sent it back. Mack told him to come to West Palm Beach, and if he made the team, he'd get more. When he proved to be one of the few healthy pitchers in camp, Mack was happy to double his original offer.

When Lou Brissie received a contract for $12,500, the same as he had earned including a bonus for the year before, he thought he deserved a raise. But he didn't want to argue with Mr. Mack. Instead of dealing with Roy, he let Art Ehlers know. Ehlers talked it over with Connie Jr. Brissie said:

> Mr. Mack had made up his mind on an amount. Connie Jr. and Arthur Ehlers didn't want to upset him, but they wanted to help make it right for me. Connie was very good about protecting his father and explaining how Mr. Mack felt about things. Art Ehlers called me to come and see him. We talked about it and the next day they told me to sign and they would pay me the additional money I wanted out of the concessions income. It was a handshake agreement—nothing in writing—and they lived up to it.
>
> I would have loved to play for a team that Connie Jr. was in charge of.

Connie Mack rolled into West Palm Beach with confidence that he had a pennant-winning pitching staff. White Sox manager Jack Onslow enthused, "Look at those pitchers. Suppose Phil Marchildon comes back. Why, Connie would have his best staff since Ehmke, Grove, Earnshaw, and Walberg. Brother, look out for Connie next year. If I can't win the pennant, there's no one I'd rather see cop it." (Onslow's assessing ability might explain why he was fired in May.)

Grantland Rice, the old sentimentalist, wasn't fooled: "The A's have little chance to crowd into the top four."

Publicly the Philadelphia writers plugged the hope more than the reality. Privately they may have been reminded of an observation by Mark Twain: "There is no sadder sight than a young pessimist, except an old optimist."

Connie Mack didn't act old. Up at seven thirty every morning, shaved and bathed and dressed for the day, a hearty breakfast, a look at the newspapers, phone calls and letter writing—always letter writing—arrival at Wright Field at ten, greeted by autograph seekers, interview seekers, photo seekers, "remember me?" seekers for an hour until practice started, standing behind the batting cage until a light lunch in the clubhouse of a sandwich or crackers and milk, then sitting beside the bench watching the practice game, back to the hotel at three for a nap, then dinner with Mrs. Mack and maybe a movie or just fanning the breeze in the lobby with anyone who approached—as he had been doing for fifty years, until bedtime around eleven or twelve.

The first day of spring training there was Mickey Cochrane, already in the Hall of Fame, catching batting practice. "How stupid can a guy get?" he joked. "Twenty-five years ago I started as a batting practice catcher. Now I'm doing it again. Is that progress?"

He and Miller and Dykes had a ball, riding each other the way they had in the good old pennant-winning years, as though they'd never been apart.

Wally Moses was supposed to double as the hitting coach. He had a pigeon-toed stance. That's all he knew, so that's all he taught. He didn't help anybody.

Stan Baumgartner speculated that the presence of Cochrane could drive the Athletics to the pennant. All they needed, he dreamed, was a key man like Kid Gleason, who had ridden herd on the 1929–1931 champions. Cochrane would "wake up" Sam Chapman, thirty-four, who had just had his most productive year since his return from the war with 197 runs and RBIs combined and 24 home runs. Cochrane's presence would, said Stan, put new life in Elmer Valo, who didn't need it, and thirty-nine-year-old Wally Moses, who was beyond it.

But Cochrane's driving license was invalid unless he was in the game. As a bench manager after he was nearly killed by a pitch in 1937, he had been too fidgety, too much of a red-flagged bull on a tether when he was not part of the action. He couldn't even sit still in the A's bullpen, often ducking out of sight under the stands for a smoke.

And there was nothing Cochrane could do to cure sore arms. Not even a trip to Lourdes could resurrect them.

Connie Mack put Hank Wyse down for 10–15 wins (he won 9, despite the worst ERA—5.85—in the AL). He counted on Alex Kellner to win 20 again. Kellner had had good success with his slider in 1949. In 1950 he confirmed the adage, "Live by the slider, die by the slider." Kellner served up 28 home runs; his ERA soared to 5.47. He pitched 15 complete games but won only 8 and lost 20.

Marchildon, Fowler, and Coleman had ended 1949 with aching shoulders. In September Coleman had fallen on his right shoulder rounding third base. Mack expected all three to be healthy for 1950. In December there had been some interest in Joe Coleman. Detroit general manager Billy Evans coveted Fain and Coleman and tried to fob off Dick Wakefield for them. (Evans finally unloaded Wakefield on the Yankees; Wakefield pinch-hit three times.) When the Yankees inquired about Coleman, Art Ehlers said, "There's not a chance in a thousand that we'd trade him."

Mack figured on 45 wins from the trio, enabling Lou Brissie and Bobby Shantz to be used mostly in relief. That cookie crumbled like a sat-on ginger snap. Instead of 45, he got 1.

Dick Fowler's bursitis, which Dr. Gopadze had nursed through two 15-win seasons, refused to surrender its grip on the Canadian's shoulder. He was of little use until he seemed to get healthy in July, pitched 2 complete games (including a 10-inning 3–2 loss), then had to give up. His shoulder was killing him. Mack sent him home.

Joe Coleman was still hurting in the spring. His fastball was missing in action. He was away for treatment more often than he was with the team. He couldn't throw strikes, and when he did, they became hits. He was 0-5 in 6 starts.

Phil Marchildon took the maximum pay cut this time without a peep. A possible trade for Yankee outfielder Johnny Lindell hinged on Marchildon's passing a physical. Doctors at Johns Hopkins told him his problem could be cured, but New York doctors disagreed. The Yankees then offered Lindell for a different pitcher, possibly Coleman. The Athletics said no.

When Marchildon couldn't throw without his shoulder aching, Mack sold him to Buffalo for $3,500. Maybe farmhand Harry Byrd, up from Savannah, would be a pleasant surprise. He wasn't.

With the Browns in St. Louis, Earle Brucker followed his former A's pitching students' travails with sorrow but not surprise. In May he said, "Connie Mack tried to get along for years with an eight-man staff. Now he's paying the penalty. Those great young pitchers are overworked and at least four have had serious arm trouble."

The Canadian right-hander Bob Hooper earned his $7,500 salary. He worked in 45 games, starting and relieving. By mid-July he was relieving several times between starts. His 15-10 record covered a 5.02 ERA.

They were so hard up for pitchers, Mack activated his batting practice pitcher, Les McCrabb, who hadn't thrown a pitch that counted for eight years. Opposing hitters were disappointed when McCrabb was deactivated after two brief appearances.

There was no bravado about spending big bucks for a first-rate pitcher—if they could find one for sale.

Dick Armstrong and Ed Hogan had put together an ambitious cymbals-clanging array of events on the golden jubilee theme starting early in the year. They lined up enough civic lunches and dinners honoring Mack to kill a mountain goat. Mack went along with all of it. Armstrong launched radio programs: *Connie Mack's Roundup* and *Here's the Pitch*. He wrote a song, "The Connie Mack Swing," which became the theme song for the season, and a poem extolling the double play exploits of the A's infield that ended:

> A long time from now, when they're telling of how
> So and so could get two with no strain,
> We'll think of the days of Connie Mack's A's,
> And of Joost and Suder and Fain.

Connie Mack had never been a shrinking violet when it came to enjoying the spotlight. He was pleased that every club in the league was planning a day to honor him.

One evening in West Palm Beach Armstrong asked Mack to go with him and club photographer Jack Snyder to Wright Field early the next morning before anyone else was there, put on a uniform, and pose in catching and batting positions. The eighty-seven-year-old Mack agreed. There were no writers present.

Armstrong sent out the catching photo with the tag: "A's sign rookie catcher." It appeared in papers all over the country.

Connie Mack had the dubious honor of explaining baseball to the Duke of Windsor when the former king of England visited Wright Field on St. Patrick's Day. To make it more confusing, the annual benefit game for the Palm Beach Police Pension Fund was being played. Mack had to explain that those old men on the field—Cochrane and Dykes and Connie Jr.—were not among his regular players. Nor was traveling secretary Benny Macfarland, who took off his shoes and went up to pinch-hit.

The parades and speeches began before the A's left the South. It was as if everybody wanted to get in a tribute before the honoree collapsed. On March 15 Mack rode in a convertible for the West Palm Beach Sun Dance Parade, trailed by Jimmie Dykes atop a huge elephant adorned with golden jubilee banners. In Savannah on April 10 a lunch and parade preceded a game against the A's farm team. Connie Mack sat in the grandstand with a Mrs. Brench, who was known locally as Mrs. Baseball.

The day before the city series opener the Junior Chamber of Commerce threw a luncheon. More than 1,200 attended, including former A's stars Rube Walberg, Joe Boley, and Joe Bush. Mack said, "The A's have a chance to win if the players went out and bustled for nine hard innings every day."

After the first city series game, Mack went to New York to appear on the radio show "We the People." On Saturday, April 15, he shivered in the forty-six-degree cold while the A's beat the Phillies, 7–4. The next day Ed Sullivan brought his popular TV show, "Toast of the Town," to the Walnut Theater, the first time it had been broadcast from outside New York, and celebrated Mr. Mack. Monday morning Mack took the nine o'clock train to Washington for a lunch honoring Clark Griffith at the Washington Touchdown Club.

After splitting the season openers at Washington, Mack was back home for a $50-a-plate jubilee dinner attended by six hundred at the Ben Franklin Hotel that raised $18,000 for a college scholarship fund. There were thirteen speakers. Mack had to stand while some of them went on and on extolling his many virtues before the presentation of a plaque. In his remarks Mack said he hoped the Phillies and A's would meet in the World Series. He was half right.

Judge Harry S. McDevitt, who had gone to Central High School with Roy and Earle and become one of Mack's closest friends despite a twenty-two-year difference in their ages, was active on the citywide jubilee planning committee, as he was on almost every celebration of his friend. McDevitt embraced his "20-to-40" nickname for his frequent pronouncements of that sentence in his courtroom, often adding to his autograph: "20 to 40 years at solitary & hard labor." McDevitt was ill and unable to attend the dinner at the Ben Franklin. On April 24 Mack dictated a letter expressing regrets that his friend had not been there: "Hope to see you before very long. Take good care of yourself for we miss seeing you around."

The letter was not mailed; Mack received word that his friend had died of a heart attack in Atlantic City on April 22.

The home opener against Boston was the official home Connie Mack Day, sponsored by the *Bulletin*. Mack rode with Mayor Bernard Samuel in a parade down Broad Street, lined with thousands, including women wearing Connie Mack blouses, which had "We all love him" printed beneath a picture of Mack.

Cold, windy weather kept the crowd at Shibe Park to a disappointing 8,184.

The *Bulletin* had sent scrolls all over the Western hemisphere—to stores, industries, military bases, Indian reservations, schools, state capitols—to be signed and returned to the paper. More than a million signatures were contained in the scrolls, piled around home plate when the parade arrived at Shibe Park at one o'clock. There were greetings from the president of the General Assembly of the United Nations, the two league presidents, and a dozen managers.

Master of ceremonies Ed Pollock called the response "one of the greatest outpourings of affection ever showered on one man."

None of them meant as much to Connie Mack or reflected the man as accurately as a letter from Charles J. McGinn: "I would like to add to the tribute to Connie Mack and I speak for thousands of boys, for whom Mr. Mack made it possible to see their first big league ball game, when the majority of us kids could not afford to see a ball game. This was not for one season, but for many years. . . . I am going back 40 years ago when Mr. Mack would take all of the boys of St. Michael's school to the game. That is why he is the grand old man of baseball."

Connie Mack thanked one and all and added, "And furthermore I hope we win today's game for you."

It was Red Sox manager Joe McCarthy's sixty-third birthday. When McCarthy shook his hand in the dugout, Mack said, "Joe, I was playing baseball three years before you were born."

The Red Sox then beat Lou Brissie, 8–2.

Two days later a rising new singer, Rosemary Clooney, sang in a light rain between games of a doubleheader.

The next night Mack was on a radio program with Joe DiMaggio.

On June 13 Edgar A. Guest, "The Poet of the People," came out with a paean to Mack. Six thousand Teen Club members had been invited to attend the June 29 game, at which bandleader Paul Whiteman would emcee a pregame show featuring stars from his TV show, members of his orchestra, and the Teen Club chorus of eighty voices singing "The Connie Mack Swing."

During the game Dick Armstrong took Whiteman up to the broadcast booth for an interview with Byrum Saam. To Armstrong's horror, Whiteman had acrophobia and could barely make it across the catwalk to the press box.

The height of the pitcher's mound must have affected the pitchers the same way that day. Bob Hooper pitched to 10 Red Sox batters, walked 6 of them, and gave up 2 hits. The four A's pitchers who followed all contributed to the 21–2 debacle. The Red Sox feasted on A's pitching all season, scoring 190 runs while winning 19 of 22.

Syndicator Christy Walsh was pitching a movie to MGM based on Mack's life, to be written by one of the studio's top writers, Howard Emmett Rogers. Rogers spent four days with Mack in St. Louis in June. Walsh arranged a press conference for Mack at the All-Star Game in Chicago on July 11, the first time, Walsh noted, in fifty years that Mack had visited a press box. The movie met the same fate as had a 1939 MGM project to film the life of John McGraw: they couldn't find a well-known actor who would be right for the part.

And there were book signings. A Philadelphia publisher, John C. Winston, brought out *My 66 Years in the Big Leagues*, ghosted by a Winston-published biographer of Lincoln and Edison, historian Francis Trevelyan Miller. The book contains a glancing history of the game, anecdotes, a smattering of biography, and lots of pictures. The cover price was $2.50; half of Mack's royalties went to the Junior Baseball Federation of Philadelphia to buy equipment for sandlot teams. Mack patiently signed books in his slow, meticulous, old-fashioned script—no hurried illegible scrawls for him.

Connie Mack's Baseball Book, published by Knopf, also tried to benefit from the hoopla. Ghosted by a writer who knew nothing about baseball, it was slapped together so poorly that Dick Armstrong had to perform major surgery: "The publisher sent me a page proof and asked me to look it over. It was full of mistakes and would have been an embarrassment to Mr. Mack. I practically had to rewrite the whole thing, but using the same number of characters, so as not to change the pagination. It was a real challenge!"

Connie Mack and the Athletics dominated the local preseason press coverage, much to the chagrin of the Phillies, who were the real contenders in town.

Then the season began. It didn't take long for the A's to go bad.

At 3-3 they said farewell to .500 on their way to 102 losses. Only once all year did they win as many as 3 in a row. On April 30 in Boston, Fowler, Byrd, and Coleman were battered in a 19–0 rout. Only Bobby Shantz, pitching the last 5 innings, was effective. Except for a few early season Sunday doubleheaders, average daily attendance dwindled to about two thousand. Many a day there were more vendors and pigeons in the stands than paying customers.

On May 10 Mack wrote to a longtime friend, screenwriter Shannon Fife, "I can't help but be worried about our club. Everything depends upon the pitchers."

The problem was more than ailing pitchers. After a 4–3 loss to Cleveland left the A's with a 7-12 record before they began a two-week road trip, Connie Jr. went into the clubhouse and walked over to Ferris Fain.

"What do you think is wrong with the club?" he asked Fain. "Why are we losing?"

"With all due respect," said Fain, "it's the Old Man. There's no leadership."

Connie Jr. knew it.

Connie Mack knew it too. Mack still seemed to be in good physical health, even though digestive problems—perhaps the old gall bladder flare-ups—had forced him to come home from Boston and cut back on his public appearances in April. (Whenever Mack had a siege of sickness, the papers would send reporters to the apartment on what they called a "death watch" assignment. More than once they sat in the kitchen all night with Mack's daughter Mary, the level of the contents of a bottle of Irish whiskey gradually ebbing.)

Mack was confined to his hotel room with similar problems in Cleveland and Detroit on the May 12–25 trip, a 4-9 disaster—during which the pitchers gave up an average of 7.3 runs per game—that left them plumbing the depths of the second division, 12 games out.

But it wasn't just digestive problems that afflicted Connie Mack. One night during the trip Mack woke up about 4 a.m. He couldn't move, not even a finger, and couldn't speak. He lay that way for a few hours and gradually regained his ability to move and talk.

A doctor later confirmed what Mack suspected: he had suffered a stroke. It was probably not the first, just the most serious.

But he stayed on the job.

While the team was away, young Connie set about making some changes. It was time—way past time, he knew—for the family business to cast off its high-button-shoes management setup. In recent years Connie Mack had divested bits and pieces of his one-man show to Mack and Shibe family members and Art Ehlers resulting in a hodgepodge of conflict-ridden crosscurrents of responsibility.

"It was crazy and sad really," Mickey Cochrane said. "We wouldn't know who we were working for from day to day. Lots of times Mr. Mack wasn't speaking to his oldest sons and vice versa. Mr. Mack stretched it a bit thin as manager, too."

Contracts might be dealt with by Earle or Roy or Art Ehlers or Mr. Mack.

The same with player deals. Successful clubs had a name for the position that handled all those responsibilities: general manager, and people like Ed Barrow, Eddie Collins, Frank Lane, Billy Evans, and George Weiss to fill it.

Connie Jr. decided the club needed two things: somebody on the bench to shepherd his dad through the rest of the season and a general manager with authority.

Jimmie Dykes was the logical person to be the assistant manager. Unlike Earle, who did what Daddy said and seldom ventured any advice, Dykes wouldn't hesitate to make suggestions. He had the respect and confidence of the players and the experience and self-confidence to assert himself. To establish Dykes as what would later be called the bench coach, Earle had to be removed from the dugout.

The A's opened a home stand with a night game against the Yankees on May 26. Before the game the visitors' dugout buzzed with rumors that Connie Mack had resigned that afternoon. Press box chatter was that Mack would soon step down if he hadn't already, Dykes or Cochrane would replace him, and Connie Jr. would become club president. Something was in the air, and it wasn't Jersey mosquitos.

That afternoon, after the team had arrived on the overnight train from Chicago, the board of directors had met, with Connie Mack observing and Earle Mack absent, at home, it was said, after feeling ill on the train. The results of the meeting wouldn't make Earle feel any better.

The late Bob Schroeder had been replaced on the board of directors by Bertram Rambo of the law firm Rambo & Mair, which had represented Mack and the Athletics for a half century. Rambo was a trustee of the Shibe estate and had represented Tom's widow, Ida Shibe, at every stockholders' meeting since Tom's death in 1937. His appointment gave the Connie Jr.–Macfarland–Shibe interests a majority on the board.

Connie Jr. went into the meeting with the full backing of Rambo and Macfarland. He proposed that Earle be appointed chief scout, to work out of an office, visit the farm clubs, and evaluate minor league players. Jimmie Dykes would replace him as assistant manager. Mickey Cochrane would leave the bullpen and become the club's first general manager, in charge of all player matters.

Where this left Art Ehlers, who was Roy's closest adviser, was unclear. Where it left Roy and Earle was very clear: powerless. Roy would be in charge of tickets and park maintenance. The erstwhile crown prince, Earle, would be out of uniform, all but out of sight. He wouldn't like it, maintaining that he wasn't about to go wandering around in the minor leagues, and would spend most of his time wandering around his office.

Dykes, Cochrane, and Bing Miller—already in uniform for that night's game—were then asked to join the meeting. The new posts were explained; no new coaches would be hired. Bing Miller would move from first to third, unless Dykes preferred to stay on the coaching line.

Cochrane went out for batting practice and spent his first night as a big league general manager in the bullpen. Afterward he stayed away from the tower offices and occupied a small office under the stands down the third base line.

Connie Mack sat in on the meeting but outside the decision making. This time he gave his wholehearted approval to the changes. There would be no surprises, no conflicting statements. Mack was probably relieved that he could now lean on Jimmie Dykes to carry him through the season. And he had complete confidence in Black Mike.

Veteran baseball writer Dan Daniel of the *New York World-Telegram* enjoyed visiting with Connie Mack each time the Yankees went to Shibe Park. When he arrived at the ballpark that afternoon, he heard the rumors of ' something afoot. He and Joe Trimble of the *New York Daily News* hurried up to the tower office.

Daniel reported his conversation with Mack:

"There is a crazy rumor around this park. They say you have resigned and Dykes is your new manager."

"Oh, it's nothing like that. But we are going to give out a story. Dykes is assistant manager, Cochrane is manager in charge of players, Earle goes out looking for ballplayers. Cochrane will be in charge of trades, he will sign the players, he will run our farm system. But they will consult me about every move they plan.

"I am not retiring as manager. I am not leaving the dugout here. I am not quitting the road. I am convinced that all the moves will turn out for the best interests of the club."

Connie Jr. was the only one in his family Mack had told about the stroke that had temporarily paralyzed him. "He seemed to recover," said young Connie, "although we noticed a decline in his ability to express himself. His mind, too, seemed to fail him at times."

Mack knew what was happening to him. But he was determined to stubborn it out to the end of the season. Nobody considered asking or persuading or forcing him to step down before then. If the idea crossed his youngest son's mind, he had only to remember the uproar over the firing of Simmons and Brucker last fall, when he was all but accused of fratricide. Ruth urged her dad to keep going: "You owe it to yourself. You wanted to last fifty years. Do it."

Besides, there were all those golden jubilee celebrations still on the schedule. When the A's were on the road, some clubs promoted "Connie Mack's 50th Year" in their game-day ads. Groups of fans from cities in the A's drawing area had their "Day" at Shibe Park circled on the calendar.

Sometimes Connie Mack seemed to have no problem knowing what was going on. Jimmie Dykes, asked later if Mr. Mack ever used bad language, first said, "Never," then hedged, using an incident in 1950 to illustrate:

> Mr. Mack called a meeting of the coaches, me and Bing Miller and Cochrane. He said he was worried about the club and had tried hard to figure out what was wrong with it. Then he didn't say anything for a minute. Finally, he spoke up again and said he had come to the conclusion that the boys were overindulging in *affaires d'amour* as the French say. But Mr. Mack did not speak French. We were shocked. We didn't say anything right away. Finally I said, "Do you mean at home, Mr. Mack?"
>
> Mr. Mack shook his head. "No, Jimmie. On trips."

He was aware of which players were dogging it—loping lazily after fly balls, loafing down the line on pop flies—in hopes of being traded. "When they get new contracts they will find a big difference in salary on account of wanting to be traded," he wrote to Fife. He was able to keep up with world news, predicting that the North Korean invasion of South Korea on June 25 would "start World War three about December."

At times there was a disconnect between his mind and his tongue. He would start to say something, and his mind would go blank in mid-sentence: "I want—uh—uh—I want . . . ," and whoever was sitting beside him would mention a name, and he would say, "Yes, that's right."

Or he would forget that a player was no longer with the team. On June 17 in Cleveland, the A's led 7–6 in the ninth, and Carl Scheib got into trouble. Mack said, "Take that man out and bring in Byrd."

Dykes said, "You can't bring in Byrd."

"Why can't Byrd pitch?"

"You sent him to Buffalo three days ago."

Scheib stayed in, and the Indians won, 8–7.

When players made mental errors or messed up a play, Mack no longer summoned them to his office to suggest how the play should have been made. He was more likely now to blurt out a sharp, often unwarranted criticism at the player in the dugout. Jimmie Dykes interceded when he could.

Mack began evading writers' casual inquiries, something contrary to his nature. His door had always been open to the press. A warm welcome awaited any new writer. He might shoot a barbed response to a dumb question from an out-of-town writer, but he had always been available for a comment or a leisurely column-filling interview. But now Ed Pollock said, "Almost every time I saw him he would tell me, 'I can't talk anymore.' I thought he meant his physician wouldn't permit him to make speeches. But what he was trying to say was that he couldn't express himself as he desired."

To shake up the team, the first thing Jimmie Dykes did as assistant manager was call a meeting and lay down the rules of discipline. Curfews went into effect. Dykes threatened to hit them with fines and make the fines public.

Ferris Fain had been in the service with Bob Dillinger for three years. He was the only player who ever saw Dillinger away from the ballpark, at home or on the road. They lived near each other and rode to Shibe Park together. Fain would tell him, "Bob, you've got to get in front of the ball," and Bob would say, "No, I'm not going to get hurt." Fain kept after him. Bob became a little more aggressive, even taking a bruise on his chest once in a while. He was hitting his usual .320–.325 but had only 5 stolen bases. Of course his opportunities were affected by his team's falling behind so early and often. But he hadn't swiped even one in over a month.

One day in early July after a game Yitz Crompton told the players to stay put; Mr. Mack was going to have a meeting. In came Mack. Fed up with their uninspired play, he stood in the middle of the room and said, "Our first baseman is the only one who's doing anything on this ball club."

Then he looked from one to another, saying, "You're not doing anything, you're not doing anything." When he came to Pete Suder, who never stopped hustling, he stammered, unsure of what to say. Finally he sputtered, "And you, Sude, you go out there and you field the ball and throw to first and that's all you do. You're too nonchalant, you don't do anything else out there."

Then he glared at Dillinger. "And you, Mr. Dillinger, cost me $100,000 and you are not worth the money we spent for you."

On the way home Dillinger said to Fain, "If that's what he thinks of me, wait and see."

Fain recalled, "From that day on you didn't see Bob get in front of any hard-hit balls. He was giving them the howdy-do and saying 'whoo-ee' at them like he'd done in St. Louis. And he 'whoo-eed' himself clear to Pittsburgh."

Dillinger's days with the A's were numbered. But first the A's had to get waivers from every other club in the league. White Sox general manager Frank Lane claimed him. Mack pleaded with Lane to drop the claim so that he could recover more of the bundle Dillinger had cost. Lane relented.

On Wednesday, July 19, new owners took over the last-place Pittsburgh Pirates. Their first move to improve the team was to give Connie Mack $50,000 for Bob Dillinger. That evening the A's lost their fifth in a row; Dillinger was 0 for 4. His average had dropped 16 points in 5 games. He hadn't stolen a base in two months.

One of batboy Frank Cunningham's postgame chores was to pick up the dirty uniforms and straighten up the lockers. There were usually some players who hung around for a few hours before they showered and dressed, and Cunningham had to wait for them to clear out. On this occasion Cunningham suddenly noticed that everybody—even the clubhouse man Yitz Crompton—had left in a hurry. Except Bob Dillinger, who was casually drinking a beer.

Connie Mack walked in.

"Hi Pop, How you doing?" said Frank.

Mack walked past him without a word, went over to Dillinger, and said, "You've been sold to the Pittsburgh Pirates."

Dillinger said, "Yes, Mr. Mack."

Connie Mack turned and walked out. On the opposite wall from where Dillinger stood was a line of sinks and mirrors with a narrow opening in the middle to get to the showers. As soon as Mack left the room, Dillinger hurled the beer can through the opening and yelled, "The only thing I hate is I'm going to have to come back to this ballpark."

Frank Cunningham thought, "That's one of the best throws I saw him make all year."

The next day Pirates general manager Roy Hamey arrived at Shibe Park to complete the deal.

A year later Branch Rickey, the new Pittsburgh general manager, peddled Dillinger to the White Sox for $10,000. By 1952 Dillinger was in Sacramento, his big league days ended at thirty-three, a .306 career hitter and fielder.

On Sunday, July 23, the A's were 32-58 and drew only 3,541 for a doubleheader against the White Sox. The Phillies, meanwhile, were battling the Dodgers for the lead in a race that would go down to the last day. It was reminiscent of thirty-five years ago, when the Phillies were winning their first pennant while the dethroned men of Mack went from first to worst. Two former Mackmen aided the Phillies' rise: George Earnshaw, the minor league pitching coach for Class B and higher farm clubs, and bullpen coach Cy Perkins.

Desperate to show they were trying to improve the team, on August 14 somebody in the A's office—presumably Cochrane—spent $10,000 to claim thirty-five-year-old outfielder Roberto Ortiz from Washington. Nobody took the credit for the purchase; Ortiz contributed 1 hit in 6 games.

The public was no longer interested in celebrating Connie Mack. Not only was Connie Mack old, the Connie Mack *Show* was old. He'd had more special days in the past five years than anybody in the history of the game. During that time, whenever Mack had appeared on the field or first entered the dugout before a game, he was greeted by cheers and applause. Now the fans were booing him when they saw him.

"It was an ignominious ending," said Dick Armstrong.

The whole team felt it. When the A's were on the field, hecklers in the stands spared no language in riding them and telling the Macks to "get out of town."

Mack's grandson Connie McCambridge and his wife were there one day, sitting behind first base. McCambridge said, "Some guy was yelling and screaming obscenities and Ferris Fain had enough and came over and fired the same language back at him and threatened to climb up in the stands after him."

Only the Browns (who casual readers of the sports pages might have thought represented some place called Lowly, Missouri, as they were more often identified as the "lowly Browns" than the St. Louis Browns) kept the A's propped up in seventh place until a 7-game losing streak in September settled the good ship Connie Mack on the bottom for the seventeenth time.

When Connie Jr. had engineered the changes on the bench and in the office in May, he had wanted to go further. He had access to much-needed capital to revitalize the business. His father was no longer up to representing the team in league meetings. He wanted a public commitment from Mr. Mack that his youngest son would succeed him as president and would be acting president in the meantime.

Connie Jr. had the votes on the board of directors to support him. But he didn't want the succession to appear to be forced and turn into an embarrassing fiasco. It was bad enough when the board had fired a few coaches. He'd be run out of town if the board fired Connie Mack as the club president. And in his heart, as much as he believed a change was necessary, he was not willing to act without his father's blessing.

So he asked Dad to agree to the plan.

Any man who has owned, operated, and managed a baseball team for fifty years will have had unlimited opportunities to make mistakes, spending big money and small on scores of flops for every high-priced or bargain star he acquired.

Connie Mack was no exception.

Now, in his eighty-eighth year, he made the worst decision of his life, one that he would live to regret.

For all his modern, far-sighted vision, somewhere in his DNA was embedded a remnant of Old World ethos.

He told his youngest son, "No. The oldest must succeed me."

Facing his father and disagreeing with him might have reminded Connie Jr. of an earlier incident that encouraged him to press his case:

Soon after I was first put on the club's board of directors, I spoke up against my father for the first time in my life.

From the time I was twelve years old and went on my first western trip with the team, Dad always treated me as an equal. After the games he would talk to me like I was a man. Over dinner, he would discuss the day's game, the strategy that worked and the things that didn't. He would talk over one particular play in great detail, and always the talk was about baseball.

At a board meeting a payroll matter came up in which I disagreed completely with Dad. I stood my ground and he stood his. He was boiling. It was my first disagreement with him in a business capacity and I wondered what he would say. I soon found out. After the meeting he came up to me with his hand extended. "That's why I put you on the board, son. I want your opinions. I shouldn't get mad. If you have anything to say, you go ahead and say it."

Now Connie swallowed hard and said what he had to say to his father: Roy and Earle were not capable of running the club or raising the necessary capital to turn the team into a contender again.

Mack was unmoved.

Connie Mack's judgment of men, which had assayed the talents of thousands of ballplayers for more than a half century, was trapped by tradition when it came to his sons. He could have lightened his load ten years ago by giving Roy and Earle more responsibility, but he hadn't. He might have realized that Connie Jr. was brighter and had some good ideas, but Connie was the youngest and therefore the last in line.

Years later Connie Jr.'s daughter Susie observed, "What happened to the A's at the end had to happen. The more I read Irish history the more it had to be. The oldest son took over the farm or the business and that's why my dad was out."

Stubbornly—blindly?—Mack continued to praise his elder sons. On August 18 he wrote to Shannon Fife, "Connie, Jr. had no faith in Roy and Earle, which will probably be news to you. I think well of both boys and do not know why Connie Jr. thinks as he does."

Chicago columnist Mike Royko later compared the decline of the Athletics to that of the Chicago Bears in the 1950s: "The Bears did not slide because [Bears founder George] Halas was cheap or because he lost his sharpness. They slid because he was human. He turned over more of the business to his sons to run and they couldn't do it. Had Connie Mack had the time to rebuild he might have done it. But the clock had run out on him. Connie Mack had three sons and they couldn't get along. The one who might have made a go of it was the youngest, born to a different mother in a different generation."

Connie Mack was aware that his sons didn't get along, though they tried to shield him from the constant turmoil that was tearing apart the organization.

Dick Armstrong was in the middle of it: "The infighting and maneuvering was fierce. It was difficult to work in that environment. The bitterness was palpable. Young Connie was friendly and approachable. Roy was like two people. Away from Shibe Park, he was congenial, a warm and welcoming host. But in the office he could be a tyrant, harsh, cruel, mean to people."

Peter J. "Jimmy" Flood had been with the A's for almost forty years, as the ticket manager and later assistant to Roy. In the fall of 1948 Roy fired him over an unspecified "disagreement."

"Maybe Roy was paranoid or insecure," said Armstrong. "If he saw me talking to Connie, afterward he'd interrogate me: why were you talking to him; what was it about; what did he say? Roy's secretary, Josephine Polo, was the same way. Earle was pretty much a nonentity who went along with whatever Roy said."

The strained relations between Connie Jr. and his older half-brothers at the office—Roy and Earle didn't particularly care for each other, either—split them away from the ballpark too. Their families rarely got together socially. Whenever Connie Jr. and his wife went to spring training for a few weeks, it was always one of his sisters—Rita or Mary (whom the kids called Mrs. Strict)—who babysat for them.

On Christmas Day four of Mack's children and eleven grandchildren surrounded him and Katherine at Ruth's home. In a letter to Connie Mc-Cambridge, he mentioned "all there but [his daughter] Rita," with no reference to the absence of his two other sons, Roy and Earle, and their families.

Connie Jr. was deeply disappointed over his father's refusal to turn over the helm to him. He never got over it. "It was very emotional for him," his son Dennis said. "He wanted to run the team. It gnawed at him."

Then young Connie made the worst decision of *his* life.

To him the only possible resolution of the split seemed to be for somebody—or everybody—to sell out. Rumors to that effect drew birds of prey like vultures to road kill. Trucking magnate James P. Clark, president of the NFL Eagles, said he had a group ready to buy the A's. As the season dragged on, other groups were rumored to be hovering over Shibe Park. They all pledged to keep Connie Mack on as manager. But that was just for show. Mr. Mack was ready to go.

An unsigned statement from the club conceded that the A's were receptive to "an attractive offer." Connie Mack was quoted that they were ready to sell "if the price is right."

Nobody expected anything to happen before the end of the season.

Art Morrow quoted an unidentified stockholder, "There have been many points of disagreement during the past fifteen years, but everyone seems agreed on this. However, we are not going to be pushed or rushed. This is not a forced sale and I, for one, do not panic."

Roy didn't want to sell unless he was assured of a job. Connie Jr. didn't want to sell. He wanted to buy. Earle wasn't crazy about the idea of being under his older brother's thumb, but he knew he'd probably be out as a coach if the club was sold.

Of the 1,500 shares outstanding, Connie Mack owned 302. Each of the three sons owned 163. The rest were held by Katherine (100), Mary S. Reach (141), Elfrida S. Macfarland (131), Frank Macfarland (5), Benny Macfarland (5), and the estate of Thomas Shibe (327, represented by attorney Bert Rambo).

Connie Jr. talked it over with his allies, who included all but his father and brothers. He believed that if they offered to buy out Roy and Earle, they would be turned down. So he suggested, "Let's give them a thirty-day option to buy us out, and if they can't, we get the option to buy them out. They'll never be able to come up with the money."

Young Connie had the backing of local Democratic power Jack Kelly, who had tried to buy control of the club earlier, a bid that had been rejected by Roy and Earle.

News of the arrangement sparked plenty of rumors, which Connie answered by denying any rift with his father. He added, "For some years I have felt we should adopt a new progressive attitude and any changes which I proposed were I felt for the benefit of the club. If any of the proposed changes have failed in their purpose I feel that it was due to lack of cooperation caused by the disagreement of policy."

His spin on offering Roy and Earle first crack at buying him out: respect for seniority.

Roy had until August 28 to find the money. At $1,950 a share, Roy and Earle would have to come up with $1,700,400. There was also the sellers' share of the concessions income up to August 28, which would come to another $52,320.

Arthur Ehlers found the money for Roy and Earle. Through Ehlers, Gordon Burlingame, a local banker representing the Connecticut General Life Insurance Company, was approached. After agreeing on a value of $3.5 million for everything the Athletics owned, from the American League franchise and Shibe Park down to the bag of batting practice balls, as collateral, the insurance giant agreed to a loan of $1,750,000 at 4.5 percent interest for ten years. Everything was in the pawn shop. The note was signed by Cornelius McGillicuddy and Earle T. McGillicuddy. The first quarterly payment of $50,000 was due December 1. The A's didn't have $50,000. The Shibe Park Concessions Company was dissolved, and the concessions privileges were leased to Jacobs Bros. Penn Sportservice for $200,000 a year, enough to cover the mortgage payments.

There may have been a hitch before all this could be concluded. The story is that Roy couldn't deliver a clear title to Shibe Park until the other stockholders were bought out, and Connecticut General wouldn't sign off on the loan without it. At least that's what Roy believed. (Burlingame later said that wasn't the case.) Roy appealed to a Main Line neighbor, wealthy construction magnate John McShain, builder of the Pentagon and other Washington monuments, who provided a bridge loan to close the deal. The announcement of the deal suggested that added capital would be obtained from "some prominent Philadelphians" to build up the team. That never happened.

The buyout resulted in Roy and Earle's owning 163 shares each and Connie Mack 302. The rest of the shares went into the treasury. For some reason—perhaps persuaded that he was no longer competent—Connie Mack signed over to Roy and Earle a three-year option on his stock at $2,000 a share. Neither son could exercise it without the other's agreement, and they rarely agreed on anything. Connie Mack was no longer free to cash in his chips no matter how things went. The option effectively tied his financial fate to that of his sons, like three mountain climbers roped together. If the boys ran the business into the ground and ran up debts that eroded the value of the collateral, Connecticut General could foreclose on Shibe Park and the stock might become worthless. On July 27, 1953, the option would be extended to 1960.

Mack, the eternal optimist, wrote to Shannon Fife: "The boys did a good job in getting the two million and we must hand it to Roy & Earle. You know the Shibe interest never thought they could raise the amount. If they had they would never give Roy the option to buy. They didn't want to sell their stock and are now sorry. Connie Jr. never expected it. Am really pleased with the new setup."

How pleased could he be?

The first thing Roy did when the sale was completed was to ask for Mickey Cochrane's resignation. Cochrane had been trying to come up with a trade to bolster interest in the club. In early August the A's were in Chicago. Cochrane called Lou Brissie to tell him, "I am working on a trade of you and Fain to the Yankees. When I get back to Philadelphia and clear it with Mr. Mack, I'll call you and let you know."

Brissie thanked him for the heads-up. Somebody—Mr. Mack or Roy—vetoed the trade.

"The next thing I knew Cochrane was gone," Lou said.

There were other casualties. Along with Connie Jr., out went club secretary Benny Macfarland, assistant treasurer Frank Macfarland Sr., and Frank Jr., the latter replaced as traveling secretary by longtime coach Dave Keefe.

When *The Sporting News* gave its "Hats Off" salute to Roy and Earle, few people in baseball doffed their chapeaus in agreement.

Among club owners, players, writers, and radio men all around the league, the consensus was: the respect for Connie Mack didn't extend to Roy and Earle. More than ten years earlier James Isaminger had written, "Connie Mack's sons became senile before Connie did."

Detroit writer H. G. Salsinger wrote, "Several years ago [Tigers owner] Walter O. Briggs said, 'The day Connie Mack turns over active command of the Athletics to his sons is the day when the league can start making arrangements to move the Athletics out of Philadelphia.'"

Ed McAuley of the *Cleveland News*: "Most of the club owners were hoping for new blood and new money in [Shibe Park]. They were disappointed when Earle and Roy were able to raise enough cash to buy control."

Arthur Daley of the *New York Times*:

In a recent issue the [*Sporting News*] skimmer was doffed to Earle and Roy Mack for purchasing the Philadelphia Athletics from their warring relatives and thus assuming control of a club which was torn by dissension. This reporter fails to share in the enthusiasm.

The older sons of Connie Mack thereby contrived to win from two competing sources. One was an outside syndicate, which was ready to buy and rehabilitate the very forlorn A's, and the other was an inside group of Junior and the Macfarland brothers, which was ready to do the same thing. It must be confessed that it came as a huge surprise to most baseball folks when Earle and Roy hit the jackpot.

If the truth must be told, the Athletics have been suffering acutely from dry rot for many years. When Connie Jr., young and progressive, assumed power a year ago, there was a great and promising internal upheaval. He shook up the high command and exiled to an unimportant scouting post his half-brother Earle, whom their 87-year-old father had long before named as his successor.

Of almost equal importance was the naming of the fiery, hustling Jimmy Dykes to Earle's old position of assistant manager and the selection of the fiery and hustling Mickey Cochrane to the position of general manager. It looked to be an ideal situation, the solution to manifold problems. . . . This certainly was the step in the right direction.

But as soon as Roy and Earle took over, Cochrane resigned. The brothers said nothing. Connie voiced automatic platitudes of regret, almost as if the old gentleman wasn't aware of what a drastic backward step Mickey's departure meant. . . .

If this sounds slightly rough on the beloved and patriarchal Connie Mack, it isn't meant to be. Connie is still the most remarkable eighty-seven-year-old in the world and this reporter's affection for him is deep and abiding. However, it doesn't spread to other members of his family. . . . Cochrane never had much chance to get the necessary reforms started. He was what the doctor ordered for a sick franchise. It will have a terrible time getting well now.

To which all of Philadelphia said, "Amen."

The A's went into Detroit on September 19. The Tigers, Red Sox, and Yankees were separated by 2 games with ten days to go. The A's lost the first game, 12–4. Wyse, Coleman, and Johnny Kucab were pounded for 4 runs each.

The next day the A's led 5–1 in the Tigers' sixth. With 2 on and 1 out, Charlie Keller hit a grounder to Fain, who threw to Alex Kellner covering first. Kellner's foot missed the bag, and Keller was safe. That led to 3 unearned runs scoring and Ferris Fain boiling.

Bob Hooper replaced Kellner to start the bottom of the seventh. The A's still led 5–4 when, with 1 out in the eighth, Keller singled and went to second on a wild pitch. Hoot Evers, a right-handed batter, bounced a grounder between first and second. Fain fielded it, saw Keller heading for third, and, while Hooper ran over to cover first, decided to get Keller. Pete Suder, playing third in place of the injured Kermit Wahl, was playing off the line. As he raced toward third, the ball sailed over Suder's head and hit the wall as Keller slid. Third base coach Dick Bartell hollered for Keller to get up and head for home. Keller scored, and Evers went to second. After Johnny Groth walked, Don Kolloway drove Evers in to give the Tigers a 6–5 lead.

The denizens of the press box tore into Fain for trying a boneheaded 100–1 chance, one that even sandlotters knew better than to try with 1 out. Get the man at first for the second out, then the man on third can't score on an out. That was sound baseball. The play was not planned; Suder and Fain had not conferred before Hooper pitched to Evers. Even if the throw had been perfect, Suder's momentum heading toward third was carrying him away from the play. He would have had to stop, reverse his direction, and try to make the tag.

Visiting writer Art Morrow commented, "Fain has made that play only once in his last six tries."

(In fairness to Ferris Fain, it wasn't always his fault. Fain: "In the first game of a doubleheader in Boston on September 9, the play comes up. Al Zarilla's on second. Buddy Rosar bunts. I pick it up and throw to third baseman Kermit Wahl. The ball bounces off his mitt into left field and the run scores. I was mad. I didn't think Wahl had given it his best shot. They gave him the error.")

While the press box was buzzing, Connie Mack was burning. So was Ferris Fain as he headed to the dugout after the third out.

What happened next was something that nobody who witnessed it ever forgot. The versions vary a little; let's go with Fain's:

> In Detroit the runway was in the center of the dugout and went down four or five steps. I headed for the runway knowing that if I stopped for one minute and started talking about it we're going to have a problem. Trying to avert that, I headed into the runway. As I'm going down the steps Mr. Mack is shouting, "Boy, boy, boy." I didn't want to listen to Mr. Mack at this point so I continue down the runway. He gets up and he's standing at the top of the stairway.
>
> "Now young man—uh—uh—I want you to know—uh—you've tried this play three or four times now and you've only completed it once."
>
> I said, "Oh horseshit, Mr. Mack. If the play worked it's a great play. It didn't, so now it's a lousy play."
>
> He continues with this "Now you've—uh—tried it—uh—uh."
>
> I interrupted. "What are you trying to tell me, Mr. Mack. You don't want me to throw that ball any more?"
>
> "Well—uh—uh—uh."
>
> I said, "Well, I'll tell you, Mr. Mack. Before I take that ball and throw it for you again, I'll stick it right in my ass."
>
> He said, "Young man, I'd like you to know that would probably be the safest place for that ball."
>
> This senile old man that we thought had lost it floored those twenty-two guys on the bench. Even I had to find some humor in that.

Small wonder a September 22 *Detroit News* photo shows a forlorn Connie Mack looking weary and haggard, bundled inside a dark overcoat and black hat in the dugout.

When Mack announced that Joe Coleman, who was 0-4 and had not started a game since August 26, would start the next day, he explained, "Shantz has pleurisy. Wyse, Kellner, and Hooper have already been used in the series."

So had Coleman: 6 hits and 2 walks in 2 innings.

The overworked Lou Brissie told the AP, "I am ready and able to pitch if called upon."

But he wasn't called upon. He was in Connie Mack's doghouse, a kennel that had seen more occupants in the past three years than the previous forty-seven.

Brissie had started in Cleveland four days ago. The A's gave him a rare gift: a 9–0 lead after 3 innings. He couldn't hold it. In the sixth inning 4 walks, 2 singles, and a wild pitch made it 9–7. Bob Hooper relieved him. When Brissie reached the dugout, Mack was up and waiting for him. He took Lou by the arm and said, "That was terrible. Were you really trying out there?"

That hurt Lou, just as the same words had hurt Nelson Potter in 1948. But it cut Lou Brissie more deeply. Ever grateful for the chance Mack had given him, he knew that winning was the most important thing in the Old Man's life, and he had always done his best to make that happen.

Brissie remained calm. "Mr. Mack," he said, "I've done everything you asked me to do. Just look at my record."

His record: 31 starts; 15 complete games; 15 relief appearances, including 8 team wins he finished; 246 innings pitched; 13 base runners allowed per 9 innings. His 19 losses included 9 by 1 run.

Mack thought Brissie's answer was "nasty."

"You're through for the year," he snapped.

If Connie Mack needed any further evidence that he was no longer capable of managing men, his attack on this wounded war veteran he admired above all others and who was so openly devoted to him was the clincher. And he knew it. A few days later, Mack saw Lou Brissie and Ferris Fain together in the hotel lobby. He went up to them and apologized. "I was upset and I was wrong to question your trying. I'm sorry."

But he didn't use him again.

Detroit jumped on Joe Coleman for 6 runs in the first inning on 4 walks and 3 hits and won, 8–2. The Tigers were now tied with the Yankees.

News tickers in the Briggs Stadium press box carried stories out of Boston and New York that fans were up in arms over Mack's use against the Tigers of a sore-armed pitcher who hadn't won all year.

After the game an AP reporter asked Mack about the reports suggesting he was favoring Detroit. The writer said Mack "bristled" when he replied:

I've always played every game to win during my long time in baseball and that's the way I played it. No one can accuse me of favoring Detroit by pitching Coleman. My pitchers are not well and he was my best choice.

If New York thinks I gave Detroit an advantage, they shouldn't feel bad because I'm planning on sending Coleman against them next week.

He did; Coleman took a 5–1 lead into the seventh, when the Yankees scored 6 runs off him. The A's rallied to win, 8–7, scoring the winning runs off Whitey Ford in the ninth to hand the rookie his first loss after 9 wins.

But by then the Yankees had clinched the pennant.

The final home stand of Connie Mack's golden jubilee season was hardly noticed by Philadelphia fans, who stayed home to follow the Phillies battle down to the last-day extra-inning wire to nip the Dodgers for the NL pennant. The first-place Yankees could attract only 2,273 for a Thursday game at Shibe Park.

Connie Mack's last game was a win—he always liked to win the season finale, even if he'd lost 100 or more, a sort of feeble but metaphorical springboard into a new year. On Sunday, October 1, rookie John Kucab pitched a 5–3 win over the fifth-place Washington Senators. The obsequies were witnessed by 1,387 mourners.

Of the 102 games the A's lost, their opponents scored 10 or more runs in 22 of them. For the year A's pitchers gave up 913 runs—a league-high 5.49 ERA. Everybody started and relieved; the staff threw a league-low 50 complete games.

The A's made 208 double plays even without Majeski; they had had considerably more opportunities than the previous year. They actually hit better than expected, fifth in slugging average. Chapman was still good for 23 home runs. Joost hit 18 home runs but little else at .233, though he walked 103 times. He set AL records of 42 consecutive games and 226 total chances without an error. Barney McCosky could not come back, hitting .240.

Paul Lehner surprised everybody by hitting .309 and 9 home runs, something he never came close to before or after. Ferris Fain laughed as he remembered him: "Paul lived at the Broad Street Hotel in South Philly and walked to the ballpark every day, stopping seven or eight times along the way for a beer. There was nothing more demoralizing for me than to be out there clear-eyed wanting to tear the cover off the ball and going 0 for 5 and he's bleary-eyed and hitting frozen ropes."

Fain tried to become a power hitter, managed to hit 10 home runs, but remained a .282 hitter. His swinging for the fences didn't lead to a lot of strikeouts: he fanned 26 times and drew 133 walks.

Joe Astroth picked the wrong year to have a career season. He batted .327, culminating on September 23 in Washington with 6 RBIs on a grand slam and a single in a 12-run sixth inning. Some of the players suggested he go up to the tower after the season and say goodbye to Mr. Mack. "Maybe he'll give you a bonus."

So Astroth went up to the office. He said, "I just wanted to come up and say goodbye, Mr. Mack. I think I had a pretty good year."

"Good, good, young man. Go home and have a good winter."

Astroth kept fishing. "Well, Mr. Mack, what did you think of my playing this year? I thought I did pretty good."

"Good, good. Go home and have a good winter."

After three "have a good winters" Astroth took the hint and left.

"I wasn't angry," Astroth said. "He had given me a raise every year. Like everybody else, I had heard how cheap Connie Mack was and I believed it. But as I got older I realized that he was a very caring man for all his players and their families. He was treating me fairly for the level of ability I had and, besides, he couldn't afford to pay me any more."

Attendance fell more than 50 percent, to 309,000, representing only 3.39 percent of the American League's total turnstile count, the Athletics' lowest contribution in fifty years. If they hadn't played thirty-two night games, it might have been half that. (For the decade 1941–1950 the A's attendance was fourteenth in the majors; only that of Cincinnati and the Browns was lower.) The Phillies drew four times as many, providing a $120,000 boon for the Athletics, who earned ten cents on each Phillies' paid admission. Even with that, the A's still reported a loss of almost $250,000. The incomes from the Phillies and Eagles, radio, and TV were the only things that kept them in business.

Connie Mack and Katherine went to New York for the World Series, which ended abruptly in four games, and they stayed a few days longer. He watched the Columbus Day Parade on Fifth Avenue with his Texas friend of more than forty years, Hyman Pearlstone; then they had lunch together, probably at Schrafft's, Mack's favorite restaurant in New York.

Jimmie Dykes was playing golf on October 17. Art Ehlers tried to reach him all day. When Dykes finally came home, Ehlers told him to get down to Shibe Park immediately.

"But it's dinner time," said Dykes

"Now," said Ehlers.

Dykes went and was told that the club had called a press conference for the next day; Mr. Mack wanted him to take over as the manager.

"They really floored me [with the offer]," Dykes said.

Some accounts say that Roy and Earle forced the retirement of Connie Mack and chose Dykes to replace him. Wrong and wrong. There was never any doubt in Connie Mack's mind that it was time—past time—for him to go and that Jimmie Dykes would be his successor. Eddie Joost said that Dykes told him, "The Old Man wants me to take his place. We won't win but I can't say no."

According to Joost, all the players were surprised. "On the last day of the season, when I had said goodbye to Jimmie, he indicated that he would not be back with the Athletics. We had understood that Lou Boudreau was scheduled to come over from Cleveland to manage the A's, while Dykes was supposed to take over the Indians. Jimmie seemed certain that was what was going to happen and so did all our players."

The next day about fifty writers and broadcasters filled the Betsy Ross room at the Benjamin Franklin Hotel for the news that was no surprise but nonetheless historic. Connie Mack, flanked by Dykes and Ehlers, stood at the head of U-shaped tables and acknowledged that he was resigning as manager. Jimmie Dykes would replace him. He would remain as club president. He said he regretted that he hadn't done better in recent years for the Philadelphia fans and blamed it on "this chain store baseball."

Smiling as he spoke, he did not stammer or steep his words in sentimental syrup. Good thing he didn't. Two of those present had known Mack almost as long as he had managed the A's: Chief Bender, first signed by Mack in 1903, looking gaunt after a recent operation, and Ira Thomas, catcher, scout, and friend for forty years. A third, Lena Blackburne, had been a coach for Mack for fourteen years through 1948. Bender was still carried as a scout, drawing $3,900 a year.

Had Mack started reminiscing, said Lena Blackburne, "I was ready to cry any second."

"Me, too," said Thomas.

Nobody in the room was smiling, not even Jimmie Dykes. They were all sorry to see Mack's remarkable tenure end, not just because of its historic length, but also because of their genuine affection for the man. Red Smith put into print what was in everyone's thoughts: "There never was another like Connie. There never will be."

Ordinarily Jimmie Dykes had no problem talking. But he wasn't smiling when he said, "This is one time in my life when I've been flabbergasted . . . to be stepping into Connie Mack's shoes which can never be filled by a guy like me. Mr. Mack taught me everything I know about baseball. Everything I've accomplished in the game I owe to him."

Connie Mack's pride and stubbornness still wouldn't allow him to admit that he could no longer do the job, not in public, not yet. When he said, "I'm not quitting because I'm too old, but because I think the people want me to," he knew better.

Nobody, his sons or anybody else, had to talk him into retiring or force him out. He knew he was being propped up and bailed out by his players and coaches. He knew the man who had chewed out Lou Brissie near the end of the season was no longer the man who had so warmly, patiently encouraged the war-torn pitcher's struggles to make it to the big leagues. For the first time in his life, he had admitted that the end of a baseball season couldn't come soon enough, writing to Shannon Fife in September that he was "really anxious for the season to close."

For the rest of his life, Connie Mack's mantra became, "I managed one year too long." He told his daughter Ruth, "I made a terrible mistake, managing that last year. I never should have done it. I could no longer talk to the players as I used to."

"I lost something in 1950," he wrote to Fife. "Even Mrs. Mack thought I should [resign]."

To Miss Helen Buque of Santa Barbara, California, who wrote to ask if it was true he was retiring, he replied, "After being manager since 1901, I felt that it was time I should pass the management on to someone else. While I have received a number of letters from different people wanting me to go on, felt that it was time I took a rest from sitting on the bench year after year."

Two months after he resigned he told the writers gathered for his birthday interview, "[The disappointing season] was my fault. I thought I could go on and on as manager and I was determined to get through that fiftieth year. At least I'm sorry now I didn't quit a year sooner. I couldn't talk to the boys any more. I was a deterrent to the team."

A week after his seventy-sixth birthday in 1948, Mack had written to a young lady who may have been one of his many namesakes: Constance Mack of Buffalo, New York: "Many thanks for the congratulations you have extended to me on my birthday. Also the splendid picture you so kindly sent me. While it will not be possible for you to be a baseball player, hope that you will grow up to be a credit to your father and mother and I'm sure that you will be all of that. Hope you had a nice Christmas and that you will have a very happy new year."

Thus began another pen pal relationship for Connie Mack.

In December 1952 he wrote to Miss Mack: "I look young in my pictures and I feel young but I forget very fast. In other words I should never [have] manage[d] the club the last year. I could not talk to the players and did not try. Something happened to me during the winter. I don't know myself what happened."

He was still saying it in the spring of 1953, when the White Sox and A's arrived in Savannah for an exhibition game. Ferris Fain had been traded to Chicago that winter. Fain said, "I truly respected and enjoyed Mr. Mack. I'm sitting in the hotel lobby and he comes in. I went over to greet him and we sat down and I asked him, 'Mr. Mack, how are you enjoying your retirement?' He remembered I had played for him. He said, 'It's a little strange. But you know, I think I managed one year too long.'"

Writers all over the country spoke their piece about the end of an era. Most emphasized Mack's physical endurance and character rather than his pennants. Only a few, like New York writer Joe Williams, were uncharitable enough to write what they all believed: "He should have done it long ago."

25 | THE ROY & EARLE SHOW, 1951 – 1953

The first thing Roy and Earle did when they gained control of the Athletics was raise their salaries from $12,000 to $25,000, Roy as vice-president in charge of the ballpark and ticket sales, Earle as secretary-treasurer. Connie Mack continued to draw $20,000 a year as the president.

The second thing Roy and Earle did was demonstrate their inability to work together.

Washington manager Bucky Harris wanted a Spanish-speaking catcher to work with his Cuban pitchers. He called Earle Mack and offered to exchange veteran catcher Al Evans for Fermin Guerra. Earle agreed.

The way Harris told the story, "I received a teletype from Earle confirming the deal, but then Roy called up and said Earle didn't have the authority to make deals, and he called it off."

Harris said he was under the impression that the A's wanted more players for Guerra, and he was "stunned" when they sold the catcher to the Red Sox in December for $25,000. (The Senators finally obtained Guerra from Boston in May for $25,000 and a minor league outfielder.)

Jimmie Dykes was probably just as surprised when Guerra was sold. In October he had told Ray Kelly, "There will be no trades unless we get what we want . . . and we don't want money."

What role Art Ehlers had in all this is unknown.

The third thing Roy and Earle did was stop speaking to each other.

Dick Armstrong pursued new promotional efforts in the wake of the golden jubilee hoopla. The Elephant Room was opened under the right-field stands as a club for season-ticket and night-plan holders to meet, have a drink and something to eat, entertain their friends, and mingle with baseball people. A grinning white elephant with upturned trunk was imprinted in the asbestos tile floor at the entrance. The room was decorated with photos that had once covered Mack's office walls and objects given to him by individuals and civic groups over the years: a bronze elephant, bats and balls made from coal, a 1911 pottery plate with a player's hands imposed on an elephant, wood carvings, a variety of miniature elephants, and silver loving cups.

Spring training 1951 was a new experience for everybody. The players had gotten to know Jimmie Dykes, and they liked him. He was part of the team, not as removed as Mr. Mack, at least in their young minds. Dykes was fifty-four, but he had still been playing when Eddie Joost and Sam Chapman broke in.

In addition to coaches Bing Miller, Wally Moses, and Chief Bender, Dykes added Tom Oliver, who had managed several of the club's farm teams in recent years and was a familiar face to many of the younger men in camp. Miller was stationed at first, Oliver at third. Dykes also lured his old trainer with the White Sox, Packey Schwartz, to come over to the A's.

Discipline was tighter. The players were expected to be up early for breakfast and out of the dining room by eight o'clock.

That didn't work for Ferris Fain. "I couldn't eat a big breakfast after being out all night, so I'd get one of the waitresses to write me up a check for a big meal and I'd sign it when I came down, then go out the back door and come around in the front like I'd been up for hours."

One morning he met Dykes at the front door. "You out last night?"

"Yeah."

"What time did you get in?"

"Skipper, I don't really know, but I bet you do."

"How about your buddies?"

"I don't know anything about them."

Dykes ran his pitchers harder than they'd ever run before. He hit fungos to them, uncannily almost always just beyond their reach. It didn't help. When the team got off to a slow start, Dykes blamed it on the pitchers' poor condition. "Then, when they did get started they lacked confidence," Dykes said.

Chief Bender worked with Bobby Shantz on throwing a knuckleball, reminding him, "If you can't change speeds, you're never going to win."

Bender told all the pitchers to slow down between pitches. "Give the batter time to think about what pitch might be coming. When he starts to think he becomes confused."

Shantz was an apt student, racking up an 18-10 season.

Carl Scheib won none of his 11 starts and wound up in the bullpen, a role in which he won 1 and lost 9 games.

Dick Fowler tried to come back and was 5-11 in 22 starts.

Eddie Joost was one who appreciated the more energetic spring training pace that had been missing. At thirty-four, he started the season in the best shape of his career and hit a career-high .289 with 106 walks. His 19 home runs put him in one of baseball's elite circles circa 1951: the 100-home-run club.)

In 1950 Ferris Fain had hit a career-high 10 home runs and began to fancy himself a power hitter. Wally Moses told him to forget it; every time he saw Fain swinging for the fences, he reminded him that he would never be a home run threat and would remain a .280 hitter. In the first week of spring training Fain developed blisters on his hands. To curtail the irritation he choked up on the bat and eased up on his swing. To his surprise line drives began leaping off his bat. He would lead the league in batting for the next two years and in doubles in '52. (Fain's career OBP of .424 is third among players not in the Hall of Fame, thirteenth overall.)

Dykes made a special project of Elmer Valo. Since 1946 Valo had been a good—a very good—right fielder, hitting around .300. Dykes wanted him to move up a notch to *great*. "If that fellow would ever stop worrying about himself, he might turn out to be the great ballplayer he is capable of being. I'm gonna have to get Elmer to relax."

Relaxed or not, Elmer kept on hitting the walls to make catches when the game was on the line and batting around .300 for another eleven years, but he never gained *great* status.

The Athletics opened the season against Washington with a night game—the first such opener in the AL. It was 40 degrees at game time, holding the crowd to 8,285. They played the next game under the lights too, before only 2,055, and lost both of them.

When you start a season 1-12, you know you're probably not going any-where. And when you score 2 or fewer runs in six of those losses, you know you need help in the hitting department. The A's had no cash to buy players and nobody to promote from the minors, so they explored the trade winds.

In Chicago Frank Lane and Paul Richards coveted Cleveland outfield-er Minnie Minoso. Dykes wanted Gus Zernial from the White Sox. Hank Greenberg in Cleveland wanted Lou Brissie. Lane did most of the telephone calling and negotiating to make it all happen.

On April 30 Dykes called Brissie into his office. "We're going to have to let you go. We need hitting. There's a three-way deal in the works with Cleveland and Chicago. I didn't want to trade you but Cleveland insisted on you." The deal would bring outfielders Gus Zernial and Dave Philley from Chicago to the A's. Minnie Minoso would pass through Philadelphia on his way from Cleveland to Chicago, taking Paul Lehner with him. (Lehner then went bar hopping to St. Louis and Cleveland before the year was over.)

Philley had played for Dykes; Zernial had not, but he'd hit 29 home runs in 1950.

"I don't want to go," Brissie said.

"Hank Greenberg wants you or it's no deal," Dykes said.

"Let me talk to him," Brissie said.

They called Greenberg. "I want to stay here," Brissie told him, "and help Mr. Mack's team."

Greenberg said, "You pitched well and couldn't help them last year. What makes you think you can help them now?"

Lou Brissie had no answer.

"I know you've had contract trouble," Greenberg said. "We'll take care of that."

Brissie had been offered $12,500, sent it back, and ultimately signed for $15,200. He would earn $17,000 at Cleveland in 1952.

Zernial, twenty-seven, became the A's most productive slugger since the days of Foxx and Simmons, leading the league with 33 home runs and 129 RBIs. He also led the league with 101 strikeouts.

Philley, thirty-one, was a reliable .260s switch hitter with 7-home-run power.

Veteran left-hander Sam Zoldak also came over from Cleveland.

Sam Chapman, now thirty-five, was not hitting in the early going. On May 10 Connie Mack sent for him. "We've traded you to Cleveland. Sorry to see you go. But it might be good for you; you might be on a winning team." (The Indians finished second in Chapman's last year.) Whoever made the deal didn't get much for him: Allie Clark, a .250-hitting twenty-eight-year-old part-time outfielder who was welcomed by Tipton and Fain into their after-hours set, and a thirty-two-year-old featherweight-hitting second baseman, Lou Klein.

Roy and Earle raised some cash to meet the payroll while unloading some expensive contracts: Bubba Harris to Cleveland for $5,000, Barney McCosky to Cincinnati for $10,000, Hank Wyse to Washington for $13,000.

In his first appearance in a home uniform at Shibe Park, Gus Zernial became the new Idol of Shibeshire when he hit 2 home runs as the A's swept a Sunday doubleheader from the Yankees on May 13 and followed it with 2 more in each of the next two games. Inexplicably he also became the hecklers' favorite target. On June 4 the A's brought back Hank Majeski, sending Kermit Wahl to Chicago. The reunited infield turned 204 double plays. From then on, Roy and Earle made no other moves to improve the team. The fans' enthusiasm over the new faces quickly vaporized. The last game of the 4-7 home stand attracted just 1,064 local stalwarts and traveling salesmen.

In Chicago on July 15 Ferris Fain popped up to shortstop in the fourth inning. Frustrated from going hitless in his last 6 at bats, he kicked the first base bag. The base didn't move; his toe did. He stayed in the game until the seventh, then was out for five weeks, during which the A's were 12-24. They sailed south, falling 28 games under .500.

As it looked like the brothers were going to take a bath and run out of hot water, birds of prey began to hover, offering to buy out either or both of them: a group in Hollywood put together by Al Horwits, and two Philadelphia groups, one headed by Babe Alexander of Adelphia Public Relations (who represented the Phillies and was probably fronting for his firm's clients) and the other by contractor John McShain. Jack Kelly was still interested. A Houston oilman, Bob Smith, pledged $250,000 if nine others in Houston would do the same to buy the team and move it

On the way north from spring training, Jimmie Dykes had told a Fayetteville reporter, "I don't say we're going to win a pennant or even crack the first division, but we're going to have some fun and make some trouble."

It took a while. In seventh place (propped up as usual by the Browns) when Fain returned, the A's suddenly became the hottest team in the league, going 25-11 to finish sixth. During that stretch they played spoilers for all the pennant contenders, knocking each one out of first place at least temporarily. Bobby Shantz put it all together, winning his last 6 starts. The revived A's drew more than 100,000 to the last 13 home dates, boosting attendance for the year above 465,000. With the aid of rental income amounting to $49,700, the loss for the year was just under $30,000.

The birds of prey all flew away.

Of such fall flourishes are future dreams forged. Earle talked about bringing his son, Earle Jr., into the business and Roy intended to do the same with his son, Connie III, a student at Penn. The house of McGillicuddy would reign forever.

The Athletics' strong finish in 1951 sparked a sharp increase in season ticket and advance sales for '52. It also sparked demands for higher salaries. Connie Mack was no longer the formidable presence confronting hungry but respectful athletes who "would play for less for Mr. Mack." None of the players was told to "sign or stay home."

Ferris Fain and Gus Zernial were the most adamant holdouts. "They both want more than we can afford," said Art Ehlers. Fain eventually signed for $25,000, a $7,500 raise. Zernial started out at $17,000; six weeks later he signed for $23,000.

Bobby Shantz had earned $7,000 in '51. His salary jumped to $12,000, matching Pete Suder's. Joost was up to $18,500, Valo to $16,500. Dave Philley rejected two offers before signing for $13,000. Sam Zoldak cost them $14,000 and didn't win a game.

Jimmie Dykes had narrowly missed a $5,000 bonus based on attendance reaching 500,000 in '51. He received no raise for 1952, but this year he would collect the bonus, thanks to Bobby Shantz.

Roy and Earle and Art Ehlers could hardly be called aggressive when it came to improving the team. They spent almost as much money—$7,000— on new uniforms and caps as they did for players. Besides drafting Kite Thomas, a twenty-eight-year-old outfielder from the Yankees' system, their biggest deal was the purchase of five Giants farmhands left at Ottawa when the Giants cut their ties with the Canadian team and the A's bought the franchise.

You never heard of any of them.

Rumors flew before the June 15 trading deadline with "sources" certain that Fain would soon be playing for the Yankees or Cleveland. Indians president Ellis Ryan reportedly offered $250,000 and two pitchers. According to one source, Art Ehlers would have accepted only Mike Garcia, Bob Lemon, or Early Wynn as one of the two pitchers.

Nothing happened.

Except that when Bobo Newsom, who had had more terms in Washington than FDR, was released on June 15, the A's signed him for $2,000 a month. Newsom, forty-four, had been down in the minors for three years. On July 15 he threw his first complete game in the AL in five years and his last for the season.

It would be hyperbolic to say that Bobby Shantz saved the Athletics. But he did postpone their demise, pitching the A's into fourth place with a 24-7 record and winning the MVP for it with 16 first-place votes. He was third in the league in ERA, shutouts, and strikeouts, second with 27 complete games, and led the league with 2.03 walks per 9 innings.

Shantz was also the most valuable member of the Athletics to Roy and Earle and the players who collected attendance bonuses (in addition to his own $3,000)—Dave Philley, Elmer Valo, Joe Astroth, Harry Byrd, Billy Hitchcock, and Cass Michaels—and fourth-place slices of the World Series melon. As Shantz's wins piled up—he was 12-1 by June 19—dates he was scheduled to pitch were circled on fans' calendars. As a pregame stunt on July 18, Dick Armstrong set up a scale at home plate and had an official of the county bureau of weights and measures verify Shantz's height and weight. The official record: 139 pounds, 12 ounces; 5 feet, 6¼ inches. On the 17 days he started at home—27 percent of the game dates—Shantz drew 48 percent of the total attendance of 627,100. Put another way, attendance on days he started averaged 17,726; the other days it averaged 6,929. Sure, his dates included some Sunday doubleheaders against the Yankees, but they also included crowds of 35,000 on midweek nights. The biggest crowd of the year—35,673—turned out on Tuesday night, August 5, to see him beat the Red Sox, 5–3, for win number 20 against 3 losses.

In the second inning of his last start on September 23, Shantz was hit on his left arm by a Walt Masterson pitch and suffered a hairline fracture.

For a change, A's pitchers gave up the fewest walks in the league. After six years' seasoning right-hander Harry Byrd finally blossomed. In 1950 he had been switched by Chief Bender from an overhand to a sidearm delivery. His 15-15 record included a 1-hitter against the Yankees on September 3 and earned him rookie of the year honors.

Bob Hooper was the bullpen. Carl Scheib and Alex Kellner had lackluster years.

Otherwise the A's were a middle-of-the-pack team in just about every department.

The offense was all Gus Zernial—29 home runs and 100 RBIs—and Ferris Fain, who had a 24-game hitting streak and led the league at .327.

The infield was no longer the double play machine of the past. Thirty-six-year-old Eddie Joost kept grinding it out, playing 108 consecutive games until a bout of intestinal flu bedded him in August. He drew 122 walks and hit 20 home runs, the most exciting a July 15 walk-off grand slam off Satchel Paige.

Dykes used four second basemen. Pete Suder was out half the time or subbing at other positions and didn't hit a lick until he woke up in mid-August. In 1948 the Tigers had invited George Kell's younger brother, Everett (known as Skeeter), to spring training but didn't sign him. Later that year the A's invited him for a look when they were in St. Louis. Connie Mack and his coaches were struck by the similarity of Skeeter's mannerisms to his brother's in the field and at the plate and offered him a minor league contract. After three years in the minors, Skeeter looked ready for the big leagues. He replaced Suder at second base on April 24 and played regularly until mid-July. He was hitting .270 on June 6; then the pitchers figured him out. He finished the year and his big league career at .215.

Art Ehlers trolled the waiver lists and picked up Clark Griffith's thirty-three-year-old nephew, Sherry Robertson, a .200 hitter, then Cass Michaels, the erstwhile White Sox all-star. The farm system cupboard was bare.

With a tailwind from the fourth-place finish and money in the bank (which, for the Athletics, meant they had sufficient cash flow to show a loss of only $20,831.54 after depreciation and farm system expenses), Roy and Earle declared they would go all out to improve for 1953.

What they did dazzled the fans like wet firecrackers. The biggest trade sent Ferris Fain to Chicago with infielder Bob Wilson for first baseman Eddie Robinson, infielder Joe DeMaestri and outfielder Ed McGhee. The premise was that while Joost and Fain were a high-percentage on-base one-two threat, nobody but Gus Zernial was behind them to drive them in. Robinson had hit 22 home runs in Chicago.

Another factor might have been that Roy and Earle knew they'd have to go high to sign Fain, and didn't even try. Fain earned $40,000 at Chicago.

Art Ehlers tried to give Bobby Shantz a little raise and had to give him a big one: a two-year contract at $25,000 a year.

Ehlers tried to *cut* Gus Zernial from $23,000 to $20,000. Zernial held out until March before signing for $24,000 and an attendance bonus that didn't pay off.

There were no more blockbuster trades. Not even a curb chipper. Here's what the McGillicuddy brothers did the rest of 1953:

• Traded veteran Billy Hitchcock for veteran Don Kolloway (released in May).

- Acquired three pitchers by drafting Giants right-hander Rinty Monahan and thirty-three-year-old lefty Hooks Iott, achiever of 3 major league victories for the Browns, and trading the 8-15 Bob Hooper for Dick Rozek. Monahan and Rozek pitched 10 innings each; Iott, none.
- Brought up thirty-year-old Marion Fricano, bought from Brooklyn in '52 and sent to Ottawa.
- Picked up Brooklyn and Washington castoff outfielder Carmen Mauro.
- Bought third baseman Loren Babe from the Yankees for $25,000; Babe hit .200.
- Sent Allie Clark on waivers to Chicago.

Red Smith, considering nobody in the league anywhere close to stopping the Yankees from their fifth straight pennant, half-heartedly picked the A's to finish third: "Bobby Shantz, Harry Byrd, Alex Kellner and Carl Scheib are first-class pitchers. Eddie Robinson and Gus Zernial can hit a ball out of sight. Philadelphia has three-quarters of an infield, no speed, and the weakest throwing arms in any major league outfield. On some days, the A's will win."

Philadelphia fans yawned.

It didn't take long for the enthusiasm or lack thereof to become evident. Only 5,599 showed up on opening day—the lowest in nine years—at the now officially named Connie Mack Stadium (a change Mack had always opposed but was no longer in a position to stop). The A's stayed among the leaders until May 3. Two weeks later, after losing 11 of 13, they were among the seven also-rans trailing the Yankees. They couldn't even entice 3,000 to several night games in June.

Phil Rizzuto was no longer an everyday player for the Yankees. During two weeks after June 16 he appeared in only two games. The Yankees, for whom there was no such thing as too much bench strength, had their eye on Eddie Joost and Elmer Valo, figuring the Mack brothers wouldn't turn down a generous cash offer for the two veterans. It didn't even have to be generous.

But Earle and Roy got greedy. They kept upping the price, reaching, according to George Weiss, $250,000, to which the Yankees said, "Forget it."

Casey Stengel said, "We woulda been swindled if we bought them."

Weiss bought Willie Miranda from the Browns instead.

A slew of illnesses and injuries brought out two intrinsic weaknesses in the A's organization: no bench and nobody ready to bring up from the minor leagues. Elmer Valo pulled a leg muscle in April, started only 6 games before mid-August, and then played with a broken finger. Eddie Joost sprained his right knee in a base-running collision on June 19 and didn't play again.

The A's fielding was poor, the hitting sporadic. Gus Zernial, who missed ten days, finished with 42 home runs; he and Eddie Robinson drove in a total of 211. That was the offense. The number five batter in the lineup, center fielder Carmen Mauro, hit no home runs and had 17 RBIs.

Alex Kellner pitched with bursitis, then broke a finger. Bobby Shantz tore a tendon in his shoulder on May 21 and won only 5 all year, none in the last two months. Carl Scheib had arm problems. So did Harry Byrd, but he kept working, pitching 237 innings with an 11-20 record. Charlie Bishop, a twenty-nine-year-old rookie up from Ottawa, finished one of his 20 starts and lost 13 of them. Morrie Martin, out most of '52 with a broken finger, was the bullpen, setting a team record of 58 appearances.

Bob Trice was the first black player to wear an A's uniform. (The A's had been signing black players since 1951, but none had made it to the big leagues.) Trice had been pitching for Canadian teams in the Provincial League and was signed by Ottawa business manager George MacDonald. He was 21-10 when the A's called him up in September. He lost his first start on Sunday, September 13, to the Browns, 5–2, but won his next two.

There were no September miracles this year. Detroit, in the cellar all year, climbed past the A's to claim sixth place. Bill Veeck's Browns, like Atlas, held up the American League. The Athletics' last ten home dates—including five doubleheaders—averaged 3,800 attendance.

On May 27 Connie Mack had written, "This year looks bad and they will lose a lot of money."

He was right. The handwriting was on the wall, not in the men's room but in the ledgers: $70,987.42 in red ink.

Back in March 1953 Bill Veeck had tried to move the Browns to Baltimore. (He really wanted to move them to Los Angeles.) Prior to the meeting to discuss the move Veeck believed he had the necessary six votes lined up. Reporters called it a done deal. But Clark Griffith and Del Webb of the Yankees were working behind the scenes against him.

According to Veeck, Connie Mack assured him that if the A's voted against the move, it was his sons' doing, not his. Veeck knew that. "Roy and Earle are more reactionary and less forward-looking than Connie Mack."

When Veeck started to make his pitch, Roy stood up and said, "I don't see why you'd want to leave St. Louis. We'd never leave Philadelphia."

VEECK: The A's will be the next to move.
ROY: Oh no, never. He then made a long speech about the great Philadelphia fans and civic loyalty, etc.

Veeck wound up with only two votes, Hank Greenberg's and Frank Lane's. He tried again in September; this time the vote was 4–4. Roy voted no again. Connie Mack's views were obviously not invited. He wrote to his niece Maudie, "Baltimore needs a major league club and they will support it very well."

Only after Veeck sold out did the league approve the move. Then Del Webb put through a constitutional amendment to expand "if it should become desirable to move to the Pacific Coast." It passed unanimously.

The Baltimore interests who bought the club invited Art Ehlers to be their general manager. Ehlers lost no time saying goodbye and good luck to Roy and Earle.

Roy Mack wanted to get rid of Jimmie Dykes, who had another year on his contract. But Roy didn't want to be on the hook for a year's salary if Dykes didn't land another job. Roy left it up to Earle to deal with Dykes and offer him an "advisory" position knowing—praying—that Dykes would prefer to take another managing job. Earle did nothing. Without telling Dykes, Roy called a press conference for November 4 and announced that Eddie Joost would be the new manager. Dykes, he said, would remain in an advisory capacity. Roy had a hard time explaining the firing of Dykes. He didn't want to admit it was a financial move. The best he could come up with was, "I don't think a manager should play eighteen holes of golf every day and come into the clubhouse at night all tired out."

Besides, he added, they wanted to go with a younger man.

(Pete Suder said the managing job was between him and Joost, but "they said I would be too easy on the players.")

At the press conference, Art Morrow observed, "Earle was the only one in the place who seemed out of place."

Connie Mack seemed out of place too. He sat there nodding his head and saying only, "I hope Jimmie will stay." Ever the optimist, he wrote to Shannon Fife, "The appointing of Joost is a good one. It looks like we will be able to get somewhere. We will get along all right. The team will make many trades during the winter and I also hope their [sic] will be good ones."

The first Jimmie Dykes heard about it was when a sportswriter told him the wire services had reported he'd been fired. He said, "I was hanging around [Shibe Park] all day yesterday and nobody said a word to me." But it was no surprise to him. He had already told Eddie Joost to expect to replace him. "But you won't win," Dykes told him. "If you finish seventh they'll say you did a good job."

Dykes showed up after the writers had left. He and Earle went into an office, where Earle presumably offered him some kind of "advisory" position. It must have been a real ordeal for Earle; when they came out he was perspiring, Dykes was joking. Jimmie already knew where he was going.

A week later Art Ehlers announced that Jimmie Dykes would be the Orioles' manager.

The A's were left with no general manager and twenty-seven-year-old Bernie Guest as the farm director. Earle Mack was scared to death to assume a general manager's responsibilities, even—or especially—with his older brother Roy's having the last word.

Asked what the club's policy would be, Roy said, "We'll go on doing the best we can with the resources at our disposal." At the same time he talked big: "We lost a million dollars on our farm system over the last six years, but we're going to add scouts and expand it." (They didn't.)

There'd be no big signing bonuses, though; Roy didn't believe in them. In 1950 Art Ehlers had given $5,000 to a first base prospect, Tom Hamilton, a 215-pound, .186-hitting pinch hitter in '53. No more of that foolishness. There were reports that no A's scout could offer more than $150 to sign a player without home office approval.

Hardly what Athletics' fans wanted to hear.

Roy went on: "We know we have a better team than we would seem to have from the standings. Even if we don't strengthen ourselves through trades or the draft . . . we figure to be better."

Show us, said the fans.

The A's signed five free agents with no future and drafted one man, twenty-eight-year-old second baseman Spook Jacobs.

Roy asked Eddie Joost to take over because Eddie was popular with the fans and respected by the players, who had picked him as their player rep. He was a smart ballplayer. And a player-manager at $22,500 was cheaper than a player and a manager.

But Roy didn't reckon with the fact that Eddie Joost was still the same man who hadn't hesitated to speak his mind to management throughout his career.

Joost began by publicly admitting the club as it stood didn't have a chance to finish in the first division. He knew the farm system was barren—there was nothing to "rebuild" with. He wasn't interested in a youth movement. He wanted players who could produce now and was willing to trade anybody but Shantz, Kellner, and "maybe" Harry Byrd. Joost considered those three the keys to his pitching staff.

All that was reported. What wasn't reported was what Eddie Joost told the author forty years later that he said in a meeting with Roy and Earle and Art Ehlers. It isn't clear when this occurred, as Ehlers had left for Baltimore a week before Joost replaced Dykes. It may have taken place after the '53 season, before the decision to replace Dykes, but if his recollection of the meeting was accurate, would he have still gotten the job? At any rate, it reflects his opinion of the Athletics' brain trust at that time.

I was asked what thoughts I had on improving the club. I said I'm going to begin with one thing. There's animosity here, and I pointed to Roy and Earle. If you two guys can get along, bury the hatchet—and I think the possibility is there—then we might have a successful season. If you guys continue as it is, there's going to be nothing but disarray. You guys have screwed this place up for years since I've been here. Earle, what do you do for this club? Roy, you're supposed to be the financial manager and know what's going on. This place has been broke for the last three years. You don't do anything about it. I turned to Art Ehlers and said as far as being a general manager, why don't you go get a broom and start sweeping the stands? You don't do anything to try to help this ball club.

Joost wasn't alone in his thinking. Arthur Daley commented, "[The change] makes no sense whatsoever. The only possible explanation is that the bickering and internal friction which has kept the blundering Athletics' front office in a turmoil ever since saintly Connie Mack released his hold on the control has erupted anew. Roy and Earle . . . see eye-to-eye on nothing. If they are now on speaking terms with each other, it's a new development."

Harry Byrd was the one A's player that other teams wanted. Boston GM Joe Cronin called Joost and offered him $250,000 for Byrd.

Joost said, "Oh, that would be great, Joe. I could play $20,000 in center field, put $40,000 on the mound. I can't use money. I need players."

If Roy heard about that conversation, he probably turned apoplectic.

The Yankees came calling too. At the winter meetings in Atlanta in early December, Joost met with Casey Stengel and Dan Topping. Stengel produced a list of six players, all minor leaguers or bench-warmers. Joost rejected all of them but one, Bill Renna, a part-time outfielder who'd hit .314. Stengel suggested other names until they agreed on a list that Joost said he would take for Byrd. All players, no cash.

Topping said, "I have to call George Weiss and run it by him."

"Forget it," said Joost. "He'll turn it down because he didn't make the deal."

They called Weiss and read off the list. Weiss exploded. "That's not going to happen."

That ended it, thought Joost.

Weiss then called Earle, who agreed to take Renna and the other players Joost had turned down. In addition to Byrd, the A's sent Eddie Robinson, Tom Hamilton, Carmen Mauro, and Loren Babe to New York for Don Bollweg, John Gray, Al Robertson, Jim Finigan, Renna, and—according to Weiss, the key player Earle insisted on—Vic Power, who had hit .349 at Kansas City. The A's also picked up $25,000.

Arthur Daley reacted the same way as Eddie Joost: "It looks like the biggest steal since the Brink's holdup. The Yankees plucked Harry Byrd and Eddie Robinson from the Athletics and gave for the two recognized stars a batch of expendable second-line ballplayers."

Art Ehlers in Baltimore sneered, "What did the A's really get? I could have gotten the same players from the Yankees for Bob Turley and Vic Wertz."

Earle was ecstatic, calling it "a wonderful deal for us. It is a good start toward a faster, younger, stronger defensive team that will return the Athletics to the first division."

Connie Mack, in Fort Myers celebrating his ninety-first birthday, cheered on his sons: "We picked up some fine young talent in line with the rebuilding program. We have a club that with a little help will go a long way."

When he said "a long way," he was not thinking 1,152 miles.

26 | M R . M A C K I N R E T I R E M E N T

Over the years, when Connie Mack was asked about his plans to retire, he often replied, "If I quit, I'd die."

Well, he quit, but he didn't die. The job hadn't killed him. Retirement wouldn't either.

Every manager struggles to maintain an even keel, not sinking too low during losing streaks nor riding too high with each come-from-behind victory. Some of them never master it, spending six months a year on a roller coaster, unable to sleep or eat during the inevitable slumps. It can shorten a man's life. Connie Mack could not have survived fifty-seven years of it if he hadn't achieved that equanimity many years ago.

Anyone who has spent his entire life doing exactly what he most wanted to do—and loving it—must feel some regret when he reaches the end of the line. Connie Mack had enjoyed *being* the Philadelphia Athletics. Sure, he had enjoyed some years more than others, but just being what he was—a baseball manager with no meddlesome owner to answer to—well, in his mind, who could ask for anything more?

Some men suffer in retirement, unable to deal with the loss of identity as a Somebody of prestige and power. Not Connie Mack. He was still the face of the Philadelphia Athletics. The rose breeder Howard & Smith saluted him by introducing the Connie Mack rose, a dark crimson bloom of mild fragrance. Even more, to baseball fans everywhere, he remained Mr. Baseball, and he took that ambassadorial role seriously. Status was important to him, more so than wealth beyond providing for his family. Wherever he went, he was feted, honored. People flocked to his presence and were flattered by his unwavering attention.

At the same time, Connie Mack was now free of the physical wear and tear of the job and the enervating frustration that had plagued him in recent years as he struggled to grind his thoughts into words and convey the words into actions. He felt healthier and stronger than he had in years. No joints ached or creaked when he spryly stood up or sat down. One day in the fall of 1951 he was at the home of his daughter Betty Nolen. Mack was walking through the living room when her ten-year-old son Jimmy came home from his first football practice. Bursting to show Pop-Pop how he'd learned to tackle, Jimmy dove and grabbed Mack's ankles. Down he went. Many years later Nolen recalled, "I felt bad about it, but he just laughed it off while we helped him up."

Mack's long stride was still so lively that younger men almost had to jog to keep up with him. His fourteen-year-old grandson Bill Cunningham (Frank's younger brother) was a batboy in 1953. "Once in a while Pop-Pop would come down to the first row beside the dugout during batting practice to talk to Jimmie Dykes. When he started to leave, Dykes would tell me, 'Go with him.' I had to run up the steps to keep up with him."

What Pittsburgh general manager Joe Brown called "the most vivid sparkling blue eyes I ever saw" still glistened. His hearing was good. Nobody in the family or working with him remembers seeing him wear glasses, even to read the newspaper.

In the weeks that followed his resignation as the Athletics' manager in the fall of 1950, much of Connie Mack's ten-to-one workday went to writing letters. He kept in touch with an extensive network of family and friends, including a distant cousin, Cornelius McGillicuddy, who had first written to him while a student at Canisius High School in Buffalo in 1937. A priest, high school coach, and athletic director for forty-four years, he was one of Mack's regular correspondents. Mack wrote often to Robert and Connie McCambridge, the sons of his first daughter, Marguerite. Connie called him Dad, and Mack sometimes signed his letters that way. Connie lived in Wilmington, Delaware, and Mack always expressed the wish that he and his family would come to see him. The McCambridge brothers had now given Mack four great-grandchildren.

In November 1950 Mack began a busy year of activity when he went to St. Paul, where the Brown & Bigelow calendar company was planning a 1952 calendar featuring him. A week later he was in Washington for a do for Clark Griffith. On December 19 he and Katherine moved to an apartment near Ruth's home—School Lane House—at School Lane and Wissahickon, a move, he said, that exhausted *her*: "Mrs. Mack is not feeling well. She has complained so much of late," he wrote to Connie McCambridge. "Am really worried about her."

It's unclear when Chuck Roberts first met Connie Mack. Roberts was the chauffeur for a Philadelphia friend of Mack's named Harry Sheets, who had a winter home in Fort Myers. It was probably January 1946, when Mr. and Mrs. Mack spent a few months in St. Petersburg before spring training opened in West Palm Beach. Sheets put Roberts and his automobile at the Macks' disposal. When spring training began, Roberts drove them to West Palm Beach, then took Mack from the hotel to Wright Field and back every day.

Mack traveled north with the team, while Roberts drove Sheets to Philadelphia. They met Mack at the railroad station and took him home. "Then I was through with him for the season," Roberts said.

The same arrangement prevailed in 1947. Then Mr. Sheets died, and Roberts went home to Jacksonville and worked as a Simonize man at a garage.

Connie Mack hadn't driven a car for many years. He'd rather ride a streetcar than get behind the wheel. Heck, he'd rather *walk* to Shibe Park than drive a car. Mack owned a green 1941 dual-carburetor Buick Special, which Katherine drove. Earle or Ruth or occasionally Ruth's husband Frank would drive him to work and home.

In the fall of '48 somebody in the family decided that Dad could use a full-time driver. They remembered Chuck Roberts. According to Roberts, Roy called and hired him to come to Philadelphia and told him to order a new car suitable for long-distance trips. The Athletics would pay for it. Roberts ordered a green Cadillac. No new cars had been built during the war. Cadillac had a backlog of orders that would take a year to fill. Frank Cunningham worked at a Buick agency and came up with a '49 Roadmaster with leather seats and all the extras. By that time the Macks were in St. Petersburg. Roberts drove the car to Florida and began his tenure as Mack's chauffeur for the rest of Connie Mack's life.

A year later the Cadillac he had ordered was delivered. It cost $4,571.25, less a trade-in allowance of $2,350 for the Buick. (Apparently the A's bought three more cars at the same time, possibly for family members; the ledgers show November 1 and 2 purchases of another Cadillac for $4,245, a blue Oldsmobile sedan for $2,235.95, and a black Olds for $2,205.95.)

As part of the golden jubilee year in 1950, on June 13 at Briggs Stadium the Ford Motor Company had presented Mack a dark blue Lincoln with a plaque on the dashboard of a gold baseball and crossed bats. Roberts took the train to Detroit to drive it home. The Cadillac was sold for $3,300.

After he retired, Connie Mack no longer traveled with the team. When he followed them on road trips, or wherever he went, Roberts drove him in the Lincoln. For the next five years a closeness developed between them: a trust and dependence on Mack's part, a reverent care-giving on Chuck's part. They covered thousands of miles and spent many long hours and days together, Mr. Mack in the front seat beside Roberts. Mrs. Mack rode with them to Florida and on some of the road trips—always alone in the back seat, which didn't please her.

There was little conversation other than occasional baseball talk. Mr. Mack often dozed off, oblivious to whatever Roberts tuned in on the radio.

"On those long trips he was completely relaxed," Roberts said. "I'd go around a curve and I had to put my hand out to keep him from tipping over on me. He never got tired. To him it was like sitting in a hotel lobby."

The car had no air conditioning. Driving through the Midwestern summer heat, Roberts sometimes was stopped for speeding. "Once Mr. Mack was about to faint from the heat in Chicago. I told the policeman that Mr. Mack was in the car and I was trying to get him to his hotel. The cop went around and talked to him and they shook hands and he let me go. Another time a cop stopped us and when I told him who was in the car, he asked for some tickets to a big game and Mr. Mack arranged it. I never got a speeding ticket."

All the ballpark cops knew them. Roberts would let Mack out at the press gate and, with some well-placed fivers, secure a parking space nearby. He had a pass to every park in the league.

How did they deal with segregation?

"Most places I was treated white," said Roberts, "because I was with him. But not in Florida. We'd pull into a drive-in and the carhop would come out to take our orders and wouldn't take mine, and Mr. Mack would say, 'Then we'll drive on,' but I knew it wouldn't be any different at the next place, so I'd tell them to take care of Mr. Mack, and I'd wait."

When he took the Macks to a store or restaurant or the movies in St. Petersburg, it didn't occur to Mack that Chuck couldn't go in with them. But to avoid trouble, Chuck would leave and come back for them.

In West Palm Beach Roberts stayed at the same hotel with the black players. On the road he would go to the biggest black church in the city and they'd recommend a good hotel. In Washington he stayed at Howard University.

One day in the spring of 1951 the Dodgers beat the A's in a game at Wright Field. Mack gave a friend a ride back to the hotel. On the way the friend said, "If it wasn't for that nigger Robinson, the Dodgers wouldn't have won today."

A few days later Mack asked Roberts, "Chuck, when you hear a fellow use that word nigger, does it bother you?"

"It's like this, Mr. Mack," he said. "I was born in the South and that's a word they used all the time and I took it as a man's ignorance."

During the winter Chuck drove Mack to the office, to lunches and dinners. Whenever they were in traffic, in town or out of town, somebody would recognize Connie Mack and wave to him. "Mr. Mack, there's a couple over there waving to you." Mack always smiled and waved back. Chuck ran errands for Katherine, sometimes took Connie Jr.'s children to school, and kept the Lincoln in shiny-like-new condition.

Chuck Roberts loaded the luggage in the car on January 13, 1951, and headed for St. Pete with Mr. and Mrs. Mack. In Florida they went to the beach every day but never to swim, just to sit on a bench. Mack played a little golf.

Retired baseball writer Fred Lieb lived in St. Pete. One day, Lieb wrote, Connie Mack rang his doorbell. He wanted a favor. "Some of my friends said that while I am still alive I should have my voice recorded—something for posterity. Could you take me to wherever I could have this done?"

Lieb took him to the city-owned radio station, WSUN, where they taped Mack's recollections of his pennant-winning teams and gave him four copies of the tapes. Nobody knows what became of them.

In February Chuck Roberts drove the Macks across the state to the first spring training in sixty-six years at which Connie Mack would be just a spectator.

Mack appreciated the predicament in which Jimmie Dykes had landed as his successor. He vowed not to interfere or second-guess Dykes. And he didn't, at least not publicly, keeping his opinions to himself. He remembered his days managing in Pittsburgh for a meddling club president. They were not pleasant memories. At West Palm Beach he refused to sit on the field or the bench, lest it look like he was interfering. One day Jimmy Burns of the *Miami Herald* showed up. "Mack was friendly and gracious with his greeting," Burns wrote, "then I asked questions about the team and he seemed embarrassed."

"Have you talked to Jimmie Dykes about the team?" Mack asked.

"Yes."

"That's good. He's the manager now. Let him give out any information about the team."

Connie Mack was anything but a forlorn figure pining for his scorecard and his cushion on the bench. He sat on the sidelines or in the first row of the bleachers. The local spectators and autograph seekers greeted him as warmly as ever.

Will Harridge was at Wright Field one day when he saw an elderly man and his wife call out from the bleachers to Mack, asking for his autograph. "As they started down the bleacher steps, Mr. Mack motioned for them to wait, saying, 'I'll come up to you, please.' He did so. As he returned sprightly to the field he received a tremendous hand from every fan in the bleachers."

Sometimes Connie Mack's thoughts were clear but his words weren't. When the Yankees came to West Palm Beach, Casey Stengel remarked to him, "It takes the Yankees to pack 'em in for you, Mr. Mack."

To which Mack replied, "Yes, but for the Brooklyn game we had seven thousand."

Stengel was puzzled; this was the first game of the spring. That evening Mack made the same comment and someone asked, "When was that game, last year?"

Mack said, "Oh no, it was the year before last."

On his eighty-eighth birthday Mack had expressed the hope that the owners would retain Happy Chandler as commissioner. He was present at the Miami Beach meeting on March 12 at which he and Griffith spoke in support of Chandler, who fell three votes short of the required nine to renew his contract. Mack thought the ten who voted against him would soon learn they had made a mistake. Later Chandler told a congressional committee, "I revere men like Clark Griffith and Connie Mack. I felt my job was to represent the fans, then the players, and lastly the owners. Mr. Mack and Mr. Griffith felt that way, too."

Mack was at every 1951 spring training game and followed the club north, missing just one game in Birmingham when the night air was too cold. In Greensboro, North Carolina, he had a grand time visiting with an old friend, Charles McCrea, who had handled the Athletics' travel arrangements for the Pennsylvania Railroad for their first twenty-five years.

"It feels good being a fan at these ball games," Mack told local sportswriter Smith Barrier at a dinner party McCrea hosted that evening. "I thoroughly enjoy it, but I don't get excited like some of the fans. There was a fellow who sat right behind us today, and he really enjoyed himself. He talked all the time. It takes fans like that to make baseball."

Mack enjoyed retelling for the umpteenth time the story of his surprise choice of Howard Ehmke to start the 1929 World Series, calling it "the finest move I ever made as manager of the Athaletics."

Once the season started, Mack followed the A's on their first western trip. On the road he was accommodated with box or reserved seats by the home team, but at home he was determined not to be a distraction by sitting conspicuously in the family box behind the A's dugout. Instead he usually sat in the mezzanine section that hung from the upper deck and could be reached by a walkway from his office. (The door to his office was not always locked, allowing inquisitive roamers to sometimes pop in on Mr. Mack unexpectedly.) The mezzanine was sparsely occupied; because of the upper deck's overhang, fans couldn't follow a fly ball through its entire journey. Between that and the scarcity of spectators, he was often alone. Some of the former park employees would sit there because they knew he would be there, and they wanted to greet him, "How are you, Mr. Mack?"

But Mack didn't go to every A's game at home or on the road. He enjoyed making the rounds of reunions, sharing the spotlight and reminiscing with old friends and foes, some of whom he hadn't seen for fifty years. On May 15 he was in Boston riding with Clark Griffith in a Model T Ford in a parade to Fenway Park marking the American League's fiftieth anniversary. Twenty-eight players from the league's first rosters were there, spinning tall tales and true, including Hugh Duffy and Cy Young of the original Boston Somersets and two from Mack's inaugural Athletics, outfielder Dave Fultz and catcher Tom Leahy. Surprisingly only 8,923 were on hand, about 3,000 fewer than had been at the first game fifty years ago.

In the game that day the old-timers learned a new wrinkle in managing from White Sox skipper Paul Richards. Leading 7–6, Richards brought in left-hander Billy Pierce in the ninth inning to pitch to lead-off hitter Ted Williams. But he did it by having Pierce replace third baseman Minnie Minoso and moving right-hander Harry Dorish from the mound to third base. After Williams popped up, Dorish returned to the mound, and Floyd Baker went to third. (Dorish then gave up the tying run, but the White Sox won it in the eleventh, 9–7.)

"Baseball's quite a game," Mack said. "You always learn something new. I haven't learned it all yet."

On June 2 Mack was in Washington for a National Celebrities Golf Tournament. He and Clark Griffith and Yale football immortal Pudge Heffelfinger—all over eighty—competed in a driving contest. Mack bowed to the 96-degree heat by taking off his coat but not his tie or vest. Griffith won with his "lumbago swing," good for 175 yards. Two weeks later Chuck Roberts drove Mack to Meriden for the weekend, during which he attended a banquet Saturday evening and on Sunday after Mass spoke to a group of two hundred inmates at the nearby Cheshire reformatory, answered questions and signed autographs, then went to Legion Park for opening-day ceremonies for the Intermediate League. From there he went to Worcester, Massachusetts, to visit Jesse Burkett, an ailing Hall of Fame outfielder Mack had played against in the 1890s.

Tipped off by Burkett's daughter, a *Worcester Telegram* sportswriter, Jack Tubert, and photographer, Buddy Meyer, both in their twenties, showed up at Burkett's home at 189 Grove Street at ten o'clock. They followed Mack up a twenty-eight-step circular staircase to the third floor, where they found Burkett, who had had his legs amputated, in bed.

"When did I see you last, Jess?" Mack said. "Wasn't it when we had that big time in Brookfield in '34 when I brought my Athletics home? George [Cohan] is dead, you know. He was the master of ceremonies."

They chewed the cud of memories—"Remember that time . . . ? Whatever happened to . . . ?"—for about ninety minutes.

"We didn't get the salaries, did we Jess?" said Mack, chuckling.

"No, we never had the salary, that's right. But we had the game, the real game. You've got a good man working for you in Dykes."

"Yes, James is a great manager. He always tends to the boys, you know."

Burkett asked him how he was feeling and what he was doing these days.

"I've got one hundred percent health. I don't bother with doctors. My appetite's good. I haven't any hobbies. I just go along signing autographs, taking pictures."

Tubert wrote, "It was time for Jesse's nap. There was a tear in his eye as they shook hands and he said, 'Goodbye, Mr. Mack.'"

It was still "Mr. Mack," even to the eighty-two-year-old outfielder.

They came down the same narrow steps, Tubert in front, Mack in the middle. Tubert felt his presence right behind him. At the bottom Tubert asked Meyer, "Did he stop at all?"

"No. He flew down, no hands on the rail."

Mack then sat patiently, hands in front of his chin, fingertips pressed together in a steeple, for his millionth interview about his biggest thrill (Howard Ehmke in the '29 World Series) and disappointment (the 1914 World Series), his predictions for the current pennant race (couldn't say— four great teams).

His parting handshake was firmer than the young writer expected.

On June 27 Mack was in Hartford for a day honoring an old friend, Bob Quinn, a club owner and general manager for more than thirty years, now the director of the Hall of Fame.

"Connie and I were talking this afternoon," said Quinn, "and both agreed if we had another chance we would do exactly the same thing [with our lives]."

July 6 Mack was in Allentown, Pennsylvania, for an old-timers event, where he had a grand visit with John Smith, who had pitched against him when Mack was a catcher for Hartford sixty-five years ago.

From there they drove to Detroit for the All-Star Game, then down to Chicago for a "McGillicuddy clan" luncheon at Phil Clarke's City National Bank, hosted by Parker Woods. Mack was in Cooperstown July 23, where Jimmy Foxx was inducted into the Hall of Fame with Mel Ott. Most of the forty-some earlier inductees were no longer living. It was the first formal induction ceremony and was followed by a game between the A's and Dodgers at Doubleday Field. The A's lost, 9–6, after Joe Coleman walked 6 in the third inning. Mr. Mack was too busy visiting and signing autographs to be upset by that.

Chuck Roberts drove Mack to Wichita, Kansas, where Mack was handed a plaque for his active promotion of youth baseball at the opening of the National Baseball Congress annual semipro tournament on August 17. More than 9,500 fans—a bigger crowd than most of the A's home audiences so far that year—turned out. Mack had a chance to visit with Hall of Famers George Sisler, Kid Nichols, and Fred Clarke. While he was there, he participated in a national memorial day for Babe Ruth on a remote pickup over New York radio station WOR.

A week later the Athletics were in St. Louis. Bill Veeck had sold the Indians and now owned the Browns. Veeck loved and revered Connie Mack. His favorite nickname for his son Mike was McGillicuddy. When Veeck had bought the Cleveland Indians and shaken up the hidebound baseball establishment with his brand of showmanship, Mack had never said a disparaging word about Veeck or his promotions.

In *Veeck as in Wreck*, Veeck wrote, "Mr. Mack was a boyhood idol of mine, and I was extremely fond of him until the day he died. Mr. Mack, alone among the Old Guard, never screamed that I was making a mockery of the game. . . . The others, like Clark Griffith, looked upon my little entertainments as a disgrace to the game."

Bob Fishel was Veeck's public relations and right-hand man for years. He recalled how Veeck had treated Connie Mack to lunch at the 1947 Yankees-Dodgers World Series:

Across from our hotel there was a very expensive restaurant called Reuben's. Veeck ordered a bunch of box lunches, about $14 each, a lot of money in those days. There were about twenty of us in the row, and he ordered lunches for Mack, Steve O'Neill, and Bucky Harris, who were sitting down in front of us, and surprised them. He paid for everything, but at the game I wanted to buy the Cokes. I sent a twenty dollar bill down the row to pay for them. Veeck was at the end. 'Who did this?' he asked, holding up the bill. 'I did,' I said. He tore up the bill and scattered it.

Now that Connie Mack was sitting in the grandstand instead of the dugout, Veeck told his office staff, "When the A's are here, I want somebody to sit with Mr. Mack and take care of anything he needs."

Bob Fishel volunteered:

I wanted to sit with him. He squinted to make out what was happening but wore no glasses. And he was still sharp when it came to recognizing the players, even if he didn't know their names. When our outfielder Roy Sievers came up to bat, he looked at the batting stance and said, "I have seen that man someplace before."

One of Veeck's stunts was a grandstand managers' day, where he had signs held up for the fans to make the managerial decisions during the game. Most of the club owners complained he was making a travesty of the game. Veeck knew that Connie Mack wouldn't object, so he asked his permission to stage it when the A's were in town. Mack agreed, and heartily joined in the activity that night along with the fans.

On September 8 it was another trip down memory lane as the Yankees brought back two teams of old-timers for a day honoring Joe McCarthy, who had joined Mack in retirement. A get-together at Jake Ruppert's brewery after the game brought together many of Mack's former players.

Wherever Mack went, friends hosted luncheon or dinner parties for him. After the season it seemed as if every organization in Philadelphia wanted to honor him. Connie Mack's "take it easy" whirlwind climaxed with the one event above all he would not have missed—the induction of his favorite player, Al Simmons, into the Wisconsin Hall of Fame on November 28, 1951, in Milwaukee. The arena was full of football, baseball, track, and wrestling heroes, including the two pitchers—Cy Young and Deacon Phillippe—and first batter—Ginger Beaumont—from the first World Series game in 1903. Beaumont had played for Mack in Milwaukee a lifetime ago.

Seated at a table with Simmons's mother, Mack left his dinner untouched as a parade of autograph seekers, including several of the inductees, from the ponderous wrestler Strangler Lewis to the svelte Green Bay Packers' end Don Hutson, kept him busy patiently signing programs. But he wasn't hungry. He was eating up all the attention and the banter, the reminiscing and the camaraderie, with his kind of people.

"I love your son," he told Mrs. Simmons. "He's been like a son to me. I have always regarded Al as my greatest player of all time."

"Thank you, Mr. Mack," she replied. "You've always been so good to my son."

Sam Levy of the *Milwaukee Journal* reported that a man approached the table and said, "How are you, Mr. Mack? I bet you don't remember me."

"Wait until I sign this program and then give me a chance to study your face."

After looking him over, Mack admitted he did not recognize him.

"Remember Jimmy Archer? I was a catcher, too." A native of Dublin, Archer had played for the Cubs against the A's in the 1910 World Series.

"Jimmy, you rascal," said Mack to the sixty-eight-year-old. "You look so young."

As the program drew to a close, the chairman, Joe Krueger, thanked Mr. Mack for being there. "It was a great honor and a thrill we won't ever forget."

Mack responded, "Don't thank me. I am the one who should be grateful for the privilege of being here. It was the finest sports gathering I have ever attended."

For Mr. Mack the first year of his long-dreaded retirement had been a ball.

In 1950 twelve-year-old Johnny Brogan and a friend had taken an A's scrapbook to Mack's apartment to try to get him to sign it. "When we knocked on the door Mr. Mack answered and invited us in. He didn't know us from the man in the moon, but he sat down and autographed every page in the book."

By 1954 Brogan was the visiting club batboy at Shibe Park. "He never knew my name," Brogan told the *Evening Bulletin*, "but he remembered me. He never failed to speak to me and he always spoke first. When we passed in the ballpark, he always said, 'Hello, how are you?'"

On the rare occasions when Mack was surrounded by fans during a game, Brogan recalled, "I used to glance up at the mezzanine. He never had much success watching the game, for he was always besieged by young and old alike for his autograph. He always obliged."

Joe Gross was a ten-year-old who lived a short trolley ride up Lehigh Avenue from Shibe Park. He'd been going to day games by himself for a few years (yes, readers, it was a different world), interested in the game but often wandering around the near-empty stadium. Several times in his roaming he saw an old man in a suit and tie and straw hat sitting alone. He waved to the man but never thought of speaking to him.

One day the Browns were in town, and that meant the upper deck was as crowded as Death Valley. As Joe ran by, the man waved him over and invited him to sit down.

"You come to so many games, you must love baseball," the man said.

"I also go to Phillies games," Joe said.

The old man smiled a little. A forlorn hot dog vendor appeared. The old man bought Joe a hot dog, then a soda. ("It was the first non-kosher meat I ever ate," Joe said. "It didn't hurt me, as I had believed it would.")

For the rest of the season, Joe looked for the old man and sat with him. Each time he was treated to a hot dog and soda. The man showed him how to keep score.

"I grew to feel he was my friend. He had a way of making me think he was happy to see me," Joe said. "I always felt he was lonely because I only once saw another person talking to him."

After every game Joe told his parents about the old man. His father became concerned about the man who bought his son non-kosher hot dogs. One day he went with Joe: "We went up to the usual spot and as we approached I can still remember my father gasping and saying, 'Oh my God.' My father shook hands with him and could hardly talk. It was only when we got back home that he told me the old man was Connie Mack. I recognized the name, and every time I saw him after that I called him Mr. Mack."

Their meetings continued throughout the next season until Joe's family moved to the suburbs. But Joe remained a Connie Mack fan for the rest of his life.

Connie Mack was still in demand as a speaker, but he was no longer the club's official ambassador. Neither Earle nor Roy was any good at that. So the players, especially Bobby Shantz and Elmer Valo, as well as Ira Thomas and Chief Bender, filled many of the speaking appearances.

For as long as he was physically able, Connie Mack remained baseball's foremost public relations man, consistently kind and receptive to old friends and strangers, young and old. He thrived on the attention, happier being on the road than at home. Wherever he went, he was instantly recognized.

Mack's granddaughter Kathleen was a Rockette at Radio City Music Hall in New York. When the family went to see the show, there were often long lines waiting. The manager usually escorted the Macks past the crowd, drawing malevolent stares. "Dad got very upset at him for doing it," said Ruth. One day he came to see Kathleen and was taken to the green room just inside the stage door to wait for her. Kathleen had never talked about her family to the other dancers. A friend of hers, Ann Kelly, came up in the elevator to the third-floor dressing room.

"Guess what?" she said, all excited. "I think I saw Connie Mack in the green room."

Kathleen said, "That's my grandfather."

Ann Kelly wouldn't let up until Kathleen introduced her to him.

Robert Langford was a greeter for teams who came to Winter Park, Florida, for spring training games and stayed at his father's hotel. Forty years later he described his most vivid memory of Connie Mack: "He loved to sit in the lobby in a big high-back chair straight as an arrow and he was delighted to have all the old ladies in the hotel come and talk to him, whereas most managers want to disappear from the public to keep away from the questions they ask. Connie Mack was delighted to talk to people. He loved to talk about the old days of baseball when he was just starting out, and he would mention some of the crazy antics of some of the old-time famous ball players."

In March 1954, during their school's spring break, a small group of thirteen-year-old A's fans was treated to a dream vacation—a week in West Palm Beach. Pat Williams was one of them. Sixty years later his memories remained vivid:

One evening my friends and I were in the lobby of the George Washington Hotel when the elevator doors opened and there he was—Connie Mack himself! He was in his nineties, yet he still walked with that tall, erect bearing. There was an amazingly youthful vigor in his step. My friends and I went over and greeted him, all talking at once, telling him how honored we were to meet him.

Mr. Mack could not have been more cordial. He shook our hands and said, "How are you boys?" He chatted with us, looking us in the eye and treating us as peers.

Later that year Williams wrote a letter to Mack asking several questions. One was, "Did Shoeless Joe Jackson really play without shoes?"

Anything that had happened fifty years ago was an easy subject for the ninety-one-year-old Connie Mack. He replied, "When Shoeless Joe was a young player in Greenville, South Carolina, he had to play a game without shoes because his cleats had given him blisters. It was only one game—but the nickname Shoeless Joe stuck "

But much of the time his mind wandered or he had little to say. His grandson Connie McCambridge recalled the last time he visited Shibe Park office: "There was a new necktie someone had sent him on the desk. He kept picking it up and saying, 'Isn't that a nice tie.' That was about it."

Mack enjoyed being with little tots too. When Jimmie Dykes ordered a workout at Shibe Park one morning, Joe Astroth showed up with his three-year-old daughter Janet. Mack volunteered to babysit her in his office and gave her a ball signed "to Jennet" that was still on display in Astroth's home fifty years later.

Connie Mack maintained an active pace in 1952. The trip north from spring training included a stop in Fayetteville, North Carolina, for the unveiling of a plaque marking Babe Ruth's first home run with the Baltimore Orioles in 1914. He was in Ottawa for the new farm team's opener; in Norwich, Connecticut, for a dinner for Danny Murphy, the second baseman on Mack's first pennant winners fifty years ago; in New York to place wreaths at the monuments for Ruth, Gehrig, and Huggins in Yankee Stadium.

Christy Walsh had sold the idea of a book on baseball's greatest lineup for the first half-century to A. S. Barnes. Walsh polled five hundred writers for their top picks in each position and turned the results over to a committee headed by Connie Mack to make the final selections. On July 7, the day before the All-Star Game at Shibe Park, Mack hosted a luncheon to announce the chosen seventeen and presented plaques to the seven who were present: Mickey Cochrane, George Sisler, Pie Traynor, Tris Speaker, Cy Young, Carl Hubbell, and Lefty Grove. (The others selected were Eddie Collins, Honus Wagner, Babe Ruth, Ty Cobb, Frank Frisch, Joe DiMaggio, Bill Dickey, Walter Johnson, Christy Mathewson, and Grover Alexander.) That evening Roy Mack threw a party for Mr. and Mrs. Will Harridge. After dinner they all watched General Douglas MacArthur's keynote speech at the Republican convention.

Rain ended the All-Star Game after five innings with Bobby Shantz on the mound.

Then Connie Mack was off to Cincinnati to take part in a salute to Hall of Famers and back to New York for another old-timers' day.

On September 4 at Shibe Park, Chief Bender, enfeebled by recent surgery, was presented a check for $6,000 and a scroll signed by 165,000 fans. Bender's old teammates Frank Baker, Rube Oldring, and Ira Thomas were there, along with Mack, who, said Bender's wife Marie, was "the only old-timer who didn't limp."

While in New York for the World Series, Mack took a bow on the Ed Sullivan and Arthur Godfrey TV shows. Sounding like a star-struck teenager, he wrote to his niece Maudie, "On the Arthur Godfrey program he shook hands with me. It's seldom that he does that."

Connie Jr. had moved his family to Fort Myers in 1951 and used the money from the sale of his stock in the A's to buy a fleet of shrimp boats. It was a wrenching change for his family. His wife, Sue, was an avid fan who sat behind the A's dugout and diligently kept score while tending to her four young children. At the same time, the move was a relief for her—most of the time—to be away from her mother-in-law.

When her in-laws came to Florida in the winter, Sue Mack was as tense as a stretched rubber band. "She went into a tailspin," her son Dennis said. "It was very stressful." Her daughter Susie said:

When we lived in Philadelphia, we never went to Pop-Pop and Granny's house for dinner. They would come to our house during the week, and go to Ruth's on Sundays. We would have meals like prime rib roast, mashed potatoes, peas, and gravy when they came. Granny insisted on beets being on the menu and made the kids eat the hated red things. Pop Pop was quiet; Granny was dominant.

When she came to our house in Florida she took over, even rearranged the furniture. She could make life difficult for everybody. Pop-Pop was just there, calm, unperturbed.

Katherine insisted a little wine or beer with dinner was good for her husband's digestion and might keep his scarce pounds on his bones. He no longer objected.

Fortunately for Sue, they stayed only a few weeks before moving to the Princess Martha Hotel in St. Petersburg until spring training began.

Granny had her generous side too. When they lived in Philadelphia and went to her apartment, there was a box of pennies on a table, and the kids could grab a handful. In Fort Myers just before Christmas, she would fold a ten or a twenty in her hand and come up to them and say, "Get yourself a gift," and press it into their hands.

Mack's grandson Connie III got up at 5:30 every morning and sat in an easy chair in Pop-Pop's room, waiting for him to wake up to help him get out of bed, but he did not go into the bathroom with him. Mack was still fiercely independent and shaved and dressed himself, still in the shirt and tie and suit. The kids helped him up and down the steps to his second-floor bedroom.

Mack might take a short walk in the neighborhood or be driven to visit friends. Otherwise he would sit in a lawn chair on the front lawn and wave when someone drove by and honked the horn and waved to him. If people stopped and asked him if they could take a picture, he never turned them down. If a man and his wife stopped, he would say, "Do you want your wife in the picture?" and stand with his arm around her waist.

By 1954 his emotions, never floridly expressed except when he was angry, were exhausted. One Christmas, when he bought bicycles for all the grandkids, he showed no more warmth or pleasure at seeing their reactions than if he had just bought a Class D pitcher.

Dennis and Connie III were in their pre-teens and early teens during those years. Dennis said:

We were brought up to be seen and not heard. When Pop-Pop was with us he never talked baseball and we didn't dare approach him and ask him anything. We would be taken in front of him, sitting with his hands steepled in front of his chest, knuckles gnarled from arthritis, but he didn't say much. When I was little I used to ask a lot of questions. One winter in Philadelphia we were snowed in for several days and I was asking my mother all sorts of questions and she said, "Dennis, if you ask one more question I'm going to go out of my mind." So of course I had to ask, "How do you go out of your mind?"

We knew who he was and all, but the curiosity had been ironed out of us. So we just didn't ask Pop-Pop anything.

When he was told that Dennis was a Little League pitcher, Pop-Pop perked up. "Denny," he said, "one day you'll be a pitcher in the major leagues." He even went to one of Dennis's games.

In the spring of 1955 the Pirates trained in Fort Myers. One day Branch Rickey took Mack, now using a cane, for a nostalgic visit to Terry Field, where the Athletics had first trained in 1925. When they returned to the house, Mack told Rickey that his grandson, Dennis, was a Little League pitcher. They went out in the yard so Rickey could watch Dennis throw to his brother Connie.

While their mother was hollering out the window that dinner was ready, Rickey showed Dennis how he taught young pitchers to throw a change-up curve.

Dennis said, "He had me come completely overhand so instead of throwing with a twist, you came straight down and the ball rolled off your fingertips and you threw it really hard so your wrist would snap and you'd finish palm up. I'd never seen anyone throw a pitch like that. Dad told me afterward to forget it and throw past my ear."

Once in a while Connie Jr. would take his dad to a high school basketball game, bringing a chair for him so he wouldn't have to climb the bleacher steps. One day Mack went for a ride on one of the shrimp boats and seemed to enjoy it.

He no longer played golf. But he would ride along in a golf cart while his son played, not always well. Dennis said, "If Dad had a bad day on the course, he'd be in a foul mood when he got home. That's one reason I didn't take up the game until I was in my sixties."

Pop-Pop would sit up close to the small flickering television screen and watch the boxing matches and the *Ed Sullivan Show*. His favorite actress was a blond bombshell, Sheree North, who appeared on many of the early variety shows. As his hearing or his cognition—or both—faded, sometimes Sue would remind him, "It's Sheree North, Dad," in a loud voice.

On the occasions when Connie Mack celebrated birthdays in Fort Myers, cards and telegrams poured in. The house was filled with floral arrangements. One year he posed blowing out the candles on a huge cake for a photographer before sneaking a finger full of frosting after the flashbulb went off. Reporters from local papers and wire services did their annual birthday interviews. The children would sit on the floor and take it all in. It was the only time they would hear the old stories, with their father helping Pop-Pop brush away the mental cobwebs.

On his ninetieth birthday in 1952 Mack talked about Bobby Shantz and Harry Byrd and extolled Joe DiMaggio as the ultimate inspirational player leading his team to victory.

Katherine Mack was beginning to show early signs of Alzheimer's. Her grandson Connie remembered coming home one night and knocking on the front door. She looked out the window and said, "Who is it?"

"It's Connie."

"Oh no, it's not. I'm not letting you in."

Dennis said, "One year Granny baked a pumpkin pie and I ate the whole pie and I became her favorite. The next time she came she baked a mince pie and I didn't like mince pie and she said, 'I'm going to take you out of my will.' She meant it. It was something about food and control."

As long ago as 1917 Connie Mack had been concerned about his wife's controlling behavior. He had put up with it just as he did wild pitchers, always reminding his children to do as she said. His affection for her never lessened, but in recent years she could make him furious at things she said or did. At one point in 1952 he briefly moved out of their apartment.

On September 3, 1952, after he returned to the apartment, he wrote to a friend, Paul Fritzinger, who lived in Ashland, Ohio, "I will not go west with the boys on this trip. Am pleased to hear from you and I was tickled to death when I got back home. I should never have left the wife and am pleased beyond words that the wife took me back."

(In his latter years, Mack's singular letter-writing style became more rambling and erratic, his lifelong skirmishes with spelling and grammar a lost cause. All his letters have been reproduced as written. His signature was no longer flourishing but flattened into a scrawl.)

As her behavior became more erratic—or more of a mystery to him—

Mack was more unguarded in his increasingly rambling letters. A week later he wrote to Fritzinger:

Am writing you that I don't know when I can see you it depends upon Mrs. Mack. I will write you at once but I do feel that Mrs. Mack will stay at home longer then I. I think Mrs. Mack will refuse to go am sorry that its this way as I would like to go but Mrs. Mack refuses to go places that I prefer to go. She is quite a nice Women but I don't think she will like to go. As she feels that she don't want to put any one out. And am sure you can understand what I mean. She is a peciulier Women but very nice and I don't want to offend her so we will not go but may see you in the South.

On July 5, 1954, Mack wrote to Fritzinger, whom he had planned to visit: "Mrs. Mack may go with me to see Mrs.–Mr. Pearlstone to Chicago and that case I will not get to see you. She wont go to see you why she wont go I have asked her a number of times and she has refused to go."

Six days later he wrote: "Will be sure and see you on the next trip and Katharine will go to Los Angeles she desired upon that she is a queer person and will tell you more about her. She is smart woman to smart for her own good."

When Roy and Earle had bought control of the Athletics in 1950, the end of the stockholders' concessions company meant that Connie Mack was no longer receiving his 20 percent share of the profits. He was still helping to support his daughters Rita and Mary, to which he alluded in this December 19, 1952, letter to Connie McCambridge, apologizing for not enclosing his annual Christmas check:

Dear Connie,

Am pleased with your letter. It was good of you to write me such a fine letter and a big one that you wrote. Shantz will sign. Byrd is a better pitcher and he will do better work than Shantz this coming year. You can bet on that. [Shantz was 5-9 in '53, Byrd 11-20]. The team did well last year and they will do as this coming year. Am not going to send you a donation this year. I don't want you to think I've forgotten you, but I don't make the money that I made in years past.

The reason why I did was the concessions money that I got I don't anymore. The boys pay it all, $50,000 a quarter, to the insurance people. Besides that I pay to Rita. She married the second time. She married Breedlove [again]. She left him and I give her 300 a month and Mary 200. Rita is at Los Angeles. Mary loved her husband and he left her, so I have to support them. That is why I cannot give you a donation. I pay out 200 more than my salary. Enough of this. Dykes did a good job this year in 1952 and assume he will do a better one this coming year as he will have the material this coming year and you can look for him to do better work than he did last year. Am really sorry that I had to write you as I did want to get it off my chest. I will write you again but I will write soon again you will understand. Best wishes to you on Christmas Day.

> Your loving [here Mack wrote
> "father," then crossed it out
> and wrote "grandfather"]

P.S. I wish Evelyn and the boy my best on Christmas Day.

Rereading the letter forty years later, McCambridge said, "Isn't that something. Imagine, he had to tell me how sorry he is cause he couldn't send me a buck. Imagine taking the time to tell me that. What a man. And he never gave up. Every time he wrote a letter he said the team was going to be better."

On September 12, 1953, he wrote to Shannon Fife, "The club is playing poorly. I don't know how they do it. It seems that they don't care. There is no interest in the club. They like Dykes but don't play as they should. The players don't seem to care whether they win or lose. I'm surprised they are not playing good baseball. They can play as well as they want to. While they can play good baseball it don't seem like they want to do it."

Two weeks later he acknowledged that he could no longer talk clearly. He asked Fife to call him at the New Yorker Hotel during the World Series: "Phone Mrs. Mack as I don't talk very well."

It is said that hindsight is 20-20. That may be true of the young, but as we age, it often becomes 20-40, then 20-60. Connie Mack was still trying to put his fingers in the dikes where his memory was leaking, but he was running out of fingers. In a letter to Maudie, he mentions his sister Nellie, who had died at the age of twelve in 1873: "Received your letter and am always thinking about you. So glad you are well again you must not have your nerves shaken again. Your vacation must have been very pleasant one and hope you will have more of them. Some time ago was Nellie she died about three years ago. It was so long that I forgot about it. You know I am in good health but forget what has happened."

But when it came to baseball, Mack remained sharp. On July 6, 1953, he was watching the first game of a twi-night doubleheader from the mezzanine when Mickey Mantle, batting right-handed against lefty Frank Fanovich, hit a grand slam in the sixth inning. Ed Pollock left the press box to go up and chat with Mack a few minutes later.

"Who was that hitter who hit the home run?" Mack asked.

"Mantle."

"Mantle? I thought he hit left-handed."

Before Pollock could reply, Mack remembered, "Oh yes, he's a switch hitter."

Shortly after the Boston Braves moved to Milwaukee, Pollock asked Mack if he thought it was a good move. Mack had managed in Milwaukee for four years before going to Philadelphia in 1901. "We had a pretty fair club, but still we didn't draw although we finished second in 1900. After the season was over I remember a man said to me. . . ."

He stopped. Silence. Seconds passed. Then, "I can't tell you what he said. I don't remember."

Mack chewed on it, and when he next saw Pollock, he said, "I remember what that fellow had to say to me. He told me I should have won the pennant." He was silent, thinking, then, "Funny, isn't it, that I couldn't remember what he said, but all along I knew I didn't like what he said."

When *New York Post* sportswriter Milt Gross predicted in January 1954, "By next year the Athletics are certain to be moved out of Philadelphia," Connie Mack was in Los Angeles with Ralph Gutzsell, making the rounds of movie studios to discuss plans for the movie of his life. (James Stewart was mentioned as a possibility to portray him.) Although he was having trouble voicing his thoughts clearly, Mack may have been briefly coherent enough (or the writer imaginative enough) to be quoted: "I love Philadelphia, but I'm heartily in favor of moving the Athletics to Los Angeles. It's increasingly difficult for more than one club to exist in the same city. I've always been against entering Los Angeles or San Francisco because I thought it would break up the Coast League, but now I'm convinced that Los Angeles should be in our league before long."

While they were there, Mack asked Gutzsell to call Al Horwits, the former Philadelphia sportswriter who was now a movie publicist, and invite him to lunch. Horwits later told Jerome Holtzman in *No Cheering in the Press Box*, "So I went down to the Town House and we had lunch together. Connie was trying to tell me something. But he couldn't get it out. The gist of it, I thought, was that he was trying to tell me what a good friend I had been and how much he appreciated it. But he had a hard time trying to express himself."

Mack's frustration showed in an April letter to Shannon Fife: "I dont know how you read my letters. I shall never forget you. Am only sorry that I cannot write. You will say this is the last I will write you why he does not write I heard him write a letter that was right although I am in perfect health, I should not attempt to write."

His inability to express his thoughts didn't stop Mack from trying whenever he saw a microphone and a cheering crowd. He was on the field in Baltimore when the Orioles had a pregame ceremony honoring Home Run Baker. Mack waved to the crowd, his left arm supported by Baker. Orioles broadcaster Ernie Harwell had been warned not to let him get near the mike as it would be difficult to stop him from babbling on and on. But when he was introduced, Mack took hold of the mike and babbled.

The Lincoln now had air conditioning, and Mack and Chuck Roberts rolled up the miles. On a western trip in July he stopped off in Carnegie, Pennsylvania, to visit with Honus Wagner before spending a few days with his friend Paul Fritzinger. On July 23 Roy Mack wrote to Fritzinger to prepare him for his father's condition: "While his health is very good, his memory is not quite so good and it is now very difficult for him to carry on a conversation. He knows what he wants to say but just cannot express himself. Whenever he attends a dinner or function here we have him under control. Under no circumstances do we let him attempt to speak as it not only embarrasses him but everyone else. He usually takes a bow while someone from the club does the talking. Last year in St. Petersburg some fresh MC made him go to a mike and he sounded like a broken record."

In August Mack was at Yankee Stadium for an old-timers' day. He posed for a photo with Cy Young and former president Herbert Hoover. Jimmy Cannon described him as standing in the Yankees dugout "feeble and stiff-jointed," asking, "Which one is Whitey Ford? He's a good pitcher," before going onto the field to be introduced. This time he didn't get near the microphone.

27 | THE PHILADELPHIA MERRY-GO-ROUND

The harbingers of the spring of 1954 didn't bode well for the Athletics.

Joe Astroth and Wally Moses were enlisted to sell season tickets and score-card ads. Roy offered them a 5 percent commission. They wisely asked for a salary of $125 a week instead.

Wherever Astroth went he was told, "I have a safe full of tickets from last year. I couldn't even give them away."

One day he called on the owner of General Steel & Brass. Instead of buying tickets, the man offered to buy the team for $1 million. Astroth told Roy, who said, "Tell him we want $2 million."

Dave Philley was the only man on the team who had played every game in '53 and the only .300 hitter. Roy conceded that he deserved a raise from $16,000 and sent him a contract for $18,500. Philley returned it unsigned. Perhaps thinking Philley had just forgotten to sign it, Roy mailed it back to him. No oversight; Philley sent it back again. The A's upped it to $19,000 and added a bonus of $1,000 if attendance topped five hundred thousand. Fat chance of that, thought Philley, and sent that one back. Let's try it once more, said Roy, and remailed the *same* contract. Philley didn't waste another stamp returning it again.

On February 19 Earle decided they would never agree on salary and sold Philley to Cleveland for $15,000, two long-forgotten pitchers, and a barrage of criticism.

Or did he?

Earle said, "Actually, the deal was not of my choosing and we hit a snag when I insisted on a player who is now fast becoming a star. Interference within our organization thwarted my efforts."

The only possible "interference" in the organization was Roy.

Eddie Joost's headaches as a manager began early and never stopped. In West Palm Beach the hotel manager called him aside one day and said, "I haven't had any money from your club." Joost told Roy they had to give the hotel something or they'd be evicted. Somehow Roy extracted $25,000 from Art Ehlers in Baltimore for catcher Ray Murray, who delivered 15 hits for the Orioles.

It didn't take long for the cash shortage to become evident to the players. When the season began, they traveled on charter flights. To cut costs they soon switched to regular scheduled flights. As things got worse, they booked red-eye flights.

Joost had enlisted Rollie Hemsley as bullpen coach and Augie Galan to replace Bing Miller. Joost soon suspected that Hemsley was undermining him with the Macks. Judy Johnson was hired as a personal coach and mentor for Vic Power and Bob Trice. The *Cleveland Call & Post* quoted Earle: "We want them to get started on the right foot. Judy should be able to give them the right advice." Chief Bender was in a wheelchair, weakened by cancer. He could no longer travel with the team.

The April 13 opener marked forty-five years and one day since Shibe Park had opened in 1909. Connie Mack sat in a box seat with three members of the 1909 team: Ira Thomas, Frank Baker, and Rube Oldring. Chief Bender was too ill to be there. On May 27 they would all be at his funeral.

Bobby Shantz started and left after 5 innings, his left shoulder aching. He pitched only 3 more innings all year.

The A's started out competitively for the first few weeks, Bob Trice winning his first four starts. Then a 2-16 stretch of reality set in and sank them.

Of the Yankee castoffs, third baseman Jim Finigan had the best year, batting .302. Nobody else hit a lick. Gus Zernial struck out 4 times for every home run. In June he and Joost had a blowup in the dugout over playing time. Joost could understand Gus's frustration; he was never a comfortable bench rider himself. But Gus wasn't producing. The defense made a ton of errors. The pitchers gave up the most earned and unearned runs in the league. Alex Kellner was the fourth A's pitcher in the last ten years to post the AL's highest ERA: 5.39. The farm system produced one pitcher, Arnie Portocarrero, who led the team with 9 wins but walked so many batters he lost 18.

In May Roy said, "The last thing we want to do is move the team out of Philadelphia. But we can't stand another year as bad as the last one."

He assured Eddie Joost that the team wasn't moving. But nobody believed it because the year was already as bad as last year and getting worse. As of July 1 the A's had drawn a total of 160,000 at home. In order to survive, they had to draw 420,000 more by the end of the season.

In 1915 Ban Johnson, speaking about struggling minor league clubs, had said, "I always have opposed the remedy of passing the hat among the businessmen of a city to raise money to keep alive a team whose cost is greater than its business justifies."

The sons of Connie Mack had sunk to passing the hat.

On July 9 Bob Carpenter and Connie Mack posed with Mayor Joseph S. Clark to launch a "Save the A's" campaign. The public took it as a "Save the Macks" campaign. It was like a drive for donations to save the liberty bell, except that the liberty bell was still popular.

Pleading with baseball fans to go to the ballpark is not the same as begging people to shop at Wanamaker's to keep the store in business. At least it shouldn't be. Baseball doesn't have customers. It has supporters, fans, constituents, lovers—assets both essential and unmatchable. The tail of a baseball team's place in the standings often wags the dog of its city's standing in the world. Ask the servicemen returning to Philadelphia from the war about the riding they had taken over their hometown's twin occupants of last place.

Roy Mack didn't understand that. The Athletics were resorting to selling civic loyalty when they should have been selling entertainment, a good time at the ballpark—beginning with an interesting, if not exciting, team on the field. Not even Bill Veeck had been able to sell a bad team with his hijinks in St. Louis, where the Browns had drawn under three hundred thousand in 1953. The only attempt at improvement the Macks made was a mid-June trade in which they sent Ed McGhee and Morrie Martin to Chicago for two guys posing as big league pitchers and a 200-pound .200-hitting outfielder—and $20,000 to meet the payroll.

The *Bulletin* invited fans to send in ideas on how to save the A's. Many responses mentioned the lack of secure parking. The automobile was rapidly replacing public transit. There was a small lot on Twenty-First Street, but very little parking on the streets around Shibe Park. Enterprising drivers created their own parking spaces by pulling in beside a fire hydrant and putting an empty garbage can over the fire plug. Since the 1940s anyone who parked on the street was immediately surrounded by kids shouting, "Watch your car?" The law left them alone; if a driver was willing to pay to have his car "watched," that was no crime—as long as the kids didn't hassle anyone who didn't want his car watched. The neighborhood had turned tougher.

The middle-class families who used to rent rooms to the players were gone. Now if a driver didn't pay up, he might find his tires cut, windows smashed, or trunk broken into—if the car was still there.

Meyer Specter, co-owner of a parking lot where Baker Bowl had stood, donated free parking to anyone with an A's ticket.

Mayor Clark asked about ninety civic and business leaders to a meeting to save the A's or lose them to another city. Jack Kelly proposed building a new ballpark with plenty of parking. Harry Sylk, president of the Sun Ray Drug Store chain, pledged to buy $50,000 worth of tickets. Another merchant pledged for five thousand tickets. That was about it. Tickets to A's games became door prizes at bingo nights.

The mayor launched a "Let's go to the ball game week." The A's lost every game—10 in a row—before dwindling crowds and landed in the cellar, never to rise again. There were many days when none of the fans' favorites—Suder or Valo or Joost or Zernial—was in the lineup. Guys named Wilson and Jacobs and Bollweg didn't inspire anybody to come out to see them.

Except the boo birds. They had turned even meaner than usual, and whenever that happened, Joe DeMaestri said, "They were meaner than anyone else. They didn't just boo. They threw beer and mustard at the players' wives from the upper deck."

On Sunday, July 11, Bob Trice pitched his last game, part of a double debacle in which the Red Sox punished them, 18–0 and 11–1, rapping out 40 hits and aided by 7 errors. It was one day Roy and Earle might have wished the 7,445 witnesses had stayed at home. So did the players.

In the ninth inning of the first game Gus Zernial dove for a fly ball in left field and broke his shoulder. When the PA announcer told the crowd, "Zernial has a broken shoulder," they booed. As Zernial was carried off the field, he heard somebody yell, "You should have broken your neck."

And Gus was the team's most popular player.

Bob Trice said, "This isn't fun," and decided he'd rather be in Ottawa. With sore arms and injuries, the roster was down to eight pitchers and twelve position players. It seemed to Eddie Joost that nobody cared, not even the Macks. "I never see anybody or hear from anybody in the front office," he said. "If there are any possible trades or somebody we could pick up on waivers, I'm not consulted. They don't even bother to criticize me. I'm the forgotten man."

The last make-or-break three-week home stand began on August 17. They didn't make; they broke, losing 14 of 20. Baltimore was the only team they could beat. They couldn't draw mosquitoes except against New York and pennant-bound Cleveland. After every game the required average attendance needed the rest of the way to reach the survival goal went up: twelve thousand, then fourteen thousand. Press box wags predicted it would soon reach forty-three thousand.

Only 1,715 showed up for the last home game, a 4–2 loss to New York.

After losing 103 games, the Philadelphia Athletics won the last game they ever played, 8–6, in New York—rookie Art Ditmar's first major league win.

To many observers, the financial failure of the Athletics had been inevitable since 1950. As Red Smith put it, "Roy and Earle Mack went broke in baseball and they did it on merit."

Later Roy blamed it on beer and Bobby Shantz—their absence, that is. He told Shantz that the little lefty's sore arm in '53 and '54 had cost the A's $500,000 at the gate, which would have been enough to save the team. Another time he said the ban on the sale of beer at Shibe Park had made the difference between success and failure.

Roy and Earle both knew the game was over long before the last home stand in August had begun. It was the only thing they agreed on. At the major league meetings in July, they sniped at each other like kids in a schoolyard:

"I'll buy you out."

"Oh yeah? I'll buy *you* out."

"Ha. Where you gonna get the money?"

"Where will *you*?"

Roy said Earle had agreed to sell to him, then reneged.

Earle said the price was agreed on, but Roy changed it in a written offer. And anyhow, "I never seriously considered selling out to Roy."

Roy admitted to Art Morrow, "We're at a very low ebb and it's management's fault that we have sunk this low. That's why we'll make a lot of changes for 1955."

Asked if that meant Earle must go, he said, "I can't say that just now, but our front office has been responsible for a lot of mismanagement and it's not going to continue."

Earle said, "Interference within our organization . . . has continued to hamper my intentions during the past few months."

Then they both denied they had said whatever it was they were quoted as saying.

For the four years they had run the Athletics, Roy and Earle had amassed a deficit of almost a quarter million dollars, equal to over $2 million today. It sounds like a trifle now—a utility infielder's salary—but when your pockets are empty and the mortgage payment is due and your credit's tapped out, it's a lot.

Connie Mack was ready to sell. Katherine Mack was *anxious* to sell. Mack's 302 shares of the Athletics was practically their entire net worth. They had maybe $50,000 in other assets and no income except Mack's $20,000 salary as the A's president. Whether he remained as an honorary president was immaterial to him. He was no longer making any decisions, and nobody asked him for advice. Never impressed with her stepsons' abilities, Katherine saw the value of their principal asset going down the tubes. Since their spat over his giving shares in the A's to his sons, Mack had assured his wife and his "girlies" that whenever his 302 shares were sold, the money would go into a trust for them. If the club landed in bankruptcy, who knew what they might salvage. But they were bound by the option on Mack's stock held by Roy and Earle and were not free to sell on their own.

The "We're not moving" chorus continued to be sung by Roy and Earle, who knew their father hoped the team would stay in Philadelphia. Some writers wondered why. The transplanted Braves and Browns were prospering in their new homes. Visions of big league status motivated people in Buffalo and Toronto to talk about building suitable stadiums. Roy fielded inquiries from Dallas, San Francisco—where a bond issue had passed to build a new stadium—and Minneapolis. Chicago insurance mogul Charlie Finley was interested. Another Chicagoan, Arnold Johnson, was talking big numbers—$4.5 million—to move the team to Kansas City, where a bond issue to enlarge Blues Stadium had passed.

Arnold Johnson and Yankees' owners Del Webb and Dan Topping were no strangers to each other. Topping was on the board of Johnson's Automatic Canteen vending machine business. In December 1953 Johnson had bought Yankee Stadium and the Kansas City Blues Stadium and leased them back to the Yankees, then sold the land underneath Yankee Stadium to the Knights of Columbus and leased it back. The deal resulted in a multimillion-dollar lower-taxed capital gain for Topping and Webb. The Yankees would exert their influence on Will Harridge and the league's directors to push Johnson's bid for the A's (not incidentally landing Webb the contract to expand Blues Stadium).

Still, there were financial heavyweights willing to try to keep the A's in Philadelphia, at least temporarily. Roy seemed determined to find them while Earle remained skeptical: "There isn't a chance of keeping the club in Philadelphia as far as finances are concerned. I'm willing to sell if Roy can raise the money. But I don't think he has a chance to meet my price. He must come up with an awful lot of money."

Connie Mack was skeptical too, if he expressed his thoughts clearly to Hy Hurwitz of the *Boston Globe* while the A's were in Chicago on August 1: "We're washed up in Philadelphia. I want to sell. Earle does, too. But I don't understand why Roy doesn't. The club is through in Philadelphia. There is no more interest in the team there."

Both he and Earle expressed a willingness to sell to Arnold Johnson.

Roy refused to give up his efforts to keep the A's in Philadelphia. He wanted to continue in an executive position and keep a place in the business for his son Connie. He clung to the belief—or persuaded himself—that the city would support a financially healthy club. During the first week in August he met with Harry Sylk and financier Albert M. Greenfield, who represented a group of sixteen civic leaders. Sylk doubted that Arnold Johnson, who had yet to make a written offer, would actually pay the $4.5 million figure he was throwing around. (Sylk was right; Johnson's eventual offer came in $900,000 lower.) Sylk's group was ready to pay $2.6 million. The Macks said that wasn't enough. Besides, Sylk made it clear that there would be no place in the business for Roy or Earle or their sons.

Then Roy called on John McShain, who had provided the temporary loan that had enabled Roy and Earle to buy out Connie Jr.'s group in 1950. We need help, Roy said. We're finished in Philadelphia without it.

He laid out the details. The year would probably end with a loss of about $120,000. A $50,000 payment was due to Connecticut General in December. The mortgage was still $1.23 million. In addition, they owed everybody from tax collectors to the Phillies a total of $861,458. (That would go up by $5,625 in back salary that Eddie Joost wouldn't see until after the team was sold.)

They had $10,000 in the bank.

Roy explained the option he and Earle held on their father's stock. McShain said he would like to see the A's stay in Philadelphia. Maybe he could put together a group to buy out Mr. Mack.

On August 11 the Athletics' board of directors discussed the various offers from other cities. Roy stated his desire to find a way to keep the team in

Philadelphia. Roy later wrote that Earle "assured me that he would support my views and would not sell to any out-of-town group." He asked Earle to go with him the next day to meet with John McShain.

Everybody came out of the board meeting all smiles, though news photographers reportedly failed in their efforts to get Roy to pose with Earle.

So Earle and Roy went to McShain's office on Thursday, August 12.

Somebody at the meeting took notes on a legal-size pad and recorded the numbers that were discussed.

Actual operating costs for 1954: $1.2 million.

REVENUE:

Phillies	$125,000
Eagles	$50,000
Radio and TV	$190,000
ABC TV	$100,000
Fights	$20,000
Colored ball games	$7,500
Concessions	$150,000
Total	$642,500

No gate receipts were noted.

Estimated revenues for 1955 were the same except that some optimist said to put down $250,000 for the concessions lease "with beer."

Subtracting the estimated '55 revenue of $772,500 from the projected operating costs of $1.2 million and estimating $300,000 in road receipts for '55, left a $237,500 deficit. Using an average of $1.10 per home admission, they divided that into the deficit and concluded that they needed only 216,000 attendance to break even. (This was unrealistic. After deducting taxes and visitors' and league shares from each $1.10, if they spent $500,000 to beef up the farm system, buy players, and have a higher payroll, they would need more than 500,000 additional attendance to break even.)

Beneath all the numbers were notes indicating that the positions of general manager, manager, and public relations director were discussed with no names listed, as well as a hint that Earle might sell his stock too, in this cryptic unfinished notation: "Earle will sell for—."

They talked about what role the investors would have in running the club—none—and who would be on the board of directors. McShain said he would form a group to buy Connie Mack's 302 shares for $604,000, pay off all the debts, and provide enough capital to improve the team. He, Roy, and Earle then signed an informal agreement along those lines.

When the Mack brothers left, John McShain dictated the following confidential memorandum:

> In a conference today, it was agreed with Earl and Roy Mack and John McShain, that John McShain would undertake to assemble a group of men who would be willing to invest a sizeable sum of money in the Athletics Baseball Team, and thereby permit the purchase of the stock now held by Connie Mack, Sr. This stock would be distributed in proportion to the number of shares held by each one of the subscribers, it being understood, of course, that Earl and Roy Mack would both retain the stock which they have.
>
> The overall purpose of this agreement is to save the Athletics from leaving Philadelphia.
>
> It also would be further understood that none of the men participating in this undertaking would have any word or direct connection with the running of the ball team, or the actual management of the club.
>
> An effort will be made on the part of both Earl and Roy to get a long extension of time on the payment of the amount of money for the stock to Mr. Mack, Sr."

McShain then began calling his friends to invite them to be part of the group.

The next day Earle discussed the meeting with one of his attorneys, Alfred Luongo, who reminded him that the numbers Arnold Johnson was tossing around might come to as much as $600,000 for Earle's 163 shares. If McShain bought Connie Mack's stock, the Johnson offer would be withdrawn, and he wouldn't get anywhere near that much if he decided to sell to McShain.

Hmmm, said Earle, or maybe, What do I do now?

Earle asked Roy and McShain to meet him on Saturday morning, August 14, at attorney Sam Blank's office. Right up to the time of the meeting, McShain was making calls to prospective investors. He was shocked when Earle told him and Roy, "I've changed my mind. I won't consent to the sale of my father's stock."

McShain suggested that if Earle wanted to sell too, they would buy him out for the same $2,000 a share. With visions of $600,000 sugar plums dancing in his head, Earle said no.

Disgusted, McShain said, "Forget it. The deal's off," and walked away. On Monday morning, he wrote to Dave Clarke, the first person he had called to join the group:

> I am dashing this note off to you to tell you that I had a meeting on Saturday morning with Earle and Roy Mack. Earle, much to my amazement, repudiated his agreement with me regarding the transaction about which I talked to you.
>
> Under the circumstances, I have dropped the matter entirely and hasten to send you this note so that you will not be forced to reach an immediate conclusion regarding this matter.

On that same Monday morning, Roy Mack drafted his own version of events and took a shot at Earle:

> Some time ago when the report was being circulated that the Club would be removed from Philadelphia, in spite of the fact that my brother Earle expressed his willingness to sell to an out-of-town syndicate, it was my belief and firm conviction that Philadelphia could afford to support the Athletics and that some citizen, or a group of citizens, would be willing to step in and aid us financially. At a meeting which I had with Earle last week, he assured me that he would support my views and would not sell to an out-of-town group.
>
> However, in view of the recent developments, I feel that for the good of the club I would be willing to sell my stock, provided, of course, that the prospective purchaser would be prepared also to purchase the stock of my father. At the present time we are negotiating with two groups who have expressed an interest in purchasing the stock of the Club, and we are hopeful that by the time of our meeting next week, we will be prepared to make an announcement of completed negotiations.

Who were the two groups?

In the September 1 *Sporting News* Art Morrow reported that "within the past week" Roy and Earle had met with Matthew McCloskey, a longtime friend of the family and another wealthy contractor who had built most of the Washington buildings that McShain hadn't built. Since the weekly paper went to press five days before date of publication, the story was probably filed no later than August 27. Morrow also wrote that McCloskey had shied away when he learned of McShain's interest to avoid getting into an auction. So it's likely that he had entered the picture after McShain dropped out.

In any event, there was great jubilation when it appeared that a deal would be made and the Athletics saved for the city; all that remained was the crossing of the t's.

Morrow later wrote that Roy was "not enthused" about McCloskey's offer.

Matthew McCloskey and John McShain were giants in the construction league. They made Del Webb look like he was playing with Legos, and they would not have been bulldozed by anybody in the American League. Either one could have outspent the Carpenters, built a new ballpark, and driven the Phillies out of town.

The other rumored group might have been led by Isadore "Speed" Sley, a parking garage mogul and friend of Roy and Earle who was an annual visitor to spring training. Or it might have been an anonymous group with an unidentified spokesman that, according to Morrow, had offered $3.5 million for the team the previous December, had been rejected, and now was said to be willing to buy out any or all of the Macks or take treasury stock, out of civic pride and a love of baseball—but for a million less.

Bob Addie of the *Washington Post and Times-Herald* reported that two Washington sportsmen, tax attorney Leo DeOrsey and Joe Tucci, a former plumbing contractor and owner of a string of race horses, had made an offer of $2,000 a share in writing to Roy on September 25. That's what McShain had offered, but it was less than Arnold Johnson's purported price.

Throughout August and September the headlines bounced between "A's Bound for KC" and "A's Saved by Philadelphia Group."

Earle and Roy were singing the old Jimmy Durante song, "Did you ever get the feeling that you wanted to go, then you get the feeling that you wanted to stay?"

<table>
<tr><td>

28

</td><td>

THE SALE OF THE A'S
A MYSTERY IN FOUR ACTS

</td></tr>
</table>

As the 1954 season crawled to its demise in Philadelphia, Roy and Earle had little to say to each other without their lawyers present and nothing to say to the press. With no resolution of the Athletics' future in sight, a bunch of baseball people became antsy. National and American League schedule makers, who coordinated their efforts, had to draw up several alternative schedules, depending on where the Athletics wound up. Would the A's remain in Philadelphia or go west? Would Baltimore remain the fourth western team with Chicago, Cleveland, and Detroit? And if the A's went west, how far west? Everything was on hold for the American Association too: would Kansas City still be in the league, and if not, who would replace it? Broadcasters, advertising agencies, and Athletics players and employees also awaited the outcome.

A 1953 change in the rules had narrowed the window of time for the approval of a club's moving into a minor league territory to between October 1 and December 1.

Hoping to decipher some answers, league president Will Harridge scheduled what he called "a clarifying meeting" for the day before the Indians-Giants World Series opened in New York. He told Roy to bring with him anyone who had made an offer for the team, especially Matthew McCloskey and John McShain, the erstwhile angels who would have breezed through any approval process. Those who hoped for them to come to the rescue of the A's were disappointed when neither showed up. McCloskey was not interested in competing against McShain for the club, and McShain had had enough of dealing with the Macks.

But Arnold Johnson and a Kansas City delegation did.

The accounts of the meetings that follow are taken from the official American League minutes.

Act 1: Meeting on Philadelphia Club Situation

HOTEL COMMODORE, NEW YORK, TUESDAY, SEPTEMBER 28, 1954, NOON

Presiding: Will Harridge, league counsel Ben Fiery, Earl Hilligan of the AL office.

Representatives: Boston: Joe Cronin; Chicago: Frank Lane, Charles Comiskey; Cleveland: Hank Greenberg, Nate Dolin, George A. Medinger; Detroit: Walter O. "Spike" Briggs Jr.; New York: Daniel Topping, George Weiss, William O. DeWitt, counsel J. Arthur Friedlund; Baltimore: Clarence W. Miles; Philadelphia: Roy Mack, Earle Mack, A's counsel J. Channing Ellery; Washington: Clark Griffith, Calvin Griffith, Gabriel Murphy.

HARRIDGE: There are reports of last few months relative to sale of the team.

Roy Mack read statement of the financial condition of club as of August: debts a little over $500,000; federal taxes owed of $150,000; $29,000 in other taxes; nothing owed to the league; mortgage now $1,223,000. "If I had $250,000 I could carry on to December first."

The A's owed Jacobs Bros. Sports Service $213,000, but Roy stressed that wasn't a factor as they weren't pressing him for it.

BRIGGS: How will you get to spring training?
ROY: A ticket drive is planned. With a new general manager and manager that I could name, we could go in Philadelphia.

Breakeven attendance would be 300,000.

Ellery said 1954 income included $125,000 from the Phillies, $50,000 from the Eagles, $90,000 from radio and TV, "which might be 20 percent lower in '55," and $150,000 from concessions. He emphatically stated that he believed the prime reason for the club's current financial status was the fact that the club mortgage had been reduced $550,000.

Roy requested a loan from the league of $250,000.

MILES: You owe $130,000 alone in taxes.
ROY: That is true.

Ellery and Roy gave a breakdown of the club ownership: 163 shares each for Roy and Earle, 302 for Connie Mack; total: 628.

ELLERY: There are only three separate proposals for purchase of the club. One is from a Philadelphia contractor, who offered $2,000 a share provided all obligations were first paid off. The second is a syndicate that offered $2,500,000 for all the outstanding stock provided all obligations were paid off. The third, from Arnold Johnson, was $3,375,000 [of which $1,675,000 would come from the Phillies' purchase of Connie Mack Stadium] and $1,700,000 for the rest of the club's assets, subject to approval to move the franchise to Kansas City. Connie Mack would receive $604,000; Roy and Earle, $436,500 each.

Clarence Miles looked at Earle. "Is the Johnson offer acceptable to you, Earle?"

EARLE: Yes, I would accept it.

Miles looked at Roy, who said, "No, I can't."

COMISKEY: What happens now?
ROY: Connie wants to stay in.
ELLERY: Mr. Mack told me yesterday that he would like to sell one half of his stock but that he would do what Roy wanted him to do. At this point, however, Connie Mack Sr. had signed a voting trust agreement with Earle to vote with Earle. I feel that Connie is trying to satisfy both of his sons.

Ellery said that he had told both Roy and Earle that they were foolish not to take the Kansas City offer but that he admired Roy's fight to keep the club in Philadelphia.

CLARK GRIFFITH: I am opposed definitely to going to Kansas City. Philadelphia is too fine a city to lose. I would ask the league to finance the A's through this period.

Will Harridge made it clear that in his opinion the American League was not financially able now to accept such a heavy obligation as financing the A's. "In emphatic language" he gave the league's financial worth currently as

$515,000, and he reminded the owners of the heavy financial obligation now being incurred through the Liberty lawsuit [a $12 million Liberty Broadcasting System anti-trust suit against thirteen major league clubs], reminding them of the importance of this suit.

After adjourning for lunch, Roy introduced his attorney, C. Brewster Rhoads, and Earle introduced his attorney, Alfred Luongo. After they spoke, Harridge asked Roy, Earle, and the attorneys Rhoads, Luongo, and Ellery to leave the room. There followed a general discussion of the situation, then Harridge brought Arnold Johnson and his attorney, Ed Vollers, into the meeting.

Johnson said he could provide a stadium holding thirty-five thousand but urged a speedy okay of his purchase of the club and its move to Kansas City: "I am not interested if this action is postponed." The stadium could be enlarged to forty-five or fifty thousand; the city would lease a six-thousand-car parking lot to him. The city council had voted 4–1 to acquire the park, and he was confident the voters would approve $1–2 million for park improvements. "I am not interested in Philadelphia because attendance for both clubs has been declining since 1947." The metropolitan population of Kansas City was 918,000, 3.5 million within fifty miles, 5.5 million within two hundred miles.

Upon request, Johnson then described his personal background.

Harridge then asked the seven-man Kansas City delegation into the meeting: councilmen, businessmen, and sports editor Ernest Mehl of the *Kansas City Star.*

"The final talk by Mr. Mehl rounded out an excellent presentation of the Kansas City plan to the owners that they would act favorably on the transfer of the franchise to their city."

Thomas Gray, representing the mayor's committee from San Francisco, was invited in and stated that in the future San Francisco would be an excellent location for a major league club and urged them to consider the possibility.

Tommy Richardson, president of the Eastern League and a member of the Athletics' board of directors since 1951, then appeared. He said his group was ready to put $800,000 into a plan to keep the A's in Philadelphia. The team needed a new manager, general manager, farm director, and well-organized ticket plan. His group would meet any offer made for the purchase of the ownership. [Now that the Johnson offer was down to $3.375 million, Richardson, who had urged the brothers to take Johnson's offer when it was higher, felt he could compete at that price.] He needed time to put together a more concrete plan.

Questioned by Miles and others, Richardson said he did not have cash on the line at this time. He would keep the A's in Philadelphia in 1955, but if it didn't work out, he would ask to move to another city in 1956. He listed a number of cities such as Toronto, Minneapolis, St. Paul, etc. but did not mention Kansas City.

Earle and Roy and attorneys Ellery and Luongo were then invited back into the meeting. [Rhoads had left the city.]

Miles moved that subject to the Macks accepting Johnson's offer, the league authorize the move to Kansas City. There was no second and no discussion.

Topping suggested the league go on record as willing to meet the Arnold Johnson offer if agreeable to the Macks, by assessment against the clubs, of $482,143 per club. There was no discussion.

Al Luongo spoke for Earle: "We will accept the Johnson offer for Earle's stock." In reply to questioning, he said, "We would sell for $450,000 under any conditions now and would assign Earle's option agreement."

Ben Fiery then asked Roy if he would accept the Johnson offer.

ROY: I am not willing to accept the Johnson offer.
FIERY: If by October twelfth you have not a definite deal, would both you and Earle sell for $450,000 each and your father's shares also?

On this suggestion, both Macks would not definitely commit themselves.

Ellery asked the league for a resolution offering a loan of $150,000 to meet the tax debts he said were extremely critical and could cause the club and the league much embarrassment, with Roy offering his stock as collateral. No motion was taken.

In answer to a question from Topping, Roy said that he would ask Johnson to keep his bid open and he would try in the next two weeks to get the $450,000 to buy out Earle.

Cronin moved the league meet again in two weeks to see if Roy had raised the money to buy out Earle's stock and go on from there.

At 7 p.m. Harridge adjourned until sometime after October 12 to give Roy time to continue his efforts to work something out for the club.

Before making his announcement to the press, Hilligan had it approved by Roy Mack, who said that the announcement met with his full endorsement.

Even if Roy Mack agreed with his brother to sell to Arnold Johnson, there was no guarantee they would have the six votes needed to move the franchise to Kansas City. Spike Briggs, who had inherited the Detroit club upon his father's death in 1952, was outspoken in his belief that the Yankees were pulling the strings and that Harridge and Baltimore president Clarence Miles were the puppets. He was saying what was generally believed. In an effort to combat that impression, Topping assumed a get-tough pose. "A year ago the Yankees were willing to waive our claim to indemnity for our Kansas City territory. Not anymore. We want to be paid for damages." Nobody bought it. (When the Kansas City move was finally approved, the Yankees waived their claim to damages.)

Briggs was determined to stop them. Clark Griffith and Chuck Comiskey called Kansas City "a step backwards." Skeptics believed the city's boosters were counting corn stalks and heifers in their population claims.

Griffith said he favored a move to the West Coast, a position that came as a surprise to Hank Greenberg, who recalled Griffith's reaction when the subject had arisen in an earlier discussion: "Clark Griffith, sitting with hat and overcoat on and cigar in his mouth, jumped up and said, 'Don't go out there. It's cold and damp out there.' Asked when was the last time he was out there, Griffith said, 'In 1905 I pitched in Portland and boy was it cold.'"

(As far back as 1946 *Variety* had reported that five oil men had taken an option on a ballpark site and put together $5 million to bring a team to the West Coast. The report noted, "The American League will be asked to nominate two franchises for the Coast, one for L.A., one for Frisco.")

Shirley Povich wrote that Griffith had previously opposed a move to Los Angeles, but his views had changed. "It's the only place for us to go," Povich quoted him. "We need some new thinking in the American League. How in the world can they overlook Los Angeles with its five million population? I'd vote for it tomorrow. We'll wake up some morning and discover that the National League has beaten us out there, and it will be the fault of some of these fuddy-duddies who won't open their eyes to the population shifts of this country."

White Sox general manager Frank Lane predicted that the West Coast would have major league baseball in two or three years, possibly through a league expansion to ten teams. "The league which gets there will be top dog, but it won't be easy to put the clubs out there," he said.

A year earlier Del Webb and Dan Topping had touted Los Angeles as a haven for the St. Louis Browns. Now, with their buddy Arnold Johnson in the picture, they had narrower priorities and raised all kinds of objections to Los Angeles: it was impractical to have only one West Coast team; it wasn't that good a baseball town; the Pacific Coast League would fight it aggressively and would have to be indemnified; it might take two years before the A's could move there.

The Mack brothers never explored the possibility.

Roy had two weeks to find a buyer who would keep the team in Philadelphia. He found eight.

Arthur Gallagher owned a trucking company. A semi-finalist in the double sculls event at the 1940 Olympics, he was president of the Penn Athletic Club, where Roy was a member. They had become better acquainted when Gallagher sold his Bryn Mawr home to Roy. Gallagher was well connected politically, active in local Republican circles while friendly with Democratic leader Jack Kelly. He had a group of friends, successful, sports-loving businessmen who had joined him in buying TV Channel 12 in Wilmington, Delaware.

According to Gallagher, Roy approached him about putting together a syndicate to keep the A's in the city. Funny you should mention it, responded Gallagher; we've been kicking the idea around for months, even before Arnold Johnson entered the picture.

Roy provided him with audited financial statements as of December 31, 1953, and what it would take to buy out the Macks and pay off the debts. He told Gallagher he wished to retain some of his stock and remain in an executive capacity. They had two weeks to put together a deal.

Suddenly the idea of buying the A's was no longer mere idle chatter and speculation among Gallagher and his friends. Some said to count them in from the start; some wanted in but would have to find the money. The lineup fluctuated. In the end, in addition to Gallagher, they included Isadore "Speed" Sley, owner of parking lots and the Viking Theater; Arthur Rosenberg, vice-president of national supermarket chain Food Fair; auto dealer John P. Crisconi; oil and auto dealer Barney Fischer; department store executive Mort Liebman; investment broker Theodore R. Hanff; and Jack Rensel, sales manager for truck-trailer manufacturer Leonard Strick and one-time public relations employee with the Phillies.

Gallagher called on John McShain, who offered to back him with as much as he needed if he bought the team, provided the Macks were completely out of the picture.

Gallagher was confident they could make it work, but there was nothing in writing when the two weeks were up and the American League met again on October 12 in Chicago. That didn't stop Jack Rensel from showing up uninvited and offending everybody by acting as though he was there to represent the syndicate and it was a done deal.

"Rensel had no authority from us to be there," Gallagher said. "He acted on his own. He was young [thirty-five] and brash, a promoter who could rub people the wrong way. He wanted to be president of the A's, but that wasn't going to happen."

Roy and Earle did not arrive in Chicago together. Roy's train was delayed by flooding in Indiana. Earle arrived first and lost no time assuring Arnold Johnson, "I'm ready to sell to you." Ernest Mehl of the *Kansas City Star* quoted him: "Before I left Philadelphia last night my stepmother told me I had to press for the sale because if I didn't, my father and myself would be broke."

Roy's late arrival delayed the meeting from eleven to one o'clock, giving him time to meet with Tommy Richardson and Calvin Griffith across the street at the Conrad Hilton, while Johnson and a sizable delegation from Kansas City paced the halls of the Blackstone. On the way to the fourth floor meeting room, Johnson pulled Roy aside to reassure him of a job in Kansas City. "Not interested," said Roy.

Act 2: Special Meeting of American League

BLACKSTONE HOTEL, CHICAGO, TUESDAY, OCTOBER 12, 1 P.M.

Roy Mack stated that he had not had sufficient time to get definite commitments for the finances. There were several groups interested in acquiring the stock. Roy said he would not sell his stock in the club and wanted it to remain in Philadelphia. Earle stated he was unwilling to sell his stock unless adequate provision was made to purchase the stock of Connie Mack Sr.

Attorney J. Channing Ellery advised that Connie Mack wanted to sell his stock, but he also wanted to cooperate with Roy. Connie Mack preferred to have at least $302,000 for half of his stock at this time.

Attorney C. Brewster Rhoads stated that in his opinion none of the additional offers matched the Arnold Johnson offer. Each offer was conditional on transfer of the franchise to some other city.

Tommy Richardson and Charlie Finley appeared. Richardson said he held checks from Mr. Finley for $450,000 to purchase Earle's stock and expected to obtain additional funds within thirty days to purchase the stock of Connie Mack Sr., pay the outstanding indebtedness, and provide funds for operations. Finley said they did not expect they could operate successfully in Philadelphia for the 1955 season and requested that in such event the American League would approve the transfer of the franchise from Philadelphia to any one of six cities.

Robert F. Thompson appeared, representing Clint Murchison of Dallas. Thompson said that Murchison wanted to purchase the club in connection with his promotion of Boys, Inc., and that he was willing to put up $1 million in cash immediately to buy the stock of Connie Mack Sr. and Earle and give three-year notes to Roy for his stock. Murchison's offer was contingent on the league's approval to move the team to Los Angeles. Two members of the Board of Supervisors of Los Angeles appeared and said Los Angeles County was willing to buy Wrigley Field in Los Angeles or acquire property to build a new stadium.

Arnold Johnson and his attorney, Edward A. Vollers, appeared. Johnson said he was offering $3,375,000 cash, which included purchase of stock and paying off outstanding debts. He said it was necessary to have a definite answer today to hold the Philadelphia National League club to its commitment to purchase Connie Mack Stadium. He intended to move the club to Kansas City for the '55 season.

At the request of Roy Mack, Charlie Finley again appeared and stated that Tommy Richardson was no longer associated with Mr. Finley in the negotiations.

Roy Mack stated that certain businessmen in Philadelphia were represented by Mr. Jack Rensel and were willing to put up $1.5 million for the acquisition of the club and provide funds. Rensel was invited into the meeting. He stated in the event Mr. Finley acquired the stock of Earle Mack, the group of Philadelphia businessmen whom he represented would provide additional funds necessary to purchase the stock of Connie Mack Sr. In the course of discussion Finley stated the proposal by Rensel was not acceptable to him.

All these proposals were discussed. The consensus was the Philadelphia club could not meet its liabilities and provide funds to operate in the '55 season.

Meeting recessed at 5:40.

During the recess, Will Harridge carried the Yankees' water. He took Roy and Rhoads aside, later telling *The Sporting News,* "Roy's primary concern was to keep the ball club so that he could turn it over to his son, Connie III. I pointed out that by the time his son was ready to assume operation of the club, there might not be anything left of it. Now he still could get out with a sizeable profit. Roy's lawyer, C. Brewster Rhoads, supported me in that contention and urged Roy to sell."

When the meeting reconvened at 6:15, Roy was not present when Brewster Rhoads told the owners that he was authorized to report that in view of the discussions that had taken place today, Roy did not feel that any of the proposals that had been submitted would permit the club to remain in Philadelphia.

After a dinner break, the meeting reconvened at 10 p.m.

Roy stated that it had always been his hope to keep the club in Philadelphia, but it looked as though he couldn't obtain the necessary financial support to continue to operate the club, and therefore, for the first time, he was willing to sell his stock and desired to accept the Arnold Johnson offer to purchase his stock and that of his father and brother, if the league approved moving the franchise to Kansas City. However, he wanted to talk the matter over with his family before giving his final answer and would not be able to do this immediately but would advise Mr. Harridge before 10 a.m. the following Monday, October 18.

Roy and his son, Connie III, then left the meeting.

Subject to the decision of Roy Mack they then voted to approve the sale and approve the moving of the club to Kansas City. [Exactly what had happened that day would later be hotly disputed.]

As far as Will Harridge was concerned, Roy Mack had just committed himself to selling the Athletics to Arnold Johnson. That's why, he said, he had called the question to move the club before any papers had been signed "to eliminate the need to call them all together again." Harridge had never asked Johnson to produce a list of his partners or their financial and background statements, and he didn't care that no offer in writing had yet been made by Johnson. He couldn't wait to welcome Kansas City into the American League as the newsreel cameras rolled and flashbulbs popped.

A writer asked him, "But Roy and Earle could still sell control to a Philadelphia group and keep the club there, couldn't they?"

"No," snapped Harridge, then hedged. "Well, they could, but that would be going back on their word. They promised Johnson they would sell to him."

That's the way it looked to the press. Wrote Povich:

At the finish, despite the fact they were probably making the league's second most important decision in the past 50 years, there were some club owners more interested in catching their trains back home than staying with their serious problem. Four of the owners, representing Washington, Chicago, Boston and Detroit, wound up voting for the Kansas City shift they had vowed to vote against.

It was another demonstration of the Yankee owners, Dan Topping and Del Webb, wagging the entire league or bending it to the Yankees' will or any metaphor you choose. Once more the Yankees put over one of their pet projects, even in the face of a declared opposition that proclaimed as the meeting opened it wouldn't bow to the Yankees.

Spike Briggs had left the meeting early to attend a press conference for his new manager, Bucky Harris. Before he left, he wrote a note giving Harridge his proxy to vote "no" on Kansas City, "yes" to keep the A's in Philadelphia for another year, or "yes" to Los Angeles "if California money was guaranteed." Harridge first said the vote was 7–0 in favor of Kansas City, and he saw no need to cast Briggs's "no" vote, but the next day he put a different spin on it: "The minutes of the meeting show that six clubs present unanimously approved both resolutions, with Washington voting in the affirmative on both resolutions. Philadelphia and Detroit were absent."

Everybody seemed to have his own version of what the minutes would show. No vote count was recorded.

Arnold Johnson believed he had just bought the Athletics. "I have been told that nothing possibly can happen now. . . . [Roy] gave his promise before all of the directors and I am sure he will keep it." He ordered his architects and engineers to proceed with plans to increase the Kansas City stadium's capacity from fifteen thousand to thirty-five thousand. He said he was too busy to think about personnel moves. "I'll pick a general manager later and with him select a field manager."

Everybody in Kansas City believed Johnson had bought the Athletics. The *Kansas City Star*'s page 1 headline read: KANSAS CITY GOES BIG LEAGUE / DEAL SEEN AS CERTAIN.

All that remained was the signing of the papers, a mere formality. The KC Chamber of Commerce envisioned hosting a World Series that might even be as big an event as the annual Future Farmers of America convention.

The Sale of the A's: A Mystery in Four Acts

The president of the American Association believed it and scheduled a meeting to pick a city to replace Kansas City in the league.

Connie Mack believed it and was described as "very upset" by his wife, who fielded the phone calls to his home. Apparently she hadn't told him she had urged Earle to sell to Johnson—if in fact she did.

Phillies president Bob Carpenter believed it and "reluctantly" set about buying Connie Mack Stadium for $1,675,000, expecting to take title on Monday, when the Macks' stock would be turned over to Johnson. "We weren't anxious to buy the park because we didn't want to get into the real estate business," he said. "But we had to buy it to ensure the Phils a place to play ball."

Calvin Griffith didn't believe it. He claimed that Will Harridge's version of the meeting wasn't the same meeting he had attended:

> A vote was taken but Washington and others do not consider it final. There were 'ifs' and 'buts' in the motion. We wouldn't have voted for it if it hadn't been hedged. Washington, Boston, Detroit still may oppose the move.
>
> Let's set the record straight. Here's what happened:
>
> The Washington team specified firstly that another year's stay of the A's in Philadelphia was its first choice; second, that a move to Los Angeles was our second choice, and that Kansas City was merely our third preference. Joe Cronin of the Red Sox made the same conditions in his vote.
>
> The Washington, Boston and Detroit votes are enough to stop any move to Kansas City, and that may still be done.

Spike Briggs agreed: "I will be a very much surprised club owner if Kansas City gets into our league."

Clark Griffith accused Harridge of "trying to railroad this thing through." He was ready to disqualify Johnson for his financial tie-in with the Yankees. He was also concerned about the competition for fans and radio and television revenues if Baltimore wound up as an eastern team with a schedule that conflicted with the Senators' home dates.

Joe Cronin denied that his vote was in any way conditional. Once Roy Mack had evidenced interest in selling to Johnson, "the vote was taken at that time to avoid another league meeting. All of us, I'm sure, wanted to make sure that Connie Mack came out all right. Voting for Mr. Johnson and Kansas City was a matter of plain economics."

Griffith, Cronin, and Hank Greenberg all wanted what was best for Connie Mack, whatever that was.

Will Harridge claimed that Calvin Griffith had his "facts garbled."

Roy Mack told me in Chicago that for the first time he had decided to sell his share of stock in the club and that he would like to accept the Johnson offer.

He requested me to have the owners vote on two propositions

1. Sale of the Athletics to Mr. Johnson.
2. Transfer of the club to Kansas City.

It was on those two propositions that Griffith, along with five other representatives, gave an affirmative vote.

When Harridge was asked what the next step would be if the Kansas City deal blew up, his personal interest broke through his usual unruffled facade: "My goodness, let's not even think about that."

Calvin Griffith conceded that "we did vote for the transfer, but only as a final alternative. If Roy Mack can't raise the money, there's nothing else to do but transfer to Kansas City. We don't want the club to go bankrupt."

Roy Mack did not believe he had sold the Athletics to Arnold Johnson. He had not been present for the last-minute rush to induct Johnson into the fraternity, but he too called Harridge's announcement "premature." He was still looking for a way to avoid moving anywhere.

When Roy had left the meeting room, reporters camped outside were struck by how harried and despondent he looked, as if his execution time had been set instead of winning a reprieve. Roy's son said his father had become so emotional about the possible loss of the team to Kansas City that he had to help him out of the room. Roy told Ed Pollock of the *Bulletin*, "I had just won a delay. I asked for it. Cal Griffith made the motion and Chuck Comiskey seconded it and it passed without a negative vote. I had been under terrific pressure. Emotions were welling up. When I knew for sure I had won a delay I cracked a little."

Harridge backed down, admitting that Roy Mack had been given until 11 a.m. Monday to decide whether to accept Arnold Johnson's offer. Not that the other club owners could do anything about it if Roy ignored the deadline. They couldn't force him to sell to anybody, and they knew it

The fat lady hadn't sung after all.

Roy Mack did not return to a quiet home at 423 Fishers Road in Bryn Mawr after the October 12 meeting. His daughter, Kathleen, was to be married to army lieutenant Clifford Kelly on Saturday, October 16. The last-minute planning for a church wedding and reception at home was in progress. A big tent was going up on the front lawn.

For Arthur Gallagher and his friends, time had about run out. From all reports, the A's appeared to be headed to Kansas City. It was time for everyone who wanted to stay in the deal to come up with the money *now* to pay for the Mack family's stock. That was the first step. They got together Thursday night, made their pledges and promises, and called Roy to tell him they were ready to meet with him Friday morning. All day Friday they parsed the details in the board room of the Tradesman's Title & Trust Company, then adjourned to Kugler's on Broad Street for dinner and more negotiating. At the end of the day the eight had pledged enough cash to buy out the Macks, pay off the immediate debts, and provide working capital.

According to one source reported by the UP, the only thing that remained unsettled was Roy's demand for a five-year contract.

Saturday afternoon during the wedding reception Roy and Earle were kept busy on the telephone with members of the syndicate, while Connie Mack danced with the bride. The prospect of the A's remaining in Philadelphia put a little extra pep in the dancers' steps. Bob Carpenter was also pleased; he would be off the hook for buying the ballpark. A meeting to close the deal was set for Sunday at 1:30 at the Walnut Street office of the syndicate's attorney, Samuel A. Blank.

For a change Roy and Earle were in agreement, although Earle's statements spun away from his repeated desire to sell to Arnold Johnson as recorded in the minutes of earlier league meetings:

Dad and I both feel the same way. We have always wanted the Athletics to stay in Philadelphia and if matters develop as we now expect, nothing can force them to leave.

I told Arnold Johnson from the beginning of our negotiations that I would sell my stock to him only if I could not dispose of it in Philadelphia.

I am free to sell to a Philadelphia group and I will go down the line with them to keep the A's in Philadelphia.

When wire reports of the Philadelphia developments reached Chicago during the day Friday, Arnold Johnson called the press to his Merchandise Mart office and issued a statement. He was "bewildered" by the news but was not giving up the fight. He described his offer of a "substantial" five-year contract and a stock interest "as big as I can make it" for Roy and a job for Connie III.

Johnson questioned why Roy would settle for less to stay in Philadelphia. The fact that none of this had been offered in writing yet and the possibilities that Roy didn't want to move anywhere and keeping the A's in Philadelphia would please Connie Mack didn't seem to occur to Johnson.

On Sunday morning, while Johnson and his attorney Ed Vollers headed to Philadelphia to settle things with Roy Mack once and for all, Earle picked up his father and they drove downtown. Reporters and photographers waited outside the conference room while the buyers and sellers and lawyers went over the terms and conditions of the agreement. Connie Mack would receive $604,000, Roy and Earle $450,000 each. (According to Art Morrow, Earle thought they should receive more per share than their father because they had, in effect, underwritten the whole club as well as their father's stock as collateral for the loans—whatever that means; that's the way Morrow reported it.) Roy would remain as vice-president at $25,000 for a year and would reinvest $250,000 for one-ninth of the stock, with a five-year option to sell his stock back to the club for the same $250,000 if he wanted to get out.

Roy Mack called Will Harridge to tell him the news. Harridge was all business. "Send me all the facts, all the names of those who will be in the new ownership." No congratulations.

The call was followed by a telegram listing the names, business connections, and financial standing of the buyers.

Roy then told the waiting reporters, "I have notified William Harridge that we have agreed to sell to this fine group of civic-minded Philadelphia businessmen. I have requested league approval. Our lawyers are now meeting and are drafting the necessary legal documents. I am very, very happy to be able to keep the A's in Philadelphia. That has always been my goal."

In reporting the news, the AP referred to "the expected league approval," after which the new owners would elect a board of directors, hire a general manager and manager, and try to find a way with the city to ease the parking problem.

The twenty-one page memorandum of agreement with twelve pages of exhibits was written by longtime A's attorneys Frank Schillp and Channing Ellery. It was dated October 18 and signed by Roy, Earle, and the eight buyers. Checks totaling $1,254,000 and the Macks' stock certificates were turned over to a representative of the Broad Street Trust Company to be held in escrow.

Several of the new owners were longtime friends of Earle, who had approached them when he sought to buy out Roy. "I'll give the new owners 100 percent cooperation," Earle said. "I am overjoyed to have the Athletics remain in Philadelphia where they belong."

Connie Mack congratulated everybody and wished them luck.

Most of them then accompanied Roy and his son to Vesper's, a private dining club tucked in an alley between Walnut and Locust Streets, for a late supper. Jack Rensel pushed himself out in front, issuing statements and getting the ink as the prime mover, but in reality it was Gallagher and Rosenberg who spoke for the club. When Arthur Rosenberg was asked why his group had done so much in three days after months of inaction, he said, "We stopped beating around the bush and finally had a meeting of minds."

The Kansas City baseball fans' roller coaster plummeted when the morning *Times* headlined: PHILADELPHIANS BUY THE A'S.

In Chicago Ed Prell of the *Tribune* asked Will Harridge whether Arnold Johnson had any recourse. Harridge replied, "I don't think so. It was a case of Roy Mack changing his mind after he had told us he was willing to sell his stock to Mr. Johnson [who] apparently had a deal on with Roy Mack that couldn't be consummated."

Harridge wouldn't say whether he would call another special meeting or use a telephone poll to vote on the new ownership until he received all the facts from Roy. But an unsigned story in the *Tribune* reported that Harridge spent Monday contacting club owners; it offered no basis for this conclusion: "Indications were that the majority of the seven other club owners favored the sale to Philadelphia interests as against the transfer to Kansas City as planned by Arnold Johnson if his bid had been accepted by the Mack family."

When Johnson landed in Philadelphia Sunday night at ten thirty, the local press was waiting for him with the news of the agreement. "It doesn't sound good to me," he said. "Roy had a much better deal with me. I was going to make him a vice president at a high salary and he would have been a key factor in the Kansas City setup."

Johnson then called Ernest Mehl. "Maybe I'll have to make a statement later," he said. "Right now I'm not sure of all the facts. I'll call Roy tonight."

Mehl, who had plenty of misinformation in his book *The Kansas City Ath-*

letics, was Johnson's chief drum beater as the sports editor of the *Kansas City Star*. So his account of what happened next probably came from Johnson.

Unable to reach Roy by telephone, Johnson and Vollers sat in a suite in the Warwick Hotel and decided to compose a telegram offering him a better deal—for *himself*. It was sent, wrote Mehl, "at 12:08 a.m. on the Monday following the Sunday meeting." Western Union was told to deliver it in person, not by telephone.

According to Mehl, the telegram began: "Dear Roy Unbelievable that you should not talk to me or let me see you before you went off the deep end."

It went on to spell out for the first time in writing the offer of a 20 percent stock interest in the Kansas City club versus the one-ninth interest Roy would receive for his $250,000 investment in the Philadelphia club. Roy would receive contracts for himself and his son. (A job for Earle's son, who had put in a year in the farm office with Bernie Guest, was no longer a factor. He was more interested in pursuing a career as an architect.)

The telegram ended, "Would appreciate courtesy of your calling me at Warwick in the morning. Suggest you do not sign until you get all the facts. Your future and your son's future are at stake."

Johnson is quoted by Mehl: "After it was all over and we had the club, Roy mentioned to me that this telegram had turned the trick."

What could have been in it that made the difference? The price for his stock was the same $450,000. Johnson had already made public his offer of a $25,000 five-year contract for Roy as vice-president and a member of the board of directors, a job for his son, and a stock interest "as big as I can make it."

What's left? Only the possibility that Johnson had put in writing for the first time a specific offer of a 20 percent stock interest in the club for Roy.

When Roy received the telegram, he and his wife discussed their options and decided that 20 percent of a new team in Kansas City could be worth a lot more than 11 percent of an old team in Philadelphia.

It's impossible to determine just when Roy Mack decided to accept Johnson's offer or when he told Johnson. Before heading back to Chicago at six o'clock Monday evening, Johnson said only that he had talked to Earle and Roy and "extended my best wishes. But I'm still puzzled about the whole thing."

Either the telegram had not yet "turned the trick" or Arnold Johnson and Roy Mack had decided to act as though Johnson's quick trip had changed nothing and they would put down a smokescreen to conceal their agreement.

There may have been other factors behind Roy's change of heart.

In the days following the signing of the preliminary agreement on October 17, some of the buyers whom Roy had met only a week ago showed up at Connie Mack Stadium acting as though they already owned the place. Arthur Gallagher said, "They caused trouble at the ballpark. They were up in the office with the secretaries talking about what they were going to do, changes they would make, before we even had the league approval. I had to tell them to stay out of there. I imagine Roy didn't like the way they acted."

Roy didn't.

Ed Sullivan invited the group to be saluted as the saviors of the Athletics on his Sunday night TV show, *Toast of the Town*, on October 24. Gallagher told him, "Ed, It's premature until the league approves the transfer. I'll take a rain check until that happens."

Four of them—Sley, Fischer, Hanff, and Crisconi—went anyhow and were introduced by Sullivan.

Whatever caused him to change his mind, Roy now had a problem: how to get out of the agreement he had signed without being sued by the Philadelphia syndicate and tarred and feathered and run out of town by the few remaining A's fans. He faced another formidable obstacle: persuading Earle to accept Johnson's offer for his own and their father's stock, on which they held a joint option, after Earle's public support of the local group.

Perhaps Johnson had not yet heard from Roy when, on Wednesday, October 21, he unsheathed his legal sword and announced that he had retained a Philadelphia lawyer to study the grounds for a suit for damages against the new owners of the Athletics: "I feel that I have been wronged by the Philadelphia group which so suddenly appeared on the scene, and propose to get my legal remedy . . . not only for the cash damages sustained by me, but also on the grounds that this group joined together to induce a breach of the contract which I made in good faith for the purchase of the A's. In view of the indicated advance ticket sale in Kansas City of almost two million dollars, the measure of my damages should be substantial."

Johnson acknowledged that no written contract existed between him and the Macks: "It was a verbal agreement, true, but it stood with me as something unbreakable—and it is part of the minutes of the American League meeting."

That was a stretch: The minutes said that Roy "wanted to talk the matter over with his family before giving his final answer."

That hardly qualified as what Johnson termed an agreement "without equivocation to sell the team to me. . . . It never was contemplated that Mr. Mack would be given an opportunity to look for other purchasers, or to do anything except to talk to his family."

Johnson may have convinced himself that "his family" would simply rubber-stamp the sale.

Johnson's statement continued: "My actions have been in complete good faith throughout, and there is certainly no doubt in my mind that I had reached an agreement with all parties in interest."

All parties in interest? Johnson had never reached any agreement with Connie Mack. And Earle's mind had changed so often even he didn't know where he stood from one meeting to the next.

Some lawyers said Johnson might have a case if he could show malicious interference with a contract, even an unwritten agreement, if there were no conditions attached to it. To this Roy Mack replied that there certainly was a condition: he would accept Johnson's offer only if the team couldn't be kept in Philadelphia. Now it appeared that it *could* be kept there.

Was the threat of what Johnson called "a long and expensive litigation" a bluff to scare the Philadelphia group into backing out, thus freeing Roy to cop a "no choice" plea in accepting Johnson's offer? Or if that didn't work, a maneuver to scare the club owners into rejecting the Philadelphia syndicate?

(At the time Johnson insisted that "this action is not directed in any manner against the American League or any club owners." Yet he was well aware of baseball's current legal woes involving the Liberty network and its historic "stay-out-of-court-at-any-cost" position. On the morning of the next league meeting Johnson's lawyer publicly threatened a suit for damages against the league "for inducing the Macks to breach their contract with Mr. Johnson. It was a verbal contract to be sure, but there were plenty of witnesses.")

The Philadelphia group spent Tuesday and Wednesday getting details sorted out, a process that involved numerous phone calls to get a consensus on the i-dotting and t-crossing. Rosenberg saw no obstacles. Everyone in the group was in good standing in the community. They had enough money— "Five more want to buy in," he said.

There was speculation about who would become the general manager and manager. Eddie Mulligan, president of the Sacramento club, said that Roy had called him about accepting the job of general manager. San Francisco manager Lefty O'Doul, who held the record for most times being mentioned as a big league manager without it ever happening, said he had been contacted too.

But Rosenberg said it was all premature; they would do nothing until they had the league's approval.

Meanwhile, the Yankees launched a campaign denigrating the Philadelphia Eight, characterizing Food Fair executive Arthur Rosenberg as a mere grocer who would demean baseball by "using the team by giving away tickets to promote the sale of groceries," which UP quoted its anonymous source as saying would be "contrary to the high professional standards of baseball."

Clark Griffith replied, "I don't care if they're grocers as long as they are good ones."

When the syndicate members met on Thursday, they shrugged off Johnson's legal threats. Their lawyers finished tweaking the agreement. They signed it and sent it to Roy, expecting it to be completed the next day, naïvely believing that once Roy had signed it, they would receive an immediate approval from Will Harridge and the other club owners and could close the deal per the agreement at two o'clock Monday, October 25.

Maybe their expectations weren't so unrealistic. Just five years earlier Bill Veeck's sale of the Cleveland Indians had been quickly approved without a meeting. (Perhaps the club owners just wanted to get rid of Veeck as fast as they could.)

Rosenberg saw no reason for a delay. "If there is any other information Harridge wants," he said, "we're not aware of it."

When they heard nothing by Friday afternoon, Rosenberg urged Roy to call Harridge and press for a decision. Roy made the call, but instead of pressing Harridge, he told the league president that he understood the need for league approval "when the proper time arrives." According to Harridge, Roy told him that in his judgment "the proper time had not yet arrived. There was still work to be done on the contract."

Asked by Philadelphia writers to comment on Harridge's statement, Roy said, "No comment."

Did Harridge take the conversation to mean that Roy was stalling, asking him to hold off on a vote? That's what it sounded like. Unlike the greased-lightning acceptance of Arnold Johnson on October 12, Harridge said he couldn't act until the agreement was "signed, sealed, and delivered." Then he insisted on more details: the terms of the agreement, how the money would be distributed and liabilities paid, who the stockholders would be, the officers and their duties—all to be studied by the league's attorneys before calling any meetings.

None of which had been asked of Arnold Johnson.

Headlined the *Chicago Tribune* on Saturday, October 23:

EXPLAIN TERMS! HARRIDGE TELLS MACKS
MOVE DELAYS LEAGUE O. K. ON A'S SALE

Outwardly Rosenberg remained patient. He understood that "it usually takes months to draw up a corporation sale agreement and we're trying to get it done in days" As for organizing and electing officers and directors, he said, "There is no sense in acting like a corporation if the stockholders have not been approved yet."

But his troops were getting restless. And suspicious. To some it smelled like Roy was looking for a way to incite the syndicate into backing out of the deal rather than make it look like *he* was the one reneging, and Harridge was abetting him by stalling. They didn't know how close they were skating to the truth. An AP story quoted one unnamed member of the syndicate that Roy had demanded 50 percent of the stock or he would sell to Johnson, a demand that infuriated some of the investors, who threatened to go public with his demands until Roy had backed down.

Everything that Will Harridge had asked for was completed on Sunday, October 24. Just after midnight Roy Mack was the last of the participants to sign off on the final agreement, knowing—hoping—praying—that he would find a way to get out of honoring what he had just signed.

Earle's lawyer, Alfred Luongo, took the earliest flight to Chicago Monday morning and put the papers in Will Harridge's hands, along with a handwritten note from Connie Mack:

Dear Mr. Harridge,

I want you to approve the sale of my stock to the Philadelphia people. I don't want the club to leave Philadelphia.

Sincerely, Connie Mack

Meanwhile, the buyers and sellers gathered in a conference room at the Broad Street Trust Company to await word of Will Harridge's approval so they could complete the exchange of money and stock by the two o'clock deadline. Connie and Mrs. Mack were there to receive their check and deposit it. Reporters and photographers waited in an anteroom.

It was up to Harridge whether to poll the club owners by telephone or telegram with his recommendation or call a special meeting. Luongo hoped that Harridge would tell him fine, everything looks in order; wait here while I call the club owners for their okay. He should have known better. What Harridge said was he'd turn it all over to the league's attorneys and set a meeting for later in the week.

It was Luongo's lot to call the anxious Philadelphians and tell them the disappointing news. Nobody revealed who took the call in the conference room.

Roy Mack could not have been surprised. The Connie Mack of five years ago would not have been surprised. But the would-be baseball moguls were shocked and confused. What did it mean? The deadline for the closing was imminent. What to do?

Somebody suggested they had no choice but to postpone the closing deadline until after the league met and approved the deal. Would the Macks agree to an extension of time?

Not a problem, said Connie Mack.

Not a problem, said Earle Mack.

Problem, said Roy Mack. I want to consult my lawyer. Let's put off a decision until tomorrow morning.

Everybody in the room was stunned. The sound of sagging spirits was almost audible. The red tide of anger on faces was clearly visible. They had all been under considerable strain for weeks, riding a roller coaster that had borne them to the emotional top when Luongo had left for Chicago with the final agreement. Now they'd been knocked off balance, as if they never knew whether a fastball or curve was coming at them.

"They didn't like that," Roy's son Connie told reporter Ray Kelly.

And they let Roy know it, so heatedly that he quickly backed down. He said he would consult his lawyer, Brewster Rhoads, without delay. Rhoads was in federal court arguing a $30 million case. Roy said he would go to Rhoads's office and wait for him and return as soon as he could. Roy sent his son Connie to the courthouse to tell Rhoads they had to talk as soon as possible. Connie found the courtroom and waited for a break in the proceedings, when he told Rhoads what had happened. "Dad's waiting for you in your office."

It was three forty-five. The bank was closed. There was nothing to do but take a break. Connie Mack and his wife left, and Chuck Roberts drove them home. As the frustrated syndicate milled about in the corridor waiting for the elevator, reporters could overhear private mutterings among the deflated group: "Maybe he's trying to back out. . . . Well, let him if he wants to. . . . I'm so mad I'd like to walk out of this thing right now. . . . Harridge must be helping Roy get out of the deal by putting us off. . . ."

Somebody said, "Let's get something to eat." They all left.

Writers for the local papers had to hang around, not knowing when the meeting would reconvene. The wire service men got a jump on them, calling in reports of a "stormy meeting" resulting in a snag in the negotiations and speculation that Roy Mack was trying to find a way to back out of the deal. This went out over the teletypes immediately to newspapers and radio stations all over the country.

When Roy asked his lawyer about granting the extension of time for the closing, Rhoads told him that since he had signed the agreement that Luongo had taken to Chicago in good faith, he was obligated to sign off on the extension necessitated by the league's delay in approving the buyers.

It's unknown whether Roy ever told the lawyer about his decision to sell to Arnold Johnson. The next morning Rhoads assured the press that the deal with the Philadelphia buyers was firm; the $4 million was "already secured. Will Harridge simply preferred not to conduct this kind of business by a telephone poll. He wanted the entire deal put on the table and discussed."

Roy may not have told his son, either. That evening, when Ray Kelly telephoned Roy's home and read to Connie III the wire reports hinting that Roy might be backing out of the deal, Connie said, "After what my father's gone through to keep the A's in Philadelphia, I don't see how anybody could get any such idea as that."

The stewing syndicate members and their lawyers returned to the bank at five o'clock and were let in by the night watchman. Roy and Connie III returned about twenty minutes later and went into the meeting room.

Arthur Rosenberg had apparently heard the AP reports. A few minutes later he came out and told the writers, "Everything's going to be all right. There will be a statement in a little while."

It didn't take long for Rosenberg to return to the anteroom with Ted Hanff and Arthur Gallagher and announce, "Roy and Earle have granted us an extension until three p.m. Friday. They cooperated beautifully."

The next day Will Harridge issued a one-sentence statement calling a meeting for Thursday in New York "to consider the sale of the Philadelphia club stock." He didn't say to whom.

To Shirley Povich, the whole business seemed peculiar—and ominous for the syndicate:

The curious aspect of the deal is that Roy Mack rejected a better offer from Johnson than he is getting from the Philadelphia group. . . .

The suspicious thing about [Thursday's] meeting is that a dozen times in the past other clubs have been sold to new owners without occasioning any formal meetings of approval. It leads to the belief that the league is not ready to sanction the group that wants to buy the A's. . . . If Harridge's investigation of the character of the Philadelphia buyers proved in their favor, he could have communicated as much over his teletype hook-up to all the club presidents and asked them to act by mail or wire on his recommendation. He didn't have to summon them to a meeting.

If the league rejects the Philadelphia group, either because of a question of integrity of character or lack of sound financial backing, it will be a carefully-worded rejection. The owners know the delicacy of impugning character, and Harridge is always three-deep in lawyers. Baseball is still shy of the courts.

None of this reached Connie Mack or Earle. On Wednesday night Mack told the *Inquirer*, "I talked to my sons and we are solidly behind the sale." With his father nodding in approval Earle said, "Dad and I want to sell to these people, nobody else."

"We all feel that way," said Mack.

The next morning Chuck Roberts bundled Connie Mack into the car at 7 a.m. and drove him to New York. Roberts helped him into the meeting room, then waited in the hall. One story has Arnold Johnson seeing Roberts in the hallway looking downcast. "I don't like what those men have done to my boss," Roberts said.

"What did they do?" asked Johnson.

"They called our house seven or eight times yesterday to insist that he make the trip over here. He's an old man and a trip like this won't do him any good."

Arthur Gallagher denied that anyone in his group had called Mr. Mack or visited him to pressure him to be there. "We never dealt with Mr. Mack."

Most of the Philadelphia Eight were outside the meeting room politicking among the other clubs' representatives before the meeting. Arthur Gallagher saw Joe Cronin and Hank Greenberg talking and introduced himself. Cronin had not forgotten Mack's support for him when he had first become a manager more than twenty years ago. He was determined to back the Old Man's wishes. The hefty Cronin, considerably more rotund than he had been in his playing days, told Gallagher, "You have our vote on one condition, that you make those seats at Shibe Park wider."

Greenberg, who realized that Connie Mack had become senile but still respected him more than he did most of the other nabobs of the league, said, "You have my vote."

Only Gallagher and Rosenberg and their attorney Sam Blank would be invited into the meeting to speak for the syndicate.

It was thirty-nine years to the day since the Federal League had met to discuss moving its Kansas City club to Philadelphia.

Act 3: Special Meeting of American League to Consider Philadelphia Club Stock

WALDORF-ASTORIA HOTEL, NEW YORK, OCTOBER 28, 1954, 10:55 A.M.

[In addition to the usual representatives, Spike Briggs was joined by Charles L. Gehringer. Connie Mack accompanied his sons and grandson Connie III. Calvin Griffith was the lone Washington presence.]

Harridge read a chronological statement of events leading up to the meeting, then said, "We have been asked to advise whether we will approve these prospective stockholders by three o'clock Friday. Mr. Roy Mack is here with his attorney, Mr. Rhoads. Mr. Earle Mack is here with his attorney, Mr. Luongo. Mr. Ellery is here representing the club and I believe Mr. Mack Senior. I think they should advise the members as to the agreement which has been made and also as to the prospective stockholders."

Roy Mack advised that he and his brother Earle had entered into an agreement dated October 18, 1954, with Messrs. Arthur Rosenberg, Arthur Gallagher, John P. Crisconi, Barney Fischer, Ted R. Hanff, Morton Liebman, Jack Rensel, and Isadore Sley for the sale of ⁴⁄₉ of the stock owned by him, all of the stock owned by his father and his brother Earle. He requested the league to approve all of the prospective purchasers of the stock and the agreement of sale. He stated the prospective purchasers were responsible businessmen of good reputation individually in Philadelphia, although some of them he had known for only a short period of time. Rhoads asked the league to approve the purchasers. He stated that he had made certain representations at the October 12 meeting, and the league had taken certain actions on the basis of those representations. But when subsequent events led to a definite contract, he felt that Roy had no alternative but to sign it.

MILES: Mr. Rhoads, do you feel that Roy Mack made a definite commitment to Arnold Johnson in Chicago?

RHOADS: He said that all other opportunities had failed him and he was requesting the transfer to Kansas City, but asked only permission to speak with Mrs. Mack.

MILES: That was the way I remembered it.

Earle Mack then urged that the club be kept in Philadelphia as his father wished and stated that Connie Mack would be honorary president. He urged approval of the agreement of October 18.

Al Luongo said that on his return to Philadelphia he felt the club was really going to leave the city and there was no alternative but bankruptcy. Then "a miracle happened," and this new group came forward. The certifications made by the group should be given credence. His partner, Fairfax Leary, had been engaged as counsel to the group.

CRONIN: What is your position in the case?

LUONGO: In Chicago we were in favor of the transfer to Kansas City.

MILES: Did you feel a commitment had been made?

LUONGO: No. Earle and I were disappointed that no definitive action had been taken. I urged approval of the sale to Johnson at that time but then the miracle happened."

RHOADS: Did Roy go back to Philadelphia thinking he could make a new deal?

LUONGO: Yes.

Several members of the league took issue with that contention.

The Sale of the A's: A Mystery in Four Acts 553

GREENBERG: Can the league pass approval on any new group?

HARRIDGE: Yes.

ELLERY: Connie Mack wants this sale. There is no doubt in my mind that Roy felt he had made no legal commitment to Johnson.

He then reviewed the individuals in the new group as he knew them and their business backgrounds.

At this point Ellery handed Harridge two letters from the prospective purchasers dated October 27, both signed by Sam Blank. Harridge handed them to Ben Fiery, who read them aloud.

The first letter stated that in the event any one of the prospective purchasers was disapproved by the league, in such event the remaining members would acquire the shares of the disapproved party, or a substitute satisfactory to the league would be designated who would agree to be bound by the same obligations. In the event of any such contingencies the approval of Roy and Earle McGillicuddy was required. The second advised that each of the purchasers under the agreement of October 18 had deposited $160,000 and that the funds were credited to the account of Ted Hanff and Isadore Sley, agents, in the Broad Street Trust Company, Philadelphia. The funds deposited in the name of Rensel would be contributed by James Anderson [president of the Union League and a friend of Gallagher's] if acceptable to the league, failing which Morton Liebman agreed to contribute the same.

RHOADS: In my opinion, the letter dealing with any change in prospective purchasers is at variance with paragraph 19 of the agreement, without which I would not have allowed Roy to sign. [Paragraph 19(a): If any one or more of Buyers is not approved by the aforesaid American League, this agreement shall then become null, void and ineffective.] In my opinion, paragraph 19 is controlling.

COMISKEY: Has all the money been deposited?

ELLERY: Each member of the new group has deposited $160,000 and plans to deposit another $90,000 each by 3:00 p.m. Friday.

At noon Arthur Gallagher, Arthur Rosenberg, and Sam Blank were invited into the meeting. Gallagher was motioned to sit at Harridge's left; the others stood.

Gallagher advised that he had been approached by Roy Mack on the purchase of his stock in the Philadelphia club upon the understanding that it remain in Philadelphia and it was their belief that they would do a good job and would be successful in operating the club.

Rosenberg reviewed the negotiations for the purchase of the stock and stated his group felt very confident they had an active group that would take an interest in the management of the club and in the promotion of the club and of the American League in Philadelphia. He said their first intention was civic and felt they had sufficient capital to do a successful job. He reviewed the financial obligations of the club and the commitments of the prospective purchasers. He stated that in his opinion the prospective purchasers had made commitments of sufficient funds to pay the current indebtedness of the club and to provide adequate working capital for operations during the current season.

During the course of Rosenberg's remarks, Connie Mack retired from the meeting. [Hank Greenberg remembered him as "sitting in the meeting with his head held high, not aware of anything that was going on, while they put pressure on Roy."]

TOPPING: How long will the team be kept in Philadelphia?
ROSENBERG: At least three or four years. [He said urgent immediate debts were about $300,000 and his group had working capital of about a half million.]
MILES: I understand the debts of the club are around $700,000.

Ellery then read some figures from a club audit saying the present obligations of the club were about $625,000.

Gallagher, Rosenberg and Blank left the meeting at 12:15.

Harridge then called the league into executive session. Everyone left the room except Earl Hilligan and AL attorney Ben Fiery and one representative from each club: Roy Mack represented Philadelphia; Calvin Griffith, Washington; Clarence Miles, Baltimore; Joe Cronin, Boston; Charles Comiskey, Chicago; Hank Greenberg, Cleveland; Walter Briggs Jr., Detroit; Dan Topping, New York.

At the request of Harridge the terms of the agreement of October 18 were reviewed and paragraphs 18 and 19 of the agreement were read in full by Ben Fiery. The certificates signed by each that the investments were his own personal investment, etc. were also read. This was followed by a general discussion of the problem. With reference to the provisions of paragraph 18b providing the buyers shall receive from Connecticut General Life written advice that the transaction is not objectionable, Roy Mack submitted a letter from Mr. Neilson of Connecticut General that was read by Fiery, in which they stated they had no objection to continuing the loan provided certain specified conditions were complied with.

Roy Mack then said, "I do not think this is the best group to bring into baseball." He went on to explain the developments that ended in his signing the contract and said that he was thinking mostly of Connie Mack Sr. when he signed and that he felt he had made a mistake in signing.

Comiskey then related a conversation he had had with Connie Mack III in Chicago and said that he had told Connie III he should have advised Roy to accept the Johnson offer; that Connie III had said, "Dad acted in haste and had made a poor move in signing"; and that Roy corroborated this.

Roy then discussed the members of the Philadelphia group. There were certain members he did not know and could not vouch for. He felt he had been deceived by Jack Rensel and that Gallagher had told him he would welcome the opportunity to withdraw from the picture [which Gallagher later denied]. He then continued to relate incidents that occurred during the negotiations, including a balloting on who would be the club president. It was his desire to be relieved of the obligation of the agreement of October 18.

COMISKEY: Do you feel you made a firm commitment at Chicago?
ROY: I would say yes.
MILES: The league should not put the stamp of approval on something that Roy himself would not approve. I have obtained considerable information on the business connections and backgrounds on members of the new group.
GREENBERG: The controlling interest in the club [Connie Mack and Earle] desire to sell to this new group.
MILES: The league would be better off with the club in Kansas City rather than Philadelphia.

There followed a general discussion as to what would be in the best interest of the league in this situation.

Fiery then reread highlights of the minutes of the October twelfth meeting.

GREENBERG: The important thing to be decided is what is good for the American League.
CRONIN: I agree.

Fiery said that if the members disapproved of the Philadelphia deal, they would be faced with the problem of Roy making a new deal and the league's approving the deal and a transfer of the franchise. Fiery told Greenberg that in the event the new group was disapproved, it was his opinion that the league should vote again on Arnold Johnson's offer and a transfer of the franchise.

MILES: Should the transaction be disapproved, would the league records show the league has voted Kansas City acceptable?
FIERY: Yes. There would have to be a motion to reconsider the Chicago action and it takes a majority vote to pass.

There followed a big discussion of how to phrase a motion to approve or disapprove the Philadelphia group. The final decision, in effect, was a motion that the transaction between the Macks, as sellers, and the new group, as buyers, be approved.
Miles agreed with that wording.
Briggs moved for passage of this resolution. Griffith seconded.

HARRIDGE: A yes vote will be to approve the motion, a no vote would reject it.

On a secret ballot, with no club names on the ballot (emphasis added), Fiery and Hilligan recorded the votes. Harridge announced them: 4 for passage, 4 for rejection. The motion was defeated. Adjourned at 1:50.
Reconvened at 2:50, still in executive session.
Roy said he would like the league to consider a Kansas City bid if Johnson was still interested. On motion of Briggs, seconded by Miles, the league took another adjournment to enable Roy to contact Johnson while the league members remained in the room. Roy returned from time to time and in one instance told the members, "I would definitely like to accept the Kansas City offer. If we talk of any other offer, the Lord knows when we would accomplish anything."
At 4:25 the league reconvened in executive session.
Fiery said he had told Connie Mack, Earle, Ellery, Luongo, and Rhoads of the league's action on the new Philadelphia group. "I told them the action was not based on individuals. Both Earle and Connie Mack said they would not sell to anyone outside of the Philadelphia group."

Roy expressed disappointment on the stand of Earle and Connie Mack.

GRIFFITH: Roy, should the league reconsider the motion that failed on a 4–4 vote?
ROY: Frankly, I would say no.
FIERY: The league can either reconsider its action or adjourn and leave the problem to the Mack family.

Griffith moved to reconsider the motion on the Philadelphia group. Briggs seconded.

On an open poll, Cleveland, Detroit, and Washington said yes. The other five (including Roy) voted no.

COMISKEY: I will not come to another meeting unless the Macks have a signed and sealed agreement as a threesome to sell to anybody and a copy of such agreement is in the league office.

It was then agreed that the press be told that the transaction presented by the Philadelphia group had failed to get a vote of approval and that the meeting was adjourned to enable the Macks to return to Philadelphia and attempt to work out their own problems.

Adjourned at 5 p.m.

Earl Hilligan came out of the meeting room and read to the press and the anxiously waiting Philadelphia group this carefully worded statement: "The transaction presented today by the Philadelphia group failed to receive a vote of approval."

"What does that mean?" someone asked.

"It means the reason the group was turned down was that the transaction wasn't approved," Hilligan clarified. He didn't say what the vote was or even if there had been a vote. He didn't say that any or all of the individuals were rejected, just the *transaction*. Before Hilligan could continue, an astonished Arthur Gallagher interrupted. "I'd like to know on what grounds our proposition was rejected."

Hilligan said Harridge would explain, then continued, "The meeting was adjourned to permit the Macks to return to Philadelphia to attempt to work out their problem."

Harridge didn't explain; he ducked. "It was a secret ballot. I cannot read the minds of the owners. The negative votes could have been on any number of grounds—maybe personal, maybe simply on a matter of business."

Asked by one of the Philadelphia lawyers how Roy Mack had voted, Harridge took an imperial umbrage-taking attitude. "You're being insulting."

That was all they were told.

Reporters are expected to turn in a story. If information is lacking, they guess. Speculation centered on the persuasive efforts of the Yankees—no secret there. Or maybe it had to do with John Crisconi's once owning stock in a race track, a matter that nobody had even brought up. Or was there some secret "bombshell" of an explanation?

There was, but it never exploded.

Arthur Rosenberg said, "I can't understand why the league wouldn't tell us, either in public or private, the reasons for the rejection."

Then he touched the heart of the matter. "Since Roy Mack attended the meeting and apparently knows what the reasons were for rejecting our setup, I think the next move is up to him."

Roy could not bring himself to admit that he was the reason they had been rejected: he had double-crossed them. He made no effort to make up a reason or double-talk an explanation. He hoped the tight brotherhood of the barons of baseball would keep his secret. All he said was, "I am truly disappointed that the deal with the Philadelphia group didn't go through." Whether he batted an eye or studied his shoes or his nose grew longer when he said it was not reported.

Asked what would happen next, he said, "I guess we'll have to operate as best as we can," a response that was met with guffaws of "With what?"

Trying to guess who voted how, the press wondered: How *did* Roy Mack vote? When Roy was asked if he had, in effect, voted "against himself," he denied it. Ray Kelly put it to him that an "excellent source" had told the *Bulletin* that New York, Boston, Baltimore, and Philadelphia had voted no. Roy said, "That's not true. How would anybody know about that? It was a secret ballot."

Precisely. A secret ballot that Roy's denial could hide behind.

Based on public comments, the consensus was that Detroit, Washington, Boston, and Cleveland had ignored Roy's plea to rescue him from the deal he had made and voted yes. It was common knowledge that New York and Baltimore were against it. The White Sox were divided. Grace Comiskey, widow of the Old Roman and still the club president, said she wanted to do whatever "the Macks" wanted. And the Macks, as far as everyone knew, all wanted the same thing. But her son, Chuck, and Sox general manager Frank Lane were Johnson supporters. With a secret ballot, Roy couldn't be sure how Chuck Comiskey would vote. It took five ayes to approve the sale. If Chicago was a fifth vote for the Philadelphia Eight without Roy, his vote wouldn't matter. He'd be a hometown hero despite his Benedict Arnold ploy. But suppose Chuck Comiskey, under the blanket of the secret ballot, voted no. Could Roy vote yes and take the chance of being the fifth vote for the Philadelphia group he had just renounced, in effect voting against his afternoon position, which was against his morning position? If he or an ally had requested the secret ballot—and it had to be requested under league rules—then he was not only shielded but blindfolded in casting his vote.

He had to vote no.

Calvin Griffith said, "I never was so surprised by anything connected with the American League as I was on the outcome of the voting."

On his way out, Chuck Comiskey made this revealing comment on Roy's pivoting position: "I will not come back to any more meetings until the Mack family has settled its own affairs among themselves. It seems they can't make up their minds."

When Earl Hilligan agreed with Comiskey's assertion about the Macks' "divergence of opinion," Gallagher and his colleagues were thoroughly confused. The Macks *had* made up their minds to sell on October 18, and nothing any of them had said publicly since then, including Roy's request for their approval two hours earlier, indicated a change of heart. Earle and Connie Mack were also puzzled. They had arrived that morning believing that they and Roy were of one mind, and Roy had said nothing to the contrary *while they were in the room.*

The attorneys, Luongo and Ellery, were confused. What "divergence of opinion" existed? To set the record straight they put together a statement: "The three Macks were united in requesting to approve the Philadelphia group and the transaction transferring the stock to the Philadelphia syndicate. If Mr. Hilligan indicated that there was any difference of opinion we believe it related solely to what should be done if the transaction of the Philadelphia group is not approved by the league."

The members of the syndicate left feeling let down, defeated, angry about not knowing why they had been rejected. "Something happened that we don't know about," was all the disconsolate group could say. Most of them. John Crisconi called it "a double cross" and "an insult" and demanded to know how the voting had gone. He was shouting into the wind.

At 3 p.m. Friday the lawyers returned the $1,254,000 worth of checks to the disheartened investors and the stock certificates to the club's attorney, J. Channing Ellery.

The Philadelphia Eight went to their graves never knowing why they had been rejected. Now their descendants know.

The next day Connie Mack was too exhausted to do any talking, but Mrs. Mack did plenty. In a statement ostensibly dictated by him but more likely drafted by her, Roy was pegged as the "real fly in the ointment, no matter what he tries to feed to the public. He's been behind everything since May, telling everybody one thing and doing something else."

She had no criticism of Earle, apparently unaware that he had been the ointment-dipped fly in John McShain's aborted rescue offer in August and the first one eager to sell to Arnold Johnson.

Then she lit into the results of the meeting.

Those good businessmen have the money and want the club, but they gave the answer that they weren't rejected—they just weren't approved.

Isn't that dressing it up a bit? Are we back in the first grade? They wouldn't get away with that stuff on me. They'd have to show me. They simply don't want those men to have the club. It's a runaround with an awful lot of pressure to take the club to Kansas City.

Mr. Mack is feeling terrible about the whole thing. It's his nature to be optimistic and he's gone through three of those meetings and been disappointed each time. He thought everything was going to be okay yesterday.

Referring to Mack's pleas in the meeting, Mrs. Mack said, "They tell me he was wonderful. (There is no record in the minutes of any comments by Connie Mack.) How those American League owners could vote against him is something I'll never be able to understand. There must be an awful lot of politics mixed up in this thing."

Her claims that the Yankees were behind the push to Kansas City were hardly news and indeed drew no denial from Dan Topping, who told the *New York Times*, "There's been no secret about our position. We think it would be best for the American League and best for us to move the A's to Kansas City."

So where did that leave everything?

Arnold Johnson and Ed Vollers left New York and headed to Philadelphia, where Johnson told Ray Kelly, "I have not tried to influence anyone in the American League. I have not tried to influence the Macks."

He would not use the word "confident"; he was just "hopeful" of closing the deal.

Will Harridge was growing impatient. He told Roy, "In fairness to the other clubs in both leagues, definite action is imperative."

Not to mention that the league had become fodder for comedians in print.

AL WOLF, *LOS ANGELES TIMES*: Trying to rationalize the zany doings of the American Leaguers, even with inside help, is about as safe as juggling triggered atom bombs.

IRVING VAUGHAN, *CHICAGO TRIBUNE*: The sale of the Philadelphia Athletics [is] a matter that has snowballed into an act good enough to prove that vaudeville is not dead.

We can only imagine what today's late show comedians would have done with the story.

Connie Mack and Earle knew there was no way the family business could survive another year—another month—in Philadelphia. Sometime between Friday and Sunday night, when Johnson returned to Chicago to vote on Election Day, November 2, and pick up a cashier's check, or on his return to Philadelphia the following Wednesday, Roy and Earle signed over their option on Connie Mack's stock and agreed to sell their own shares to him.

Johnson spent much of Wednesday conferring with the attorneys—six in all—representing the Athletics, Connie Mack, Roy, Earle, and Katherine and her daughters.

That evening he called Ellery's partner, Frank Schillp, and arranged to pick him up at 8:30 a.m. to go to Connie Mack's apartment.

On the way to School Lane Johnson said, "I have a $500,000 cashier's check in my pocket."

Schillp said, "I don't think that's enough."

"Is there a stationery store around here where I can buy some blank checks?"

"No, but I have a personal check. I always carry one with me. You can borrow it and strike out my name and my bank."

They went up in the elevator and did not see anyone in the lobby. Connie Mack was sitting up, dressed, in a deep chair in the bedroom. Mrs. Mack and their daughter Rita were there. Despite reports to the contrary, Frank Schillp did not place Earle Mack or his attorney, Alfred Luongo, in the apartment while he and Johnson were there.

Johnson said he was prepared to give Mack $2,000 a share. Connie Mack said, "That is satisfactory."

Johnson scribbled through Schillp's name and address on the end of the check, crossed out "Provident Trust Company," wrote in "City National Bank & Trust Co of Chicago," and made out the check for $604,000. Either Mrs. Mack or Johnson—thirty-five years later Schillp wasn't sure—suggested calling the Chicago bank for assurance that the check would go through. Johnson made the call and explained that he would be returning the certified check and had written a check for $604,000. Assured that the check would be honored, he handed it to Connie Mack. "It was about ten a.m.," Schillp said. "Nothing else changed hands. No receipts or papers of any kind. The stock certificates were delivered some time later. Then we left."

Mack endorsed the check; Chuck Roberts and Rita took it to the bank. Rita then went to the offices of Stradley, Ronon, Stevens, and Young. Richard Stevens had drawn up a trust, with the Provident Tradesmens Bank as trustee. Funded with the net proceeds of the sale of the stock after taxes, it provided for a monthly income of $500 each for Connie Mack and Katherine and $300 a month for each of their four daughters. (When Katherine died in 1972, the trust was split into four separate trusts for the daughters and the net income from each paid annually. Ruth, the last surviving daughter, received income from the trust into the 1980s.)

Rita probably brought the trust to the apartment; Connie Mack signed it on Saturday, November 6.

Several factors make it likely that the scenarios put forth of "a race to get to Connie Mack first to buy his stock" and Chuck Roberts leading Johnson and Schillp up the back stairs to beat the local bidders waiting in the lobby are fiction. Katherine Mack might have said the first one there at noon or nine or any other time would get the prize; if she did, she didn't know what she was talking about. She may have been told that four of the local syndicate might show up with four checks to buy Mr. Mack's stock and may have said, "I like one check better than four." When John Crisconi had said that he and three other diehards from the syndicate—Sley, Liebmann, and Hanff—would go to see Connie Mack in a last-ditch effort to obtain the franchise, they made Don Quixote look like a supreme rationalist. Earle never frantically called any of the locals with a last-ditch "Where are you guys?" plea. They couldn't have bought the stock anyhow. Roy and Earle had already signed over their option on their father's stock to Johnson. Otherwise, Frank Schillp would never have abetted Johnson in the transaction with Connie Mack.

According to the AP, when Johnson left the apartment, he said he'd have a statement in an hour. "I think it will be of interest."

> AP: Then came Earle, along with his attorney, Alfred Luongo. Both wept. Earle faced the Philadelphia hopefuls and said, "We lost. The club is sold to Johnson."

Earle knew the club was lost the minute he and Roy had signed over their option to Johnson. Maybe the burning fuse to the finality of it had taken until now to reach Earle's tear ducts.

About an hour later, after calling Will Harridge to tell him the news, a grinning Arnold Johnson stood before a room full of reporters and photographers, waving a contract he said covered his purchase of all the stock of Roy and Earle in addition to his purchase of Connie Mack's 302 shares: "All of the Macks have signed a letter to the American League requesting approval of the transaction at the earliest possible date."

The letter was dated November 4. Since all three signatures were ostensibly witnessed by Mrs. Mack and Rita Breedlove, it's likely that the letter had been written by Schillp or Ellery and brought to the apartment that morning for Connie Mack to sign, and Earle and Roy had either signed it earlier or in the time between Johnson's leaving the apartment and the press conference, where the letter's contents were released.

Johnson announced that he would hold at least 51 percent of the stock.

Will Harridge immediately called a league meeting for ten thirty Monday, November 8, in New York.

Ed Delaney wrote in the *Philadelphia Daily News*, "Title to the Athletics was conveyed in shame today to New York, signed, sealed and delivered with the stamp of a broken family."

That night the kind of cold, hard rain poured down on the city that in better times would have meant "Game called." Now the Philadelphia skies wept for "Team called."

But the fat lady was still clearing her throat. In addition to an approval of the sale of the club to Arnold Johnson, there remained the approval of the move to Kansas City, which required six votes. Johnson's purchase had been contingent on the move. If it was not approved at the next meeting, the money would be returned. Nobody knew what would happen in that event.

Clark Griffith had not wavered in his opposition to the move. Spike Briggs was on record that he would vote against it, preferring a move to Minneapolis or the West Coast. Hank Greenberg still hoped to find a way to keep the team in Philadelphia for at least another year. Failing that, he preferred a move to the West Coast. Joe Cronin was noncommittal, saying he would wait to hear the details.

Apparently somebody opposed to the move to Kansas City—maybe Spike Briggs—had not given up. Charles Johnson, executive sports editor of the *Minneapolis Star and Tribune*, reported that he received a call on Friday, November 5, from an unidentified American League club owner hoping to head off the move to Kansas City. The caller asked him if anyone in the Twin Cities could raise $1.5 million to buy the Athletics by Monday. If it could be done, the caller said, the league would keep the A's in Philadelphia another year, then move them to St. Paul, where funds for a new ballpark had already been approved.

The newspaperman said he couldn't find anybody over the weekend.

The Minneapolis territory was owned by the Giants and St. Paul by the Dodgers. The scuttlebutt was that the National League would welcome the plan since it would leave California untouched until the National League was ready for its conquest.

Will Harridge, driving the Yankee steamroller with Clarence Miles riding shotgun, remained confident that the Kansas City move was finally a done deal.

Until they hit a bump.

Act 4: Special Meeting of the American League on Philadelphia–Kansas City Transaction

COMMODORE HOTEL, NEW YORK, NOVEMBER 8

Present:
Boston: Joe Cronin, Jack Hayes
Baltimore: Clarence W. Miles
Chicago: Charles Comiskey, Frank Lane
Cleveland: Hank Greenberg, Nate Dolin
Detroit: Walter O. Briggs Jr.
New York: Dan Topping, George Weiss, J. Arthur Friedlund
Philadelphia: Roy Mack, Earle Mack, Connie Mack III, Brewster Rhoads, Alfred Luongo, Channing Ellery

Washington: Clark Griffith, Calvin Griffith, Gabriel Murphy, club attorney John Powell

Harridge convened the meeting at 11:00 a.m. He read a letter dated November 4:

> Dear Mr. Harridge:
>
> This letter is being sent to you by Cornelius McGillicuddy, Earle T. McGillicuddy and Roy F. McGillicuddy to inform you that we have made an agreement with Arnold M. Johnson to sell all of the outstanding stock of the American League Baseball Club of Philadelphia. This agreement contemplates a transfer of the franchise to Kansas City, Missouri. We are now united in our desires and we hereby request the American League to approve the above, and would appreciate it if such approval would be obtained by you at the earliest possible date.
>
> > Very truly yours [signed
> > by the three Macks and
> > witnessed by Katherine A.
> > McGillicuddy and Rita T.
> > Breedlove]

A discussion of the landlord-tenant relationship between the Arnold Johnson Corporation and the Yankees involving Yankee Stadium followed.

AL counsel Fiery said the landlord-tenant relationship was not in conflict with the constitution, reorganization agreement, or major league rules. There was a debtor-creditor relationship and the league should act on that. He recommended that the league should act on the sale of the club to Johnson first, then on the Yankee Stadium lease relationship.

CLARK GRIFFITH: The league should be protected in case of default of the lease.

BRIGGS: I understand Johnson owns a part of a restaurant-club in Chicago.

Fiery read a letter from Johnson saying if any conflict arose he would divest himself of any interest in Yankee Stadium. He had no connection with the Yankee club. He and Topping were stockholders in Automatic Canteen Company. He would comply with all American League rules. If necessary, he would divest himself of any interest in the Arnold Johnson Corporation or the Kansas City club.

During a discussion of Johnson's qualifications, Harridge read a letter praising Johnson from a Chicago banker. Fiery then repeated that they should vote first on the sale of the Athletics, then on the Yankees relationship, then on the transfer to Kansas City.

GREENBERG: We should vote on the Yankees situation first.

Powell summed up his objections to the Johnson-Yankees relationship.

Miles and Weiss said the league should not forget the practical aspects of the situation and harm itself by splitting hairs.

Calvin Griffith moved that the debtor-creditor relationship between the Arnold Johnson Corporation and Topping and Webb involving the sale and lease of Yankee Stadium and other property be consented to. Frank Lane seconded.

A roll call vote produced 4 yeas, 4 nays. Failed.

Recessed at 12:30.

[The AP reported that during the recess "there were numerous huddles in the corridors and an adjoining dining room as Johnson talked fervently with the owners. He and his attorney did their best to convince Greenberg and Cronin that he was not closely associated with the Yankees just because he owned Yankee Stadium."]

Reconvened at 2:45.

Johnson and Vollers were invited into the meeting. Johnson said to divest himself of all interest in Yankee Stadium would mean a substantial loss to him of around $200,000, maybe as high as $600,000, over 8–10 years, but he would reduce the loss by putting his funds into some other investment. He reviewed his efforts to obtain the club and transfer, assured the field would be ready, explained he had met Topping not more than a year ago, and had purchased Yankee Stadium as a good investment. He described his personal background, denied he had any interest in a night club, was proud of his associates, whom he named: J. Patrick Lennan, Joseph Briggs, Nathaniel Leverone, and his brother Earl Johnson, all of Chicago. He said he had resigned from the board of the Chicago Blackhawks, had never had anything to do with boxing, knew [Chicago Stadium and Blackhawks owner]

Arthur Wirtz personally but had no business ties with him, and if he was given ninety days he could make a deal to divest himself of Yankee Stadium. He wanted the Kansas City acquisition to go through and would definitely dispose of his Yankee Stadium interest if it would help him acquire the club. It would be an arms-length deal if necessary, not to a family member. He said he had one million ticket orders in Kansas City and would not operate in Philadelphia. Kansas City Mayor Kemp had assured him it would be put in his lease that if the club failed to average one million attendance for three years, they could leave Kansas City.

Following a discussion of scheduling problems, etc., Johnson finished by reiterating his commitment to divest himself of any interest in Yankee Stadium in ninety days.

At this point Roy and Earle Mack stated flatly that they were committed to selling their stock to Johnson. [The first time in years they had agreed on anything.]

CLARK GRIFFITH: My club would be harmed by conflicts with Baltimore playing on the same date.

MILES: I will vote for whatever is best for the league.

GRIFFITH: Other people still wish to buy the club.

ROY MACK: I am not going to sell to that bunch out there.

COMISKEY: The principal question is to leave the club in Philadelphia or go to Kansas City. Let's vote on the transfer. Johnson is sincere. I favor the move. Los Angeles is not ready now and Kansas City is. The White Sox are opposed to making a loan to help the Athletics remain in Philadelphia.

Comiskey moved, second by Miles, to approve the sale of the Athletics to Arnold Johnson.

Miles sang the praises of Johnson.

GREENBERG: I want to make the position of the Cleveland club clear. I believe that the coast is a better objective and a move to Kansas City is not in the best interests of the league.

ELLERY: Connecticut General Life has given the Macks until last Thursday to enter into an agreement to sell the club with the threat of calling the mortgage.

[According to a report in the *Chicago Tribune*, after the Philadelphia group was not approved, the insurance company, which had consented to the new buyers assuming the mortgage, had called in the loan because of dereliction in interest and principal payments.]

Fiery amended the original motion approving the sale to Arnold Johnson, adding that Johnson had agreed to comply with league provisions by disposing of the Arnold Johnson Corporation within ninety days.

Rhoads then emphasized that Roy urged that the deal with Johnson be consummated and he was definitely committed to Johnson and definitely would not go out and try to refinance with any other group. This was echoed by Luongo on behalf of Earle.

Poll of members on the motion carried unanimously.

Briggs then moved, second by Comiskey, to authorize transfer to Kansas City. Roll call vote was 6–2 in favor.

[There was no breakdown on the vote. Cleveland and Washington voted no.]

Comiskey moved the league prepare a suitable memento to Connie Mack in recognition of his long years of service to the league. Griffith seconded. Passed unanimously.

Adjourned at 4:15.

The difference maker was Spike Briggs, who had gone into the meeting determined to vote no and wound up making the motion to approve the move to Kansas City.

Briggs explained his switch: "I wanted harmony in the league. I was sick and tired of all the wrangling. I knew if I voted against the move, we'd be back where we started from and the wrangling probably would go on all winter and into the next season. I think now we'll be straightened out once and for all."

Clark Griffith was gracious in defeat. "The Washington club took a beating today, but I congratulated the winner." His fears of conflicting TV dates with the Orioles proved to be unfounded. Each team televised only about thirty games a year, and both had the same sponsor.

Looking back in 1956 Roy told Cy Peterman, "I don't think [Dad] ever really accepted [the move to Kansas City]. At times I thought sure he didn't know the truth. He just vaguely wondered what had happened."

Others disagreed. Mack knew what was happening; he just couldn't do anything about it. His daughter Ruth said, "That piece of him going away was difficult for him."

"Two things stand out in retrospect," wrote Peterman. "Mr. Mack did not want to lose the club for Philadelphia, nor did he want to relinquish entirely his contact with it. Secondly, the members of his family were determined to have their shares. The old man's wishes in that struggle were thrust rather ruthlessly aside. When the toll was counted it was Mr. Mack who paid."

One thing the sequence of events does is turn on its head the spin that Earle was the one consistently, tearfully begging for someone to step up and keep the Athletics in Philadelphia so dear old Dad could go to the office every day, while Roy was the cold-hearted one eager from the start to desert Dad and the city for his own benefit.

As it turned out, they both fumbled the ball that Kansas City recovered. Neither Roy nor Earle had been honest and aboveboard in everything each had said and done. Their public statements seem to reflect more of a priority to be contrary to each other than to honor their father's wishes or the fans' interests. Earle had been responsible for scuttling John McShain's rescue attempt, then had been the first to favor selling to Arnold Johnson, while Roy was determined to keep the club at home. Later, after killing the bid by the Philadelphia Eight, Roy said he was ready to sell to Johnson, then Earle said no.

Roy never quit sniping at Earle. Six months later he wrote to Paul Fritzinger, "You have no idea what [my father] went thru last December—all on account of my brother Earle with one of his daughters [Rita] and his wife."

No wonder the press, even those who considered Kansas City a poor choice, said "Good riddance to the Mack brothers."

In the end, Spike Briggs may have saved Connie Mack's financial hide as well as Roy's and Earle's. The Athletics were finished in Philadelphia. Without the move, one of two things probably would have happened. Either the league would have bought the club, if it wanted Connie Mack to come out whole, and operated it for a year before finding a buyer to move it somewhere. Or Connecticut General would have foreclosed and taken over the team and all its assets, and the Grand Old Man of baseball might have died broke.

29 | LAST OF THE NINTH

It looked like the American League might have to present Connie Mack's commemorative book posthumously. Dr. Gopadze said, "Before the last meetings were held and by the time the final signatures were made, I really thought we were going to lose him. The realization that the A's were gone became more of a shock than this famous, almost shock-proof man could stand."

The turmoil of the last three months had debilitated him. He had become unsteady on his feet, falling at least twice. He walked with a cane or holding onto Chuck Roberts's arm for support. His normally slow pulse became weaker. His blood pressure dropped from about 140 to 108.

In early December Mack was driven to his son's home in Fort Myers. Mrs. Mack stayed in Philadelphia, making it a more relaxed winter for everyone.

On February 4, 1955, Connie Jr. wrote to Paul Fritzinger:

Dad asked me to write to you and thank you for your very nice letter and to tell you he hopes that he will see you this summer.

I am sure that you will be pleased to hear that Dad has been improving steadily since his arrival here some eight weeks ago. About the time of the sale of the ball club Dad had a couple of bad falls and when I went to Philly to get him he was in very poor health. He has been wonderful the past two weeks. We have been going to the movies and to the local high school basketball games. He understands everything that is going on but unfortunately cannot always express himself as well as he would like to. I am afraid his writing days are over so I know you will understand if you do not always receive an answer to your letter. We will try to have someone keep up with his correspondence as long as he is able to take an interest in his mail, which we all hope will be for many years to come.

Thanking you for your very kind interest in my father, I am

Sincerely yours,
Connie Mack Jr.

That same week Roy wrote to his cousin Maudie:

Dear Maudie,

This is to inform you that your Uncle Connie is not in very good condition both mentally and physically. He failed very much during September, October and November at which time he could not walk alone. However, after we engaged two male nurses for him he started to improve. He was then taken to Ft. Myers, Florida to stay with Connie Jr. and expects to go to Palm Beach later.

He is not capable of doing any reading or writing. We hope that he will improve so that he can send you a note upon his return in April, however, I doubt this very much. I do know that he has been thinking about you.

Connie Mack celebrated his ninety-second birthday in Fort Myers. The house was filled with elaborate floral creations, newsmen, and photographers. "It looks as if the one hundred mark will be easier to reach than I thought," said the eternal optimist. He did not mention the sale of the team except that he was now a rooter for the Kansas City Athletics. He had intended to go to West Palm Beach for the Athletics' spring training but was not up to it. His son drove him to one exhibition game.

Watching boxing matches on television and taking short walks and rides around town were his main activities, along with bouncing his newest grandson, three-month-old John Sheppard McGillicuddy, on his knees.

Ira Thomas was among the early casualties of the transfer of the Athletics to Kansas City. Now seventy-three, Thomas had been on the Athletics' payroll for forty-five years. He was in bed recuperating from an automobile accident when he received a telegram: "Your services will no longer be required." Thomas scouted for the Yankees for a year and died in 1958.

Eddie Joost was the next to get the ax. "Arnold Johnson assured me I'd be part of the club. Then I picked up the newspaper and learned that Lou Boudreau had been named the manager. I was out."

Joost finished his career as a utility infielder and pinch hitter with the Red Sox.

Charles "Shots" Monaghan, the visiting club custodian since 1920, died on January 19, 1955, the day before two moving vans pulled up at Connie Mack Stadium and barrels of uniforms; ledgers; ivory elephants; and large portraits of Connie Mack, Home Run Baker, Rube Waddell, and other stars of yesteryear were carried off to Kansas City. On Bob Carpenter's orders, nothing was removed from Connie Mack's office.

Howard "Yitz" Crompton helped pack up the trophies, photos, and bric-a-brac stored in what had been the Elephant Club. He had been the visiting club custodian for the Phillies beginning in 1931 and, since 1940, the clubhouse boss for the A's. But he was more than that; he and his wife Caroline had been babysitters, money lenders, and, in Lou Brissie's words, "good to all of us, willing to do anything for you, outgoing and pleasant, very popular." Having lived all his life within two blocks of Shibe Park, Yitz went with the club to Kansas City but didn't like it. A year later he was back in Philadelphia. Without baseball he was lost. He hanged himself on August 23, 1956.

Said Brissie, "I was shocked when I heard he had killed himself, but I guess it was like losing his whole family when the A's left Philadelphia."

Farm director Bernie Guest and traveling secretary Dave Keefe went with the franchise in those same positions. Lena Blackburne scouted for Kansas City for a year, then retired. Jack Coombs, now retired as Duke's baseball coach, maintained his ties to the Athletics until he died in 1957.

Earle Mack left baseball and went into the pre-fab construction business with his son. Earle died February 4, 1967.

In addition to his duties with the Athletics, Roy Mack signed a three-year contract with Bob Carpenter to guide the Phillies' new stadium maintenance supervisor Andy Clark. Arnold Johnson asked him to supervise the training camp at West Palm Beach in the spring. Otherwise Roy had few real responsibilities. He and his wife continued to reside in Philadelphia. His son Connie worked in the Athletics' public relations office until he resigned in 1961.

Roy Mack died on February 10, 1960. Arnold Johnson died three weeks later. Roy's 20 percent stake in the Athletics was left in a trust for his sons, Tom and Connie, provided there were enough other assets to provide for his daughters, Kathleen and Dorothy. Their mother, Margaret, was the trustee. In December 1960 the Johnson heirs sold their 52 percent interest to Charlie Finley for $1.975 million. When the other stockholders sold out to Finley two months later, Margaret McGillicuddy decided to sell too, for about $791,730. (Finley paid a total of $1.9 million for the remaining 48 percent; her stock represented 41.67 percent of that.)

The Kansas City A's died and went to Oakland in 1968.

Connie Mack, accompanied by Roy and a nurse, flew on a private plane to Kansas City for the April 12 opener and sat with former president Harry Truman while Alex Kellner won the new Athletics' first game, 4–2. Mack stayed for the second game, then went home.

On May 9, 1955, Roy Mack wrote to Paul Fritzinger:

> This is to advise you that my father is not capable of carrying on any correspondence. He is able to walk with the aid of a cane but is physically failing in health. He looks pretty good, but mentally—not so good. He has no worries now but he thinks he does and it is difficult at times to get him on the right path. . . .
>
> We went to K. C. on a private plane and he stood the trip fairly well—with the aid of a male nurse. No doubt that will be his last trip, except of course a trip to Fort Myers next winter. My father can still sign his name but cannot write a letter. That is out of the question.

It was not Connie Mack's last trip. He returned to Kansas City for an all-star Athletics reunion on July 20. Eight of his boys were there—Grove, Cochrane, Barry, Baker, Foxx, Simmons, Haas, Miller, and Eddie Collins Jr.—all saddened by what they saw. Jack Barry said, "The poor man had failed considerably since I had seen him before. In fact, when I went and spoke to him I told him who I was and he was glad to see me and the next day Bing Miller said to me that Connie told him that afternoon that he was sorry he didn't recognize me."

Chuck Roberts occasionally drove Mack and Bill Cunningham to Baltimore for a doubleheader. After the first game they would go into the clubhouse to meet the players. They never stayed for the second game.

Once in a while Mack went to Connie Mack Stadium accompanied by a male nurse to see the Phillies play. Sportswriter Joe Tumelty recalled, "His mind was gone. I'd ask him questions like, 'Who do you think will win the

National League pennant,' and he'd say, 'Pittsburgh,' and they were always around last place in those days."

Mack had digestive problems, gall bladder problems, urinary infection problems.

At some point during this time, Connie Mack and his wife left their School Lane apartment and went separate ways. Katherine took an apartment downtown. Connie Mack moved in with his daughter, Rita Breedlove, in her tiny apartment at 724 Wolcott Road in Chestnut Hill. (He was still paying her $165 monthly rent.)

That's where Connie McCambridge saw his grandfather for the last time in the fall of 1955. "He was sitting in a wheelchair," McCambridge said. "He recognized me and patted my hand and said, 'Everything's going to be all right.' He always said that, whether it was about the team or himself."

On the afternoon of Saturday, October 1, Mack awakened from a nap. Chuck Roberts was in the living room watching Game 4 of the Yankees-Dodgers World Series. He heard Mack stirring.

"Mr. Mack, do you want any help?" Roberts asked.

"No, you watch and let me know what happens."

"All right, but don't get up by yourself."

A few minutes later Chuck heard a thud. He rushed into the bedroom and found Mack on the floor. He had slipped trying to get out of bed. Roberts tried to help him up. "It hurts," Mack said. Rita called Dr. Gopadze, who ordered an ambulance to take Mack to nearby Chestnut Hill Hospital for X-rays. Mack's right hip was broken. Dr. Gopadze ordered Mack transferred to Presbyterian Hospital, where, four days later, he operated on his ninety-two-year-old patient, using metal fasteners to pin the pieces together, and drew accolades from the medical world for a successful outcome. Two days later Mack was sitting up, cheerful and uncomplaining. He was in the hospital for three weeks then went back to Rita's apartment to recuperate.

Clark Griffith, Mack's oldest and closest friend in baseball, died on October 27, 1955, at eighty-five. Both had come from poverty and made baseball their lives with a passion that had never dimmed. Both had risen from players to managers to club owners. Both have been tarred indelibly and inaccurately with tags of tight-fistedness and miserliness; both were chronically generous to down-and-out former players, extended families, and strangers in ways unknown to the public.

Griffith never softened his disdain for the industrial magnates who bought into baseball—the "bushwhackers" who had no understanding of the game on the field or in the clubhouse. Mack welcomed and admired successful businessmen and more readily accepted innovations he thought were good for baseball.

Connie Mack was not told of his friend's passing, nor of the deaths of Cy Young on November 4 and Honus Wagner on December 6.

When Roy and his wife returned from a forty-five-day Mediterranean cruise in December, Mack was moved to their spacious home.

More than three hundred turned out at the Warwick Hotel for the Reciprocity Club's annual Connie Mack birthday party, but the guest of honor was unable to attend on doctor's orders. Mack's former players Bing Miller, Frank Baker, and Howard Ehmke spoke. Dr. Gopadze read from a letter he had received from an unnamed man who had played thirteen years for Mack: "Baseball owes me nothing because of my association with a great man."

Of the hundreds of birthday greetings he received, the one that touched Mack the most came from Fred Haynes, who had been a batboy for the Athletics in 1905.

Mack seemed content at Roy's home. But it wasn't a good arrangement for Roy's family or Chuck Roberts, who was uncomfortable going there to take him for a drive. "Roy's wife wanted to make a houseman out of me, doing things that weren't my job, and I refused."

So Connie Mack was moved again, to a second-floor bedroom in Ruth's home at 7014 Anderson in Germantown. He had two male nurses, Arthur Brady during the day and Harry Starts at night. Ruth hired a registered nurse, Miss Weatherly, for daytime duty, and a cook. Unknown to the others, the night nurse was working two jobs. Sometimes he fell asleep in the chair in Mack's room. Independent and stubborn as ever, Mack would sooner do for himself than wake him. One night he reached for a urinal and it fell and cut his nose.

Frank Cunningham's bedroom was on the third floor. He was now a student at LaSalle University. "Every morning before I went to school I would stop in and say good morning. I thought he was just going through a recovery, not that he was dying. In the evenings I would sit and chat with him, sometimes briefly, sometimes for a while, depending on how he felt. He no longer had much interest in winter sports; we'd talk about something in the news. Sometimes his responses were alert and sometimes, especially in early February, his reaction was more of an acknowledgment with his eyes; he didn't say much."

Chuck Roberts came to the house every day to take him for a drive. Arthur Brady carried Mack to the car like a bundle of bones wrapped in an overcoat.

In the middle of January Mack stopped eating and had to be fed intravenously. He was ready to go.

On Sunday, February 5, Chuck Roberts arrived to take him for a drive. Ruth's daughters, Kathy and Alice, went with them. Soon Mack complained of not feeling well and asked to go home.

The next morning Dr. Gopadze came by and saw that his old friend was slipping fast.

On Tuesday night Harry Starts was dozing. Mack reached for something and fell out of bed. Sixteen-year-old Bill Cunningham was in the next room and heard him fall. When he opened the door, Starts woke up and they lifted the Old Man back into bed.

The next morning Frank stopped in to see him before going to school: "I walked in and to my surprise he was sitting up in a chair. I went over to him and said, 'Hi Pop, how are you?' He looked me straight in the eye and clear as a bell said, 'Frankie, I want you to take care of your mother.' I said, 'Sure, Pop, sure.' He grabbed my hand. I said, 'I'll see you after school.'"

Ruth felt that it was time to call for a priest. The Reverend Joseph A. Cavanaugh of Holy Cross Church in Mt. Airy came at noon and administered the last rites. Connie Mack asked for Katherine. During the last several months, he had seldom seen her. Occasionally Frank would pick her up and bring her home for Sunday dinner or take a meal to her. She was going downhill mentally.

Calls went out to Katherine and the rest of the family, except Earle, who had suffered a stroke.

Betty and Mary arrived. Ruth went upstairs shortly after three. Nurse Weatherly said to her, "He's going."

Arthur Brady protectively thought Ruth didn't need to hear that: "Don't tell her that!"

By the time Betty and Mary went up, Connie Mack had peacefully passed away at 3:20.

Bill was in his room. He went into Pop-Pop's room and looked at death for the first time.

When Frank came home, Betty met him in the living room and told him. After seeing his grandfather sitting up so alert that morning, he was shocked. When he thought about it, he realized, "Pop knew he was departing the planet. That's why he said what he did to me."

Alice was a fifth grader. Told that Pop-Pop had passed away, she later recalled, "I felt so sad, but I didn't know what to do with my sadness."

When Katherine finally arrived, having ridden the bus to the house, she said, "Is he gone?"

Told that he was, she turned around and left.

The Oliver Bair funeral home had four viewing rooms on the second floor. In view of the anticipated crowd, all four were reserved for Mr. Mack's visitors, and they were all needed. A line of people waiting in the rain to get in went down the street for blocks well into the evening.

Inside, cameramen asked Ruth's children to line up and walk to the open coffin and kneel down. Years later Alice remembered, "I was kneeling there with Mom, saying goodbye and looking at his face. Then I almost fainted and Mom took me to sit down."

Frank was thinking, "I'm just doing this for show. I'm sad but I feel that Pop had had a long and exciting life. He had died and that was okay, the natural way for things to happen."

Connie Mack was buried on February 11, 1956, at Holy Sepulchre Cemetery, where he had bought two lots on June 29, 1929, for $2,000. It was Katherine's birthday. Years later Ruth recalled that they could have held the funeral on a different day. "Somebody slipped up there."

Frank Cunningham and Connie McCambridge never forgot that day.

Connie remembered, "It was cold and wet, very wet. That didn't deter hundreds of people of all ages from standing outside to see the procession of baseball magnates and old-timers entering St. Bridget's, then watch as a police escort led the procession through Fairmount Park on the way to the cemetery. After a brief service, the family went to Betty and Jim Nolen's home. Even the police escort was invited."

It was a real Irish wake, "a great big party," said Frank, "and I thought, 'Gee, this is neat. Everybody's having a good time.'"

Not quite everybody.

Katherine stayed only a short time, then found Connie and Frank. "Take me home," she said. Connie drove them to her apartment building. She got out of the car. "Come with me, Connie," she said.

Frank said, "Don't you want me to come, too?"

"No, I don't want you, just Connie."

They climbed to her third-floor apartment. She took a photo of her husband from the mantle and thrust it at Connie. "Take that out of here," she said.

Recalled McCambridge, "She said what a terrible old man he was, took him up one side and down the other. I don't know why. I couldn't believe what I was hearing. I took the picture and left."

Several years later Katherine's granddaughter Susie visited her. "She was affectionate but there was still that sternness about her. Shortly after the last time I saw her she was put in a very nice nursing home. Of course she hated it, said how horrible it was."

Katherine died November 28, 1972, at ninety-five.

The tributes to Connie Mack began with President Eisenhower and came from all over baseball and the country.

Roy received a letter from J. Edgar Hoover: "It was with deep regret that I learned of the passing of your father. The world has lost a true gentleman and America one of its unforgettable figures. As long as the game is played, our countrymen will recall with deep admiration the great Connie Mack."

Branch Rickey said, "I'm all upset. Griff is gone. Ed Barrow's gone. Honus Wagner's gone. Now my greatest baseball friend is gone."

Ty Cobb: "We sort of expected him to pass on but it's still a shock when you hear it's happened. I loved Mr. Mack. You know, a man can love another man. I'm pretty old myself and I just can't help crying at hearing that he's gone. I thoroughly enjoyed my years with Mr. Mack. I never enjoyed playing any more than for him."

Ruth received a letter from Texas that bore this address:

Mrs. Frank Cunningham
Daughter of Connie Mack
Grand old man of baseball
Germantown Philadelphia

It came from Connie Mack Luce, who had been named for Mr. Mack fourteen years earlier. It ended: "I have always wished I could be another 'Connie Mack.' Now I know there will never be another one. So many people are grieved, I know, but we shouldn't be, as he aimed his dream at a star and won. God bless him."

Another letter arrived from a fifth-grade class at PS 39 in New York City, written in pencil on lined notebook paper by Carmen Soto on behalf of the class: "We were very sorry when we heard of the death of your father. We talked about his life. Today we made some mathematics problems that you might like to see. Our teacher showed us your father's autograph and the picture that was taken at the Hall of Fame. We send sympathy to your whole family."

Enclosed were seven problems in addition and subtraction based on Connie Mack's life.

Connie Mack's one-page will, signed on August 10, 1955, and witnessed by Roy and Frank Schilpp, was filed for probate on February 16. The value of his estate was $60,377.40. Taxes and expenses took it down to $46,332. The bulk of the estate was a $38,000 life insurance policy. The will left one-third of his possessions to his wife, $5,000 each to the McCambridge boys, A's auditor Stoughton Sterling, and attorney J. Channing Ellery. (After taxes and expenses the McCambridge boys received about $3,926.90 each and the attorneys about $2,500.)

The rest went to the four daughters.

The executors were Roy, Ellery, and the Provident Trust Company.

A striking aspect of the estate was the number of worthless stocks and unpaid loans. Sixty-three shares of Philadelphia Life Insurance Company, worth about $9,000, were the only positive investment. A lot in Lake County, Florida, was sold for $200. Loans for $1,800 to Robert and Laureen Fitzgerald, dated May 7, 1950, and $4,500 to Alice Drennan Trump, scout Mike Drennan's daughter, on July 13, 1946, were written off.

It took until 1959 to settle the estate. One matter of contention concerned whether a federal tax of $39,828.31 should be taken from Mack's 1954 trust or the estate. If the latter, it would have left very little to distribute. The taxes eventually were charged to the trust.

Red McCarthy, sports columnist for the *Philadelphia Times*, summed up Connie Mack:

He was the acme of politeness, a man of graciousness, a man humble. Yet his was a popularity that not even presidents, kings nor movie heroes could approach.

Looking back on a career of successes and heartaches, and he had so much of both in 93 years, you find three R's in the life of Connie Mack—Respected, Remarkable and Ridiculed. . . .

Ridicule was the only taint on Connie Mack's career. Ninety-nine percent of it was unjustified.

The miserly reputation hung on Connie Mack that continues to be repeated bears no resemblance to the man. During his lifetime he did little to try to correct it What his critics wrote about him was usually immaterial to him.

Members of the family who drove him home after games in the 1930s and '40s related similar experiences: "Sometimes when we were on the way home he'd direct me through the streets of row houses around the ballpark, and he'd say, 'Stop here.' He'd run up to the door and ring the bell and an older woman would open it and he'd hand her an envelope. Sometimes I could see they were crying. He did that so many times; nobody knows how many checks he gave to individuals. But I know, because I drove him to so many places."

After Mack's death, Cy Peterman quoted an unidentified "business adviser":

That talk about his being a tough, hard old man with players and fans is not deserved. Nine out of ten years he was paying as well or better than the average, and usually he had a higher payroll than two or three other second division clubs. He had to make ends meet, to be sure. He had to provide for the members of his family. But he did not, as some critics loudly proclaimed, let down the fans because he was tight or didn't care. He cared for his club. He cared most of all for the game that he dignified. It was because he tried to keep his club and still remain solvent that things became so difficult and forced his hand.

As a businessman, Connie Mack genuinely detested haggling over salaries with players, not because he was loath to part with the money. If they played well, he wanted to pay them well. He knew, during his lean years, that he could not afford to pay them what they were worth. At the same time, he was reluctant to pay them more than he thought they were worth or the Athletics could afford. That was business. He had a budget and stuck to it. There are more zeroes in the numbers today, but baseball clubs in the twenty-first century operate the same way.

So what if his teams lost more games than they won in fifty-three years? Among baseball managers there are no geniuses, just varying degrees of failure. In the long run the difference between winning and losing just over half the time is meaningless. No manager of any lengthy tenure has ever won as many as 5 out of every 8 games he managed.

Connie Mack admitted that he was a poor manager of a losing team. If he didn't have a contender, as during his long treks through the rebuilding wilderness, his teams lost plenty of games while he experimented, trying out trainloads of prospects. The future was more important than that day's final score.

What Connie Mack did do was build two of the greatest teams in history, winning seven pennants and five World Series with them—and two other pennants besides.

Not bad for an eighth-grade dropout.

In the end, the measure of Connie Mack's life is not the number of pennants or games won and lost but the lasting effect he had on the men he managed and the minds and hearts of those whose lives he touched.

In 1936 Dr. Albert C. Barnes, an eminent art collector and commentator, said in a lecture at Philadelphia's Central High School that Connie Mack was the greatest artist Philadelphia had ever produced:

> Let me reconcile this apparently wild assertion with the facts of the case. Connie Mack would not accept a recruit who would not rather play baseball than do anything else in the world. He gets teamwork out of men who are concerned primarily with their own excellence. When Connie Mack is successful, his team has the attributes which all aestheticians agree are the indispensable requisites of great art—unity, variety, individuality, and the production of aesthetic pleasure in others. . . . Connie Mack has given honest aesthetic pleasure to more people than anybody I know of in a lifetime spent in Philadelphia.

Many of his players took some of him with them when they became managers and college coaches. A player for Holy Cross said of Jack Barry, who coached the New England college team for forty years, "As a coach, he was like Connie Mack on the bench. If you made a mistake—and you made them—when you came in there was always a seat next to Barry. He'd tell the player sitting next to him to move, or you knew to move if you were sitting there, and the player who made the skull would sit next to him and he'd tell you what you did wrong in a calm way."

Connie Mack earned the love and respect of those who knew him well—family, friends, players, Shibe Park employees—and not so well.

Ray Beck was a member of the St. Louis Cardinals Knothole Gang and the Browns Boys Brigade in the 1930s, which provided free admission to youngsters under fifteen. Fifty-five years later he remembered:

> Before and after games I collected autographs on baseball cards and in an autograph book. I was twelve in 1934. Following a game between the Athletics and Browns at Sportsman's Park, Mr. Mack was seated in the front passenger's seat of a long, black limousine outside the ballpark signing autographs for a group of boys that included myself. He sat patiently in the heat, signing autographs, wearing his usual dark suit, white shirt, and tie and the ever-present straw hat. One by one he accommodated us, slowly and carefully inscribing his name for each boy in turn as he spoke kindly to each of us. Although I had rooted mightily for my beloved Cardinals against the Athletics during both the 1930 and 1931 World Series, thereafter I was inclined to wish for his future success although he, of course, never won another pennant.

Mack's nature was reflected in his letters. He invariably asked about family members and wished them well, or he expressed pleasure in meeting a son or relative or friend of his correspondent and gratitude for hearing from him or her.

On January 16, 1953, Mack wrote to Constance Mack of Buffalo, with whom he had corresponded for fifteen years:

> Your letter came tonight and was pleased to hear from you. You don't mind writing to one who is ninety years old. The story of the dog is a good one and can understand just how you felt when you found your dog was lost to you when one is young that happens.
>
> With best wishes
>
> P.S. Have no picture that would want to give you, won't until I get home and will send. I love that picture of you and you must be good looking. The picture is a dear one and I will look at it often. May I keep it I would like it very much.

His grandson, Senator Connie Mack III, summed up Mack's life:

> The interesting thing about my grandfather is that, no matter where I have gone in this country, people recognize the name Connie Mack. A lot of them will get into a discussion about baseball and that 1929 team and I mean name the players, position by position.
>
> Thinking about it today, the thought that has hit me is that, even though he spent his entire life in baseball, managed the Athletics for fifty years, I think that the message, the impression that he left was more about who he was as far as character, his attitude toward his fellow man, his integrity—there are more things mentioned about my grandfather as far as how he treated people as opposed to how many games he won or lost in the years he managed. He left for me a pretty challenging goal of living up to the standards of life that I perceive that he lived as a result of things that people said to me.
>
> One that immediately comes to mind is the guys who would drive the busloads of people to the game and the buses would be lined up alongside Shibe Park and my grandfather walked by and saw them sitting in the buses and said, "What are you sitting out here for?" They said, "We can't afford to go to the game every time we drive people here." He said, "Come with me," and would take them in and get them seats. It was that kind of story. It got to the point where I said to somebody, "I'm still looking for the first person who's going to tell me they paid to get into Shibe Park."
>
> That is what comes across to me about him, not wins and losses, but character, caring for people, kindness.

Doc Cramer put it more succinctly: "Whatever you want in a man, Mr. Mack was it."

Connie Mack has not been forgotten.

On the evening of April 16, 1957, just prior to the Phillies-Dodgers opening game, an eight-foot statue atop a five-foot base was unveiled across the street from Connie Mack Stadium by two of Mack's descendants, Earle III and Bob McCambridge. The public contributed $20,000 toward it. The sculptor was a lifelong A's fan, Harry Rosin. The statue has Mack's right arm raised, a scorecard in his hand. His eight-point sportsman's creed is carved into the base.

League presidents Ford Frick and Will Harridge led the speakers, who included Leo Durocher. Among the letters and telegrams read was one from Jack Coombs in Texas, who wrote, "I'm sorry I can't be with you tonight." Coombs died on April 15.

That same year a new twenty-two-story Sheraton Hotel opened in downtown Philadelphia. Dozens of celebrities, including eight of Mack's former players, were on hand for the dedication of the Connie Mack Room. A Residence Inn near City Hall still has a Connie Mack Room for meetings, weddings, and dances.

One of the luxury suites in the Rittenhouse Hotel near City Hall bears his name.

In 1958 a springer spaniel named Connie Mack won the national field trials.

In 1970 a Phillies-Athletics old-timers' game at Connie Mack Stadium reunited the A's from as far back as Grove and Earnshaw through the 1950s. In 2000 the Oakland A's honored an A's all-century team and invited Mack's baseball-loving "girlie," Ruth, to throw out the first pitch. Oakland manager Art Howe brought out the lineup card wearing a blue suit and straw hat.

Connie Mack is remembered today in his birthplace, East Brookfield,

Massachusetts. In 1970 then congressman Connie Mack III spoke at the unveiling of a plaque at the house where Pop-Pop was born. The playing field and a main street were renamed for Mr. Mack.

In 2012 the town of two thousand celebrated the 150th anniversary of Mack's birth with a two-day lineup of events, including a ball game played in 1880s style.

When Bob Carpenter bought Connie Mack Stadium from Arnold Johnson in 1954, everything went with it, including a box set in concrete several feet beneath home plate that contained some coins that Jim Fitzgerald had buried when he supervised the laying out of the Shibe Park playing surface in 1909.

In 1961 Carpenter sold the ballpark to a group of New York real estate developers who intended to build an industrial park on the site. Three years later the owners of the Philadelphia Eagles bought it. The Phillies continued to lease the park until 1971.

The largest crowd of the year—31,822—turned out for the last game at Connie Mack Stadium on Thursday, October 1, 1970. It was the wildest night at a ballpark since Bill Veeck's Demolition Derby, but instead of phonograph records, the ballpark was demolished. Before the game the Phillies' management handed out slats from the wood seats as souvenirs. The slats became hammers. Some fans had come with pockets filled with tools. They didn't wait until the game was over before they started chipping and chopping and tearing apart whatever pieces of the old ballpark they could free and carry away. Seats were torn out unless someone was sitting in them. The place shook like an unending earthquake was wrecking it. When the game ended, thousands descended onto the field and ripped up handfuls of sod and tore down the outfield walls.

On August 20, 1971, the statue of Connie Mack was rededicated after it was moved to Veterans Stadium. During the luncheon that followed, it was announced that the remains of Connie Mack Stadium were burning.

Today the site is occupied by the Deliverance Evangelistic Church. The statue stands on the west side of Eleventh Street across from Citizens Bank Park.

Connie Mack Jr. knew what it was like to be the son of a famous man. He told his children, "Never be apologetic that your grandfather is a famous person, but never believe that it entitles you to anything. It might open a door but you're the one who's got to walk through that door."

A successful businessman in his own right, Connie Jr. later lived under a different shadow. His son, Connie III, became a congressman and two-term senator from Florida (1989–2001). In the 1990s Connie Jr. was invited to throw out the first ball at a Florida Senior League season opener. The local newspaper referred to him as "son of the legendary manager and owner of the Philadelphia Athletics, and father of U. S. Senator Connie Mack."

He told his son, "I've gone through my entire life being known as Connie Mack's son. Now they're referring to me as Connie Mack's father. I'm having one hell of an identity crisis."

Today, in every ballpark from Little League to Yankee Stadium, the spirit of Connie Mack is in the stands, on cold spring days huddled in his black overcoat, in the dog days of August with a rolled handkerchief between his long scrawny neck and high stiff collar. And when the music isn't blaring or the crowd roaring, you can hear him saying, as he did so often, "This is a great game, a fine game. It makes people happy, makes them live longer."

APPENDIX

CONNIE MACK'S RECORDS

Batting Record

	G	AB	R	H	2B
1886 WAS NL	10	36	4	13	2
1887	82	314	35	63	6
1888	85	300	49	56	5
1889	98	386	51	113	16
1890 BUF PL	123	503	95	134	15
1891 PIT NL	75	280	43	60	10
1892	97	346	39	84	9
1893	37	133	22	38	3
1894	70	231	33	57	7
1895	14	49	12	15	2
1896	33	120	9	26	4
Totals 11 years	724	2698	392	659	79

3B	HR	RBI	BB	SO	SB	AVG
1	0	5	0	2	0	.361
1	0	20	8	17	26	.201
6	3	29	17	18	31	.187
1	0	42	15	12	26	.293
12	0	53	47	13	16	.266
0	0	29	19	11	4	.214
4	1	31	21	22	11	.243
1	0	15	10	9	4	.286
1	1	21	21	14	8	.247
0	0	4	7	1	1	.306
1	0	16	5	8	0	.217
28	5	265	170	127	127	.244

Managing Record

	G	W	L	PCT	FINISH
1894 PIT NL	23	12	10	.545	7
1895	135	71	61	.538	7
1896	131	66	63	.512	6
1901 PHI AL	137	74	62	.544	4
1902	137	83	53	.610	1
1903	137	75	60	.556	2
1904	155	81	70	.536	5
1905	152	92	56	.622	1
1906	149	78	67	.538	4
1907	150	88	57	.607	2
1908	157	68	85	.444	6
1909	153	95	58	.621	2
1910	155	102	48	.680	1
1911	152	101	50	.669	1
1912	153	90	62	.592	3
1913	153	96	57	.627	1
1914	158	99	53	.651	1
1915	154	43	109	.283	8
1916	154	36	117	.235	8
1917	154	55	98	.359	8
1918	130	52	76	.406	8
1919	140	36	104	.257	8
1920	156	48	106	.312	8
1921	155	53	100	.346	8
1922	155	65	89	.422	7
1923	153	69	83	.454	6
1924	152	71	81	.467	5

1925	153	88	64	.579	2
1926	150	83	67	.553	3
1927	155	91	63	.591	2
1928	153	98	55	.641	2
1929	151	104	46	.693	1
1930	154	102	52	.662	1
1931	153	107	45	.704	1
1932	154	94	60	.610	2
1933	152	79	72	.523	3
1934	153	68	82	.453	5
1935	149	58	91	.389	8
1936	154	53	100	.346	8
1937	120	39	80	.328	7
1938	154	53	99	.349	8
1939	62	25	37	.403	7
1940	154	54	100	.351	8
1941	154	64	90	.416	8
1942	154	55	99	.357	8
1943	155	49	105	.318	8
1944	155	72	82	.468	5
1945	153	52	98	.347	8
1946	155	49	105	.318	8
1947	156	78	76	.506	5
1948	154	84	70	.545	4
1949	153	80	73	.523	5
1950	149	51	98	.342	8
Totals 53 years	7750	3730	3944	.486	

World Series Record

	G	W	L
1905 PHI A	5	1	4
1910	5	4	1
1911	6	4	2
1913	5	4	1
1914	4	0	4
1929	5	4	1
1930	6	4	2
1931	7	3	4
Totals	43	24	19

Source: Records courtesy Retrosheet.org.

INDEX

Brancato, Al, 216, 243, 263, 269, 326
Brandt, William, 58, 62–63
"break up the Yankees" rule, 226
Breedlove, Rita, 289, 513–14, 562–64, 566, 575
Bridges, Tommy, 76
Briggs, Joseph, 567
Briggs, Walter O., 192, 196, 237, 472
Briggs, Walter "Spike," Jr.: Athletics sale and Johnson as buyer and, 533, 538, 539, 565, 566, 569, 570; Athletics sale and Philadelphia Eight as buyers and, 555, 557, 558
Briggs Stadium, 418
Brissie, Leland "Lou," 258–59; 1947 season, 386; 1948 season, 401–2, 403, 404, 405, 408, 410, 414; 1949 season, 421, 424, 429; 1950 season, 455, 471, 475; contract of, 453; on Crompton, 573; Tipton and, 447; trade of, 483–84; in WWII and injuries from, 290, 367–69
broadcast programming, radio, 204–5
Brogan, Johnny, 505–6
Broun, Heywood, 91
Brown, Joe. E., 203, 233
Brown & Bigelow calendar, 496
Brubaker, Wilbur J., 290
Brucker, Earle, 135, 455; as Athletics coach, 244, 247–48, 258, 287, 308, 362, 376; as Browns coach, 436; Christopher and, 308, 366; firing of as Athletics coach, 432–41, 443; as a player, 135, 144, 145, 172, 191
Brucker, Earle "Gidge," Jr., 415–16
Bryant, George, 428
Bucci, John, 447–48
Budwitz, Joe, 310–11, 385
Bull Durham, 244
bullfights, 138
Bullock, Red, 120
Buque, Helen, 479

Burgo, Bill, 291, 302
Burkett, Jesse, 79, 502
Burlingame, Gordon, 470, 471
Burnes, Robert L., 345, 390
Burns, Jimmy, 499–500
Burns, Joe, 321, 329
Burr, Harold C., 202, 205
Busch, Ed, 295, 302, 306, 317
Byrd, Harry, 455, 459, 487, 490, 494, 513
Byrd, Richard L., 66

Caesar, Irving, 202
Cain, Sugar, 39, 47, 69, 72–73, 75, 97–98
Caligiuri, Fred, 255, 263, 272
Cameron, Stuart, 115
Camilli, Dolf, 175
Campbell, Bill, 369–70
Cannon, Jimmy, 124, 166, 225, 341, 516
Cardenas, Lazaro, 138
card playing, 48, 268, 304, 422
Carillo, Leo, 233–34
Carlsbad CA, Athletics in, 247
Carmichael, John P., 90, 313
Carpenter, Robert, Jr., 519; Connie Mack Stadium and, 539, 541, 573, 586; as Phillies president, 288, 349–50, 391, 448; Wilmington club and, 230–31
Carpenter, Robert, Sr., 230–31, 280, 288, 391
Carter, Art, 353
Carter, Boake, 213
Carter, Pat, 79, 385
Cartwright, Al, 310
Cascarella, Joe, 61, 69, 73, 75, 87, 98
Case, George, 118, 317
Casey, Daniel, 176
Caster, George, 70, 135, 137, 144, 190, 222, 240
catchers, 71–72, 135, 192, 322, 340, 378, 419

Powell, John, 567

Power, Vic, 494, 518

Power Boating, 129

Prell, Ed, 543

press, the: bashing of Athletics and Phillies, 174–78; Connie Mack and, 5, 105, 125–27, 190; Earle Mack and, 165; rumors of, 82–83, 105. *See also specific sportswriters*

Priddy, Gerry, 449–50

Prohibition repeal, 28, 54, 56–57, 68

Provident Tradesman Bank, 563

Provident Trust Company, 580

public opinion, 352–53, 448

public relations, Athletics, 264–65, 344, 443–44, 447

Puccinelli, George, 116, 117

Quinn, Bob, 29–30, 151, 278, 313, 503

Quinn, John, 361–62, 363

race riots, 354

Radcliff, Rip, 62, 72

radio, baseball on, 201–13; advertising and sponsorships of, 202–3, 206, 207–11; American League and, 203, 204, 206, 207–11, 212–13; announcers of, 202, 203, 207, 211–13; beginnings of, 201–2; bootlegging and pirating play-by-play broadcasts, 202, 205, 207–11; Mack and, 206–7, 211; minor leagues and, 203–4, 205–6, 418; play-by-play regulations for, 212–13; programming of, 204–5

Radio City Music Hall, 507

Rags, 95–96

Rambo, Bertram, 461, 470

Ray, Bob, 89, 231

Reach, Mary S., 470

Record. See Philadelphia Record

Red Cross, 66

Reiss, Steve A., 24

Reninger, Jim, 191

Renna, Bill, 494

Rensel, Jack, 534–35, 536, 543, 552, 554, 556

rental income for Athletics, 187–88, 309, 350, 388, 477, 485, 524, 529

Reporter (Eureka UT), 89

retiring, Connie Mack's views on, 89–90, 122, 153, 425, 439

reunion of Athletics, 574

revenue sharing, 44

Reynolds, Allie, 348, 378, 427

Rhoads, C. Brewster, 531, 535, 537, 549–50, 552–54, 557, 569

Rhodes, Gordon, 102, 121

Rice, Grantland: on Athletics, 144, 145–46, 395, 453; broadcasting of, 202; Doyle and, 144; on Mack, 236

Rice, Sam, 7

Richards, Dick, 27–28

Richards, Paul, 97, 142–43, 483, 501

Richardson, Tommy, 161, 251, 278, 531–32, 535, 536

Rickard, Tex, 202

Rickey, Branch, 62, 159; with Cardinals, 76–77, 180–81; Connie Mack and, 278, 354–55, 579; Dennis Mack and, 511; as Pirates general manager, 466; player integration and, 354–55; polling players and, 396; sale of Browns and, 195–96

Rittenhouse Hotel, 585

Rizzuto, Phil, 225, 489

Roberts, Chuck, 497–99; assistance to Mack family, 334, 551, 563, 571, 575, 576; driving of, 502, 503, 516, 550, 551, 574, 576–77

Roberts, Robin, 416

Robertson, Al, 494

Robertson, Sherry, 488

Salisbury MD, 203–4
Salsinger, H. G., 131–32, 200, 434, 472
Samuel, Bernard, 457
sandlot players, 71
San Francisco: as potential home for
    Athletics, 259, 531; Connie Mack in,
    234
San Francisco Chronicle, 234
San Francisco Seals (PCL), 364–65
Sargent, Jim, 148
Saturday Evening Post, 99, 100, 180, 264
Savage, Bob: 1942 season, 273–74; 1946
    season, 340; 1947 season, 386; 1948
    season, 402, 404; contracts of, 398;
    on Rosar, 337; in WWII, 289–90
"Save the A's" campaign, 519–20
Savino, George, 102
Scallen, John P., 186–87
Scarborough, Ray, 301, 446
Schaefer, Bob, 16
Scheib, Carl, 286, 293; 1943 season,
    286–87; 1947 season, 372, 375–76,
    379; 1948 season, 404, 411, 413, 414;
    1949 season, 422, 427, 430–31; 1950
    season, 463–64; 1951 season, 483;
    1952 season, 487; 1953 season, 490;
    Mack and, 329
Schillp, Frank, 542, 562–64
Schroeder, Bob, 22, 130, 136, 434, 435,
    437
Schultz, Howie, 409
Schwartz, Louis A., 37, 38, 54
Schwartz, Packey, 482
scoreboards, 96, 256
scorecards, income from, 23–24, 130, 188
scouting system of Athletics, 159, 161,
    183, 191, 258, 339, 356, 359, 398. *See
    also specific scouts*
Sedgwick, Hubert, 230, 314, 460
segregation and Chuck Roberts, 498–
    99

Selective Service Act, 338
Seminick, Andy, 350
Sewell, Joe, 4
Shannon, Paul, 68
Shantz, Bobby: 1949 season, 421–22;
    1950 season, 459, 475; 1951 season,
    482, 485; 1952 season, 487; 1953 sea-
    son, 490, 513; 1954 season, 518, 521;
    contracts of, 486, 488
Shaughnessy, Frank, 42, 44, 71
Shaw, John, 384
Sheets, Harry, 497
Sheppard, Morris, 78
Sheppard, Susan, 78
Shibe, Ben, 23, 160
Shibe, Ethyl, 128, 245
Shibe, Ida, 113, 377
Shibe, John, 23, 24, 112; Athletics trades
    and, 57–58; on beer sales, 28; death
    of, 128; gate receipt skimming and,
    129; Johnson and, 35; Mack relation-
    ship with, 129–30; politics and, 37;
    press and, 83, 126; private side of,
    128–29; radio and, 207–11; Shibe
    Park and, 92, 187
Shibe, Tom, 57, 102, 112–13, 129–30, 160,
    470
Shibe Park: concessions, 23–26, 28–29,
    187, 220, 437, 470, 513, 524; lighting
    at, 199, 220; maintenance and reno-
    vation of, 92–93, 130–31, 220, 391,
    417–18, 437, 448; name change of,
    257, 489; parking at, 519–20; Phillies
    rental of, 187–88, 309, 350, 477, 524,
    529; police duty at, 29; press box at,
    130; stockholders and, 471. *See also*
    Connie Mack Stadium
Shibe Park Concessions Company, 24,
    470
Shook, Ken, 291
Shore, Frank A., 4

618   *Index*

Shoriki, Matsutaro, 81

Siebert, Dick, 268; 1938 season, 180–81, 185–86, 188; 1939 season, 218, 221; 1940 season, 243; 1941 season, 251; 1942 season, 274; 1943 All-Star Game and, 286; 1944 season, 302, 303–4; 1945 season, 329–30; contracts of, 262, 315–16; Fox and, 292; trade and quitting of, 336

Sievers, Roy, 449–50

signals, 387

signing bonuses, 492

Simmons, Al, 41, 82, 306; 1932 season, 11–12, 16; 1933 season and All-Star Game, 46, 49; 1943 comeback attempt, 279; 1944 season, 301–2; as Athletics coach and pinch hitter, 229, 243, 264, 303, 372; Athletics firing of as coach, 432–36, 438–41; contracts and salary of, 3, 18; Mack and, 318, 328, 331, 373, 425; in old-timers' game, 429; pitcher razzing of, 252–53; with White Sox, 76, 104; in Wisconsin Hall of Fame, 505

Simmons, Curt, 421, 448

Sisler, George, 168, 503, 509

Skaff, Frank, 310

Sley, Isadore "Speed," 527, 534, 545, 552, 554

Smith, Bob, 485

Smith, Edgar, 137, 147, 151, 200, 252–53

Smith, John, 503

Smith, Mayo, 316

Smith, Red, 31, 234; on Athletics, 121–22, 489; on Christopher, 301–2, 308; on Earle and Roy Mack, 165, 521; on gamblers, 306; on George and Rue conflict, 323–24; on Heusser, 241; on Mack, 5, 122–23, 153–54, 227, 233, 284–85, 355, 479; on Moses, 172, 173; on Newsom, 297; night games and,

201; salary of, 31, 315; on Simmons, 432, 435, 436; at spring training in Mexico, 137, 138; Valo and, 266–67; on Werber, 142

smoking by players, 31, 146

sobriety clauses, 94–95, 135, 396

Society for American Baseball Research (SABR), 262

Socony-Vacuum, 207

Soto, Carmen, 580

Southworth, Billy, Jr., 290

Spalding, 283

Spalding, Hughes, 156

Speaker, Tris, 67, 168, 203, 279, 285, 509

Specter, Meyer, 520

speedboat racing, 128–29

Spink, J. G. Taylor, 30

spitters, 403

Spoelstra, Watson, 342

sponsorships of radio broadcasts, 203, 206, 207–11

Sport, 184, 390

Sporting News: on Athletics sale, 526, 537; baseball profits and, 23, 24; black players and, 352; on firing of Simmons and Brucker, 440–42; on game attendance, 44; on Grove, 68; on Mack, 106–7, 278; on polling players, 396; radio announcers and, 212; rating managers poll of, 311; on Roy and Earle Mack, 472; on Yawkey, 30

Sportsmanship Brotherhood award, 225

Sportsman's Park, 44, 196

sportswriters, 31, 73, 352. *See also specific sportswriters*

spring training and Athletics: 1912, 192–93; 1933, 27–28; 1934, 67–72; 1935, 93–94; 1936, 111–12, 113–17; 1937, 133–39; 1938, 169–74; 1939, 214–19;